1777

The Year of the Hangman

GEORGE WASHINGTON
C. W. Peale
COURTESY OF THE PENNSYLVANIA ACADEMY OF FINE ARTS

1777

The Year of The Hangman

JOHN S. PANCAKE

The University of Alabama Press
Tuscaloosa & London

This book is for
John and Connie

Library of Congress Cataloging in Publication Data

Pancake, John S.
1777, the year of the hangman.
Bibliography: p.
Includes index.
1. United States—History—Revolution, 1775–1783
—Campaigns and battles. I. Title.
E233.P27   973.3'33   76-30797
ISBN 0–8173–0687–0

Copyright © 1977
The University of Alabama Press
Tuscaloosa, Alabama 35487–0380
All rights reserved
Manufactured in the United States of America

First Paperbound Edition 1992

Contents

Preface

ANYONE WHO HAS READ THE HISTORY OF THE WAR OF INDEPENDENCE CANNOT fail to be fascinated by the campaign of Gentleman Johnny Burgoyne. The story evokes pictures in the mind's eye: scarlet-coated Englishmen; the green and blue uniforms of the German mercenaries; the flash of brass and silver and steel accoutrements; the swarms of Indians in their war paint; the whole moving through the green forests or sailing the blue waters of lakes and rivers. Even the names have a lyrical tone: Richelieu, Champlain, Oriskany, Ticonderoga, and La Chine. Not the least part of the fascination is the fact that the fate of the expedition marked a turning point in the history of the war.

It is not surprising that there has been a host of chroniclers, scholars, and novelists, and those who fall in a category somewhere between because their artistry bridges the gaps that footnoted facts cannot, and so allows some scope for imagination (and may teach more history than the rest).

It is this fascination that has been partly responsible for the present writer's exploration of this particular part of the history of the war. There was also the fact that no scholar since Hoffman Nickerson in his *Turning Point of the Revolution* (1926) has attempted a detailed study of the British invasion from Canada, although there has been a vast amount of literature on specific aspects of the campaign.

Nor has any study to date attempted to link the Canadian expedition to the concurrent operation of General Sir William Howe in Pennsylvania in such a way as to present a complete story of the campaign of 1777 from the point of its inception and launching by the American Secretary, Lord George Germain, to the point where it was reduced to a shambles at the end of the year.

There is another gap which needs to be filled. As T. Harry Williams has reminded us, wars are won and lost by men who fight each other on the battlefield. But war also intrudes itself into the lives of the whole people of a nation, and the present study attempts to show this, if only in a limited way. It would be highly instructive, for instance, to present more about the state of mind of the English people, the social and economic factors that resulted in less than a full commitment of Britain to the suppression of the American rebellion.

On the American side it would be of great interest to find out to what extent this was truly a people's war.

So at the end of an investigation of this sort one is left with more questions than at the beginning—and a devout wish that some day he or others may answer them.

As I have noted elsewhere, anyone who says "I wrote a book" states considerably less than the truth. *We* wrote this book, and this includes: my wife, Frances, who had the frustrating experience of typing much of the manuscript in such odd sequences that she professes to know nothing about the campaign of 1777; Boyd Childress and Bruce Ellis, students *par excellence*, who were splendid research assistants, and who just may know more about the source materials than I do; Hugh Rankin of Tulane University, who generously read the manuscript (in record time) and who corrected many errors; Howard Miller of the Psychology Department of The University of Alabama, who enthusiastically took on Sir William Howe as an outpatient; John Ramsey of the History Department of the University of Alabama, who was kind enough to advise me on the French alliance; Richard Brough of the Art Department of the University of Alabama, who reproduced the map of the northern theatre of operations; Douglas Jones, Dean of the College of Arts and Sciences, who wangled a special leave of absence.

I am also indebted to the long-suffering staffs of the libraries of The University of Alabama, the University of Virginia, Washington and Lee University, Virginia Military Institute, The Chicago Historical Society, the city of New York, the New York Historical Society, and the William L. Clements Library at the University of Michigan.

The New York Historical Society, the New York Public Library, and the William L. Clements Library have generously allowed me to use quotations from manuscripts in their collections.

This work would not have been possible without the generosity of the Research Grants Committee of the University of Alabama, enabling me to take time off from my teaching duties.

For any errors of fact or aberrant conclusions I take full responsibility.

University, Alabama   JOHN S. PANCAKE

1777

The Year of the Hangman

"I left Congress on the 11th of November, 1777, that year which the Tories said, had three gallows in it, meaning the three sevens."
—John Adams

Prologue

IF GEORGE WASHINGTON AND HIS CONTEMPORARIES HAD BEEN TOLD THE American history books would have contained sections entitled: "The American Revolution: 1763 to 1789" they would have been amazed. Washington remarked on his return to his farm at the end of the Seven Years' War that "we are much rejoiced at the prospect of peace which 'tis hoped will be of long continuance." For the frame of the colonial mind had as yet conceived of no serious quarrels with the mother country, much less the notion of American independence.

Yet what Professor Lawrence Gipson has called the Great War for Empire had given England a preponderance of power which ultimately proved her undoing. France and her allies were dismayed at the drastic shift in the balance of power and anxious for an opportunity to redress it. As Benjamin Franklin noted, "Every nation in Europe wishes to see Britain humbled, having all in turn been offended by her insolence." When her American colonies revolted England's enemies welcomed the opportunity, and their aid was crucial to the success of the War of Independence.

For the Americans in 1763, there was relief that the threat of New France which had hovered over the Northern horizon for more than a century was finally gone, although they did not perhaps perceive that they thereby became less dependent on the mother country. Loyalty is rooted in mutual needs and common hopes and fears. At the beginning of the eighteenth century 200,000 colonists were strung along the Atlantic littoral from Massachusetts to the Carolinas, a thin rim of Britain's empire. Their existence was vitally dependent on support from England. By 1763 the population had exploded to two million and the colonies were not only prosperous but remarkably self-reliant.

It might be noted in passing that their self-confidence generated a myth: that they, not the redcoats, had won this war, and veterans' tales of Louisbourg and the Plains of Abraham lost nothing in the telling in the years after 1763. For such men of valor British regulars posed no serious problem when it came time to assert American rights by force of arms.

In fact, at the beginning of the French war, Americans had been extremely reluctant to aid the British army. Not a single colony came near meeting the quotas of men and supplies which the home government requested. Pleas and threats alike fell on deaf ears, for colonial assemblies controlled taxes and appropriations, including the salaries of the governors. Many a faithful servant of the crown, faced with royal displeasure 3,000 miles away or the wrath of the colonial assembly just across the street, was bludgeoned into submission by the power of the legislative purse. General Edward Braddock, on the eve of his fateful march to the forks of the Ohio, complained that Pennsylvania and Virginia "promised great matters and have done nothing, whereby instead of forwarding they have obstructed services." Only when the war government of William Pitt, driven to desperate measures, agreed to reimburse the colonies for wartime expenses, did colonial patriotism become as swollen as colonial purses. Royal officials had the uneasy feeling that one of the badly wounded casualties of the war was British authority in America.

England emerged from the war staggering under an enormous national debt, and a program of imperial retrenchment was inaugurated. George Grenville, a capable administrator but sadly lacking in imperial statesmanship, was the first of a series of ministers who attempted to set Britain's economic house in order. He began by instructing customs officers to begin enforcing the trade laws, a proposal which was not only startling but financially disastrous to crown officials who had been thriving off the bribes of colonial merchants. Under Grenville's whip they had no choice but to turn on their erstwhile benefactors and recover their former affluence by zealous— and often fraudulent—enforcement of intricate and complicated customs laws. Customs officials were entitled to a percentage of confiscated goods and cargoes, and their legal racketeering outraged colonial merchants.

Lord Grenville also began to cast up the accounts on the colonial books. He discovered that the administrative cost of the American colonies was several times as great as the revenue which they contributed. To Grenville's orderly mind this was an untidy situation and he set about to remedy it through taxation. To his credit, he asked for advice, even consulting that foremost expert in American affairs, Benjamin Franklin. The solution which Grenville hit upon was the Stamp Act of 1765 which levied a tax on all kinds of legal and commercial paper—newspapers, contracts, invoices, wills, and the like.

The reaction in America was as violent as it was unexpected. In Virginia, Patrick Henry declared that "taxation of the people by themselves . . . is the only security against burthensome taxation, the distinguishing characteristic of British freedom, . . ." and lit the fuse which exploded into colonial defiance. Protest groups called the Sons of Liberty held torchlight parades and hanged Grenville in effigy. Colonial boycotts were declared against British goods, and nine colonies sent representatives to a Stamp Act Congress in New York to address a petition to the Crown. Colonial newspapers rallied public opinion: "Taxation without representation is tyranny!"

Two things are worth noting about the Stamp Act crisis. Although there were virtually no precedents to guide them, Americans displayed a remarkable talent for revolutionary techniques of protest. Whig editors showed an immediate appreciation of newspapers as weapons of propaganda. The Sons of Liberty not only organized popular support but injected an atmosphere of enthusiasm—and, not incidentally, thoroughly terrorized the opposition. The boycotts added the reality of economic pressure to constitutional arguments of principle. Considering the slowness of communications and the diversity of colonial interests it was an amazing performance. From the passage of the Stamp Act by Parliament in March, 1765, only seven months elapsed before the Stamp Act Congress published its protest.

The second point was less apparent in both America and England. In protesting the constitutionality of the Stamp Act, the colonists were raising serious questions about the nature of the British Empire. They seemed to be assuming the existence of a sort of federal structure in which a considerable degree of self-government belonged by right to their own colonial assemblies. If Parliament lacked the most fundamental of all powers, the power to tax, what authority did it have? Perhaps it was fortunate that the colonies did not press the point in 1765. Parliament vehemently denied any limitations on its powers in the Declaratory Act of 1766, but since it was accompanied by the repeal of the Stamp Act, few Americans bothered to dispute the issue. In England the Stamp Act and its repeal were minor issues, which were quickly dismissed by members of Parliament who knew little and cared less about the American colonies. But as the controversy with the mother country grew in the years that followed, it became increasingly clear that what the colonies insisted were English rights and English liberties had acquired a distinctive brand which read "Made in America."

For example, when the Stamp Act Congress spoke of being taxed only "with their own consent, given personally or by their representatives," Englishmen were not only irritated but puzzled. A member of Parliament felt that he represented the whole empire—he certainly did not consider that he was the spokesman for the populace of the "rotten borough" from which he was elected. But Americans had developed a republican system; that is, a representative conceived of himself as the voice of the people who had elected him, and as being responsible to them.

As with the political system, so it was with other American institutions. Jefferson attacked the established church in Virginia, not because of religious intolerance, but because established religion was an anachronism which violated the rule of reason. With thousands of Baptists, Presbyterians, and Methodists peopling the Virginia back country it seemed ridiculous to maintain in law what did not exist in fact. Americans deplored the English "rotten boroughs," not because people in the colonies could not vote, but because, even with property qualifications, a substantial number of adult males could and did vote. The Stamp Act and the Townshend Acts which followed two years later they considered to be a corruption of English constitutional principles, and they insisted in all sincerity that their cause was the cause of English liberty. Theirs was an Enlightenment philosophy overlaid with the imprint of New World experience. In short, Americans were preaching what they were already practicing.

So it was that as late as 1773 few colonists were thinking in terms of American independence. Indeed, the explosive clash between soldiers and citizens in 1770 known as the Boston Massacre was followed by a period of calm which dismayed radical agitators like Sam Adams. But Lord North, the latest of a succession of ministers through whom George III attempted to rule, managed to revive the dispute. At his request Parliament passed the East India Company Act, better known as the Tea Act, which attempted to aid the great corporation by granting to it a monopoly on the sale of tea in America.

The Act itself was not onerous, but by this time the colonists were convinced that it presaged an attempt to revive Parliamentary authority. Committees of Correspondence were soon busy organizing colonial resistance. The confrontation came in Boston a few days after Christmas, 1773. The Boston Sons of Liberty boarded one of the East India Company ships and dumped its cargo of tea into the Boston harbor. The reaction of Parliament was swift and severe for George III, through Lord North, now commanded a majority in Parliament for the first time since 1763. There was no question of Parliament's belief in its authority. The port of Boston was closed until the tea was paid for; the Massachusetts assembly was prorogued and courts were authorized to issue changes of venue so that persons charged with serious crimes could be tried outside the colony; and army commanders were authorized to quarter their troops on private property (although not in private residences, as Sam Adams alleged). The authority of government was concentrated in the hands of the royal governor, General Thomas Gage, who was also commander-in-chief of the British Army in America.

Action and reaction followed in rapid succession. By the fall of 1774 half a hundred delegates from the colonies had organized the First Continental Congress in Philadelphia. They professed their loyalty to the Crown, but on terms which were hardly compatible with England's concept of the empire. John Adams framed the proposition:

> . . . The foundation of English liberty, and of all free government, is a right in the people to participate in their legislative council: and as the English colonies . . . cannot be properly represented in the British Parliament, they are entitled to a free and exclusive power of legislation in their several provincial legislatures, where their right of representation can alone be preserved, in all

cases of taxation and internal polity, subject alone to the negative of their sovereign. . . . We cheerfully consent to the operation of such Acts of the British Parliament as are . . . restrained to the regulation of our external commerce, for the purpose of securing the commercial advantages of the whole empire. . . .

Adams' proposal was essentially the principle of dominion status by which Britain later held together her far-flung empire. But such proposals were lost on the government at Whitehall. Among other things, it seemed to suggest that Americans considered themselves the equal of Britons, a notion as dangerous as it was outrageous.

Though they denied the authority of Parliament the colonists insisted that they were loyal subjects of the King. Their relationship was defined by their colonial charters, granted by authority of the Crown and consisting of a contractual relationship between the colonists and the King. This idea had its roots in the philosophy of John Locke, who had justified the Glorious Revolution on the basis of a "social contract" that existed between the rulers and the ruled. Such a contract could only exist between equals, and the logical corollary was that the people could call the ruler to account if he violated the terms of the contract. The dispute between the colonies and the mother country was thus founded in the tradition of English Enlightenment philosophy, but by no means accepted in English practice: that government is in its nature an agreement between equal contracting parties and that the rulers are accountable to the ruled.

The First Continental Congress did not stop with a petition of protest. The members adopted resolutions of nonimportation, nonexportation, and nonconsumption. They also created a Continental Association which provided for committees throughout the colonies to see that the resolutions were enforced. The Congress then adjourned, but not before its members agreed to meet again within a year to deliberate on further action which might be necessary.

The meeting of the First Continental Congress was a momentous step along the road to independence. In adopting its restrictive resolutions the Congress had enacted what amounted to legislation, and it had provided the machinery to enforce it. These were functions normally exercised by governments; and, like a government body, Congress provided for its own continuity by agreeing to meet again.

Probably Americans did not themselves appreciate the full significance of what they had done. Certainly it did not penetrate the limited vision of Parliament, the ministry, or the King. Lord North's reaction was to frame a reply to Congress' petition which was designed to hoodwink the colonists and at the same time assuage the sensibilities of Parliament. Its blatant trickery outraged some members of Parliament and deceived the Americans not at all. The ministry's bad faith is revealed in the instructions to General Gage in January, 1775, which urged him to take "a more active and determined part" in dealing with troublemakers in Massachusetts.

When the Second Continental Congress met in May it found that further steps had indeed been taken. New England militia had fought British troops at Lexington and Concord, and so began a civil war which was to last eight years.

Congress made a last appeal to the King in the summer of 1775, mostly to satisfy Whig-Loyalists, Americans who fervently supported the cause of liberty, but hoped against hope that a solution could be found which would not force them to renounce their country. The King's Proclamation confirmed their worst fears. It declared the colonists to be rebels and soon afterward Parliament ordered the interdiction of American trade. Thus the King, who had been appealed to as "the party of the first part" in the social contract, had betrayed his trust. For many Americans the problem had been reduced to its simplest terms. Either they must submit and abandon their fight for liberty, or take the only other avenue left open to them—independence. And the clarity with which they perceived the choices made many colonists aware of what they had already intuitively sensed: that somewhere along the way they had become more American than English.

ONE

The War Begins: 1775

In 1842 Captain Levi Preston, a ninety-one year old veteran of the War of Independence, was interviewed by the historian, Mellen Chamberlain. Captain Preston, it turned out, had never read Sydney or Locke, never drunk tea, nor did he recall ever having seen a stamp. But he was very explicit about why he had fought. "Young man, what we meant in going for those red-coats was this: We always had governed ourselves and we always meant to. They didn't mean we should."

The Appeal to Arms

General Thomas Gage is a familiar name to anyone who has read about the War of Independence. After all, Gage started it by sending his redcoats to Lexington and Concord on April 19, 1775. Yet Thomas Gage is a faceless shadow-man who only gave the orders which sent the soldiers on their desperate mission. He was not at the head of those men when they faced Captain John Parker's militia on the Lexington Common nor when the battered, bloody ranks staggered back to Boston, ripped apart by swarms of minute men. In the American tradition Gage is a villain, but he conjures up no remembered personality. The tall, swarthy Howes, "Sir Billy" and "Black Dick," fat-faced George III, swaggering "Gentleman Johnny" Burgoyne, savage Cornwallis who could turn cannon on his own men to win a battle—these men make pictures in the mind's eye. Gage gave his fateful orders and a few months later left America forever.

Yet Gage ought to be remembered if for no other reason than that he had a thoroughly sound appreciation of the situation of the colonies in the spring of 1775. He had served in North America for twenty years, twelve of them as commander in chief of the British army in America. He had survived frequent clashes with civilians and had displayed a resolute composure in the face of petitions, protests and as bad language as Whig editors could muster, which was bad indeed. In 1773 he had gone to England on leave and had returned in the spring of 1774 not only as commander in chief but as governor of Massachusetts. His first duty was to put into effect the Boston Port Bill, closing the city to all trade until its citizens paid for their very expensive tea party of the previous December.[1]

As tension increased in Boston and the surrounding countryside Gage reiterated to the ministry warnings which he had been sounding ever since his return. He was never hostile toward nor contemptuous of Americans (his wife was a native of Brunswick, New Jersey); but he was positive that the authority of the Crown must be firmly asserted. "If you yield to [colonial] menaces there is an End of your Sovereignty; and I shall expect they will very soon make laws for you, and take the same method to enforce them," he wrote in June, 1774. He was also convinced that an overwhelming demonstration of authority "should be effectual at the beginning. If you think ten thousand Men sufficient, send Twenty, if one Million [pounds] is thought to be enough, give two, and you will save both Blood and Treasure in the end." And finally, in December, 1774, mindful that his regulars numbered only about 4,000 men, he urged the ministry to "send me a sufficient Force to command the Country, by marching into it and sending off large detachments to secure obedience through every part of it." Instructions from the Earl of Dartmouth, Secretary of State for the Colonies, arrived in Boston on the 16th of April, 1775. They left no doubt that the ministry expected action and that Gage was free to pursue his own inclination to take a hard line. But there was no mention of twenty thousand men, or even ten.[2]

In dispatching troops to Lexington and Concord on the 18th of April Gage's ostensible purpose was to arrest some of the most notorious Whig leaders and to seize stores of arms which the militia were said to have collected. But his real purpose was undoubtedly to scotch the rebellion by a display of force, "to command the country by marching into it." Before the bloody day was over Gage had to commit one third of his entire force of which seventeen percent were casualties. The Patriots not only turned out by the thousands but pursued the troops to the very outskirts of Boston.

The story of New England farmers springing to arms and besieging the British in Boston is a well-known one.[3] (It also gave birth to the myth that the nation would always turn out enough volunteer citizen-soldiers to fight its wars. American leaders from George Washington to George Marshall knew differently.) To Gage mobs of angry New Englanders were a familiar story. But this time there was a shocking difference. Instead of venting its spleen and dispersing, this mob stayed and its members steadily increased. By early June there were between 12,000 and 15,000 men surrounding Boston and they were loosely organized into an army. It might not have been much of an army by Gage's precise British standards, but every night for six weeks sentry fires winked relentlessly from Roxbury to Chelsea. General Hugh Earl Percy, who had fought the militiamen on April 19, commented, "Whoever looks on them as an irregular mob will find himself very much mistaken."[4]

By early June the first reinforcements had arrived from England. These included parts of six regiments and brought Gage's total effective force to about 6,500 rank and file. The reinforcements also included three major generals, William Howe, Henry Clinton, and John Burgoyne whom the ministry had sent as "advisers" to Gage. Of these the senior was General Howe. He had seen previous service in the Seven Years' War and it was rumored that he might succeed Gage. This created a situation which was both frustrating and embarrassing to Gage, since he had as his junior officer the man who might be promoted in rank and possibly was his successor.

In response to instructions from the ministry and in a last attempt to avoid the cataclysmic course of events, Gage issued a proclamation declaring martial law but offering amnesty to all rebels except the ringleaders, the Adamses, John Hancock, and Joseph Warren. Whatever hopes Gage had for a reconciliation may well have been extinguished when General Burgoyne, sometime London playwright, offered his literary talents in composing the proclamation. The resulting combination of bombast and insult was a literary and diplomatic disaster, "replete with consummate impudence, the most abominable lies, and stuffed with daring expressions of tyranny," according to the *Pennsylvania Journal.*[5]

It was Burgoyne who had reacted to the idea that the British were besieged by saying, "Well, let *us* get in, and we'll soon find elbow room." After Bunker Hill he seemed to resent the fact that soldiers on both sides dubbed him "General Elbow-Room," but then Burgoyne was a slow learner on the subject of America and Americans. Henry Clinton, a man of more sober and meticulous mind than Burgoyne, also urged more elbow-room and Howe seems to have concurred. By the second week of June the coterie of generals agreed that their force was too small to break out of the encirclement, especially since there seemed to be no feasible objective beyond the American lines. But the situation did seem to call for the occupation of the two peninsulas, Charlestown and Dorchester, which jutted out into the harbor to the north and south of Boston.

At the American headquarters at Cambridge General Artemus Ward heard rumors from Boston of the British plans. A veteran of the Seven Years' War, Ward had risen from sickbed to take command of the militia after Lexington and Concord. If he appeared cautious and indecisive to some it was because he stubbornly refused to risk his fragile "army" of untrained, undisciplined troops in any madcap offensive. The line he had established from Winter Hill around to Dorchester was formidable, and his bluff, no-nonsense attitude earned him the respect, if not the adulation, of the conglomeration of officers and men who came to (and often left) the crowded camps.

On June 16 Ward finally yielded to the urgings of his subordinates and sent Colonel William Prescott to occupy Bunker Hill on the Charlestown Peninsula. When Prescott reached the ground he decided to fortify Breed's Hill, and by daylight on the 17th his men had entrenched themselves on its crest. Later in the morning the line was extended on the left to the Mystic river where Connecticut militia under Captain Thomas Knowlton hastily threw up a "breastwork" consisting of fence rails, rocks, and hay. About noon Knowlton was joined by Colonel John Stark's New Hampshire militia, bringing the total of Prescott's command to about 1,500 men.[6]

General William Howe took charge of 2,500 redcoats and by early afternoon he had crossed to the peninsula. Howe intended to make short work of this rabble of upstart farmers who were finally offering to make a stand-up fight. He sent half his force under General Hugh Pigot against the redoubt on Breed's Hill, while he himself led an attack on the rail fence defended by Knowlton and Stark.

It was still the age of picture book wars and this battle had thousands of spectators watching from the hills and housetops in Boston. Through the eddying smoke of the British bombardment the double line of redcoats could be seen moving forward, sunlight flickering on bayonets and accoutrements, "one of the greatest scenes of war that can be conceived." As Pigot's line reached the crest of Breed's Hill Prescott's men "rose up and poured in so heavy a fire upon us that the oldest officers say they never saw a sharper action." The British line staggered to a halt and then retreated.

Out of view of the spectators in Boston, beyond the curve of the hill, Howe's right wing was advancing against the rail fence. In a surprising display of discipline most of the militiamen held their fire until the British were within easy musket range. Then "an incessant stream of fire poured from the rebel lines. It seemed a continued sheet of fire. . . . Our light Infantry were served up in companies against the grass fence and without being able to penetrate. . . . Most of the Grenadiers and Light Infantry at the moment of presenting themselves lost three-fourths, and many nine-tenths, of their men. Some had only eight and nine men a company left, some only three, four and five." The red line recoiled, "fell into disorder" and retreated.

It was a mind blowing experience for William Howe—"*a moment that I never felt before.*" But he did not waver from his purpose. He pulled his battered lines together and launched a second attack. Again the troops met a shattering fire which "put the regulars to flight who once more retreated in precipitation."

But Prescott, Knowlton, Stark and the militiamen were done. The third assault, reinforced by 400 men under Clinton, found many of the Americans out of ammunition, although a handful met the British bayonet charge with clubbed muskets. Even in retreat the militia "continued a running fight from one fence, or wall, to another," noted Lord Rawdon of the Grenadiers.[7]

General Burgoyne watched the battle from Boston, and said "the day ended with glory," and Rawdon reported that "we have . . . given the rebels a signal defeat." But to William Howe it was "what I call this unhappy day. . . . The success was too dearly bought." Howe was an eighteenth century general whose doctrine was to fight his regulars "under circumstances the least hazardous to the royal army; for even a victory attended by a heavy loss of men

on our part, would have given a fateful check to the progress of the war. . . ."
The price Howe paid at Bunker Hill was devastating. Of something more
than 2,500 men engaged 1,050 had been killed and wounded including 92
officers. This was forty-two percent of his force, a prohibitive loss in any era
of warfare. Howe confessed that "when I look to the consequences of it . . . I
do it with horror." A week after Bunker Hill the British army could muster
only 3,400 rank and file, present and fit for duty.

For Thomas Gage it was the final blow to his American career. Lord George
Germain, soon to be appointed Secretary of State for the Colonies, had already
expressed the opinion that "General Gage . . . finds himself in a situation of
too great importance for his talents." After the news of Bunker Hill orders
were issued for his recall and he returned to England in October, although he
was not formally relieved of his command until the spring of 1776. Yet his
report to Lord North contained the clearest perception of the significance of
this first full-dress battle of the war. Gage's grammar was bad and his blunt
language probably either offended or amused his superiors. But Gage knew
Americans and he understood the enormity of the crisis. "These people show
a spirit and a conduct against us they never showed against the French, and
every body has judged of them from their former appearance and behavior
when joyned with the King's forces in the last war; which has led into great
mistakes.

"They are now spirited up by a rage and enthousiasm as great as ever people were possessed of, and you must proceed in earnest or give the business
up. . . . I have before wrote your Lordship of my opinion that a very large
army must at length be employed to reduce these people. . . . or else to avoid
a land war and make use of your fleet. I don't find one province in appearance
better disposed than another. . . ."[8]

THE BIRTH OF THE AMERICAN ARMY

The Second Continental Congress convened on May 10, 1775, three weeks
after Lexington and Concord and a little less than six weeks before the battle
of Bunker Hill. Its members were preoccupied with many problems and complexities, not the least of which was that they were in a state of armed rebellion against the Crown while some of its most influential members were convinced that reconciliation could still be achieved. Whig-Loyalists like John
Dickinson, James Duane, and Robert Morris could not easily bring themselves to renounce their loyalty to Britain.[9] The radicals, that is, those who
were beginning to think of independence, were inclined to move slowly lest
they alienate these conservative supporters. It must be remembered that the
Congress was an illegal body and the Whig movement which sanctioned it
represented a minority of the American people. To propose such a portentous
issue as independence its advocates had to be sure, not just of a majority vote,
but of virtual unanimity in Congress. It was not until a year had passed that

Jefferson, the Adamses and other radicals were to feel confident enough to propose separation from England.

Meantime, there was the war. Congress, which had originally assembled for the purpose of confronting the home government with an organized protest, found itself willy-nilly forced to govern. It is a commentary on the rising spirit of American nationalism that the members never considered leaving the conduct of the war to the individual colonies. John Jay went so far as to advocate that the "Union depends much upon the breaking down of the provincial Conventions."[10]

From the beginning the Massachusetts assembly and the Committee of Safety assumed that Congress would take over the responsibility for the army, and on May 16 a petition was dispatched to Philadelphia urging "to your consideration the propriety of your taking the regulation and general direction of it, that the operations of it may more effectually answer the purpose designed for it." There is no record of formal action by Congress, but on June 17 James Duane noted that "Congress have agreed to raise, at the Continental expense, a body of fifteen thousand men," and the next day John Hancock referred to a Congressional appropriation for "a Continental Army."[11]

Having adopted an army Congress next set about selecting its commander. In later years John Adams remarked somewhat petulantly, that when the history of the American Revolution was written, "The essence of the whole will be that *Dr. Franklins electrical rod smote the Earth and out sprang General Washington.*" If Adams was then perturbed that his own career would be lost in the giant shadow of the father of his country he might reflect that he had only himself to blame, for it was he who proposed that Washington command the new army. In 1775 Adams was not so much concerned about creating America's first authentic hero as he was with finding a commander in chief who was both capable and politically acceptable. No one was more aware than Adams that colonial unity was a fragile thing, and the new general and his army would be the principal instrument through which this unity would be forged and strengthened. He, more than any one else, would personify the American cause.

So Adams' keen political eye singled out Washington. It would be a Southerner and a Virginian who would command an army of New Englanders. Washington's patriotism was unquestioned, but he was no radical. He was a planter and an aristocrat, but his massive frame and rugged features suggested a man of great physical power and endurance. He was a superb horseman and he had "an easy, soldier like air and gesture." It may well be that the big Virginian's most important asset was that he *looked* like a commander in chief.

Washington's military experience was limited. He had served four years in the French and Indian War, much of it with the British commanders, Braddock, Forbes, and Bouquet. He was therefore well acquainted with army routine and administration. He had also served for two years as commander of the Virginia militia guarding a frontier which stretched three hundred and fifty miles from Fort Cumberland in Maryland to Fort Bedford in southwest Virginia. Undoubtedly Washington regarded this as the most thankless and unrewarding duty of his early career, but it must have taught him invaluable lessons. Here he learned that while legislatures might vote troops for duty, any resemblance between the number authorized and the number that appeared in the field was usually coincidental. He experienced the frustration of relying on untrained militia who might flee in panic at the mere rumor of the approach of the enemy. He learned that neither militia nor legislators could be ordered about, but must be handled, each in their own fashion, with delicate care. Considering the choices which confronted Congress it had chosen a man who was somewhat limited in military qualifications, but who was especially attractive politically and personally. Whether he could measure up to the enormous task remained to be seen. Washington himself declared "with the utmost sincerity, I do not think myself equal to the Command I am honored with."[12]

Having chosen the commander in chief Congress then selected five major generals and eight brigadiers. Of these Nathanael Greene was to prove indispensable. Four more could be said to have rendered valuable services and two died before their fine promise could be realized. Israel Putnam never achieved the success expected of this most famous veteran of the French and Indian War, and four others were clearly incompetent. If one recalls the dubious quality of the generals at the outset of most of the wars of the United States, the conclusion is that the men at Philadelphia did very well. If nothing else, they used unerring judgement in selecting the commander who would lead the army to victory.

Washington left the capital on June 23, 1775, and nine days later he arrived at army headquarters in Cambridge. There he found "a mixed multitude of people . . . under very little order or government." He was informed that there were 20,000 men on the rolls, but when he asked for a return of those present and fit for duty (a process which took eight days) the number had shrunk to 13,743.

For the next six months Washington struggled to create an army out of the chaos around Cambridge. "I dare say the men would fight very well (if properly officered) although they are an exceeding dirty and nasty people," he noted soon after his arrival. The general himself soon earned the respect, if not the affection, of the army. It discovered that the commander in chief was a severe disciplinarian and a hard task master. "The strictest government is taking place and great distinction is made between officers and soldiers. Everyone is made to know his place and keep it. . . ."[13]

Autumn brought the first crisis, but not from the threat of the British in Boston. Most of the American soldiers had agreed to serve for eight months, or until approximately the end of the year. Washington feared that a "Dissolution . . . of the present Army will take place unless some early Provision is made against such an Event." The enlistments of the Connecticut regiments were due to expire on December 10 and most of the troops prepared to go home. The officers made strenuous efforts to reenlist the men for an additional year but by the end of November Washington was so discouraged that "I should not be at all surprised at any disaster that might happen." In desperation he appealed to Massachusetts and New Hampshire for temporary replacements. The response was enormously gratifying. Into the lines on December 11 marched the first regiments of 5,000 militia—boiling mad at being called from their firesides in the dead of winter. As the Connecticut troops marched off "through the lines they were so horribly hissed, groaned at, and pelted that I believe they wished their aunts, grandmothers, and even sweethearts, to whom . . . they were so much attached, at the devil's own place." The pace of reenlistments quickened and Washington marvelled at having had "one army disbanded and another to raise within the same distance of a reenforced enemy." By January, 1776, the army numbered about 15,000 men of whom one third were militia.[14]

General Howe replaced Gage in October but made no move to leave the security of Boston. Some reinforcements had arrived from England but his army still counted less than 10,000 men present and fit for duty. As winter advanced life in the besieged city deteriorated. Supplies ran short and "Death has so long stalked among us that he is become less terrible . . . than he once was." Soldiers plundered to such an extent that Howe ordered "the provost to go his rounds attended by the executioner with orders to hang upon the spot the first man he shall detect. . . ."

By the New Year Washington was becoming impatient. He admitted that "to have the eyes of the whole continent fixed, with anxious expectation of hearing some great event, and to be restrained . . . is not very pleasing." His hopes for an offensive were emboldened by the arrival of a train of artillery.[15]

The genius behind this achievement was a twenty-five year old artillery colonel named Henry Knox, who had been ordered to bring in the guns from Ticonderoga, which had fallen to the Americans in May. Possessed of a booming voice, a huge girth, and a vast amount of energy, Knox contrived to transport the guns across winter ice and snow on forty-two sleds drawn by eighty yoke of oxen. Although a mild winter provided less freezing weather than he would have liked, by early January Knox had bulldozed his way across Lake Champlain and down the Hudson to Albany. The distance from Albany to Boston is today traversed by 165 miles of the Massachusetts Turnpike. In 1776 Knox delivered fifty-two cannon and fourteen mortars to the artillery park in Cambridge in eighteen days.[16]

Washington now decided to fortify Dorchester Heights and threaten Howe's position in Boston. The American movement was made under cover of darkness on March 4. If the little redoubt on Breed's Hill a year earlier had surprised the British, the sight of the elaborate works on Dorchester Heights on the morning of March 5 left them dumfounded. Howe is said to have exclaimed, "Good God! Those fellows have done more work than I could have made my army do in three months."

On March 7 Howe announced that he intended to evacuate the city, and ten days later, accompanied by over 1,000 Loyalists, he embarked his troops for Halifax. The British made no move to destroy the city and the American guns were silent. As Washington's troops approached cautiously toward the town they saw that the lines were apparently manned by British sentries. Closer inspection revealed that they were dummies, and on one of them was a placard which read, "Welcome, Brother Jonathan."[17]

So a year after the war began the British army had been driven from American soil. It was true that the ministry had agreed with Howe that Boston should be abandoned. But Washington had forced the enemy to leave at a time of his choosing, not theirs, and his threatening guns had forestalled any inclination on the part of the redcoats to sack the town. The evacuation of Boston was a tremendous boost to American morale.

In the process the new commander in chief had showed himself fully capable of his responsibilities. If his actions had not been brilliant, the fact that he had methodically carried out his task, overcome serious obstacles and made no mistakes, constituted a kind of brilliance. Most of all he had convinced both Congress and the army that he was to be trusted.

TWO

The American Secretary

ENGLAND'S MILITARY SYSTEM WAS ENTIRELY CONSISTENT WITH EIGHTEENTH century rationalism. Because weapons systems were not very destructive and because economic considerations limited the size of armies, the eighteenth century accepted war as a necessary element in the international order of things. Eighteenth century statesmen tacitly admitted that behind the moral poses of diplomacy and the elaborate language of treaties there lay the threat of brute force as the ultimate sanction of international law. The revolution which began in America in 1775 caught the British government off guard, not only in the inadequacies of its military establishment but in the narrowness of its imperial vision.

GERMAIN AND THE STRATEGY OF RECONQUEST

He was the son of a peer of the realm and at the age of four he was entitled to be called Lord George Sackville. His father was briefly lord lieutenant of Ireland and the son was a lieutenant colonel of cavalry by the time he was thirty-four. A year later in 1741 he was elected member of Parliament and so became one of those soldier-politicians who were familiar figures in late eighteenth century England. His military career in the War of Austrian Succession was outstanding and on the eve of the Seven Years' War he was promoted to major general.

In 1758 Sackville was assigned as second in command under the Duke of Marlborough in the British expedition sent to the continent in support of the Prussian army, and on Marlborough's death he became the British commander. At the battle of Minden in 1759 he was accused by the Prussian commander in chief, Prince Ferdinand, of being dilatory in obeying an order to attack. Sackville's pride was stung and he returned to England demanding a court martial which would justify his conduct. It is probable that if he had been less insistent the government would have been happy to drop the whole matter, since at one point Sackville was asked to specify the grounds on which he wished to be charged. But he conceived that his honor had been impugned and he was finally accused of disobedience of orders. A more astute politician would have foreseen that the scales of justice were too heavily weighted by politics, for now the affair became a political football between contending factions headed by the King and William Pitt on the one side and the young prince who was to become George III on the other. But Sackville's stubborn— even arrogant—belief in the justice of his cause led him to persist. He was convicted and the vindictive old monarch, George II, ordered the verdict posted in every regiment of the army, and had Sackville's name struck from the list of Privy Councillors.

Eighteenth century British politics was constituted not only of a vast amount of corruption but of bitter feuds in which elegant language furnished only a thin veneer for slashing insults and outrageous personal attacks both in and out of Parliament. Although Sackville had been convicted only of disobedience to orders in a trial which was admittedly shot through with political prejudice, he found himself the target of slurs and insults which questioned both his courage and his honor. This must have been insufferable for a man whose overbearing manner gave evidence of deep-rooted pride. In the five years of political banishment which followed the court martial his self-control and composure were severely tested.

George II died in 1760 and young George III succeeded to the throne. In the confusion of factions, cliques and blocs which had shattered England's traditional two-party system the young King made slow headway. He recognized that Sackville had been a casualty of political warfare, but even the King had to move warily in rehabilitating the man who was already plagued by the "Ghost of Minden." In 1765 during the debates surrounding the Stamp Act Sackville took a strong stand in Commons in support of the Declaratory Act which asserted Parliamentary supremacy over the colonies. At about this time he received a minor appointment as vice-treasurer of Ireland and had his name restored to the Privy Councillors' list. These were insignificant marks of recognition, to be sure, but they brought an end to his political exile.[1]

It was not until 1770 that George III was able to stabilize his executive control. The head of his ministry was Lord North, an amiable, conservative man who handled the political and financial affairs of the Crown. He was likeable and level-headed, though he often appeared indolent and inattentive during Parliamentary debates. But from this somnolent air of studied indifference his lordship could deliver a sudden thrust which was as acute as it was unexpected; or the opposition might find its argument punctured by a barb of sarcasm and wit which left the House roaring with laughter. By 1775 the North ministry had achieved a degree of durability and permanence. Yet despite his shrewdness, and his skill at picking his way through the political swamps and jungles, North was deficient in both originality of thought and resolution of purpose.

When the colonial calm in America was broken by the dispute over the Tea Act Lord North welcomed the support of Sackville (who had taken his aunt's family name of Germain as a condition of inheriting her fortune in 1770). The passage of the Intolerable Acts found him supporting North along the same lines that he had taken in 1766. When the question of the repeal of the Intolerable Acts was brought before the House early in 1775 Germain made it clear that conciliation must be on the ministry's terms. He would listen to American petitions, he said, but not to American demands for rights which they did not possess. By the time the news of Lexington and Concord reached London in the summer of 1775 Germain had established himself as one of the ablest spokesmen for the ministry on the American question. He was frequently consulted by the members of the cabinet, especially by William Eden, under-secretary for the Southern Department. Germain's advice was detailed and emphatic. Gage must be recalled and military and naval forces must be concentrated immediately. "As there is not common sense in protracting a war of this sort, I should be for exerting the utmost force of this Kingdom to finish this rebellion in one campaign." He also recommended that Howe replace Gage and that New York be occupied as the center for British naval and military operations.[2]

The sentiments expressed by Germain fully accorded with the policy which had been developing for more than a year. When the meeting of the First Continental Congress in September, 1774, gave clear evidence that the colonies intended to resist the Intolerable Acts, George III wrote Lord North that since "the New England governments are in a state of rebellion, blows must decide whether they are to be subjects of this country or independent." With the King striking the key note the subsequent line of ministerial policy was to subdue the rebellion in the colonies by military force, and only then to consider what changes in colonial policy might be advisable.

An important factor in the development of this policy was a serious misunderstanding of the strength of the Loyalists. The government acted on the assumption that the trouble in America was the work of a small number of dissident radicals who had no considerable popular support, and who were confined largely to New England. This was an understandable miscalculation and was not a serious misreading of intelligence from America. What was much more serious was the assumption that the overwhelming majority of Americans would actively respond in the crisis and vigorously support the home government in its suppression of the rebels. The King and his ministers failed to recognize that in the beginning many Americans were apathetic to both sides, and that the Whigs had been unusually effective in scotching the organization of Loyalist support.

Lord Dartmouth, soon to be supplanted by Germain as the American Secretary, was probably not aware of the perceptiveness of his admonition to William Howe when the latter was informed of plans for a military expedition to South Carolina in the fall of 1775:

> In truth the whole success of the measure His Majesty had adopted depends so much upon a considerable number of the inhabitants taking up arms in support

of government, that nothing that can have a tendency to promote it ought to be omitted: I hope we are not deceived in the assurances that have been given, for if we are, and there should be no appearance of a disposition in the inhabitants of the southern colonies to join the King's Army, I fear little more will be effected. . . .[3]

Dartmouth had already expressed his desire to be relieved as Secretary for the American Colonies and it is probable that North had decided to elevate Germain to the post by the end of the summer of 1775. As usual this involved complicated arrangements at which Lord North excelled. Dartmouth must be placated by suitable rewards, both pecuniary and honorary. Germain must be given enough authority to execute policy without offending the Secretaries of the Northern and Southern Departments who showed signs of resenting an upstart commoner who headed a newly created (1769) department. But Germain was finally installed less than a month after Parliament convened in the fall of 1775.

At the time of his appointment Lord George was fifty-nine years old. He was a tall, imposing figure of a man with a strong face dominated by keen blue eyes. He had a rather haughty manner which many found formidable and even forbidding. His subordinates knew him as a driving, insistent task-master who could still be considerate and courteous. He took little part in the social life of London, partly because he put in long hours in the American Department and partly because he had few friends. In fact, it was this lack of influential intimates or strong family connection that made his position a difficult one. His views on American colonial policy were popular, but Lord George was not. He had no difficulty finding support both in the ministry and in Commons, but there was no very wide margin for error. He must succeed or convey the appearance of success if he were to remain in power.

On October 26, 1775, less than a month before Germain took office, Parliament assembled to hear the King's decision to seek a military solution to the American rebellion. It is doubtful if George III or his ministers were aware of its full implications. The decision was the culmination of a series of actions, or perhaps reactions, that had occurred over the past year. Gage had sent his troops to Lexington and Concord in response to instructions from the ministry urging "a more active and determined part." By the summer of 1775 George III had issued a proclamation of rebellion in which he directed "all our officers, as well civil as military . . . to use their utmost endeavors to with stand and suppress such rebellions."

Now, in October, the King asserted that the colonies had begun the war "for the purpose of establishing an independent empire," and announced his intention to "put a speedy end to these disorders by the most decisive exertions." Alexander Wedderburn, a member of the cabinet, led the support of the King's policy in the House of Commons. "Sir, we have been too long deaf; . . . faction must be curbed, must be subdued and crushed; Our thunders must go forth; America must be conquered." The Opposition protested the use of force to no avail. Young Charles James Fox thought that Lord North was "the blundering pilot . . . [who] had brought the nation into its present condition." And the rabble rouser, John Wilkes, now Lord Mayor of London viewed the war as "fatal and ruinous to our country. . . . An human mind must contemplate with agony the dreadful calamities and convulsions which are the consequence of every civil war, and especially a civil war of this magnitude and extent." With prophetic insight Sergeant Adair insisted that the policies advocated by the ministry, whether "they are followed by defeat or success, . . . will, almost with equal certainty destroy the power, the glory, the happiness of this once great and flourishing empire. It is my opinion that we cannot conquer America; I have no doubt that we cannot acquire or maintain a beneficial sovereignty over her by violence and force." But the majority was unimpressed and regarded the idea of serious American resistance as ridiculous. When the debate was over the House voted 176 to 72 to support the ministry's war policy.[4]

King, Lords, Commons, generals and ministers all concurred in the decision to subdue the rebellion by force and only then to work out a policy of conciliation. It would be unjust to say that the decision was heedless, that George III and his ministers blundered mindlessly into disaster. It is true that there was little understanding of the depth of American resistance and of the quickening spirit of colonial unity. It is perhaps ironic that part of the failure to appreciate the rise of American nationalism was the fact that England's own national pride was outraged by the audacity of colonial resistance. The idea that an illegal Congress would deny the supremacy of Parliament was as obnoxious as the notion that an American "rag, tag and bobtail" should defy British regulars.

Moreover, Britain and its king were not prepared for what Professor Robert Palmer has called The Age of Democratic Revolution. This was the first colonial war of independence in modern history and the first rebellion which had a popular base. The political and military minds of the late eighteenth century were conditioned by the Age of Limited Warfare in which armies were finely tooled instruments of national policy. Marlborough and Frederick the Great did not allow the glories of military victory to obscure diplomatic objectives. Wars were concluded, not with the conquest and ruin of nations, but at the point where one nation had had its military and economic strength strained to the extent that it would agree to concessions. A treaty might demand from the vanquished a piece of territory, a trade concession, or even a change of dynasties, but nations were rarely required to give up their national existence. The Treaty of Paris of 1763 which ended what Professor Lawrence Gipson called the Great War for Empire was the result of a delicate negotiation in which demands on France were pushed to the farthest tolerable limit — but no farther. Britain's own resources had been stretched to the point where the national debt was almost insupportable. To provoke France into a renewal of the conflict was unthinkable.

Yet George III and his ministers saw no correlation between the diplomacy of limited warfare and the American rebellion. In demanding that the Americans submit to Parliamentary authority and, after July, 1776, to renounce independence, England was committing herself to the kind of war to which eighteenth century statesmen were not accustomed, a war of conquest which could be ended only by destruction of the enemy. As the king had earlier noted, "The dye is now cast, the colonies must either submit or triumph."

THE GREAT TROOP LIFT

"There was at once an end to all circumlocutory reports and inefficient forms, that had only impeded business, and substituted ambiguity for precision; there was. . . . no trash in his mind." So a minor official described Lord Germain's assumption of the office of American Secretary. The task that faced him was formidable. If the ministry was to realize its hope for a swift and decisive suppression of the rebellion the first step was the transportation of an expeditionary force to America. This of itself posed monumental logistical and administrative problems. The governmental system through which the war effort must be executed was shot through with antiquated bureaucratic procedures, and conflicts which were rooted not only in politics but in petty personal jealousies, family rivalries, and the greedy quest for sinecures and patronage.

To act with efficiency and dispatch in such circumstances would tax the energies and even the courage of the stoutest leader. Policy was shaped in the Cabinet whose members were constitutionally spokesmen for the King. In reality the King took the initiative only in matters of broadest policy and then only if he could be sure that his policies would be supported in Parliament. As the direction and execution of policy evolved from the Cabinet the King's role became one of advice and suggestion, although such suggestions were rarely ignored. For example, the plan for Burgoyne's expedition of 1777 was given in initial form by Germain in consultation with, and approval of the Cabinet. It was then laid before the King who suggested certain alterations or attached certain conditions. These were incorporated into the final plan and the American Secretary then became responsible for its execution.

In carrying out war plans Germain had to deal with several executive departments. The most important—and the most amorphous—was the army. The King, as Captain-General, was the head of the army and George III, like all Hanoverians, took great pride in his knowledge of military matters. He was familiar with every regiment in the army, its reputation and that of its commander, and he preferred to control the army directly. He was assisted by a secretary at war but this minor official was responsible only for administrative details and finance. Not until 1778 was a military man, Lord Jeffery Amherst, named commander in chief. For all practical purposes the operational control of the army was exercised by the American Secretary, and he was also responsible for its manpower requirements and the deployment of forces. Since the largest military unit was the regiment, training was left almost entirely to the regimental commanders.

The navy was a far different matter. The First Lord of the Admiralty, the Earl of Sandwich, was a powerful and independent figure and the Lords Commissioners of the Admiralty Board were professional officers who also had a great deal of political influence. The Admiralty exercised control over a fleet of several hundred vessels and a vast administrative and logistical machinery that included shipyards, storehouses, naval bases scattered all over the world, a vast purchasing system, and a recruiting service. Its control of operations was such that no military strategy could be carried out without the First Lord's advice and consent.

Supply and transport were even more complex. The navy had its own Victualling Board through which it secured supplies and hired ships to carry them. Army supplies were procured by the Treasury which also hired ships for their transportation. Troop transports were hired by the Navy Board. Artillery and ordnance for both services as well as army engineers were furnished and transported by the Board of Ordnance which was completely independent of both the army and the navy. Germain had also to keep in mind the military and naval requirements of the Northern and Southern Departments. The government was aware from the beginning of the American rebellion that there was the threat of French intervention. The Secretary of the Northern Department, whose responsibility included Europe and the North Atlantic, had to be constantly concerned about the security of the Channel and the threat of a sudden descent by the French upon the coast of England.[5]

In such a situation the need for energetic and unifying leadership was essential. Lord North could handle the complexities of patronage and soothe the frictions of political rivalries, even manage the defense of the ministry in Parliament, but he could not provide resolution and cohesive administration. The King could bring the considerable weight of his prestige to bear, could lend his stubborn determination to the support of his ministers, but he could not exercise the kind of sweeping powers that absolute monarchs had wielded in the past. The very fact that he was king made it necessary for him to proceed with caution lest he arouse the ancient Whig animosities against arbitrary royal power. If the administrative maze was to be penetrated, if the ponderous machinery of government were to generate energy, the American Secretary must provide the driving force.

The first task confronting Germain was manpower. It was obvious that requirements were far in excess of what the King and his ministers had imagined when the crisis in America first developed. General Gage may have been thought facetious when he suggested before Bunker Hill, "If you think ten thousand men sufficient, send Twenty . . ." but by the fall of 1775 Howe was requesting 11,000 reinforcements to supplement the 9,000 men he already had in Boston. Germain planned not only to meet this request but to send an additional 10,000 men to Canada. By the beginning of 1776 it was known that American forces had successfully invaded Canada and were besieging Quebec. Germain proposed not only to lift the siege but to send Governor-General Carleton enough troops to enable him to take the offensive.

At first glance such numbers seemed out of the question. The total strength of the British army in 1775 was less than 50,000 men. Lord Barrington, the Secretary at War, held out a gloomy prospect for recruiting and his pessimism was confirmed by reports of recruiting officers. "Never did the recruiting parties meet with such ill success in every part of this Kingdom as at present, so invincible is the dislike of all ranks of people to the American service. . . ." The government had hoped to hire large numbers of troops from Russia but Catherine II rebuffed the British in the summer of 1775. Germain then turned to the German states of central Europe for help. By March, 1776, he had concluded agreements for 4,636 men from Brunswick, 12,000 from Hesse-Cassel, and 668 from Hesse-Hanau, a total of 17,304. Of these 5,000, mostly Brunswick troops, were sent to Canada and the remainder to General Howe in New York. From England Germain allocated nine British regiments and McLean's Highland Corps, about 5,000 men, to Carleton. Howe was to have a detachment of the Guards and a Highland corps, which, together with the Germans and the force which he had at Halifax, would bring his total strength to more than 25,000 men.

The assembling of troops was only the beginning of the task; transports and escorting warships must be organized to make the voyage across 3,000 miles of ocean. In the early part of 1776 Germain discovered that not only was the campaigning of armies seasonal but so was the Atlantic crossing. The governors of North and South Carolina had reported that large numbers of southern Loyalists were prepared to rise against the Whigs and needed only to be supported by regulars to put down the rebellion in the South. Germain had an expedition of 2,500 men ready on December 1, 1775—except for the Ordnance Department which did not have its store ships ready until the middle of the month. Then a northeast wind locked the ships in the Thames estuary for two weeks. Not until the first of the year was Sir Peter Parker able to collect his ships at Spithead. He then sailed for Cork to pick up the Irish regiments where another five weeks were lost. The convoy finally put to sea in the middle of February, only to be scattered by a North Atlantic gale. The ships were painstakingly reassembled and again set out for their rendezvous off the coast of North Carolina. During the crossing the fleet was again scattered and it was not until May that the expedition reached Cape Fear, too late to support the Loyalists who had been defeated at Moore's Creek Bridge. General Clinton, commanding the expedition, was persuaded by the naval commander, Sir Peter Parker, to lead an abortive attempt against Charleston, and it was not until the middle of July that the expedition finally reached New York, with nothing to show as to results.

One of the most disillusioning of Germain's discoveries was the fact that almost all of the supplies for the army must come from England. These included not only arms, uniforms, tents (with pegs and poles), axes, kettles, and all the myriad items of housekeeping equipment, but also food and forage. The fact that the army was largely confined to coastal bases meant that only a limited amount of food could be foraged from the countryside or purchased from Americans. In 1776 alone one hundred and five ships carried to New York 912 tons of beef, 3,500 tons of pork, 4,900 tons of bread, 800 tons of oatmeal and rice, and 390 tons of butter. At least that was the amount the government contracted for. Not only was there enormous wastage but contractors were notoriously careless about packaging and storage of supplies. A combination of venal government inspectors, profiteering contractors, and the long sea voyage made serious inroads on the quantity and quality of foodstuffs. ". . . I have had the mortification to see Butter taken out of Firkins and Stones etc., put in lieu to compleat the weight," wrote a commissary general in Canada. A soldier noted, "The pork seemed to be about four or five years old. It was streaked with black toward the outside and was yellow farther in, with a little white in the middle. The salt beef was in the same condition. The ship biscuit was so hard they sometimes broke it up with a cannonball, and the story ran that it had been taken from the French in the Seven Years' War. . . ."

To organize and implement the complex elements of this troop lift required an enormous amount of administrative skill and sheer energy from Lord George Germain. Ordnance, Admiralty, and Treasury had to be simultaneously coaxed and bullied to furnish ships for ammunition and guns, troops and supplies. The Highlanders must be embarked on the Clyde, the Germans at North Sea ports on the Continent, the Guards at Spithead, the Irish regiments at Cork. Howe had requested landing craft, Carleton needed prefabricated ships for Lake Champlain, wagons must be built for hauling ordnance. Embarkation orders to regimental commanders had to be coordinated with orders to naval escort commanders; sailing instructions issued to transport captains; camp equipment for twenty-nine battalions must arrive at its destination at the same time as the regiments. Admiral Palliser, who bore the burden of the work of the Admiralty, began to sense the enormity of the task.

> It seems the demands from the small army now in America are so great as to be thought impossible to furnish. The waggons and draft cattle [horses] is prodigious. If this is the case, what will it be when we have another army there above 20,000 men, if they can't make good their quarters, and command carriages and cattle, and subsist and defend themselves without the aid and defence of the fleet, who, whilst so employed can perform no other service? I think some people begin to be astonished and staggered at the unexpected difficulties we are in.[6]

It was shortly after this that poor Palliser discovered that another 10,000 troops were destined for Canada. Yet it should be noted that despite the unprecedented task required of it the Admiralty met the prodigious demands of the American Secretary.

Germain's tireless efforts, his air of certainty and optimism, infused the ministry and its bureaus and boards with an energy and vitality that had not been known since the days of William Pitt. Confident that one bold stroke would bring an end to the revolt in America and finally establish his own reputation, Germain prepared to send overseas the greatest trooplift in modern history until the twentieth century.

News from Canada revealed that American forces had driven all the way to Quebec where they were besieging the slender forces under Governor-General Carleton. Relief for the northern provinces was therefore given top priority and early in March eight British regiments and 2,000 Brunswickers sailed for the St. Lawrence. In just two months, an amazingly short time for a westward crossing, the vanguard of this force crashed through the melting ice of the spring thaw and delivered reinforcements to Quebec. Accompanying the force was General John Burgoyne who was to direct the field operations of the troops under Carleton's command.

Early in May the first contingents of troops for General Howe left England: 3,500 Highlanders, 1,000 of the Guards, and 8,200 Hessians. The shortage of transports delayed the departure of 4,000 more Hessians until July. Thus it would be well into the summer before Howe's force would be assembled and organized for the campaign. But the General was nevertheless greatly impressed "at the decisive and masterly strokes for carrying such extensive plans into immediate execution as has been effected since your Lordship has assumed the conduct of the war."[7]

THE HOWE BROTHERS

By the time Germain came into office in the fall of 1775 William Howe had already been picked for the American command. In 1775 he was forty-six years old and he had spent twenty-eight of those years in the army. He was just under six feet tall with heavy, swarthy features; not a handsome man, but genial and pleasant, well liked by his officers and respected by his men. He had had an outstanding career, most notably as colonel of the 58th Regiment under Wolfe during the Seven Years' War. He had fought with distinction at Louisbourg in 1759, and had led the "forlorn hope" up the heights to the Plains of Abraham outside Quebec, enabling Wolfe to achieve his great victory.

He became a member of Parliament after the war while continuing on active service with the army. His political career was not notable and it was said that the first speech that he ever made in Parliament was in 1778 when he defended the conduct of his campaign in America. He was promoted to major general in 1772 and shortly afterward he was placed in charge of training light infantry. These were lightly equipped, highly mobile troops who could act as regimental scouts and skirmishers, and maneuver in open or extended formation. Howe had just completed this assignment when the fighting began in America.

He was obviously not a man of strong political convictions. He told his Nottingham constituents that he opposed the ministerial policy of coercion, saying he would resign his commission if asked to serve in America. But when he realized that the army was to be employed on a large scale he privately notified Lord North that he was available for assignment. This was welcome news because many senior officers, including Lord Jeffery Amherst, had declined service in the colonies. The fact that much of Howe's service had been in America and that he was an expert in light infantry tactics made him the logical choice for the command. Germain had indicated his approval even before he took office, noting that "Nobody understands that discipline [light infantry] so well as General Howe who had the command of light troops, and who will . . . teach the present army to be as formidable as that he formerly acted with." Germain was aware of Howe's record on conciliation but probably did not consider the general as having a great deal of political weight. Or perhaps he recognized that Howe's announced views had behind them very little conviction.[8]

Lord Richard Howe, William's older brother, posed an altogether different problem. The Howes had powerful family connections and the oldest brother George Augustus Viscount Howe had died a hero's death at Ticonderoga in 1758. George Howe was one of the few British officers who did not despise colonial militia and at his death he became an American hero. The Massachusetts assembly voted two hundred and fifty pounds for a statue to his memory which stands in Westminster Abbey. Whether the younger brothers' sympathy dated from these events or not, Richard, now Viscount Howe, had on several occasions spoken in Parliament in favor of conciliation.

He was three years older than William and his swarthy, craggy features gave him a rough-hewn appearance that befitted a man who had spent thirty-five years in the Navy. He had had an excellent record in the Seven Years' War, establishing a reputation of unquestioned personal courage and as a commander who took care of his men. "Give us Black Dick and we fear nothing," was said to be the toast of the sailors, a recognition of their respect for his skill as a fighter and their regard for him as a captain. By 1775 he had been promoted to admiral, held the sinecure of treasurer of the navy, and had served on the Board of Admiralty.

Richard Howe carried considerably more political weight than his brother. He was an active member of Parliament, especially where naval affairs were concerned, and he was accorded the deference due the head of a family with powerful connections. He regarded the rebellion in America as a tragedy; he believed that a solution could be found and that he himself might be the instrument through which reconciliation could be achieved.

Here he found a sympathetic supporter in Lord North, who was determined to create a peace commission if for no other reason than to placate the opposition. Yet North also shrank from the idea of a long and bloody conflict which would leave Englishmen and Americans angry and embittered. The hard-line policy advocated by Germain and the King, and Parliament's insistence that the colonies acknowledge its supremacy as a precondition for settling the imperial relationship did not bode well for colonies contented and useful to the empire.

If Lord Howe was to achieve his purpose he must first secure a position of power. And to do this he must mask his conciliatory attitude from Germain and George III. His ambition was aided by the fact that the King had as much difficulty in finding candidates for the naval command as he had had in supplanting Gage.

George III had an almost unlimited constitutional power to wage war, but the workaday world of English administration and politics was a maze of complexities. There is an aprocryphal story that early in his reign the King's mother had admonished him, "George, *be king.*" The son took the admonition seriously, but he was wise enough to realize that, in the political realities of eighteenth century England, he must contrive to rule by building a combination of political forces that could execute his will. From a politician's point of view the decade of the 1760's was a bedlam through which there moved an array of cliques and factions—the "Bedford Gang," the Grenvillites, the "Hero of the Mob," John Wilkes, and a host of others. It was not until 1770 that the King found in Lord North a minister and a coalition that would do his bidding.

Intricately interwoven into the political fabric were the personal ambitions of individuals whose loyalties and family connections the King dared not ignore. To these complications must be added the fact that many high ranking military and naval officers were Members of Parliament. (In addition to the Howes, Lord Cornwallis and Lord Rawdon, Clinton and Burgoyne were M.P.'s.) In order to command support for his American policy George III and his principal ministers, North and Germain, had always to control the myriad threads of this political and military tapestry so that the pattern would produce the desired results. The fact that the King was able to do so and adhere steadily to his American policy for seven years is a commentary on his skills as a political leader. George III may have been stubborn, but he was not the bumbling oaf so often depicted in American histories. Like his brother William, Lord Howe began to make himself more acceptable to the ministry by appearing to concur in the military policy advocated by Germain. At the same time he maneuvered through his friends in and out of Parliament to secure the command of naval forces in North America.

At this point chance intervened to give Howe unexpected leverage with Lord North and the ministry. The death of Sir Charles Saunders created a vacant lieutenant-generalcy of marines, a sinecure awarded to naval officers which carried a salary of £1,200 a year. North awarded the post to Admiral Hugh Palliser—and was immediately confronted by Lord Howe, who reminded North that the post had been promised to him. Howe threatened to resign unless the injury to his pride and his pocketbook were not repaired. There now began an intricate and time-consuming game as Lord North tried to extricate himself. He simply could not afford to lose the support of Lord Howe, a man with powerful family influence who was also a distinguished naval officer and a responsible member of Parliament, qualities which were in short supply in 1775. It was not long before Admiral Howe was openly demanding not only a fleet command but the position of American peace commissioner. North's task was complicated by the fact that the Earl of Sandwich, First Lord of the Admiralty, disliked Howe, and Germain still suspected that Howe favored conciliation. In the weeks that followed, North's twistings and turnings included an effort to get Palliser to resign, a quarrel with Admiral Keppel, and a strenuous effort to placate Germain and Sandwich. More than two months later, early in February, 1776, Lord Howe was appointed commander in chief of the North American fleet and named peace commissioner. As a sop to Germain's suspicions, William Howe was also appointed a commissioner, presumably to prevent the admiral from indulging any leniency toward the colonies.[9]

The episode is interesting from several viewpoints. Certainly the ministers were influenced by political and family pressures into appointing to a position of great sensitivity a man that none of them thought particularly well-qualified. Certainly Lord Howe had indulged in a kind of blackmail to further his own ambitions. But it was precisely his rare reputation as an outstanding seaman and able member of Parliament that forced the ministry to succumb. And if Howe was driven by a desire for position and fame, there is no reason to doubt that he was equally moved by the belief that in his dual role he would be in a unique position to save England her American empire.

It was in these circumstances that Howe and Germain, after a bitter wrangle, finally reached an agreement on the instructions of the peace commission. Still suspecting that Howe was too inclined to conciliate, the American Secretary determined to place such strictures on the mission as to leave no room for appeasement. Lord Howe was given no powers to negotiate a permanent peace nor was he to acknowledge Congress as representative of the colonies. He was directed to declare each colony, county, or town "at peace" only after all revolutionary assemblies were dissolved, all armed bodies disbanded, and royal officials once more established in office. He was not to discuss terms or conditions of settlement of any sort until an area had been declared "at peace." In short, the colonists were to lay down their arms and submit; only then would they learn the bases for settling their differences with the mother country.

These stipulations vexed Lord Howe. He especially objected to the requirement that the colonies acknowledge the supremacy of Parliament "in all cases whatsoever," the language of the Declaratory Act. He recognized that this was the essence of the quarrel with the mother country and that to flaunt this in the face of colonial opposition would stifle any spirit of compromise. He insisted that the odious requirement be dropped and finally succeeded, but the concession was meaningless. Germain was careful to keep a firm hand on the peace commission, and to insure that it was stipulated that when the commissioners declared a colony at peace their action would have to be ratified in London before further terms of settlement could be negotiated.

Admiral Howe's success as fleet commander was deemed much more important in ending the trouble in America. In addition to lending support to the army Howe was expected to enforce the Restraining Acts by interdicting colonial trade and destroying colonial shipping; to carry the war to the ports and harbors of the American coast; to seize all military supplies and even impress seamen into the navy. In a word, the ministry expected his lordship to rely on the vigorous application of force to bring peace in America.

The strangulation of colonial commerce was designed to complement the objectives of the British armies. As previously noted General William Howe had been ordered to move from Boston to New York in the autumn of 1775, but he had thought it best to spend the winter in Massachusetts. The first move for 1776, then, would be to occupy New York City and establish it as a base of operations. From this point several prospects appeared feasible. It was expected that the sizeable force sent to Canada would allow Carleton and Burgoyne to go over to the offensive. This suggested the possibility of coordinating an invasion from the north with a movement by Howe up the Hudson. Massachusetts and the rest of New England would then be open to attack from the west. The seizure of Rhode Island would also offer possibilities both as an important naval base and as an entering wedge to New England. But Germain had no intention of dictating details to his American commanders. "These operations must be left to your judgement and discretion," he wrote in identical letters to Howe and Carleton, "as it would be highly improper, at such a distance, to give any positive orders, especially as so much confidence is placed in your knowledge and military experience."[10]

The plans for 1776 were not very specific because the parts of the machinery were not in place. At the end of April Quebec was still besieged by the Americans, Howe was still in Halifax, and the first elements of his reinforcements had barely cleared English waters. Germain had perforce to depend on his commanders in America to seize opportunities as they were presented and shape their strategy to the occasion. And in addition to the geographic objectives there was, as General Howe pointed out, the need to deal a blow which would shatter American morale, "to check the spirit which the evacuation of Boston will naturally raise among the rebels." He thought that "it is probable that the leaders, urged on by the people and flushed with the idea of superiority, may be the readier brought to a decisive action, than which nothing is more to be desired . . . as the most effectual means to terminate this expensive war. . . ."[11]

Lord George Germain had come a long way from the court martial which had convicted him of disobedience—the gossips still whispered "cowardice"—at Minden. He had assumed direction of the first great imperial crisis that England had faced since 1763. He at once grasped the dimensions of the problem posed by the decision to suppress the rebellion by force of arms. If the decision itself ultimately proved to be fatal, Germain staked his reputation on it, and he brought to the war effort a single-minded determination and a display of driving energy not seen since the days of the great Pitt. In drawing the comparison some discrepancies are obvious. Haunted by the "Ghost of Minden" Germain could never assume the heroic stature that inspired such patriotic fervor in the followers of Pitt. Perhaps this was impossible in a war in which Englishmen were fighting Englishmen. And Germain did not have at hand an Amherst or a Forbes or a Wolfe to execute his will.

THREE

Dress Rehearsal: 1776

FROM HIS BASE AT HALIFAX SIR WILLIAM HOWE WROTE TO LORD GERMAIN on April 26, 1776:

> There is not the least prospect of conciliating this continent until its armies have been roughly dealt with; and I confess my apprehensions that such an event will not be readily brought about, the rebels get on apace, and knowing their advantages in having the whole country, as it were, at their disposal, they will not be readily brought into a situation where the King's troops can meet them on equal terms. Their armies retiring a few miles beyond the navigable rivers, ours cannot follow them from the difficulties I expect to meet in securing land carriage. It cannot be denied that there are many inhabitants in every province well affected to the Government, from which no doubt we will receive assistance, but not until His Majesty's arms have a clear superiority by a decisive victory.[1]

William Howe does not get high marks for brilliance in the history of the War of Independence, but this is as clear and concise a statement of the military problem as was ever expressed by an English or ministerial leader.

The day before Howe wrote his dispatch the American Secretary had issued instructions to his brother, Admiral Lord Richard Howe. As noted, the admiral was not only given command of naval forces for the campaign in America but had been named, along with his brother, as peace commissioner to receive the colonies' submission. Yet this last title was misleading, for what Germain envisioned was a decisive victory which would smash American armed resistance and be followed by a dictated peace. On May 11 Lord Howe's flagship HMS *Eagle* set sail for America.[2]

THE CANADIAN OFFENSIVES

While the American army had been forcing the British out of Boston Congress had taken under consideration another military objective. It was not surprising that both Massachusetts and Connecticut should focus their attention on Ticonderoga, located at the upper end of Lake Champlain.

Ever since Samuel de Champlain had accompanied the Hurons south against the Iroquois in 1609 the Richelieu river-Lake Champlain-Hudson river depression had been a pathway for Indian and white warriors alike. As England and France struggled for supremacy in North America during the Seven Years' War this natural highway took on an immense strategic importance. At its upper end (that is, southern end) the lake narrows to a width of less than half a mile where it is joined by the swift unnavigable waters from Lake George. Fort Ticonderoga was situated at this strategic point and was considered the key to the invasion route.

The idea of seizing Ticonderoga occurred almost simultaneously to Benedict Arnold and Ethan Allen. Captain Arnold had marched to Cambridge with his company of Connecticut militia when the New England troops gathered after Lexington and Concord. At his request the Massachusetts Committee of Safety early in May authorized Arnold to recruit 400 men to take the fort and its artillery, which numbered over a hundred guns.

In the meantime a motley force of Connecticut and New Hampshire troops had assembled at Castleton in the "Hampshire Grants" (Vermont) and had elected Ethan Allen as their colonel. Allen was a lean, tough frontiersman who had become notorious as the leader of the Green Mountain Boys during the hotly contested boundary dispute between New York and New Hampshire. There had been several armed clashes with the New Yorkers and Governor Tryon had put a price of £100 on Allen's head.

When Arnold heard of the gathering of Allen's men he hurried to Castleton, presented his commission and claimed the command. The Boys declared that they would march with no one but Allen. After a furious exchange of words the two commanders finally reached an agreement to share authority, probably because each recognized in the other a stubbornness that matched his own. The joint expedition of about 200 men reached the lake opposite Ticonderoga on May 10, 1775. Early the next morning about half of them crossed under cover of darkness and burst upon the handful of British soldiers manning the works. Allen brandished his cutlass over the head of Captain Delaplace, the fort's commander, and demanded his surrender "in the name of the great Jehovah and the Continental Congress." At least, so Allen later wrote in his version of the adventure; it was strange language from a man who had no authority from Congress and who had written a pamphlet on deism.[3]

The Americans pressed northward in the days that followed. Arnold and Allen each led raiding parties all the way to the Richelieu, but by early June the troops were back at Ticonderoga. The fortress was stripped of its guns and it was at first decided to abandon the Lake Champlain position. But the public outcry, especially from New York and New England, caused Congress to reconsider. It was reported that the British were urging the Indians of the Iroquois Confederacy to attack American forts and settlements and Congress was reluctant to relinquish its hold on Lake Champlain. It therefore appointed Major General Philip Schuyler to organize and command a Northern Army.

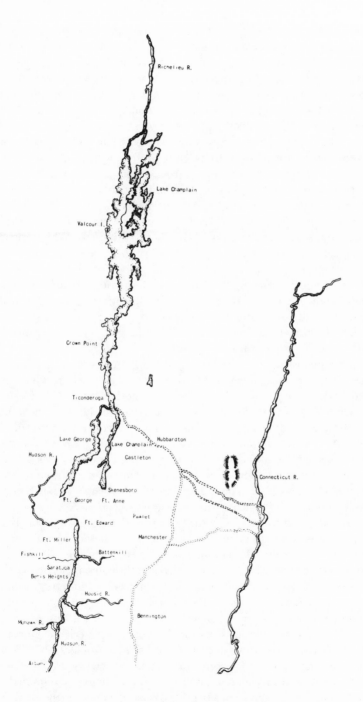

THE CANADIAN INVASION ROUTE

At about the same time Congress received a dispatch from Benedict Arnold, who had been replaced as commander at Ticonderoga and was on his way back to Massachusetts. Arnold reported that Sir Guy Carleton, the governor-general of Canada, had only a corporal's guard with which to defend the whole province. A force of two thousand men, said Arnold, could not only clear the enemy from Lake Champlain but should be able to capture Montreal and threaten Quebec. This opened a glittering prospect to Congress, and at the same time confronted it with the paradox of its position. The delegates would, a few weeks later, vote a petition to the King professing their loyalty and asking for reconciliation with the mother country. Although this would be done primarily to placate the Whig-Loyalists, could the colonies, while professing to be fighting in defense of their liberties, undertake what amounted to a campaign of conquest? Moreover, it was by no means certain that the Canadians were prepared to receive the blessings of liberty, American Whig style, since the latter had only recently inveighed against the Quebec Act which confirmed Catholicism as the approved religion of the French *habitants*. Yet the prospect was alluring and if the Canadians were not persuaded it would at least deprive the British of a base for military operations against the northern colonies. Accordingly, Schuyler was ordered to take the offensive against "St. Johns, Montreal and any other parts of the country." The general and his staff went to Ticonderoga on July 18.[4]

Philip Schuyler was the scion of one of the Dutch patroon families of the Hudson Valley and he had married Catherine Van Rennselaer, whose family was even more prominent and wealthy. His mother was a Van Cortlandt, and so Schuyler was typical of the landed gentry of the Hudson River Valley whose family connections and vast land holdings enabled them to rule New York. He had been a member of the New York Assembly since 1768 and was a man of considerable influence in the clannish, factional politics of the colony. The revolutionary New York Provincial Congress had nominated him to Congress for the rank of major general in 1775, probably as much in deference to his political influence as to his military experience.

Arnold had urged the necessity for prompt action against Canada but this was more easily said than done. At Ticonderoga Schuyler found a garrison of about 600 men, many of them ill, most of them undisciplined. These and other troops in the area were badly supplied and the enlistments of many were about to expire. New York had voted additional troops, but the assembly had noted that "they have no arms, clothes, blankets or ammunition, the officers no commissions, our treasury no money, ourselves in debt. It is vain to complain. . . ." It was the sort of situation with which American commanders would soon become painfully familiar. In addition, Schuyler, a New Yorker, did not have the capacity to inspire confidence in the New Englanders. He was an aristocrat and a patroon whose large land holdings and dignified manner made him an object of considerable skepticism among the democratic militiamen and their officers. Schuyler was honest and brave, an able administrator, and unselfishly devoted to the Patriot cause. But his health was chronically poor and all during the campaign he was plagued with a "bilious fever and violent rheumatick pains."

It was not until the middle of August that a northern army was finally assembled, but even then Schuyler delayed to attend a conference of Indians at Albany. In his absence General Richard Montgomery, his second in command, decided to wait no longer. The antithesis of Schuyler when it came to action, the young brigadier was convinced of "the necessity of a vigorous and speedy effort to crush [the British] naval armament before it got abroad." On August 28 he embarked 1,200 men and eight days later, on September 5, he reached St. Johns on the Richelieu, where Schuyler rejoined the command. After some confusion and a brief retreat the Americans besieged St. Johns and finally forced its surrender. But the ill-conducted operation had taken fifty-five days and not until the first week in November was the way to Montreal open. By the 13th Montgomery had forced the capitulation of Montreal, although Governor-General Carleton managed to escape down the St. Lawrence to Quebec.[5]

In the meantime a second striking force against Canada had been organized under the command of Benedict Arnold, who had been promoted to brigadier general. With 1,100 men Arnold had started from the mouth of the Kennebec river in Maine on September 19, 1775, intending to penetrate the wilderness by way of Lake Megantic and the Chaudiere river and descend on Quebec. Among the units of Arnold's force was a company of riflemen under the command of Daniel Morgan, Indian fighter and veteran of the French and Indian War.

Arnold's march to Quebec was an epic of hardship and bravery. Beset by bad weather, bad maps and hunger, Arnold's force was reduced to making porridge out of barber's powder and moccasin leather. When they reached the headwaters of the Chaudiere the men collapsed, but the tireless Arnold drove ahead to the nearest Canadian village and brought food back to his men. The command emerged on the St. Lawrence opposite Quebec on November 8. The march had taken forty-five days instead of the anticipated three weeks and they had come 350 miles instead of 180.

But the worst of bad luck foiled the expedition. A message sent to Montgomery fell into the hands of the British and the defenders of Quebec were warned. Montgomery finally arrived on December 3 bringing the total force of the invaders to about 2,000 men. Despite the cold of Canadian winter, sickness, lack of supplies and expiring enlistments, the Americans kept the city in a state of siege. On December 30 they launched a desperate assault under cover of a driving snowstorm. In the bitter struggle Montgomery was killed, Arnold was wounded, and the giant Morgan was captured. The attackers were finally beaten off, but they did not lift the siege. Held to their task by the iron determination of the wounded Arnold they stayed before the city until spring. Despite the pleas of Schuyler to Congress and Washington the first reinforcements did not reach Arnold until April 1, 1776. By that time it was too late. Soon afterward Carleton began to receive the first of the reinforcements from England and, early in May, he drove off the Americans in such confusion that many of their supplies and the wounded had to be abandoned. Altogether the Americans had lost about 100 killed and wounded and 400 captured. It was a dismal ending to the hopes for the conquest of Canada.[6]

By the time the American retreat had reached St. Johns, Washington and Congress had at last begun to send significant numbers of men and supplies. On the first of June General John Sullivan was sent to the Northern Army in command of about 8,000 men. With characteristic optimism Sullivan decided that the course of the campaign could be reversed and he launched a reconnaissance in force of 2,000 men against Trois Rivieres on the St. Lawrence. But General Carleton had now received the full complement of his reinforcements from England which consisted of 10,000 men and General John Burgoyne. The American attack on Trois Rivieres ran squarely into the main body of Carleton's force advancing up the St. Lawrence and was smashed and scattered. What had begun as an American offensive suddenly became a scrambling retreat. The Americans barely escaped to Isle-aux-Noix at the northern end of Lake Champlain. Temporarily out of reach of the British, the army was now attacked by an even more deadly enemy, smallpox. By the end of June Sullivan's force had been reduced by more than half, and what was left was ill-fed and ill-equipped. Malaria and dysentery now struck down many who had escaped the pox and Isle-aux-Noix became a filthy pest hole. Early in July the sick, dispirited army finally returned to Crown Point, their point of departure ten months before.

When Carleton arrived at the Richelieu he considered that naval control of Lake Champlain was a necessary condition to a further advance southward. Since no vessels had been sent from England he began to build a fleet. He was also preoccupied with his duties as governor of Canada and as the summer dragged on he was frequently absent at Quebec reorganizing the provincial government. He seems to have felt no urgency in pressing his advance, for he turned down a proposal by Burgoyne to make a diversionary attack from the west by way of Lake Ontario and the Mohawk Valley. It was not until the first week in October that Carleton finally launched his fleet on Lake Champlain to seek out a hastily assembled little force commanded by Benedict Arnold. Arnold fought his usual stubborn and skillful battle off Valcour Island but his guns could not match the weight of the British metal. He brought his badly mauled boats out of action under the cover of darkness and fog, but two days later Carleton caught up, completely destroyed the remnant, and occupied Crown Point. By October 27 the British advance parties were probing the defenses of Ticonderoga.[7]

The campaigning season was now well advanced and Carleton was forced to make a decision. Should he seize Ticonderoga and press on southward? Should he hold Crown Point as an advance base, or should he withdraw to the St. Lawrence? To the dismay of Burgoyne Carleton decided to abandon Crown Point and pull back to Canada. "I think this step puts us in danger . . . of losing the fruits of our summer's labor & autumn victory," said Gentleman Johnny.[8]

From Carleton's point of view there were good reasons for his decision. He was, after all, governor of Canada and the political affairs of the province were still in a tangle. A winter campaign over a long supply line was out of the question, since Howe, in New York, had given no indication that he intended to move up the Hudson. Even a decision to hold Crown Point would necessitate a lengthy line of communication and supply if it were not to suffer the same exposure that led to the fall of Ticonderoga.

A more important question is why Carleton delayed the entire summer in preparing for his advance southward. The ease with which he brushed Arnold aside suggests that the naval problem was not very serious, and the confusion and discouragement of the American forces would have made them vulnerable to a determined attack or even a reconnaisance in force. Yet Carleton showed no sense of urgency and indeed seemed to be pointedly ignoring Germain's instructions to support Howe.

Without reaching any firm conclusions, some tentative explanations may be put forward. Despite his autocratic manner and haughty bearing Carleton was a genuinely humane man. He treated American prisoners captured at Quebec with every consideration "to convince all His Majesty's unhappy subjects that the King's mercy and Benevolence are still open to them."[9] He saw to it that the wounded were treated and paroled home when they recovered. He paroled several captured American officers including Daniel Morgan—and may well have regretted it a year later when the "Old Waggoner" led his riflemen against Burgoyne at Saratoga. All this suggests that Carleton considered reconciliation to be the solution to the American rebellion as opposed to the hard line military policy of Lord Germain.

As previously noted, he was concerned about political and administrative problems created by the Quebec Act and he made frequent trips back to the capital during the summer of 1776. If the ministry considered that the rebellion was the major concern of the governor-general, Carleton obviously did not. His commission as major general was senior to Howe's, and he despised Lord George Germain. Under the circumstances Carleton felt free to judge for himself where his duty lay, and he was, on the whole, well satisfied with what he had accomplished. In desperate circumstances he had saved Canada from conquest and had driven the enemy from its borders, for which the King awarded him the red ribbon of a Knight of the Bath. From the point of view of continental strategy Carleton may have missed a golden opportunity. But from the citadel of Quebec the governor-general had a different view.

THE MISSION OF THE HOWES

On June 29, 1776, Daniel McCurtin, an American soldier on Staten Island, "was upstairs in an outhouse and I spied as I peeped out the Bay something resembling a wood of pine trees trimmed. I declare, at my noticing this, I could not believe my eyes, but keeping my eyes fixed on the very spot . . . in about ten minutes the whole Bay was full of shipping as ever it could be. I declare I thought all London was afloat." The sight which distracted him was the arrival of General Howe and his army from Halifax. (Unfortunately, "Just about five minutes before I see this sight I got my discharge," and the journal ends; future generations were thus deprived of the subsequent views of Rifleman McCurtin on the backside of American history.) With the arrival of substantial reinforcements, Howe had decided to make New York his base for the campaign of 1776. On July 12 HMS *Eagle*, flying the pennant of Admiral Richard Lord Howe, arrived off New York after nine weeks at sea.[10]

The dates are important. Lord Howe's peace commission had been the subject of discussion in the colonies for months. Whig-Loyalists in and out of Congress still hoped for a reasonable offer of settlement by the Crown. By alternately holding out expectations of reconciliation and the spectre of military conquest they had hoped to stem the radical movement for independence. Robert Morris, wealthy financier who abstained in the final vote for independence, had succinctly stated the dilemma of Loyalists in April: "Where the plague are these Commissioners, if they are to come what is it that detains them; it is time we should be on a certainty and know positively whether the liberties of America can be established and secured by reconciliation or whether we must totally renounce connection with Great Britain and fight our way to total independence."

Yet winter ended and spring came in with General Howe's army still at Halifax, so there was not a single regiment of the British army on American soil when Richard Henry Lee introduced his resolution on June 7, "that these United Colonies are, and of right out to be, free and independent States. . . ." The great debate began, although it was less a debate than a period when the delegates awaited instructions from their provincial governments. Members of Congress were thorough republicans and they did not intend to vote on such a momentous question until they were directed to do so.[11]

If General Howe saw any relationship between his arrival at New York and the decision which was being reached in Philadelphia, he gave no sign. He prudently put his troops ashore on Staten Island on July 3 and awaited the reinforcements which Germain had promised him. Even so, the appearance of the British brought radical activity in New York to a halt, and its delegates in Philadelphia abstained from voting for independence on July 2. When the *Eagle* dropped anchor on July 12 the United States was ten days old.

This is not to say that spirited action by General Howe or an earlier arrival by his Lordship would have forestalled completely the vote on July 2. Admiral

Howe and Lord Germain were thinking in terms of submission followed by reconciliation at a time when the colonies were debating independence. Yet a fuller appreciation of the intentions of the radicals and a better understanding of the issues involved might have enabled the Howes to employ both military and diplomatic means to weaken support for the radicals. It was not until the last week in June, for example, that New Jersey denounced Governor William Franklin and instructed its delegates to join the other colonies in declaring independence. Considering how quickly the Whigs of New Jersey collapsed five months later, it is interesting to speculate on what their reaction would have been had Howe lodged his army in New York instead of Halifax during the winter, or if he had put a few regiments ashore at Sandy Hook when he finally arrived on the 25th of June.[12]

As it was Lord Howe proceeded as if the Declaration of Independence had never occurred. Officially, of course, he refused to acknowledge the existence of the United States and, in seeking an interview with Washington, insisted on addressing him as "George Washington, Esq., etc., etc." The commander in chief's reply was simply to convey "my particular compliments" to the Admiral and the General. Within a few days a packet of dispatches from Lord Howe was intercepted by American soldiers and sent to Congress. From these documents, which included instructions to royal governors and letters to private individuals, it was clear that, however eager the peace commissioners might be to open negotiations, there was simply nothing to negotiate. Aside from issuing pardons to individuals and receiving submission of the "colonies," the Howes had no authority. These revelations, which were published in the Whig press, snuffed out the last hope of the waverers.[13]

Lord George Germain, believing from the beginning that a military solution was necessary, did not stint in his support of the plans for 1776. He had urged General Howe to move his base from Boston to New York not only to rid himself of the hornet's nest of New Englanders, but also because New York had the best port facilities in America and because its geographic position made it an ideal center from which Howe's operations could be conducted. Centrally located on the Atlantic coast, it lay at the southern end of the Richelieu-Lake Champlain-Hudson trench which would provide a communications route to Canada. In addition New York City was thought to be a center of Loyalism and it was believed that neighboring New Jersey and Pennsylvania might be easily won over if Loyalists in those areas were given military support.

General Howe told Germain that, once he had established himself in New York, his principal objectives would be to win a decisive victory over the American army and isolate New England. The latter might be accomplished either by the occupation of Rhode Island or a move up the Hudson to link with Carleton, or both. By early spring, then, Germain, Carleton, and Howe had all agreed on the general plan, and had announced their intentions to make it operational at the earliest possible moment. The American Secretary had conceded to his commanders that, as noted above, they must exercise their own "judgement and discretion" in the execution of their respective phases of the plan.

For the campaign of 1776 Howe estimated that a total of 20,000 men would be needed for his operations in New York and New England, plus 2,000 men to garrison Halifax. This meant that Germain would have to more than double Howe's force of something less than 9,000 men which the latter had brought to New York. If Carleton was expected not only to beat back the American invasion but go over to the offensive he would need a force of 10,000 men. Considering the fact that the total strength of the entire British army in 1775 was less than 50,000 men this constituted an enormous demand on the American Secretary as well as on the Admiralty which would have the job of lifting these troops overseas.

As noted above, Germain authorized a force which not only equalled Howe's estimates but exceeded them. The sudden demand for manpower was met by hiring mercenaries from the German states, principally Hesse-Cassel and Brunswick. Twelve thousand Hessians were sent to Howe along with 3,500 Highlanders and 1,000 volunteers from the Guards, bringing his total force at New York to nearly 26,000 men. Of the 10,000 man force sent to Carlton, half were Germans.[14]

But the hopes for an early beginning to the campaign, for that "decisive Action . . . to terminate this expensive War" soon vanished. Howe's Halifax force did not arrive until the end of June. An expedition of 3,500 men under General Henry Clinton had been diverted southward in the vain hope of supporting Loyalist risings in the Carolinas. The British attack was repulsed at Charleston and Clinton finally rejoined Howe at New York at the end of July. The main body of reinforcements, the Guards and the Hessians, did not arrive until August 12. William Howe was an orderly man. Not until he had assembled his entire force with all its supplies and equipage, did he begin his offensive. Even then he avoided a direct attack on Manhattan.[15] On August 22 he began landing 15,000 men on Long Island.

This ended a long period of watchful waiting for George Washington. After the evacuation of Boston he had correctly guessed that the next move of the enemy would be against New York, and he shortly sent General Charles Lee to Manhattan to supervise the erection of fortifications. The island was surrounded by navigable waters on three sides; Lee's pessimistic conclusion that the city could not be defended was hardly surprising. But he did believe that the Americans could punish the British severely by a vigorous resistance. Subsequently, when Washington arrived in New York in mid-April, he directed the construction of two forts, Washington and Lee, on either side of the Hudson at the northern end of Manhattan to guard the approaches to the upper Hudson valley. Remembering the British experience in Boston, Washington also fortified Brooklyn Heights on Long Island which overlooked the southern tip of Manhattan across the East River. To him this may have appeared to be another Dorchester Heights, from which the British guns could make the lower end of Manhattan untenable and open the East River to the British fleet. Finally he stationed some militia across the river at Amboy in New Jersey to guard against a landing there. Washington had thus attempted to provide for all contingencies, but in reality none of them could be adequately met considering the meager and undisciplined force at his disposal.

When the British landed on Long Island Washington hurried to the scene. He already knew that General Greene, who commanded on Long Island, was ailing and he had delegated John Sullivan to take charge. During the next four days there was fitful movement on both sides, a cautious sparring, as Howe planned his attack. Washington was still fearful that the British might storm Manhattan directly, but he filtered more regiments across to Brooklyn until about half his force, 10,000 men, was committed. On the 24th came still another change of command. General Israel Putnam, veteran of the French war and senior to Sullivan, pleaded with Washington to be given charge on Long Island and Washington acceded to his request. "Old Put" was still regarded as the most seasoned of the generals and it seems not to have occurred to the commander in chief that Putnam was not familiar with the fortifications or the terrain. The most prominent feature was an escarpment of wooded hills which formed a natural defensive position about a mile and a half east of the fortifications in Brooklyn. Sullivan was placed in command of an advance force of 3,500 men manning this height. The right wing was anchored on the south shore at Gowanus Bay and was commanded by William Alexander, a self-styled Irish peer who claimed the title of Lord Stirling. The center was commanded by Sullivan himself while the left or northern end of the American line simply petered out—in military terminology, it was "in the air." Washington inspected these dispositions on the 26th and made no suggestions. Putnam took his post in the fortifications in Brooklyn.

On the morning of August 27 General Howe launched his attack. About 5,000 men, mostly Germans, advanced directly against the American position and began to skirmish along Stirling's front while 10,000 men under Clinton and Cornwallis swung to the north and circled the unprotected American left flank. The envelopment was a complete surprise and the British fell on the rear of the American line like a clap of doom. Complete disaster was avoided when Stirling swung his Delaware and Maryland troops ninety degrees to the north, and rammed them straight into the van led by General Cornwallis. It was a measure of Stirling's determination and the courage of these raw troops that the British vanguard was halted and temporarily thrown back, allowing many of Sullivan's command to escape. The Maryland and Delaware regiments lost 250 men and both Stirling and Sullivan were captured. The British pursued the fleeing Americans into the outer works of the fortifications at Brooklyn, at which point Howe called off the attack.

Did he miss a golden opportunity to destroy the American army and capture its commander in chief? Clinton thought so and so did innumerable critics of Howe after he was recalled in 1778. Howe later admitted that he could have carried the fortifications at Brooklyn, but "the loss of 1,000 or perhaps 1,500 British troops, in carrying those lines of the enemy, would have been but ill-repaid by double that number of the enemy." It has often been said that Howe's memory of the slaughter on Breed's Hill had instilled in him a fatal caution which he carried with him for the rest of the war. But there are reasonable explanations for his decision. There was no evidence that Howe knew of Washington's presence on Long Island and, more important, no reason at this point for Howe to recognize the enormous value of Washington's indomitable leadership to the American cause. Nor did Howe's decision allow the Americans to escape. They were still tightly pinned between the British and the East River from which Howe believed there was no escape, especially since the fleet would shortly be able to move up the river and seal off the way to Manhattan. "The most essential duty I had to perform was not wantonly to commit his majesty's troops where the object was inadequate." Howe had, after all, struck his decisive blow and he may well have expected the rebellion was about to collapse.

For two days, August 28 and 29, the Americans held their position, but it became increasingly clear to Washington that he had not only been defeated but that the Long Island detachment, more than half his force, was in dire peril. Only a northeast wind, which had blown steadily down the East River for the past several days had prevented Admiral Howe from interposing his vessels across the line of retreat. In the darkness and fog of the night of August 29–30 Washington ferried his entire force to the safety of Manhattan. It was a magnificent maneuver and it showed the commander in chief at his best. Planning and discipline—and luck—had made possible the evacuation of over 9,000 frightened, wet, dispirited men with so much dispatch and so little noise that the British did not react until the last elements of sentries and the small covering force had pushed out into the stream. Even the artillery, except for the heaviest guns, was brought off.[16]

THE RETREAT FROM NEW YORK

The defense of New York presented Washington with formidable problems. He was faced with an enemy that had overwhelming superiority in numbers and experience of its soldiers. British naval support enabled the Howes to land troops and give fire support to any spot of their choosing. Yet the American commander had not done well in his first test of battle in the field. He had divided his force for understandable reasons, but he expected too much of both his troops and his generals. Sullivan might be blamed for the stunning success of Howe's envelopment but Washington had himself inspected the lines and had made no move to protect the exposed flank. He had been present during the battle but had issued none but routine orders during the course of the action. Of the principal subordinates (Greene excepted) Putnam had shown no capacity at all; Sullivan and Stirling had proved themselves to be hard fighters, but incapable of controlling a battle field or even a considerable part of it. There was one small bright spot in the otherwise dark picture of the engagement. In the morning hours of the 27th there was sharp skirmishing along the center and right while the British waited for Clinton to reach his flanking position. During these sporadic fire fights the Americans stood up well and displayed considerable poise in the presence of the enemy. In addition when Stirling counterattacked, William Smallwood's Marylanders and John Haslet's Delaware Continentals behaved like veterans; and "General Lord Stirling fought like a wolf."

But this did nothing to dispel the pall of gloom which descended over Washington's headquarters and over the entire army. Once more militia began to leave for home. Enlistments fell off sharply, and despite some replacements, Washington's strength fell below 20,000 by the end of the first week in September. The commander's soldierly sense of propriety was outraged by breaches of discipline especially among militiamen, whose officers were obviously incapable of controlling the men in the presence of the temptations of the "big city." Colonel Laommi Baldwin wrote his wife that in his duties as officer of the day, "going the grand round with my guard of escort, [I] have broke up the knots of men and women fighting, pulling caps, swearing, crying 'Murder' etc., hurried them off to the Provost dungeon by the half dozens, there let them lay mixed till next day. Some are punished, some get off clear— Hell's work. . . ."[17]

Fortunately for the dispirited and disorganized army, the Howes chose this moment to resume their role as peace commissioners. The two prisoners of war, John Sullivan and Lord Stirling, found themselves guests of Admiral Lord Howe aboard the *Eagle*. His Lordship avowed his friendship for America, declared that the war was most unwise, and gave his guests to understand that Parliament would ratify whatever terms he could arrange with the "colonies." He urged Sullivan to convey these sentiments to Congress so that a conference could be arranged. Sullivan agreed and on September 2 he came to Philadelphia, insisting that Howe was willing to negotiate with Congress and make concessions. Hopes rose among the moderates and the radicals were afraid to refuse the invitation. They gambled that the Admiral was overstating his authority, since to negotiate with Congress would be, in effect, to recognize its legitimacy and that of the new independent nation. Benjamin Franklin, John Adams and Edward Rutledge, the latter a moderate, met with Lord Howe on Staten Island on September 11. Franklin and Richard Howe "had been in long habits of friendship and intimacy," so the discussion was amiable, but the Americans soon discovered that Howe had nothing to offer. As John Adams put it, "The whole affair . . . appears to me, as it ever did, to be a bubble, an ambuscade." It was the end of the peace commission. Patriots, Loyalists, moderates and the Howes themselves finally and fully understood

George III's self-fulfilling prophecy, now more than two years old, "The colonies must either submit or triumph."[18]

While Congress played out the game with Lord Howe, Washington gained a two-week respite. It finally became evident that New York was untenable and he began to make plans for a slow withdrawal. His inclination was to put the town to the torch and thus reduce its usefulness to the British, but Congress instructed that "no damage be done to said city by his troops, on their leaving it." On September 13, the withdrawal began.

The decision was made barely in time to avert disaster. On September 15, Howe landed 9,000 redcoats and Hessians at Kip's Bay on the eastern side of Manhattan. It is doubtful if the thinly held American defenses could have seriously impeded the operation, but the militia abandoned their trenches without firing a shot and their panic quickly spread. Washington arrived at the scene and he and his subordinates tried desperately to rally the fugitives. As the soldiers continued to flee in blind panic, the frustrations and disappointments of the past weeks which were bottled up beneath Washington's monumental calm and composure at last exploded in a towering rage. "The General was so exasperated that he struck several officers in their flight, three times dashed his hat on the ground, and at last exclaimed, 'Good God! Have I got such troops as those?' It was with difficulty his friends could get him to quit the field, so great was his emotions."

Two circumstances saved Washington from disaster. The first was the fact that, pursuant to the decision of the Council of War three days earlier, the army had already begun to move to a defensive position at Harlem on the northern end of Manhattan. The second factor was another inexplicable pause by General Howe. The last of the Americans, about 5,000 men under Putnam's command, were hurrying north along the west side of the island, but Howe made no attempt to cut them off; instead he turned north along the East River. At one point his leisurely march paralleled Putnam's sweating militia, separated only by what is now Central Park.

By the evening of the 15th the two armies faced each other at Harlem Heights, the last of Putnam's fugitives safe within the American lines, although there had been a heavy loss of supplies and artillery. Washington's position was a strong one and he seems to have been confident of his ability to bloody Howe "if the generality of our troops would behave with tolerable resolution." When the British conducted a reconnaissance in force on the morning of the 16th the Americans checked them; then, as each side fed more troops into the fight, the Americans drove the British, including eight companies of the famous Black Watch regiment. Washington broke off the engagement after each side had lost about 200 men, killed and wounded. Among the dead was Thomas Knowlton who had defended the rail fence at Bunker Hill. It was no more than an oversize skirmish but coming as it did on the heels of the disgraceful scene at Kip's Bay, "you can hardly conceive the change it made in our army. The men have recovered their spirits and feel a confidence which before they had quite lost." And, most gratifying of all Howe left Washington alone for almost a month.[19]

It was a month of disappointments and frustrations. Malingering, lack of discipline, desertions, and thievery testified to the most critical weakness of the army, lack of capable officers. Colonel Stephen Moylan confessed that he was not qualified as quartermaster general and was replaced by General Thomas Mifflin. Any kind of training was impossible because militia units came and went so often that by the time they learned the rudiments of duties and drills their enlistments expired. Even the Continental troops had only three more months to serve. ". . . Such is my situation" wrote Washington, "that if I were to wish the bitterest curse to an enemy this side of the grave, I should put him in my stead with my feelings."

In the middle of October Howe moved again, this time with another amphibious flanking maneuver, but again conducted with such indecision and at such a leisurely pace that Washington had ample time to withdraw to White Plains. This time Howe risked an attack on October 26 and in the engagement which followed Washington was outmaneuvered and thoroughly beaten. But again Howe did not press his advantage. (It should be remembered that on October 27 Carleton was before Ticonderoga, and was making his decision to withdraw to Canada. Did Howe consider pushing Washington aside and penetrating up the Hudson? Despite the fact that the operational plan discussed by Howe and Germain had referred to isolating New England by "an operation on the Hudson" and the instructions to Carleton indicated cooperation with Howe, there is no evidence that Howe considered a move northward after the battle of Long Island, nor that he and Carleton ever communicated on the subject.) Instead, Howe turned his attention southward to the two American fortresses, Lee and Washington on opposite sides of the Hudson. The American commander decided that the forts should be abandoned, since he was now in no position to support them, but he allowed himself to be dissuaded by his generals. Putnam and Greene were convinced that Fort Washington, east of the Hudson, could withstand a British attack. On November 14 the British stormed it and Colonel Robert Magaw, who had sworn he could hold "till the end of December" surrendered the fort and its garrison of nearly 3,000 men before nightfall. Six days later an alert American patrol's timely warning allowed Greene to escape from Fort Lee, with 1,000 men of its garrison.[20]

Even before the loss of the Hudson forts Washington had once more divided his army. To General Lee he designated a force of 7,000 men to operate in the neighborhood of White Plains. General Heath was allotted 2,500 and left at Peekskill to guard the Hudson Highlands. Washington himself with less than two thousand men moved down the west side of the Hudson to Newark, New Jersey. He counted on the garrisons of the fallen forts and the New Jersey and Pennsylvania militia to augment this slender force but, as noted, only about 1,000 men from Fort Lee had escaped, and the militia response was negligible.

By the 28th of November he was forced out of Newark by the approach of a British force under Lord Cornwallis. At Brunswick he was joined by Lord Stirling with his division of 1,000 men. The hard drinking, hard fighting Irishman was a welcome sight but his men were "broken down and fatigued—some without shoes, some had no shirts." The soldiers, as always where the opportunity offered, were addicted to "Barrel Fever" which had its own peculiar symptoms, and "which differs in its effects from any other fever—its concomitants are black eyes and bloody noses."[21]

Now came the first signs of lack of confidence in the commander in chief. Repeated and urgent requests to Charles Lee to bring his 7,000 men to join Washington were answered by a variety of excuses and justifications which only thinly concealed Lee's conviction that "a certain great man is most damnably deficient." Even Washington's long-suffering adjutant, Joseph Reed, was writing to Lee, "You have decision, a quality often wanting in minds otherwise valuable. . . ." There was no difficulty in making a decision now. Tired, hungry and cold though they might be, the little army of 3,400 men was driven out of Brunswick on December 1, passed through Princeton and arrived at Trenton on the Delaware on the 3rd. Again Washington was granted a respite as Howe came down from New York to snap the leash on Cornwallis. It was four days before the British again took up the pursuit. By this time the Americans had stripped the left bank of the Delaware of every boat and scow they could find, and had crossed over into Pennsylvania.[22]

In self-governing states where responsibility is divided it is not very difficult for war leaders to report failure as success, and in so doing they are frequently led into self-deception. Germain had been chosen, in the face of considerable opposition, to preside over the reestablishment of British authority in the colonies. He had, in turn, chosen Sir William Howe to succeed Gage in the confident expectation that he would destroy the rebel army. Since Parliamentary support was necessary if the American Secretary and his commander were to retain their positions and reputations, it would have been surprising if either had admitted failure. On the contrary, the enemy, said Sir William was "much depressed at the success of His Majesty's arms," and Germain noted that Howe "finishes his campaign most honorably for himself and most advantageously for the country." The King indicated his approval by awarding the American commander the Red Ribbon of the Bath.[23]

During 1776 Lord Germain's enormous energies had produced a troop lift overseas the magnitude of which was unparalleled in military history until the twentieth century. Yet neither Germain nor Howe was very explicit as to objectives and priorities. Scattered through the welter of their correspondence from the autumn of 1775 through the summer of 1776 were four ob-

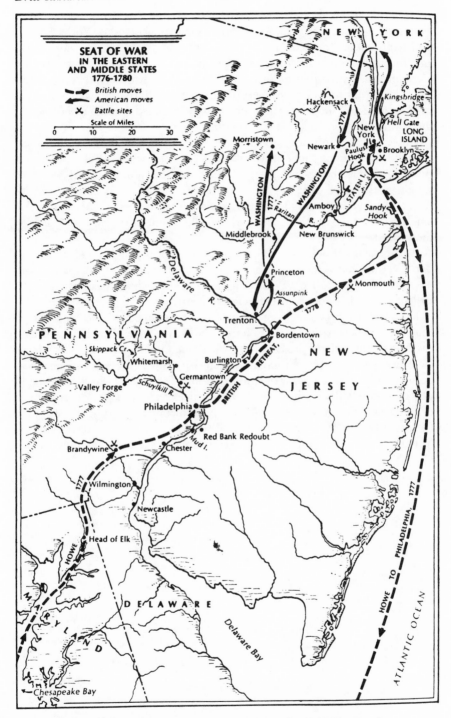

© Mark Boatner, III, *Encyclopedia of the American Revolution*, David McKay Co., Inc.

jectives to which both had agreed: the occupation of New York; striking decisively at the American army; a juncture with Carleton's northern force; and the occupation of Rhode Island. A fifth objective had been undertaken by Germain, the expedition to South Carolina, which had been driven off. Finally, in the autumn of 1776, Germain had suggested that Howe "pay a visit to Philadelphia," and Howe indicated that he intended, "in the disposition of the winter cantonments," to occupy New Jersey.

Howe had certainly accomplished the occupation of New York and he had brought Washington "to a decisive action" at Long Island. But whether his subsequent maneuvers had been designed "as the most effectual means to terminate this expensive war" is a question that has been debated by critics then and now. Howe himself reported on September 25, ten days after his landing at Kip's Bay, that there was "not the slightest prospect of finishing the contest this campaign. . . ."

As for the other objectives, Howe had made not the slightest effort to support Carleton nor did he show any interest in a "visit to Philadelphia." And not until late December was Clinton dispatched to Rhode Island, where the British succeeded only in occupying Newport.

In his dispatch of August 10 Howe had mentioned, almost as an afterthought, the occupation of New Jersey. Now, in November, having driven the Americans beyond the Delaware, he decided to leave a chain of garrisons to secure the state. There is no indication that Howe gave any thought to an occupation policy except for the promulgation of an amnesty to all who would declare their loyalty to the Crown. The choice of Hessians to comprise most of the occupation force seems to have been dictated by nothing more than the usual British tendency to give the dirty chores to their mercenary allies. Yet the success or failure of this objective may have been the most fateful of all.[24]

FOUR

Crisis in New Jersey

IT WAS PERHAPS THE DARKEST HOUR OF THE WAR. EVEN IF THE REMNANT OF the forces under Lee and Heath joined him Washington's army could count less than 10,000 men. Already, on December 1, some militia enlistments had expired and many more were simply walking out of camp and going home. The Continental troops would end their term of service on the last day of the year. Congress had fled from Philadelphia to Baltimore without offering any prospect of reinforcements. Confidentially, Washington wrote to John Augustine Washington: "*If every nerve is not strain'd* to recruit the New Army with all possible expidition, *I think the game is pretty near up.* . . . ." But his discouragement did not break the iron will. Dr. James Thacher reports a remark which may be apocryphal but not out of character. "My neck does not feel as though it was made for a halter," said the commander in chief. " . . . We must retire to Augusta County in Virginia, and if overpowered, we must cross the Allegheny Mountains." But Washington was not yet ready to take to the back country. He still had an army, even if only for a few more weeks.[1]

Meanwhile, Howe retired to New York for the winter. But he reiterated his intention to "quarter a large body of troops in that [New Jersey] district." He therefore left a chain of cantonments stretching across the state from Perth Amboy to the Delaware. It was the first attempt by the British to establish and maintain control of an area from which they had driven the enemy. In many respects it was a crucial test of England's ability to carry out its program of reconquest, and if it was successful it would constitute a long stride toward ending the war.[2]

THE REVOLUTION IN NEW JERSEY

The struggle between Whigs and Tories in New Jersey followed much the same course as the revolutionary movement in the other colonies. Its people developed the same American identity and the same stubborn resistance to Parliamentary authority. Most of the Anglican clergy defended the Crown while Presbyterians and most other dissenters made cause with the Whigs. In the southern part of the state the Society of Friends, impelled by conscientious objection to violence, stolidly refused to take sides in the war. Gen-

scientious objection to violence, stolidly refused to take sides in the war. Generally speaking, debtor groups tended to join the Whigs since they were waging a constant battle against the conservative propertied classes.

The situation was complicated by the legacy of the original New Jersey charter, the Council of Proprietors. The proprietors had long since ceased to function as recruiters and promoters of colonization and confined their activities to selling property, recording and notarizing land titles, and collecting quit rents. Yet the proprietary holdings were still considerable and in 1775 a twenty-fourth share of a proprietary right was worth £1,200 a year. Not only did the farmers protest the payment of quit rents but they frequently challenged the proprietary titles. They brought suits attempting to show that the only valid titles were those granted under royal patents or those derived from Indian purchases. There were riots in 1770 in the course of which the demonstrators raised the cry of "Liberty and Property" directed, not against the Crown, but against the proprietors and their detestable henchmen, the lawyers.[3]

The Council of Proprietors formed the nucleus of a coterie of powerful land holders and colonial officials who were known as the "Perth Amboy Group." Prominent among them were Courtland Skinner, a proprietor and the attorney general of the colony, and Frederick Smythe, chief justice of the colony. Peter Kemble, father-in-law of General Gage, was president of the Governor's Council and his son, Stephen, was an officer on General Howe's staff. Altogether there were some twenty or thirty families who represented the economic, social, and political elite of the colony.[4]

Any attempt to make hard and fast distinctions of economic or class interests inevitably produces important exceptions. William Paterson, an outstanding lawyer, became attorney general of the revolutionary state government. William Livingston, whose family was prominent in New York, became New Jersey's first revolutionary governor. John Witherspoon, the brilliant Scot who was president of Princeton, was one of the most vocal supporters of the Whig cause. His students made a point of attending graduation exercises in American made clothes and, after Lexington and Concord, they formed a military company (in which, appropriately, all were officers). Francis Hopkinson, a former member of the Governor's Council, was elected to both Continental Congresses and Lord Stirling, another Council member, was one of Washington's commanders.[5]

The guns of Lexington and Concord precipitated a revolutionary upheaval in New Jersey. In the summer of 1775 the Whigs seized the initiative by electing a Provincial Congress which adopted an "Association" of the people which "forms a social compact." The Congress ordered the establishment of local Committees of Inspection (also called Committees of Observation) in every county and town. These committees circulated the "Association" for signatures by the inhabitants and sometimes rather rudely brought recalcitrant individuals and districts into line.

British authority in the colony was represented in the person of Governor William Franklin, illegitimate son of Benjamin Franklin. This handsome, affable gentleman was also a skilful politician and he courageously attempted to maintain Royal authority. But as the revolutionary movement grew, as committees and congresses were organized, Franklin found himself helpless to oppose them. One reason was that he had no police force. Regular troops had been withdrawn from the area some years before, and the Whigs in New Jersey had followed the example of other colonies in getting control of the militia.[6]

A more important reason was the failure of the Loyalists to take a firm stand alongside the governor. While Franklin remained at his residence in Perth Amboy, refusing to acknowledge the authority of the Provincial Congress, prominent members of the colonial establishment made every effort to avoid committing themselves. Courtland Skinner, who later raised a Loyalist regiment, gave evasive answers to a Committee of Inspection and it was not until December, 1775, that the Whigs intercepted one of his letters which revealed his Loyalist sympathies and forced him to flee. Chief Justice Smythe, a cautious man, avoided antagonizing the Whigs until 1777 when he finally went into the British lines. Stephen Skinner's views were so misunderstood that he was elected to the Provincial Congress in the spring of 1775 and was not arrested as a Loyalist until more than a year later. Peter Kemble, sometime Council president whose son was serving with the British army, managed to trim his sails to the political winds enough to avoid Whig reprisals, and he was a gracious host to American officers when the army wintered near his estate in 1775–1776.

The Provincial Congress was soon requiring loyalty oaths, even of its own members, and it passed a treason law which provided for barbaric penalties for offenders. Estates of Tories who had "deserted" to the enemy were confiscated and those of dubious loyalty were required to give paroles. Families of Loyalists in the vicinity of New York were moved to the interior of the state and Patriot militia did short terms of "Tory hunt service." On July 2, 1776, the Provincial Congress adopted a constitution for the independent state of New Jersey. Governor Franklin was arrested and imprisoned.

But the summer began with the arrival of Howe's fleet and army in New York. Staten Island, the initial British base of operations, was only a cannon shot across the water from the farms of Middlesex and Essex counties. Resentful Tories who had endured the high-handed Committees of Inspection became bolder in the proximity of this military might. Armed clashes broke out in Hunterdon and Monmouth counties and Tory raiders began to collect in the Great Cedar Swamp in the south. Although local Patriot militia prevented a concerted uprising militiamen were reluctant to leave their homes for service in the army, and Washington released some of his New Jersey regiments to defend Powle's Hook (modern Paulus Hook) and Newark.

The British victory on Long Island and Washington's retreat had a devastating effect on the Patriot cause. The wealthier Tories sought refuge inside the British lines and the boldness of the Tory partisans increased. As Washington abandoned New York and retired into New Jersey he brought in his wake the British advance commanded by Lord Cornwallis, creating "a great to Do of Moveing of Goods and talk of hideing Earthly treasure."[7]

Washington was deeply disappointed at the failure of the militia to rally to his support, but he understood their frame of mind. "When danger is a little removed from them, they will not turn out at all. When it comes home to them, the well-affected, instead of flying to Arms to defend themselves, are busily employed in removing their Family's and effects, while the disaffected are concerting measures to make their submission [to the British], and spread terror and dismay all around."[8]

The "disaffected" lost no time in turning on their tormenters. Northern New Jersey quickly fell to the Loyalists who hunted down their enemies as savagely as had the "Tory hunters." John Hart, speaker of the Assembly, fled to the Sourland Hills after the Tories murdered his wife and ransacked his home. The state legislature decamped from Trenton, met briefly at Burlington, and then disbanded until spring. "The State," wrote General Alexander McDougall on December 22, "is totally deranged, without government, or officers, civil or military, in it, that will act with any spirit. Many of them are gone to the enemy for protection. . . ."

On November 30 General Howe proclaimed a pardon for all who would take an oath of allegiance within sixty days, and it was now the turn of the Tories to "persuade" their fellow-citizens to declare their loyalty. Samuel Tucker, former president of the Provincial Congress, was taken prisoner, but obtained his release by accepting Howe's pardon. Two other members, John Covenhoven and Henry Garritse, also accepted British protection along with thousands of less prominent inhabitants who found it expedient to side with the winner.

Courtland Skinner, powerful leader of the Amboy Group, was commissioned a brigadier general with authority to raise five regiments, a total of 2,500 men. But Tories proved to be no more eager for long-term enlistments than their Whig counterparts. They preferred to enlist in the Loyalist militia "Associations" which enabled them to draw muskets and ammunition to harass their Whig enemies.[9]

By the middle of December it appeared that the British conquest of New Jersey was complete. As Howe prepared to go into winter quarters he decided to secure the state by a line of garrisons extending from Perth Amboy, opposite Staten Island, through Brunswick and Princeton to the Delaware river towns of Trenton and Bordentown. "My principal object," said Howe, "in so great an extension of the cantonments was to afford protection to the inhabitants, that they might experience the difference between his majesty's government, and that to which they were subject by the rebel leaders."

There was indeed a difference, but not of the kind Sir William meant. Redcoats and Hessians were much more thorough and efficient in their looting than the Americans, and they made no distinction between Tory and Patriot. They "carried off their furniture . . . and piled up looking glasses with frying pans in the same heap, by the roadside. The soldier would place a female camp follower as a guard upon the spoil, while he returned to add to the treasure." Young Stephen Kemble, a native of New Jersey and a member of General Howe's staff, attested to the fact that the British incursion was "marked by the Licentiousness of the Troops, who committed every species of Rapine and plunder."

Both Howe and Cornwallis issued stern orders against looting but both were back in winter quarters in New York. It was not long before more serious breaches were being committed. A committee of Congress reported *"inhuman treatment of those who were so unfortunate as to become prisoners,"* and *"the lust and brutality of the soldiers in abusing women."* Such reports were no doubt exaggerated but the indignation of the Loyalists confirmed the fact that there was considerable substance to the charges.

The severity of the Tory reprisals and the indiscriminate looting by the soldiers was fatal to Howe's hopes for a peaceful conquest. The British invasion laid the ground for a bitter internecine struggle that lasted until the end of the war. By the middle of December, 1776, the Whig partisans had unleashed a fierce guerilla counter-attack that kept British and Tory nerve ends raw. On December 11 a member of Howe's staff reported the theft of 700 oxen, 1,000 sheep and hogs, 400 cattle, and 8 baggage wagons. During the next week parties of militia on their way from the north to join Washington's army captured 75 Tories. A Hessian officer reported that it was "very hard to travel in New Jersey." Rebels hid their weapons "in some nearby bushes, ditches or the like; when they . . . see one person or only a few, they shoot at their heads, then thrown their muskets away . . . and act as if they know nothing about it." Colonel Johann Rall, commanding the Hessians at Trenton, lost so many dispatch riders that he decided to bring the problem to the attention of General James Grant, commanding at Brunswick, by sending his dispatches under an escort of 100 men and two guns. General Grant does not seem to have been either amused or impressed.[10]

Yet these were sporadic and uncoordinated harassments. If they drove the Hessians to distraction and irritated the British command, they did not threaten British control of the state. Moreover, the ebbing of American fortunes was not confined to New Jersey. Washington was painfully aware that the entire American cause was in grave peril. He must have wholeheartedly agreed with Joseph Reed when the latter wrote: "We are all of the opinion, my dear General, that something must be done to revive our expiring credit, [and] give our cause some reputation. . . . Even a failure cannot be more fatal than to remain in our present situation. In short, some enterprise must be undertaken . . . or we must give up the cause."[11]

THE GUNS OF TRENTON

On the western bank of the Delaware above Trenton, Washington began to collect the remnants of what had been, less than four months before, an army of 20,000 men. He ordered General Gates to bring in the regiments of Continental troops which had been sent to the northern army, and only reluctantly decided to leave Heath's little command at the Hudson Highlands. For more than two weeks he had been urging Charles Lee to join him in accordance with the plans made when the army left New York, but Lee had other ideas. Dispatch after dispatch went out from headquarters and the answers from Lee were equivocal and argumentative. Lee had been given 7,000 men comprising the best regiments in the army, but Washington's urgent request "to hasten your march as much as possible" drew from Lee a vague suggestion that "it will be difficult I am afraid to join you; but cannot I do you more service by attacking their rear? I shall look about me tomorrow and inform you further."

On December 12 Lee carelessly rode out of his lines near Basking Ridge to White's Tavern "for the sake of a little better lodging." The next morning a British patrol captured him as he finished a leisurely breakfast, and he remained in enemy hands until the summer of 1778. The loss of this most experienced of Washington's subordinates added to the gloom that was descending on headquarters. John Sullivan, Lee's successor, brought in the vagrant command on the 20th, but only 2,000 men paraded for the commander in chief's inspection, and Gates' seven "regiments" had shrunk to 600 rank and file. Again it was the militia that brought Washington's army up to something resembling respectability. Nearly 2,000 Maryland and Pennsylvania troops came in commanded by General John Cadwalader and Colonel James Ewing, so that as of December 20 the force west of the Delaware numbered about 7,500 men. But the enlistments of the Continental troops would expire at the end of the year. Unless there were reenlistments or replacements the Continentals would be reduced to less than 1,400 effectives. "This handful, and such militia as may choose to join me, will then compose our army."[12]

In addition to collecting his troops Washington needed to collect his wits. The man who had always advocated concentration of forces had divided his army, and had allowed himself to be talked into decisions that had lost the two forts on the Hudson with their invaluable men and supplies. Even when he reached Trenton, on December 3, he had made as though to attack the pursuing British although he was outnumbered almost two to one. Once across the Delaware he had attempted to spread his regiments over a twenty-five mile front which left him weak at all points. By carefully destroying or bringing off all the boats on the east bank of the Delaware, he had temporarily thwarted the enemy's pursuit, but Washington dreaded a hard freeze which would allow the British to cross the river into Pennsylvania and threaten Philadelphia.[13]

The most feasible way to regain the initiative seemed to be to strike a blow against Howe's tenuous line of cantonments. The idea probably occurred to others besides the commander in chief. The keys to the success of such a movement would be surprise and concentration of forces which would give the Americans a decided advantage in numbers. Intelligence reports placed the enemy force in Trenton at about 2,000 men, all Hessians, commanded by Colonel Johann Rall. About six miles further down the river at Bordentown was another contingent of some 1,500 men commanded by Colonel Von Donop. Three more regiments were reported quartered at Princeton. This information was fairly accurate although the estimate of Hessian strength at Trenton was exaggerated by about twenty-five percent.

Above all, there must be secrecy. Washington did not call a council of war, as he usually did before a major operation. He did not even issue the orders for the attack until the morning of the 25th, the day when the troop movement was to begin. These orders called for a main force of 2,400 men to attack the garrison at Trenton. General Cadwalader was to cross at Bordentown to distract Von Donop. Colonel Ewing was to take 700 men across the river below Trenton to seal off the enemy's escape downriver.[14]

On a bitter cold Christmas night Washington's main force began its embarkation. Colonel Henry Knox, the stout artillery chief whose voice was as big as his girth, acted as "beachmaster," his stentorian commands reaching above the blustery northeast wind as he directed men and equipment into the boats. Eighteen guns were manhandled aboard, more than three times as many as were usually employed with such a force of infantry. Knox's artillerymen were an elite corps, well trained and confident. Washington was undoubtedly well aware of their quality and of the special value of artillery in bad weather.

John Glover's regiment, composed largely of seamen from Marblehead, Massachusetts, manned the forty-foot "Durham boats." These were flat-bottomed craft drawing less than two feet of water, used to haul iron ore and grain on the Delaware, and they could hold 100 men. They were pointed at both ends and propelled by four pole-men who sank their long poles in the river bottom and then "walked" the boats forward. For three hours the Marblehead men battled the wind and floating ice as the boats passed back and forth, and it was not until 3 a.m. that the last of the men and guns were across to New Jersey. Only four hours of darkness remained and their objective was still nine miles away. It was obvious that the army would not be in a position for a dawn attack, as Washington had planned. The troops set off down the road to Trenton, measuring their pace to the progress of the guns.

About halfway to Trenton Washington divided the command, sending Sullivan along the river to attack the lower town while he rode with Greene's division toward the upper end. Each division was accompanied by nine guns,

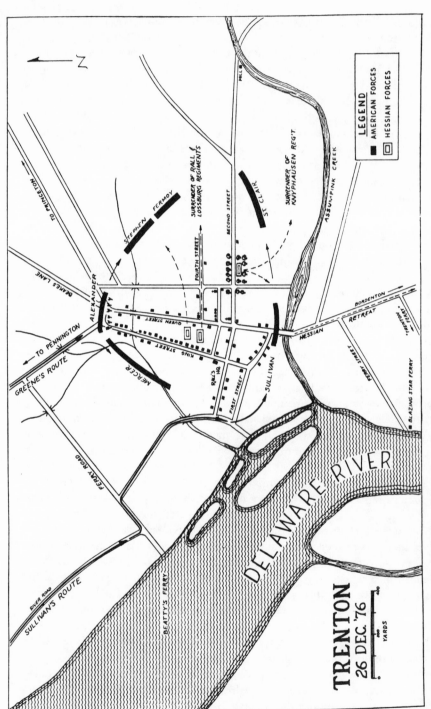

TRENTON
26 DEC. '76

DELAWARE RIVER

© Mark Boatner, III, *Encyclopedia of American Revolution*, David McKay Co., Inc.

four at the head of each column. Daylight came and both wings were still short of Trenton. The wind now carried rain and sleet which glazed the road and numbed the thinly clad soldiers. It was almost eight o'clock when Greene's van approached the first Hessian pickets posted along the Pennington Road.

This road came into Trenton from the northwest, ran across the northern edge of the town and continued northeast toward Maidenhead and Princeton. The two principal streets, King and Queen, ran south from this road and perpendicular to it. The head of these two parallel streets was Greene's objective. At the far end of Trenton, King and Queen Streets merged to cross a bridge over Assunpink Creek, this being the only easy exit to the south. The Assunpink bridge was Sullivan's objective.[15]

Much has been said about the slothfulness of the Hessian commander, Colonel Rall, and the fact that his soldiers were suffering from massive hangovers as the result of their Christmas celebration. There is no question but that much of this is true. But all the Hessians were not asleep. Lieutenant Andreas Wiederhold was in charge of the outposts on the night of December 25–26 and he attended to his duties. At daybreak he sent patrols up both the Pennington Road and the River Road. With the coming of full light the patrols returned and reported that all was quiet. If Washington had been able to keep his schedule both his columns would probably have been discovered. As it was, about eight o'clock Wiederhold stepped out of the building housing the pickets to get a breath of fresh air and saw Greene's vanguard about one hundred and fifty yards away.

Driving in the Hessian outpost the Americans broke into a stumbling, sliding, sprawling run. Urged on by Washington they poured into the upper end of King Street, then slipped between the buildings and into alleyways, pressing the enemy toward the center of the town. Shots from the other end of King Street signalled the simultaneous arrival of Sullivan. But the driving snow and sleet rendered many of the muskets useless. Quickly the way was cleared for the guns, vents kept dry by leather plugs and powder charges encased in starched cloth smeared with tallow. Young Captain Alexander Hamilton swung two six-pounders into action at the head of King Street. As the Hessians attempted to form the American guns boomed into their ranks and broke their formation. Captain Thomas Forrest posted six guns at the head of Queen Street and fired salvos into the flank of an attack that was forming against Sullivan, who was seizing the Assunpink bridge.

Meantime, Hugh Mercer's Virginians pressed into the town from the western side of King Street and linked up with Sullivan's left. Lord Stirling's brigade advanced down King and Queen Streets in the wake of the artillery fire. As Stirling, Mercer, and Sullivan squeezed the Hessians they retreated to the eastern outskirts of Trenton. Greene, however, had not committed his whole command and he now sideslipped the regiments of Adam Stephen and Roche de Fermoy out along the Princeton road to the northeast. Rall's men were now surrounded but the Hessian commander bravely attempted to rally his men. He placed himself at the head of one of his regiments and ordered a charge but his troops were driven back and Rall himself was shot from his horse, mortally wounded. Major von Dechow, the second in command was also killed. A little before nine o'clock the last of the Hessians grounded arms, the officers raising their hats on the tips of their swords to indicate surrender.

Twenty-two of Rall's men were dead and 948 were captives. About 500 escaped to Bordentown or Princeton. Two Americans had been killed, possibly frozen to death, and only a handful were wounded, among them Lieutenant James Monroe and the commanding general's cousin, Captain William Washington.[16]

Included in the spoils were forty horses, six field guns, 1,000 muskets and bayonets, and enough trumpets, clarinets, and hautboys for two bands. There were also forty hogsheads of rum which the commander in chief ordered staved in. But one must suppose that these veterans had learned all the arts of war and there must have been a few cases of "barrel fever." At least one group managed to salvage not only a cask of rum but also a hogshead of sugar. The whole was dumped into a rain barrel, stirred with a fence rail, and punch was served using shoes for cups. What gastric and cerebral effects this had on poorly fed soldiers who had marched and fought in the bitter cold for twelve hours is not recorded, but the imagination boggles.

There had been no news from either Cadwalader or Ewing, so Washington decided to cross back into Pennsylvania. In fact, Cadwalader had gotten part of his men across but could not land his guns, and so abandoned the attempt. Ewing made no effort to brave the storm and the river. But the threat to the Hessians at Bordentown was nonetheless achieved by a stroke of good fortune. On December 22 a detachment of militia had moved up from Philadelphia and skirmished with Hessian outposts not far from Bordentown. On the 23rd Von Donop reacted by pursuing them to Mount Holly, some ten or twelve miles southeast of Bordentown, and was thus too far away to help Rall. By early morning of the 27th Washington's men were back in Pennsylvania, worn to exhaustion and anxiously awaiting supplies which would restore their strength.

The battle had been a marvel of tactical neatness, considering the lack of training of both officers and men in offensive battlefield maneuvers. When the two columns divided on the way to Trenton Washington had had the officers set their watches with his. Whether he really believed that the attack would be so closely coordinated, the fact was that Greene and Sullivan had struck within minutes of each other. Greene had displayed fine judgement in keeping Stephen and Fermoy clear of the melee and then moving them out to snap the trap shut on the enemy retreat. But the outstanding performance of the day was surely that of young Henry Knox. Each attempt by the Hessians to rally their forces had met a blast from the guns, especially effective on

a day when many of the soldiers' muskets failed to fire. Knox was promoted
to brigadier on December 27.

There was indeed ample honor for all and when Washington reported to
Congress he said simply that "were I to give preference to any particular
Corps, I should do great injustice to the others." The men were enormously
pleased with themselves. Pennsylvania soldiers said in lofty disdain that
"engaging the English is a very trifling affair—nothing [being] so easy as to
drive them over the North River." Somewhere on the long road from Brooklyn Heights to Trenton this little army had become part of that rare breed
called "veterans."[17]

<h2 style="text-align:center">PRINCETON</h2>

The effect of the victory at Trenton was electric. Washington had "pounced
upon the Hessians like an eagle upon a hen. . . . If he does nothing more he
will live in history as a great military commander." In Baltimore, "This affair
has given such amazing spirit to our people that you might do anything or
go anywhere with them." From the President of the Pennsylvania Council
of Safety came encouragement of a more tangible sort. "We are sending off
reenforcements of militia, in hopes this very important blow may be followed
up. . . . Our militia are turning out by degrees, but this will give them new
stimulus. . . ."

Washington was greatly encouraged and hoped to continue his offensive.
He remained west of the Delaware only because supplies had not arrived to
feed his tired men. He was further encouraged by news from Cadwalader,
who was no ordinary militia general. He reported his failure but added that
he still intended to take his force into New Jersey which "would cause a diversion that would favor any attempt you may design in future. . . ." Cadwalader
added that the militia "are in good spirits and enlist very fast."[18]

But militia could not replace Continentals. Washington must retain a substantial number of his hard-bitten veterans as the nucleus of his army. There
was no way for him to launch an offensive before the first of the year and
by that time the enlistments would expire. Much as he hated speech-making
Washington resolved to make a personal appeal to these troops who "were
absolutely necessary to lead on the more raw and undisciplined."

The Continental regiments were paraded and, after offering a ten dollar
bonus for six weeks additional service, he told them plainly that they had done
all that he had asked them to do, "but we do not know how to spare you." The
drums rolled and, after an agonizing interval, "one said to another, 'I will
remain if you will,' . . . A few stepped forth, and their example was immediately followed by nearly half who were fit for duty. . . ." When an officer
asked if the men should be enrolled Washington's answer was, "No! Men
who will volunteer in such a case as this need no enrollment to keep them to
their duty."

He was ready to challenge the enemy again. Cadwalader and the other militia commanders were summoned and for the third time in five days the army crossed the Delaware. He was in Trenton on New Year's Eve when dispatches arrived from Congress at Baltimore informing Washington that he had been made virtual dictator for six months. He was authorized to raise troops "in the most speedy and effectual manner from any or all of these United States . . . to displace and appoint all officers under the rank of brigadier general . . . to take, wherever he may be, whatever he may want for the use of the army, if the inhabitants will not sell it, allowing a reasonable price for the same. . . ." This grant of "powers . . . of the highest nature and almost unlimited extent" could be viewed as a vote of confidence, but it also meant that Washington would receive all the blame if he failed. He answered by saying, "Instead of thinking myself freed of all *civil* obligations by this mark of confidence, I shall constantly bear in mind that as the sword was the last resort for the preservation of our liberties, so it ought to be the first to be laid aside when those liberties are firmly established. . . . I shall instantly set about making the most necessary reforms in the Army."[19]

By New Year's Day Cadwalader had come in with 2,100 men and 1,600 more Pennsylvania militia raised by General Thomas Mifflin had arrived. This brought his forced to somewhat more than 5,000 men along with the whole of Knox's artillery train, forty guns.

He now learned that Lord Cornwallis himself had come out from New York to deliver a counterattack. With a swiftness that was uncharacteristic of the British his lordship routed the New Jersey garrisons from their winter quarters and, five days after the news of Trenton reached New York, Cornwallis was in Princeton. Leaving 1,500 men in the college town and another 1,500 at Maidenhead the British pressed toward Trenton.

The movement caught Washington napping. Instead of scattered garrisons spread across the state he was faced with 5,000 regulars under a commander who obviously did not intend to waste time in getting to the business at hand. Hastily the American commander pushed out a reconnaissance in force along the Princeton road commanded by Colonel Edward Hand who made contact with Cornwallis about noon on the 2nd. Hand fought his men tenaciously and harassed the enemy to such an extent that he forced them to abandon their marching formation and advance the last few miles in line of battle. It was not until about four o'clock that Hand finally pulled his men into the American lines on the south side of Assunpink Creek across from Trenton. As the British approached, Knox's forty guns greeted them, and Daniel Hitchcock's Rhode Island Continentals defended the bridge with a steady rifle fire. Cornwallis withdrew to Trenton for the night and Knox's howitzers continued to lob an occasional shell into the town.

Washington now found himself squeezed into much the same kind of cul-de-sac as he had himself fashioned for Rall. One soldier remembered that "our army was in the most desperate situation I had ever known it; we had no boats to carry us across the Delaware . . . to cross the enemy's line of march between this and Princeton seemed impractical . . . [in] the south part of Jersey there was no support for an army. . . ."

In fact, there was a way "between this and Princeton." Cornwallis had not taken care to close the back roads which led off to the right of the American lines, roads which Colonel Reed and General Cadwalader knew well. Having decided that the odds were too great to risk a battle, Washington sought advice from a council of war. Probably he had already made up his mind to slip off by the right flank since patrols reported that the way was clear. However, unseasonable weather had thawed the ground and muddy roads would make slow going for the soldiers and monumental work for the gunners. The council readily agreed that a retreat to Princeton was the solution and the troops began to move at midnight.

Five hundred men were left behind to keep the campfires burning and make appropriate noises with pick and shovel. Three guns continued to send an occasional shell across toward the enemy camp. The rest of the men moved out silently, careful not to rattle their arms, the wheels of the guns muffled with rags. Washington's incredible luck was still with him, for the wind shifted to the northeast and the temperature dropped sharply. By two o'clock on the morning of January 3rd the muddy roads had frozen solid. It was another cold, slow night march but the weather was clear. As always, the soldiers had to adapt their pace to the guns, "frequently coming to a halt, or stand still, and when ordered forward again, one, two, three men in each platoon would stand, with their arms supported, fast asleep." Daylight came "bright, serene, and extremely cold, with a hoar frost which spangled every object." About eight o'clock the vanguard arrived at a Quaker meeting house about a mile and a half from Princeton. Here a back road led off to the right toward the town, along which Washington intended to make his attack by flanking the British defenses. Parallel to this road and about three-quarters of a mile ahead to the north lay the main Post Road from Trenton to Princeton. Hugh Mercer with about 350 men was to push ahead and destroy a bridge at Worth's Mill to prevent reinforcements to the enemy from Trenton.[20]

A few minutes after Mercer had started on his errand and Sullivan's division was filing off on the back road, firing was heard to the north in the direction of Worth's Mill. Colonel Robert Mawhood, commanding the British garrison at Princeton, had taken the Post Road for Trenton shortly before eight o'clock at the head of the 17th and 55th regiments. As he passed Worth's Mill Mawhood spotted Mercer's force coming up to his left and turned on it, driving the Americans back toward the main body. Mercer rallied his men and checked the British advance momentarily, but as the superior enemy force increased its pressure Mercer and Colonel John Haslet of the Delaware Continentals were both shot down. The men broke and were pushed back

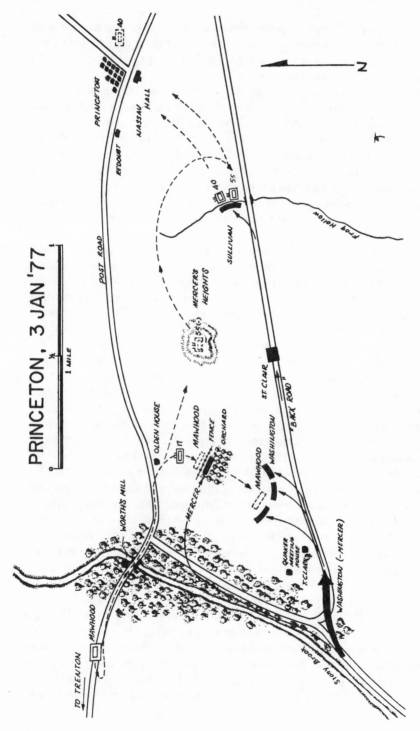

PRINCETON, 3 JAN '77

1 MILE

N

© Mark Boatner, III, *Encyclopedia of the American Revolution*, David McKay Co., Inc.

into the advance elements of Cadwalader's Pennsylvanians. The raw militia panicked and for a brief time it looked as if another Kip's Bay was developing.

But the panic was not universal. In the midst of the melee the gunners of Captain John Moulder's battery cooly swung their "long" four-pounders into action and slammed charge after charge of grape and canister into the advancing British. Washington's towering figure loomed through the smoke a scant thirty yards from the enemy line as he rallied the Pennsylvanians and directed Hitchcock's veterans into line. He built up the formation with Hand's tough riflemen. The line advanced with Washington at its head and he himself gave the order to halt and fire. The British broke and the big Virginian could not restrain himself. "It's a fine fox chase, my boys!" he roared and spurred his horse in pursuit of the flying redcoats.

The remainder of the Princeton garrison was surrounded and captured. Washington estimated the British losses at 400 men of whom 100 were killed. His own losses were 40 killed and wounded. But among the dead were General Mercer, an officer of proven ability, and John Haslet, whose Delaware Continentals had performed so brilliantly at Brooklyn Heights, and had been in virtually every action since then. It was a tribute to the young colonel that long after his death the regiment continued to be called Haslet's Continentals.

After helping itself to the scanty stores of food and blankets the army moved out. Cornwallis could be expected to be close on their heels, so Washington abandoned an attack on Brunswick. There were simply no more swift marches left in these exhausted, hungry men. From Princeton the commanding general led them northwest out of the path of the pursuers. A veteran sergeant made a rather clinical report on what had obviously been his own extensive study of the psychology of facing the enemy: "In this battle and that of Trenton there were no ardent spirits in the army, and the excitement of rum had nothing to do in obtaining the victories. As I had tried [gun] powder and rum on Long Island to promote courage, and engaged here without it, I can say that I was none the less courageous here than there."

On January 6, twelve days after the Christmas embarkation on the Delaware, the little army went into winter quarters in Morristown.[21]

"The unlucky affair of Rall's Brigade has given me a winter campaign," General Howe wrote to Germain on January 8, ". . . our quarters were too much exposed, and it is necessary to assemble our troops; that is now done and all is safe." What Sir William was saying, as delicately as possible, was that New Jersey had been abandoned by the British except for a garrison at Perth Amboy, across from Staten Island, and another at Brunswick, ten miles further inland. Even these two posts were harassed by the Americans in the months that followed. A British officer at Brunswick noted almost casually that "our Foraging Parties meet with the Rebels as usual, and a Man or two Killed now and then;" and a Hessian at Elizabethtown complained, "One can no longer lie down to sleep without thinking: this is your last night of living."[22]

More important than the failure in New Jersey was the fact that the Howes had missed their chance to bring the war to an end. From Long Island to the Delaware there had been one opportunity after another to bring Washington "to a decisive action" and most of these had been lost, not so much by Washington's skill as by Sir William's indolence or stupidity. Even the victories at Trenton and Princeton were impressive only against the background of dark despair that had fallen on the American cause. Granted that Washington had displayed magnificent courage and determination, and had managed the little campaign with great skill, he would have been a poor general indeed if he had failed to rout Rall's 1,500 men with his own force of 2,500. At Princeton, with more than four times the strength of his opponent, he had barely escaped disaster before he finally drove the enemy.

But the stunning success of the campaign could not be denied. On January 20 Howe was somewhat more frank with Lord Germain: "I do not now see a prospect of terminating the war but by a general action, and I am aware of the difficulties. . . ." But, as always, he found an excuse, albeit a rather lame one. ". . . The Enemy moves with so much more celerity than we possibly can with our foreign troops who are too much attached to their baggage. . . ."

Germain was not at all pleased with the news of Trenton and Princeton, although he perforce defended Howe's conduct publicly. He informed Howe that he disapproved of the leniency which had provoked the proclamation of November 30 and reminded the general that "it [is] necessary to adopt such modes of carrying on the war, that the Rebels may be effectually distressed, so that through a lively experience of Losses and sufferings they may be brought as soon as possible to a proper sense of their Duty." In short, Sir William was to wage war, not peace.[23]

The gloom in the British camp was shared by the Loyalists. "The minds of the people are much altered," wrote young Nicholas Creswell. "A few Days ago they had given up the cause for lost. Their late successes have turned the scale and now they are all liberty mad again. Their Recruiting parties could not get a man . . . no longer since than last week, and now the men are coming in by the companies. Confound the turncoat scoundrels and cowardly Hessians together. . . . Volunteer Companies are collecting in every County on the Continent, and in a few months the rascals will be stronger than ever. Even the parsons . . . have turned out as Volunteers and Pulpit Drums or Thunder or whatever you may please to call it, summoning all to arms in this cursed babble. D——— them all."

From one end of the country to the other Patriot despair changed to jubilant hope. "Washington retreats like a General and acts like a hero," trumpeted the *Pennsylvania Journal*. "If there are spots on his character, they are like spots on the sun. . . ." The *Freeman's Journal* urged that "whilst we are united in our sentiment, vigilant in our duty, and active in our operations, we need not dread the thunder of cannon, nor tremble at the names of heroes arrayed in all the splendor of a corrupt court, or crowned with faded laurels which have been plucked by the hands of tyranny."[24]

So the dark crisis of 1776 passed. The Americans had not yet won this war. But Britain had lost an irretrievable opportunity to win it.

FIVE

Arms and Men

THE CREATION OF THE AMERICAN ARMY MARKED A MILESTONE IN THE HISTORY of modern warfare. Until 1775 eighteenth century wars were fought by relatively small armies composed of highly trained soldiers. The American army, of necessity, was made up of citizen soldiers who were mustered into the ranks, given the barest minimum of training, and often sent almost immediately into battle.

In 1790 the War Department reported that there had been 396,000 enlistments of all kinds in the national and state armed forces between 1775 and 1783. This included, of course, a large number who had enlisted more than once. Considering the fact that there were probably no more than 250,000 men of military age available for duty a fair estimate would seem to be that about 100,000 men bore arms at one time or another during the War of Independence. Less than one third of this number, about 30,000, were under arms at one time. The largest return of the regular, or Continental army under Washington's command was in October, 1778, when the commander in chief reported 18,742 men present and fit for duty.[1]

The myth persists to this day that the soldiers who defeated the British regulars were veteran Indian fighters, crack shots who harried the redcoats from ambush with their deadly long rifles. In fact, probably ninety percent of the American soldiers were recruited from areas east of the Appalachians and were a generation or more removed from the frontier. Most of them had never seen a wild Indian in their lives and few had ever fired a shot in anger. Most of them were familiar with fire arms, for most were farmers and hunters, so their fire was somewhat more accurate than their British counterparts. But their weapon was a smoothbore musket which had a maximum effective range of seventy-five yards and took from twenty to thirty seconds to reload. On the battlefield a fire delivered at pointblank range (twenty-five to thirty yards) rarely inflicted more than ten percent casualties.[2]

The close-ordered ranks of British regulars were the subject of much derision by Americans then and since, but eighteenth century generals knew what they were about. Only when soldiers were organized into disciplined ranks so that their limited fire power could be concentrated and controlled could an army be effective. American derision changed to terror at Brooklyn Heights when the serried ranks of redcoats advanced against the Americans, halted to deliver a fire at thirty paces, and then charged with levelled bayonets. General Washington insisted that his army be trained according to the practice of European military science, and the first occasion on which his Continentals met the British on something like equal terms (i.e., without benefit of fortifications or superior numbers) was at Monmouth Courthouse in 1778. It was an army which had been trained the previous winter by the Prussian drill master, Baron Von Steuben.

THE REDCOATS

"The success was too dearly bought," said General Howe after the battle of Bunker Hill. His dismay reflected not only his awareness of the limited number of soldiers in Boston, but the fact that the entire British army in 1775 numbered only about 45,000 men. Of this number 20,000 were committed to Ireland, Gibraltar, and other outposts of Britain's vast empire.

The basic unit of the British army was the regiment. Regiments were sometimes combined into brigades, divisions, wings or corps, but these were usually temporary organizations for special purposes or limited time periods. Lord Cornwallis' force that came out of New York to attack Washington at Trenton was referred to as both a corps and a division. A brigade of the Guards that served in America consisted of fifteen men from each of sixty-four companies of the King's household troops.[3]

The infantry regiment consisted of ten companies, eight of regular infantry and two flank companies. One of these consisted of grenadiers, so called because when they were incorporated into the regiments in the seventeenth century the men were selected for the size and strength necessary to throw grenades into the enemy ranks. By 1775 the grenades had long since disappeared but the tall, rugged grenadiers were still regarded as elite troops. The other flank company was composed of light infantry. These men were lightly built, active and quick-moving, and were usually picked for their marksmanship.

If several regiments were combined into a corps or there was an especially difficult assault to be made the flank companies were sometimes detached from their regiments and formed into a special regiment. At Bunker Hill Howe formed a regiment from eleven light infantry companies to attack the rail fence on the left of the American line.

Each company consisted of a captain, two lieutenants, two sergeants, three corporals, and thirty-eight privates. The total, including a drummer, was forty-seven officers and men. The regimental staff included a lieutenant-colonel, chaplain, two surgeons and, of course, the colonel commanding. It should be noted that reports of troop strength (or casualties) were made in terms of "rank and file," which meant the total of privates and corporals. A colonel who reported his regiment at full strength would therefore be accounting for 410 men.[4]

The standard weapon for the infantry of both armies was a smoothbore musket approximately four and a half to five feet in length with a calibre range from .69 to .80. A recruit was trained in the complicated loading procedure until he could fire every twenty seconds. If this were done on command twelve separate orders were necessary to complete the evolution.

Powder and shot were made up into paper cartridges. These were carried in a cartridge box made of wood and leather which afforded some protection from dampness, but were not proof against heavy rain. In loading his weapon the soldier extracted a cartridge, bit off the end of the paper spill, and poured a few grains of powder into the priming pan. He then closed the pan and poured the remaining powder and the ball into the muzzle of the musket, using the paper as a wad, and ramming the whole firmly into place. He then pointed his weapon in the general direction of the enemy and fired, bracing himself against the vicious recoil. When he pulled the trigger the hammer or cock, which held a bit of flint, fell upon the lid of the pan (called the frizzen) creating a shower of sparks and flipping up the frizzen to expose the powder. The resultant flash ignited the propellant charge through a touch hole bored through the barrel.

It is not surprising that these crude weapons often failed to fire. A worn flint, damp powder, a clogged touch hole—all these could cause a failure. There was also human failure. An enemy fire delivered at thirty yards while a soldier was reloading was not conducive to steady hands and cool nerves, especially when the enemy might at any moment burst through the dense cloud of smoke with his deadly bayonet levelled. If the soldier were under fire for the first time his performance usually left a great deal to be desired. It was not remarkable to see a number of ramrods sailing through the air when a volley of counterfire was delivered. And in the crash of musketry it was hard to tell if one's own weapon had fired. So it was commonplace after a fight to find on the battlefield muskets loaded to the muzzle with unexpended charges.[5]

The field artillery of the British army was organized into four battalions (or regiments) of eight companies each. Although their total company strength was only 116 there were, for this specialized army, six officers and eight non-commissioned officers. Nine bombardiers, eighteen gunners, and seventy-three matrosses (privates) completed the complement. Field guns ranged in size from enormous 24-pounders to tiny 3-pounders. A 12-pounder required ten to twelve horses to haul its 3,200 pounds of dead weight so that 6- and 9-pounders were increasingly used by both armies as a concession to the bad roads and rough terrain of the American countryside. Gun teams were handled by civilian drivers who were hired by the army.

All field guns, regardless of size, had approximately the same range of about 2,000 yards, but were generally not effective beyond 1,000 to 1,200 yards. The standard piece fired a fairly flat trajectory and used solid shot, grape, or canister. Grape consisted of clusters of iron balls about two inches in diameter. Canister was, as the term implies, simply an iron container filled with musket balls. A 6-pounder had a bore of about 3.6 inches and the gun tube was about five feet long. The gun was trained by a long pole called a tiller or handspike which was inserted through a ring in the gun trail, so that the entire gun and carriage was slewed to left or right. The range was set by an elevating screw or wedge.

In addition to the regular field guns there were also mortars and howitzers. Mortars were stubby, massive pieces mounted on flat, immobile beds at a fixed angle of 45° to 70°. They fired high-trajectory explosive shells, the range determined by the size of the powder charge. Howitzers were the compromise between regular field guns and mortars. They were mounted on wheeled carriages, but the short trail and stubby barrel enabled them to fire high-trajectory explosive shells as well as the standard solid shot, grape, and canister. Although their effective range was decreased by the short barrel length they were very versatile guns.

It was the usual practice to allot two guns to each regiment, although by the time of the War of Independence commanders on both sides were beginning to use much higher ratios and to employ massed artillery operating independently of the infantry regiments. The rate of fire achieved in both armies was remarkable considering that the loading was similar to, though less complicated than loading a musket (a gun could be primed and loaded at the same time). Captain George Pausch, an artillery officer of the Hesse-Hanau regiment, gave a demonstration for General Burgoyne and his officers during which his gunners fired twelve rounds per minute.[6]

Mounted troops were traditionally divided into two categories: cavalry, that is, troops trained to fight from horseback; and dragoons, who were technically mounted infantry who rode to the battlefield and then dismounted and fought on foot. In practice, the dragoons performed as cavalry and the two terms were often used synonymously. There were only four regiments of cavalry in the British army and none served in America until the end of the war. Dragoons were used for outpost duty, scouting and reconnaissance, and especially to harry a retreating enemy whose formations had been broken. Since horses were in short supply there was almost never a sufficient force of dragoons available to appear in battle formations. There were Hessian dragoons with Burgoyne's army but they had no horses and were therefore relegated to infantry duty.

Despite their public assurances to the contrary the ministry and the King did not make the mistake of planning for a short war. As already noted, when General Howe asked for 20,000 men for the campaign of 1776 Germain not only exceeded his request but sent an additional 10,000 troops to Canada. Before the war was over 56,000 men had been sent to North America and the West Indies.[7]

Peacetime enlistment in the British army was for life, and it was obvious that the expansion of the army, as well as the navy, would never be accomplished under the normal peacetime conditions. "Sad work everywhere in recruiting," wrote the British adjutant-general, Edward Harvey, late in 1775. "In these damn times we must exert zeal."

The most usual way to enlarge the army was for the King to grant a commission to a regimental commander, who in turn recruited his men, for which he received a bounty, and pay and subsistence for his men. George III was reluctant to incur the additional expense of raising new regiments until the existing ones had been brought up to strength. But enlistments were encouraged by an order of December, 1775, which provided that volunteers would receive a guinea and a half bounty and could be discharged at the end of three years or the conclusion of the war, "at the option of His Majesty." In addition, vagrants, smugglers, and those convicted of minor crimes might enlist as a means of escaping imprisonment. It is not surprising that jails and prisons became a favorite haunt of recruiting officers. By 1779 additional inducements had been added, among them doubling the bounty and allowing the conscription of convicted criminals. [8]

The obvious conclusion is that those who were enlisted were for the most part riffraff and vagrants, and those whose earning power was so low that a guinea and a half bounty was irresistible. From such "disorderly persons" and "incorrigible rogues" the ranks of the army were filled, scarcely "such Recruits as a Battn. might choose to take in times of profound Peace." But under hard-eyed sergeants these recruits became soldiers, and whatever identity they might have had as civilians was lost as they merged into and became a part of the regiment. This new identity led to the development of a fierce pride and loyalty that was so intense that it could become explosive. Soldiers of Fraser's famous 71st Highlanders were threatened with transfer to another regiment, which would have forced them to stop wearing their kilts. They mutinied and thirty of them were killed before they could be subdued.

A private's pay was eight pence a day but so much of this was deducted for various "off-reckonings" that the soldier rarely received any hard cash. As one contemporary observed, ". . . when all deductions are made, for clothing, for necessaries, for washing, for the paymaster, for the surgeon, for the multiplied articles of useless and unmilitary fopperies (introduced by many colonels to the oppression of the soldier for what they call the credit and appearance of the regiment) there is not sufficient surplus for a healthful subsistence; and as to the little enjoyment and recreation, which even the meanest rank of men can call their own in any country, the brave, the honorable veteran soldier, must not aspire to."[9]

So the army existence was desperately hard. But then in the eighteenth century all life among the lower classes was harsh, and punishments, even for petty crimes, were cruel and brutal. Similar brutalities existed in the disciplinary code of the army. Petty offenses such as malingering or failing to pass inspection might bring confinement to barracks on bread and water for a week. Serious breeches of discipline brought drastic penalties. Striking an officer was a court martial offense punishable by a sentence of 800 lashes. Delivered full force with a cat-o'-nine-tails such punishment might kill a man, and would certainly cripple him for weeks.

The poverty of the average soldier made him a chronic thief. Thomas MacMahan and his "wife" were convicted of theft, he being sentenced to 1,000 lashes, she to "100 lashes on her bare back, at the Cart's Tail, in different portions and most conspicuous Parts of the Town, and to be imprisoned for three months." Two soldiers convicted of robbing a storekeeper were shot.

Drinking, gambling, and women provided most of the diversions for the British redcoat. That estimable chronicler of army life, Sergeant Roger Lamb, relates that privates would often gamble away their uniforms, and be forced to borrow clothes from their comrades in order to muster for inspection. Women were commonplace with the army. It was said that Burgoyne's army was accompanied by 2,000 women when he invaded New York, and Sir William Howe issued a general order authorizing six women per company in the campaign of 1776, a total of 2,776 women and 1,904 children. Some few of these were undoubtedly wives, and there is convincing evidence that many of the women, wives or not, were remarkably loyal to their men, some even accompanying the troops to the battlefield.[10]

All in all the British regular soldier, despite his miserable existence, proved to be a formidable opponent. Trained as he was in monotonous drill and rigid formations, he moved when he was supposed to move with predictable precision and speed. Because he performed as he was expected to perform he was, man for man, the superior of his American counterpart on the battlefield. Burgoyne paid tribute to the courage of his infantry: "Men of half [your] bodily strength and even Cowards may be [your] match in firing; but the onset of Bayonets in the hands of the Valiant is irresistible. . . ." English officers lost a good many battles in the War of Independence but almost never because of the failure of the redcoat.[11]

Officers owed their positions to two factors, social rank and money. It was not very difficult to become an officer if one came from an upper or middle class family. Younger sons of the nobility who sought army careers were placed in a regiment at an early age, ordinarily sixteen. A subaltern's commission could be purchased in most infantry regiments for £1,200. From that point the officer advanced by finding a vacancy created by death or retirement and purchasing it. If he rose from ensign to lieutenant-colonel in his regiment, the total cost was £3,500. Usually the senior subaltern was given preference for vacancies up to the rank of major. Above that rank the officer encountered stiffer competition, since the rank of lieutenant-colonel might carry with it a regimental command. It became necessary for the aspirant to find a sponsor from the higher military ranks or from a patron in the government. He might find himself favored because of his excellent record, but he was more apt to be promoted for family or political reasons.[12]

At first glance the system appears impossible as a means of producing capable and competent commanders. In the peace-time establishment senior officers only occasionally saw duty with the troops, preferring instead to enter politics or to indulge in the games society played. A regimental colonel might be in his seventies, for there was only half-pay retirement for officers too infirm for active duty. But the coming of war usually eliminated the physically and mentally disabled. Sponsors rarely backed a candidate who was a proven incompetent, for if the officer failed his disgrace discredited the man who recommended him. It is doubtful if William and Richard Howe would have received their American commands if they had not had excellent records, since their failure could (and, in the event, did) adversely affect those who had backed their appointments.

In the absence of any professional schooling it is difficult to see how officers could be better trained than simply by serving with a regiment. A lad of sixteen, if he were not a complete dullard, would likely be a capable lieutenant by the time he was twenty-one. The truism that senior sergeants are the backbone of the army was no less applicable in the eighteenth century, and an erring young subaltern could usually be guided through the first years by the tactful wisdom of non-commissioned officers.

Unless he had an independent income the junior officer was rarely able to live much above the level of a middle class tradesman or mechanic. If the purchase system blocked his way to advancement he found an outlet for his energies in perfecting the efficiency of his platoon or company. He was often widely read in the military literature of the day and occasionally gained a reputation as a military scholar. An officer was a gentleman and was accepted as a peer by his fellows, even those who might have titles of nobility; "off parade . . . It ought to be the characteristic of every gentleman neither to impose, nor submit to, any distinction but such as propriety of conduct, or superiority of talent, naturally create." In short, the major must not assume an overbearing attitude toward a lieutenant—especially as the lieutenant might turn out to be properly addressed as "M'lord."

The highest ranking generals and admirals were often from families of the nobility. Francis Lord Rawdon, Hugh Earl Percy and Lord Cornwallis, for all their patrician background, were hard and skilful fighters. Not a few officers earned titles in the performance of their duties. Guy Carleton, as noted, was knighted for his defense of Canada in 1776 and ten years later he became Lord Dorchester. The large number of officers of the nobility was not surprising, for eighteenth century Britons had not forgotten the Civil War which had brought Cromwell to power, and other unsuccessful rebellions against the Crown. What better way to preserve order and secure property than to entrust control of the military to the landed gentry?

It should also be noted that at the beginning of the war there were twenty-three members of Parliament who held commissions in the armed forces, and that among their number were both Howes, Clinton, Burgoyne, and Cornwallis. This may seem strange to Americans who have traditionally kept the military carefully separated from politics. But Britain during the period of her great empire undoubtedly benefitted from the mutual understanding of the military and political problems of imperial control. The United States in the twentieth century has come to understand that politicians and generals have difficulty solving global problems if each operates in isolation from the other.[13]

If in hindsight the British officer corps seemed shot through with inefficient fops who held their positions through a capricious system of selection, it should be remembered that every system before and since has had its share of bumblers and nincompoops. If William Howe appears inordinately lazy and dull, if "Gentleman Johnny" Burgoyne comes on as a braggart and a blunderer, their counterparts have appeared in other times and circumstances. It is too much to expect that every war will produce a Wolfe or a Wellington.

THE CONTINENTALS

Two days after Lexington and Concord the Massachusetts Committee of Safety began enlisting men into a provisional army. The soldiers took a rather simple oath to obey their officers and to submit to orders and regulations. They agreed to remain in the army until the end of the war, and so were known as the "Eight Months Army." Congress adopted it in the middle of May, 1775, and General Washington took command of it a year and a day before the Declaration of Independence.

In the weeks that followed Washington labored to organize the inchoate assemblage into an effective fighting force. Uniforms were scarce although Congress promised "a suit of clothes" for those who reenlisted. The shortage of arms constituted another problem but almost any of the muskets which these first volunteers often brought with them were as effective as the British "Brown Bess." Artillery was much more difficult to acquire, but some was obtained from colonial arsenals and more from forts abandoned by the British. Soon significant supplies of arms of all sorts came in from abroad, especially from France.[14]

By the spring of 1776 Washington had come to believe that a standing army of regular soldiers was a necessary requirement for winning the war. Congressional leaders thought that the war would be a short one, and they shared the traditional Whig aversion to standing armies. "We already see the growing thirst for power in some departments of the army," Elbridge Gerry remarked darkly in the fall of 1775, "which ought to be regulated so as to keep the military subservient to the civil in every part of the United Colonies." The subsequent history of the United States has provided so little ground for such fears that there is a tendency to smile at the Founding Fathers for their paranoia. But politicians in 1775 were students of history and they cited examples from Caesar to Cromwell to demonstrate their point. Indeed, the dreary history of Congressional procrastination and political malingering in the states suggests that a commander in chief with only a little less patience and patriotism than George Washington might have changed the course of revolutionary history as profoundly as did Napoleon.[15]

It was these considerations which led Congress to limit the enlistments of the "Eight Months Army" and the policy was continued for 1776. Not until Washington was driven from New York and the army was at the edge of disaster did the leaders awake to the fact that their theoretical fears were wasted in the reality of the imminent collapse of the revolution. Belatedly Congress authorized an army of eighty-eight regiments to be enlisted for three years or the duration of the war. But by this time the first flush of patriotic ardor had cooled and those who felt the call to duty found it more convenient to enlist in their state militia for terms of from two to six months. The army that was recruited in the winter of 1776–1777 was the real beginning of the "regulars."

When recruiting first began in 1775 the adjutant general directed that officers were prohibited from enrolling "any deserter from the ministerial army, nor any stroller, negro or vagabond." By 1777 a more realistic attitude dictated the acceptance, not only of such undesirables, but slaves and convicts. This was often the result of state laws which permitted men called to duty to furnish substitutes, and if the price was right recruiters accepted almost anyone, even "miserable sharp looking Caitiffs, [and] hungry lean fac'd Villians." It was true that some substantial citizens joined the ranks in the early days of the war, shopkeepers, farmers, and artisans who were moved by a sense of duty and patriotism. But by the beginning of 1777 the Continentals were reduced to less than a thousand men consisting of what must have been the toughest bodies and spirits in the country.[16]

By the spring of 1777 Congress had turned the problem of recruiting over to the states by assigning to each a quota and providing for the payment of a fee for each enlistment in the Continental army. Both Congress and the states had long since resorted to bounties to persuade men to serve in the ranks. In fact, during the early years offers of bounties to serve in the state militia often exceeded those offered by Congress. By the Act of 1776 privates who agreed to enlist in the national army received twenty dollars and one hundred acres of land. Local townships and counties offered additional bounties of their own in order to meet their quotas.

Such inducements make it clear that while some few of the troops may have joined the army because they felt an obligation to do their duty such high-minded motivation did not suffice for most. It must be remembered that patriotism is an outgrowth of history and tradition, of which the new nation had almost none. Loyalty was much more strongly rooted in the states and even in regions of the states. Soldiers often adamantly refused to serve in regiments from other states and they even objected to "foreign" officers as their commanders. Some may have responded to the romantic appeal of the recruiting broadsides "to see this beautiful country" but the thought of leaving home was probably a stronger deterrent. A lad from the Hampshire Grants who travelled to Boston found himself in surroundings as strange as if he were on the other side of the world. Homesickness was the most widespread of the diseases of the camps. It was sometimes only a few weeks after enlistment that the soldiers felt "such an unconquerable desire of returning to . . . their homes, that it not only produces shameful, scandalous Desertions among themselves, but infuses a like spirit in others."[17]

By 1777 Washington was writing that "we may fairly infer that the country has been pretty well drained of that class of Men whose tempers, attachments and circumstances disposed them to enter permanently . . . into the army. . . ." Whatever mixture of motives there may have been to enlist and remain in the service, it is fair to assume that an essential ingredient was material reward of money and land. And it must be supposed that a large proportion of the men were those very vagabonds and strollers against whom recruiters had earlier been warned.[18]

But is there any reason to suppose that they were bad soldiers? As human raw material they were certainly no worse than the recruits of the British army. Is it not fair to assume that the Continental soldier also came to regard his regiment as "home," that to him the army, with all its hardships and privations, afforded the kind of security and companionship that he had not found on the outside?

In the case of one group of soldiers motives are somewhat easier to define. With the organization of the army the new nation faced the oldest of American dilemmas, the black man. Both Congress and General Washington opposed the enlistment of Negroes in 1775, and both were forced to swallow their prejudices in the face of the realities of war. Although neither gave any formal sanction, at the end of 1775 the commander in chief issued a general order which read: "As the General is informed, that numbers of Free Negroes are desirous of inlisting, he gives leave to recruiting officers to entertain them, and promises to lay the matter before Congress, who he doubts not will approve it." Rhode Island, New York, and Maryland had, by 1777, authorized the recruitment of regiments of Negro slaves.[19]

But the reality of the enlistment of black soldiers had little to do with the law. The combination of whites who wanted to avoid service by furnishing black substitutes and recruiting officers who were under pressure to fill their quotas resulted in the appearance of considerable numbers of black Americans in the Continental ranks. Officers might rail at "the strangest mixture of Negroes, Indians, and whites, with old men and children, . . . [whose] nasty lousy appearance make the most shocking spectacle," but the regiments had to be filled. It has been estimated that about 5,000 identifiable black men served in various branches of the armed forces during the War of Independence. In August, 1778, Washington's adjutant general reported 755 black troops serving in fourteen regiments of the New York Continental Line; if these were typical regiments Negroes constituted about ten percent of their strength.[20]

The assumption that all black soldiers were freemen (slaves being disbarred from enlistment unless by the consent of their masters) must have been a powerful incentive for fugitive slaves seeking refuge. Once accepted into the ranks it became very difficult for masters to recover them. Dr. Israel Ashley of Westfield, Massachusetts, was drafted into the service. He intended to provide his slave, Gilliam, as a substitute but to his dismay he found that Gilliam had already enlisted for three years. The doctor's appeal to General Gates for the return of his property fell on deaf ears. Attempts by masters in Virginia to reclaim their slaves after the war led Governor Benjamin Harrison to appeal to the General Assembly, "not doubting that they will pass an act giving these unhappy creatures that liberty which they have been in some way instrumental in securing to us." The governor had his way.[21]

For the free Negro the security of the army—food, clothing, and shelter—offered considerable attraction. He was still subjected to the degradation accorded a Negro at any level of society. He was usually given the most undesirable duties, orderly, cook, teamster, and every other dirty work which is the lot of men in the army. But he nonetheless enjoyed the status of being a soldier. The bounty of money and especially of land were rewards which he found difficult to obtain elsewhere. There was little inducement for him to desert and he usually served out his full enlistment. For the slave the reward for honorable service was freedom. It might be several years away but he had long since learned that to endure was to survive.

Serious as were the problems of recruiting, they must sometimes have seemed insignificant beside the problems of training and discipline. These were especially difficult at the outset of the war because there was no cadre of veterans to teach the men the most fundamental facts of camp life. So the general orders of the commander in chief himself were taken up with such elementary details as reminding officers "to keep their men neat and clean," and "to see that they have straw to lay on." Time and again it was necessary to repeat "Orders that have been given against the firing of small arms, it is hourly practised." Similarly, "There is a bad custom prevailing of the Non-Commissioned Officers and Soldiers absenting themselves from Guard, under the Pretense of going for Provisions." The men had not only to be instructed in personal cleanliness but in the necessity for keeping the camps clean. "One Man a Company to be appointed Camp Colour man, from every Company in every Regiment in the Army, whose particular duty it must be . . . to sweep the Streets of their respective encampments, to fill up old Necessary houses and dig new ones, to bury all Offal, Filth, and Nastiness, that may poison or infect the health of the Troops . . . and by persevering in the constant and unremitting Execution thereof, remove the odious reputation, which (with too much reason) has stigmitized the Character of American troops." Washington was trying to make the army *respectable*.[22]

The most serious disciplinary problem was desertion, and Washington never solved it to his satisfaction. Some soldiers left because of hunger or homesickness, others because they were impatient with the boredom and drudgery of camp life. Should these men be severely dealt with? Would a few exemplary executions or long prison terms have a salutary effect? Or would such stringent measures discourage enlistments and keep the repentent from returning?

In the first months of his command Washington was inclined to be lenient. Where simple desertion was the charge thirty-nine lashes became the standard penalty. As the army began to take shape, as he attempted the "new modelling of it," to make it "in every point of view entirely Continental," discipline became more severe. Deserters were executed, or sentenced to serve "on an American frigate" for the duration, or tarred and feathered and forced to run the gauntlet of their companies. By the time the army went into winter quarters at Morristown in 1777 he had again come around to a more lenient point of view. Severe punishment for one deserter was accompanied by pardons for ten, and in April, 1777, he issued a blanket pardon for all deserters who would come in within a month.[23]

Breakdown of discipline could usually be traced to two sources. One was lack of the basic rewards which every soldier had a right to expect, food, prompt pay, and clothing. The army seldom had enough of any of these. The other serious flaw lay in the failure of the officer corps. Men accused of drunkenness or malingering and disorderly behavior could scarcely be expected to respond when officers were guilty of the same offenses. One may well imagine the circumstances which produced the charge against Private James McDaniel, accused of "foregoing an order of General Putnam's to obtain a quart of rum, and for abusive language." Of 900 officers who served at one time or another with seven New York regiments during the war 135, or over fifteen percent, deserted. All too frequently officers were drunkards or cowards, cheated the men of their pay, and in general fell far short of the standards set by the commander in chief:

> . . . At a time when everything is at stake, It behooves every Man to exert himself. It will not do for the Commanding Officer of a Regiment to content himself, with barely giving Orders, he should see (at least know) that they are executed. He should call his men out frequently and endeavor to impress them with a just sense of their Duty, and how much depends on subordination and discipline. Let me therefore not only Command, but exhort you and your Officers . . . to Manly and Vigorous exertion at this time, each striving to excell the other in the respective duties of his department.

Washington made it clear that he preferred officers who were gentlemen. He was appalled at the New England custom of electing their commanders and he insisted that an officer must set himself apart from his men; otherwise they would "treat him as an equal; and . . . regard him as no more than a broom-stick, being mixed together as one common herd; no order, nor no discipline can prevail; nor will the Officer ever meet with that respect which is essential to due subordination."[24]

The quality of the officers was probably neither better nor worse than the citizenry of the nation has always furnished in time of war. The trouble was that, like the men in the ranks, they seldom stayed for very long. For those who did not desert, resignation provided an honorable way of quitting the service. Officers who were gentlemen were also those who had the most to lose by an extended tour of duty. By April, 1778, Washington was complaining that officers' resignations were being submitted at the rate of two or three a day.

A case in point is the career of Samuel Smith, a young officer of the famous First Maryland regiment. Son of a wealthy merchant and engaged to a Baltimore belle, Smith served faithfully through the campaigns from 1776 through 1778. He commanded the defenses of the Delaware forts in 1777 for which Congress voted him a sword, an honor not lightly given. By 1778 he was a lieutenant colonel, but the rather considerable fortune of his father had been wrecked by the war. In the fall of 1778 he resigned his commission and went home to run the family business. He served in the Maryland militia and rose to the rank of brigadier general. He also restored the family fortunes, mostly through contracts with the state and with Congress to supply the army. Far from being considered a slacker he was called "General" Smith for the rest of his life and was a charter member of the Society of the Cincinnati.[25]

By the end of January, 1777, Washington's force at Morristown had been reduced to 3,000 men of which less than a third were Continentals. It was at least some consolation that there were not so many mouths to feed, and the army did not suffer as it did the next winter at Valley Forge, or when it returned to Morristown in 1779. Even so, much of the army's food was forcibly seized in the surrounding countryside by foraging parties, who frequently clashed with British detachments on similar errands. Washington justified this on the basis of the grant of extraordinary powers from Congress in December and because it denied supplies to the enemy. But he tried to proceed with caution. He was well aware that the heavy hand of the military would arouse deep resentment among some civilians, and he recognized that the popular support of the revolutionary cause must not be jeopardized. A year later, under similar circumstances he pointed out, "To acts of legislation or civil authority [the people] have ever been taught to yield a willing obedience, without reasoning about their propriety; on those of military power, whether immediate or derived originally from another source, they have ever looked with a jealous and suspicious eye."[26]

As spring came in so did the recruits, but enlistments still fell short of expectations. In addition to the eighty-eight battalions which Congress hoped to raise in the states Washington himself was authorized to recruit sixteen regiments. plus three of artillery, 3,000 dragoons, and a corps of engineers. Had the entire authorized force been raised, the total would have been 75,000 men. As it was, by the middle of May forty-three regiments of about 200 men each had been assembled at Morristown. Almost as important, as the ranks began to fill, supplies came from France: 20,000 muskets, 1,000 barrels of powder, 11,000 flints, and an assortment of other supplies, notably clothing and blankets. Although it was to be another year before France became a formal ally, the French foreign minister, the Comte de Vergennes, had seized the opportunity to weaken an ancient foe, and for more than a year unofficial aid had been making its way across the Atlantic.

The army that began to prepare for the summer campaign was far short of the 20,000 men with which Washington had begun the campaign of 1776, but his efforts to create a "fixed and settled force" had made him less dependent upon "the practice of trusting the Militia." Counting dragoons, artillery, and engineers, the Continentals numbered over 9,000 men. Never again would the commander in chief be reduced to the shadow force which had brought him to the edge of extinction in the winter of 1777.[27]

THE MILITIA

Early in 1776 Francis Lord Rawdon, despite his baptism of fire at Bunker Hill, was still convinced that "we shall soon have done with these scoundrels, for one only dirties one's fingers by meddling with them." It was a continuing source of amazement to the British that American citizen-soldiers could constitute a serious threat to the British army.

This was in part due to the low opinion of colonial militia that English officers had acquired during the Seven Years' War. Wolfe thought Americans were "the most contemptible cowardly dogs you can conceive. There is no depending on them in action." In his more pessimistic moments Washington would have been inclined to agree, but he noted that "a people unused to restraint must be led, they must not be drove, even those who are ingaged for the War must be disciplined by degrees."

English officers tended to regard all soldiers as the lowest level of English society. They expected, and got, servile respect from the ranks, and they assumed that Americans were simply "a set of upstart vagabonds, the dregs and scorn of human society." Colonel (later General) James Grant, who had served in Florida and therefore qualified as an expert, stated categorically in Parliament, "They would never dare face an English army and did not possess any of the qualifications of a good soldier."[28]

Political leaders accepted the army's verdict. Alexander Wedderburn told the Commons in 1774, ". . . Our thunders must go forth; America must be conquered." And Richard Rigby, M.P., assured the members that tales of colonial resistance "was an idea thrown out to frighten women and children."

There were other observers who were more discerning. Hugh Earl Percy, who had met the Massachusetts militia one April morning in 1775, remarked, "They have men amongst them who know very well what they are about." Thomas Gage, who had observed Americans in two wars, reported to the ministry that "in all their wars against the French they never shewed so much conduct attention and perseverence as they do now."[29]

When American revolutionary leaders found themselves faced with "the Necessity for Taking up Arms" they were not especially perturbed by the lack of an army. Some were deluded by the myth of the American victory over the French and Indians, but their more tangible expectations were based on the existence of the militia organizations. The militia tradition had its origins in the early years of English colonization to take care of the exigencies of the expanding frontier. First the Indians and then the French and the Dutch had threatened the tiny settlements, and the mother country had never sent troops to defend her outposts overseas until the latter part of the Second Hundred Years War.

Left to fend for themselves the colonial assemblies enacted laws which created militia organizations. In 1631 Massachusetts Bay required that all men between the ages of sixteen and sixty be supplied with arms, and local officers were made responsible for compliance. Two years later the Plymouth colony decreed that every man must have a musket, sword, cartridge box, powder, and ball. In the same period Virginians were required to take their muskets to church on Sunday so that they would be ready for drill after the service.

By the 1760's the militia had pretty much deteriorated into a semisocial organization which met a few times a year, and gave the men folks an excuse for fun and games. The ranks on parade were liable to be ragged as much from an excess of rum as a lack of discipline. But there was a tradition that every man should own a weapon and that every man had an obligation for military service. What may have passed unnoticed in England was a phenomenon remarked on by Governor Berkeley of Virginia at the time of Bacon's Rebellion: "Unhappy is the man who governs a people who are poor, indebted, discontented, and *armed*."[30]

As the crisis with England grew more serious in the 1770's there was a revival of militia activity. Muster days became more frequent and a serious air pervaded the farmers who assembled for drill. The threat against which they were obviously preparing was not from a foreign foe but from the authority of the Crown. Although colonial governors were nominally in control of the militia by virtue of their office of commanding general, in colony after colony the Whigs began to gain control of the militia organization, especially in New England where officers were elected.

The most famous of the militia units—and the most short-lived—was the "minute men." Each regiment in Massachusetts designated one third of its number to be prepared to "come in at a moment's warning," and it was these troops that harassed Gage's redcoats on their expedition to Lexington and Concord. Many of the "minute men" stayed on and fought in the battle of Bunker Hill. Many joined regiments and enlisted in the "Eight Months Army." Others simply went home when they felt that the emergency was over. They left a name and a legend in American military history, but by summer's end they had disappeared.[31]

Following the colonial pattern the states organized their militia primarily for defense against an invading enemy, and to "keep the peace" locally. This meant providing enforcing authority for the local committees of safety who were charged with suppressing "enemies," that is, Loyalists. The militia were also expected to march to the aid of Washington's army when Congress or the commander in chief thought it necessary.

In colonial times a sort of conscription system existed in the sense that local officers were responsible for seeing that able-bodied men were armed and ready to deal with emergencies. The new state governments made custom and practice more explicit. In Connecticut all males between the ages of sixteen and sixty were required to enroll, with exceptions which are surprisingly similar to those of today. Exempted were state and national officials, ministers, students and teachers at Yale, Negroes, Indians and mulattoes. Officers were elected and it was possible to purchase a substitute, or, if none could be found, to pay a fine of £ [32]

North Carolina passed a similar law in the summer of 1776. To the usual list of exemptions was added the Quakers, but they were required to pay a fee of £10, presumably for the expense of hiring a substitute. The state was divided into five military districts, each under the command of a brigadier general. The men were divided into five classes: the first, consisting of men over fifty years of age, who were not required to serve on active duty; the other four to be called in rotation for a term of service of not more than sixty days.

In Pennsylvania the first Militia Act was passed as a result of pressure from the Pennsylvania Association, a volunteer group that was political as well as military. The Associators insisted that those who did not contribute to the cause by volunteering for service be required to pay a fee, and a sum of £3/10 was levied. All adult males between the ages of eighteen and fifty (not excepting Negroes and Indians) were eligible. Sons between the ages of sixteen and eighteen might serve in place of their fathers. There were the usual occupational exemptions and provisions for hiring substitutes.

Each county was to enlist a regiment of from 440 to 680 men under the supervision of county lieutenants and sub-lieutenants. Officers were elected, but all colonels and majors had to be property owners and all officers had to be qualified voters. Each regiment was divided into eight classes to be called to service in rotation for no more than sixty days. County lieutenants were authorized to hire substitutes the expense for which the state would presumably collect a fee from delinquents who failed to turn out. Despite the sweeping nature of the system recruitment was not very effective. In 1777 Captain

Thomas Askey's Cumberland County company turned out only forty-four men, of whom ten were substitutes and thirteen were hired by the county lieutenants.[33]

The service of the militia as reinforcements for the army left more than a little to be desired. Washington delivered his low opinion of these troops frequently and at length, of which one in the fall of 1776 was typical:

> To place any dependence upon Militia, is, assuredly, resting upon a broken staff. Men just dragged from the tender Scenes of domestick life; unaccustomed to the din of Arms; totally unacquainted with every kind of Military skill, when opposed by Troops regularly train'd, disciplined and appointed, makes them timid and ready to fly at their own shadows. Besides, the sudden change in their manner of living, (particularly lodging) brings on sickness in many. . . . Men accustomed to unbounded freedom, cannot brook Restraint which is absolutely necessary to the good order and Government of the Army; without which licentiousness, and every kind of disorder triumphantly reign. To bring Men to a proper degree of Subordination, is not the work of a day, a Month or even a year; and unhappily for us and the cause we are Englaged in, the little discipline I have been laboring to establish in the Army . . . is in a manner done away with by such a mixture of Troops as have been called together within these few months.[34]

Yet in spite of their presumed worthlessness Washington could not have kept an army together without the militia. The 5,000 men who turned out in December, 1775, got him past the critical termination of the "Eight Months Army" and two-thirds of the skeleton force at Morristown in the early part of 1777 was composed of militia. If they had failed at Trenton they had responded magnificently at Princeton where Cadwalader's Pennsylvanians had held the line at the crisis of the battle. On many other occasions they were to display a splendid elan, especially when they were led by capable officers and supported by veteran Continentals.

A word should be said about the riflemen, since they achieved a fame in some degree unwarranted in the history of the army. These men were Indian fighters from the frontier whose accurate fire astonished all who witnessed it. But the frontiersmen posed problems. Products of the back country settlements and conscious of their elite status, they did not take to army discipline. In the fall of 1775 Pennsylvania riflemen precipitated a riot at Prospect Hill near Boston and thirty of them were arrested for "disobedient and mutinous behaviour."

On the battlefield another weakness of the riflemen was exposed, one inherent in the weapon which made them famous. The accuracy of the rifle stemmed from the fact that the ball was tightly fitted into the barrel which was rifled; that is, there were spiral grooves cut on the inner surface which gripped the tightly seated ball and gave it a spin, giving it greater accuracy and a range three times that of the musket. The tight seal of the ball was achieved by fitting a greased patch over the muzzle when the ball was rammed, and this increased the reloading time. Furthermore, the rifle barrel could not be fitted with a bayonet. The result was described by Colonel George Hanger, a British officer who was captured at Saratoga:

> When Morgan's riflemen came down to Pennsylvania from Canada, flushed with success gained over Burgoyne's army, they marched to attack our light troops under Colonel Abercrombie. The moment they appeared before him he ordered his troops to charge them with the bayonet; not one man in four had time to fire, and those who did were given no time to load again; the light infantry not only dispersed them but drove them for miles over the country.[35]

The riflemen were to be found in both the militia and the Continental line, but at the peak of their strength they never constituted more than ten percent of the armies to which they were attached. They constituted a valuable weapon—Hitchcock's Rhode Islanders at Trenton and Morgan's brigade at Freeman's farm—but the rifle was scarcely "the gun that won the Revolution."

The militia in general proved to be a source of disappointment as adjuncts to the regular army. The system of rotation used in most states meant that even the few months of discipline and drill with the army were largely wasted. By the time the raw troops had learned the rudiments of march and maneuver their time was up and their replacements had to be trained anew. More important, most of them had never seen action in battle and if they did participate in a campaign this experience, too, was lost when the regiments were rotated home. So it was not surprising that, as Washington concluded, "Men who have been free and subject to no controul cannot be reduced to order in an Instant . . . and the aid derived from them is nearly counterbalanced by the disorder, irregularity and confusion they occasion."[36]

A far more important effect of the militia may well have been in areas outside the main theatres of the war. Much has been made of guerrilla warfare and its effects on enemy supply and communication lines, and certainly this had its impact. But the real prize of the American Revolution was the allegiance of a majority of the people who, in the early stages of the war, did not commit themselves. The winning of independence was, in the final analysis, a numbers game. The objectives were not so much New York or Charleston or the Hudson River Valley but control of the civilian population. When Germain and the King talked, at first confidently and then wistfully, of the rising tide of Loyalism which would eventually take over the task of reconquest, they dimly perceived the real issue over which the war was being fought. But the Patriots understood far better that "loyalty" was in most cases to be read as "interest" and that while "life, liberty and pursuit of happiness" made a fine catch phrase, it had to be understood in concrete terms.

The percentage of the population devoted to either the Patriot or Loyalist cause at the beginning of the war thus becomes relatively unimportant. Standing between them was a large majority of Americans, probably as great as Patriots and Loyalists combined, who were undecided and neutral, who did not want to risk their lives and fortunes on any cause. They may or may not have understood the issues involved but they rather naively believed that they could continue to pursue the even tenor of their lives. Yet these people found their opinions altered, and indeed their whole lives changed when the war came to their doorstep. "The war" did not necessarily mean the marching ranks of Continentals and redcoats. John Hart, whose wife was murdered by Tory renegades, found the war suddenly very real. When Patriot committees of safety, backed by militia, offered a choice between military service and possible imprisonment as suspected Torys, "liberty" took on a special meaning. When Hessians plundered barns and corncribs the "pursuit of happiness" became difficult, to say the least. A thousand local clashes, betwen militia and Tories, acts of mob violence, even petty annoyances, all of which might be peripheral to campaigns and battles, had a decisive effect in destroying the illusions of that segment of the population who had begun by thinking that they could stand aloof from the conflict. The political education of many Americans may have begun with the exhortations of Whig editors and pamphlets like *Common Sense*, but the lessons were driven home when the county lieutenant appeared to make up the militia muster list. The very act of enrollment and participation in drills forced most adult males to declare themselves. This may have been the reason why the law in many states required a man to turn out for muster in person, even though he intended to provide a substitute when he was called to active duty.

This does not mean that military operations were not important. New Jersey was firmly in Patriot hands until Howe's invasion of 1776, but upon his approach the Patriot militia disintegrated and local leaders went into hiding. Loyalists, emboldened by the appearance of the redcoats, organized their own militia and were soon harrying the countryside. They in turn collapsed after the American victories at Trenton and Princeton caused Howe to withdraw his garrisons. Even after the military theatre of operations moved elsewhere, the bitter struggle in New Jersey continued until the end of the war. The history of New Jersey was repeated in one form or another until the end of the war.

As Professor John Shy puts it: "In this sense, the war was a political education conducted by military means, and no one learned more than the apathetic majority as they scurried to restore some measure of order to their lives."[37]

In a way, the warfare of the eighteenth century represented the ideal employment of what Clausewitz called "the ultimate weapon of diplomacy." Though it was cluttered with rules and conventions that amuse the modern military scientist, wars were narrow in scope, seldom touching the civilian population with mass destruction or atrocities. Even the casualties were small. The diplomatic objectives were reasonable and limited. Warfare was thus the epitome of that enlightened rationalism on which the eighteenth century prided itself. Campaigns were conducted in warm weather and battles were avoided in place of chess-like maneuvers. The perfectly conducted campaign would place the enemy in such a hopeless tactical position that he would refuse to risk a battle, withdrawing from the field and leaving his objective to the superior general.

Washington revealed early in the war that he was not only a student of eighteenth century warfare but a disciple as well, thereby revealing his own failure to appreciate the special nature of a war of revolution: ". . . It is impossible to forget," he wrote in the fall of 1776, "that History, our own experience, the advice of our ablest friends in Europe, the Fears of the Enemy, and even the Declarations of Congress demonstrate, that on our side the war should be defensive. It has even been called a War of Posts. That we should on all Occasions avoid a general action, or put anything to the Risque, unless compelled by a necessity into which we ought never to be drawn."[38]

Eighteenth century wars should be understood in their social and economic setting. A considerable cleavage existed between the British army and the society which it served. The gap was less distinct in the officer corps because the purchase of commissions led inevitably to an increasing number of officers from the middle class. But the rank and file were filled with large numbers of the unproductive elements of the lowest level, the English classes, and it was here that the distinction was most marked.

The industrial revolution was just beginning in England but there was already an enormous demand for productive workers, especially skilled artisans. If Great Britain did not support the American war with her full resources—meaning especially man power—it was because her politicians did not think it necessary or proper to sacrifice her economy to inflated notions of national pride. Why conscript productive workers into a national army and so drain the very labor force which was in short supply? Citizen-soldiers were of considerably less value than citizen-workers. This was the rationale which limited conscription to vagrants, "strollers," criminals and "public idlers," rather than those who were gainfully employed. Volunteers were tempted by bounties, but these were not high enough to appeal even to an apprentice who had regular employment. Rather than tap this useful class the government considered hiring German mercenaries as a superior investment.

For Americans the war posed a different problem. While England could and did lose the war without catastrophic consequences to her position as a world power, the outcome would determine the very existence and survival of the United States. The full resources of lives and fortunes were to be called forth to win independence—that is, to avoid the alternative of unconditional surrender. Yet despite the exhortations of the leaders in Congress and in the states, the American army which emerged was cast in much the same mold as other eighteenth century armies. Not because of government policy, but in spite of it. The Continental ranks were filled from the lowest levels of American society. Even the words which describe the recruits, "lean fac'd caitiffs," "worthless dogs," the "meanest, idlest, most intemperate and worthless," are the same as those used by British recruiters. This was because those who could afford it sent substitutes and those who could not enrolled in the militia so that they would not have to absent themselves from farms or businesses for long. A soldier of some means and substance who did enlist for a long term could rarely resist an appeal for help from home occasioned by family distress or hardship. If he was not granted leave he simply went home.[39]

There is, of course, no way of knowing how many soldiers of the Continental army served from a sense of duty and how many were society's "losers," for whom the army, miserable as it was, provided a security that was better than none. But, taking into account the number of substitutes, the honorable alternatives (an officer's commission or militia service), and the fact that bounties became more and more generous in order to induce enlistments, it seems fair to infer that a relatively small number of Continentals were what could be called "solid citizens." But, as in the case of the redcoats, there is also reason to agree with General Washington that "in a little time we shall work these raw materials into good stuff."[40]

The militia constituted an unknown quantity in the eighteenth century military equation. European theory was based on waging war between two or more armies of known strength. The quality of arms, the presence or absence of fortifications, the quality of generalship, and other factors could be calculated with some precision. But how was one to calculate an unknown number of soldiers of unknown quality who might reinforce Washington's army, or suddenly appear to harass outlying posts, or whose presence created a countryside of hostile civilians?

British leaders who were used to wars waged between governments only dimly perceived that in dealing with a popular revolution they were waging war on the American people.

SIX

Germain and
the Generals

THE BRITISH PLAN OF CAMPAIGN FOR 1777 WAS QUITE SIMPLY AN EXTENSION
and elaboration of the campaign of 1776. It did not originate with any particular person nor did it contain any startling new ideas. From the point of view
of Lord George Germain, at least, it commended itself because it would be
coordinated so as to lend maximum effectiveness to British military power in
North America, and because troops and commanders were already in place
on the western side of the Atlantic. The stupendous overseas lift of men and
supplies which had preoccupied so much of his and the ministry's effort in
1776 would not have to be repeated. The invading Americans had been cleared
from Canada, and the possession of New York gave the Howe brothers a central base from which they could achieve maximum flexibility of naval and
military operations.

The focus of the plan was the axis of the Richelieu river, Lake Champlain,
and the Hudson. A force from Canada would fully exploit the objectives that
Carleton had failed to achieve in 1776 because of the lateness of the season
(or, as Germain thought, Carleton's slothfulness). It would penetrate to Albany and there be joined by an offensive force from New York. Control of
the Hudson-Lake Champlain line would prevent the American movement of
large bodies of troops and supplies between New England and the rest of
the colonies. Control of the Hudson Highlands, Albany, and Ticonderoga
would give the British bases in the interior of the country from which they
might penetrate especially into New Hampshire and Connecticut. As a memorandum in the Germain papers puts it:

> By our having the entire command of the communications between Canada
> and New York, which is both convenient and easy, being almost altogether
> by water, the troops from both these provinces will have it in their power to act
> in conjunction, as occasion or necessity may require. In consequence whereof,
> the provinces of New England will be surrounded on all sides, whether by
> His Majesty's troops or navy, and liable to be attacked from every quarter,
> which will divide their force for the protection of their frontier settlements,

while at the same time all intercourse between them and the colonies to the southward of the Hudson's River will be entirely cut off.[1]

THE PLAN GERMINATES

On November 30, 1776, as the British pursued Washington's retreating army across New Jersey, Howe wrote to Germain recounting what he intended to do during the remainder of 1776: send Clinton to occupy Rhode Island; and occupy New Jersey by establishing a chain of posts from Perth Amboy to the Delaware.

He then launched into a detailed proposal for the campaign of 1777. Clinton's conquest of Rhode Island would pave the way for a force of 10,000 men which would advance "into the country towards Boston and, if possible, reduce that town." Another force of 10,000 men was to advance up the Hudson to Albany to join with an army moving south from Canada. Five thousand men were designated for the defense of New York city, and a third "defensive army" of 8,000 men, commanded by Lord Cornwallis, was to cover New Jersey "to keep the southern [Washington's] army in check, by giving a jealousy to Philadelphia, which I propose to attack in the autumn, as well as Virginia, provided the success of other operations will admit an adequate force." For this grandiose plan Howe requested 15,000 additional reinforcements to bring his army to a total of 35,000 "effective men."

As Clinton was designated for Rhode Island and Cornwallis for New Jersey it must be assumed that Howe himself would lead the expedition "up the North [Hudson] River to Albany." Since he believed the northern invasion force would not reach Albany "earlier than the month of September" it is difficult to understand how he then expected to attack Philadelphia "as well as Virginia."[2]

But the November 30 letter is worth careful notice because in it Howe's attention was directed in general to the north and New England, and the focus of his own movement was up the Hudson to Albany and a junction with the army from Canada.

On the same day that he wrote to Germain Howe issued his proclamation of pardon. As noted previously considerable numbers of people in New Jersey accepted it in the hope that they would be protected from the pillaging and looting of British and Hessian soldiers as they pursued Washington to the Delaware. Howe was still hoping to fulfill his role as peace commissioner and he was greatly encouraged by the response to his offer of amnesty. There were also reports of "the opinions of the people being much changed in Pennsylvania," which may account for the subsequent changes in his own thinking about the campaign of 1777.

On December 20, six days before the disaster at Trenton Howe sent a supplemental dispatch to Germain. He reported the increasing strength of Loyalist opinion "in which sentiment they would be confirmed by our getting possession of Philadeliphia [.] I am from this consideration fully persuaded the principal army should act offensively on that side where the enemy's chief strength will be collected." He went on to propose that the New England expedition be deferred until reinforcements arrived from England. And the joint expedition against Albany was now reduced to "a corps to act defensively upon the lower part of Hudson's River to cover New Jersey on that side, as well as to facilitate in some degree the approach of the Army from Canada." These objectives could be attained with his present force of about 20,000 men, although he urged Germain to send "every augmentation of troops . . . to this port [New York]. . . ."

The most significant aspect of this last dispatch was the shift in priorities. In the original plan of November 20 Philadelphia was almost an after-thought and a main striking force of 10,000 men was designated for Albany. By December 20 Howe had become afflicted with that most chimerical of all British delusions, the rising of the Loyalists. It had lured Clinton's expedition to South Carolina in the summer of 1776 and it was to become the most fatal of all the British miscalculations about the war for America. But in the euphoria surrounding the flight of Washington from New York across New Jersey, and the wholesale applications for pardons, Howe's optimism was understandable. He became convinced that Loyalism was rampant in Pennsylvania and that possession of the American capital was the key to British success.

Before Germain could fully digest the varied diet which his American commander was serving up there arrived still another dispatch from Howe, dated January 20, 1777. This was written, of course, after Trenton and Princeton had forced the British to abandon most of New Jersey, wiping out the gains of the December campaign. There was a tone of deep pessimism in this addendum to the plan for 1777. It was clear that Howe was keenly conscious of his failure in New Jersey although he made a half-hearted attempt to blame the Hessians and their dead commander. He now said that 20,000 reinforcements would be necessary if his campaign were to have any chance of success and expressed the fear that the capture of Philadelphia might not be as decisive as he had hoped. (Howe surely could not have really expected a reinforcement greater than the one he had received in 1776; an impression is conveyed of a commander preparing to defend a future failure by having his request a matter of record.)[3]

Germain's reaction to his American commander's proposals was curious. Replying to Howe's November 20 dispatch Lord George spoke of "your well digested plan," a phrase he may have regretted when he received the proposal of December 20 and the gloomy forebodings of mid-January. He was, he said, "really alarmed" by the size of the request for reinforcements. The most that Howe might expect would be about 8,000 men, a figure that was subsequently reduced to slightly less than 6,000.

After considering Howe's latest proposals Germain replied on March 3. The King, he said, had approved "your proposed deviation from the plan which you formerly suggested, being of opinion that the reasons which have induced you to recommend this change . . . are solid and decisive." Lord George said nothing in this letter about the expedition from Canada, although he had spent several weeks planning the campaign in detail with Burgoyne and had received the King's approval of it only three days before.[4]

The omission is striking. Although Howe knew that a northern invasion was planned he had deliberately downgraded his own part in support of it to the point that it barely received mention in the December 20 projection of his movements for the coming campaign. It is possible that at this point Howe was not aware of the elaborate nature of the Canadian expedition or of Germain's high hopes for it. But the astonishing fact is that Lord George's letter, in which he gave Howe official notice of the King's approval of his plans, contained not the slightest mention of the British invasion from Canada.

GENTLEMAN JOHNNY

Six days before he sent George III's assent to Sir William the American Secretary received a long memorandum from General John Burgoyne entitled "Thoughts for conducting the war from the side of Canada." If Germain had not read it when he wrote to Howe, he knew that it contained a detailed summary of the plan for a British offensive from Canada, and that Burgoyne would be its commander.

John Burgoyne had reached the climax of a colorful and tempestuous career. It was rumored that he was the illegitimate son of Lord Bingley because he had made Burgoyne's mother a major beneficiary of his estate. Burgoyne himself eloped with Lady Charlotte Stanley, daughter of the Earl of Derby, which forced the young couple to live for a time in genteel "exile" on the continent. But the marriage ultimately provided him with the powerful family connection so necessary to either military or political preferment. At the age of twenty-one Burgoyne purchased a commission in the Royal Dragoons and by the beginning of the Seven Years' War he was a captain.

He distinguished himself in the campaigns in Portugal where he served under General Wilhelm von der Lippe who was regarded as one of the finest artillerymen in Europe. It may have been in Portugal that Burgoyne acquired his belief in the importance of artillery. He seems to have been a better than average student of military science and he produced several treatises, especially on the psychology of discipline. He came to believe that English soldiers were more intelligent than those of most European armies and that officers should appeal to the reason and sensibilities of their troops as well as to their pride and patriotism. Burgoyne practiced what he preached, and it was because he earned the respect and affection of his men that he was dubbed "Gentleman Johnny."[5]

He was fairly typical of his time and class. He became a member of Parliament, he gained a reputation as a gambler and *bon vivant*, and he developed some talent as a playwright. But beneath the surface of the urbane, convivial gentleman was a streak of hard ruthlessness. London gossip had it that he was not above "taking his stand at gaming table, and watching with soberest attention for a fair opportunity of engaging a drunken young Nobleman at Piquet." Gentleman Johnny had a driving ambition for fame and place.

When the war began in America he was fifty-three years old and a major general. He was sent to Boston with Howe and Clinton to "assist" Gage, but the fact that he was the junior of the generals convinced him that this was a dead end. By the end of 1775 he had returned to England, voicing his opinions of the war in America, subtly disparaging Gage, and pushing his claims for recognition and promotion. He published a treatise early in 1776 suggesting the idea for an invasion from Canada, and this may have been responsible for his assignment as Carleton's second in command when troop reinforcements were sent to Canada in the spring. His wife was desperately ill at the time and Burgoyne had protested that only his duty to King and country had forced him to leave her side (she died while he was in America).

Burgoyne was home once more in December, 1776, unhappy with his role and pushing for a high command. His timing was fortuitous. A smouldering quarrel between the American Secretary and Sir Guy Carleton had exploded when Germain was sharply critical of Carleton's mismanagement of the expedition on Lake Champlain in 1776. He even went so far as to suggest that the defeats at Trenton and Princeton were indirectly attributable to Carleton's bungling. The Governor-General replied in a tone of aspersion and resentment that even shocked the King.

Aware of the friction between Carleton and Germain Burgoyne again suggested an offensive from Canada and he did not hesitate to urge "a more enterprising Commander." In February his plans were nearly ruined by a dispatch from Sir William Howe. Sir William assumed that Clinton would be given the Canadian expedition and asked that Burgoyne be assigned to New York, presumably as Howe's second in command. The King approved the suggestion.

Burgoyne did not intend to be shouldered aside. It was primarily to promote his own fortunes that he had composed the "Thoughts" and its comprehensive detail was designed to demonstrate his familiarity with the problem. Lord Germain was sympathetic. Even so, Clinton's senior rank would probably have won him the Canadian command. He was back in England in February and there were hints from several of the ministers that he had only to ask and the assignment was his. But Clinton was of that odd sort who refuses to grasp at opportunity—and afterward complains resentfully about how they were victims of slights and discriminations. He did not ask and Burgoyne and Germain were vastly relieved.

Henry Clinton was a study of conflicting qualities and emotions. He had perhaps the best military mind of all the British generals. Time after time his analyses of military problems sorted out the central kernel from the chaff. Yet he possessed a diffidence, a lack of confidence which all too often prevented him from acting with decision. He counted Burgoyne his friend and the numerous letters which passed between the two indicate that the friendship was mutual. But Burgoyne would scarcely have allowed friendship to stand in the way of his ambitions. Clinton, on the other hand, had "a delicacy upon those matters that would not permit me to do anything of that kind [push his claims]." Besides, he pointed out, Burgoyne was familiar with the country, "knew better what to do and how to do it."

So in the end Clinton went back to the very job from which he had hoped to escape. His relations with Howe had become abrasive and bitter, and the commander in chief seldom accepted his suggestions. Clinton had come home determined either to secure another command or resign. It was typical of him that he did neither. He was assuaged by the Red Ribbon of the Bath and returned to New York for his last and bitterest quarrel with his commander.

The plan that Burgoyne submitted to Germain was, as noted, not original with him. During the French and Indian War British and French forces had attacked and counterattacked in both the valley of the Mohawk and the route of Lake Champlain and the Hudson. Fort Stanwix, Ticonderoga, and Crown Point had stood for years as monuments to the importance that both nations had attached to these routes. What Burgoyne proposed was a two-pronged attack utilizing both lines of advance. The principal thrust was to be by way of Lake Champlain and the Hudson, with an army of no less than 8,000 men. The expedition down the Mohawk would be a token force of Canadian rangers and Indians designed to protect the western flank of the main body, suppress any local threats from Patriot militia, and enlist the support of the Tories who were reported to be numerous in the Mohawk Valley. The objective of both forces was Albany, some ten miles below the confluence of the Mohawk and the Hudson.

"These ideas," said Burgoyne, "are formed on the supposition, that it be the sole purpose of the Canadian army to effect a junction with General Howe, or after cooperating so far as to get possession of Albany and open communication with New York, to remain upon the Hudson's River, and thereby enable that general to act with his whole force to the southward."[6]

No doubt Burgoyne knew of the ambiguous nature of Howe's plans which encompassed both the taking of Philadelphia and supporting in some way the northern army. The statement above may have been an implied question. Was he to expect a junction with Howe or was he merely to "open communication?"

When the plan was submitted to the King, George III made a number of comments. He took pride in the fact that he was well informed on military affairs and his notes justify the claim. One of his comments gave the answer to the question implicit in Burgoyne's statement of objectives: "As Sir William Howe does not think of acting from Rhode Island into Massachusetts, the force from Canada must join him at Albany." When Germain drew up the order to put the plan into execution he directed Sir Guy Carleton (nominally the command link between Germain and Burgoyne) "to give him [Burgoyne] orders to pass Lake Champlain, and from thence, by the most vigorous exertion of the force under his command, to proceed with all expedition, to Albany, and put himself under the command of Sir William Howe."

By the widest latitude of interpretation, this could mean either that Germain expected Howe himself to arrive at Albany to take command of the joint force, or that Howe would be back in New York in time to assume jurisdiction over Burgoyne when he "opened communications."

Yet Germain's method of notifying Howe of what was expected of him in the coming campaign was merely to send him an information copy of his instructions to Carleton. Howe later claimed that, prior to his departure for Philadelphia, he did not receive any order from Germain positively directing him to support Burgoyne, and technically he was correct.[7]

But what was happening was a gradual and subtle shift of authority without either Howe or Germain being fully aware of it. A change had come over Sir William since he had first begun formulating his plans in November, 1776. At that time Washington's army seemed on the point of either destruction or disintegration. Another year's campaigning, a concerted strategy that would strike devastating and coordinated blows at the rebels and the war would be over. Howe's tone was as hopeful and enthusiastic as he had ever allowed himself to be. But at the turn of the year came the disasters at Trenton and Princeton and the rebellion revived. The reverse had bitten deep, the characteristic pessimism had reasserted itself. And with the pessimism came a great stubbornness. Convinced of the revival of Loyalism to the southward, lured by the prospect of the capture of the American capital, Howe fixed his eyes steadfastly on Pennsylvania. He would erase the Trenton blunder; ". . . by the end of the campaign we shall be in possession of New York, the Jersies, and Pennsylvania." By March, 1777, Sir William had become oblivious to Germain's attempts to control or restrain him. It was not insubordination in the sense that he defied Germain's orders. He simply ignored them.

In England Howe's demands for reinforcements dismayed Germain and he flinched at the idea of going to Parliament for additional money and men. His enormous efforts of 1776 had made deep inroads on the ministry's political capital. Beset by increasingly sharp attacks from the opposition in Parliament, grumblings from his colleagues in the cabinet, and the fragile sensibilities of Burgoyne, Clinton, and Carleton, Germain shrank from any gesture or reproof which might alienate his American commanders.

In fact, one of those unfortunate episodes involving family sensibilities and court favors may have complicated matters for the American Secretary. The treasurer of the navy Sir Gilbert Elliot had died in January leaving vacant a position which carried a salary of four thousand pounds a year. Lord Richard Howe had previously held this sinecure and was considered likely to receive it again—so thought Lady Caroline Howe. She was the widow of George Howe, oldest of the brothers, who had been killed in America during the

Seven Years' War. Lady Howe was the jealous guardian of the family interests at court and she made it clear that, though Lord Howe would not solicit
the post, he would certainly accept it if offered. Lord North, immersed as
usual in the impenetrable maze of obligations owed and favors due, awarded
the office to Welborn Ellis. Caroline Howe and other powerful family friends
were soon at pains to inform all and sundry of exactly how an ungrateful ministry had slighted those who were its most faithful servants.[8]

The Howe brothers had been brought forward for the American command
at considerable political cost on the confident assertion by Lord Germain that
their abilities would insure a victorious conclusion to the rebellion. He had
backed his favorites to the hilt and he had no recourse now but to defend their
conduct and give them his confident support. To have dismissed Howe would
have been to sink himself. But in dealing so gently with Sir William the American Secretary had unwittingly become Howe's prisoner. Viewed as a whole,
the correspondence between Germain and Howe conveys the impression that
the general was giving the orders—with a bewildering array of modifications—and the minister was almost supinely acquiescing.

If this was true, Germain gave no overt sign. The great plan was now complete. With the posting of orders to Governor-General Carleton (copy to
Sir William Howe) Lord George confidently expected that Britain's great
engine of war would roll forward inexorably and crush the American rebellion. To provide additional assurance that the operation would not falter Germain sent Major Nisbet Balfour to New York as his special emissary to prod
the British high command to action.

Spring Comes To America

After the withdrawal from the New Jersey interior in January the British
army was divided for the remainder of the winter, about half quartered in
New York city and the other half encamped along the Raritan at New Brunswick and Perth Amboy. Despite the pall cast over headquarters by the failure
in New Jersey (and a dispatch from Germain calling it "extremely mortify-
ing") Howe did his best to provide entertainment for his officers and important
citizens of the town. Although he was gloomy about the prospects for the coming campaign Sir William did not allow this to suppress his naturally gre-
garious nature and his expansive social tastes. There were balls and fireworks,
dinners for prominent Loyalists, receptions for generals and admirals, and
"play at Vingt et Un." Howe had discovered the charms of Mrs. Joshua
Loring, wife of the commissary of prisoners, and their dalliance led one young
Loyalist to decide that the campaign against the rebels would begin "whenever
he shall think proper to leave Mrs. Lorain and face them."

For the rank and file it was not so easy. Confinement to winter quarters was
always a dispiriting experience. With no fresh food available the soldiers

subsisted on weevily biscuit, worm-eaten peas, and maggoty beef. The troops in New Jersey were even more miserable. Crowded into makeshift quarters they were subjected to the added indignity of constant harassment by coveys of Continentals and militia that roamed the countryside. Parties of redcoats who attempted to forage outside their lines rarely did so with impunity. One contingent of nearly 500 British soldiers returning from a raid was set upon by Pennsylvania militiamen who scattered the raiders and recovered forty wagons of plunder and 200 horses and cattle. The Hessians were especially guilty of indiscriminately looting Tories and Whigs alike. Thus were many converts made to the American cause.

Washington took great pains to defer to civilian sensibilities. After Trenton he had distributed the Hessian baggage to those who were victims of enemy pillaging; he himself issued orders for severe punishment for looting by American soldiers. And he saw to it that accounts of British depredations received full coverage in the Pennsylvania and New Jersey press. When Howe's deadline for accepting pardons expired on January 30, 1777, Washington promptly countered with his own proclamation. Those who had accepted British protection had thirty days in which to renounce their allegiance to the Crown or go into the enemy lines. Those who did neither would be considered enemies of the country. It certainly did not improve Howe's spirits when, soon after the expiration of Washington's order, a dispatch arrived from Germain criticizing his amnesty policy and reproving him for acting so leniently toward the rebels.

The British commander, nonetheless, decided to try again. On March 15 he issued another proclamation which again offered a pardon, but on much more stringent terms. This time those who accepted were not allowed to return to their homes but must either enlist in one of the Loyalist regiments or be returned to England. This new order proved to be more successful and there were numerous desertions from Washington's army into the British lines.

But as spring came and the weather grew milder Howe made no move to bestir himself. The only spark of energy came from the Earl of Cornwallis. American outposts had pushed to within seven miles of Brunswick where a force of about 500 men under General Benjamin Lincoln was posted at Bound Brook. On April 18 his lordship suddenly debouched from his cantonment with 2,000 men, crossed the Raritan, and drove for Lincoln's outpost. Militiamen supposed to be watching the river crossing failed to warn the Americans and they barely escaped encirclement. There was a brisk skirmish in which Lincoln lost his guns and suffered about seventy-five casualties before Nathanael Greene brought up his division and forced Cornwallis to retire.

All this was somewhat confusing to the American commander in chief. A few weeks earlier an enemy raiding party had attacked an American supply depot at Peekskill in the Hudson Highlands. This had lead Washington to believe that Howe might be starting northward, and he had ordered John Sullivan to reinforce the river forts with eight newly recruited regiments. Now Cornwallis' demonstration in New Jersey seemed to warn of a movement toward Pennsylvania.

Later in April Howe sent Governor William Tryon with 2,000 men to raid Connecticut. The objective was a large American supply depot in Danbury. The British landed at Fairfield and marched unopposed to Danbury where they burned not only a large quantity of supplies but a good part of the town.

As the raiders retreated an American force hastily gathered by Benedict Arnold attempted to cut them off. Although his 600 men were only about one third the size of the British, Arnold boldly threw them in against the redcoats, stubbornly contesting their retreat. But his force was too small and the raiders escaped.

Arnold was in Connecticut because, despite his proven reputation as perhaps the hardest fighter in the army, five junior brigadiers had been promoted over his head to major general. Arnold had left the army in disgust, and only a tactful appeal from General Washington had prevented his resignation. The coincidence that placed him in the vicinity of Danbury was a fortunate one, for Congress finally acknowledged his abilities by promoting him to major general. Arnold was mollified sufficiently to return to General Philip Schuyler's northern command.[9]

Washington puzzled to fit all these events into some kind of pattern that might indicate Howe's intentions. But the British commander's strategy was as obscure to some of his own subordinates as it was to the Americans and what Howe had in mind was outside the range of Washington's speculations. It certainly must have come as a shock to Lord George Germain.

Under the date of April 2 Howe informed Germain that he had abandoned his plan for an overland march from New York to Philadelphia because of "the difficulties and delay that would attend the passage of the Delaware . . . I propose to invade Pennsylvania by sea, and from this arrangement we must probably abandon the Jerseys. . . ."

By sea! However ambiguous Howe may have been about his cooperation with the Canadian expedition the fact that his army would be between Washington and Burgoyne afforded willy-nilly some assurance of support. If Washington followed Howe's march toward Philadelphia or moved to block him this would remove the American southern force from any position from which it could threaten Burgoyne. If the American commander ignored Howe and moved toward the Hudson Sir William would know it instantly and take the necessary precautions.

But to go to Philadelphia by sea was to leave Burgoyne entirely on his own. Not only would Howe be out of position to support the northern army, he would even be out of communication with it, especially while he was at sea.

If any doubt remained in Germain's mind of Howe's aberration it was dispelled by a dispatch that Howe had written to Carleton, a copy of which accompanied his letter to Germain. To the Governor-General Sir William wrote: "Having but little expectation that I will be able, from the want of sufficient strength in this army, to detach a corps in the beginning of the campaign to act up Hudson's River consistent with the operations already determined upon, the force your Excellency may deem expedient to advance beyond your frontiers after taking Ticonderoga will, I fear, have little assistance from hence to facilitate their approach, and as I shall probably be in Pennsylvania when that corps is ready to advance into this province, it will not be in my power to communicate with the officer commanding it, as soon as I would wish; he must therefore pursue such measures as may from circumstances be judged most conducive to the advancement of his Majesty's service consistently with your Excellency's orders for his conduct."

The most that Howe could offer in the way of assistance was to "endeavor to have a corps upon the lower part of Hudson's river sufficient to open communication for shipping thro' the Highlands." What may have been most significant about this latest communication was the aura of pessimism which pervaded it. "Restricted as I am from entering upon more extensive operations by the want of force, my hopes of terminating the war this year are vanished."[10]

And what of Major Balfour, who was aware of the ministry's expectations and whose mission it had been to represent those wishes to the commanders in New York? Balfour's influence on Howe's decision may be deduced from the latter's letter to Germain on May 22, two weeks after Balfour's arrival in New York. Howe merely reported Tryon's raid on Danbury and the news that Burgoyne was expected to be on Lake Champlain in June. His own army, he said, was encamped on the Raritan and he gave no hint of when he expected to move on Philadelphia.

The only reference to any of the suggestions conveyed by Balfour was in a dispatch of June 3. To the ministry's suggestion that a raiding expedition into New England might discourage recruiting for Washington's army, Howe again referred to his lack of reinforcements and noted that such an expedition would interfere with the major operations "that have received royal approbation and which are already too curtailed by the want of land force. . . ."

In the meantime Germain had gone to the King with the news of Howe's April 2 dispatch containing the latest deviation from the plan of campaign. The result of their conference was an instruction to Howe (May 18) which, once more, can be understood only on the assumption that Germain and the King were, in effect, at the mercy of the whims of their commander in chief in America. The King, wrote Germain, "does not hesitate to approve the alteration which you propose, . . ." But he added the important condition that "it will be executed in time for you to cooperate with the army ordered to proceed from Canada and put itself under your command." There was every indication, both in Howe's April 2 letter to Germain and in his letter to Carleton which he enclosed, that Howe did not intend to do more than "endeavor" to open the lower Hudson to "communicate" with Burgoyne. Nevertheless, Germain's dispatch on May 18 closed with the notation that "his Majesty entirely approves of your letter to Sir Guy Carleton."[11]

Perhaps Germain was resigned to the fact that there was nothing he could do at this late date to alter Howe's course of action. If his dispatch took the usual eight weeks to make the westward crossing of the Atlantic Howe would not receive it until mid-July when he would presumably be fully launched on his sea voyage (in fact, Howe did not receive it until August 12). If Howe and Burgoyne were successful Germain would have given no offense. If the great campaign fell apart because of lack of cooperation, he, like Howe, had his justification on the record.

There was still a faint hope. Sir Henry Clinton had left late in April to resume his duties as Howe's second in command. He was thoroughly conversant with Burgoyne's plans and with the ministry's views. He was himself convinced that victory depended on the coordination of British forces. Moreover, Sir Henry never hesitated to speak his mind to his chief, although seldom with any success.

Cat And Mouse In New Jersey

With the coming of warm weather the army in New York became restless yet the British commander seemed in no hurry to begin the campaign. To the ministry he pointed out "the delays which may attend the evacuation of the Jersies" but he issued no orders to the army on the Raritan. April passed into May and now Sir William complained that he had not received sufficient tents to take the field. Finally, having talked of delays in getting the army out of New Jersey, he began a series of maneuvers *into* New Jersey, presumably either to disguise his intentions or to force Washington out of his position behind the mountains at Morristown. Howe evidently hoped to maneuver him into open country and bring the Americans to battle.

Washington had already concluded the obvious, that Howe would either take his army up the Hudson or strike overland for Philadeliphia. At the end of May he moved his army south to Middlebrook, about ten miles northwest of New Brunswick where he could keep an eye on the road to Philadelphia and still be in a position to fall back into a defensive position in the Watchung Mountains.

In the second week in June Howe made his first feint. Marching west from New Brunswick he seemed to be offering Washington a chance to get between the British and New York. But reports came into headquarters at Middlebrook that Howe had left his heavy baggage in Brunswick and that he had no boats for crossing the Delaware. The further Howe advanced, the further he was separated from his base but Washington simply waited. New Jersey militia and Morgan's deadly riflemen now began to harass the redcoats, picking off stragglers and snapping at outposts and detachments.

After about a week Howe suddenly withdrew his army toward New Brunswick, simulating a hasty retreat. The Americans followed with the divisions of Nathanael Greene and "Mad Anthony" Wayne closing on the rear of the British column. The pursuit continued to New Brunswick but the American units had trouble coordinating their movements and Washington cautioned his commanders not to press too hard. As the British continued their withdrawal toward Amboy the Americans broke off the pursuit, but the move had succeeded in drawing the American commander out of his defensive positions at Middlebrook.

On June 26 Howe tried to close the trap. Marching swiftly out of Amboy in two columns he attempted to cut the Americans off from Middlebrook and the sanctuary of the New Jersey hills. But the effort was too great for his men. The heavily clad troops suffered from the intense June heat, and small parties of sniping militiamen stung the lumbering column. Lord Stirling, commanding the advance American division, briefly found himself in serious trouble. The belligerent Irishman further imperilled his position by standing and fighting. The British column under Cornwallis smashed him and almost cut him off but the long march and the hot, humid weather halted the pursuit. Washington was amply forewarned and withdrew to Middlebrook, leaving the two armies in the same positions they had occupied three weeks before. Howe refused to risk an attack and the American commander in chief would not be drawn from his prepared defenses.[12]

Having already decided to take his army to Pennsylvania by sea Howe pulled back through New Brunswick to Amboy and on June 30 ferried the entire force across to Staten Island. It was, of course, a logical move, one that was in fact long overdue if the British were to make the most of the remainder of the summer. But it had an unfortunate effect on the army. After the frustrations and confinement of winter quarters officers and men had had high hopes for the spring. Their spirits had lifted as they began what many thought would be the final campaign of the war. Now, in the first week of July, a month's campaign had not only been fruitless but aimless. New Jersey was abandoned, the army was back in New York, and the commander in chief had fallen into another of his strange lapses of torpid inactivity.

It was a dispirited and idle army that Sir Henry Clinton found when he arrived in New York on July 5. He was alarmed that the summer was so far advanced for he knew that Lord Germain and the King expected two results from the coming campaign: that Philadelphia would be captured, and that Howe would have made a junction with Burgoyne. He now learned for the first time that Howe planned to go to Philadelphia by sea. Sir Henry was dismayed. He had earlier expressed to Germain his doubts that there would be time for a campaign to Pennsylvania and a return to the Hudson to assist Burgoyne. Now he was certain of it.

Clinton and Howe had never gotten along well, although it was part of Clinton's paradoxical personality that he could sincerely admire his superior. All

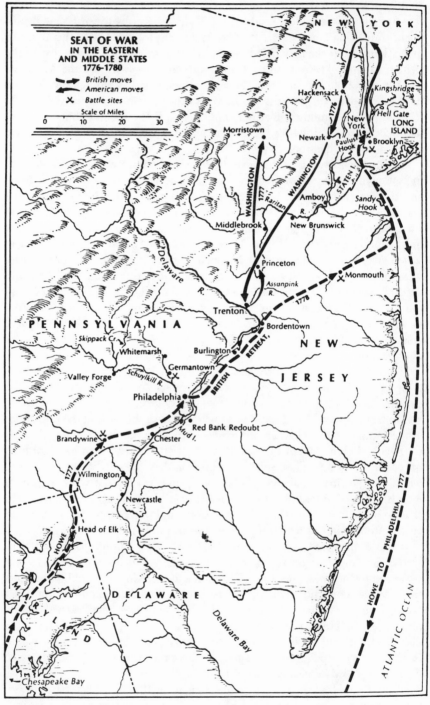

© Mark Boatner, III, *Encyclopedia of the American Revolution*, David McKay Co., Inc.

through the campaign of 1776 they had disagreed, Clinton expressing his opinions with a forcefulness and frankness that was surprising in view of the diffidence he had lately displayed at court. During 1776 he had insisted that it was Washington's army, not the occupation of territory that was the real objective (Did he now remind Howe that he had spent a month pursuing that same army in New Jersey when he should have been on his way to Pennsylvania?). He had proposed a flanking movement to cut off Washington's army during the American retreat of December, 1776. He steadfastly refused to believe that much reliance could be placed on the Loyalists.

Now, in the summer of 1777, Clinton vehemently denounced the strategy proposed by his commander. In going to Philadelphia by sea, he argued, Howe could not possibly bring the Americans to a decisive engagement unless Washington wished it. Holding Pennsylvania and New Jersey at the end of the campaign would require an army of occupation as well as extensive support from the Loyalists in whom Clinton had no more faith than he had had a year ago. In such circumstances support for the army on the Hudson became impossible.

Howe professed (not withstanding Germain's dispatch to Carleton) that he did not understand the purpose of Burgoyne's expedition and that he had no specific instructions to support it. Clinton removed his doubts. "I told him [the] government did not seem to hold that language, but freely declared—too freely—I thought this [movement by sea] must finish it. He stared." Was it possible that Howe never really grasped the ministry's intention, that he had not realized the importance Germain attached to Burgoyne's invasion? Clinton seemed to think so. Having relegated the Canadian army to a minor role in his own thinking it never crossed Howe's opinionated mind that Germain and the King might disagree.

But if Clinton's emphatic assertion of the ministry's view came as a surprise to Howe it did not alter his fixed intention. He finally silenced Clinton with what, to his involuted logic, must have been an unanswerable argument: ". . . he had sent home his plan, it was approved, and he would abide by it." But Germain and the King had not approved a sea voyage to Philadelphia.

To Clinton, Howe's decision was simply unbelievable. By mid-July Burgoyne was reported at Ticonderoga, and Sir Henry, at the moment of Howe's sailing, flatly told his chief that *he intended to deceive us all, and, though he was pleased to say he was going to sea . . . I should expect to see him return with the first southerly blast and run up the North River.*[13]

On July 23, with his troops finally embarked, Howe and the fleet disappeared beyond the southern horizon.

SEVEN

The Suppression of
the Loyalists

IN APRIL, 1776, THE BALTIMORE COUNCIL OF SAFETY ORDERED A DETACHMENT of militia to Annapolis to arrest Governor Robert Eden on the charge of giving aid to the enemy. Major Mordecai Gist, the detachment commander, reported to the State Council of Safety before proceeding with his mission. That august body sent the detachment back to Baltimore and shortly afterward issued a reprimand to the Baltimore council chairman, Samuel Purviance, for exceeding his authority. Two months later Governor Eden was allowed to take his departure peacefully. The fact that the Baltimore Council of Safety had acted on the recommendation of the Continental Congress carried no weight with the state council of Maryland.

The episode is illustrative of the dilemmas presented by the problem of Tory or Loyalist subversion. Eden was one of the few colonial governors who made a genuine effort to reconcile the conflicting views of the colonists and the home government in the crisis of 1775. His moderation had earned him the respect of the colonists, especially those in the more conservative eastern counties, and he was personally popular in Maryland. His friends, some of whom were members of the state council, were shocked at the idea of humiliating him by placing him under arrest.[1]

When the war came in 1775 enthusiastic Whigs throughout the colonies began a campaign to "overawe the disaffected." Mobs harassed notorious Tories, breaking into their homes, terrifying their families, and often subjecting the victims themselves to tar and feathers or other physical abuse. Yet on the whole there was surprisingly little bloodshed. Alexander Graydon recalled that a Tory who had shouted out his allegiance to George the Third was given mild treatment compared to the bloody vengeance of the French Reign of Terror twenty years later; ". . . his bravado would unquestionably have brought the offender to the lamppost and set his head on a pike."[2]

The irony of rebels suppressing disloyalty by attacks on people who proudly called themselves Loyalists was lost on most of the Whigs. But they realized that the success of the Revolution depended not merely on winning adherents but in stifling the opposition. Who, then, were the opponents of the Revolution? Among Americans who had voiced their opinions since 1763 almost all had expressed disapproval of one or another of the measures of the home government that became known collectively as the "new colonial policy." When the Whigs shifted the focus of their struggle from the defense of their liberties as Englishmen to independence, they lost a sizeable number of supporters. Joseph Galloway, a prominent member of the First Continental Congress, became one of the leading supporters of the Crown after 1776. John Jay, Robert and Gouverneur Morris, and James Duane were also opposed to independence, hoping for reconciliation even after July, 1776. Yet in the end they remained faithful to the Whig cause. John Dickinson, author of the famous *Letters from a Pennsylvania Farmer*, was so torn by his deep-rooted loyalty to England that he could not bring himself to sign the Declaration of Independence. Yet he served in the Delaware militia and was sent back to Congress by his Delaware constituents in 1779.

Thus distinctions were blurred and this greatly complicated the Whig problem of what today we would call internal security. Moreover Americans prided themselves on the fact that they were men of reason who could conduct an orderly revolution.

THE MOBS

It is important to remember that those who eventually came to be judged as enemies of the Revolution were themselves American and an integral part of the community in which they lived. As the Whig movement progressed from protest to resistance to independence the differing loyalties put a serious strain on the social fabric of these communities. When these men—and their families—many of whom had been respected leaders of their county or town, found their homes surrounded by mobs threatening them with violence, the shock was sometimes overwhelming, and the trauma deep and lasting.

The period of greatest confusion and perplexity over the division of loyalties came in the initial stage of the war. Although Americans were in a state of rebellion against Great Britain it was more than a year after Lexington and Concord before they had governments, either state or national, that possessed some kind of legitimacy. The first act of the Maryland revolutionary convention which met in April, 1775, was to swear allegiance to King George. The members then proceeded to elect delegates to the Second Continental Congress.[3]

Most of the interim governments were hastily formed and were primarily concerned with raising and fitting out troops and meeting other problems created by the emergency of war. The regular processes of government were left largely to local governments, along with the problem of the suppression of the Tory opposition.

The most obvious potential enemies were royal officials. Some had used their positions to bully and tyrannize, but these were probably the exception rather than the rule. After all, even royal officials were mostly Americans and had lived peaceably with their neighbors all their lives. As the revolutionary movement gained momentum their positions became increasingly difficult. As holders of royal office they were committed to uphold Crown authority. When, as most believed, the rebellion was suppressed, and they had compromised their loyalty they would be called to account. In the meantime there was the question of survival.

Lieutenant Governor Thomas Oliver of Massachusetts was confronted by a crowd of 4,000 angry citizens of Cambridge on September 2, 1774. Oliver was a respected land owner and leading citizen but he had accepted his appointment under the Massachusetts Government Act, which had dissolved the assembly and virtually ended self-government in the colony. This made him the focus of attention for the aroused Whigs. The crowd did not appear to be in a dangerous mood so Oliver addressed them, answered some of their questions, and persuaded them to disperse. Shortly afterward a rumor spread that troops were being sent to Cambridge from Boston and the crowd reappeared, some of its members armed. Five spokesmen "of decent appearance" were admitted and presented a demand that Oliver resign his office. Fearful for his family, Oliver agreed to sign a resignation, although he entered a notation that he had done so in the face of threats. Some of the crowd objected to this but moderates among them persuaded the rest to go home. The next day Oliver and his family fled to Boston where he resumed the duties of his office. Even though he had acted under duress, the lieutenant governor was disturbed by the fact that he was breaking an oath. He finally concluded, ". . . I still had it in my power to die or to make the promise. I chose to live."[4]

Other marked men were members of the Anglican clergy. Many of these churchmen were politically naive and extremely conservative in their views. Most regarded defiance of authority as a mortal sin and it would not have been unusual to hear sermons from their pulpits defending the divine right of kings.

Jonathan Boucher, an Anglican clergyman from Annapolis, announced that he would preach a sermon in which he would instruct his parishioners that "they could not be sure they were right and doing good; and so their truest wisdom as well as duty . . . was, as the Prophet advised, to *sit still*." When Boucher arrived he found his church filled with 200 armed men. He grimly determined to deliver his message and started to mount to his pulpit, "my sermon in one hand and a loaded pistol in the other." He was suddenly seized by "one of my good friends," who urged him to desist, saying that men had been ordered to fire on him if he entered the pulpit. After some scuffling and arguing, Boucher concluded "that there was but one way to save my life. This was by seizing Sprigg [the leader of the armed men] . . . by the collar and with my cocked pistol in the other hand, assuring him that if any violence was offered me I would immediately blow his brains out. . . ." The two marched to Boucher's horse—Sprigg "had the meanness" to order his drummers to play the "Rogue's March"—and the sturdy minister escaped.[5]

American revolutionaries were the first to recognize that the press could be a powerful weapon in promoting their cause. The obvious corollary was that the Tory press must be silenced. Here the Whigs ran into an ideological conflict that obviously disturbed them, for the tradition of a free press was strong in the colonies, and it was not easy to reconcile attacks on Tory editors with the struggle for liberty. James Rivington, editor of the *New York Gazetteer*, at first made a sincere effort to steer a middle course, inviting expression of opinion from both sides. But by 1775 his obviously Tory sympathies led to his condemnation by a Whig meeting and his press and offices were destroyed by the New York Sons of Liberty. Young Alexander Hamilton, although he had already attracted attention as a radical pamphleteer and orator, remarked, ". . . I cannot help condemning this step." The New York Provincial Congress investigated the charges against Rivington and exonerated him upon his pledge to sin no more. Nevertheless he sailed for England early in 1776 and did not return until the British occupied New York.[6]

The local work of suppressing the Loyalists fell to the old Committees of Correspondence or the more recent committees created by the Continental Association (to enforce the nonintercourse resolutions of the First Continental Congress). These constituted themselves as committees of safety at both the county and state levels. Since there were no statutory codes to guide them the committees had to decide cases on the basis of their own notions of justice. In small rural communities the suspect's local reputation and character might count as much in his defense as the evidence. Committeemen were usually aware that in such a heated atmosphere old personal scores might be paid by bringing charges based on false testimony, and that a witch hunt might result. They were also conscious of the fact that their verdicts were as often based on a sense of the feeling of the neighborhood as their own sense of justice.

Difficult problems arose in that gray area where an accused might have spoken out against the Whig cause without having advocated support of the Crown or the measures enacted by Parliament. In late 1774 and early 1775 there were many who believed that radical Whigs were leading the colonies down the road to war and that bloodshed must be avoided at all costs. In June, 1775, Elisha Adams, Timothy Hammant, and Jonathan Cutler were accused in Medway, Massachusetts, of being "unfriendly and inimical to the just rights and liberties of America and measures for recovering the preservation of the rights, liberties and constitution thereof." The evidence consisted of one's protest against bloodshed, another's prediction of a race riot in Boston, and the sinister fact that the third had sold his horse two days before the battle of Lexington and Concord.

The three were asked to unite with the community in opposing British tyranny. When one replied that he could not "see any reason nor justice in riotous actions in the later times" the committee allowed that such an opinion did not conflict with his pledge to "exert myself in a just and constitutional way. . . ." The charges against the accused were dismissed.[7]

Such leniency was the rule rather than the exception in most of the proceedings of the committees from 1774 to 1776. The exceptions could usually be found in those areas where tensions were high and where overt hostilities by one side or the other outraged the people of the community. In Virginia the Nansemond Committee of Safety decreed that the Reverend John Agnew be ostracized for persisting in preaching obedience to the Crown. The stubborn Anglican refused until a mob forced him to stop preaching entirely, but except for the original judgement of the committee he was not punished further. However, when the royal governor, Lord Dunmore, decided to raise an armed force to oppose the Whigs, and especially after he offered freedom to any slaves who joined him, the temper of the area changed sharply. The aroused Virginians defeated Dunmore outside Norfolk in December, 1775, and then burned the town, forcing its inhabitants, Whig and Tory alike, to flee. Once the threat of Dunmore was removed, Virginians relaxed their vigilance to an extent that alarmed some Patriot leaders. James Madison complained that although Benjamin Haley's words and actions "gave abundant proof of his being an adherent to the king" he was only fined twelve shillings and sentenced to one hour in jail.[8]

From first to last the most troublesome problem for the Pennsylvania Whigs was the Society of Friends. Their militant pacifism forbade them from participating directly or indirectly in the war. Although many of them were wealthy and politically powerful they aroused a good deal of resentment, especially among the westerners who accused the self-righteous Quaker merchants of putting guns in the hands of the Indians, and now were enriching themselves by trading with the British. Yet religious diversification in American society, and the strong hold that religion of whatever faith had on community life in the colonies precluded any systematic attack on the sect. North Carolinians and Rhode Islanders seem to have adopted much the same view toward the Friends in those colonies.

Most of the Quakers attempted to follow a policy of reconciliation. The Philadelphia Meeting of the Suffering early in 1775 urged its members to "demean themselves as peaceable subjects and to discountenance and avoid every measure tending to excite disaffection to the King as the supreme magistrate or to the legal authorities of government."

Moses Brown, a wealthy merchant of Rhode Island, became a member of the Society of Friends in 1773. He urged Rhode Islanders to seek reconciliation, but his ostentatious pacifism became somewhat tainted after the British seized one of his ships and arrested his brother. Brown went to Boston and secured the release of both in return for which he agreed to use his efforts to curb hostilities in Rhode Island. For the moment the tensions were relaxed between the Patriots and the Friends, and Brown and his fellows earned a grudging respect for the extensive program that they carried on for the relief of refugees and other destitute people during 1775 and 1776.[9]

THE LAW

In August, 1776, Asa Porter of Haverhill, New Hampshire, was jailed for plotting to induce the British to send troops from Canada to invade New Hampshire. Porter, it was alleged, was organizing a band of armed Tories to cooperative with the invaders. The Haverhill Committee of Safety passed the case to the New Hampshire assembly. The evidence against Porter was not very substantial, but the accused defended himself on quite a different ground.

He challenged the constitutionality of the whole proceeding against him. He pointed out that in American legal practice "it doth not consist with the liberties of the people that the same body which hath the power of making laws should also have the power of executing the laws or determining causes of individuals." Moreover the legislature, even if it had judicial power, was determining treason without having passed a law that defined it. Finally it was examining evidence without a formal charge having been brought and was denying Porter's right to trial by jury. Porter was paroled and rearrested several times, but he continually bombarded the assembly with appeals and petitions, and their refusal to hold him in custody may have indicated that the members were sufficiently troubled by his arguments to bury them in procedural red tape.[10]

In the absence of constitutional or legal sanctions the colonies tended to follow English common and statutory law and to operate through their colonial court systems. In most of the New England and middle colonies revolutionary provincial congresses were elected, but constitutions were somewhat slow to take shape. In Virginia a constitutional convention was in session in the summer of 1776, but it was some months before the frame of government was complete. Massachusetts did not ratify a constitution until 1781. The Second Continental Congress in Philadelphia, though it assumed responsibility for the army and other functions of a national nature could only make suggestions to the states. Lacking constitutional authority to tax, to conscript troops, or, indeed, to take any measures without the consent of the states, it is not surprising that Congress avoided the perplexing problem of Loyalist subversion.

The American rebels were obviously having a difficult time defining treason. It was not until a few days before independence that Congress finally faced the problem. On June 24 it passed a resolution suggesting criteria for disloyalty. Those who levied war against the "united colonies," were adherents to George III, or gave aid and comfort to the enemy should be adjudged guilty of treason. It was six months to a year before most of the states responded. Maryland passed an act providing for the death penalty for "adherents to Great Britain" on July 4, 1776, but New York did not legislate against treason until 1781, relying instead on English common law. It passed a test law—a law providing for the administration of an oath as a test of loyalty—in December, 1776.

Most states also specified lesser crimes of subversion. Those who encouraged recognition of the sovereignty of George III, who discouraged enlistments in the army or advised against resistance to Britain, who disseminated false information, or maintained communications with the enemy were liable to less severe punishments. Two of the most widespread crimes were counterfeiting and trading with the enemy (the former was considered subversive as well as criminal).

Edward Perry, a Maine lumberman, supplied masts under contract to the royal navy in Nova Scotia. Perry was required by the local committee to post a bond of £2,000, but there was little the committee could do about "seizing" the huge mast timbers. After some hesitation it released Perry (who had displayed no other signs of disaffection) but ordered him to move to an inland town.

By 1777 most of the states came to the conclusion that there had to be some means of identifying the "disaffected." In short, the Patriots were driven to the axiom that those who were not for them must be against them. The means employed to effect this was the test oath.

The wording varied from state to state but in general the person taking the oath swore that he renounced his allegiance to the Crown, would do nothing that would compromise the freedom and independence of the United States, and would report to the authorities any conspiracies or treasonable acts of which he had knowledge. It should be noted that rarely did test oaths require any positive action, although in some states the test oath was administered by those who made up the militia rolls, so that swearing to or signing the test oath made one liable for militia conscription.[12]

In the early stages of the war committees of safety were often loath to convict suspects when there was only the flimsiest kind of evidence. The test oath bound the suspect to future good conduct and in effect put him on notice that he was being carefully watched by the authorities. The committees now had recourse to deterrence rather than punishment as a means of checking disaffection.

By 1777 many states, on Congress' recommendation, were calling on all inhabitants to take the oaths, thereby inaugurating a sweeping campaign of intimidation (New Hampshire, New York, North Carolina, and Georgia required test oaths only of civil and military office holders). In the twentieth century many Americans are outraged and insulted at the idea of loyalty oaths, but it must be remembered that large segments of the population in America in 1776 were in the process of switching allegiances. Many of the stoutest supporters of the Whig cause had held civil or military office under the Crown and thus welcomed the opportunity to proclaim their loyalty to the new nation. As Professor Don Higginbotham has suggested, an analogy might be drawn between the Patriots and the twentieth century immigrant who is proud of his new citizenship when he becomes naturalized. Those who refused to take the oath were disarmed and deprived of some of their rights, such as the right to vote, to run for office, or to bring civil suits in court. In some cases they were exiled, either to the British lines or to some destination outside the United States. In two states, Delaware and New Jersey, property of nonjurors was seized, and in New York, Maryland, and Delaware their taxes were doubled or trebled.[14]

Those who refused to take the oath were kept under surveillance especially during military crises. In the fall of 1777 after Howe occupied Philadelphia those who refused to take the oath were jailed without bond. When the British shifted their major military effort to the South in the latter years of the war and invaded the Carolinas penalties became increasingly severe. South Carolina nonjurors were banished and threatened with death if they returned. Georgia had no test oath until 1781, but those who refused to take it were automatically adjudged guilty of "high crimes and misdemeanors."

By the end of 1777 all the states except New York had enacted laws for the suppression of loyalism, although time and experience made necessary additions and modifications. In all states except Delaware and Georgia test oaths were established to separate friend from foe. It had taken almost two years for the Patriots to translate their concern over subversion into law. Yet on the whole the record was not bad, especially if one compares the American Revolution with other revolutions of the eighteenth and early nineteenth centuries which were often characterized by witch hunts and mass executions.[14]

THE ENFORCERS

The administration of both laws and test oaths was carried out by the committees of safety in cooperation with local justices of the peace. These officials usually had at their command the local militia who hunted down and arrested suspects, and who were occasionally called on to deal with armed bands of Tories who were so bold as to try to raise the standard of counterrevolution. The militia, then, performed as a sort of local constabulary in addition to preparing themselves for service with the army. As noted above, administering test oaths and drawing up militia rolls was often done at the same time, usually by the county lieutenant. In many states conscript laws specified that all who were subject to military duty were required to appear in person for drills and other militia training. Thus every man publicly identified himself as a supporter of the Revolution, even though he might have a substitute ready to serve in his place when the regiment went to active duty.

Suspects were brought before the local justice of the peace and the charge, with supporting evidence, was presented. The justice might himself dispose of the case if the charge was not serious. Mrs. John Davis of Woodbury, Connecticut, came under suspicion after her husband left home and joined the British army. Several people of the town presented affidavits attesting to Mrs. Davis' unquestioned adherence to the Patriot cause and the local justice dismissed the charges. A year later Davis deserted from the British and returned home. He was believed when he said that he was a convert to the American cause and the local justice of the peace instituted a petition to the General Assembly to grant him a pardon.

In more serious cases the justices of the peace held what amounted to preliminary hearings. In Fairfield, Connecticut, the local constable delivered John Cannon to Justice Thaddeus Betts, charging Cannon with coming from the British lines with a pass signed by the former governor of New Jersey, William Franklin. Since Cannon might be a British spy, Betts ordered him jailed to await trial in Superior Court. In Massachusetts courts of special session, composed of three to five justices of the peace, tried persons accused of treason, spying, and other serious crimes of subversion. In most states defendants who were convicted were allowed to appeal to the state assembly or the highest state court.

Punishments ranged from fines and the posting of bonds for good behavior in cases of minor offenses to banishment and imprisonment for serious crimes. Prison sentences were limited because there were simply not nearly enough jails. In New England, especially, the courts seem to have been more concerned about future behavior of the accused and neutralizing subversion than in reprisals against the Tories themselves. There was only one execution in Connecticut during the entire war.[15]

The middle states differed somewhat from New England because the problem of disaffection was much more widespread and the percentage of Loyalists was much higher. New York city became a haven for Loyalists from all parts of America, and sizeable numbers were enlisted in provincial corps of the British army. It was here that Major Robert Rogers, the famous ranger of the French and Indian War, organized raiding parties that terrorized Patriots on Long Island and the Connecticut coast. Here also Burgoyne's invasion in 1777 raised the hopes of enthusiastic Loyalists on the lower Hudson and in the Mohawk Valley, and frightened many others into fearful neutrality.

Under these circumstances local committees of safety often proved unequal to the task of checking subversion and aid to the enemy. Early in 1777 the New York Convention authorized the trial of traitors by military courts martial. The previous year a state Committee and Commission for Detecting and Defeating Conspiracies had been set up; now, assisted by a militia corps, the commission began to sweep the state, using the militiamen to round up suspects, and organizing courts-martial. In April and May, 1777, eighteen accused were convicted and sentenced to death. The Convention approved fourteen of these. During the three years of its existence the commission heard over a thousand cases of disloyalty. In 1778 New York passed a test oath law and failure to take it was punished by banishment or imprisonment. By this time local committees of safety had become merely administrative arms of the state committee, rarely deciding any cases on their own or exerting much influence.[16]

A similar pattern developed in New Jersey. Here the state's executive body, the state Council of Safety was given virtually complete control of detecting and punishing disloyalty. Its energetic attorney general, William Paterson, soon had the council travelling throughout the state, conducting its own prosecutions and rendering judgements. Such action was highly suspect so far as constitutional theory was concerned, but constant incursions of British troops during 1776 and 1777 disrupted the regular court system and the Whigs had to exert the full force of their authority to check the rather sizeable number of Tories and waverers.[17]

The effect of troop movements and military campaigns on the fortunes or misfortunes of the Loyalists was nowhere better illustrated than in Delaware. This smallest of the states had perhaps the highest percentage of Loyalists, and Patriots frequently had to call on their neighbors in Maryland and Pennsylvania for militia to help contain Tory uprisings.

Howe's invasion of Pennsylvania in 1777 brought hopeful Loyalists into the open, and when the British fleet appeared in the Delaware Loyalist pilots were on hand to guide the ships upriver and armed bands were ready to join forces with the redcoats. When Howe announced his decision to go to the Chesapeake, Loyalists were bitterly disappointed. One of them, Thomas Robinson, went aboard the flagship and begged Howe to put 500 regulars ashore in Delaware. This gesture, he said, would bring out 5,000 Loyalists who were ready to fight. Although Howe had been attracted southward by word of widespread Loyalist support, Sir William headed for the Chesapeake and what he believed to be prospects for greater support in southern Pennsylvania. With his departure went the best opportunity for a counterrevolution in Delaware.[18]

Pennsylvania, like New York, relied principally on state authority vested in a touring committee of safety. The problem of the Society of Friends proved just as nettlesome after systematic procedures had been established as before. The Whig majority—if indeed it was a majority—dared not completely antagonize this considerable body of militant neutrals, who steadfastly refused to aid either the American or British war effort. There were enough unscrupulous merchants masquerading under Quaker guise to antagonize the Patriots and in the summer of 1777 the Continental Congress urged the state to disarm and arrest the "disaffected," a measure obviously aimed at the Friends. Eleven prominent Quakers were arrested by the militia and, after interminable legal proceedings, they were exiled to Winchester, Virginia, where they lived under surveillance until the end of the war.

Enactment of a test oath met with equally stubborn resistance, not only from the Society of Friends, but from lesser sects like the Dunkards and Mennonites. The latter especially became victims of vigilante groups, notably where their numbers were small. Pennsylvania was one of the first states to use confiscation laws to suppress disaffection, and gangs of outlaws masquerading as militia descended on isolated communities and literally stripped the inhabitants bare. Eventually the Friends were forced to accommodate themselves to reality. They ceased condemning the American cause and, in effect, claimed only such consideration as might be given any religious group. They intensified their program for the relief of refugees and the destitute, and thus an uneasy truce was established between Friends and Patriots.

The fate of the Loyalists in Philadelphia during and after the British occupation of 1777 and early 1778 points up the frustration and impotence that they so frequently experienced with the British army. During the winter of 1777–1778 Joseph Galloway secured an appointment as Superintendent of Police. Using his powers broadly Galloway restored order to the city, suppressed trade with the enemy, and restored civil government. In a remarkably short time the city was flourishing, foreign trade had resumed, the Loyalist exiles had returned.

Then, in the spring of 1778, Sir Henry Clinton, the new commander in chief, announced that the British were evacuating the city. In vain, Galloway urged the British to retain the city, if for no other reason than as a model for what could be accomplished by the restoration of English rule. But Clinton was adamant and Philadelphia instead became an example of the fate of Loyalists who put their trust in the British army.[19]

In all the states the militia were an essential ingredient in the enforcement of state authority. Governor Clinton of New York thought that suppression of disaffection was the militia's most important duty and General Schuyler frequently called on them for such purposes. As we shall see, he used them to hold the Indians of the Six Nations in check, and he smashed an incipient rising of Highland Scots in Tryon county in early 1776. In Fairfield county, Connecticut, Whig militia nipped a Loyalist rising in the bud in the fall of 1776, and it was roving bands of militia between the lower Hudson and Saratoga that were to play havoc with communications between Burgoyne and New York during the campaign of 1777. We have already noted how militia harassed outposts in the vicinity of British bases, ambushing foraging parties and killing or capturing stragglers. In such situations it was difficult for the redcoats to extend their influence to Loyalist sympathizers in the surrounding countryside.[20]

The failure of the Loyalists to make a more significant contribution to the cause of England's reconquest of America can be attributed to several factors. The most obvious is the thoroughness and swiftness with which the Whigs in the states set up measures for controlling and neutralizing Tories and would-be Tory sympathizers. The dispersal of power among the states undoubtedly hamstrung the American war effort in general, but it was a blessing in disguise for counteracting subversion. Congress passed this problem to the states by default and it would appear that the states, with their local court systems, committees, and militia already in place, were much better equipped to meet the problem.

Whig leaders early realized that it was important to get control of the militia, the only organized "police force" in the colonies, and they were successful in getting Whig officers elected or appointed, and in using the militia organization as a means of promoting the revolutionary cause. Equally important was the fact that committees of safety were, in general, careful to avoid witch hunts and campaigns of terror. Certainly there were many unjust convictions, innocent people who were victimized, and property illegally and arbitrarily confiscated. All too often militia units were covers for outlaw gangs who pillaged and looted friend and foe alike. But by and large the committees exercised admirable restraint, giving those who were accused every opportunity to recant their loyalty to the Crown. By 1777 even those against whom the evidence of treason was overwhelming were tried under proper legal procedures and their rights were safeguarded. The Tory argument that Whig rule was mob rule was effectively answered, and waverers were encouraged to believe that the newly independent state governments were capable of creating an orderly society.

The failure of the British authorities to support and encourage the Loyalists more successfully may be attributed to both circumstance and negligence. It was soon apparent that Howe's strategy of extending British authority over large areas by the use of occupation troops was beyond the capacity of the forces under his command. The British abandonment of Philadelphia in 1778 was dictated not by lack of concern for the Loyalist, but by strategic considerations growing out of the entrance of France into the war.

Yet those Loyalists who actively and enthusiastically supported the Crown were usually met with indifference or downright contempt. Loyalist regiments were often badly equipped. Their officers were given provisional rank and they were never fully accepted by the British officer corps. Burgoyne, Howe, and Clinton all shared the basic disdain of Englishmen for Americans and they consistently expressed their lack of faith in the Loyalists as effective soldiers.

Germain and his generals continually overestimated the strength of the Loyalists, especially in terms of the numbers available for military duty. Expressions of loyalty to England did not necessarily mean active participation, and there were probably as many summer soldiers and sunshine Loyalists as there were Patriots.[21]

In the final analysis, then, the Loyalists never had a base from which to launch a counterrevolution. Almost everywhere those who might have been emboldened to raise the King's standard found themselves surrounded by neighbors who were either hostile or apathetic. Given the rapidity and thoroughness with which the states implemented the machinery of suppression, by 1777 any hope that Germain and the ministry may have had for Americanizing the war was at an end.

EIGHT

The Northern Invasion

FOR THE THIRD TIME IN TWO YEARS JOHN BURGOYNE CAME TO NORTH AMERICA. He had achieved the hope of every general, an independent command, and orders for a campaign that would make him a national hero. England was tired of the Howes and Clinton, commanders whose campaigns were unlucky and inconclusive. Burgoyne was the new star in Britain's firmament and the colorful, flamboyant Gentleman Johnny was fully prepared to take the center of the stage in the war for America.

"THIS ARMY MUST NOT RETREAT"

The army that assembled at Montreal was, at first glance, a polyglot of nationalities and even of races. Yet its elements had been carefully specified by Burgoyne and Germain. The regular troops consisted of an almost equal number of redcoats and German mercenaries, most of whom had been sent to Canada in the great troop lift of 1776. They had had a year to become accustomed to the climate and other vicissitudes of America. Of the allotments of reinforcements which Germain made for 1777 only 1600 were consigned to Canada.

The British force consisted of seven regiments: the Ninth, the Twentieth, the Twenty-First, the Twenty-Fourth, the Forty-Seventh, the Fifty-Third, and the Sixty-Second. Three other regiments were left as a garrison for Carleton, less their flank companies which were detached to the invading force. On his July 1 return of troops Burgoyne listed "total rank and file (sick included)" of these regiments as from 542 (9th) to 524 (47th). If these figures are correct their strength was from twenty-five to thirty percent greater than the normal British regiments. As was customary when a large number of regiments was serving together, the flank companies were combined into two regiments of grenadiers and light infantry. These, together with the 24th Regiment, formed the "advance corps" commanded by Brigadier General Simon Fraser.

Fraser was a hard-bitten Scot who had served under Wolfe at Louisbourg and Quebec in the 62nd Royal Americans. He had subsequently been named colonel of the 24th and had come to Canada with it in 1776 where he had been given the "local rank" of brigadier general. The grenadiers were commanded by Major John Acland whom the Baroness Riedesel described as "a plain, rough man, and was almost daily intoxicated; with this exception, however, he was an excellent officer." The light infantry was commanded by Major the Earl Balcarres who was often the commanding general's late night companion at cards and drink, but this did not seem to impair his ability to get into the thick of every fight.

The remaining British force was divided into two brigades. The 9th, 47th, and 53rd regiments comprised the first brigade commanded by Brigadier General Henry Powell; Brigadier General Hamilton commanded the second brigade made up of the 20th, the 21st, and the 62nd. The British troops were designated as the right wing of the army and were commanded by Major General William Phillips. Phillips was a violent-tempered artilleryman of thirty years' service who had distinguished himself in the Seven Years' War. As an artilleryman he would normally have never gotten an infantry command, but Burgoyne was so impressed with his aggressiveness that he had named him second in command as an "emergency measure."

Burgoyne's artillery park contained 138 guns ranging from huge 24-pounders to 4.4-inch mortars. Knowing that his first major objective was Ticonderoga he assembled a train of two 24-pounders, four 12-pounders, eighteen 6-pounders, six howitzers, and twelve smaller pieces, altogether forty-two guns. The British right wing totalled about 3,600 infantrymen and 400 artillerymen.

The left wing consisted of the Germans, mostly from Brunswick, commanded by Major General Friedrich von Riedesel. The Baron was thirty-nine years old and had spent twenty years in the armies of Hesse-Hanau and Brunswick. His good looks and hearty, jovial manner were infectious, and he was an intelligent, quick-witted commander. His force consisted of the Regiments Rhetz, Riedesel, Specht, Barner, Hesse-Hanau, a regiment of grenadiers, and a regiment of dragoons (who had no horses). There was also a company of Hesse-Hanau artillery commanded by the redoubtable Captain Pausch.[1]

The German mercenaries were the ministry's answer to England's troop shortage. For almost a century the rulers of the central European states had used their armies as a lucrative source of income. Although American propagandists and the Opposition in Parliament professed to be shocked that "the German slave had been hired to subdue the sons of Englishmen and freedom," Great Britain had often employed such troops during the Second Hundred Years' War. In fact the availability of these troops was one of the reasons why England and other nations were able to maintain such small standing armies.

The treaty that was concluded with the Duke of Brunswick in January, 1776, was fairly typical. The soldiers were hired at the rate of £7.4s:4½d. per man plus an annual subsidy of £11,500 and a payment of £46,000 when the troops had completed their service. The Duke was also to be compensated "at the rate of the levy money" for every soldier who was killed or wounded. Altogether the 5,700 troops furnished from Brunswick cost the royal treasury about £150,000. During the entire course of the war nearly 30,000 German troops served in America.

The soldiers from the German states were recruited and trained much like those of the British army, although the pressure of the despotic dukes and princes on recruiting officers made them more indiscriminate and heavy-handed. The regiments contained not only the usual number of unemployed vagrants and drifters but "foreigners," that is, those not native to the dukedom or principality. A student travelling from Leipzig to Paris found himself impressed into a regiment of Hesse-Cassel along with "a bankrupt tradesman from Vienna, a fringemaker from Hanover, a discarded secretary of the post-office from Gotha, a monk from Wurzburg . . . a Prussian sergeant of hussars, [and] a cashiered Hessian major. . . ." Yet, like the British regular, the German recruit became a disciplined, tough, efficient soldier.

The Brunswickers in Burgoyne's army included a company of jägers who were armed with short, heavy rifles; there was also a considerable number of musicians. The latter were considered very important for the morale of the troops and the soldiers often marched into battle not only with bands playing but with the soldiers themselves singing lustily.

It was natural that there should be some friction between the British and the Germans. Captain Pausch thought it was because "the Devil of Jealousy has been aroused because the English see that my men drill quicker and more promptly, and because, also, the spectators do us the justice publicly to acknowledge this to be the case." There were occasional fights between the two nationalities, and at one point an order was issued forbidding the Germans from carrying side arms. Captain Pausch entered a strenuous protest "since were they to depend on boxing for protection, some would return to Germany cross-eyed and some blind." General Riedesel and Burgoyne seem to have gotten along well enough although the German complained that Burgoyne did not consult him or keep him informed of plans and operations.[2]

The total of Burgoyne's regular rank and file, then, numbered about 6,600 men. To cover the two wings of the army and to provide scouts, artificers and other auxiliaries Burgoyne hoped to recruit 2,000 Canadians and Loyalists and 1,000 Indians. British expectations were, as usual, far beyond reality. The French *habitants* were impassively apathetic, "awkward, ignorant, disinclined to the service, spiritless." Only 150 could be enlisted and to these were added about 100 Loyalists. This force was to act as a screen for Phillips' right wing.

Riedesel's screen was made up of Indians. Burgoyne expected to recruit a large force of warriors and on the surface this appeared to be a reasonable expectation. Western New York was the homeland of the powerful Iroquois Confederacy whose allegiance to the British dated back to the first European settlements in North America. Samuel de Champlain had accompanied a war party of Algonquins against the Iroquois in 1609 and thus the struggle between England and France for control of North America paralleled the hereditary hostility between the Iroquois and the Algonquins.

In more recent years Sir William Johnson, the Indian superintendent for the Northern Department, had cemented the alliance by marrying Molly Brant, sister of the Mohawk chief, Joseph Brant. Sir William had spent a lifetime in close association with the Indians. He knew their ways, was sympathetic to their interests, and had taken care to see that they received continuous government subsidies. He had built a fortress-like "castle" on the upper Mohawk which became known as Johnstown, and at his death in 1774 his son, Sir John, assumed his father's duties. He was assisted by Guy Johnson, a distant relative, Daniel Claus, Sir William's son-in-law, and John and Walter Butler. All were Loyalists and all held commissions in the militia of Tryon County, which included the whole Mohawk Valley west of Schenectady.

Yet this seemingly powerful hold on the Six Nations was seriously weakened soon after the outbreak of the war by the genius and determination of General Philip Schuyler. The Butlers and Guy Johnson went to Canada at the outbreak of hostilities, but Sir John remained at Johnstown surrounded by a guard of 150 Mohawk braves. In January, 1776, Schuyler marched on Johnstown with 3,000 militiamen at his back and arrested the Indian superintendent. He convinced the Indians that their territory would be respected if they would stay out of the white man's fight. Overawed by the militia, the Indians agreed. When Johnson was released on parole he fled to Canada. All this damaged British prestige severely and the Indians were in a dubious frame of mind when Burgoyne called them to a council at St. Johns on the middle of June, 1777. Here he issued a proclamation calling on them to "go forth in the might of your valour and your cause;—strike at the common enemies of Great Britain and America;—and disturbers of the public order, peace and happiness; destroyers of Commerce; parracides of the state."

It may have been the idea of Indians restoring law and order in America that reduced Lord North to tears of laughter when the proclamation was read in Parliament. Or it may have been when Burgoyne insisted that the Indians give "most serious attention to the rules" which forbade the killing of women, children, prisoners, and the aged. "You will receive compensation for the prisoners you take," continued Gentleman Johnny, "but you shall be called to account for scalps."[3]

The proclamation elicited a sonorous response from Indian orators at the Council and enthusiastic whoops from the assembled warriors, but only 400 of the expected 1,000 responded. Only after the word had spread to the far western tribes did another 400 drift in, lured by the prospect of loot. The Indians, in fact, became a chronic source of irritation to Burgoyne who was constantly pestered by demands for money, supplies, and ammunition, and their irregular comings and goings made them difficult to control. Their leader was

St. Luc de la Corne, a sixty-five year old French Canadian, veteran of the frontier wars who had just served fourteen months in a Yankee prison.

Taken together Burgoyne's total effective force of Indians, provincials, and regulars was about 7,500 rank and file. But there was another way of looking at the invasion force which might well have given its commander a pause. Adding officers, non-commissioned officers, civilian employees, and camp followers, Burgoyne had over 10,000 mouths to feed. As was usual with British armies there were a number of women, and not only camp followers. Several officers' wives and their women servants accompanied the army. Among these were the Baroness Riedesel, with her three children aged one to six, and Lady Harriet Acland who was pregnant.

Artillery, supplies, and equipage necessitated a tremendous amount of transport. Burgoyne's commissary general estimated that it would take 1,125 carts to haul rations for the entire force for 30 days. Carleton had neglected this phase of the expedition's preparation and Burgoyne waited a month after his arrival at Quebec before he requested 400 horses for his artillery train and another 1,000 animals to draw 500 carts carrying his provisions. The carts were hastily built of green wood and the quartermaster procured less than half the number of horses which had been requisitioned. This was not thought to be serious at the time since the principal objective of the army was Ticonderoga at the upper edge of Lake Champlain and could be approached by water. Burgoyne expected that once this American strong point was reduced the way to the Hudson and Albany would be open. Transportation between the lake and the river was a problem which would be met in due time. The distance, after all, was only twenty miles.

By the middle of June the army was assembled at St. John's on the Richelieu, and Carleton came up from Montreal to take formal leave of Burgoyne. On June 14 a review was held under the royal standard, a banner rarely displayed except in the presence of the monarch. It bore the three golden lions of England, the red lion of Scotland, the harp of Ireland, and the *fleur-de-lis*, that quaint symbol of the ancient claims of English sovereigns to the throne of France. After appropriate rounds of wining and dining and the firing of salutes Carleton returned to Quebec and Burgoyne embarked his army.

By June 21 the various contingents of soldiers, Indians, sailors and camp followers had made their way up the Richelieu and debouched into the lower end of Lake Champlain. There they formed into a spectacular column, the Indians leading in their big war canoes. Then came two ship-rigged schooners, *Royal George* and *Inflexible*, followed by a long line of bateaux crowded with colors: red-coated British infantry; the green of the jägers; the blue coats of the Brunswickers, with their glittering cap plates; "in such perfect regularity as to form the most complete and splendid regatta you can possibly conceive." A closer scrutiny would have revealed that the red coats had been trimmed down to jackets by cutting off the skirts, that many of the Brunswickers were ill shod, and that the whole army was somewhat threadbare after a year in Canada. But the soldiers were in good spirits from the generals down to the German privates who strained at the oars of the bateaux. "At first they made bad work with it; but after a while they rowed nicely," observed Captain Pausch.

By June 30 the invaders had reached Crown Point, fifteen miles north of Ticonderoga. Here Burgoyne issued the last of his exhortations, an order to the army. For once he was brief and to the point:

> The army embarks tomorrow, to approach the enemy. We are to contend for the King, the Constitution of Great Britain, to vindicate the Law, and to relieve the oppressed—a cause in which His Majesty's Troops and those of the Princes his Allies, feel equal excitement. The services required of this particular expedition, are critical and conspicuous. During our progress occasions may occur, in which, nor difficulty, nor labor, nor life are to be regarded. This Army must not Retreat.[4]

TICONDEROGA

Ticonderoga was built on a high bluff overlooking the narrow neck of water at the upper end of Lake Champlain. Stretching to the south and east an arm of the lake continued for almost twenty miles to Skenesboro. Lake George formed a parallel arm to the west connected to Lake Champlain by an unnavigable creek.

The fort was commanded by Major General Arthur St. Clair. As a twenty-two year old ensign in the 60th Regiment he had fought with Wolfe at Quebec. After the Seven Years' War he had settled in America and become a wealthy Pennsylvania land owner. He served in Canada in 1776 and had commanded a militia regiment at Trenton. Promoted to major general he was sent to the Northern Department in June to replace Gates as commander at Ticonderoga. Although the fort had undergone considerable repairs since its capture by the Americans in 1775, its defense still posed a number of problems.

In order to understand the geography of Ticonderoga it should be remembered that Lake Champlain makes a turn to the west so that a vessel sailing through the narrows to the upper arm of the lake is heading only one or two points south of due west. The headland on which the fort was located lay less than half a mile from the opposite shore which was dominated by a hill called Mount Independence. Since it was within cannon shot of Ticonderoga it had to be fortified. The American garrison had connected Mount Independence with the fort by a boat bridge and had constructed a log and chain boom across the narrows. They believed that this would effectively block the passage of vessels into the upper arm of Lake Champlain. They had also cleared a rough track through the forest from Mount Independence eastward to Hubbardton to link with the main road to the Hampshire Grants in Vermont. To the southwest of Fort Ticonderoga another hill called Sugar Loaf rose 800 feet above the lake. Although it was only 1800 yards from the fort its slopes were considered too steep and rugged to allow guns to be mounted. The land approaches from the west were protected by a crescent-shaped series of trenches and redoubts called "the old French lines." Finally, to the northwest was Mount Hope which guarded the road and the stream from Lake George. Altogether Ticonderoga and its supporting positions constituted 2,000 yards of lines, fortifications and outworks.

The fort had been built originally by the French in 1755 and subsequent occupants had added to and refined it along lines dictated by European military engineers. Because it had figured so prominently in the military history of North America Ticonderoga had acquired an impressive mystique as the "Gibraltar of North America." Its complex of lines and ramparts epitomized the kind of strong point which figured so prominently in the European doctrine of strategic posts guarding important geographic areas. The British were sure that Ticonderoga was the key to the conquest of New York, if not the entire continent, and Americans, including General Washington, thought so too. Their political ideology might be revolutionary but American military strategy was orthodox European.[5]

The very complexity of the fortress was its greatest point of weakness. The French, the English, and now the Americans found that establishing and maintaining a garrison large enough to man the entire works presented formidable problems in logistics. This was why the fort had fallen so easily to the Americans in 1775, and it may well have been the consideration that led Carleton to abandon the upper end of Lake Champlain in 1776.

A garrison post imposes an especial strain on discipline. Although General St. Clair put the American soldiers to work repairing and strengthening the trenches and block houses, they complained that this was not proper duty for soldiers. Long weeks and months in this distant outpost were tedious and the troops became bored and quarrelsome—and sick. "Our men are harassed to extreme weakness by fatigue. . . . what can be expected from a naked, undisciplined, badly armed, unaccoutred body of men? . . ." The New York legislature, despite the nagging insistence of General Schuyler, was no more willing to furnish supplies in 1777 than they had been in 1776. Schuyler in desperation dispensed $10,000 of his own money, and his reward was to be charged with mishandling of government funds. During the winter of 1776–1777 Congress had yielded to blandishments of the friends of General Horatio Gates by making him commander of Ticonderoga, semi-independent of the command of the Northern Department. Schuyler blew up and went to Philadelphia to demand an investigation. By late spring the issue was apparently resolved to Schuyler's satisfaction. Gates refused to serve under Schuyler and St. Clair succeeded him, arriving at Ticonderoga on June 12, 1777.

There he found what was left of ten Continental and two militia regiments, some of only forty-five men, the largest 265. Major Benjamin Whitcomb had nineteen scouts, Thomas Lee about the same number of rangers and there were perhaps 375 artificers. Altogether the garrison numbered about 2,500 men present and fit for duty. Had they manned the entire position from Mount Independence to the old French lines there would have been about one man per yard. St. Clair had three brigadier generals as subordinates, the Frenchman Roche de Fermoy, John Paterson of Massachusetts, and Enoch Poor of New Hampshire.

General Schuyler arrived on June 19 to confer with St. Clair. Although Burgoyne had complained that "the whole design of the campaign" had been published in Canada "almost as accurately as if it had been copied from the Secretary of State's letter," the news had not reached St. Clair. Congress had heard that the Canadian army would move by sea, presumably either to Boston or New York. Schuyler himself was dubious about the feasibility of defending Ticonderoga but "without orders from Congress, he dare not undertake on himself the responsibility of a measure [retreat] which would create a great outcry." So reported young Colonel James Wilkinson who had been appointed deputy adjutant by Gates and continued to serve under Schuyler. On June 20 a council of war was held. It concluded that both sides of the lake should be defended but that if they were attacked by a major force of the enemy, "the number of troops now at this post, which are under 2,500 effectives, rank and file, are greatly inadequate to the defense; . . ." and that "we think it would be imprudent to expose the army to be made prisoners by the enemy; and that, therefore, it is prudent to provide for a retreat." The council recommended that the retreat follow two lines, by the road east to Hubbardton and Castleton, and by boat southward up Lake Champlain.[6]

Although Schuyler was present at the council his views are not recorded. He left Ticonderoga and shortly afterward appealed to Washington for help. Washington, threatened by Howe's army in New Jersey, could only agree to "hold in readiness" four regiments in the Hudson Highlands. In the midst of all this uncertainty only General Gates, whose many faults did not include bad military instincts, predicted that Burgoyne would move south in force to link up with Howe and control the Hudson.

By the last week in June St. Clair knew that a British force was on the lake. Although Major Whitcomb was a seasoned veteran of frontier warfare he and his scouts could not penetrate the screen of Indians under the skillful leadership of St. Luc de la Corne. The American commander finally concluded that the slowness of the enemy's advance was caused by his hesitancy in attacking the fort; he therefore must have a small force. It seems not to have occurred to St. Clair that a very large force, with its artillery and baggage, would also move slowly.

Burgoyne reached Crown Point in the last week in June and set up a temporary base. From there he moved his troops to a point about three miles from Ticonderoga and began to disembark. Fraser's advance corps and the British right wing were assigned to the western side of the lake with Riedesel and the Germans on the east. On July 2 Burgoyne ordered the advance. Riedesel's command was to move against Mount Independence and seal off the road to Hubbardton. Fraser was ordered to circle to the west and attack the old French lines. He also expected to cut off the garrison at Mount Hope, but St. Clair forestalled him. Early on the morning of the 2nd the garrison set fire to their works and hurried into the American lines.

Fraser's attack was a comedy of errors on both sides. The British advance was screened by Indians directed by Captain Fraser, the general's nephew. The Indians were drunk, and, their courage thus emboldened, they dashed helter-skelter toward the American positions, sweeping Captain Fraser and some of the regulars along with them.

General St. Clair took personal charge of the American defenses. He ordered his inexperienced men to sit down on the firing step and wait for his order, hoping that their inability to see the advancing enemy would keep them from firing (or running) prematurely. But it was his own adjutant, the ubiquitous Colonel Wilkinson, who spoiled the game. As a few British skirmishers moved within musket range the eager young colonel took it upon himself to order a sergeant to fire at one of the exposed redcoats. At the sound of the shot the defenders, officers and men alike, sprang to their feet and discharged a thunderous fusillade. Most of the muskets were pointed "at an elevation of twenty degrees, and the artillery without any direction." When the heavy cloud of smoke finally eddied away the attackers were running like mad, but only two Indians and one soldier had fallen before the awesome volley. The light infantryman whose reckless exposure had provoked Colonel Wilkinson was one of the fallen, but he was found to have succumbed to liquor rather than lead.[7]

It was this prisoner, in fact, who gave St. Clair his first real knowledge of what he was up against. Placed in confinement, the soldier was deceived by a fellow "prisoner" who posed as a Tory and St. Clair was apprized of the fact that he faced an overwhelming force of regulars. If he needed further convincing a new development soon made his situation critical.

The evacuation of Mount Hope gave the British access to the Sugar Loaf. One of Burgoyne's engineers, Lieutenant Twiss, reported to General Phillips that he thought a battery could be gotten to the summit. The old artilleryman was quick to seize the opportunity. "Where a goat can go a man can go and where a man can go he can drag a gun," he said and turned his furious energy to the task. By the morning of July 5 the British had a battery mounted which commanded both the interior of the fort and the narrows of the lake.

St. Clair did not hesitate. He paused only long enough for a hasty council of war to confirm his decision and then ordered a retreat. The baggage, the sick, and a guard of 600 soldiers were loaded into boats and evacuated up Lake Champlain towards Skenesboro. The rest of the army crossed the bridge under cover of darkness to Mount Independence. Scouts reported that the road to Hubbardton was still open so the army began its withdrawal. So silently did the Americans move that not until almost daylight did General Fraser realize they were gone.

Without waiting for orders the commander of the advance corps hastily assembled 750 men and took the road in pursuit. Burgoyne ordered Riedesel to follow with a supporting force. But St. Clair was moving too fast. By late afternoon of July 6th he had reached Hubbardton where he left a rear guard under Colonel Seth Warner to delay the pursuit. St. Clair and the rest of his force pushed on to Castleton. Altogether it was a highly creditable performance. St. Clair had marched almost thirty miles in a day losing only about fifteen percent of his force as stragglers, many of whom caught up with Warner. The July heat brought Fraser to a halt three miles short of Hubbardton.

Warner's force camped for the night, a violation of St. Clair's orders to follow the main force to Castleton. Moreover the inexperienced colonel failed to post pickets, although he must have known that the British were close on his heels. His rear guard consisted of three undermanned Continental regiments which, together with the stragglers, amounted to about 800 men.

At dawn on July 7 Fraser surprised the Americans at breakfast and drove Nathan Hale's New Hampshire regiment right out of the fight. But Warner recovered quickly and established a line that checked the British advance with a galling fire. The British took more than twenty casualties including Major Grant of the 24th killed and the Earl of Balcarres who was wounded. Fraser sent his grenadiers clawing and scrambling up the steep hill overlooking the American left flank, but was soon threatened on his own left by Colonel Turbott Francis' Massachusetts regiment. As the fight raged back and forth Riedesel's German advance guard arrived, a company of jägers and eighty grenadiers and light infantry. Fraser was on the point of launching a bayonet attack in a desperate effort to stop the threat to his right flank. Riedesel drove the jägers straight in to his support and swung the rest of his small force up the hill against the opposite flank. Warner's men wavered and then broke as Colonel Francis was shot dead. Warner ordered his troops to disperse and rendezvous at Manchester.

The little battle, the first real encounter between Burgoyne's invasion force and the troops of the Northern Department, was notable for several reasons. It was a bloody business, for the combined British and German losses were 198 killed and wounded, including fifteen officers. This was more than twenty percent of their force. The American losses were 325 killed, wounded, and captured. After the initial panic of Hale's troops Warner's men had done well, firing from cover and severely punishing Fraser's command. This was the kind of fighting they understood best, but it could not cope with Fraser's aggressiveness. In the end, discipline and bayonets drove the Continentals from the field. Finally, although the British chronically complained about the ponderous slowness of the Germans, Riedesel's troops had kept pace with Fraser's advance corps, and the little German had shown unerring judgement in directing his 120 men to the key points to break the American line.

The noise of the battle reached St. Clair at Castleton. He sent his aides to direct two militia regiments who were within supporting distance to go to Warner's assistance. The militia declined and St. Clair's own troops displayed a mutinous reluctance to join the fight. Wearily, the general turned eastward toward Schuyler's headquarters on the Hudson.

Meantime, the remaining Americans with the baggage and sick were making their way up the southern arm of Lake Champlain. Believing the log boom would deter pursuit by water, they arrived at Skenesboro and began leisurely unloading their boats. But the British were only a few hours behind. A few well-aimed cannon shots had broken the boom and the enemy followed hard on the heels of the fugitives. Their attack sent the small American force flying to the southeast where they took refuge at Fort Anne, a tumble-down stockade halfway to the Hudson. Here they stood off a small force of British pursuers and then made their way to Fort Edward on the Hudson where they found General Schuyler with a corporal's guard of 700 men.

The pursuit of the Americans had left Burgoyne's army scattered all over the landscape between Ticonderoga, Hubbardton, and Skenesboro. Troops were separated from their baggage and commands were dispersed. Riedesel brought his advance corps in on July 8 and the next day Fraser's chewed up brigade came up with over 200 American prisoners. The wounded on both sides had been left on the field at Hubbardton. By July 11 Burgoyne had reassembled his scattered forces at Skenesboro. The great American fortress at Ticonderoga had fallen and the way to Albany was open.[8] There was, however, one small fly in Burgoyne's ointment. He had expected that Carleton would garrison Ticonderoga, but the governor-general pointed out that he had positive orders from Germain that he was to have no authority over the expedition once it left Canada. Burgoyne was forced to leave more than 900 redcoats and Brunswickers to man the defenses of the fortress.

THE SPIDER AND THE FLY

The fall of Ticonderoga generated shock waves in England and America. Its exaggerated importance as the key to the continent produced unwonted despair in Philadelphia, and jubilation in Whitehall. When the news reached London George III is said to have rushed into the Queen's chambers (surprising her in her chemise) exclaiming, "I have beat them! I have beat all the Americans!"

Across the channel in Paris the news reached Benjamin Franklin early in September. The French foreign minister, the Comte de Vergennes, had been under increasing pressure from the British to call a halt to the aid being furnished to the United States. Whitehall was particularly incensed that Vergennes permitted American privateers entry to French ports. The French and their Spanish allies were beginning to bristle as much at English arrogance as at English demands. Franklin hoped that Louis XVI was reaching the point where he could be persuaded to redress the European balance of power by depriving England of thirteen of her American colonies. The news of Ticonderoga brought such expectations to an abrupt halt.

In Philadelphia there was dismay on all sides and savage denunciations of Schuyler, especially from the New Englanders. They now felt vindicated in their support of Gates for command of the Northern Department. "I think we shall never be able to defend a post until we shoot a general," exclaimed John Adams. For General Washington the news was "an event of chagrin and surprise, not apprehended nor within the compass of my reasoning. . . ." This stroke is severe indeed, and has distressed us much."

Schuyler protested that "not the most distant Hint of such an Intention [to withdraw from Ticonderoga] can be drawn from any of my Letters to General St. Clair," but he was silent about the council of war on June 20. Nor could he show any positive order for St. Clair to defend the fort in the face of a superior enemy. St. Clair himself did not quibble. "It was done," he said, "in consequence of a consultation with the other general officers . . . and had their opinion been contrary to what it was, it would have nevertheless taken place, because I knew it would be impossible to defend the post with our numbers. . . . I may have the satisfaction to experience that although I have lost a post I have eventually saved a state."[9]

As the clamor over his behavior swelled Schuyler went to Fort Edward to do what he could to restore the situation. Twenty-three miles separated him from Burgoyne's base at Skenesboro. Although the region divided the basin of Lake Champlain from the valley of the Hudson there were no mountains or even high hills to mark the watersheds. In 1777 the land was heavily wooded and crisscrossed by streams which meandered sluggishly through swampland which covered much of the country. A single rough track led from Skenesboro along Wood Creek to Fort Anne, the tumble-down relic of the Seven Years' War. Here the fugitives from the retreat had checked the British pursuit on July 7 before withdrawing the remaining ten miles to the Hudson.

Schuyler reached Fort Edward that same day, and for almost a week he boldly held his position with less than a thousand men. Finally St. Clair came in from Castleton and Colonel John Nixon arrived from Peekskill with 600 Continentals. This brought Schuyler's command to just under 4,500 men, a mixed body of 2,800 Continentals and about 1,600 militia.

Schuyler did not intend to make a stand at Fort Edward, but he did want to make life as miserable as possible for the British. Emboldened by the fact that Burgoyne sent no advance parties to secure the route to the Hudson the American commander sent a thousand axmen back into the woods and swamps. They systematically destroyed every bridge and causeway. They dug ditches to divert streams and turned stretches of the road into muddy bogs. For days their axes rang through the virgin timber, felling huge trees so that the branches interlaced to create a nightmare tangle along the road.

Schuyler urged the few settlers to drive off their livestock and burn their crops so that there would be no forage or food for the invaders. The axmen pressed as far north as Fort Anne but except for occasional harassment by Burgoyne's Indians the British made no attempt to halt their work.

Having created a veritable jungle to delay the enemy Schuyler abandoned the ramshackle works at Fort Edward and withdrew his force down the Hudson to Saratoga. There he halted and sent out urgent pleas for reinforcements, but he was losing men by desertion almost as fast as he gained recruits. On July 24 Wilkinson reported that "in the short space of five days, our continental force was reduced to less than 3,000, and our militia to about 1,300 men . . . the greatest part badly armed, and both men and officers half-naked, sickly and destitute. . . . Our troops . . . instead of recovering confidence, lost spirit; and the panic became more general than ever."

By August 3 Schuyler had retreated again, this time to Stillwater, twenty-five miles south of Fort Edward. The constant withdrawal in the face of the enemy was calculated to make Burgoyne's line of communication at Ticonderoga more tenuous, but it nevertheless fueled the criticism of Schuyler which had been mounting ever since the abandonment of Ticonderoga. His appeals to Washington for help placed the commander in chief in a dilemma. General Howe had embarked his army on transports on July 23 and disappeared over the Atlantic horizon; with his destination unknown Washington hesitated to send more reinforcements northward. In an effort to stimulate militia response in New England he dispatched Benedict Arnold and Benjamin Lincoln to report to Schuyler.[10]

Arnold was the most experienced combat officer in the army. His knack for inspiring loyalty in the men under his command suggested that he might instill some of his own fighting spirit into the troops on the Hudson. Arnold's quarrelsome, abrasive personality kept him in constant hot water with Congress and his military superiors, and was probably responsible for the delay in his promotion. But he respected and admired George Washington, and his service under Schuyler in 1776 had resulted in mutual confidence and a curious affinity between this tough, hard fighter and the aristocratic patroon.

Washington had at first probably judged Benjamin Lincoln too much by appearances, but finally recognized that he "was an abler man than his great bulk and loose jowel would indicate." Lincoln had caught the commander in chief's eye while serving as a general in the Massachusetts militia. Washington had paid him the compliment of mistakenly recommending him for promotion to major general of the Continental Line and Congress had complied. Lincoln reported to Schuyler who promptly dispatched him to New England to recruit militia.

Schuyler's delaying tactics began to bear fruit, unpopular though they were. Burgoyne was now at the point where he had to make some critical decisions. He must now abandon the easy water communication with Ticonderoga and Canada. He might have retraced his steps to the foot of Lake

George and moved south by this western arm to a point only nine miles from the Hudson. But this would have involved hauling his bateaux and artillery across the portage below Ticonderoga. According to Captain John Money, Burgoyne's quartermaster, "it would have taken a fortnight to transport 400 bateaux from Lake Champlain to Lake George. . . ." The British commander accordingly decided to move his troops directly from Skenesboro to Fort Edward and use the Lake George route for his provisions and supplies.

Burgoyne also decided to take most of his artillery, for which he was later severely criticized. But he reasoned that "artillery was extremely formidable against raw troops." Also the Americans might be expected to adopt defenses "at which they were beyond all other nations expert . . . that of entrenchment covered with strong abbatis, against which the cannon, of the nature of the heaviest described [24-pounders], and howitzers, might often be effectual, when to dislodge them by any other means might be attended with continued and important losses." And artillery would be necessary for "the intention of fortifying a camp at Albany."

It took the British several days to collect their scattered forces and their baggage after their headlong pursuit of the Americans. By July 10 they had begun the laborious task of clearing away the ruin left by Schuyler's axmen. It was heavy work and the engineering parties were harassed by the sultry summer heat, and clouds of gnats and mosquitoes. At the outset a causeway two miles long had to be constructed across the worst of the swamp. Heavy rains made the streams run full and British working parties were obliged to build over forty bridges. Axmen, most of them Canadians, struggled to clear the tangle of trees, their branches so densely matted that they could not be hauled aside, but had to be cut through. Nearly a week was consumed in opening the road to Fort Anne and it was not until July 24 that the road to Fort Edward was finally clear. Burgoyne took four days to move fourteen miles to Fort Anne. On the 28th, Fraser's advance corps was sent forward and two days later the British right wing occupied Fort Edward. Bringing up the rear Riedesel's Germans came in and by August 9 Burgoyne's entire force was finally assembled on the Hudson.[11]

There now ensued another delay. Ammunition and stores for thirty days had to be assembled and bateaux dragged across from Fort George, for Burgoyne intended to use the river to transport his supplies. It was to be almost a month before the British were prepared to cut their communication with Canada and make the final dash to Albany.

Meantime the general and his officers were enjoying what ease they could find in the North American wilderness. ". . . Burgoyne liked having a jolly time of it and spending half the night singing and drinking and amusing himself in the company of the wife of the commissary, who was his mistress and, like him, loved champaign." There seems to have been plenty of food and drink although Burgoyne had ordered that "officers are depended on not to encumber the service with more baggage than shall be absolutely necessary."

But headquarters did not stint and Baron Riedesel found himself the recipient of occasional cases of Madeira. The Baroness Riedesel and Lady Acland joined the army in the middle of August. "The surrounding country was magnificent" related the little baroness, ". . . when it was beautiful weather we took our meals under the trees. . . . It was at this place I eat bear's flesh for the first time, and found it of capital flavor."[12]

On August 3 Burgoyne received a dispatch from Sir William Howe, dated July 17: "My intention is for Philadelphia, where I expect to meet Washington; but if he goes to the northward, contrary to my expectations, and you can keep him at bay, be assured I shall soon be after him to relieve you. . . . Sir Henry Clinton remains in command here [New York], and will act as occurrences may direct." Burgoyne does not seem to have been perturbed by this news. Nor did he show any alarm over the delays which daily consumed his supplies and cost him wear and tear on his transport. Having spent more than a month on the road from Skenesboro to Fort Edward, he appeared unconcerned at the prospect of abandoning his supply line with thirty days provisions to reach an objective more than fifty miles away.

Whether the idea of drawing the British farther and farther from Ticonderoga and Canada before engaging them was a preconceived strategy of the American high command is an open question. But by midsummer its merit was obvious. General Washington gave it expression in mid-August when he advised:

> Independent of the Inconveniences that attend a Situation, where the Rear and Flank are constantly exposed to the insults of light parties which may be at every moment harassing them; the necessity of never losing sight of the means of a Secure Retreat, which ought to be the first object of an Officer's Care, must be exceedingly embarrassing where there is a Force in such a position as to endanger it. If a respectable Body of Men were to be Stationed on the Grants, it would undoubtedly have the effect intimated above, would render it not a little difficult for Mr. Bourgoigne to keep the necessary Communication open, and they would frequently afford opportunities of intercepting his Convoys.[13]

LORD GEORGE GERMAIN
Joshua Reynolds
COURTESY OF THE CLEMENTS LIBRARY,
UNIVERSITY OF MICHIGAN

GEORGE THE THIRD
Allan Ramsey
COURTESY OF COLONIAL WILLIAMSBURG

JOHN BURGOYNE
Joshua Reynolds
COURTESY OF THE FRICK COLLECTION

SIR WILLIAM HOWE
C. Corbutt
COURTESY OF THE CLEMENTS LIBRARY,

DANIEL MORGAN
C. W. Peale
COURTESY OF THE INDEPENDENCE
NATIONAL HISTORICAL PARK

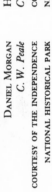

HORATIO GATES
C. W. Peale
COURTESY OF THE INDEPENDENCE
NATIONAL HISTORICAL PARK

PHILIP SCHUYLER
John Trumbull
COURTESY OF THE YALE UNIVERSITY ART GALLERY

HENRY KNOX
Gilbert Stewart
COURTESY OF THE MUSEUM OF FINE ARTS, BOSTON

SIR HENRY CLINTON
A. H. Ritchie
COURTESY OF THE CLEMENTS LIBRARY,
UNIVERSITY OF MICHIGAN

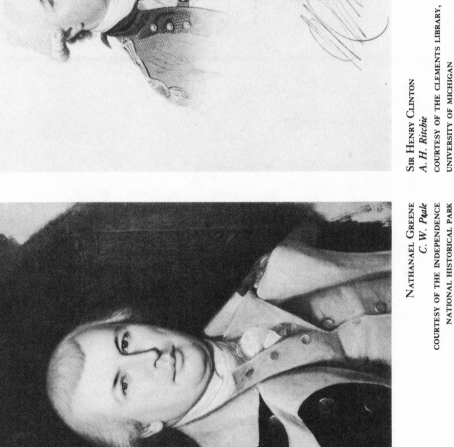

NATHANAEL GREENE
C. W. Peale
COURTESY OF THE INDEPENDENCE
NATIONAL HISTORICAL PARK

1. " . . . handle cartridge"

2. " . . . tear cartridge"

Firing a Musket

3. " . . . prime"

4. " . . . close frizzen"

5. " . . . load"

6. " . . . ram"

7. " . . . full cock"

8. " . . . fire!"

9. A "soldier" of the 42nd Highlanders

" . . . those dear, ragged Continentals."
Trego
COURTESY OF THE VALLEY FORGE HISTORICAL SOCIETY

NINE

The Gathering Storm

As he paused on the Hudson, preparing his army for the final drive on Albany, Burgoyne was confident. Ticonderoga had fallen and the enemy was scattered into the hills of Vermont. Only Schuyler's little army, not much more than half his own numbers, stood in his way, and it appeared doubtful if they intended to stand and fight. There were rumors that the Loyalists were increasing in strength and boldness, "and I have certain intelligence that the country around Fort Stanwix is in alarm." Burgoyne shared with Germain the assumption that the populace of northern New York awaited only the appearance of his triumphant army to display their loyalty to the Crown.[1]

The Crisis in New York

New York was a prime example of the geo-politics of the American Revolution. The entire length of the Appalachian ridge from New England to the southern coastal plain is broken in only two places and both are in New York. One is the Champlain basin. The other is the Mohawk Valley, not as well travelled by the armies of the eighteenth century, but destined to become vastly more important as the transportation link between the Hudson and the Great Lakes. The state itself lies like a wedge between New England and the states to the south. This geography gave New York a political and imperial importance beyond that of any other region in the United States. On the upper Mohawk river in Tryon County Sir William Johnson and his son, Sir Guy, presided over the affairs of the Six Nations of the Iroquois Confederacy and of all the tribes of the Northern Department. At the confluence of the Mohawk and the Hudson Albany was the *entrepôt* for the fur trade. At the mouth of the Hudson New York city was already gaining recognition as potentially the greatest port in North America. Here were not only the headquarters for the British army and navy but the center of supply contractors and merchant factors for British trading firms which gave the city closer ties with England and Europe. Its population of 25,000 was twelve percent of the population of the entire state, and it dominated the Lower Counties.

The first test of strength in the revolutionary crisis came in the wake of the meeting of the First Continental Congress. That body's passage of resolutions for nonimportation, nonexportation, and nonconsumption of British goods was accompanied by a recommendation that each colony create "associations" to urge the enforcement of the resolutions. Collectively these were known as the Continental Association.

This recommendation was duly considered by the Committee of Fifty-One of New York city originally set up in the spring of 1774 as a committee of correspondence. Although the group was committed to opposing ministerial and Parliamentary policy, especially the Intolerable Acts, it contained a considerable number of conservatives who eventually could be called Whig-Loyalists. The committee passed Congress' recommendation along to the towns and counties for action, but the response of local leaders was apathetic. The more conservative group was centered around the DeLancey family while the moderates looked to the Livingstons for guidance. These two factions may well have been contending as much for power as for principle, and it is confusing to label them as radicals or conservatives. The Tory party (DeLanceys) included many who accepted the idea of the Association but who were reluctant to sacrifice their financial interests or to entertain any idea of disloyalty to the Crown. The true radicals, mostly in New York city, denounced the Committee of the Fifty-One for foot-dragging and accused DeLanceys and Livingstons alike of being obstructionist and delaying the implementation of the boycott. The moderates gave in to the pressure by inducing the colonial assembly to send petitions of remonstrance to the King.

The critical point was reached in the spring of 1775 when the Whigs called on the legislative assembly to vote approval of the actions of the First Continental Congress and to choose delegates for the Second Continental Congress which was about to convene. The assembly refused, and the Whigs thereupon abandoned the legal machinery of the colony and elected their own Provincial Congress. The DeLancey group lost considerable prestige, but continued to lend at least token support to the struggle for American rights. Whig-Loyalists such as John Jay, William Duane, and Isaac Low continued to carry considerable weight with the moderates, while the radicals led by Isaac Sears and Alexander McDougall attempted to force the revolutionary movement into more militant opposition to the home government.[2]

Yet the radicals were unable to seize the initiative, to overwhelm the conservatives as the Adamses had done in Massachusetts, or Patrick Henry and Thomas Jefferson in Virginia. There were several reasons for their failure. Perhaps most important was the fact that the DeLancey faction did not take an adamant stand of unqualified support for the Crown. They retained their influence on the new Committee of Sixty and their presence probably accounted for the lack of a viable network of county committees of safety. Moreover, the Committee of Sixty, the dominant revolutionary organization in the colony, was beset by internecine frictions and quarrels which constantly threatened its facade of unity.

Another factor was the intelligent leadership of Governor William Tryon and his deputy, Cadwallader Colden. Tryon had already served as governor of North Carolina when he came to New York in 1771. He was a capable administrator and a good politician, and in the beginning he announced that he "would not be dealt with or crossed for Party Purposes." He judiciously courted the Livingston group through appointments and other political favors and maintained a nice balance between amiability and tolerance on the one hand, and firm assertion of authority on the other. By coincidence he returned from a leave of absence in England on the same day that General Washington passed through New York on his way to command the troops at Boston. The citizenry greeted the general enthusiastically on the morning of his arrival and "huzzaed for Tryon in the evening." A few days later, in July, 1775, the radicals moved to arrest Tryon. Philip Schuyler, recently appointed a major general by Congress, intervened and produced an order from Washington forbidding Tryon's arrest.

One of the most effective weapons in the governor's hand was his influence in granting land patents. The colonial secretary, Lord Dartmouth, wrote Lieutenant Governor Colden in 1774: "Their [land speculators'] Pretensions will meet with every Countenance and Support that can be shewn consistent with Justice; for I can with truth say that the conduct of that Province in general . . . has been such as justly intitles its well disposed and peaceable Inhabitants to His Majesty's particular Favor and Indulgence." Tryon and Colden secured approval for grants totalling 433,000 acres from April, 1775, to July, 1776, of which 275,000 went to prominent Tories.

Over 300,000 acres of this land lay in the area east of Lake Champlain. In fact, one of the largest grants went to Colonel Peter Skene, the Loyalist who attached himself to Burgoyne's staff. The Colonel received a patent for 120,000 acres and was commissioned governor of Crown Point and Ticonderoga. These grants, of course, exacerbated the quarrel between the great land barons of the Upper Hudson (of whom Schuyler was one) and the settlers in the Hampshire Grants. It is not too much to say that this dispute had a powerful influence in promoting radicalism in the Vermont area and a countervailing propensity toward loyalism among the inhabitants of the Upper Hudson.[3]

Another powerful source of royal influence, especially in the vast region of the upper Mohawk Valley embraced by Tryon County was Sir Guy Johnson. His influence with the Six Nations has already been noted. Johnson was also a large landholder whose numerous tenants might be expected to rally to his leadership. Although the Tryon County Committee was industrious in attempting to organize the Whig forces, their efforts were not notably successful. In the elections to the Second Provincial (New York) Congress in the fall of 1775 the county elected two delegates. One resigned to become chairman of the County Committee. The other departed for the meeting of the Congress in New York City but two months later he had not arrived. Although the committee promptly chose new delegates the incident was perhaps illustrative of the problems of organization in the widely scattered rural areas.

The First Provincial Congress which met in the fall of 1775 was still lukewarm in its support of the Whig cause. It professed support of the Association but it was laggard in providing for the raising of troops and in carrying out its own resolution for the suppression of Tories. By November so many members were absent that the Provincial Congress dissolved. October elections for a new Congress, with voting limited to freeholders, brought confused results. Apathy and factionalism took their toll and in three of the fourteen counties elections were delayed for several weeks. Two counties did not elect any delegates and when the Second Provincial Congress finally met early in December, 1775, only half the countries were represented.

Meantime, royal authority had suffered two set-backs. Guy Johnson, the Butlers, and Daniel Claus had retired to Canada, leaving only Sir John at Johnson Hall with his corporal's guard of Mohawks. In New York City Governor Tryon found it expedient to move his quarters to a British warship in the harbor. Even so, the new Provincial Congress moved slowly. The reasons for its hesitancy were not hard to find. Anchored in New York harbor were HMS *Asia*, a ship of the line, and her consorts whose menacing guns threatened Manhattan. Her captain had orders from Admiral Samuel Graves to bombard the town if the ships were molested and there were rumors that Lord Dartmouth would order reprisals against any town that raised troops for the rebel army.

By the end of the year the New York Whigs found themselves like a nut in the jaws of a nut-cracker. The King's Proclamation of 1775 declared the colonies to be in a state of rebellion and ordered a naval blockade of the Atlantic ports. This was ample demonstration of the radical contention that the government did not intend to relax its restrictions against the American colonies. But it was also common knowledge that General Howe was to be reinforced and that he planned to seize New York City as his base of operations for 1776. When General Charles Lee was sent to New York in January, 1776, to fortify the town against attack the Committee of Safety was in a panic. Many Tories fled the city and "you would scarce see any person or but few in the streets carts and waggons all employed in carrying out goods and furniture. . . ."[4]

Although the committee protested that heavy-handed tactics would convert many people to Toryism Lee refused to be cowed. He began removing cannon and stores from the city forts and threatened retaliation against the Tories if the fleet interfered. By April his belligerence had so alarmed the city fathers that they protested to General Washington. Lee was transferred shortly afterwards, but the commander in chief delivered a stinging rebuke to the New

York authorities for allowing communications between the British naval vessels in the harbor and people in the city.

While the Whigs thus vacillated the Tories failed to take advantage of the situation. They too were caught between threats, the Sons of Liberty on one side and royal authority on the other. Both sides undoubtedly recognized that the King's Proclamation reduced the choices to independence or unconditional surrender to whatever settlement the home government decided to make with the colonies, but neither wanted to make an overt commitment. In the last elections of the colonial assembly the Whigs won a heavy majority, and Governor Tryon predictably prorogued it almost as soon as it convened.

During the first four months of 1776 most of the Whig Loyalists moved into the ranks of the revolutionaries. After a year of war, as John Jay observed, ". . . it is natural to suppose that the Sword must decide the Controversy — and with a View to that object our Measures should in great Degree be taken."

The elections of the Fourth Provincial Congress in April chose 101 delegates from all fourteen colonies. County committees of safety were now becoming more effective at turning out voters. The state committee cut off supplies to British naval vessels and warned the people to prepare for sterner measures. But, as Washington began to move his troops into the city, the lame duck Third Provincial Congress failed to raise the quota of troops fixed by Congress. It was accused of leniency towards Tories, a charge underlined by General Washington's discovery of a Tory rebellion plot on Long Island.

The introduction of Richard Henry Lee's resolution for independence in the Continental Congress on June 7 drove New York Whig-Loyalists to their last desperate strategem. Jay proposed that discussion of independence be postponed until the new Provincial Congress could convene. This was unanimously approved in the dying days of the Third Congress. The New York delegation in Philadelphia was therefore without instructions on independence and so abstained from voting on July 2.[5]

In New York Lord Richard Howe's vast fleet came over the horizon and the Provincial Congress hastily adjourned to White Plains. It was there that its successor, the Fourth Congress, convened on July 9. Gouverneur Morris may have given the most honest explanation for New York's tardy acceptance of independence: "*We are hellishly frightened but don't say a word of that* for we shall get our spirits again. . . ." Once committed the Whigs did indeed begin to recover their spirits. As Robert Livingston put it after the disastrous battle of Long Island, "I am amazed at the composure I feel tho' I have everything at stake, & the enemy are already in possession of one third of my income."

The British occupation of the city and the lower Hudson valley was greatly encouraging to the Loyalists. As in neighboring New Jersey the Whig movement collapsed and Tory militia turned on their erstwhile tormenters. Governor Tryon and royal authorities had their hands full administering loyalty oaths. Many who had been prominent on Whig committees in the lower countries hastily departed. Others professed that they had been coerced into cooperating with the rebels, and now took the oath of allegiance to the Crown. By October, 1776, Loyalist refugees who had fled to escape the American army streamed back into the city. The Provincial Congress, now rid of its anxieties about New York, was emboldened to take energetic measures for the suppression of the Tories on the Upper Hudson. In the fall of 1776 the state committee of safety sent a special investigating committee to Albany to cooperate with General Schuyler. County and local committees were urged to disarm potential enemies and directed to use the militia to suppress any Tory uprisings.

Burgoyne's invasion had a disastrous effect on the revolutionary cause in the early summer of 1777. There was never any serious danger of a real Tory uprising, but the fall of Ticonderoga and Schuyler's retreat down the Hudson in July had a serious effect on his enlistments. The country was not prepared to welcome Burgoyne with open arms, but neither was it prepared to risk its collective lives and fortunes. "I am exceedingly chagrined at the pusillanimous spirit which prevails, . . ." said the commander of the Northern Department in mid-July.

As July came to a close a crisis had been reached that was not only military but political. The success of Burgoyne's invasion would not only mark a triumph of British strategy. There was also every reason to think that the Whigs would collapse before a successful military conquest just as they had in New Jersey in 1776. The revolutionary movement in New York was about to be decided by the outcome of the clash between rebels and redcoats.[6]

BENNINGTON

Although he did not realize it, Burgoyne's passage from the Lake Champlain watershed to the Hudson marked more than the crossing of a geographical divide. From the time of his arrival on the Hudson Gentleman Johnny's luck began to run out.

He had foreseen that his supply problem would be a serious one since he was now 185 miles from Montreal. Moreover, Sir Guy Carleton, obedient to the letter of his orders from Germain, refused to furnish a garrison force for Ticonderoga. This meant that in order to guard his supply line—possibly a line of retreat—Burgoyne felt obliged to garrison the fort with the 53rd Regiment and the Brunswickers of the Regiment Prince Frederick, about 900 men in all. Having decided to assemble thirty days' supplies at Fort Edward for his final drive to Albany, it might be supposed that Burgoyne would cut himself loose from his tenuous link with Canada. But eighteenth century doctrine, with its emphasis on fortified posts and lines of communications, would not permit it.

Burgoyne's situation was complicated by lack of horses. He had expected to be furnished 1,500 animals in Canada but had received only 500. The poorly built carts with which he had been equipped had broken down badly in the rough country between Lake Champlain and the Hudson. Finally, there was the sad state of Riedesel's dragoons. Clad in their heavy leather britches and huge cocked hats they were still horseless, clumping along in their jack boots and spurs. Riedesel had been urging Burgoyne to find mounts for them and now, at Fort Edward, Burgoyne decided to send an expedition into the Hampshire Grants where he was told livestock was fat and numerous. Since horsemen would be needed to round up and drive the 1,300 or so animals that were needed Burgoyne chose Lieutenant Colonel Friederich Baum's Brunswick dragoons for the raid. Fifty German jägers (riflemen), 100 grenadiers, fifty British regulars, and 300 Canadians, Loyalists and Indians brought the force to about 700 men. One of the Loyalists was Colonel Philip Skene, who was to recruit Tories in the region and act as a sort of aide and emissary for Baum, who spoke no English.

The German commander's instructions were detailed and covered a whole range of objectives. In addition to collecting draught animals and wagons Baum was to "try the affections of the country, to disconcert the councils of the enemy," to gather intelligence, and even "to tax the several districts." The specific objective was Bennington, about thirty-five miles to the southeast. British headquarters received a report just before Baum's departure that the rebels had established a supply depot there, and Burgoyne changed Baum's orders at the last moment in order to avail himself of this windfall. The only obstacle to Baum's advance was thought to be the remnant of Seth Warner's command which had been scattered at Hubbardton.[7]

It is obvious that Burgoyne's intelligence, which was gathered by Indians and Tories, was beginning to falter, for it failed to report the existence of a force of 1,500 men assembled by a veteran commander, John Stark. In the middle of July the settlers in Vermont had appealed to New Hampshire for help against the enemy invasion. The New Hampshire assembly had generously responded by an appropriation of funds and an authorization for Stark to raise a corps of militia. Stark was another of the Continental officers who had been offended by the Congressional promotions of January, 1777. Although he had fought with distinction at Bunker Hill, in Canada, and at Trenton, he had been passed over for brigadier general and had resigned his Continental commission in disgust. Understandably stiff-necked about his treatment and typically New England in his distrust of "them"—meaning Schuyler, New Yorkers, Congress or anything else south and west of the Green Mountains—Stark insisted that he be accountable only to the legislature and that he be authorized "to act separately for the protection of the people or the annoyance of the enemy."

By the last week in July Stark had raised 1,500 men and marched them to Manchester, about twenty-five miles north of Bennington where he was joined by Seth Warner. A few days later General Benjamin Lincoln arrived with orders from Schuyler to move part of this force to the Hudson. Stark displayed his orders from the sovereign state of New Hampshire and declared that he, not Schuyler or Lincoln, was giving the orders. The politic Lincoln agreed to try to work out a plan which would allow the New Englanders to remain between the invaders and their homes and at the same time cooperate with Schuyler. Lincoln went back to report to headquarters on the Hudson and Stark moved to Bennington, leaving Warner at Manchester. So it was that the late intelligence that directed Baum to Bennington failed to report that it was occupied by a force over twice his numbers.

The German commander left the Hudson on August 11. Two days later he reached the little village of Cambridge and the next day, August 14, began to move south to the Walloomsac river where he made his first contact with the Americans. Stark, equally ignorant of the presence of an enemy, had sent out a force of 200 men in response to a report of "a party of Indians." The Americans delayed Baum by destroying a bridge and for the first time the German commander became aware of the size of Stark's force. He sent a report to Burgoyne on the morning of August 14, and later in the day a second dispatch requested reinforcements, although Baum was confident and apparently unconcerned about the safety of his force. At about the same time Stark learned that he had more than an Indian raid on his hands, and sent orders to Warner to bring in his corps from Manchester. That afternoon Baum made his approach to Bennington and Stark formed a defensive line, but since it was late afternoon the German commander went into camp on high ground overlooking the western approach to the village. Stark withdrew about two miles to the east.

Now the weather intervened. Rain came in a steady downpour. All day on the 15th the two forces huddled in their camps, soaked to the skin, their weapons useless. At Burgoyne's headquarters at Fort Miller Lieutenant Colonel Heinrich von Breymann with a body of 550 men moved out on the road to Bennington although there was no urgency to his mission; he was simply supporting an operation that was apparently going well but might encounter unforeseen trouble. From Manchester Warner's men were also on the march, but making slow progress over bad roads and rough country. The rain continued throughout the night and into the morning of the sixteenth.[8]

About noon the weather began to clear and Stark decided to launch an attack. Baum's position represented a tactical compromise. His main force occupied a commanding hill where he constructed a redoubt. But he also wanted to defend the bridge across the Walloomsac about a half a mile away. Here he posted a force of grenadiers and Canadian rangers. The two positions were loosely linked by three detachments between the hill and the river. Still another detachment guarded the rear.

These scattered elements would probably have had difficulty supporting each other against a simple frontal assault, especially by a force as large as Stark's. But the American commander, with Warner's force about to come up, decided to attack Baum's detachments in detail by flanking parties. He was aided by the fact that the Brunswicker made several bad guesses. In igno-

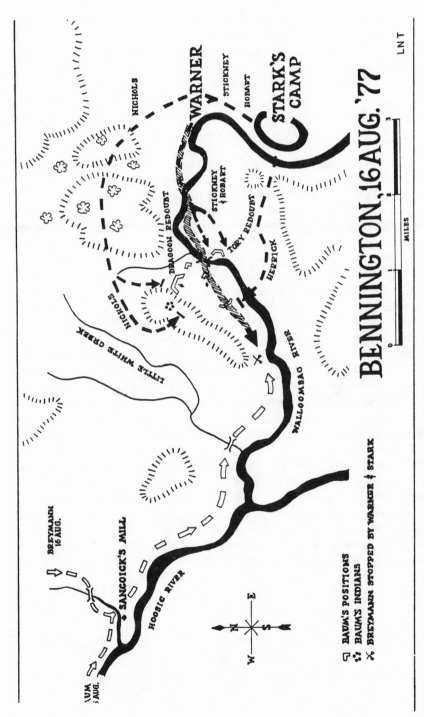

BENNINGTON, 16 AUG. '77

© Mark Boatner, III, *Encyclopedia of the American Revolution*, David McKay Co., Inc.

rance of the fact that he was opposed by an experienced commander Baum
noticed but failed to realize the threat of Stark's flanking parties. He concluded
that they were leaderless fragments who were probably retiring.

Colonel Skene persisted in his assurances that the countryside contained
many Loyalists. Skene had circulated the word that when they came in to
join the British they were to wear pieces of white paper in their hats as identification. The Americans picked up this bit of information and several parties
of them displaying scraps of paper, infiltrated among Baum's scattered positions before they were recognized.

About three o'clock the Americans opened fire and the British suddenly
found themselves assailed from all sides. Considering that over 1,000 untrained militia had been widely deployed the coordination of the attack was
remarkable. The separated parts of Baum's command collapsed under the
fierce attack and the detachments were soon surrendering or trying to escape
into the surrounding forest. As the Americans began to close on the German
strong point at the redoubt, a sheet of fire and a thunderous roar marked the
destruction of Baum's ammunition wagon. This was the signal for the final
assault which drove the dragoons from the hill. Baum and a few followers
almost hacked their way clear with their cavalry sabres, but the German commander was finally cut down by musket fire and the fight ended.

The militiamen began to scatter, some pursuing the escaping enemy, most
of them looting the baggage and equipment. It was into this confusion that
Seth Warner finally brought his command. Simultaneously Breymann appeared from the west, unaware that Baum was even engaged since the jumble
of mountains and valleys had deadened the sound of firing. As the German
light infantry collided with the first elements of Stark's men they drove the
Americans back on the main body. Stark seems to have favored retreating in
the face of this new threat but the timely arrival of Warner's men halted Breymann's advance. Suddenly alive to his danger Breymann drew up into a defensive position and beat off a sharp attack by the Americans. Both sides were
exhausted by the sultry heat and the day's marching. Soon the Germans
began to run short of ammunition and Stark and Warner got more men into
action. Breymann began a fighting withdrawal and darkness finally ended the
engagement. Breymann pulled his battered column back toward the Hudson.
Twenty-five percent of his force had been killed or wounded and he had lost
his guns.

Bennington was a disastrous combination of bad luck and bad judgement
for the British. Chance had placed Stark at Bennington, and chance had allowed the weather to clear before Breymann could join Baum. With the two
forces combined Baum's position would have been a tough nut for the Americans to crack even with the addition of Warner's brigade. (It should be noted
in passing that the Germans, ridiculed by their British allies and by historians
for their lumbering, heavy-footed marching, covered the twenty-five miles
to Bennington in the same time that it took Warner's men to march the same

distance from Manchester.) Burgoyne's force was now reduced by nearly 1,000 men of all ranks. The British left 207 men dead on the field at Bennington and 700 officers and men prisoners of the Americans. Counting Breymann's wounded, the missing, and deserters the loss was fourteen percent of Burgoyne's force, of which half were regulars.[9]

The defeat seems not to have seriously dampened the morale of Burgoyne's men. "We shall soon be in a position to move on toward Albany," wrote a Brunswick soldier on August 18. "The unhappy occurrence . . . has not dispirited us." But it did dispirit the Indians. Shortly after Bennington they held a council and most of them decided to go home. Only eighty of the 500 or so who had accompanied Burgoyne as far as the Hudson now remained. Of the Loyalists "I have about 400 (but not half of them armed), who may be depended upon. The rest are trimmers merely actuated by interest." These departures seriously handicapped the British reconnaissance. Before Ticonderoga the Americans had great difficulty penetrating the screen of Indians and Loyalists to secure information about enemy numbers and movements. After mid-August it was the British who lacked intelligence of the enemy.

If the spirits of the troops were unimpaired a shadow of doubt began to nag Burgoyne. "Had I latitude in my orders, I should think it my duty to wait in this position, or perhaps as far back as Fort Edward"—was he already preparing the record for failure?—"where my communications with Lake George would be perfectly secure; . . . but my orders being positive 'to force a junction with Sir William Howe' I apprehend I am not at liberty to remain inactive longer. . . ."

Still, said Gentleman Johnny, "I do not yet despond." But before the week was out he was again overwhelmed by bad news, this time from the west.[10]

DRUMS ALONG THE MOHAWK

The key to the American defense of the Mohawk Valley was Fort Stanwix, guarding the portage between the Mohawk River and Wood Creek leading to Lake Oneida and thence to Lake Ontario. Built by the French during the Seven Years' War, the geometric precision and elaborate outworks of its eighteenth century military engineering presented an odd contrast to the primitive forest surroundings. The fort was located on the only dry ground between the two waterways; except in its immediate vicinity the area was heavily wooded and marshy. A road down the Mohawk forded the river a short distance below and followed the left bank eastwards to Fort Dayton and Albany. By the spring of 1777 the fort had fallen into a bad state of repair and reflected the apathy of the local militia. A handful of troops garrisoned the tumbled-down works and the Tryon County Committee of Safety reported, "More than half of our inhabitants are resolved not to lift up arms in defense of their country."

In April General Schuyler ordered Colonel Peter Gansevoort and his 3rd

New York Continentals to occupy Fort Stanwix and that energetic young officer immediately set about repairing the fortifications. In May he was joined by his second in command, Lieutenant Colonel Marinus Willett, who had been a radical firebrand in the early days of the Revolution and had fought with Montgomery in Canada. The two young officers fell to work repairing the works and drilling the garrison. They cajoled and wheedled supplies from Albany and urged that more reinforcements be sent. Warnings from the Oneida Indians, one of the Six Nations that took sides with the Americans, convinced the commanders that the fort was in danger. By mid-July they had definite news of St. Leger's expedition and they redoubled their efforts to get the fort in a condition of readiness.[11]

Colonel Barry St. Leger was the commanding officer of the 34th Regiment which had been left on garrison duty in Canada. His selection as commander of this flanking foray was no accident for Burgoyne had designated him in the initial planning of the campaign. He had spent half of his forty years in the army and had won a reputation as a frontier fighter under Abercrombie and Wolfe in the Seven Years' War.

St. Leger's command left La Chine, just above Montreal, on June 23. Indian scouts reported from the upper Mohawk that Fort Stanwix was in ruins and manned by less than 100 men. The expedition included 100 men each from St. Leger's 34th Regiment and the 8th Regiment, eighty jägers of the Hesse-Hanau Regiment, and thirty artillerymen who served two 6-pounders, two 3-pounders, and four 4.4. inch mortars. There were also 350 Tories of the King's Royal Americans commanded by Sir John Johnson, dubbed the "Royal Greens," and a company of John Butler's rangers. About 100 Canadian bateaumen and axmen were hired as workmen. The total rank and file of St. Leger's white troops was about 750 men.

The first leg of his journey was up the St. Lawrence, 140 miles to Lake Ontario. This strenuous stretch was made in bateaux, thirty to forty feet long, which could be propelled by poles, sails, or oars and were sufficiently seaworthy to withstand turbulent rapids or windy weather on the lakes. As the main body toiled up the river Daniel Claus and Sir John Johnson went ahead to rally the Indians of the Six Nations. By July 14 they were at Oswego on Lake Ontario where they were joined by Joseph Brant. Now began the task of persuading the warriors assembled at Oswego to join St. Leger.

The Indians were suspicious of all white men, American or British. Only nine years before, the Treaty of Fort Stanwix had established an Indian boundary at Unadilla Creek (near Utica), and already the whites were pushing beyond it. The Iroquois understandably did not want to get involved in a white man's fight unless there was something in it for them. Probably Joseph Brant persuaded them that if Fort Stanwix fell they could drive the white settlers back beyond the Treaty line.

The Indians needed other assurances. They wanted it understood that the whites would fight with them, that there would be no heavy casualties, and that there would be plenty of loot. Claus pointed out how easily the great fortress at Ticonderoga had fallen; ". . . when I come before that fort [Stanwix]," he said, "and the commanding officer shall see me, he . . . will not fire a shot, but will surrender the fort to me." Whether impressed by the oratory or by the promises, about 800 Iroquois, most of them Mohawks, agreed to accompany the British.

By the time St. Leger reached Oswego at the end of July a scouting party had come in with prisoners taken near Fort Stanwix. From them St. Leger learned that the fort was "garrisoned by upward of 600 men; the repairs far advanced, and the rebels expecting us, and were acquainted with our strength and route." Another party reported that a convoy of supplies was on its way up the Mohawk toward Stanwix. Speed was now essential and St. Leger detached a force of thirty regulars and 200 Indians under Brant to invest the fort and intercept the supplies. They reached Stanwix late on August 2 only moments after the supplies had been landed and hauled inside the walls.

St. Leger brought the main force in two days later, between 1,500 and 2,000 troops and warriors. He established two camps, one on Wood Creek for the white troops and an Indian encampment at what was called the Lower Landing on the Mohawk. In between he set up a loose picket line of Indians. Warriors and German sharpshooters kept up a desultory fire on the fort.[12]

St. Leger was confronted with a situation not at all to his liking. Fort Stanwix was not only adequately defended but the timely arrival of supplies had furnished "provisions sufficient to support the garrison [for] six weeks." He must therefore settle down to a siege which would delay his advance and would without doubt try the patience of Brant and his warriors. Despite his experience in frontier warfare St. Leger was too thoroughly conditioned by eighteenth century military dogma to consider bypassing the American fort. He sent out axmen "for opening Wood Creek (which the enemy with the indefatigable labor of one hundred and fifty men . . . had most effectively closed up) . . . for a present supply of provisions and transport of artillery."

Meanwhile Tryon County was at last bestirring itself. The committee of safety had been warned by a half-breed Oneida named Thomas Spencer on July 30 that "there is but four days remaining of the time set for the king's troops to come to Fort Schuyler [Stanwix]. . . . one resolute blow would secure the friendship of the Six Nations, and almost free this part of the country from incursions of the enemy." The chairman of the committee of safety, Nicholas Herkimer, was also commander of the militia. He was a stolid, softspoken German who several months before had held a conference with Joseph Brant in an effort to persuade the Indians to remain neutral. It was rumored that Herkimer had allowed himself to be faced down by the Mohawk chieftain. Nor did it help matters that the general's brother was a ranger captain with St. Leger.

Nevertheless 800 militia answered General Herkimer's muster order and assembled at Fort Dayton on August 4. Perhaps it was the threat of Brant's

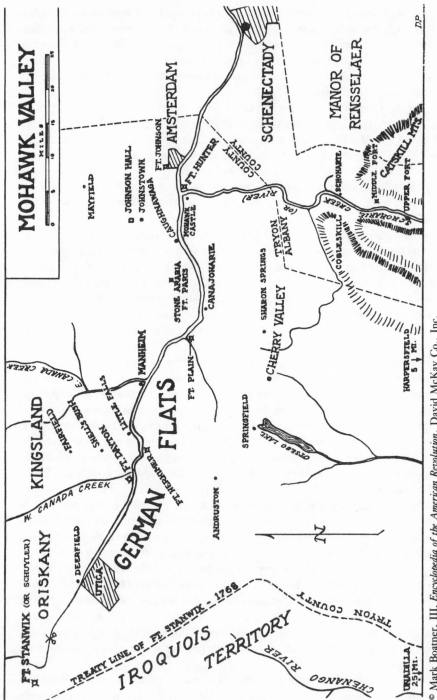

© Mark Boatner, III, *Encyclopedia of the American Revolution*, David McKay Co., Inc.

Indians, perhaps a determination "not to make a Ticonderoga of it," but the Tryon county men were full of fight and anxious to get at the enemy. The party set out, divided roughly into three regiments, and accompanied by a number of ox carts carrying their provisions. Despite their lack of discipline the militia made good time and by the evening of August 5 they were encamped about ten miles down the river from Fort Stanwix. Herkimer now sent several messengers to make their way through the Indian lines to the fort. They were to tell Gansevoort to make a diversionary attack from the fort, signalling his sally by firing three cannon shots. Herkimer would then move to his relief.[13]

The messengers got through but not until late in the morning. Herkimer's men were astir before daylight of the sixth and still spoiling for a fight. When the commander insisted on waiting for the signal from the fort their impatience mounted. A stormy council of war ensued, Herkimer advising that they should wait for the signal guns, the regimental commanders urging an immediate advance. There were ugly imputations, first of the general's courage and then of his loyalty. Finally the little German's temper snapped and he ordered the advance. With a screen of Oneidas in the van the militia moved out, 600 of the main body leading the way followed by the provision carts, and then a rear guard of about 200.

St. Leger's "discovering parties" brought him news of Herkimer's approach on August 5. It caught him at a bad time. ". . . I had not two hundred and fifty King's troops in camp, the various and extreme operations . . . having employed the rest, and therefore could not send above eighty . . . rangers and troops included, with the whole corps of Indians." Sir John Johnson was placed in command, accompanied by Joseph Brant and Butler's rangers. They moved down the river about six miles and laid an ambush on either side of a narrow defile.

About ten o'clock on the morning of the sixth Herkimer's van reached a point not far from the Indian village of Oriskany. The militia column was strung out for nearly a mile along the road as the forward companies moved into the narrow ravine and crossed a log bridge spanning a transverse gulley. It was approaching a second bridge, the rear of the column not yet fully into the defile, when the impatient Mohawks opened fire.

Why the Oneidea scouts did not discover the ambush is a puzzle, but the surprise was complete. Probably a hundred Americans were cut down in the first rush of the Indians and rangers. The militiamen scrambled out of the road and up to some high ground on the north. Herkimer's horse was shot from under him and he was badly wounded in both legs. He ordered his men to place him on his saddle against a tree and proceeded to rally his men in a loose circle on the hill above the road.

At this point a violent thunder storm broke, the wind and rain so intense that men on both sides were driven to cover. During the interlude, Herkimer posted his men in pairs so that one could protect the other during reloading.

When the battle resumed the militiamen had recovered from their panic. There were savage exchanges, not only of musket fire, but of hatchets and bayonets and knives and clubbed muskets. The fighting raged for the better part of four hours before the toll taken by the Americans finally discouraged the Indians and they broke off the fight. They had lost about thirty killed and forty wounded, including several of their chieftains. Herkimer's men also had paid a bloody price. Seventy-five of them were killed and as many more were wounded. Perhaps fifty of them were taken prisoner. There was now no question of relieving Fort Stanwix. The wounded, including the courageous commander, were placed on crude litters and the little army made its painful way back to Fort Dayton.

While militiamen and Indians fought at Oriskany Gansevoort made his diversion, though not in time to affect Herkimer's desperate situation. He sent Colonel Willett out of the fort at the head of 250 men to attack the nearly deserted Indian encampment at the Lower Landing. Willett and his men made a swift descent, driving off the few defenders. They then thoroughly looted the camp of its provisions, blankets, clothing, muskets, and camp kettles, altogether several wagon loads of spoil. By the time St. Leger could react Willett was back inside the fort. When Brant and his Indians returned from Oriskany, gloomy over the number of their people lost in the fight, they were outraged to find that St. Leger had allowed their camp to be plundered.

So although Herkimer had failed to relieve Fort Stanwix St. Leger's situation was not a happy one. He found that his 6-pounders made no impression on the walls of the fort and the range was too great for the shells from his mortars and howitzers to reach its interior. The British commander tried to bluff Gansevoort into surrender by threatening to massacre the garrison if it continued its resistance. The defenders were not impressed, and Willett denounced the threat as "a stigma upon the name of Britain." St. Leger's only alternative was to begin the slow work of digging parallels to bring his guns within effective range of the fort.[14]

Gansevoort's problem was ammunition. Though the fort was well supplied with provisions of food constant skirmishing with the Indians had obliged the defenders to burn a good deal of powder. Gansevoort decided to send for help and on the night of August 10 Willett and a companion slipped through the enemy lines and started down river.

At his headquarters at Stillwater Schuyler was aware of the critical situation at Fort Stanwix even before Willett's arrival. Despite the menace of Burgoyne's advance and the fact that there were less than five thousand troops in the American camp Schuyler called a council of war on August 12 to discuss a relief expedition. The meeting was the final bitter episode in the last days of his command of the Northern Department. The officers, with one exception, adamantly opposed the relief of Fort Stanwix and there were mutterings that Ticonderoga was about to be repeated. The exception was Benedict Arnold who had just returned to the army after his promotion to major general. When

Schuyler overruled his dissident officers Arnold volunteered to lead the relief force and within five days he was at Fort Dayton with 700 Continentals. Here he paused, hoping to strengthen his force with militia, but Oriskany had taken the heart out of the Tryon County men.

Finally Arnold tried a desperate stratagem. Among the Tories arrested by the committee of safety was Hon-Yost Schuyler, who had been sentenced to be executed as a spy. Hon-Yost had some kind of mental illness, possibly epilepsy, which made him highly respected by the Indians. (White men attributed mental illness to the baneful influence of the devil and put such people in dungeons. The barbarian viewed them as touched with the Great Spirit and treated them with consideration and respect.)

In return for his life Hon-Yost was induced to go to St. Leger's camp with an alarming story of swarms of Americans approaching under the command of the general whom the Indians called "The Dark Eagle." Friendly Oneidas followed Schuyler and added their elaborations. It is questionable whether such stories convinced Brant's Iroquois, but they were looking for an excuse to abandon St. Leger. The fighting had not been easy and they were still angry over the looting of their camp. The siege had now lasted three weeks and St. Leger's parallels were not yet complete; the warriors had little taste for such tiresome maneuvers. When St. Leger called a council of war on August 21 nearly 200 of his red allies had already drifted away. "In about an hour they insisted that I should retreat, or they would be obliged to abandon me." On the 22nd he lifted the siege and began a retreat to Lake Ontario, his column occasionally harassed by his erstwhile warrior allies. "[They] seized upon officers' liquor and clothes . . . and became more formidable than the enemy we had to expect."[15]

Even before the news of St. Leger's failure reached him Burgoyne had written a gloomy assessment to Germain:

> I am afraid the expectations of Sir J. Johnson greatly fail in the rising of the country. On this side I find daily reason to doubt the sincerity of resolution of the professing loyalists. . . . The great bulk of the country is undoubtedly with Congress, in principle and zeal; and their measures are executed with a secrecy and dispatch that are not to be equalled. . . . The Hampshire Grants in particular, a country unpeopled and almost unknown in the last year, now abounds in the most active and rebellious race on the continent, and hangs like a gathering storm on my left.

On August 20 Nicholas Herkimer lay in his bed at his home in German Flats, cheerfully smoking his pipe, and bled to death.

TEN

Saratoga:
The First Battle

THE MORE OF HISTORY THAT WE READ THE MORE IT IS APPARENT THAT HEROES must to a considerable degree be endowed with what the eighteenth century called presence and what today is called image. Suppose that George Washington had been short, dumpy, and bald and John Adams had been six feet two and a splendid horseman. Might not the latter rather than the former have been the Father of His Country?

A case in point is Horatio Gates. Middle-aged, stoop-shouldered, near-sighted, he was not only consumed with ambition but his egotism and vanity were so obvious as to be offensive. His supporters in Congress spoke of the admiration and adulation that he inspired in the troops, especially New England militia. But there is little evidence from the soldiers themselves that Gates was any more than a welcome change from Schuyler's arrogance and pessimism. Yet Gates had a sound military mind and his victory over Burgoyne may have been the most important of the war. History has been niggardly in its praise and this is perhaps simply because Gates cannot pass history's physical exam, cannot project the image that history requires of its heroes.

THE COMMAND OF THE NORTHERN DEPARTMENT

The Northern Department was created soon after Congress assumed direction of the war in the summer of 1775. Its evolution was the natural outgrowth of the New England expedition that seized Ticonderoga and the Congressional decision to launch an invasion of Canada. It was treated almost as a separate command and even after General Washington was named commander in chief, "I have never interfered further than merely to advise, and to give such aid as was in my power. . . ." Philip Schuyler, who was one of Congress' four original appointments to the rank of major general, was placed in command. As related above, Schuyler directed the Canadian offensive and he was still in command fifteen months later when the American forces were shattered and driven back to Ticonderoga in 1776.

By that time Schuyler had experienced a number of difficulties which were to plague him for the rest of his military career. Although he could be a gracious and urbane gentleman Schuyler had a strong streak of arrogance and irascibility—perhaps in even greater degree than could be expected from one of his standing and background. He was sensitive to any challenge to his authority or criticism of his motives. And his chronic illness undoubtedly contributed to his displays of bad temper.

In June, 1776, General Gates had been appointed to replace John Sullivan after the disaster at Trois Rivieres and the retreat to Lake Champlain. Gates leaped to the assumption that his command was independent of Schuyler's authority. The confusion was a combination of Gates' ambition and Congressional bumbling. Sullivan's appointment in 1776 to "the American army in Canada" had been designed to give him discretionary authority, since it would have been difficult for him to communicate from the St. Lawrence to Schuyler's headquarters in Albany. By the summer of 1776 Sullivan's (now Gates') command was no longer in Canada but Congress had never formally restored it to the jurisdiction of the Northern Department. Schuyler was furious at what he regarded as Gates' effrontery and he vented his spleen in several angry letters to Congress. After some hesitation that body decided that Ticonderoga and its garrison was part of the Northern Department and affirmed Schuyler's authority, but the episode was a forewarning of strained relations between Philadelphia and Albany.

Another source of Schuyler's troubles was the long-standing quarrel over the disputed boundary between New York and New Hampshire. Part of Schuyler's large land holdings lay in this area and he had been prominent among the Hudson land barons in their efforts to evict settlers from New England, who from Schuyler's point of view were squatters and land pirates. The Yankees were slow to volunteer for service in an army commanded by a New York patroon. So, at least, ran the argument of the New England members of Congress, who set out to displace Schuyler after the failure of the Canadian campaign. It might be added that the cantankerous, willful Yankee troops irritated Schuyler as much as his patrician hauteur offended them.[1]

Horatio Gates, champion of the New England Congressmen in Philadelphia, was in his fiftieth year. Somewhat older than most of Washington's generals, he was the son of lower middle class English parents. His mother was a housekeeper and his father held a minor civil service post, but they managed to catch the eye of the Walpole family who saw to it that young Gates secured a commission in the army. He was assigned to Nova Scotia in 1749 and remained in America until the close of the Seven Years' War. He was badly wounded at Braddock's debacle on the Monongahela in 1755, and after his recovery he held a series of staff positions until the war ended.

With little money and no social position Gates was doomed to retirement at half-pay. His tenuous connection with the Walpoles and his wife's family position (she was an army officer's daughter) allowed him a place on the outer fringe of English society, but this was perhaps merely frustrating to a man of Gates' ambition. He came to America in 1772 and bought a small estate in Western Virginia. He counted George Washington his friend and he became an outspoken supporter of the Whig cause. Congress welcomed the services of this regular army veteran and appointed him a brigadier general.

His first assignment was as Washington's adjutant general and he rendered important service to the commander in chief during the first months of the organization of the American army. He was promoted to major general in May, 1776, and was assigned to the Ticonderoga command where he had his first skirmish with Philip Schuyler. Gates had a profound respect for the British army and a thoroughly realistic appreciation of the limits of American military capabilities. Perhaps even more than Washington he advocated a cautious and defensive strategy.

In the latter part of 1776 Congress ordered eight regiments detached from Schuyler's command to meet Washington's critical situation in New Jersey. Fearful that the British would attack from Canada over the winter ice on Lake Champlain, Schuyler castigated Congress for its neglect of the Northern Department, but he complied with the order. Gates seized this opportunity to leave Schuyler's headquarters as commander of the detachment, but he did not remain with Washington after he delivered the troops. Instead he went to Philadelphia where it must be presumed that he made the most of the opportunity to further his own advancement. It was suggested that he resume the position of Washington's adjutant general but Gates protested that he "had last year the honor to command in the second post in America. . . . After this, to be expected to dwindle again to the adjutant general requires more philosophy on my part than could be expected."[2]

By mid-March Gates' backers in Congress had instigated a movement to censure Schuyler for disrespect of Congress, a charge not difficult to substantiate from some of the northern commanders' scathing remarks in his correspondence with that august body. The result was a Congressional vote of reprimand. The Gates faction now pressed its advantage and induced Congress to order Gates back as commander of Ticonderoga with authority to appoint his own subordinate officers. The strategy was clear. By giving Gates the semiautonomous position it had denied him the previous summer the New Englanders hoped to provoke Schuyler into resigning. They mistook their man.

When the rumors that Gates was to supplant him reached Albany Schuyler decided it was high time that Congress heard from him directly. But he did not intend to appear as a supplicant. Before leaving for Philadelphia he arranged for the New York legislature to name him as a delegate to Congress.

He then, in effect, abdicated his command leaving Gates to take over the Northern Department (and to learn that procurement of men and supplies was more easily said than done). Schuyler arrived in Philadelphia in mid-April, 1777, and demanded an investigation of the charge of disrespect of Congress. His prestige was considerably enhanced by an invitation from the governor of Pennsylvania to take charge of that state's military forces. Schuyler accepted the position and worked diligently at it during his brief stay. He also served on a Congressional committee to reorganize the Commissary Department.

All the while he and his New York colleagues, William Duer, James Duane, and Philip Livingston were mounting a counteroffensive. They pressed for action on Schuyler's reprimand and demanded an investigation of the gossip that whispered that Schuyler had embezzled government funds. Late in May they were successful. Congress voted to withdraw its censure and expunge it from the records. The investigation of finances in the Northern Department was a source of considerable chagrin to Schuyler's enemies. It revealed that the government owed Schuyler $3,750—in specie. On May 22 Congress voted a resolution declaring that "Albany, Ticonderoga, Fort Stanwix, and their dependencies, be henceforth considered as forming the Northern Department." Schuyler was ordered to resume his command and Gates was given the option of remaining as Schuyler's subordinate or reporting to Washington for further assignment. The vote was six states to three, with two states divided and two absent.

It turned out to be a hollow victory for Schuyler. He returned to Albany in June to find the Northern Department much as he had left it two months before. Despite the claims of Gates' admirers that his name would attract volunteers and militia the ranks were not filled and there were still shortages of provisions and equipment. Before another two months had passed Ticonderoga had fallen, the forces of the Northern Department had collapsed before Burgoyne's onslaught, and Schuyler had retreated to the mouth of the Mohawk. Although the British had been checked at Bennington and Fort Stanwix little of this redounded to Schuyler's credit. Stark, Gansevoort, Willett, and Arnold were the heroes of the hour. Not much notice was taken of the fact that Schuyler had gotten supplies to Stanwix in the nick of time and that it was his stubborn insistence that had sent Arnold's expedition to disperse St. Leger.

During the intervening weeks Horatio Gates had not been idle. By mid-June he was not only back in Philadelphia but managed to gain the floor of Congress to promote his case. It was not an auspicious occasion. For some time Gates harangued the members, not only about his qualifications for command but his entire life history. His voice querulous, his spectacles resting on the end of his nose, "peering over his scattered notes," his delivery "incoherent and interrupted with frequent chasms," he rambled on until he was finally interrupted by several members who demanded that he leave the floor.

In the ensuing debate "Granny" Gates stood by unembarrassed, "interrupting several times in the debates which arose. . . ." At last he withdrew and Congress voted that he "not again be admitted on the floor."

Congressional sensitivity being what it was the episode should have been the end of Gates' ambitions. Most members, according to Duane, "declared that there was no room for supposing it [the Northern Department] ever had been invested in him." But all this was before the gloom of Ticonderoga and the retreat down the Hudson. It appeared that Burgoyne would sweep down to Albany unopposed. John Stark refused to bring his men in and it was said the New Englanders would never fight as long as Schuyler commanded (some New Yorkers said *they* would not fight if he did not). Congressional critics recovered from their embarrassment at Gates' performance. The attack on Schuyler intensified. "It is indeed droll . . . to see a general not knowing where to find the main body of his army!" said Sam Adams, and even Pierre Van Cortlandt was "disgusted, disappointed and alarmed."[3]

Clearly Schuyler's days were numbered. His reputation declined further when he made an unsuccessful attempt to win the governorship of New York. He was defeated by George Clinton and it was said that his failure was due to a special law passed by the Provincial Congress that allowed the soldiers to vote. His bad temper, his stormy relations with Congress, above all the fact that around him was an aura of defeat and bad luck—all these doomed him. The opposition in Congress demanded an investigation of the loss of Ticonderoga and on August 1 General Schuyler was ordered to report to Philadelphia. General Washington was directed "to order such general officer as he shall think proper, immediately to repair to the northern department, to relieve Major General Schuyler in his command there. . . ." The commander in chief refused to become involved in the squabble. It was clear that Congress intended to get rid of Schuyler and that it wanted Gates to have the command. Washington had no wish to participate in Schuyler's humiliation. "The present situation of that department is delicate and critical, and the choice of an officer to command may involve very interesting and important consequences," was his non-committal answer to Congress. On August 4 Congress named Gates.and two weeks later he relieved Schuyler of the command of the Northern Department.

Young James Wilkinson, who had been appointed deputy adjutant by Gates and had continued to serve under Schuyler may have given the best evaluation. Gates' appointment, he said, came "precisely in season to profit by the reverse of fortune, which radically affected the physical forces of the adverse armies; and to engross all the eclat which attended that conspicuous change. . . . Schuyler . . . was obliged to resign the fruits of his labours. . . ."[4]

THE ARMY OF THE NORTHERN DEPARTMENT

One of the factors that upset British strategy in 1777 was the difficulty of ascertaining the strength of the armies that would oppose Howe and Burgoyne. This is not surprising since neither Congress nor Washington was ever very sure how many men would be recruited, or how many of these could be retained in the ranks. The situation of the Continental Line had improved somewhat after Congress authorized three-year enlistments; at least commanders were now able to reckon the approximate strength of Continental regiments. But there was still no knowing what militia reinforcements would be raised in the states although in many instances the commander in chief was pleasantly surprised at their response to his appeals.

The exaggerated importance that both sides attached to Ticonderoga and the ease with which Burgoyne overwhelmed the American garrison had, as noted, produced elation and perhaps overconfidence on one side and despair on the other. For a time Burgoyne believed that there was virtually no American opposition between Lake Champlain and Albany. Yet between the first week in July and the third week in September a formidable force larger than his own appeared in Burgoyne's path and destroyed his army. Having watched the swarms of militia that had appeared around Boston in 1775 the British commander believed that he was the victim of similar spontaneous rising of American farmers. "Wherever the King's forces point," he wrote Germain, "militia, to the amount of three or four thousand, assemble in twenty-four hours; they bring with them their subsistence, &c., and, the alarm over, they return to their farms."

History has tended to take the general's word at face value. In its pages the Saratoga campaign is the story of Yankee militia rising, as it were, from the ground, stirred to righteous wrath by the presence of an invader accompanied by alien mercenaries and red barbarians. The real story of the army of the Northern Department is not quite so simple.

Of the American army of 10,000 men that was sent north for the spring offensive into Canada in 1776 less than half could be mustered when Governor-General Carleton withdrew that same fall. For most of the winter Schuyler lived in constant fear that the British would resume the offensive when Lake Champlain froze and sleds could be used to transport men and supplies. During the mild winter of 1776–1777 the lake never froze but Schuyler could keep only about 2,500 men at Ticonderoga. Another 1,500 were dispersed in small garrisons from Skenesboro to Fort Stanwix. It was difficult to recruit men to serve at Ticonderoga, for it was widely known that the troops there had suffered severe losses, mostly from sickness, and that the garrison was ill-clothed and badly fed.

By the end of the spring of 1777 the situation had not significantly improved. As noted above, the principal reason that St. Clair abandoned Ticonderoga was that there were simply not enough troops to man the fortifications. On June 28, just a few days before the enemy appeared, the troop return of the deputy adjutant general, Colonel Wilkinson, showed ten undermanned Continental regiments totalling 2,066, two militia regiments of 225 men each,

229 artillerymen, and 183 rangers and engineers (whatever one may think of the subsequent career of this "tarnished warrior" it was Wilkinson's job to keep track of troop strength and there seems to be no reason to question his figures). It might be noted that during the two-month tenure of General Gates (April and May) the situation of the northern army remained virtually unchanged.[5]

As the army retreated to the Hudson after the fall of Ticonderoga Schuyler hurried to Fort Edward to pick up the pieces. St. Clair brought in what was left of the Ticonderoga garrison and Schuyler decided to leave Seth Warner in the Hampshire Grants with his 600 men to threaten Burgoyne's flank. Warner held a Continental commission but most of his men were Green Mountain Boys who were probably as reluctant as Stark's militiamen to serve under "them." Schuyler was in a desperate situation. He warned Washington that "with less than three thousand continental troops and not quite a thousand [New York] militia, I am faced with a powerful enemy from the north." Thanks to Schuyler's industrious axemen and his subsequent withdrawal down the Hudson, his army was granted almost six weeks' respite. But the outlook was grim. "Desertion prevails and disease gains ground; nor is it to be wondered at, for we have neither tents, houses, barns, boards or any other shelter except a little brush. . . . We are in want of every kind of necessities, provisions excepted."

Washington was plagued by the uncertainty of Howe's intentions but he sent General John Nixon with nearly 600 Massachusetts Continentals and by mid-July Schuyler could muster 4,500 men present and fit for duty. Of these, five brigades of Continentals totalling 2,842 men composed the nucleus of his army. New York militia, almost all from Albany County, amounted to 1,625 rank and file. "With this small body we have to encounter a much more numerous body of the enemy, well-appointed, flushed with success, and daily increasing by the acquisition of Tories. . . ." Schuyler's appeals for militia brought little response; New Englanders still professed an unwillingness to serve under him. The western districts of New York, according to Wilkinson, were intimidated because "hostile Indians let loose by the British commander . . . penetrated the frontier settlements, committing murders and spreading terror all over the country."[6]

On July 27 occurred one of the most notorious atrocities of the war. Jane McCrae, reputedly tall, lovely, and fair, had arrived at Fort Edward and taken up residence with a Mrs. McNeill. Jenny was to meet her fiance, Lieutenant David Jones, a Tory serving with Burgoyne. As the British advanced from Skenesboro toward the Hudson the local residents fled, but Jenny and her hostess, who was a cousin of General Fraser, remained at Fort Edward. On the morning of the 27th a party of Indians drove off an American picket, seized the two women, and hurried them off. What happened to Jenny is uncertain, for the captives were separated. According to an American soldier who had also been captured by the Indians, Jenny was murdered, scalped, and her body mutilated. In any event, the Indians appeared in the British camp with a scalp that both Mrs. McNeill and Lieutenant Jones identified as Jenny's. General Burgoyne ordered St. Luc de La Corne to hand over the murderers for punishment, but the hard-bitten old frontiersman pointed out that the Indians were already restive under the restrictions imposed on them. Any reprisals for the murder might result in further desertions by Burgoyne's red allies. The British commander relented and the red fiends went unpunished.

This, in bare outline, is the story of Jenny McCrae. It has been both embroidered and debunked, but as with most such episodes, the legend is more important than the fact. As the historian Christopher Ward has put it, "That the Wyandot Panther killed Jenny McCrae is just as certain as that Hamlet stabbed Polonius." The story was believed and it was said, then and later, that New Englanders were outraged by the atrocious crime and turned out by the thousands to seek revenge on Burgoyne and his savage horde. And it is just here that that legend runs into trouble.

One suspects that Yankee farmers might not be especially enthusiastic about avenging the sweetheart of a Tory, rather inclining to the view that Jenny got what was coming to her. Moreover there is evidence that although the story was widely circulated in New York and New England, it evoked almost no response. It should be remembered that John Stark had drummed in his 1,400 militiamen by July 24, four days before Jenny was killed. Seth Warner's brigade numbered the same 600 men at Bennington (August 16) as when Schuyler detached it to the Grants on July 10. If the militia turned out, they did not march to Schuyler's headquarters for the army he turned over to Gates on August 19 had no additional militia units. Where, then, did the army that faced the British at Bemis Heights in September come from?[7]

Although Schuyler's appeals to state officials fell on deaf ears, those to Washington did not. He was alive to the crisis in the Northern Department, especially after the news of the fall of Ticonderoga. Although Washington was still puzzling over Howe's intentions, his concern for the northern frontier led him to detach several regiments to Peekskill and to direct General Israel Putnam, who was guarding the Hudson Highlands, to release "four of the strongest Massachusetts regiments [who] will proceed immediately to Albany." Putnam sent John Glover's veteran brigade of 750 Continentals and they reported to Schuyler on August 1. On August 22 two New York Continental regiments, Philip Van Cortlandt's 2nd and James Livingston's 4th, came in and were sent to support Arnold's expedition up the Mohawk (thus accounting for the fact that Arnold set out with 800 men and returned with 1200). By this time Washington finally had certain word that Howe's expedition was in the Chesapeake, so he detached Daniel Morgan's riflemen, 331 tough Indian fighters who arrived on August 30. Finally, on September 6, Major Henry Dearborn noted in his journal that a force of Connecticut militia reached the American camps. These must have been the regiments of Colonel Thaddeus Cook and Colonel Jonathan Latimer who were added to Poor's brigade. If they were average militia regiments their total was not more than 300 rank and file (a return of Poor's seven regiments for October 4 lists 831 men present and fit for duty).

In summary, then, Wilkinson's return of July 20, seven days prior to the murder of Jenny McCrae gives Schuyler's force a strength of almost 4,500 men, including Nixon's brigade which had come up from Peekskill on July 10. On August 1 Glover's Massachusetts Continentals arrived, probably about 750 men (the October 4 return shows 918). On August 22 the 2nd and 4th New York regiments, 400 strong came in and were sent up the Mohawk. They returned with Arnold's command on August 31, the day after Morgan's 331 riflemen arrived. This brings the total of the northern army to 6,280 men. On September 8, according to Wilkinson, "the American army, about six thousand strong, began to retrace its steps toward the enemy . . . and reached Stillwater the next day." Of this force, seventy percent were Continentals, and of these forty-five percent had been ordered forward by the commander in chief after Ticonderoga. It was the Continental Line, not the militia that "turned out" to face Burgoyne's invaders.[8]

As the American army moved up the Hudson, General Gates cast his professional eye about for suitable ground on which to make his stand against the British. He had the able assistance of Colonel Thaddeus Kosciuszko, a Polish engineer who had been with the Northern Department since early spring. Kosciuszko was one of the few who had foreseen the disastrous consequences of leaving the Sugar Loaf undefended at Ticonderoga and he had remained as Schuyler's lieutenant during the long summer on the Hudson. Gates halted the army at Stillwater where Schuyler and Kosciuszko had earlier laid out some field works, but the position afforded no protection to the west. On September 13 the army moved north again, this time to Bemis Heights where heavily forested hills pushing to within two miles of the river afforded an anchor to Gates' left flank. He sited his right on the bluff overlooking the river and the road along its bank which led down to Albany. From here Kosciuszko laid out a line that stretched in a convex arc north and west. The center occupied Bemis Heights, a broken elevation rising about 300 feet above the river. Linking the two segments of the works was a barn which was converted into a rude fortress. The line then extended to the west, curving back to the south where it was anchored on a steep knoll. The chord of the arc thus formed was about a mile long.

Kosciuszko and his sappers fell to work with the troops and by September 17 a line of entrenchments and breastworks of logs, trees, and fence rails had been constructed, along with revetments for the guns. Commanding the right wing was General John Glover with his own brigade and those of Nixon and Paterson. The left was commanded by Benedict Arnold and consisted of Ebenezer Learned's brigade and Enoch Poor's oversize brigade of seven regiments. On the extreme left, outside the entrenchments and masking the

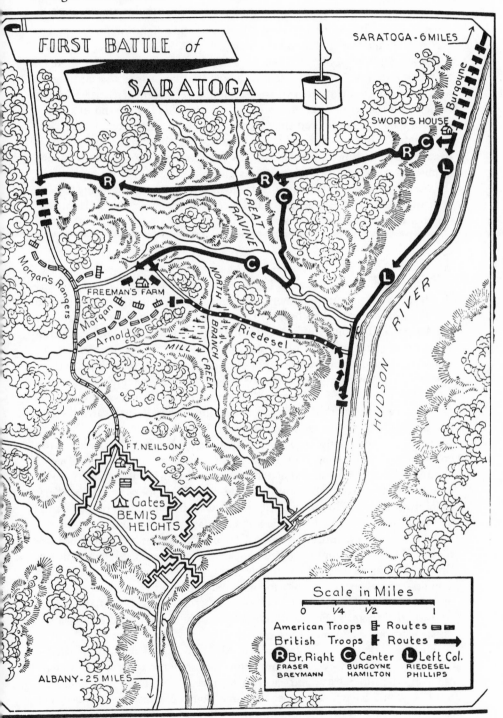

FIRST BATTLE of SARATOGA

Lynn Montross, *The Story of the Continental Army*, Harper and Row, Publishers, Inc.

western flank, was Morgan's corps of riflemen and a light infantry regiment commanded by Major Henry Dearborn.

On the morning of the 18th Gates was heartened by the arrival of General Stark who had finally been persuaded to join the main army. The addition of his 1,500 men would give the American commander a decided numerical superiority, and the army "was animated by the arrival of [this] band of citizen-soldiers who had conquered the Germans and killed their commander near Bennington." But it was quickly evident that Stark and his men were only passing through. The militia enlistments expired that very day and by noon, despite the vehement urgings of Gates and his officers, it was obvious that the New Hampshire men were determined to go home. Stark seems to have done little to try to dissuade them, and by early afternoon they had departed; "neither officer nor private was left behind."[9]

FREEMAN'S FARM

To the north of the American lines for the next few miles the country was rough and wooded, cut by numerous ravines and creeks meandering from the western hills down to the Hudson. One of these lay immediately in front of the American position. Another, called the Great Ravine, cut a deep gash from west to east about two and a half miles to the north. Where these and lesser water courses led to the river they cut the Albany road. With their usual thoroughness the Americans had destroyed all the bridges, making tedious work for Burgoyne's engineers. The woods between Bemis Heights and the Great Ravine were interspersed with a few clearings around small farms whose owners had long since abandoned them.

On the day that Gates began to dig in on Bemis Heights Burgoyne's army crossed the Hudson from Fort Miller to the west bank at the little village of Saratoga. He had now accumulated his store of provisions for thirty days, most of which moved on bateaux down the river. The troops and the artillery train crossed on a boat bridge and once it was dismantled Burgoyne broke his last link with Lake Champlain and Canada; "from the hour I passed the Hudson's river and proceed towards Albany, all safety of communication ceases." The news from Howe was almost two months old at which time the British commander in chief had told him only that "my intention is for Philadelphia," and assuring him of support if Washington turned north. Clinton in New York could be counted on only to "act as occurrences may direct." Knowing his friend as he did Burgoyne probably did not expect substantial assistance from the lower Hudson.

But he was determined to press forward; ". . . I had dislodged the enemy repeatedly, when in force and more strongly posted; my army was conscious of having the superiority, and eager to advance. . . ." Had he not gone forward he would have fallen under the same stigma of caution and indecision that had threatened the reputation of his fellow generals. Whether he really believed that his orders left him no choice, his flamboyant nature and his driving ambition would scarcely have permitted him to retreat until he had "tried a battle with the enemy." Besides, Gentleman Johnny was a gambler. Unfortunately, there was somewhat more than a drunken young nobleman contending for the stakes.

The army that moved down the Hudson was lean and spare compared to the grand parade that had ascended the Richelieu almost four months before. The English troops were nearly intact except for the regiment left behind to guard Ticonderoga. Three hundred recruits had joined at Fort Edward bringing the redcoat rank and file to 2,900 infantry and 150 artillerymen. Riedesel's Germans had suffered more severely. One regiment was detached at Ticonderoga and nearly 400 of his regulars had been lost at Bennington. With Captain Pausch's gunners the Baron mustered 1,800 rank and file. All but about 100 of Burgoyne's Indians had vanished into the forest and his Canadian and Tory provincials did not exceed 500 men. As the army moved down the right bank of the Hudson its total strength was about 5,500 men.[10]

Ever since Fort Edward Burgoyne's reconnaissance had been deteriorating. On August 4 St. Luc de La Corne had presided over a council at which the Indians had again insisted on a free hand in the conduct of their operations. When this was refused the Indians began to desert in droves thus depriving the British of "scouts and outposts, and all the lesser but necessary services for giving due repose to the Camp." The few Indians who remained, perhaps sensing the changing fortunes of the campaign, became less enterprising and more cautious. From the time he crossed the Hudson Burgoyne was uncertain of both the numbers and the position of his opponent.

The Americans, conversely, became bolder, especially after the arrival of Morgan's men. These forest-wise frontiersmen constantly harassed Burgoyne's pickets and advance parties, restricting the range of his scouts so that they had little opportunity to obtain information. On the east bank of the river parties of American militia were also able to keep track of enemy's movements.

On the 16th the British moved down river and Burgoyne conducted a limited reconnaissance that moved as far as Sword's Farm about four miles from Bemis Heights. He made no contact with the Americans and during the next two days the entire force with its baggage and artillery was brought up. Bridges were repaired and the road improved for the next forward movement. Toward evening of the 18th "regiments of the enemy with banners, could plainly be seen."

These troops were undoubtedly part of a scouting force led by Arnold. They surprised an enemy party digging for potatoes and gathering forage. The Americans opened fire killing and wounding several redcoats but then withdrew to the American lines. This was the first contact between the British and the army of the Northern Department since the retreat from Ticonderoga.

On the morning of September 19 a thick fog delayed the British until the

late forenoon. Burgoyne mustered his troops in three divisions for a reconnaissance in force which he expected would bring on an engagement. Fraser's
advance corps contained the flank companies (grenadiers and light infantry)
of all the British regiments, plus the 24th Regiment, the Brunswick grenadiers
and light infantry, and the few remaining Indians and provincials. Altogether
Fraser had with him nearly 2,000 men. His task was to move to the right as far
as the line of hills west of the river and attempt to flank the American left. The
center under General Hamilton consisting of the English 9th, 20th, 21st, and
62nd Regiments also moved away from the river and then turned south forming on Fraser's left. Burgoyne accompanied this force of about 1,100 men.
Riedesel and the Germans moved on the road which followed the right bank
of the Hudson, making repairs in the bridges and fills, clearing the way for the
rear elements which guarded the baggage. The German wing consisted of
Regiments Rhetz, Specht, and Riedesel, and mustered 1,100 bayonets. From
his artillery train Burgoyne had allocated eight guns to the advance corps and
six to Hamilton's center; eight guns of Captain Pausch's Hesse-Hanau artillery accompanied Riedesel's command. Altogether the strike force had about
five guns per thousand men. By noon the British force was deployed and ready
to move south, but its component parts were separated by the woods and the
rough terrain. This seems not to have disturbed Burgoyne; he merely ordered
Fraser to await the firing of three guns as the signal for a general attack.[11]

   Word that the British were on the move reached American headquarters
from scouts sent out early in the morning. Gates' inclination was to sit tight
and let the enemy come to him. But General Arnold strongly objected. Up to
this point there seems to have been little trouble between the two major generals. The argument this morning over tactics seems to have been vehement
but not ill-tempered. Arnold urged that in the forest the Americans would
be able to employ the kind of harassing tactics at which they excelled. He also
argued that it would be folly to allow Burgoyne to bring up his guns unopposed to batter the American fortifications.

   Gates' decision was a nice compromise. Morgan's corps was directed to
advance and make contact with the enemy. The rest of Arnold's wing was held
in readiness to support Morgan. The riflemen and the light infantry moved
out and after marching a little more than a mile they reached a clearing about
seven or eight hundred yards long and almost four hundred yards across. This
was Freeman's farm. Burgoyne's center had crossed the Great Ravine and was
drawn up just north of the clearing waiting for Fraser to get in position farther to the west. A British picket had been sent forward to occupy a small shed
on the edge of the woods. One of Morgan's detachments spotted the enemy,
advanced, and opened fire. Since they were well beyond musket range the
British skirmishers probably did not take cover, for the rifle fire hit them with
telling effect. They hastily retreated and Morgan's men pursued them—
squarely into the main British line. A volley of musket fire slammed into the
Americans and they took to their heels. Colonel Wilkinson, riding forward to

ascertain the progress of the advance, found the riflemen scattered, Morgan almost alone and, according to Wilkinson, sobbing in frustration. More likely the "Old Waggoner" was filling the forest air with a special brand of frontier profanity. But he was soon sounding his turkey call and pulling his command back together.

In the meantime Poor's brigade had been sent forward in support. Its leading regiments. Cilley's and Scammell's, drifted off to the left and struck Fraser's corps on the British right. The grenadiers and light infantry counterattacked vigorously and the American advance was brought to a halt. At this point Poor's men tried to drive between Fraser and Hamilton. They were checked and driven back as the 24th Regiment and Breymann's Brunswickers extended into the gap and formed on Hamilton's right. By about three o'clock the battle, which had begun at the break between the right and center wings, had shifted to the clearing opposite the English regiments composed, from right to left, of the 21st, the 62nd, and the 20th, with the 9th in reserve. Some of Learned's men were now fed into the American line although some of the Massachusetts brigade drifted off to the left. The Americans now advanced across the clearing of Freeman's farm and drove the enemy back into the trees north of the open ground. They even overran the British guns but the redcoat artillerymen had prudently carried off their linstocks, so that their guns could not be turned on them. The British reformed and came surging back, counterattacking with the bayonet and driving the Americans back across the open ground.

The seesaw battle of advance and retreat raged for the next three hours. The British, outnumbered on this part of the field by about two to one, fought stubbornly. Their guns played havoc with the American attacking line and drew the concentrated fire of every assault. Captain Jones, commanding the battery, and four other officers were killed, and thirty-six gunners were cut down by the Americans. Lieutenant Hadden, the only officer who had not been hit, called on General Hamilton for men to serve the guns but the hard pressed infantry could not spare them. Before the day was over these four regiments would lose thirty percent of their force, 76 killed, and 250 wounded. With most of its guns silenced, with the 62nd reduced to 60 or 70 men, the British line was on the edge of disaster.

Along the river General Riedesel was making his way unopposed except by broken bridges and washouts. All afternoon he had listened to the sound of firing which rolled down from the heights to the west, but no orders came. Finally Riedesel sent one of his own officers to find out what was happening. About five o'clock the officer returned with orders from Burgoyne to reinforce the line on the left. Riedesel did not hesitate. Snatching up the nearest troops, two companies of Regiment Rhetz and two of Pausch's guns, he hurried up the bluff ordering his own Regiment Riedesel to follow. He rushed through the woods until he came to the flank of the hard-pressed 20th. Without waiting for his own regiment he threw the two Rhetz companies in against the Americans and Pausch's guns opened with grape. In a few moments Regiment Riedesel came up and the Baron sent them scrambling across an intervening ravine and up the far side to attack Poor's men. The Americans were driven back, and in the gathering darkness the British line reformed, now bolstered by Riedesel's fresh troops.

This was the turning point of the battle. Morgan and Poor pulled back their regiments, Learned disengaged on the left, and the battered redcoats retained possession of the field. They had lost 140 killed and 360 wounded. The Americans had suffered substantially less, 65 killed and 254 wounded and missing.

Although the American withdrawal was orderly there was no elation of the sort that usually accompanies a victory. That night anxiety over the possibility of an attack kept most of the army from generals to privates awake and standing to arms. The plain fact was that the Americans believed that they had been beaten and that as soon as the British caught their breath they would storm Bemis Heights. The next morning there was a good deal of confusion; "we were badly fitted to defend [our] works," reported James Wilkinson. The troops of the left wing had expended most of their ammunition and it had not been replenished. Indeed, the whole army was short of powder and shot. Again a morning fog concealed the approaches from the north. A deserter from the 62nd regiment reported that the British were about to renew the attack. Anxiously the men peered into the fog expecting redcoats to loom out of the mist at any moment. Then, about nine o'clock, the sun burned away the mist and there was no enemy in sight. The deserter's report lost some of its credibility, and the Americans finally began to persuade themselves that they had delivered an effective blow against the invaders. Yet for the next four days the soldiers looked anxiously northward from their trenches and breastworks; "we hourly Expect a General Battle," said Major Dearborn on the 22nd.[12]

American fears of an impending action were not unfounded. Burgoyne wrote to General Powell commanding at Ticonderoga, "We have had a smart and very honorable action, and are now encamped in front of the field, which must demonstrate our victory beyond the power of even an American newswriter to explain away." He was prepared to follow up this success and actually deployed his regiments on the morning of September 20. But he had second thoughts undoubtedly induced by the severe casualties suffered by his best regiments. Burgoyne decided to postpone the attack, and on the 21st he received a message from New York. Sir Henry Clinton was bestirring himself and the dispatch asked if a diversion on the lower Hudson might not be welcome. Burgoyne immediately replied, urging "an attack, or the menace of an attack. . . . Do it, my dear friend, directly." Thus heartened, the British dug in to wait for help.[13]

On the whole, the action of September 19 was a curious one. Of the two commanding generals Gates had clearly demonstrated his superiority. Knowing that time was on his side he had prudently pursued his defensive strategy. He permitted the left wing to deliver its attack but despite Arnold's urgent pleas Gates refused to commit any more reinforcements after Poor and Learned went into action. Nixon, Paterson, and Glover remained firmly in place on Bemis Heights against the possibility of a disaster at Freeman's Farm. On the battlefield itself the American command did not distinguish itself (Arnold's precise role is not clear). The attempt to split the gap between Hamilton and Fraser was sound, but thereafter no overall command was exerted over the various brigades. Continuous charges across the clearing unsupported by artillery was playing the British game. After all, Burgoyne was committed to the advance. If the Americans had, for example, held to the woods south of Freeman's Farm and employed the flexible tactics at which they were allegedly expert, they could have received the British attack across a clear field of fire while protected themselves by the cover of the forest. Instead they repeatedly threw themselves against the devastating fire of the British guns and infantry—and painfully learned what history has to teach about "the thin red line."

If American leadership was faulty Burgoyne's was deplorable. In rough and broken country he divided his force so that coordinated action was impossible (one wonders if he would have sent for help from Riedesel if the German had not sent his own messenger to offer it). But the most shocking lapse was Fraser's. Not only did he have the elite regiments, the grenadiers and light infantry, but he had almost as many troops as the other two corps combined. It was his right wing that was to deliver the decisive blow and turn the American flank. Yet after repulsing the initial American attack he stood fast in his position while the center absorbed the full weight of the American assault. For this Burgoyne must share the blame, for when he finally called for help he sent to Riedesel who was a mile and a half away while Fraser could not have been more than a third that distance to his right. Whatever the reason for Fraser's strange immobility, it was buried with the fearless Scot on October 8.

What happened on the field at Freeman's Farm, then, was that Burgoyne, who was committed to an offensive designed to dislodge Gates from his blocking position, stood on the defensive. The Americans, whose task was simply to check Burgoyne's advance, hurled themselves against the British line until they had spent their energy and were driven from the field. Yet as Lieutenant Anbury observed several days later, "Notwithstanding the glory of the day remains on our side, I am fearful the real advantages resulting from this hard-fought battle, will rest on that of the Americans, our army being so much weakened by this engagement, as not to be of sufficient strength to venture forth and improve our victory, which may, in the end, put a stop to our intended expedition. . . ."

On the American side young Henry Dearborn grasped the full significance of the battle more clearly than anyone. The major's journal is terse and to the point, the daily entries often limited to a phrase or two. Although he was in action for seven continuous hours on September 19 his account runs to only 300 spare words, concluding with the laconic comment, "on this Day has Been fought one of the Greatest Battles that ever was fought in America. . . ."[14]

ELEVEN

Philadelphia
Takes Howe

IF SIR HENRY CLINTON WAS BAFFLED AND DISBELIEVING OVER GENERAL HOWE'S decision to take ship for Pennsylvania, George Washington was completely disconcerted. Even after the British fleet was reported in Delaware Bay Washington professed:

> I am now as much puzzled by their designs, as I was before; being unable to account, upon any plausible Plan, for General Howe's conduct in this instance or why he should go Southward rather than cooperate with Mr. Burgoyne. The latter appeared to me so probable and of such importance and still does, that I shall with difficulty give in to a contrary belief, till I can be obliged by some unequivocal event.[1]

BY SEA TO PHILADELPHIA

There had never been any doubt in Howe's mind about his destination for the summer campaign of 1777. Yet, as always, the British commander moved as though time meant nothing. He had shifted his headquarters to his brother's flagship, the *Eagle*, on June 24, but it was a full month before the fleet finally weighed anchor. The army, 13,000 strong, was embarked on July 9 but Sir William so far acknowledged his responsibility for Burgoyne as to say he could not leave without some word from the upper Hudson. His concern was somewhat odd in view of the fact that he had made up his mind to sever his connection with the northern army.

On the 15th he received a dispatch from Burgoyne written as the latter was preparing to attack Ticonderoga. The next day Howe sent his own dispatch to Germain, a typical hodgepodge of self-justification and bad logic. Sir William noted that Washington was moving toward the Hudson for the purpose of "preventing a junction between this and the northern army, which will no further affect my proceeding to Pensilvania. . . ." If this movement of the enemy represented a threat to New York city "I shall . . . strengthen Sir Henry Clinton still more by the reserve which is already ordered to remain here. . . ." (Three days later, over Clinton's protests, he detached a full brigade from the New York garrison and added it to his own force.)

Should Washington move against Burgoyne Howe thought the northern commander would have sufficient forces "to leave me no room to dread the event," despite the fact that Washington and Schuyler between them would outnumber Burgoyne more than two to one; "but if Mr. Washington's intention should be to retard the approach of General Burgoyne to Albany he may soon find himself exposed to an attack from this quarter." If by "this quarter" Howe meant Clinton's command, Sir Henry himself noted that his garrison force had been reduced to a point that "would leave no surplus whatsoever for offensive operations." If Howe meant that he himself would go to Burgoyne's assistance it is difficult to see how he would have timely news of Washington's movements if he were at sea en route to Philadelphia.[2]

Having thus, in his own mind, prepared for all possible contingencies Howe took another week to tidy up his affairs, including, no doubt, a fond farewell to his mistress, Mrs. Loring. On July 23 Lord Richard Howe's fleet, 267 sail in all, cleared Sandy Hook and turned south. For a week the great task force plodded down the Atlantic and on July 30 entered Delaware Bay. Here Captain Andrew Snape Hammond, commanding HMS *Roebuck* which patrolled the Bay, reported to the *Eagle*. He recommended to Howe that the troops be disembarked on the western shore at Reedy Island, about twelve miles below Wilmington. Here Howe would have been thirty-five miles from Philadelphia.

To Hammond's astonishment Howe announced his intention to go on to Chesapeake Bay. He was, he said, afraid the rebels would oppose his landing with floating batteries and fire ships; besides, a landing at the head of the Chesapeake would put his army between Washington and American supply depots at York, Reading, and Carlisle.

The reaction of the officers of the expedition to Howe's decision ranged from puzzlement to outrage. Even Admiral Howe entered a mild demurrer, a rare occasion, for his Lordship meticulously refrained from interfering with his brother's military decisions. But keeping men and animals jammed aboard the transports for additional weeks in the August heat was bound to be extremely debilitating. Lord Howe's staff secretary, Ambrose Serle, remarked, "May GOD defend us from the Fatality of the worst Climate in America. . . ."

A glance at a modern map will show that the two sites are at approximately the two ends of the Chesapeake-Delaware Canal, less than twenty miles apart. A landing at the head of Chesapeake Bay would cut the American army off from its supply bases only if Washington wished it so. But Sir William was adamant. Once more the fleet put out into the Atlantic, a move so puzzling to Washington that he halted his movement toward Philadelphia.

The appearance of the fleet off Cape Henlopen had appeared to confirm Philadelphia as Howe's objective. Until this news reached Washington he had prudently kept his army near New York so as to be in position to contest a thrust up the Hudson. Howe's embarkation and southward course had in-

duced Washington to move cautiously toward Philadelphia, but he was fig-
uratively looking over his shoulder, suspecting a feint that would find Howe
back on the Hudson to cooperate with Burgoyne. The report of Howe's
appearance in Delaware Bay caused him to start the whole army southward,
and he himself rode to Philadelphia to inspect its defenses. When the British
again put to sea there seemed reason to believe that Howe was indeed playing
a foxy game, so on August 10 the commander in chief started the army on a
slow march back toward New York. Finally, on August 22 came definite news
that the English fleet was in Chesapeake Bay. With a feeling of vast relief
Washington again reversed the army's march and started for the capital, now
certain that Howe "must mean to reach Philadelphia by that Route, tho' to be
sure it is a very strange one." What with all the marching and countermarching, the men in the ranks must have thought their own commander's route
equally strange.[3]

Washington's decision to defend the capital was based partly on political
considerations, so he decided to put the army on display en route to his meeting with the British by parading it through Philadelphia. In the course of campaigning in the first half of 1777 the haphazard organization of the Continental
Line had become more stabilized. Both the regiments and Washington's generals had acquired experience, not only in combat but in troop movement and
administration. The army was now organized into divisions, and several major
generals were beginning to emerge as competent commanders. Already
marked as the ablest tactician and strategist of them all was Nathanael Greene.
Not only was his division the best organized but when the army formed for
battle Washington always gave him command of that part of the field where
the danger seemed greatest.

William Alexander, who refused to abandon his Irish title of Lord Stirling,
had emerged as one of the hardest fighters in the army. He had also earned a
reputation as one of its hardest drinkers, but no one ever accused him of being
drunk in combat. His division contained two outstanding regiments, Smallwood's Marylanders and Haslet's Delaware Continentals. John Sullivan had
had the misfortune to command the American left at Long Island, and he had
also briefly commanded the disastrous American expedition to Canada in
the summer of 1776. But he had performed brilliantly at Trenton and, despite
a botched affair at Staten Island in August, he still enjoyed Washington's
confidence. When Congress voted to relieve him in order to investigate his
conduct, the commander in chief refused to release him in the face of the imminent threat of Howe's invasion.

Adam Stephen, a Virginian, was so given to exaggerated reports of his
prowess that Washington finally had to tell him flatly that one of Stephen's
reports of "an orderly retreat" was, in fact, "a disorderly rout," and that "the
disadvantage was on our side, not the enemy's." Like Stirling, Stephen was
fond of liquor but, unlike the Irishman, there was growing evidence that the
Virginian was beginning to rely on the bottle to stiffen his resolution in battle.

Washington tolerated him because they had fought together in the Seven Years' War, and because there were simply not enough major generals available. The fifth division was Benjamin Lincoln's and in his absence the command fell to "Mad Anthony" Wayne. The nickname should be taken in its eighteenth century context when it often meant fiery or impulsive. Wayne was thirty-two years old and had fought in the Canadian campaign of 1776. He had preceded Gates as commander of Ticonderoga and had been promoted to brigadier general in February, 1777. He commanded the Pennsylvania Line and had impressed the commander in chief as an able administrator, but he had not had combat experience as a division commander. Wayne was belligerent and pugnacious in battle, but not mad.[4]

The grand parade through the capital was led by General Washington, as always an impressive and heroic figure. There were bands and the clattering hooves of the mounted troops, led by Colonel Theodorick Bland's First Virginia Dragoons; the rumbling wheels of Henry Knox's guns, and the tramp of rank on rank of infantry—14,000 officers and men. "The best clothed men were the Virginians and the smartest looking troops were Smallwood's Marylanders." The regiments passed in files of twelve and the long column took two hours to pass through the center of the city. John Adams, self-styled military expert, watched with a critical eye. "Our soldiers have not yet quite the air of soldiers," he noted. "They don't step exactly in time. They don't hold their heads quite erect, nor turn out their toes exactly as they ought. They don't all of them cock their hats; and such as do, don't all wear them the same way."

One untoward episode marred the scene toward the end of the display, and Washington, at the head of the column, was probably not aware of it. He had ordered that "not a woman belonging to the army is to be seen," so the rather considerable number of camp followers were "spirited off into quaint little alley ways and side streets." As they tramped along parallel to the army's line of march they seethed with resentment. It was *their* army and *their* men. Somewhere in the middle of the city their resentment exploded. They "poured after their soldiers, their hair flying, their brows beaded from the heat, their belongings slung over one shoulder, chattering and yelling in sluttish shrills as they went, and spitting in the gutters." So the women made it their parade, too.

Riding at Washington's side at the head of the column was a young Frenchman whose name was destined to pepper the American landscape with place names. The Marquis de Lafayette had arrived from France a few weeks before, one of the cloud of foreign officers whose ambitious pretensions were usually inversely proportionate to their abilities. But the twenty year old marquis was an altogether different case. Scion of one of the truly old and aristocratic families in France, he offered to serve without salary or expenses. He accepted the rank of major general but did not ask for a command. He had come, he said, only to learn, and he impressed the commanding general, who had come to loathe most of the foreign officers foisted on him by a Congress eager to gain sympathy abroad. Lafayette's modesty, his quick intelligence, and his eagerness to learn earned him, first Washington's regard, and then his respect and affection. Lafayette's modest charm extended to the rest of the officer corps and ultimately to the men in the ranks. And the young Frenchman's admiration for Washington developed into an extreme case of hero worship.

The army moved on from Philadelphia to Wilmington where Washington established his headquarters on August 25.[5]

It took the British fleet two weeks to reach Cape Henry, for the ponderous armada could only proceed as fast as the slowest ship. Ten days were consumed sailing up the great bay to the Head of the Elk. Twenty-five days from Delaware Bay Howe landed his army—ten miles farther from Philadelphia than if he had landed at Reedy Island. Altogether it had taken the British commander thirty-three days to bring his army some twenty miles closer to Philadelphia than it had been at Perth Amboy in June. Moreover, it was an army whose men were exhausted from more than a month at sea in the summer's heat. The army's horses—those that survived—were physical wrecks.

But the most severe blow was the fact that there were virtually no Loyalists to welcome Howe. Many farms and villages were deserted and in some cases the people of the neighborhood had burned their crops to prevent the enemy from using them. No more than a handful of people came forward to greet Sir William and pledge their allegiance to the English cause. So the hope of a Loyalist rising in Pennsylvania and a campaign that would end with the conquest of the middle states secured by an occupation force of provincial troops disappeared in the smoke of the burning fields. Howe abandoned his intention of seizing the supply depots (if indeed he ever had such intention) and ordered his victualling ships back to the Delaware—presumably to brave the fire ships and floating batteries which he had earlier avoided. He would, he told Admiral Howe, allow ten days for them to reach New Castle, by which time he expected to be in position to destroy the rebel army.

On August 30 Howe finally replied to Germain's May 18 dispatch which had approved the movement to Pennsylvania by sea on condition that Burgoyne was properly supported. Howe had received this on August 12 while he was still at sea. Now his belated reply revealed between its lines the ruin of Sir William's strategy. He would, he said, be unable to cooperate with Burgoyne; and "the prevailing disposition of the inhabitants [of Pennsylvania] . . . I am sorry to observe, seem to be, excepting a few individuals, strongly in enmity against us. . . ." He reminded Germain that his previous request for reinforcements had not been met, and that "in the present extended situation of the King's southern army" the American Secretary should not expect the war to be ended by the present campaign. Read out of context Howe's dispatch makes it appear almost as if Germain were responsible for the deplorable state of affairs. Sir William had by now become quite accomplished at laying his faults on others.[6]

The one bright spot in this otherwise gloomy prospect was the news that Washington's army was only a few miles away, and from the disposition of the American troops it was obvious that they were looking for a fight.

As soon as Howe's landing was reported to headquarters at Wilmington Washington began to call in his various detachments: Sullivan, from his "unlucky" attack on Staten Island; Colonel George Baylor, who was recruiting for the dragoons; and most of all, to the militia regiments from Pennsylvania, Maryland and Virginia. "It is to be wished that every Man could bring a good Musket and Bayonet into the field, but in times like the present, we must make the best shift we can, and I would therefore advise you to exhort every Man to bring the best he has." Washington also ordered the formation of a regiment of light infantry made up of 100 men from each of the nine brigades of Continentals to be used for such special duties as reconnaissance, advance guard, and covering force. The command was given to Colonel William Maxwell who had served as a provincial officer with the British army in America for twenty years.

On the 27th Washington and his staff rode southwest to find the British. It was obvious that his fox hunter's blood was up and his eagerness brought him within sight of the enemy, although he could make no satisfactory estimate of its numbers. On that day and the next he rode the countryside trying to familiarize himself with the terrain. By the 29th he was back in Wilmington where he ordered out Maxwell's light infantry "to be watchful and guarded on all the Roads."[7]

By this time Howe's command had sufficiently recovered from its sea voyage and begun to stir itself. The British force consisted of about 13,000 men divided between eight German regiments and seventeen regiments of redcoats. Mounted troops were scarce although raids through the countryside had procured enough horses for the artillery and a few dragoons for reconnaissance. But Howe still lacked a sufficient force of mounted troops that could be used to perform the classic functions of screening and pursuit.

Howe divided his force into two "grand divisions." One of these, composed of four German regiments and nine of redcoats, numbered about 5,500 men commanded by the Hessian general, Baron Wilhelm von Knyphausen. The other division was led by General Cornwallis and consisted of twelve English regiments and three of Hessians. It included a brigade of the Guards and seven regiments of grenadiers and light infantry. Its total strength was 7,500 rank and file.

On September 8 the British army broke camp. The early hours before dawn were lit by the eerie northern lights, the aurora borealis, as the regiments filed off to the northeast. Howe's intelligence had reported the enemy across his path, obviously ready to dispute his passage to Philadelphia. The British moved toward the American right flank causing Washington to shift to the northwest. He took up a position along the left bank of Brandywine Creek at Chadd's Ford. The Brandywine was not a formidable obstacle, but its deep sharp banks compelled the British to use its fords. These were numerous and Washington's decision to defend Chadd's was because it was on the principal road to Philadelphia, and because rough country to the southeast would make it possible to hold his left flank with militia.

By September 10 the British army was encamped at Kennett Square, six miles west of Chadd's Ford and twenty-six miles from Philadelphia.[8]

THE BRANDYWINE

William Howe may not have been a military genius, but he was perfectly at home on the battlefield. Although he was fighting in the enemy's country his knowledge of terrain and road networks was invariably superior to Washington's. He used his information to good advantage and his execution was nearly flawless. In the pre-dawn darkness of September 11 Howe's army was in motion along the Nottingham Road which led toward Chadd's Ford. About five miles west of the Ford this road intersected the Great Valley Road which led northward toward West Chester. Howe planned a wide turning movement against Washington's right flank, so when the British reached the intersection Cornwallis' division, accompanied by General Howe, swung left and filed northward, while Knyphausen's division continued directly eastward on the Nottingham Road. About a mile beyond where the two divisions separated, Knyphausen's van, Major Patrick Ferguson's Queen's Rangers, came to Welch's Tavern. There some American videttes were refreshing themselves in Welch's tap room, and they barely escaped by dashing out the back door.

From Washington's post at Chadd's Ford the Brandywine flowed from the north slightly to east of south toward the Delaware, ten miles away. Above Chadd's, at about one mile intervals, were Brinton's Ford, Wistar's Ford, Jones Ford and Buffington Ford, the latter located at the forks of the Brandywine. These names and other local landmarks were not thoroughly familiar to Washington or his generals, and he seems not to have taken the precaution of having at hand someone who knew the countryside. His army was formed into three wings. Downstream the left was guarded by 1,500 militia posted at the one usable ford. Rough terrain and the widening of the river as it approached the Delaware seemed to preclude any danger in this sector. Greene and Wayne, with their divisions, were in the center with Sullivan on the right. Stirling and Stephen were in support, prepared to reinforce either Greene or Sullivan. The American right extended beyond Jones Ford, and Sullivan had been told by the people of the neighborhood that above Jones there was no usable ford for twelve miles. Colonel Moses Hazen, guarding Jones Ford on Sullivan's right, was ordered to scout to the north and west. A perusal of the orders and dispositions issued by Washington and his generals indicates that they were quite vague about the geography of the area. In fact, during the battle the commander in chief needed a guide to take him from one part of the battlefield to the other.[9]

As reports of Knyphausen's advance began to come in Washington ordered Maxwell's regiment across the Brandywine to establish contact with the enemy. It was the videttes of the light troops that Ferguson's Rangers flushed at Welch's Tavern. Supported by the jägers, the Rangers pushed the Americans back until they came within sight of Chadd's Ford. There Maxwell's men stiffened and their stubborn fighting brought the British van to a halt. Three more regiments of redcoats had to be brought up before the 800 light infantrymen could be dislodged. Washington ordered Maxwell back to the east side of the Brandywine as the rest of Knyphausen's division came up and began to deploy. By about 10:30 the British had formed a line opposite the Ford and a desultory artillery duel began; ". . . the [American] balls and grapeshot fell right among us, [but] this cannonade had little effect because the battery was placed too low." Howe and Cornwallis were almost to Trimble's Ford, six miles upstream on the West Branch of the Brandywine. Here the flanking column turned eastward.

Eleven o'clock came and went and there was no movement from Knyphausen. Washington became increasingly uneasy as memories of Long Island began to plague him. He had earlier ordered Colonel James Ross and a small party of Pennsylvanians to reconnoiter west of the Brandywine, and all of the light dragoons were patrolling to the north of Sullivan. He had finally found a man who was familiar with the neighborhood, Major James Spear of the Pennsylvania militia, and had sent him off to scout the British movements.

The first warning came from Colonel Hazen who commanded what was known as the "Canadian Regiment" on Sullivan's right. He reported a strong British column to the west headed toward the forks of the Brandywine. Soon afterward a message from Colonel Ross reported a column of at least 5,000 men on the Great Valley Road at about 11:00 o'clock. Ross was hanging on the rear of the column and some of his men had skirmished with the British rearguard.

Here was the answer to the curious inactivity of the British across Chadd's Ford. Howe was repeating the maneuver of Long Island. This offered a great opportunity, for if Howe had as many as 5,000 men Knyphausen, with only slightly more than half the strength of the American force, was vulnerable. Washington began issuing orders. Colonel Bland and his dragoons were to reconnoiter and confirm the flanking movement. Stirling and Stephen were to move into a blocking position at the Birmingham Meeting House, two miles beyond Jones Ford, and check Howe's flanking column. Greene, Sullivan, and Wayne were to prepare to cross the river and smash Knyphausen. It was now about noon.

At this point a message arrived from Sullivan at Brinton's Ford:

Since I sent you the message by Major Morris I saw some of the Militia who

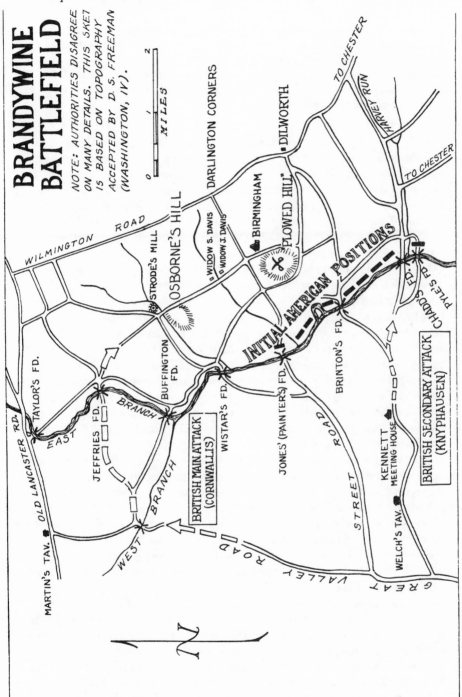

BRANDYWINE BATTLEFIELD

NOTE: AUTHORITIES DISAGREE ON MANY DETAILS. THIS SKETCH IS BASED ON TOPOGRAPHY ACCEPTED BY D. S. FREEMAN (WASHINGTON, IV).

MILES

TO CHESTER

HARVEY RUN

TO CHESTER

DARLINGTON CORNERS

DILWORTH

"PLOWED HILL"

BIRMINGHAM

WIDOW S. DAVIS

WIDOW J. DAVIS

INITIAL AMERICAN POSITIONS

OSBORNE'S HILL

STRODE'S MILL

WILMINGTON ROAD

CHADD'S FD.

PYLE'S FD.

BRITISH SECONDARY ATTACK (KNYPHAUSEN)

BRINTON'S FD.

BUFFINGTON FD.

BRANCH

EAST

JEFFRIES FD.

WISTAR'S FD.

TAYLOR'S FD.

OLD LANCASTER RD.

BRITISH MAIN ATTACK (CORNWALLIS)

JONES' (PAINTER'S) FD.

WEST BRANCH

KENNETT MEETING HOUSE

STREET ROAD

MARTIN'S TAV.

WELCH'S TAV.

GREAT VALLEY ROAD

N

© Mark Boatner, III, *Encyclopedia of the American Revolution*, David McKay Co., Inc.

came in this morning from a tavern called Martins on the forks of the Brandywine. The one who told me, said that he had come from thence to Welches Tavern and had heard nothing of the Enemy above the forks of the Brandywine
and is confident that [sic] are not in that Quarters. So that Colonel Hazen's Information must be wrong. I have sent to the Quarter to know whether there is
any foundation for the Report. . . .

   The information came from the Pennsylvania militia officer, Major Spear,
and it may be that he himself brought Sullivan's dispatch to Washington. This
might explain why Washington believed this report in the face of those of
Hazen and Ross. What Spear did not make clear, and what Washington failed
to perceive because of his vague knowledge of the neighborhood was that
Martin's Tavern was not "on the forks" of the Brandywine, that is, at Buffington's Ford, but three miles up the West Branch and a mile above Trimble's
Ford where Howe and Cornwallis had turned east. Howe's column was probably at Trimble's Ford about the time that Spear reported to Sullivan. Spear's
information was undoubtedly correct. But neither Washington nor Sullivan
asked the crucial question: *When?* When had Spear made his ride, and at what
time had he intersected Howe's presumed route? The British column had covered a huge circuit of ten miles, crossing the West Branch at Trimble's Ford
and continuing east to Jeffries' Ford which it reached about 2:00 p.m. Spear
had evidently ridden from Martin's Tavern past Trimble's Ford early in the
morning. He then continued downstream, checking each ford as he went until
he arrived at Welch's Tavern. There had been some fog earlier in the day
which might have obscured sound as well as sight of the British from Spear as
he moved along the river east of the Great Valley Road.
   Washington's lapse was understandable, if unfortunate. What was not
understandable was why he credited the report of a militia officer (who knew
nothing of the tactical situation or the troop dispositions) and refused to believe
the reports of two experienced Continental officers, one of whom had actually
skirmished with the British column.
   But Washington concluded that Howe's entire force faced him across the
Brandywine. Previous orders must be countermanded. Greene and Sullivan were to halt their movements and pull back to the high ground above the
creek. Stirling and Stephen should halt where they were and be ready once
more to support the center and right.
   Whether there were other reports seeming to confirm Spear or not, there
was one that contradicted him. About 2:00 in the afternoon an excited man
named Thomas Cheney arrived at headquarters. The big, black-eyed farmer
shouldered Washington's aides aside and insisted on seeing the commander
in chief. The army, he told Washington, was nearly surrounded. He himself
had seen a huge column on the eastern side of the Brandywine. Washington
refused to believe him, but he seems to have been doubtful enough to start
off to see for himself. At this moment a dispatch arrived from Bland who had at

last discovered the enemy north of the Birmingham Meeting House. A message from Sullivan confirmed the bad news. Washington ordered Stephen and Stirling to resume their march at once. Sullivan was sent in support and given overall command of the right wing.[10]

Sullivan immediately took the road and soon met Hazen coming down from Wistar's Ford. For the first time the division commander learned the full import of the contradictory reports, and the fact that he was faced with an enemy who was in great strength. Hurriedly he pressed on toward the Birmingham Meeting House where Stirling and Stephen were already in position. In his haste Sullivan overshot, for as he deployed his troops into line he found the other two divisions to his right and rear defending a strong position on a plowed hill. Only the fact that Cornwallis insisted on resting his men for a full hour after their seventeen mile march allowed Sullivan to come up. His appearance was the signal for the British to go into action. Cornwallis attacked toward the American right, causing Stephen and Stirling to shift their positions and further disrupting Sullivan's attempt to form on Stirling's left. Despite the confusion the American position on the hill overlooking the Meeting House held for nearly three-quarters of an hour. But Sullivan's men never got their line stabilized and under the pressure of the British assault the division broke and began to retreat in confusion.

Washington now made the decision which may well have saved his army. He ordered Maxwell and Wayne to fend off Knyphausen who was now advancing to the attack across the Brandywine. He sent Greene's division hurrying north to stem the disaster on the right, and followed them himself to be present at the critical point. As Greene's van, George Weedon's 3rd Virginia brigade, neared the Meeting House they met Sullivan's men retreating in disorder. Weedon's men calmly opened ranks to let the fugitives through, then closed and threw a hard check into the British advance. The fighting was violent and chaotic, and the tangle of American formations dictated a withdrawal southward to Chester. But the combined efforts of the American divisions had checked Cornwallis for the better part of two hours. Although he was in the thick of the battle, Washington was untouched. Young Lafayette got a bullet in the leg but continued at Washington's side, helping to rally and steady the troops.

The battle became almost as confusing to the British as to the Americans. Said one officer, "Describe the battle. 'Twas not like those of Covent Gardens or Drury Lane. . . . There was a most infernal fire of cannon and musquetry. Most incessant shouting, 'Incline to the right! Incline to the left! Halt! Charge!' etc. The balls plowing up the ground. The trees cracking over one's head. The branches riven with artillery. The leaves falling as in the autumn by grapeshot. . . . The misters on both sides showed conduct."

At Chadd's Ford Wayne and Maxwell fought a stubborn holding action, but they were hopelessly overmatched. "The enemy's [American] left flank began to fall back, and we took the battery. Our regiments, which pushed across one by one, gained one height after another, from which the enemy withdrew. They withstood one severe attack behind some houses and ditches. . . . Had not darkness favored their retreat we might have come into possession of much artillery, munitions and horses." But Wayne had done his job, holding off Knyphausen until the retreating army could pass to the south.[11]

The aftermath of the battle found many of Washington's formations badly disorganized. The roads along which the soldiers retreated were jammed, men separated from their commands, blundering along in and out of the ranks of regiments who were trying to keep their own troops in order. But there was little panic, none of the blind flight that had followed Long Island and Kip's Bay.

Not until midnight when the army reached Chester did officers bring some sort of order out of the chaos. Morning muster on the 12th seemed to indicate that losses in the battle had been heavy, but as the day passed more and more men straggled into camp. General Greene set the losses at between 1,200 and 1,300 men, killed, wounded and missing, slightly more than ten percent of Washington's force. The British lost 575. But the most significant aspect of the defeated army was its equanimity. Washington reported to Congress, "Notwithstanding the misfortune of the day, I am happy to find the troops in good spirits. . . ." Nor was this wishful thinking. Captain Enoch Anderson of Haslet's Delawares observed that "there was not a dispairing look nor did I hear a discouraging word. . . ." 'Come, boys, we shall do better another time,' sounded throughout the little army." Congress itself took heart—at least to the extent of voting thirty hogsheads of rum to be dispensed to the soldiers.

Perhaps the best proof was the fact that within two days the army had pulled itself together, crossed the Schuylkill to Germantown, and stood once more between Howe and the capital, its commander ready for a fight.[12]

THE CAPITAL FALLS

Philadelphia lies at the tip of a peninsula bounded on the east by the Delaware river and on the west by the Schuylkill. The latter was fordable in several places but the former was not. Washington, encamped at Germantown, five miles north of the city, was faced with a difficult problem. On the one hand he was still determined to defend the capital. On the other, his principal supply depots had been established outside the capital so that the priceless stores would not be lost along with the city. In fact, it is probable that Washington never intended to defend Philadelphia at the risk of a defeat that would leave him pinned against the Delaware with no line of retreat. Nor must he allow Howe to get too far to the north between him and the stores, the nearest of which was at Reading. In short, to move northwest from Germantown to cover his supplies would expose the capital. To take a strong position before Philadelphia was to uncover the route to Reading. Washington therefore concluded that he must once more seek out Howe and attack in order to gain the initiative. On September 14th he led the army back across the Schuylkill at Swede's Ford (modern Norristown) and advanced along the Lancaster Road, throwing out Wayne and Maxwell as an advance guard.[13]

Howe had spent four days tidying up after the battle of September 11 and was now once more on the road. On the 16th the two armies came within sight of each other and occupied adjacent heights. At this moment a northeast gale of unusual violence struck the two armies. The driving, soaking rain "came down so hard that in a few moments we were drenched and sank in mud up to our calves."

So the two armies faced each other unable to fire a shot. If the British generals considered an attack with the bayonet, the gusting northeast wind which drove sheets of rain into the faces of Howe's men discouraged the notion. Washington was forced to withdraw because the inadequate cartridge boxes his troops carried could not protect ammunition against such a deluge. Four hundred thousand rounds of powder were ruined.

The nearest ammunition depot was at Reading Furnace (modern Warwick) twenty-one miles away. The army had left its baggage east of the Schuylkill so, hungry, soaked, and as usual badly shod, the army slogged off in the rain (Colonel Alexander Hamilton was sent to Philadelphia to requisition shoes but the merchants hid them against the day when they could sell them for British gold). After replenishing their cartridge boxes at the Furnace the troops turned back toward Philadelphia, and by the 19th Washington was again between Howe and the capital. The soldiers had marched fifty-two miles in a little more than forty-eight hours. Warned by Washington, the Continental Congress had packed its records and evacuated the city, moving briefly to Lancaster before settling in at York.[14]

Washington detached Mad Anthony Wayne west of the Schuylkill to screen the army's movements. Wayne attempted to conceal his little force near Paoli Tavern, hoping to ambush some unwary British detachment. Whether enemy scouts discovered him or whether his presence was reported by Loyalists, the hunter became the prey. On the night of September 20–21 Wayne's sleeping men were surprised by Major General Charles Grey at the head of five British regiments. Grey ordered a bayonet attack with unloaded muskets. Wayne's sentries got off warning shots but the redcoats were into the American camp before the troops could form. The "massacre" cost Wayne 150 men killed and wounded and was widely reported as the slaughter of defenseless men. But the fact was that Wayne was caught napping. And the "English brutes" were careful to see that forty of the American wounded were left in homes in the neighborhood to be cared for (Mad Anthony was humiliated and his resentment smoldered until he vented it on the British garrison at Stony Point two years later).

But all this maneuvering and fighting was to no purpose. On the day after the fight at Paoli Howe turned north toward Reading Furnace. Washington moved northwest to guard his stores and in the night Howe countermarched, crossing the Schuylkill and made for Philadelphia. By a simple feint Howe had again outmaneuvered his opponent. Four days later Cornwallis' van entered the city, half deserted because not only Congress but most of the Patriot residents had taken a hasty leave. Howe's long delays, both before and after the Brandywine, had allowed the removal of all military stores and other public property. The British and their German allies saw "a lovely city of considerable size . . . laid out with parallel streets. The public squares are beautiful. For the most part, ordinary houses are moderately large and built of brick in the Dutch style. Classical architecture and its embellishments are met with only in the churches and in a few public buildings. . . ."[15]

Ever since the battle of September 11 Washington had been calling for reinforcements. General Putnam, guarding the Hudson Highlands, was ordered to send 2,500 Continentals, and when General Alexander McDougall arrived with only 900 Washington lashed out at "Old Put." He was directed to send 1,600 more men without delay. "That you may not hesitate about complying with this order, you are to consider it as peremptory and not to be dispensed with." General William Smallwood was urged to bring up his Maryland militia and harass Howe's rear as he made for Philadelphia. President Thomas Wharton of Pennsylvania had already called out additional regiments of Pennsylvania militia and General Philemon Dickinson brought 1,200 men to Washington's camp, about thirty miles north of Philadelphia. By the 27th of September with the arrival of 1,000 additional Continentals from Putnam, Washington's army was at full strength, nearly 11,000 rank and file.

The next day came glorious news. Burgoyne's army had been repulsed at Freeman's Farm on September 19. Dispatches from General Gates to Congress—but not to the commander in chief—informed Washington, with some exaggeration, of "the total ruin of Burgoyne." Washington ordered the soldiers paraded, cannon to fire a thirteen-gun salute and an issue of a gill of rum to every man in the ranks.

With the cloud of worry and doubt about the northern invasion removed Washington was now free to set in motion a strategy he had been contemplating for some days. Howe had indeed taken Philadelphia, but could not this be turned to the American advantage? For in all the marching and countermarching one important fact had not escaped Washington's notice. Lord Howe's fleet was still down the Delaware from the city and must penetrate the river defenses and obstructions erected by the Americans to block its passage. Here was a great opportunity. ". . . Genl. Howe can neither support his Army in Philadelphia, if he is cut off from Communication with his ships, neither can he make good a retreat should any accident befall him."[16]

Washington had already ordered Colonel Samuel Smith to take a contingent of the crack 1st Maryland to strengthen Fort Mifflin, a fortification on an island in the middle of the Delaware. On the Jersey shore at Red Banks was Fort

Mercer, occupied by Rhode Island Continentals and New Jersey militia under Colonel Christopher Greene.

In Paris Doctor Benjamin Franklin, head of the American diplomatic mission in Paris, heard the news of the defeat at the Brandywine and the fall of the capital. He did not join in the lamentations of the Americans on his staff. Instead, the venerable philosopher pointed out that "instead of saying Sir William Howe had taken Philadelphia, it would be more proper to say, Philadelphia has taken Sir William Howe." As September drew to a close Washington advanced his headquarters closer to the capital and watched for an opportunity to prove Dr. Franklin's point.[17]

Sir William Howe's southern strategy had turned out to be a debacle. He had expected two results. The fall of their capital city would, he thought, discourage the Americans and sap their will to resist. But the capture of Philadelphia had been dreaded for so long that the actual event made comparatively little impact on American morale. Wrote one observer, ". . . I am satisfied at all times, that the loss of a battle or of a town will detract nothing, finally, from the Americans; and the acquisition of victories and territories will serve only to weaken General Howe's army, and to accelerate the period when America shall establish her freedom and independence. . . ."[18]

The second objective had been to lend support to a Loyalist rising and thus pave the way for the conquest of the middle states. It was this conviction fostered by men like Loyalist Joseph Galloway, who were undoubtedly over-enthusiastic in their exaggerated reports of the sentiments of Pennsylvania, that led Howe to abandon Burgoyne. Only when it was too late to assist the northern army did Howe discover the reality of a hostile or indifferent populace.

The campaign had once again demonstrated Howe's singular indolence. For six months he had corresponded with Germain, proposing and modifying a plan of campaign. Yet when the time came to execute he seemed to flinch from plunging into action, making one impromptu maneuver after another, and finally leaving himself no alternative but the hollow conquest of Philadelphia.

Yet this indolence and indecision seemed to vanish once Sir William reached the battlefield. At the Brandywine he acted with a promptness and certitude that brought his army a victory, as on every occasion when he himself was in personal command.

Washington, by contrast, had demonstrated a considerable talent for overall strategy. His movements in the face of the bewildering confusion of Howe's movements were sound and only at the end of the Pennsylvania campaign had he been outmaneuvered. But on the battlefield Washington still showed his lack of experience, his inability to analyze a situation and respond quickly to changing conditions. Above all, he was inclined to ask too much from his commanders and expect too much from his men.

The most notable development of the campaign was in the quality of the American army. The Brandywine has often been compared with Long Island, since Howe had flanked Sullivan on both occasions. But at the Brandywine the reconnaissance had been good—only the analysis of it at headquarters had failed. And even though errors were made Sullivan had come very close to retrieving the situation on the right. The men had fought well and although they finally broke, it was not the kind of blind, disruptive panic that had so often marred the soldiers' performance. The conduct of Wayne and Maxwell at Chadd's Ford at the end of the day received little notice (then or later in the history books). Faced by Knyphausen's attacking force which was twice as large as his own, Wayne fought off the British division for two hours, that is, as Major Baurmeister testifies, until "darkness favored their retreat." And in the aftermath what was remarkable was not the number of desertions (mostly militia), but the number who finally came straggling into camp at Chester, twenty-four and even forty-eight hours later. Three days after the battle Washington was able to write, "Our Troops have not lost their spirits and I am in hopes we shall soon have an Opportunity of Compensating for the disaster we have sustained. . . . We brought the army to this place [German-town] . . . and are just beginning our march to return towards the Enemy." The Continentals had developed a certain toughness of spirit which is the mark of veteran soldiers.[19]

TWELVE

Saratoga:
The Forlorn Hope

ON THE UPPER HUDSON THE AUTUMN AIR WAS BRINGING A CHILL TO BURGOYNE'S army. Parties of Americans hovered just beyond the lines, and "not a night passed without firing, and sometimes concerted attacks on our picquets. . . . By being habituated to fire, our soldiers became indifferent to it, and were capable of eating and sleeping when it was very near them. . . ." It may have been so. But as the men shivered in their blankets surely their sleep was troubled by the howling of wolves, drawn to the battle field by the odor of corpses hastily buried in their shallow graves.[1]

THE HUDSON HIGHLANDS

On September 21 as the British worked at entrenching their positions they were alarmed by the sudden booming of guns from the American lines. Hastily the redcoats stood to arms but there was no movement from the enemy. Not until several days later did Burgoyne learn that the firing was in celebration of the news that troops commanded by Benjamin Lincoln had won victories on Lake Champlain.

By mid-September Lincoln had persuaded between 1,500 and 2,000 militia to come in to his headquarters at Pawlet in the Hampshire Grants (although they refused to go west of the Hudson). He dispatched three regiments to attack Skenesboro and Ticonderoga. Colonel John Brown made a surprise attack on the Lake George portage south of Ticonderoga and drove in the German and British outposts although he could not dislodge General Powell from Ticonderoga itself. But he captured 300 of the enemy, freed 100 American prisoners, and seized 200 batteaux and a sloop. Another American force attacked Mount Independence with indifferent success. Brown then attempted to seize a British post at Diamond Island on Lake Champlain but was driven off. The Americans also occupied Skenesboro after it had been abandoned by the British. In themselves these actions were of little importance but the fact that small detachments could roam at will behind the British made it clear that the road back to Canada was very nearly closed.

So Burgoyne was forced to rely on the slender hope that Clinton might somehow extricate him. While he waited the British commander fortified his camp. On the right farthest from the river at the northwestern edge of Freeman's Farm the German grenadiers under Breymann were posted in a redoubt. They were supported on the left by another redoubt manned by the light infantry under the Earl of Balcarres. Next came the main line of British troops extending toward the river where Burgoyne constructed a strong work called the Great Redoubt, which guarded headquarters and the army's stores.[2]

Sir Henry Clinton, left in command of New York city after General Howe put to sea, had spent two months in virtual idleness, although his inactivity was not accompanied by peace of mind. His garrison force of 7,700 men, half of them Loyalists, was barely sufficient to guard the city surrounded as it was by "an extended coast, of nearly two hundred miles altogether." He beat off a token attack on Staten Island by the Americans in mid-August and Clinton himself sallied into New Jersey in a brief and ineffective show of British force. But mostly Sir Henry waited. He waited for news from Burgoyne who had told him on August 6 that he would be in Albany by the 23rd. News of Bennington worried him and no news from Howe worried him even more.

By the middle of September Clinton became restless. For some time he had had his eye on the Hudson Highlands forty miles to the north. Here two forts, Montgomery and Clinton, guarded the approaches to the upper Hudson. General Israel Putnam commanded an American force of about 1,500 men at Peekskill on the eastern side of the river opposite the forts. Although Clinton had no idea of penetrating to Albany or even of occupying the Highlands he did believe that he might make a swift ascent up the river, drive off Putnam, and destroy the two forts. Two things were necessary, more troops and an excuse to leave New York, since the defense of the city was his primary responsibility.

It was this latter that inspired the letter that Burgoyne received on September 21. If Washington was now preoccupied to the south and Burgoyne asked for help, surely Clinton could not be faulted for responding and furthering the ministry's intention to open communication with the northern army. So the inquiry as to whether General Burgoyne might "be in want of some little diversion" was designed to elicit a request for help, furnishing thereby the excuse Sir Henry needed to attack the Hudson forts.

It took ten days for Clinton's message to reach Burgoyne. The country between Saratoga and New York swarmed with suspicious militiamen, and several British couriers travelling between the two commands were caught and hanged as spies. Each dispatch was sent by two couriers and sometimes three in order to make sure of delivery. If the dispatches were of special importance the messengers were officers. By September 29 Clinton had Burgoyne's answer and its tone of urgency was underscored by the officer messenger who reported that less than thirty days' provisions remained and that the line of retreat to Canada was threatened.[3]

Five days earlier a reinforcement of 1700 men had arrived in New York from England, providing Clinton with the additional troops he needed. For once a British commander wasted no time. By October 3 Sir Henry had embarked 3,000 men and two days later he landed at Verplanck's Point, three miles below Peekskill. Putnam took to the hills frantically seeking a defensive position from which he could defend against the superior British force. Clinton's landing was a feint and its effect was exactly what he had hoped for. The troops were reembarked and, under cover of a fog, landed on the west bank at Stony Point. Marching inland through the rugged hills he split his force and launched simultaneous attacks on the two forts. By October 8 Forts Clinton and Montgomery were overrun and the British were in possession of the Highlands.

Sir Henry had every right to be pleased with himself. He had sustained virtually no losses, his action had been a model of neatness and daring precision, and he had delivered his promised diversion. But it was not enough. Captain Alexander Campbell brought news from Burgoyne that his army was only 5,000 strong, that Gates had cut his line of retreat to Ticonderoga, and that militia pouring into the American camps had almost doubled the numbers of the enemy. (Now that the Americans sensed that Gates' army was a winner, the militia turned out in droves.) Burgoyne still believed that he could force his way to Albany (this may have been inserted for the benefit of the Americans should his dispatch be intercepted), but suggested three alternatives: attack Gates again; remain where he was; or retreat to Lake Champlain. To Clinton's amazement Burgoyne asked for "most explicit orders" as to which course he was to pursue.

It was obvious that the northern commander was desperate and looking for someone on whom he could lay at least a share of the responsibility for his situation. Having previously contended that his orders gave him no latitude but a direct advance to Albany, Burgoyne now asked for modifications from a man whom he knew was not authorized to give them. His suggestion that he should have been supported from New York was justified but he had known for weeks that Howe had gone to Pennsylvania and had never before intimated that he needed help to reach Albany.

Clinton's reply was coldly formal. "Sir Henry Clinton cannot presume to give any orders to General Burgoyne. General Burgoyne could not suppose that Sir Henry Clinton had any idea of penetrating to Albany with the small force he mentioned in his last letter." Yet Clinton, irritated as he was, would not abandon his friend. The dramatic success of his expedition led him to hope that if Burgoyne could reach Albany Clinton might be able to push through a relief expedition. His formal refusal to take responsibility for Burgoyne's action was followed by a series of encouraging personal messages: "I sincerely hope that this little success . . . may facilitate your operations;" on the 10th he noted that Sir James Wallace was taking a squadron up river; "the Commodore and I [will] do our utmost to force a communication . . . and supply . . . provisions." Not a single message reached Burgoyne.[4]

In the American camps recruits were finally beginning to swell the ranks. Most were fed into the existing regiments increasing their strength by about thirty percent. By the first week in October Gates had over 7,000 men present and fit for duty at Bemis Heights. Stark had finally returned with 1,000 New Hampshire men and was sent up the eastern side of the Hudson to threaten the British rear. Lincoln and Seth Warner also brought their men in.

It was inevitable that the uneasy truce between those two towering egos, Gates and Arnold, would eventually erupt. The occasion was Gates' report of the action of September 19 which did not mention either Arnold or the brigades of Poor and Learned which he had commanded. The victory, said Gates, was due "entirely to the valour of the Rifle Regiment and the corps of Light Infantry under the command of Colonel Morgan."

It was, intentional or not, a gratuitous insult to Arnold. Gates, a regular army man, knew that after such a victory a commander was normally either generous in his praise for everyone who had participated or omitted reference to any individuals, thereby implying that the glory was shared by all. Arnold was infuriated. He exploded into Gates' headquarters and vented his wrath in no uncertain terms. Gates replied with equal asperity, and it may be presumed that the volume, if not the words, of the altercation was heard for some distance in the vicinity of the commanding general's quarters. The quarrel brought into the open the resentment that Schuyler's friends had felt towards Gates ever since August 19. Richard Varick and Henry Brockholst Livingston, former aides to Schuyler who had attached themselves to Arnold, added fuel to the fiery controversy, and so did Gates' adjutant, Colonel Wilkinson. Arnold retired to his tent and then erupted in a blast of correspondence to Gates, the tone of which was that his gallant services were not appreciated by the commander of the Northern Department. He called on Gates to explain why he had been treated "with affront and indignity, in a public manner" and demanded "an opportunity of vindicating my conduct." He ended by offering to resign.

To his amazement and considerable discomfiture Gates acquiesced and issued a pass for Arnold and his aides to go through the lines. Arnold, his bluff called, declared his intention "to sacrifice my feelings . . . to the public good and continue in the army at this critical juncture, when my country needs every support." Gates allowed him to remain but he relieved Arnold of the command of the left wing and replaced him with Benjamin Lincoln. Colonel Wilkinson, despite the fact that he was a Gates partisan, may have had the last word. It was, he said, "traced to official presumption on the one side, and an arrogant spirit and impatience of command on the other."

The source of all the trouble, Philip Schuyler, had all the while remained at Albany, using his quartermaster's talents to keep supplies moving up the river to Bemis Heights. By the end of September Gates' command had full cartridge boxes and plenty of provisions.[5]

BURGOYNE CASTS THE DIE

In the British camp the soldiers went on half rations October 3. His outposts constantly harassed, his soldiers threadbare and shivering, his supply line closed, Burgoyne's situation was rapidly becoming intolerable. Anxiously he waited for word from Clinton but no couriers came up from the south. His efforts to reconnoiter Gates' position to get some idea of the size and deployment of the American army was unsuccessful. Although some of his wounded had recovered there was still a sizeable hospital which precluded rapid movement. Without really knowing, he sensed that the enemy was growing stronger every day.

On October 4 Burgoyne called his first council of war. It appeared that Gentleman Johnny was about to take a high-risk gamble for big stakes. To Phillips, Fraser, and Riedesel he proposed another attack. This time he would leave only 800 men to guard the baggage and boats. With 4,000 men he planned to strike again at the American left in an attempt to gain the flank and rear of the fortifications on Bemis Heights. It was a bold and audacious plan but it was also a desperate one. Yet considering the cold courage of his infantry and the cool efficiency of his gunners one wonders what would have been the outcome if Burgoyne had managed to throw the full weight of his force in against the Americans.

His subordinates were appalled. To leave the entire store of provisions under such light guard was to invite its destruction. Even if the attack succeeded it would leave the army separated from its supply base and the river. Its success depended on the ability of the British not only to flank a force nearly twice its size but to drive it into disorder. Burgoyne's generals persuaded him to postpone the decision. The next day Riedesel proposed a more limited action, a reconnaissance in force to test the American left; ". . . if it were impossible to get in the enemy's rear in one day, it would be more adviseable to recross the Hudson and again occupy their old position on the Battenkill [Fort Edward]." Burgoyne at first refused to discuss any plan involving a retrograde movement, but he was finally persuaded to "undertake another great reconnoitering expedition against the enemy's left wing to ascertain . . . whether it would be advisable to attack him. . . ." If the results were negative it was agreed to retreat to Fort Edward. The attacking force would consist of the 24th Regiment, Balcarres' light infantry, Acland's grenadiers, the flank companies of Riedesel's command, and Breymann's jägers. The total numbers of this force would be 1,500 men.[6]

This decision risked both too much and too little. To repeat the maneuver of

September 19 with less than half as many men served no purpose other than as a hollow gesture of defiance. Burgoyne's original plan, even though the odds against it were astronomical, promised dazzling rewards. But by this time "the Gamester," as Gates called him, had lost his gambler's nerve. He settled for the "reconnoitering expedition."

Late in the morning of October 7 Burgoyne, accompanied by all three of his major generals, led his reconnaissance force out of the British lines. Moving south across the western edge of Freeman's Farm the British and Germans moved to within less than a mile of the American position on Bemis Heights. Of the ten guns accompanying the column two were 12-pounders. About one-thirty in the afternoon Burgoyne halted his column and deployed into line with Balcarres and the light infantry on the right, the German flank companies under Lieutenant Colonel Speth in the center, and Acland's grenadiers on the left. For the next hour and a half the command remained in position, strange behavior for a force whose purpose was "to ascertain definitely his [Gates'] position and whether it would be advisable to attack him." Nothing could be seen of the American troops or their fortified line. It was as if Burgoyne had thrust out this slender force and invited the enemy to attack it. If this was indeed his intention the Americans soon obliged.

The British movement was observed almost as soon as it began and reported to Gates' headquarters. Colonel Wilkinson was sent forward to locate the enemy and found them just as they were forming their line. According to Wilkinson, the redcoats then "sat down in double ranks with their arms between their legs and I soon after observed several officers, mounted on the top of a cabin . . . endeavoring to reconnoiter our left." When this was reported to Gates he ordered out Morgan.

The "Old Waggoner" noted the exposed British position and moved to make a wide circle of the enemy right. Enoch Poor directed his brigade against the enemy left and Learned led his men against the center. This would bring a total of 2,100 men against Burgoyne's 1,500. Before the day was over Gates would commit another 3,000 to 4,000 men, but it was the three brigades of the left wing that bore the brunt of the fighting.[7]

About three o'clock the first elements of Learned's brigade, which had the shortest distance to go, collided with the Germans of Burgoyne's center but did not press its attack. Within half an hour Poor's men struck at Acland's grenadiers across a shallow ravine. The grenadiers met the attack with musket and artillery fire. Their volleys, directed downhill may have been high for they failed to check the Americans. The New Hampshire men drove forward up the slope and the grenadiers fell back under the pressure. Acland, galloping furiously among his men trying to reform the line, went down, shot in both legs. The fight raged back and forth but the grenadiers were finally overwhelmed and broken. Wilkinson rode up in time to see Colonel Cilley astride a British gun, shouting with excitement; a surgeon dressing the wounds of a British officer and exclaiming, "Wilkinson, I have dipt my hands in British

SECOND BATTLE of SARATOGA

N

SARATOGA. 6 MILES

SWORD'S HOUSE

GREAT RAVINE

HUDSON RIVER

BRIDGE of BOATS

FT. NEILSON

Gates
BEMIS
HEIGHTS

Scale in Miles

0   1/4   1/2   1

American Troops — Routes
① Morgan ② Learned ③ Poor

British Troops — Routes →
❶ Balcarres' Red. ❷ Breymann's Red.

ALBANY. 25 MILES

Lynn Montross, *The Story of the Continental Army*, Harper and Row, Publishers, Inc.

blood;" a fourteen-year old lad aiming his musket at Acland as he lay helpless in the angle of a rail fence. Two of his soldiers had tried to carry the burly major to the rear, but he had finally been left behind and was taken off by the Americans.

Meantime Learned's Massachusetts men had attacked the center. The 300 Brunswickers cooly beat back the five regiments of the American brigade. Captain Pausch's battery, slightly in advance of his line, poured salvo after salvo into the advancing ranks. He emptied three wagon loads of ammunition and his guns became too hot to touch. His crew was reduced to four gunners and a single subaltern but Pausch still fired his 6-pounders. After nearly an hour the Germans began to feel the pressure on their left as the Americans exploited the flank exposed by the retreat of Acland's men.

By this time Morgan had delivered his assault on Balcarres' light infantry and the 24th Regiment. Since Morgan was almost directly west of the British position and threatening to turn it Balcarres was forced to refuse his flank. This in turn put severe pressure on the Brunswickers. Seeing the danger Simon Fraser rode forward to rally the British on the right. He directed part of the 24th to the support of the Germans in an effort to restore the line. At this point Morgan ordered his riflemen to direct their fire at Fraser. Tradition has it that an Irishman named Tim Murphy posted himself in a tree and shot Fraser out of his saddle. The fall of the veteran Scot ended the British resistance on the right. Unsupported on both sides, the Germans in the center collapsed. Pausch, forward of his line, "looked back towards the position still held as I supposed, by our German infantry, under whose protection I, too, intended to retreat—but not a man was to be seen." The tough Hessian captain barely escaped capture, but he brought off one of his guns. In his report to Germain (Oct. 20) Burgoyne did not mention the Germans except to note that they occupied the center. It was perhaps too much to expect that Gentleman Johnny would acknowledge that the Brunswickers held their part of the line until the collapse of the British on both flanks compelled them to retire.[8]

Burgoyne ordered a withdrawal to the right wing of his main position at Freeman's Farm where he hoped to make a stand at the field works called Breymann's and Balcarres' redoubts. The American commanders probably would have broken off the fight at this point since they knew that headquarters was committed to the defensive. But at this moment a short, compact man on a big bay horse came storming onto the field. It was Benedict Arnold.

Arnold had been alternately sulking and raging at headquarters ever since Morgan's troops had marched out to battle. He was without a command but he could not resist the music of the gunfire. Whether, as one account has it, he secured Gates' reluctant permission, or whether he simply mounted and rode to the front with one of Gates' aides in pursuit, he reached Learned's brigade as the British began their retreat.

Arnold rounded up some of Learned's regiments and placed himself at their head as the pursuit reached the British main line. Urging the Massachusetts troops forward Arnold struck at Balcarres' redoubt, but the light infantry did not budge and the attackers were thrown back. Arnold then shifted to the left, picked up some men from Morgan's corps, and drove between Balcarres and Breymann, routing a force of Tories and Canadians who held the gap between the two redoubts. He then turned his attention to the log breastworks of Breymann's redoubt. Furiously Arnold rammed his men against the Germans and swept into the enemy position. Breymann was shot down (some said by his own men) and at almost the same moment Arnold's horse fell and rolled, breaking its rider's leg. In the gathering darkness the attack spent itself. The tired men returned triumphantly to Bemis Heights bearing their disabled general, six captured guns, and 240 prisoners.[9]

Baroness Riedesel, whose breakfast that morning had been disrupted by the sudden departure of her husband and his staff, had nonetheless prepared a dinner party for that evening. But "in place of the guests who were to have dined with me, they brought in to me, upon a litter, poor General Erazer (one of my expected guests), mortally wounded. Our dining table, which was already spread, was taken away, and in its place they fixed a bed for the general." By nightfall when the rest of the army returned "the entry and the other rooms were filled with the sick. . . ." The little baroness spent a fitful night and early in the morning General Fraser died in the adjoining room.

In the battle of October 7 the British lost about 600 killed, wounded, and taken prisoner; the American losses were about 150. The effect on Burgoyne's command was devastating. Altogether, since Ticonderoga (where he had left a garrison of 900 British and German troops) he had lost 730 of his regulars killed or taken prisoner. Riedesel's command had lost 750. On October 8 Burgoyne had over 700 wounded and sick in his hospital. Thus of the 7,250 infantry and artillerymen who had left Canada he now had no more than 4,100 men present and fit for duty. Losses in the officer corps were especially severe. The British had lost 50 officers dead or captured including General Fraser, Major Acland, and Burgoyne's senior aide, Sir Francis Clarke. Riedesel's command had lost 40, including Colonel Baum and Colonel Breymann.

On the night of October 8 a heavy rain began to fall. At nine o'clock Burgoyne's command began to move north toward the Fishkill and the little village of Saratoga.[10]

THE SURRENDER

At the Highlands of the Hudson Sir Henry Clinton refused to abandon Burgoyne. He had still not received any word from Howe as to the situation in Pennsylvania but he felt that he had enough troops to hold the Highlands position as long as it seemed likely that he could assist the northern army. At about this time General Pigot, commanding the British forces in Rhode Island, offered to make 1,000 men available to New York. For Clinton this represented unlooked-for abundance. He hurried to Manhattan and ordered six months provisions for 5,000 men loaded on transports. By October 13 he was back at the Highlands where he detached General Sir John Vaughan and 2,000 men, ordering them to feel their way toward Albany. Clinton was determined to leave no stone unturned in his attempt to open communications with Burgoyne.

His efforts were finally frustrated from two directions. From the north came word from Vaughan that the increasing difficulty of navigation made it impossible to go further up the river. American militia were beginning to join Putnam and there were now 6,000 of the enemy swarming along both banks of the Hudson. Vaughan was still forty-five miles from Albany. Clinton was nonetheless determined "to retain the footing we are now possessed of in the Highlands." But from Pennsylvania the long arm of his commander in chief reached out to frustrate even this hope. Although Howe had defeated Washington and was safely ensconced in Philadelphia he ordered Clinton "without delay" to detach 4,000 men and start them to Pennsylvania. Only if he were "on the eve of accomplishing some very material and essential stroke" was he to delay, and even in that event he was to allow only "a few days" before releasing the troops—"for what purpose, after all the victories we heard of, he best knows," remarked Sir Henry sourly.

Howe's insistence on immediate compliance is interesting as indirect evidence of his attitude toward Burgoyne's expedition. He actually sent two dispatches to Clinton, the first before and the second after he had received news of Burgoyne's precarious situation (i.e., the dispatch of September 21 and the officer who carried it, both of which Clinton had forwarded to Howe). Howe's second dispatch underscored the peremptory tone of the first. In other words, if Clinton were in the midst of an operation which would relieve pressure on Burgoyne he was to conclude it within a few days after which he must detach more than one third of his command. This would have forced Sir Henry to abandon any such operation and return to Manhattan, as it did. It hardly mattered. By October 17, the day Clinton received Howe's orders, Burgoyne was surrendering his army.[11]

The British retreat ground to a halt at Saratoga on October 10 after a number of delays. General Riedesel thought that a swift march to the Battenkill might have given the army time to cross the river and try for Fort George. On the 11th the column was completely bogged down by the rain and mud. The Americans had now not only occupied the east bank but had patrols west of the river between the British and Lake George.

The British came under almost constant fire not only from enemy muskets but from artillery. Baroness Riedesel and her children took shelter in the cellar of a house filled with wounded. As the American bombardment became heavier, cannon shot began to fall on the house and "threw us all into alarm. Many persons . . . threw themselves against the door [of the cellar]. My children were already under the cellar steps, and we should all have been crushed, if God had not given me the strength to place myself before the door, and with extended arms prevent all from coming in. Eleven cannon balls went through the house, and we could plainly hear them rolling over our heads."

Patrols and outposts skirmished constantly and "the army was under constant fire the whole day, both front and rear." Riedesel proposed abandoning the baggage and wounded and retreating up the west side of the Hudson, crossing above Fort Edward, and fighting through to Fort George. "Burgoyne, however, could not make up his mind that evening [the 11th], but allowed the precious moments to pass unimproved. . . . Every hour the position of the army grew more critical, and the prospect of salvation grew less and less."[12]

On October 12 Burgoyne called a council of war to which he invited Brigadiers Hamilton and Gall as well as the major generals. He noted that the American army was now estimated at 14,000 men. British boats and wagons had been almost entirely destroyed or captured, and even by cutting rations again the army could not last more than thirty days. He proposed three alternatives: forcing a passage northward, with or without baggage; attempting to fight southward to Albany; or staying where they were and waiting "for coming fortunate events." Riedesel reiterated his belief that without the encumbrance of baggage they could cut their way through to Fort George, and this was finally agreed to. A delay ensued while six days' rations were distributed among the troops. The task was completed about ten o'clock in the evening, but when Riedesel asked for the order to march he was told that the movement had been postponed. "That evening the retreat was possible. A movement of the enemy made it impossible the following day." Colonel Skene sardonically suggested that Burgoyne scatter his baggage "at proper distances and the militia will be so busy plundering that you and the troops will get clean off."[13]

The next day the Americans finally slammed the door on the escape route to the north. John Stark and his New Hampshire militia were finally persuaded to cross the Hudson and take a blocking position north of the Fishkill. Thousands of militia were now pouring into the American camps, some in organized regiments, some in platoons and companies, roaming the enemy flanks under no orders but their own (Wilkinson would report 18,000 three days later). Burgoyne called another council, this time including all the field officers. They were unanimously of the opinion that the army had no alternative but to surrender. A flag of truce was sent to Gates' headquarters.

There now began the intricate formalities of arranging surrender terms. Gates, a former British regular, went through the ritual, but beneath his air of triumph there were nagging worries. He had intercepted Clinton's messages to Burgoyne and he was aware of the threat to his rear. Moreover, Israel Putnam, panicked by Sir Henry's swift and overwhelming thrust, had sent exaggerated reports telling of defeat and disaster. So when Gates presented his terms to Captain Kingston he was not as confident as his bearing indicated. The American terms, which amounted to unconditional surrender, were rejected by Burgoyne who then made a counterproposal. The British would march out with "the honors of war," surrender their arms, and be returned to England "upon condition of not serving again in North America during the present contest." In other words, Burgoyne was avoiding surrender by asking that the army be paroled back to England where they could relieve other troops which could replace them. It was Burgoyne's last gamble, a magnificent bluff against long odds. And Gentleman Johnny saw his opponent fold. Gates accepted the terms. Although he had more reassuring news from Putnam and Governor George Clinton, he was still worried about the threat from the south. In accepting the terms Gates set a deadline. The acceptance must be complete by three o'clock on the 15th and the army must lay down its arms two hours later.

The alacrity with which Gates accepted the terms and the deadline gave Burgoyne food for thought. If he read the signs correctly Gates was worried about something. The British commander decided to push a little. He asked for a further delay so that the details of the "convention"—rather than surrender—could be worked out by representatives of the two commanders. Again Gates agreed. All day on the fifteenth the officers from both headquarters worked on the provisions and stipulations and by evening the terms were settled. The British would march out under arms; they would not surrender their colors or their equipment, only their shoulder arms and guns; they would be marched to Boston where they would be transported to England on parole.[14]

That night a Tory arrived at Burgoyne's headquarters. He brought news at last of Clinton's movement to the Highlands, and reported erroneously that a British advance corps was in Albany. Burgoyne called a council of war the next morning and announced the news to his officers. He proposed that the American terms be rejected and that they should hold out until help could arrive from the south. By a vote of fourteen to eight the officers decided that the terms of the convention had already been agreed to and that they could not honorably be repudiated. Even if the report was true the army could hold out only a few more days.

Burgoyne refused to accept the decision. He informed Gates' aide, Colonel Wilkinson, that he believed that large numbers of the Americans had left their camps. He demanded that a British representative be allowed to count the American troops in order to be assured that his army was hopelessly outnumbered.

But Gates' patience was at an end. Wilkinson was sent to announce that the negotiations were broken off. He did so and was returning to the American lines when he was called back. Gentleman Johnny had finally had his hand called. The British agreed to capitulate.

On the morning of October 17 the British and German soldiers of Burgoyne's army marched out of the mud and stench of their camp. The drums beat "The Grenadiers' March." The women straggled after their men as they moved past the silent ranks of the Americans to stack their arms. General Gates received General Burgoyne's sword and gallantly returned it.

A German soldier described the army that had defeated him and his comrades:

> . . . nature had formed all the fellows who stood in rank and file so slender, so handsome, so sinewy, that it was a pleasure to look at them, and we were all surprised at the sight of such finely built people. And their size! . . . [The soldiers] had their musket with bayonet affixed in hand, and their cartridge box or powder horn slung on their backs; they had their left hands on their hips and their right foot advanced slightly. . . . I must say in praise of the enemy regiments that there was not a man among them who showed the slightest sign of mockery, malicious delight, hate, or other insult; it seemed rather as if they wished to do us honor.

Philip Schuyler had come up from Albany. While Gates entertained Burgoyne, Phillips, and Riedesel, General Schuyler escorted Baroness Riedesel and her children to his tent where they had dinner. "Never," said the baroness, "have I eaten a better meal. I was content."[15]

On August 20 Burgoyne had complained of the fact that his orders left him no latitude, "being positive 'to force a junction with Sir William Howe.'" This ignored a clause in Germain's original instructions (delivered through Sir Guy Carleton) "that they [Burgoyne and St. Leger] act as exigencies may require and in such manner as they shall judge proper. . . ."

On October 20 Burgoyne, in his report to Germain, was still justifying his actions on the ground that he was bound by his orders, "that . . . a passage to Albany was the principle, the letter, and the spirit of my orders." On the same day he wrote to a friend, "If the State thought it necessary to devote a corps of troops for general purposes, it was no more within the General's duty to decline proceeding, upon motives of prudence . . . than it would be justifiable in a sergeant who heads a forlorn hope at the storm of a breach to recede because his destruction was probable—mine was a forlorn hope with this difference that it was not supported."[16]

THIRTEEN

Stalemate

To those who sought to compare Washington to the Roman general, Fabius, who carefully kept his army out of reach of the enemy, the weeks following the battle at Chadd's Ford posed a serious contradiction. For he continued to seek out the enemy and he called at least one council of war to suggest an attack on Philadelphia. The officers voted him down, ten to five. Yet Washington was convinced that "Gen'l Howe's Situation in Philadelphia will not be the most agreeable; for if his supplies can be stopped by Water, it may easily be done by land. To do both, shall be my utmost endeavor, and I am not yet without hope that the acquisition of Philadelphia may instead of his good fortune, prove his Ruin." It may well be that his pride was stung by the contrast between his own failure and Gates' repulse of Burgoyne on September 19, but he said only, "I am in hopes, it will not be long before we are in a situation to repair the consequences of our late ill-success, and give a more happy complexion to our affairs in this quarter."[1]

GERMANTOWN

By September 28 Washington had moved his command within twenty miles of Germantown. It was obvious that Howe was becoming concerned about his naval support from the fleet commanded by Lord Howe, for he had begun to send detachments to escort supplies that were landed below the river defenses and brought by wagon to the city. This was only a temporary expedient, which could provide neither the volume nor the security of a permanent winter supply line.

Howe's main force was encamped at Germantown, five miles north of Philadelphia. Intelligence reports indicated that the British troops were rather loosely deployed, their outposts just north of the village. Howe had erected no fortifications or entrenchments and most of his guns were in his artillery park rather than distributed with the regiments.[2]

All this convinced Washington that this was the opportunity he had been seeking. For the third time in less than a month he decided to attack. There is no record of a council of war and Washington did not refer to one in his report to Congress, saying only that "I communicated the Accounts to my General Officers, who were unanimously of the Opinion [a rare event in a council of war], that a favourable Opportunity offered to make an Attack upon the Troops, which were at and near Germantown." Washington's fighting blood was up, and it may be that he decided not to risk an adverse vote of a council, choosing to persuade the senior officers individually. On October 1 he moved the army to within fifteen miles of Germantown, close enough to make a night march to the enemy's lines, but not so close as to alarm him.

Since Washington and his officers had been in and out of Germantown several times during the last weeks there appeared to be no problem so far as knowledge of terrain and roads was concerned. No doubt the success of his coordinated attack on Trenton was in his mind as he laid out a plan that called for converging columns moving down on the enemy by different routes. The brunt of the fighting, the attack on the center would be delivered by Sullivan and Greene, with Washington accompanying the unwary Sullivan to insure against "bad luck." Greene would command his own and Stephen's divisions, and on his left flank would be General Smallwood with nearly 2,000 Maryland militia to envelop the British right and rear. Sullivan, with Wayne's division, would be to the right of Greene and on the extreme right would be General John Armstrong with 1,500 Pennsylvania militia to turn the British left. Stirling's division would be the reserve, moving behind Sullivan.

From Washington's camp at Pennypacker's Mill the direct route to Germantown led down the Skippack Road. Two miles to the west, close to the Schuylkill, was Manatawney Road, and about the same distance to the east was the Lime Kiln Road. In the center of Germantown was a cross street called School House Lane to the west, and Church Lane to the east. Sullivan's command, coming down Skippack Road, was to be supported by Greene advancing on the Lime Kiln road to Church Lane and then turning west toward Germantown. Armstrong's militia would close by way of the Manatawney Road and School House Lane. Smallwood was to complete the encirclement by striking Church Lane east of Greene and coming up in support.

It was a complicated plan, one that would have taxed the energy and skill of officers and men far more experienced than Washington's Continentals. The distance across the whole American front from Armstrong on the right to Smallwood on the left was seven miles.[3]

Washington put the army in motion on the night of October 3 hoping to get into position before dawn and rest the men prior to the attack. But it was daylight before Wayne struck the British advance guard—daylight which was shrouded by "a low vapour lying on the land which made it very difficult to distinguish objects at any considerable distance."

Wayne's division drove through the enemy pickets, swarming into the camp of the 40th Regiment and the 2nd Light Infantry. The British quickly discovered that these were Wayne's men, for there were shouts of "Have at the bloodhounds!" and "Paoli! Paoli!" After a hot exchange of fire the redcoats

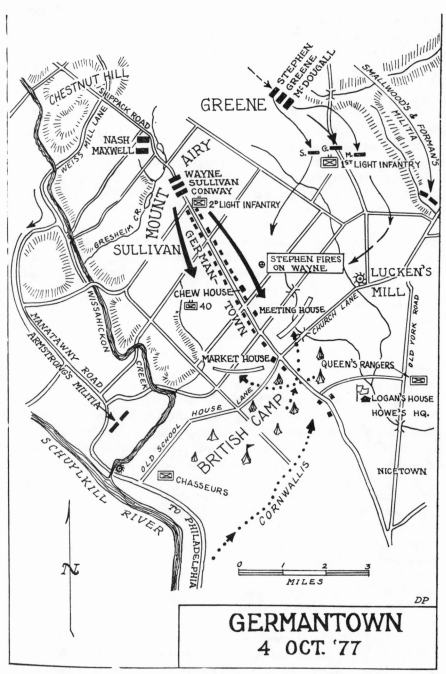

GREENE

STEPHEN
GREENE
McDOUGALL

SMALLWOOD'S & FORMAN'S MILITIA

CHESTNUT HILL

SHIPPACK ROAD

WEISS MILL LANE

NASH
MAXWELL

MOUNT AIRY

WAYNE
SULLIVAN
CONWAY

2ᴰ LIGHT INFANTRY

S.   G.   M.

1ˢᵀ LIGHT INFANTRY

GRESHEIM CR.

SULLIVAN

GERMAN-TOWN

STEPHEN FIRES
ON WAYNE

LUCKEN'S
MILL

CHEW HOUSE

40

MEETING HOUSE

CHURCH LANE

OLD YORK ROAD

WISSAHICKON

MANATAWNY ROAD

ARMSTRONG'S MILITIA

CREEK

MARKET HOUSE

HOUSE LANE

OLD SCHOOL

QUEEN'S RANGERS

LOGAN'S HOUSE

HOWE'S HQ.

BRITISH CAMP

CHASSEURS

CORNWALLIS

NICETOWN

SCHUYLKILL RIVER

TO PHILADELPHIA

N

0   1   2   3

MILES

DP

GERMANTOWN
4 OCT. '77

© Mark Boatner, III, *Encyclopedia of the American Revolution*, David McKay Co., Inc.

fell back toward Germantown with the Americans at their heels. Despite the efforts of the officers to stop them, Wayne's men ruthlessly bayonetted the British who tried to surrender and even some of the wounded.

Behind Sullivan, Stirling's division suddenly struck a snag. British Colonel Musgrave's 40th Regiment had put some men into a large stone mansion owned by Judge Benjamin Chew, from which neither musket fire nor cannon could dislodge them. For more than half an hour Washington tried to reduce what Knox called "a castle in our rear" (Knox was doing it by the book). Finally it was decided that the position posed no threat and the attack moved on.

Sullivan and Wayne now made good progress despite the blinding fog. Wayne shifted his division to the left, grouping for contact with Greene. By now the sound of firing aroused the British main camp and General Howe himself rode out to the fight; ". . . seeing the battalion retreating, all broken, he got into a passion and exclaimed, 'For shame, Light Infantry. I never saw you retreat before. Form! Form! It's only a scouting party.'" At that moment Sullivan's column came out of the fog. At its head were three guns which greeted Sir William with a blast of grape. The light infantry "all felt pleased to see the enemy make such an appearance and to hear the grape rattle about the Commander-in-Chief's ears. . . . He rode off immediately full speed." But the rest of the British main body was up, and as the regiments of Grant and Agnew began to put pressure on Sullivan's right, the American attack was checked.

In the meantime Greene's advance was lagging since the left assault column had further to go and had briefly lost its way. However, by the time Sullivan reached the crossroad Greene had reached Church Lane and was coming up on Sullivan's left. Fog still shrouded the field. As Greene's troops groped their way forward Private Joseph Martin remembered,

> The curs [muskets] began to bark first and then the bull dogs [guns]. . . . We saw a body of the enemy drawn up behind a rail fence on our right flank; we immediately formed into line and advanced upon them. Our orders were not to fire until we could see the buttons upon their clothes, but they were so coy that they would not give us an opportunity to be so curious, for they hid their clothes in fire and smoke before we had either the time or leisure to examine their buttons. . . . The enemy were driven quite through their camp. They left their kettles, in which they were cooking their breakfasts, on the fires, and some of their garments were lying on the ground, which their owners had not had time to put on.[4]

The thrust of Greene's attack drove deep into the enemy's lines—so deep that Muhlenburg's Pennsylvanians were momentarily in the British rear and had to counterattack in the opposite direction in order to rejoin Greene. On Greene's right Stephen was extending toward Wayne when he heard firing, so he thought, in his rear. Possibly it was from the Chew house; in any case, Stephen changed his line of advance further toward the north and probably lost his sense of direction in the fog.

At this point the attack suddenly collapsed. Some of the other regiments may have been rattled by bursts of musket fire in the rear. Stephen's division, moving toward the Skippack Road, came up on the left rear of Wayne's flank. In the confusion of the fog the two commands fired on each other. At the same moment, Sullivan's men were not only under heavy pressure from the British but their ammunition began to run short. For one or all of these reasons the troops between Sullivan's left and Greene's right suddenly broke and ran.

Washington was riding exultantly forward to press home a general attack when out of the fog in front of him burst the wild-eyed, panicky fugitives. In vain he and his aides attempted to halt the fleeing men, but there was no stopping the frightened soldiers. The wave of dispair that engulfed the commanding general can only be imagined, for there was no outburst, as at Kip's Bay, and his subsequent report of the battle only emphasized the nearness of victory. Nor was the panic universal. Private Martin, at age seventeen already a veteran of two campaigns, "never wanted to run (if I am forced to run) further than to be beyond the enemy's shot, after which I had no more fear of their overtaking me than an army of lobsters. . . ." Citizen Tom Paine, who observed the withdrawal, found that "the retreat was extraordinary. Nobody hurried themselves. Everybody marched at his own pace."

Instead of pursuing the fugitives the British were forced to turn their attention to Greene's disciplined men. Although he had hit the British hard the Rhode Islander's attack soon lost its momentum. Smallwood had not come up on his left. Stephen's division was lost in the fog, its men in a panic, its commander thoroughly drunk. Cornwallis and Grant now had twelve regiments in action and Greene felt the full force of the British counterattack. He was forced to retreat, pressed hard by the British, but with his regiments preserving their formations. By ten o'clock the fight was over. Tired and hungry, exhausted by almost three hours of fighting, the men managed a twenty-four mile march back to their camp at Pennypacker's Mill.[5]

Here it was evident that the army still retained that remarkable resilience it had somehow acquired in this, the third year of the war. Washington reported to Congress, "Upon the whole it may be said the day was unfortunate rather than injurious. We sustained no material loss of Men and brought off all our artillery except one piece. . . . The Enemy are nothing better by the event; and our Troops, who are not in the least dispirited by it, have gained what all young Troops gain by being in Actions." Whether the loss of 600 killed and wounded, and 400 prisoners could be considered "no material loss," Washington, as usual, was being his most optimistic when the outlook appeared most dismal. He continued to believe that victory had been snatched from him by the accident of the fog and the inexplicable panic of the men.

Intelligence from the enemy camps seemed to confirm this. A report from Philadelphia related that "in my presence several British Officers who had returned from the action of the 4th Instant Confessed that they had never met with so severe a Drubbing since the Battle of Bunker Hill, that the Attack was made with great Judgement and Supported with equal Bravery. . . ." The British loss in the battle was nearly 500 men and 34 officers killed and wounded.

This time Sullivan could not be blamed. He had put his men into action promptly and had fought his division well. The fog and the shortage of ammunition he could not help, and the confusion of the formations was as much Wayne's doing as his. General Stephen was another case altogether. He was found asleep in a fence corner, and it may have been that his collapse was as much from exhaustion as from drink. But he had led his division astray and had been totally confused in the direction of his men. That he had been drinking heavily was later attested to, and when he was cited for a court martial Washington would not defend him. Stephen was convicted of "unofficerlike behavior" and dismissed from the service. Washington gave command of his division to Lafayette.[6]

Of the many factors in the defeat the one least mentioned may have been the most obvious and the most important. It was succinctly expressed by the French engineer, General du Portail, who told Washington, "Your Excellency, in that instance, really conquered General Howe, but his Troops conquered yours." Though they had been surprised and driven, the redcoats did not panic. Their commanders formed them for a counterattack and delivered it with coolness and precision. The American army had developed neither the skill of command nor the steadiness under fire that could bring them to victory in the open field against an opponent nearly equal in strength to their own. The Continentals could be counted on to win only when they had a clear tactical superiority of either numbers or position.

Yet it remained a fact that Washington's confidence in the ability of the soldiers to maintain their spirits seemed to be justified. What was obvious was that, with Howe on the defensive, American numerical superiority became increasingly important. So the commander in chief continued to send out calls for militia. But his principal reliance was on the return of his veteran Continentals from the Northern Department. The battle at Freeman's Farm seemed to demonstrate that Gates now had Burgoyne well in hand. Washington believed that the time had come to press home his strategy of pinning Howe to Philadelphia and the Delaware while denying him the support of Lord Howe's fleet.

Ten days before Germantown, when Washington had asked Gates to return Morgan's corps, Gates replied that since the British still occupied the ground at Freeman's Farm "Your Excellency would not wish me to part with the Corps the Army of General Burgoyne are most afraid of." If Washington recognized an incipient insubordination, he gave no sign.

But the failure of the militia at Germantown underscored the fact that a serious challenge to Howe made necessary the return of the regular regiments from the north, for these amounted to almost 3,000 seasoned troops. Nor was there any question of Washington's authority to order them back to Pennsylvania. On August 23, in answer to a query about his relationship to the Northern Department, Congress had passed a resolution "that Congress never intended . . . by the Establishment of any Department whatever to Supersede or Circumscribe the powers of General Washington as the Commander in Chief of all the Continental Land Forces within the United States."

It was news from the Northern Department that now brought a surge of hope for the American cause. On October 16 Washington received a report (premature, but, as it turned out, accurate) that Burgoyne's army had surrendered. This incredible news sent a shock wave of jubilation throughout the entire country. No single event of the entire war so galvanized American spirits. General orders for October 18 directed that "*Thirteen* pieces of cannon are to be discharged at the park of artillery to be followed by a *feu-de-joy* with blank cartridges. . . ."[7]

The victory also meant that virtually the whole of Gates' army would be available for reinforcements in Pennsylvania. Confirmation of the victory came on the 20th—but not by direct communication from Gates to headquarters. It was beginning to appear as though Gates had drunk deeply of the heady wine of victory. He asked Congress to promote Wilkinson to brigadier general, presumably for nothing more outstanding than bringing Congress the terms of the surrender convention—a feat that took Wilkinson two weeks. Although this rankled the senior colonels, Congressman Nathaniel Folsom pointed out, "I was glad Gates asked no more at this time, for assured I am that if he had it would have been granted. . . ." Congress was indulging in that paradoxical behavior that was to characterize it for the next two hundred years—denouncing standing armies and the influence of the military, while fatuously fawning over hero-generals. Gates' arrogance eventually strained even Washington's monumental patience to the limit.

Adding to his problems were the continuous demands of foreign officers for rank and command. One especially unpleasant affair involved a French artillery officer, Phillippe du Coudray to whom Silas Deane in Paris had promised command of the army's artillery corps with the rank of major general. The problem was happily solved in mid-September when the arrogant Frenchman's horse threw him overboard from a ferry and he was drowned. It was, of course, important that cordial relations be maintained with foreign nations, especially France. Yet the promotion of an officer like Thomas Conway over the heads of brigadiers who had fought and marched through two years of hard campaigning had a devastating effect on the morale of Washington's generals.

Conway was an Irish-born Frenchman who had spent twenty years in the army of Louis XVI. He had been made a brigadier general in the summer of 1777 and commanded a brigade at Germantown. His courage and capabilities were obvious, but Washington questioned his tendency to substitute his own discretion for orders from his superiors. After Germantown Conway pressed for a promotion and proclaimed his superior qualities to all who would listen. Washington characterized him as having "that after kind of sagacity which qualifies a Man better for profound discoveries of errors, that have been committed and advantages that have been lost [rather] than for the exercise of . . . foresight and provident discernment. . . ." He came to despise Conway as he did no other man, but for the moment he was only concerned that Congress might undermine his generals by yielding to Conway's threat to resign unless he was promoted.

All this did not divert Washington's attention from his basic strategy: Hold the Delaware defenses until his regiments could return from the north. With a superior force of Continentals at his back, and Howe cut off from his supplies, the war might be won now, this year.[8]

THE FIGHT FOR THE DELAWARE

When Colonel Samuel Smith and his handful of Maryland Continentals arrived at Fort Mifflin on September 27 they found that post in a sorry plight. It was occupied by 40 militiamen whom Smith immediately detached as unfit for duty, along with 30 of his own men who were either sick or worn down by exhaustion. This left him with less than 200 men. His subordinates were Major Simeon Thayer of Rhode Island and Captain Samuel Treat, an artilleryman. Soon afterward a French engineer, Major the Marquis de Fleury reported for duty. Fleury was one of a number of officers granted leave from the French army to enlist in America, but who were expected to return to the French service when the war ended. Fleury's performance at Fort Mifflin proved him to be, in Colonel Smith's words, "a Treasure that ought not to be lost." Fleury had already fought at the Brandywine and Germantown, and he was to win one of only nine Congressional medals awarded during the entire war. He had supervised the defenses of the Delaware which consisted of three strong points. A fort at Billingsport several miles down river was abandoned by its militia garrison at the first threat of the British advance. On the New Jersey side of the river near Red Bank was Fort Mercer, manned by a Rhode Island regiment commanded by Christopher Greene. Fort Mifflin lay in the middle of the Delaware on an island which was not much more than a mud flat thrown up by the current of the Schuylkill as it flowed into the Delaware.

The two forts were so placed that their guns guarded a two-tiered line of *cheveaux de frise* which blocked the main channel between Fort Mifflin and the Jersey shore. *Cheveaux de frise* were made of heavy spars ballasted on the river bottom at a forty-five degree angle, their sharpened, iron-shod tips pointing downstream about four feet below the surface. They could rip the bottom out of any ship that tried to pass up the channel, and the guns of the two forts guarded against any attempt to raise them. To the west of Fort Mifflin was a low, marshy mud flat, separated from the Delaware shore by a slough. It was dignified by the name of Province Island but it offered only limited sites for enemy guns. Commodore John Hazelwood, commander of the Pennsylvania state naval forces on the river, assured Colonel Smith, "A mosquito could not live there under the fire of my guns." Hazelwood's force consisted of an assortment of row galleys and floating batteries, and two small frigates, one of which had already run aground and been destroyed.[9]

Smith and his men set to work repairing the dilapidated works. In addition to the masonry wall which faced the main channel and masked the principal batteries, blockhouses mounting four guns each were built at the four corners of the fort. An open platform mounting a 32-pounder was erected to bear on Province Island. Walls of pine logs and earth were erected connecting the batteries, and revetments were constructed to protect the men when they were not manning the guns.

All this took a great deal of effort. Living conditions in the fort were miserable and the men were short of every sort of supplies and equipment—shoes, clothing, and blankets. The soldiers became so sickly that Smith was constantly detaching men and asking for replacements. It is doubtful if one third of the troops who garrisoned Fort Mifflin at the beginning of October served until the end of the siege.

Soon after the battle of Germantown the British established a battery on one of the few dry hummocks on Province Island, unhindered by Hazelwood's naval batteries. When Smith asked the commodore to attack the battery Hazelwood refused. In exasperation Smith procured the use of some of the gunboats and led the assault himself, driving off the redcoats and nearly capturing the guns. But by October 14 the British were back. This time they quickly threw up an earthwork behind which they mounted a battery. Smith's force had been reduced to 156 men so he could not risk an attack. Fort Mifflin was soon being bombarded by the guns from Province. The little garrison hung on, although "at least 60 of our small force are without breeches, many of whom have scarce so much as to cover their nakedness."

By the third week in October the British had raised the obstructions at Billingsport and their frigates moved into a position just below the *cheveaux de frise* at Fort Mifflin. Until they could breach these, the fleet ferried a trickle of supplies by night in small boats up the shallow channel between Province Island and Fort Mifflin. Smith called on Hazelwood to use his small vessels to block this line but the cautious commodore explained that a single shell would wreck one of his little ships. The indignant Smith retorted, "Yes, and [a shell] falling on your head or mine will kill, but for what else are we employed or paid? . . ."[10]

Nonetheless, the blockade of the river was a serious matter for the Howes. Supplies brought up Province Channel and what little could be brought overland from New Castle would not suffice for a garrison that intended to winter in Philadelphia.

Fort Mercer was located on the New Jersey side of the Delaware opposite

Fort Mifflin. The distance between them was almost 2,000 yards, too far for mutual fire support, but close enough so that the guns of both could rake the main channel which lay between them. Fort Mercer, like so many of the European designs in America, was too large to be properly defended by the 400 Rhode Islanders under Christopher Greene, but another French engineer, the Chevalier du Plessis, had built an interior wall across one section of the fort thereby reducing the defense perimeter. Greene had fourteen guns of which five were mounted on the walls facing inland.

The Howes seriously underestimated the strength of the American positions. On October 22 the 64-gun *Augusta*, the frigates *Roebuck*, *Vigilant*, and *Fury*, and the sloop *Merlin* moved in to take Fort Mifflin under fire. At the same time Colonel Karl von Donop led a mixed force of 2,000 English and Hessians against Fort Mercer. He divided his force and sent storming columns against opposite sides of the fort. One penetrated the ditch and the abatis without drawing a shot. The other swept over the north wall—and found itself in the dead space formed by du Plessis' interior wall. Only then did the Americans open fire. The soldiers sent their volleys into the British at thirty yards. The guns slammed charges of grape into the close packed ranks. The walled-off interior of the northern redoubt became a slaughter pen. When the British finally withdrew they left 500 killed, wounded, and captured including their Hessian commander who died three days later. The American loss was 38 killed and wounded.

The British had also fared badly in the attack on Fort Mifflin. The five ships were met by furious fire from the fort and from Hazelwood's small craft. Hazelwood claimed much of the credit for repulsing the British but Colonel Smith had noted earlier that "so general a discontent and panic runs through that part of the fleet . . . they conceive the river is lost. . . ." It seems likely that it was the fire of the fixed guns of the fort that threw the British into confusion. As they retired downstream both the 64-gun *Augusta* and the sloop *Merlin* went aground and were eventually destroyed.

The British unwittingly did Sam Smith a favor. The Baron d'Arendt, a tall, imposing Pole, had arrived to take command of Fort Mifflin a few days before. His arrogance and bad judgement had already led Major Fleury to remark, "Par dieu! C'est un poltroon!" When the British guns opened fire the Baron panicked and Smith had to take command. As the *Vigilant* drifted down stream at the end of the engagement she loosed a final broadside. One shot hit a wall near d'Arendt and sent a fragment of brick smashing into his groin. He was promptly evacuated and Fort Mifflin knew him no more.[11]

At headquarters Washington waited anxiously for news of the regiments which should be on their way from the north. It was now clear that Gates considered himself an independent commander since he was making his reports directly to York. "Congress having been requested immediately to transmit copies of all my dispatches . . . I am confident your Excellency has long ago received all the good news from this quarter," he announced grandly in one of only three letters he wrote Washington during November.

By this time Washington's patience had run out. On October 30 he dispatched his aide, Colonel Hamilton, to Saratoga to see to the return of the troops. On his way Hamilton met Morgan's Corps but by the time he reached headquarters it was obvious the Hero of Saratoga had no intention of giving up his army without a struggle. By the first week in November Hamilton had pried loose "near five thousand, rank and file, Continental troops, and twenty-five hundred Massachusetts and New Hampshire militia." These troops, however, struck a snag when they reached Putnam's headquarters at Peekskill. "Old Put," suddenly in command of 9,000 men, conjured up the glorious vision of an attack on New York. Hamilton was wild with exasperation. "Indeed, Sir . . . every part of this gentleman's conduct is marked by blunders and negligence, and gives general disgust." By November 12 Putnam's orders had been overridden and Paterson, Glover, Learned, Poor, and Parsons had started their brigades for Pennsylvania. But "the disposition for marching, in the officers and men in general, of these troops, does not keep pace with . . . the exigency of the occasion."

Three weeks had passed since Burgoyne's surrender.[12]

The victory of October 22 could not disguise the precarious condition of the forts. By the first of November British batteries on Province Island pounded away at Fort Mifflin at a range of 600 yards. Naval vessels just below the *cheveaux de frise* at 1,200 yards added to the cannonade. The fort kept up a steady answering fire and the men settled down into a sort of routine, taking shelter from enemy shells by day and turning to under cover of night to rebuild walls and blinds that had been uprooted and dislodged during the daylight hours.

Like soldiers everywhere they discovered diversions. The 32-pounder facing Province Island had no solid shot. Across the channel the British batteries also mounted a 32-pounder. "The artillery officers offered a gill of rum for each shot fired from that piece. . . . I have often seen from twenty to fifty men standing on the parade waiting with impatience the coming shot, which would be seized before its motion had full ceased, and conveyed off to our gun to be sent back to its former owners. When the lucky fellow who had caught it had swallowed his rum, he would return to wait for another. . . ." (And since the British batteries were equally difficult to supply, is it too much to imagine the same shot passing endlessly back and forth between the rebel and redcoat batteries?)

Early in November an autumn gale lashed the eastern seaboard bringing heavy rains that raised the river level. A good part of Fort Mifflin was submerged under two feet of water. The men, miserable from lack of clothing and bad food, were now denied fires because all the space above water was either built of wood or being used for powder storage. General Varnum, who was acting as senior officer to Greene and Smith, authorized the confiscation of clothing from the nearby towns but, said Colonel Smith, "I fear it will be a very poor Resource—the Garrison must be well cloathed or they will perish."

Boatloads of supplies continued to pass up Province Channel to Philadelphia without interference from Hazelwood. "The Commodore says he cannot prevent the Enemy Boats from passing up and down the River, as they are covered by their Batteries," reported Varnum; ". . . the Commodore appears to be a very good kind of a Man; but his extreme Good Nature gives too great a License to those under his Command."[13]

By November 10 the British began to intensify their bombardment of the battered little fort. Several floating batteries had been built and moved into Province Channel to add to the fire power of the island batteries. Major Fleury wrote almost casually in his journal, "The 24 and 18 pound shot from Batteries No. 16 and 17 broke some of our Palisades this morning, but this does not make us uneasy—they save us the trouble of cutting them to the height of a man. . . ." The storm of shells inflicted surprisingly few casualties and the garrison kept up its spirits. Fleury showed only annoyance as the enemy now "kept up a firing part of the night—their shells greatly disturb our workmen and as the moon rises opposite to us, her light discovers to the Enemy where we are. . . ."

On November 11 a shell crashed into one of the few remaining brick chimneys of the fort. It collapsed on Colonel Smith, temporarily paralyzing him. He had to be evacuated but four days later he was back on his feet. "My Arm will this Night permit me to take the Command at Fort Mifflin. I was there last Night, it is now one Heap of Ruin & must be defended with musketry in Case of Storm. . . . With 600 men I think we could defend it as an Island."

But the fort's hours were numbered. General Varnum reported on the 16th: ". . . last evening we were obliged to evacuate Fort Mifflin. . . . *Vigilant* lay within one Hundred Yards of the Southwest part of the Works [*Vigilant*'s shallow draft enabled her to work her way past the *chevaux de frise*], & with her incessant Fire, Hand Grenades, & Musketry from the Round Top, killed every man that appeared on the Platforms.—The Commodore gave positive orders to six Gallies to attack, and take that Ship. . . . I am just told the Gallies . . . did Nothing."

With the fall of Fort Mifflin Fort Mercer lay exposed. It was also evident that General Howe was acutely concerned about the river blockade, for he sent from Philadelphia a column of 3,000 men under Lord Cornwallis. On November 20 General Varnum ordered Mercer evacuated. The Delaware was now a British river.

For seven weeks Christopher Greene and Sam Smith, with a combined force that never counted more than 700 men had effectively scotched the junction of the British army and its supporting fleet. Washington was powerless to capitalize on the situation. Not until additional regiments from Gates gave him a decided superiority of numbers could he even consider attacking the trenches and breastworks that Howe had strung across the northern face of the city from the Schuylkill to the Delaware. He did send Greene after Cornwallis, urging his subordinate to attack and destroy the British detachment. But Cornwallis, moving by interior lines, outmaneuvered the Rhode Islander. Despite Washington's urgent desire for a fight, Greene refused to do so without positive orders "under these Disadvantages." Greene then elaborated:

> . . . Your Excellency has the choice of but two things, to fight the Enemy without the least Prospect of Success, upon the Common Principle of War, or remain inactive, & be subject to the Censure of an ignorant & impatient populace. In doing one you may make a bad matter worse, and take a measure, that if it proves unfortunate, you may stand condemned for by all military Gentlemen of Experience; pursuing the other you have the Approbation of your own mind, you give your Country an opportunity to exert itself to supply the present deficiency, & also act upon such military Principles as will justify you to the best Judges in the Present Day, & to all future Generations.

When Fort Mercer was evacuated on November 20 the brigades of Morgan, Glover, Paterson, and Poor had not yet reached Trenton.[14]

Valley Forge: End and Beginning

Sir William Howe was at last secure in the rebel capital, his defensive line drawn from the Schuylkill to the Delaware, his supply line open and guarded by Admiral Howe's fleet. But General Howe did not regard his achievement as the conclusion of a successful campaign. If he did, dispatches from Germain would have disillusioned him. Between August and December the King and his ministers waited anxiously for word of the outcome of this, their second campaign of the war. Not since the news of the fall of Ticonderoga had there been anything to relieve their anxiety. Through July the American Secretary remained optimistic, although by this time it was known that Major Balfour and Clinton had failed to deter Sir William from his sea voyage.

By August no news was bad news. Germain's indulgent tone in his dispatches to the Howes was replaced by sarcasm. He complimented Admiral Howe on his indulgence in allowing American fishermen to ply their trade (his Lordship had said that if they were allowed to fish they would not join the American navy), and agreed with General Howe that popular opinion was no substitute for sound strategy. But, said Germain, despite Admiral Howe's benign wisdom, there seemed to be enough hands to man the swarm of American privateers crowding into French ports; and Lord George professed to Sir William, "I shall be happy in seeing you meet with the Applause and Admiration of the Ignorant, as well as the abler judges of military merit." The American Secretary was becoming disillusioned with his commanders even before the news of Burgoyne's disaster and the fruitless Pennsylvania campaign reached London. Only the fact that Germain's own fortunes were harnessed to those of the Howes prevented him from openly denouncing their leadership.

By the first of December word of Burgoyne's defeat had reached England, and a dispatch from Howe complained as usual of lack of reinforcements. Burgoyne, he said, should not have expected support, since Howe had warned him that the army in New York was going south. Then came Sir William's final effrontery: "From the little attention, my Lord, given to my recommendations since the commencement of my command, I am led to hope that I may be relieved from this very painful service, wherein I have not the good fortune to enjoy the necessary confidence and support of my superiors. . . ."

And on the last day of November, with the surrender of Burgoyne now confirmed, came the denouement: ". . . I candidly declare my opinion, that in the apparent temper of the Americans, a considerable addition to the present force will be requisite for effecting any essential change in their disposition, and reestablish the King's authority; and that this army, acting upon the defensive, will be fully employed to maintain its present position."

Acting upon the defensive! This was the sum of Howe's strategic thinking as the year came to an end. Although Washington did not so consider it, in the lexicon of eighteenth century military thinking, the ultimate victory was achieved by maneuvering the adversary into a situation where he had to yield his ground, because it became impossible to defend it. Howe's avowed objective had been the conquest of the middle colonies, but he had yielded all but the empty shell of the rebel capital, and for its defense "this army . . . will be fully employed."[15]

Howe made one last defiant and empty gesture. On December 4 he marched out of Philadelphia and brought his army north to Chestnut Hill where he faced Washington in a strong, entrenched position. There was sporadic skirmishing, but Howe did not deliver an attack. The British withdrew to Philadelphia and settled in for the winter.

Washington was reluctant to end the year with what was to him an inconclusive campaign. The regiments from Gates' northern command had finally come in, too late to attack Howe while the river was still blocked. Gates' behavior had been very close to insubordination, but Washington was painfully aware that questions of military command were deeply enmeshed in Congressional politics.

The more immediate questions were whether a winter offensive could be undertaken; if not, what were the strategic considerations for locating the army's winter quarters. The former question was posed by the Congress, its members still convinced that a more vigorous policy was needed. To this the opinion of Washington's generals was an emphatic "No!" After reading the statements elicited by a poll which included everyone from Nathanael Greene to Colonel Henry Lutterloh, the deputy quartermaster general, the members of Congress agreed. Despite the increase in the army's strength, there were still the lack of training, the shortage of equipment, "the present temper of the soldiery,"—all these precluded any offensive maneuver. John Sullivan pointed out that "of your Army one third of whom at Least are now confined to their cold Tents & unwholesome Hutts for want of Shoes, Stockings & other Cloathing, a very Large number of them unable Longer to endure the Severity of their Situation have retired (sick) to the Hospitals or to the Country Houses." Many officers were on the point of resigning and another failure would break their spirit.[16]

Some of the officers were aware that Washington was sensitive to the growing criticism but, warned General Weedon, a failure would open the floodgates to those "who want nothing more to blast reputations than a miscarriage, without inquiring into its causes. . . ." How serious this criticism had become was revealed by a letter from Lord Stirling reporting a conversation with James Wilkinson in which the young aide had quoted General Conway as defaming the commander in chief. For the moment Washington contented himself with a brief note to Conway which read:

> A Letter which I received last Night contained the following paragraph.
> In a Letter from Genl. Conway to Genl. Gates he says: "Heaven has been determined to save your Country; or a weak General and bad Councellors would have ruind it."

This and nothing more. It brought a spate of protestations from Conway; Gates heard of it and angrily hinted that Colonel Hamilton had snooped in Gates' files when he was at Saratoga. Washington let them stew for the time being, not even bothering to tell Gates that the source of the leak was his own aide, Wilkinson.[17]

Congress began flexing its muscles. It created a new Board of War composed of men outside of Congress, and named Gates as its president. Also named to the Board was General Thomas Mifflin who had become one of the foremost critics of the commander in chief. Congress also made Conway a major general, but as a staff officer in the capacity of inspector general. Some members undoubtedly hoped that these affronts would induce Washington to resign, but it is doubtful if the majority would have voted to accept his resignation. (When Conway arrived at headquarters Washington, with cold formality, asked to see orders specifying his duties. When Conway confessed that he had none Washington informed him that he would have no duties until instructions from Congress were received.)

Meantime the army prepared to go into winter quarters at Valley Forge, a bleak stretch of country on the west side of the Schuylkill near Kelly's Ford (modern Norristown). There had been talk of furloughing the army home but Washington considered that a fatal step. Another consideration was to break it up into cantonments scattered through Pennsylvania, New Jersey, and Delaware. In this way foraging would be easier and the inhabitants would be protected from British marauders. This was also rejected. Howe must be watched and some effort must be made to harass British detachments around Philadelphia. Scattered cantonments brought to mind the fate of the Hessians at Trenton. So it was to be Valley Forge, close enough to keep an eye on the redcoats in Philadelphia, but safe enough from a sudden sally by Howe, since the Schuylkill would guard against a surprise.[18]

The suffering of the army during the winter of 1777–1778 has made Valley Forge a symbol of hardship and privation. A detailed study of the army in that grim winter is not properly part of this study, but a few observations are worth noting. The winter weather was not especially severe, and Pennsylvania and New Jersey had ample food and forage for at least the minimal needs of the army. Washington and his men believed that it was the lack of patriotic spirit among the Pennsylvanians, especially the Quakers, that led them to withhold supplies, preferring to sell them for hard money to the British.

Yet foraging parties sent out from Valley Forge had considerable success. Private Joseph Martin was assigned to this duty. "I do not remember," he says, "that during the time I was employed in this business, which was from Christmas to the latter part of April, ever to have met with the least resistance from the inhabitants, take what we would from their barns, mills, corncribs or stalls. . . . I had to travel far and near, in cold and in storms, by day and by night, and at all times to run the *risk* of abuse, if not injury, from the inhabitants when *plundering* them of their property. . . . But I will give them the credit of never receiving the least abuse or injury during the whole time I was employed in this business."

The real root of the problem was in the army organization. Able men for positions in the quartermaster's department were hard to find. Officers quickly found out that the army offered no financial rewards, which meant that motivation for continuing in the service was confined to patriotism or the rewards of a hero's acclaim. And as General Greene noted, "No body ever heard of a quartermaster, in history."[19]

Even so, early in the war Washington was fortunate enough to find a splendid administrator for the position of quartermaster general. Thomas Mifflin of Pennsylvania proved to be not only an able organizer but a skilful recruiter, and the militia turnout for the Trenton campaign owed much to his silver-tongued oratory. His fine performance earned him rapid promotion and by February, 1777, he was a major general and a close confidant of the commander in chief. His friendship and admiration for Washington began to deteriorate in the summer of 1777 when it was said that he believed Washington was not sufficiently concerned about the defense of Pennsylvania and Philadelphia. By the end of the campaign Mifflin had not only become one of Washington's severest critics but was beginning to neglect his duties as quartermaster general. He finally asked to be relieved for reasons of health (he recovered miraculously when he was appointed to the Board of War), and Congress did not replace him. His duties devolved upon his senior deputy, Colonel Henry Lutterloh, who had neither the rank nor the capacity for the job. The result was that the administrative apparatus for collecting and distributing supplies had collapsed. No preparations had been made for stockpiling supplies for the winter months or for setting up collection depots for foraging parties. Obviously, if Private Martin's experience was typical, the supplies gleaned from "barns, mills, corncribs or stalls" were not reaching the men in the huts at Valley Forge.[20]

Even before the soldiers had built their permanent quarters for the winter they had begun to feel the pinch. Standard fare was "Firecake and water, sir." Firecake was simply unseasoned flour and water mixed into a dough that could be cooked over an open fire, or perhaps flattened on a heated rock and "baked" enough to be edible. In mid-December, after a week without a ration of beef, the hills and valleys around the Forge began to ring with the chant of "No meat! No meat!" The din was interspersed with crow caws and owl hoots until the whole encampment was engulfed in a cacophony of sound. Yet there was no edge of violence in the uproar. "See the poor Soldier . . . —if his food is bad, he eats it notwithstanding with seeming content—blesses God for a Good Stomach and Whistles it into digestion."

The situation was not helped by a Congressional reorganization which had established a maze of red tape for the commissary general's office. Joseph Trumbull, who held that post until the summer of 1777, insisted that his subordinates must be paid by commission rather than by salary. Only on that basis could he induce competent men to serve. When Congress refused to change the system Trumbull resigned. His duties were taken over by William Buchanan who, to put charitably, was not equal to the task.

The army was not only starving but it was freezing. Of all the services that of clothier-general was the most inefficient. This was an army that was seldom fully clothed, much less in uniform. With the approach of winter the situation was desperate. General Sullivan reported that officers who wanted to resign their commissions "assigned as a Reason for not waiting on me that they were so naked they were ashamed to be seen. . . ."[21]

Two days before Christmas Washington sent a dispatch to Congress that must be read in its entirety to understand fully the seething indignation that gripped the commander in chief. Poor Captain Granberry, the aide to whom it was dictated, was the recipient of a veritable flood of words which he never did get into proper sentences. Part of it reads

> . . . since the 4th Instt. our Numbers fit for duty from the hardships and exposures they have undergone, particularly on Acct. of Blankets (numbers being obliged and do set up all Night by fires, instead of comfortable rest in a natural way) have decreased near 2000 Men. We find Gentlemen without knowing whether the Army was really going into Winter Quarters or not (for I am sure no resolution of mine would warrant the remonstrance) reprobating the measure as much as if they thought Men were made of Stocks or Stones and equally insensible of frost and Snow and moreover, as if they conceived it practicable for an inferior Army under the disadvantages I have describ'd our's to be wch. is by

no means exagerated to confine a superior one (in all respects well appointed, and provided for a Winters Campaign) within the City of Phila., and cover from depredation and waste in the States of Pensa., Jersey, &ca. but what makes this matter still more extraordinary in my eye is, that these very Gentn. who were all apprized of the nakedness of the Troops, from occular demonstration thought their own Soldiers worse clad than others, and advised me, near a Month ago, to postpone the execution of a Plan, I was about to adopt (in consequence of a resolve of Congress) for seizing Cloaths, under strong assurances that an ample supply would be collected in ten days agreeably to a decree of the State, not one article of wch., by the bye, is yet come to hand, should think a Winters Campaign and the covering these States from the Invasion of an Enemy so easy a business. I can assure those Gentlemen that it is a much easier and less distressing thing to draw remonstrances in a comfortable room by a good fire side than to occupy a cold bleak hill and sleep under frost and Snow without Cloaths or Blankets; however, although they seem to have little feeling for the naked, and distressed Soldier, I feel superabundantly for them, and from my Soul pity those miseries, wch. it is neither in my power to relieve or prevent.

It was probably during this dreadful time that Washington developed a real affection for what his aide, John Laurens, called "those dear ragged Continentals." And the soldiers recognized that the big, weary general was not entirely responsible for their plight. At the end of a horrible week in February when no rations at all were issued, the men finally protested, but respectfully, "as if they had been humble petitioners for special favors." Later when rumors circulated that Washington might be replaced, the word that came from the soldiers was "Washington or no Army."[22]

So it may be that here at Valley Forge the army won its greatest victory. It survived.

With the men finally in some kind of permanent winter quarters Washington now turned his attention to his American enemies, real or imagined. Shortly after the first of the year he became embroiled in a new dispute with General Conway over the matter of his duties as inspector general. On Washington's part the correspondence was almost prim in its formality; on Conway's there was a lofty pretentiousness that young John Laurens thought was inexcusably insolent. What Colonel Laurens thought might have been inconsequential but his father had just been elected president of Congress. Henry Laurens had at first been inclined to join the critics of Washington, men like Congressman James Lovell of Massachusetts and Thomas Mifflin; but reports from his son and from committees of Congress who had visited Valley Forge led the elder Laurens to an increasing appreciation of Washington's towering stature as the personification of the whole American cause. In this latest controversy with Conway the commander in chief's solution was to lay the whole correspondence before Congress.[23]

At about the same time came Gates' reaction to the "weak General and bad councillors" letter. Gates was disturbed that his private correspondence was being promiscuously circulated, and he notified Washington that he was transmitting a copy of his complaint to Congress. Washington professed to be astonished. Did not Gates know that the source of the letter was Gates' own aide, Colonel Wilkinson? It had been conveyed to him, said Washington, in such a way as to lead him to believe that Gates was warning him against Conway. He had hoped to keep this whole affair "in the family" but since Gates preferred to lay the matter before Congress the commander in chief would do the same with his own correspondence.

As these dispatches reached York the august members of Congress were buffeted from another direction. Nine brigadier generals from seven states wrote to protest the promotion of Conway to major general. A similar blast came from more than forty colonels protesting the promotion of Wilkinson to brigadier. While the members might be sensitive about the authority and dignity of Congress few of them ever forgot that they were also politicians.[24]

With the furor out in the open the air was soon filled with protestations of innocence. Gates brought Conway's offending letter to York and showed a copy of it to President Laurens. The offending phrase quoted by Washington did not appear, but Laurens pronounced the rest of the letter "ten times worse." The letter, it turned out, was a critique of the battle of the Brandywine and probably was filled with much of Conway's "after kind of sagacity." If Gates expected that his arrival at York would promote his cause he was sharply disappointed. On the contrary, it was obvious that Washington's critics were more vocal than numerous, and that Gates would do well to muffle his pretensions. As for Conway, Washington simply gave him the silent treatment, refusing to answer any of his protesting letters. Conway withered on the vine until April, when he once again incautiously threatened to resign. To his dismay Congress accepted with alacrity.

The new Board of War also sank into oblivion. It planned and ordered a winter invasion of Canada. Bypassing Washington's headquarters completely it ordered Lafayette to take command of the expedition with Conway as his second in command (and thus the guiding genius behind the inexperienced young general). But Lafayette scotched this maneuver by refusing to serve with Conway and threatening to return to France. Conway's prestige could scarcely match that of the marquis. The Canadian expedition was, in Washington's words, "the child of folly," and when Lafayette reached Albany at the end of January neither supplies nor troops were at hand, so the invasion was aborted.

The affair ended with professions of loyalty from Gates and a gracious acknowledgement from Washington urging that "those matters which have been the subject of our past correspondence makes me willing to close with the desire . . . of burying them hereafter in silence."[25]

It is idle to say that there was no Conway Cabal. It existed in the minds of men in 1777 and in the histories of the War of Independence ever since. The real question seems to be whether such a term is justified in describing the anti-Washington movement that grew and flourished in the latter part of 1777.

Opposition to Washington came from three principal sources. Congress, imbued with a "new broom" spirit, was determined to assert itself to show its bumbling predecessors how to win the war. As with many of their spiritual descendants they were soon disillusioned and came to appreciate the magnitude of their task (it is notable that not once did Washington visit Congress to plead his cause; instead he invited its committees to the camps—and the effect was invariably devastating). Gates and Conway were simply out to exploit the circumstances to promote their own vaulting ambitions.

To say that these constituted a conspiratorial group of plotters or intriguers is to ignore the bumbling of Gates and Conway, and the ease with which Washington finally disposed of his critics. The conspirators, if such they were, had neither the cohesiveness nor the will to deserve the name.

In the aftermath of recriminations as the participants tried to justify themselves, Wilkinson was appointed secretary to the Board of War. After his complicity in the Conway affair was revealed Gates, the president of the Board, refused to allow him to serve, and Wilkinson was forced to resign his position and his commission (March, 1778). A dual between Gates and Wilkinson was barely averted. Conway could not avoid one with hard-bitten John Cadwalader, the Pennsylvania militia general who had managed to fight in every battle from Trenton to Germantown. They met on July 4, 1778 and Cadwalader, appropriately, shot Conway in the mouth. The Board of War soon sank into that limbo which so often overtakes committees whose members are reluctant to serve and seldom attend.[26]

From the standpoint of personal achievement Washington, who had started the year on a high note of victory, ended it with the bitter taste of defeat in his mouth. His enormous pride was undoubtedly deeply stung, especially as it seemed to him that his very position as commander in chief was being threatened. He had not proven to be the general that the nation—and perhaps he himself—had imagined him to be. His greatest failing was that he could not recognize the limitations of both his men and his officers. He refused to acknowledge that, for the time being, his soldiers, man for man, were not the equal of the redcoats in the field.

Yet in his pessimism he may have failed to give himself sufficiently high marks for achievement. If he bothered to cast his mind back twelve months, he might note that, though this was a tatterdemalion army, it was much more truly a fighting force than in December, 1776. Then he had written, ". . . By the first of next month, then, we shall be left with five [Continental] Regiments of Virginia, one of Maryland, General Hand's and the remains of Miles; reduced by so much sickness, fatigue, &ca. as in the whole not to exceed but fall short of 1200 men;" in December, 1777, "our whole strength in continental troops . . . amount to no more than 8200 In Camp fit for duty."

One accomplishment Washington would not be aware of for some time.

The Year of the Hangman

The great victory over Burgoyne has always been cited as a telling point in convincing the French government to conclude its alliance with the young republic. But John Adams, who had gone to Paris to assist Benjamin Franklin in the negotiations (and had joined the chorus of Washington's critics before he left) made an interesting observation:

> General Gates was the ablest negotiator you had in Europe; next to him, General Washington's attack on the enemy at Germantown. I do not know, indeed, whether this last affair had not more influence on the European mind than that of Saratoga. Although the attempt was unsuccessful, the military gentlemen of Europe considered it as the most decisive proof that America would finally succeed.[27]

FOURTEEN

Epilogue:
The French Alliance

TWO YEARS HAS PASSED SINCE GEORGE III HAD DECLARED BEFORE PARLIAMENT his intention to "put a speedy end to these disorders by the most decisive exertions." Since that time the colonies had declared independence and created an army to resist the authority of the Crown. One of the results of the campaign of 1777 was a document whose words had perhaps a greater significance for the history of the war than those of the great Declaration itself:

> . . . and his most Christian Majesty guarantees on his part to the united states, their liberty, Sovereignty, and Independence, absolute and unlimited. . . .[1]

PARIS

As noted above, the upset in the balance of power occasioned by England's great victory in the Seven Years' War had been a serious blow, not only to France's overseas empire, but to her pride. The intervening years had done little to assuage French sensibilities. She had been forced to stand idly by while two of her former allies, Poland and Turkey, had been dismembered by the powers of eastern Europe, Russia, Prussia, and Austria. The Duc de Choiseul, the French foreign minister, saw in a brief span of ten years the loss of much of France's colonial empire and the shift of the power center of continental Europe to the east. His efforts to revive French military and naval power were therefore aimed at two objectives. The more obvious one was to be ready to take advantage of whatever fissures or cracks appeared in Britain's far-flung colonial empire. The other was to restore French prestige on the continent of Europe, to make the court at Versailles once more a power to be reckoned with.

Choiseul labored under two disadvantages. One was the pacific and phlegmatic person of Louis XV who, unlike his great-grandfather, had no desire to impose the Bourbon will on all of Europe. His successor, Louis XVI, was at heart a man of simple piety who disliked disorder and controversy. He believed firmly in the reduction of his government's extravagant spending and in the reordering of the financial chaos into which his kingdom had fallen. In this he was supported by his principal advisor, the Comte de Maurepas, and his comptroller-general, Anne Robert Jacques Turgot. The King opposed an aggressive foreign policy, with its attendant mounting costs for military expenditures and dangerous diplomatic consequences. But Choiseul's successor and protege, the Comte de Vergennes, was no less determined to achieve Choiseul's objectives. The difference was that Vergennes brought to his office tact, patience, and subterfuge which he had developed in a lifetime of diplomatic service.

Both Choiseul and Vergennes believed that the most vulnerable spot in Britain's empire was her North American colonies, and as early as 1764 French agents had been sent to America to take soundings of public unrest and dissatisfaction. The reports were disappointingly accurate. There was ample evidence that the colonists were chafing under some of the restrictions of the British colonial system, but no discernible signs of colonial disloyalty. At this early date Americans were still contending for their rights as Englishmen.[2]

The mounting crisis of 1774–1775 was vastly encouraging to Vergennes. He was soon at work setting up a system through which covert military aid could be channeled across the Atlantic to America. With the help of Caron de Beaumarchais, sometime playwright and man about Paris, Vergennes let it be known that if French merchants would like to engage in arms traffic with the new republic certain arrangements could be made. It was all to be very quiet and unofficial, for France must not give offense to England by meddling in the latter's domestic affairs.

Meantime, even before the Declaration of Independence Congress had created a secret Committee of Correspondence—a committee on foreign affairs— which was soon actively engaged in seeking help from England's enemies. One of the reasons why the radicals pressed for a vote for independence was the fact that they wished to be able to deal with foreign nations as an independent state. By the time Silas Deane, the first American representative to France, arrived in Paris the initial success of his mission was assured. Although the French government carefully avoided official acknowledgement of the presence of an American commissioner, the astonished Deane received a steady parade of French merchants to his door, anxious to press upon him contracts for supplying the Americans with arms and munitions. The arms were available because Vergennes had seen to it that the arsenals of the government were open—strictly to French merchants, of course. And payments for the weapons was assured because Vergennes quietly circulated the word that American credit was good. The subsequent flow of arms and munitions to the United States was crucial to the American war effort in 1776 and 1777. It has been estimated that eighty percent of the powder burned by Washington's army from Bunker Hill to the end of the campaign of 1777 came from France.

The next step in Vergennes' program was to promote an alliance, and here he was confronted with a stubborn Louis XVI. Military supplies to America were not especially costly, and besides French merchants were turning a nice profit. But the King's passion for economy would not brook the possibility of a war with England. Nor was this the fanciful whim of a wilful monarch. One of the ablest of Louis XVI's ministers was Turgot, the comptroller-general of finance, who was not only a capable administrator but a *physiocrat*. He had inveighed against unofficial aid to the Americans in 1775 and 1776; Vergennes, he said, was going back to the old system of overseas empire with the attendant expenses of a fleet and an army to defend it. Not so, replied Vergennes. France claimed no aspirations for territory overseas (American ministers and Congressmen take note). It was England's trade with her colonies that was the key to her wealth, not the possessions themselves. Deprive her of those colonies and divert the trade from the new republic across the Atlantic to France; the profits from this lucrative free trade area would restore prosperity to France and bring disaster and humiliation to England. It was the sort of argument that should have appealed to a *physiocrat*, but Turgot the financier refused to yield to fine-spun theories. The new commercial and industrial imperialism might be the wave of the future but Turgot was concerned with the here and the now. He insisted that Vergennes' policy would lead to another expensive war and that this would be fatal to the financial structure of the kingdom. Fortunately for Vergennes, Turgot was dismissed in 1776 for reasons unconnected with foreign policy. Still the King declared that he was unwilling to make any commitment to the Americans, at least until there was stronger evidence of a favorable outcome of the war.

Only one other concession could Vergennes wring from the King. This was that the government would tacitly allow vessels of the United States to enter French ports. These included privateers, who were not only allowed port facilities but could dispose of their prizes at auction. The British government protested vigorously claiming that a mere declaration of independence did not constitute a fact of international law. The privateers were especially galling to the British. Lightly gunned, swift, and highly maneuverable, they could slip out of French ports, descend like hawks on fat English merchantmen, and be back in Le Havre or St. Nazaire before patrolling British men-of-war could possibly intervene.[3]

The Earl of Sandwich, the First Lord of the Admiralty, was caught in a strategic bind. General Howe's demands on his brother's fleet, especially during the troop lift to Philadelphia in 1777, taxed the navy beyond its capacity. Had the privateers been forced to operate from bases in America or the West Indies they obviously would not have posed a serious problem. As it was, the talk at the coffee tables at Lloyd's was of insurance rates increased by thirty percent, and ship losses in the last eight months of 1777 were set at nearly £5,000,000. Nor had Lord Howe been successful in significantly interfering with the flow of French supplies to America.

Last, but by no means least, Sandwich reminded Germain of the direct threat of the French fleet across the channel. Although diplomats and their agents and spies played their intricate games both London and Paris were pretty well informed about each other's actions, and could make shrewd guesses as to intentions. Thus in making military and especially naval dispositions the Admiralty was not likely to forget that it was an English Admiral

Boscowan who had delivered a sneak attack on Belle Isle prior to a declaration of war in 1756. It was to be assumed that the French had not forgotten it either. This anxiety was reflected in the increasingly sharp warnings of the British ambassador, Lord Stormont, that the flagrant violations of international law were endangering the peace of Europe.

The arrival of Benjamin Franklin in Paris in December, 1776, was not calculated to placate his lordship. Franklin had been a colonial representative in London for some years before the war and his devious ways had earned him the public censure of Parliament. Stormont warned Vergennes that England would regard any dealings with Franklin as an unfriendly act.[4]

Yet the *haute monde* of Paris could no more ignore "Poor Richard" than it could the Deluge. He became the darling of the aristocracy that surrounded the court at Versailles. His simple dress, his unpowdered hair, his lumpy, aged frame moving through the pomp and glitter of Parisian society had a devastating effect. Here was the rustic from the new republic of mankind who was, in fact, no rustic at all, but a renowned scientist and man of letters. The philosophy of the Enlightenment which had pervaded Europe for more than a century had suddenly found the personification of Rousseau's child of nature. Benjamin Franklin became a Paris fashion in the midst of a world that made a tyranny of fashion. Young ladies were "ready to eat him up" and, to borrow John C. Miller's phrase, Franklin was, even at seventy-one, no mean dish.

And it was a triumphant commentary on both his erudition and his charm that the Franklin fashion was not a sometime thing. During the seven years of his stay in Paris his popularity was undiminished until his own declining health forced him into semiretirement.

To say that the alliance with France would not have come about without Franklin's presence in Paris is obviously to overstate the case. His great contribution was that he made the alliance popular with the *aristoi* who by instinct and breeding could scarcely have been expected to welcome republicanism bred in revolution.

The news of the failure of the British campaign of 1777 and the surrender of Burgoyne's army began to filter into Paris early in November. When rumor became fact the wave of enthusiasm that swept through Paris made it appear as though the long sought alliance was now a foregone conclusion. But the King and Maurepas still hesitated. It seemed to Louis XVI that the United States might be capable of winning its independence without the necessity of French intervention. One of the factors in his hesitancy was the tie with Spain in the form of the Family Compact, an agreement between the two Bourbon monarchs to lend mutual support to each other. Only five years before Spain had become involved in a dispute with Great Britain over the Falkland Islands, and had been forced to back down when France had refused its support. Spain, with her far-flung colonial empire in the west, had not the least interest in supporting a colonial war of liberation. Louis was hesitant to give too great offense to his one close ally.

These arguments failed to impress Vergennes. France, he urged, must not lose this opportunity to recover prestige and influence by humiliating Great Britain; if the United States won independence on its own it might still retain its commercial ties with England. Only by positive action on the part of France could the young republic be persuaded to break all ties with the mother country and make France the beneficiary of its trade. There was also the danger that the British, now fully awake to the possibility of losing the war, would make such generous concessions that the Americans would abandon the vicissitudes of war in favor of "a family compact, that is to say, a league against the House of Bourbon."

Franklin was well aware of the objections being raised to the alliance and he shrewdly played on Vergennes' hopes and fears. After the first wave of jubilation over Burgoyne's surrender had subsided Franklin suddenly became less importunate in seeking to open negotiations, and hinted that the United States' position was now radically altered. It must now seek the best terms for a settlement, whether from Paris or London. He carefully nurtured rumors that he and members of his staff were holding secret meetings with English agents.[5]

Two circumstances finally broke the deadlock that seemed to be developing. The first was that Vergennes convinced the King that if an alliance with the United States did lead to war—as it almost surely would—Spain would be forced willy-nilly to honor the Family Compact from the sheer necessity of having to protect her Latin American possessions. The second factor was that it was well-known that the North ministry was ready to present a plan of reconciliation when Parliament reconvened late in January. If Britain came up with a definite and generous proposal while France held aloof, at worst, the Americans would accept; at best, Franco-American relations would be badly damaged.[6]

On December 6 the first formal meeting of American and French representatives took place, although it was a secret session since France was not yet ready to recognize the United States officially. Franklin assured Vergennes that the Americans were not engaged in any conciliatory negotiations with England, but warned that unless France moved quickly, at least concluding a treaty of friendship and commerce (which would be tantamount to recognition), the United States might "be forced by the people into measures with the Power with whom they should most fear any connection."

As rumors and reports ran rife through the diplomatic underground of Paris the advocates of alliance became increasingly strident. Beaumarchais, the playwright whose energetic—and often comic—efforts in behalf of secret aid to America had made him an ardent advocate of intervention, was near despair. "—Promptly enchain the Americans by a treaty," he insisted; "seize the last moment at which they can still say with noble pride; France has been the first to honour our successes by treating with us on an equal footing. . . ." Probably what broke the deadlock was the knowledge that in London Parliament was about to convene and it was certain that the North ministry was ready to present a peace plan for its immediate action.

At a meeting between the American commissioners and Conrad Gerard (who was to become the first French minister to the United States) Franklin applied the final pressure: ". . . The immediate conclusion of a treaty of commerce and alliance will induce the Deputies to close their ears to any proposal which should not have as its basis entire liberty and independence, both politial and commercial." Gerard agreed, and two weeks later, on February 6, 1778, the treaties were concluded.[7]

LONDON

As the autumn of 1777 came to an end an air of deep pessimism pervaded the ministry in London. The word from Stormont in Paris was that France and Spain had no intention of withholding aid from the Americans; on the contrary, there was every indication that their efforts would be redoubled. By the end of October news came from Burgoyne of the reverse at Bennington and the inconclusive battle at Freeman's Farm on September 19. Howe reported from the Head of the Elk that Loyalism was not rampant in the middle colonies as he had supposed and his gloomy prediction that the war could not be ended without another campaign seemed to Germain and the King a masterpiece of understatement. News of the battle on the Brandywine and the occupation of Philadelphia raised no hopes. Washington's army was still very much alive and Lord North was heard to say that "the best we can make of it is to get out of the dispute as soon as possible."

Then, early in December, came a veritable avalanche of disaster: Burgoyne's army surrendered; Howe cut off from the fleet by the Delaware blockade; Washington's army not only intact, but aggressively seeking out his opponent. All this meant that the ministry must completely reshape its policy.

Germain must consider whether Parliament would support the expenditures for another campaign. Certainly such a proposal would be difficult to support unless the Howes were relieved of their commands. This in itself distressed Germain not at all but he foresaw that to accept their resignations (Lord Howe had also offered to resign) could scarcely be done without blaming the Howes for the failure of the ministry's policy. This, in turn, would raise a political storm from their powerful family and friends. Nevertheless, early in February, 1778, Germain informed Sir William that the King "was graciously pleased to signify to you his royal acquiescence to your request to resign your command. . . ." Admiral Howe did not resign until the following summer, but the storm that Germain foresaw continued for the next two years, marked by Parliamentary investigations and bitter recriminations.

Germain also needed to revise the military strategy of the war in America. He suggested to Clinton that the army's role be essentially a passive one, used offensively only in conjunction with the navy in conducting raids along the New England coast and perhaps attacks on French and Spanish possessions. Lord Howe should conduct a tight naval blockade and concentrate his efforts on reducing privateering and cutting off the flow of supplies coming to the United States from France. It was now almost certain that there would be war with France, probably allied with Spain. This meant England must now think in terms of survival, for the rebuilding of the French army and navy during the ministry of Choiseul had not gone unnoticed. What had begun as a rebellion of colonial farmers had now blossomed into a full-scale war as dire in its significance as those conflicts that had been known collectively as the Second Hundred Years' War. Germain and his colleagues agreed that military conquest as a means of solving the American problem was no longer viable. So ended, for the time at least, the policy which ministers, King, and Parliament had so enthusiastically and confidently launched two years before.[8]

Finally, Lord North saw that if anything was to be salvaged from the wreckage of England's American policy a high order of diplomacy was called for— not the kind of deceptive trickery that he had practiced in 1775, but meaningful concessions that would somehow persuade the Americans that empire was preferable to independence. And it was here that North encountered formidable obstacles. He must prepare his proposals in the face of the virtual certainty that France would offer the United States an alliance. To achieve reconciliation England's terms must grant a wide degree of autonomy to the colonies, one that would make them coequal partners in the empire. This was a bitter pill to swallow. Yet both Lord North and the King recognized the gravity of the situation, and both steeled themselves to the task of winning support, not from the opposition, but from the members of their own party in Parliament who had consistently advocated bringing the colonies to a state of submission. In short, any proposition that was acceptable to the Americans was sure to meet with violent and indignant protest from the ministry's own supporters.

Nowhere is the chasm between American and English thinking better illustrated. Americans believed that, while they might still be country bumpkins in many ways, they had developed a political system that was superior to Britain's. Most wars of colonial liberation were waged to win rights and privileges which had their existence only in the hopes and aspirations of the revolutionaries. American goals were not mere fine-spun theories but, in many cases, accomplished fact. They already had representative assemblies, freedom of worship, voting rights. Their struggle for "liberty" in the decade from 1765 to 1775 was against what they considered to be encroachments on these rights by Parliament. The Stamp Act, the tea tax, the Coercive Acts—these the Americans regarded as acts designed to undermine and destroy a system that they had firmly established.

When members of Parliament expressed outrage that Americans should ever consider themselves as the equals of Englishmen, the American answer was, "We already are!" And Englishmen, blinded by national pride, found this beyond belief.

It was this attitude that Lord North encountered when he prepared to present his solution to the House of Commons when it opened its session in January, 1778. His program was embodied in two acts: "An act for removing all doubts and apprehensions concerning taxation by the parliament of Great Britain in any of the colonies; . . ." and an act authorizing the King to appoint a commission to negotiate with the colonists, it being understood that what they were to offer was essentially a return to the conditions prior to 1763. What North was proposing, in effect, was to trade a policy of colonial taxation for a return to the old mercantile system as embodied in the Navigation Acts. Under questioning Lord North expressed his belief that the tax on tea, the Restraining Acts, and the Coercive Acts would all probably have to be repealed. But he did not wish to make concessions prior to negotiations.

The tumult that Lord North had foreseen erupted. There were bitter denunciations and dire predictions of the decline of the empire. But in the end Parliament—even the Lords—choked down the vile thing. By mid-February it was almost certain that a Franco-American alliance had been concluded. No time must be lost. The attitude of most Englishmen was probably akin to that described in the Commons following North's presentation: "A dull melancholy silence for some time succeeded. . . . It had been heard with profound attention, but without a single mark of approbation. . . . Astonishment, dejection, and fear, over clouded the whole assembly."[9]

YORK AND PHILADELPHIA

The Congress of the United States has always been a very deliberate body, seldom allowing the pressure of events to hasten its measured—and sometimes maddening—pace. The Continental Congress was no exception. The nation's first important debate on foreign policy took place late in 1776 when Washington was being pushed out of New Jersey and almost out of the war. The occasion was the nomination of Benjamin Franklin to be an American commissioner to Paris, and the question was over whether or not he and his colleagues were to seek an alliance with France. Congressional pride in its newly declared independence at times almost matched the arrogant nationalism of Parliament. "It is a cowardly Spirit in our Countrymen," said John Adams, "which makes them pant with so much expectation after a French war. I have very often been ashamed to hear so many Whigs . . . Whining out their ears that We must be subdued unless France should step in." It must be remembered that Americans shared the age-old English hatred of all things French, and, as English colonists, they had engaged in the colonial counterparts of the Second Hundred Years' War. Suspicion was rife that France would use an

American alliance to reestablish New France in North America. It was not to be expected that Anglo-American fear of French imperialism, Catholicism, and absolutism would vanish overnight.

Yet such a revolution of opinion did in fact take place in the succeeding months. Despite the persistence of a good deal of Francophobia in Congress the American delegation in Paris became convinced that France was truly aiming at the humiliation of England and an entree to the trade in North America, and that this was the limit of her aspirations. Moreover Franklin and his colleagues succeeded in convincing Congress. This was due in no small part to the steady stream of supplies and munitions that flowed across the Atlantic in 1777. This was accompanied by a somewhat less welcome tide of French officer volunteers. As noted, American privateers found a safe haven in French ports from which they launched their forays against English shipping. Despite all his devious maneuverings and subtle gestures, when Vergennes proclaimed that France's motive was *revanche*, he meant it.[10]

The first packet of dispatches from Paris which was supposed to contain news of negotiations was opened in York and found to contain thick packets of blank paper. Paul Wentworth, a Loyalist agent, and Dr. Edward Bancroft, Franklin's confidential secretary who was also an English spy, were undoubtedly responsible for this admirably clever theft. They hoped that by delaying Franklin's report of the opening discussions of the alliance they would enable the British government to sow the seeds of discord among the Americans. Indeed the essentials of North's proposals to Parliament reached America before the French treaties since North had sent his plan of reconciliation to America even before it had been approved by Parliament. The terms were distributed throughout the states, and the Whigs shrewdly made no effort to suppress them. In fact, they assisted in giving them the widest possible circulation along with their own pamphlets denouncing the proposals as another perfidious offer which Parliament would renounce as soon as the Americans laid down their arms. Lord North's chickens of 1775 had come to roost. It was carefully noted that the bills had not passed Parliament and there was no assurance that they would not be drastically altered in the process.

Loyalists were quick to point out that America was being conceded everything that had been asked for in 1775. In effect, the mother country was renouncing taxation for revenue and going back to a system under which the colonies had flourished before 1763. But Loyalist arguments were to no avail. Too much blood had been spilled, too many dreams for future of the new nation had been born, too many people thought of themselves more as Americans than as Englishmen.

Congress' reply to North's proposals was a demand that either independence be recognized or all British forces be withdrawn from the states as a precondition for opening negotiations. Already news of an alliance with France was filtering across the Atlantic. On May 2 Simeon Deane arrived at York bearing the official treaties, the terms of which exceeded the fondest hopes of the members of Congress. Not only did France specifically renounce any pretensions to territory in North America, but "they mutually engage not to lay down their arms, until Independence of the united states shall have been formally or tacitly assured. . . ."[11]

It was not until June 6 that the Earl of Carlisle and his fellow commissioners arrived in Philadelphia to attempt to implement the settlement with the mother country. Though empowered to grant generous terms Carlisle was supposed to yield these point by point. Yet if pressed to the limit he was authorized to offer what would have been, in a later era, dominion status. But the Carlisle commission was far too long in reaching America. On his arrival his lordship found that General Clinton and Admiral Howe were on the point of evacuating Philadelphia. Orders to this effect had been issued even before the commissioners had left England. Carlisle was outraged. Though he was a novice at diplomacy, even the young earl knew that diplomats can only operate if they have some kind of leverage. How could he possibly convince the Americans when the British army was in retreat? "It appears that we were to be deceived because the cheat could not otherwise be put upon the nation," remarked his lordship bitterly; "by an imposition of this nature the public is wounded thro' us, and those who contrived the cheat, must answer for the consequences."

On March 23 the King was formally notified of the existence of the French alliance with the United States. The same day George III made recommendations to Lord North that clearly expressed the ruin of England's American policy:

> The paper delivered this day by the French ambassador is certainly equivalent to a declaration and therefore must certainly overturn every plan proposed for strengthening the Army under the Command of Lieut. Gen. Clinton with an intent of carrying on an active War in North America . . . it is a joke to think of keeping Pensilvania for we must form from the Army now in America a corps sufficient to attack the French Islands and two or three thousand men ought to be employed with the Fleet to destroy the Ports and Warfs of the Rebels.

And a few days later:

> . . . I think it so desireable to end the War with that country [the United States], to be enabled with redoubled ardour to avenge the faithless and insolent conduct of France that I think it may be proper to keep open the channel of intercourse with that insidious man [Franklin].[12]

FIFTEEN

The Campaign of 1777: Success and Failure

THE STORY OF THE CAMPAIGN OF 1777 IS DOMINATED BY THE PERSONALITIES OF
five men: Lord George Germain, Sir William Howe, John Burgoyne, George
Washington, and Horatio Gates. Some histories, especially biographies, have
been centered on the "great man" theory, that is, that the great events and
epochs of history have been caused or decisively shaped by great men. This
has at times been amended to say that there are no great men; there are only
great challenges which ordinary men are called upon to meet, which suggests
that there is greatness in many men if the challenge is strong enough to call
forth the best that is in them.

However valid these ideas may be it is surely obvious that history can be
drastically altered by men in positions of power who are weak or incompetent
when confronted by crises. So it seems proper to try to answer several questions as to why the campaign of 1777 turned out as it did in the context of the
failures as well as the successes of the men who had the greatest power to
control events.

One should always be aware that these dominant figures are surrounded
by a host of lesser individuals who played their roles in the outcome. In England George III loyally backed his subordinates and Parliament was a factor
that Germain had constantly to reckon with. In America Washington was
acutely and at times painfully aware of his accountability to Congress.

William Howe and John Burgoyne could not win fame and glory without
the redcoats and their German allies, and the American "rag, tag, and bobtail"
marched and fought through thousands of miles of bitter winter cold and
stifling summer heat. And it may well be that the outcome of the campaign
of 1777—indeed, of the whole war—was determined by those nameless
but deadly little struggles that took place between small parties of Tories and
Patriots. As Professor John Shy has pointed out, most Americans in 1776 only

dimly perceived the issues of which so much was made in speeches, newspapers, and pamphlets of the time, and in the histories that have been written since. We would do well to heed his admonition that "the war was a political education conducted by military means. . . ."

Yet one is constrained to believe that Americans were inclined to climb aboard the most attractive band wagon, so that military campaigns and battles do assume great importance in determining public opinion. Tom Paine's *Common Sense* may have stimulated the movement for independence in the early months of 1776, but a more important factor may have been that on July 2 there were no British troops on American soil. It is doubtful if Paine's *Crisis* series in the latter part of 1776 would have had much effect without the American victories at Trenton and Princeton. So it becomes important to find out why the leaders and their grand plans failed or succeeded because in the final analysis the War of Independence was won by men who fought each other on the battlefield.

Had the King and his ministers decided to treat the rebellion as a diplomatic and political problem one can go through a whole range of speculation and prediction about the fate of England's American empire. (In fact, both Troyer Anderson and Ira Gruber, in their splendid studies of the Howe brothers, emphasize the efforts of the British commanders, in their roles as peace commissioners, to use just such an approach.) But the fact was that King, ministers, and Parliament never seriously considered anything other than a military solution to the American problem prior to 1778. Imbued by a nationalism that amounted to arrogance, it never occurred to them that a similar sense of national identity had developed in America and that English arrogance would be met by a stiff-necked Yankee pride as stubborn as their own.

So the great campaign was launched that would bring the colonies to heel and end the rebellion. Lord Germain, with the full support of the government, set the ponderous British military machine in motion, a prodigious feat for which he has only recently received recognition.

THE BRITISH HIGH COMMAND

The plan for the campaign of 1777 was essentially a simple one. Using the forces from Canada and the lower Hudson moving toward each other along the axis of the Richelieu river, Lake Champlain, and the Hudson river, British armies would separate the New England colonies from the middle Atlantic area so that the rebel forces would be divided and isolated.

Over the years a great deal has been written about whether such an objective was possible, whether indeed the control of the lake and river line could have effectively crippled the Americans and brought about their defeat. Some modern military strategists have insisted that such a line was far too long to be maintained by the limited forces available to the British command.[1]

It should be noted that this was an offensive plan (much like the Union plan for severing the Confederacy by controlling the Mississippi) that envisioned a chain of posts from which raids could be made especially into western Massachusetts and New Hampshire. American supply and troop movements to and from New England, if they could not be entirely interdicted, would be seriously disrupted. A basic tenet of eighteenth century military doctrine was to conduct a "war of posts" from which the enemy could be harassed — e.g., Ticonderoga, Albany, and the Hudson Highlands.

More to the point, whatever latter day theorists believe is really of little relevance. The fact is that those who planned and fought the campaign believed that it was feasible. There are two extensive memoranda in Germain's papers, one directed to him in 1776 and the other Germain's "Own Account of Plans for the Campaign of 1777," that spell out the objectives and their expected results. And not only the British but the Americans believed that the Hudson river and Lake Champlain were of crucial importance. Even as Washington's army reached its last extremity in December, 1776, he insisted that troops be kept at the Highlands of the Hudson. Forts Clinton and Montgomery and later the fortification at West Point guarding the great chain across the river attest to the fact that Washington shared the British conviction that the river line was an all-important element in the strategy of the war. The historian is primarily concerned with why people did what they did and his judgements are rendered on the basis of discernible results. Only then may he indulge in the "might-have-beens" or the "should-not-have-beens."

Even before the British launched the campaign of 1777 serious flaws were apparent. There were early indications that Germain was not firmly in control of either the planning or execution of the campaign. As Howe's alterations and deviations reached London Germain seemed quite willing to acquiesce, even to the point of accepting Howe's final aberration to virtually abandon Burgoyne and concentrate on Philadelphia and Pennsylvania. It is all very well to say that commanders in the field should be allowed a certain latitude in order to deal with changing circumstances. But overall objectives should have been clear cut and agreed upon by Germain and his generals. Even though communications between England and America were tenuous and time-consuming, the planning for 1777 began late in 1776, and both Burgoyne and Howe's second in command, General Clinton, had opportunities to confer personally with Germain.

Why, then, was not such agreement reached? One explanation is that political leaders from that day to this have proven singularly inept at controlling the military. By this is not meant the acquiescence to military domination that raises *juntas* or military dictatorships, but the kind of accommodation to military wishes and opinions that little by little alters and distorts objectives. This, in turn, stems from the fact that the public—or in this case Parliament— becomes infatuated with generals and the heroic aura that surrounds them, so that political leaders hesitate to bring pressure on these popular demigods for fear of political repercussions (one is reminded of Lincoln and McClellan,

Lloyd George and Sir Douglas Haig, President Truman and General Mac-
Arthur). Thus control of overall strategy gradually slips from the grasp of
political leaders and military policy becomes an end rather than a means.
If someone had raised the question in the spring of 1777 in the cabinet: What
terms are to be imposed on the colonies once the war is won, the babel of conflicting views would have revealed that there was little or no agreement as to
the answer. The fact that the King immediately relegated the American war
to secondary status after France entered the conflict of 1778 suggests that the
government's policy of applying a military solution to the American rebellion
was simplistic and shortsighted.

If one is to blame Germain as a major architect for the failure of the campaign of 1777 it must be done in the knowledge that he had to work within the
framework of British politics. He rose to power because he was a strong advocate of forcible suppression of the American rebellion and the Howes were
his chosen instruments for the execution of his policies. In terms of political
influence it is rare that even the most influential politician can match the
glamor of generals and admirals. This was doubly difficult for Germain who
was seldom allowed to forget the cloud that hung over his own military career. Having created the command of the Howe brothers the American Secretary found that he could not get rid of them. There is evidence that as early as
midsummer, even before the results of the campaign were known, Lord
George had become thoroughly disillusioned with General Howe and only
slightly less so with the admiral.

It may have been that Germain realized that Sir William's arbitrary alterations in the basic objectives of the plan for 1777 would make its success doubtful and that the American Secretary's position and prestige were doomed
unless he could rid himself of the incubus of his American commanders. Certainly General Howe's gloomy dispatch from the Head of the Elk late in
August must have warned Germain that the high hopes for 1777 were at an
end. When the Howe brothers finally did resign, the political cost to Germain
and the ministry was severe. But Germain had lost his grip on the control of
the campaign when he failed to impose his will on General Howe and insist
that he adhere to the broad strategic concept which had been laid down as the
basis for its success.

William Howe continues to be an enigma and the command of the Howe
brothers has provoked at least two brilliant studies which are basic to an understanding of the campaign of 1777. While the reasons cited in these studies
are worthy of serious consideration there would appear to be other factors
that need emphasis.[2]

Two characteristics of General Howe seem so obvious that they scarcely
need to be pointed out. The first was that he was seemingly devoid of any
sense of an overall strategy. He never really understood that he was a commander in chief, and therefore responsible for all the King's forces in America.
His statement before Parliament in 1779 that Germain had never actually

ordered him to cooperate with Burgoyne is ample testimony to his utter lack of comprehension of the scope of his responsibility. His almost casual disregard for the northern army may have been rooted in a subconscious fear that Burgoyne's success would overshadow his own reputation, and the Pennsylvania campaign may have been an effort to outshine the rising star of Gentleman Johnny (although there is little evidence to support this assumption). Only when he received Germain's admonitory dispatch in August did Howe finally seem to realize that he had failed in his obligation to Burgoyne.

The second factor was Howe's incredible indolence. One hardly needs to reiterate the series of interminable delays that characterized the entire two and a half years of his command: the delay in moving his base from Boston to New York in 1775–1776; the seven weeks that elapsed between the time he put his first troops ashore on Staten Island in the summer of 1776 and August 27 when he finally brought Washington to battle at Brooklyn Heights; a delay of eight more weeks until he again caught up with Washington at White Plains. In 1777 Sir William made his decision to go to Philadelphia by sea in early April, but not until the third week in July did he finally sail for Pennsylvania and not until September 11 did he engage Washington on the Brandywine (it might be noted that in the summer of 1778 Clinton took the army back to New York in twelve days).

When the army was not on the march Howe's predilection for rounds of social events, his fondness for the bottle—and for the charms of Mrs. Loring—were the subject of much bitter comment, especially among junior officers and Loyalists. Yet all this may be simply an outward sign of an inner weakness, perhaps an abhorrence of launching a campaign with all its attendant responsibilities and risks. This is not to say that Howe lacked courage. Once on the field of battle he displayed more than adequate tactical skill and his bravery under fire is unquestioned.

Thus in immediate circumstances William Howe performed well. When presented with limited responsibility (such as development of the light infantry tactics) his accomplishments seemed exemplary. It was when broader planning and wider responsibility, with their long-term consequences were involved that his performance became deficient.

Like many others, but unlike truly great military leaders, Howe responded far better to immediate rewards than to delayed gratifications. He gave little evidence throughout his career of a genuine commitment to overriding and far-reaching goals, often deferring to personal pleasures and aggrandizement. His political convictions were conspicuous only by their absence. His adherence to the policies of the Crown were less than steadfast and his strongest efforts seem to have been expended in events of the moment, leaving little for the long term.

While these traits may have been insufficiently pronounced to consider Howe as a disordered personality they certainly precluded the kind of iron-willed persistence displayed by great military leaders. In another profession

Sir William might have been highly successful, but his personality simply did not meet the demands of a commander with his far-reaching responsibilities.

Finally, Howe lacked the killer instinct, the intensity of purpose that leads successful commanders not only to defeat an opponent but to drive him relentlessly until he is destroyed. One may imagine what Napoleon, or Robert E. Lee, or Erwin Rommel would have done in the aftermath of Brooklyn Heights or the Brandywine.

In the annals of 1777 John Burgoyne is usually depicted as the epitome of British futility. After all, he lost an entire army and in the military lexicon glory or disgrace rests squarely on the shoulders of the commanding general. Yet on the whole Burgoyne seems the least culpable of them all. Vainglorious and flamboyant he may have been, and his struttings and bombast make him at times appear almost a character out of comic opera. But of the three principals in the British high command he alone held steadfastly to the task that had been assigned to him. He had been ordered to take his army to Albany and he never swerved from that purpose. Part of his failure was due to bad luck (the appearance of Stark's force at Bennington, the unexpected state of readiness at Fort Stanwix), and part of it was due to his own ineptitude, especially his tactical failures at Saratoga. Yet if Howe and Carleton had given him their unstinted support, if the British commander in chief had even harassed Washington persistently during the summer of 1777, Burgoyne would not have had to fritter away his limited force and Gates would not have had those invaluable Continental veterans from Washington's army around which he built the force that checked and then mated the northern invasion.

THE AMERICAN HIGH COMMAND

The resounding American victory at Saratoga and the subsequent alliance with France have tended to obscure a very important question. Having gone to great lengths to explain why the British failed it would seem logical for history to ask why the Americans did not win the war in 1777. By the spring of 1778 the Carlisle Commission was authorized to grant the colonies virtual autonomy in their domestic affairs and the ministry admitted privately that the American rebellion was secondary to defense against France and other potential enemies who would surely go to war with England. It is not logical to suppose that if Howe's army in Pennsylvania had met with a major setback, this, coupled with the destruction of Burgoyne, would have convinced the government that the suppression of the American rebellion was hopeless, and that by granting the colonies their freedom England would avoid a dangerous and expensive war? In short, would not the government have acknowledged in 1778 what it finally did conclude after Yorktown? Even as events stood, in March, 1778, George III gave serious consideration to granting the Americans their independence in order to assure the safety of British possessions in the West Indies and Canada.[3] It therefore seems pertinent to examine the reasons for the American failure in Pennsylvania where success might have profoundly altered the course toward independence.

By 1777 George Washington had become the personification of the American cause. Among the commanders of both armies he alone seems to have had the clearest grasp of the scope of the war. He alone appears to have thought in terms of truly continental strategy. His generalship on the whole is difficult to evaluate for he was harassed by logistical problems such as few generals have had to cope with. His superiors were the members of Congress and enough has been said of their ineptitude to make it clear that few generals have operated with such a millstone around their necks. One never fails to wonder at his infinite patience with the vagaries of Congressmen, his deference to their opinions and orders, and his insistence on one of the most basic of Whig principles, civilian control of the military. More than any other military leader, Washington recognized the political nature of the war and even when Congress granted him dictatorial powers he seldom used them to the fullest extent. It was a corollary of that intensely developed sense of duty which made him a truly great commander and, by 1777, he was the embodiment of the American struggle for independence.

On the battlefield Washington's abilities were not of a very high order, although in the first thirty months of his command he had obviously developed as a field general. One has only to compare Brooklyn Heights and Kip's Bay with the Brandywine to realize that he had developed the very important ability to keep control of a defeated army and restore it rapidly to a state of readiness.

Far from being a Fabius, during 1777 Washington showed himself to be aggressive and even belligerent in seeking out the enemy. Only the restraining counsel of his officers saved him from disaster on more than one occasion. His principal flaw in battle was that he expected too much of the officers and men under his command.

Although he was not as remiss as Howe, Washington also failed to function as a true commander in chief (unlike Howe, he did feel responsible for, and gave significant help to his commander in the north). He had not been able to weld his subordinate officers and their disparate commands into an organizational team that could execute mutually coordinating strategy. Although his mandate from Congress was clear, that he was the commander of all the land forces of the United States, Washington tended to make almost deferential requests rather than positive orders to senior generals like Charles Lee and Israel Putnam. It should be noted in passing that very few eighteenth century armies had achieved the kind of structured chain of command that was established by Napoleon and became fundamental to the organization of the armies of the nineteenth and twentieth centuries.

Nevertheless, it was this inability to work his will on his subordinates that was a major factor in the failure of Washington's campaign against Howe in the latter part of 1777. When Burgoyne surrendered at Saratoga on October 17

Colonel Wilkinson's returns showed the army of the Northern Department as having a total strength of 18,000 men. This was probably exaggerated to impress Burgoyne but certainly Gates' army numbered close to 13,000 and included in these were 5,000 Continentals of which ten regiments had been detached from Washington's command and sent to Gates' assistance.

Washington's strategy after Howe occupied Philadelphia was obvious. Pen up the British and block the Delaware, denying Howe support from the fleet. The battle of Germantown was more than just a show of belligerence. It was an attempt to deal a severe blow to the British commander and pin him down with his back to the Delaware.

With the surrender of Burgoyne it appeared that at last Washington would have available an abundance of Continentals and militia which would give him the kind of decisive superiority needed to mount a successful siege and, if not defeat Howe, at least lock him up in Philadelphia as tightly as he had confined him in Boston two years before—but without an escape route to the sea. With high hopes, Washington called on Gates for reinforcements, explaining the situation and the opportunity it offered.

Gates, justifiably proud of his victory over Burgoyne, was reluctant to give up all or any part of the superb army under his command. Against whom or what he intended to use it he did not say. That he hoped that his splendid success would result in his displacing Washington is quite likely; that he actively conspired to achieve Washington's removal is doubtful. But it was clear that the Hero of Saratoga had soaring ambitions and his swollen ego led him to snub the commander in chief in a manner that was as offensive as it was insubordinate.[4] Only after Washington had sent a member of his staff to Saratoga was he able to pry loose even those regiments that had originally come from his own command. Had these veteran troops been available while the Delaware blockade held Washington might have punished Howe severely.

The failure must be attributed both to Gates' insubordination and to the commander in chief's refusal to insist on compliance. If Washington held back because he feared the political consequences of a confrontation with Gates, the result was the loss of an opportunity such as would not recur until four more weary years of war had passed.

Notes

The number of notes for each chapter has been kept to a minimum in order to distract the reader as little as possible. Each note cites the source material (including quotations) in the order in which it appears in the text. Occasionally more than one source has been cited for the same material where it was felt that confirmation was needed.

Because some sources have been cited with unusual frequency throughout, the following abbreviations have been used to conserve space.

AA, 4th ser. Peter Force, ed., *American Archives: Fourth Series, Containing a Documentary History of the English Colonies . . . to the Declaration of Independence of the United States.* 6 vols. Washington, 1837–1846.

AA, 5th ser.·———, *American Archives, Fifth Series, . . . from the Declaration of Independence, July 4, 1776, to the Definitive Treaty of Peace with Great Britain, September 3, 1783.* 3 vols. Washington, 1848–1853.

AHR American Historical Review.

CL William L. Clements Library, University of Michigan, Ann Arbor, Michigan.

Geo. III Sir John Fortescue, ed., *The Correspondence of King George the Third, from 1760 to December, 1783.* 6 vols. London, 1927–1928.

HM Historical Magazine.

JCC Gaillard Hunt, ed., *Journals of the Continental Congress.* 34 vols. Washington, 1904–1937.

LCC Edmund C. Burnett, ed., *Letters of Members of the Continental Congress.* 8 vols. Washington, 1921–1936.

LTGW Jared Sparks, ed., *Correspondence of the American Revolution; Being Letters of Eminent Men to George Washington. . . .* 3 vols. Freeport, N.Y., 1853.

MHM Maryland Historical Magazine.

MHS Massachusetts Historical Society.

NJA Documents Relating to the Colonial, Revolutionary, and Post-Revolutionary History of the State of New Jersey. Newark, N.J., 1880–19––. Commonly cited as *New Jersey Archives.*

NJHS New Jersey Historical Society.

NYHS New York Historical Society.

PMHB Pennsylvania Magazine of History and Biography.

SS Report on the Manuscripts of Mrs. Stopford-Sackville. Historical Manuscripts Commission. 2 vols. London, 1910.

State John Burgoyne, *A State of the Expedition from Canada as Laid Before the House of*

Commons, With a Collection of Many Circumstances Which Were Prevented from Appearing Before the House by the Prorogation of Parliament. London, 1780.
WGW George Washington, *Writings*, John C. Fitzpatrick, ed. 39 vols. Washington, 1931–1944.
WMQ William and Mary Quarterly.
In citing printed correspondence, addressor, addressee and date have been included only when such data seemed significant.

CHAPTER ONE

1. For Gage see John Richard Alden, *General Gage in America* (Baton Rouge, La., 1948).

2. Gage to Lord Barrington, June 26, Nov. 2, and Dec. 14, 1775, Thomas Gage, *Correspondence*, Clarence E. Carter, ed. (New Haven, Conn., 1931–33), 2, pp. 650, 653–59, 663; John R. Alden, "Why the March to Concord?" *AHR*, 49 (1944), pp. 449–50.

3. Harold L. Murdock, *The Nineteenth of April* (Boston, 1923); Allen French, *The Day of Concord and Lexington* (Boston, 1925).

4. No one, including Ward and the Massachusetts Congress, knew how many men were in the American camps before Washington took command. Allen French, *The First Year of the American Revolution* (New York, 1934), Chaps. V and VI; Hugh Earl Percy to Edmund Harvey, April 20, 1775, *Letters . . . from Boston to New York, 1774–1776*, Charles K. Bolton, ed. (Boston, 1902), p. 48.

5. French, *First Year of the Revolution*, pp. 737–39; Christopher Ward, *The War of the Revolution* (New York, 1952), 1, pp. 59–62; Peter Force, ed., *American Archives: Fourth Series . . . to the Declaration of Independence of the United States* (Washington, 1837–1846), 2, pp. 967–70; Frank Moore, ed., *The Diary of the American Revolution, from Newspapers and other Original Documents* (New York, 1876), 1, p. 94.

6. French, *First Year of the Revolution*, pp. 201–02, 48–49. Security in both armies was extremely lax, although Washington took strict precautions after he took command. Rumors of British plans were out soon after the decision on June 12–14. The Massachusetts Committee of Safety received a warning on June 13. Howe to Germain, June 22, 1775, *Reports on the Manuscripts of Mrs. Stopford-Sackville*, Historical Manuscripts Commission (London, 1910), 2, p. 3; *AA*, 4th ser., 2, pp. 979, 1352, 1040, 1373.

Nomenclature becomes a problem when one talks about the British army. Its forces were almost always a mixture of nationalities, English, Scottish, and Germans, and the latter sometimes contained more than one nationality. I have tried to use the term "British" to denote all troops of whatever nationality who fought under the standard of Great Britain. I have used "redcoats" and "English" to designate troops who came from the British Isles, although I am sure this will offend latter day Scots whose ancestors fought so gallantly in the Highland regiments. The term "Hessian" has been commonly used to describe all German mercenaries, but I have tried to avoid using it unless the units referred to were predominantly soldiers from Hesse-Cassel or Hesse-Hanau.

7. French, *First Year of the Revolution*, Chaps. XV and XVI; Burgoyne to _____, June 25, 1775, *AA*, 4th ser., 2, p. 1094; Rawdon to the Earl of Huntingdon, June 20, 1775, *Report on the Manuscripts of the Late Reginald Hastings*, Historical Manuscripts

Commission (London, 1930, 1947), 3, p. 155; Rev. Peter Thacher, "Narrative," *HM*, 2nd ser., 3, pp. 382–84; "A British Officer to a Friend in England," MHS *Proceedings*, 45 (1910–1911), pp. 101–02; Howe to _____, June 22 and 24, 1775, Sir John Fortescue, ed., *The Correspondence of George III from 1760 to December, 1783* (London, 1927–1928), MHS 3, pp. 220–24; Rawdon to Huntingdon, June 20, 1775, loc. cit., p. 155.

8. Burgoyne to Lord Stanley, June 25, 1775, *AA*, 4th ser., 2, p. 1095; Rawdon to Huntingdon, June 20, 1775, loc. cit., p. 154; Howe to _____, June 24, 1775, *Geo. III*, 3, p. 224; Sir William Howe, *Narrative . . . in a Committee of the House of Commons . . .* (London, 1780), p. 19; Gage to Barrington, June 26, 1775, *Gage Correspondence*, Carter, ed., 2, pp. 686–87.

9. "Whig-Loyalist" is a term applied by William Allen Benton in *Whig-Loyalism: An Aspect of Political Ideology in the American Revolution* (Rutherford, N.J., 1969), to such people as are here described. Some remained loyal to England, others finally supported the American cause. Radical Whigs, as I have used the term, denote primarily those who earliest and most vigorously supported the movement toward independence. Here and elsewhere I have used the terms "Whig" and "Patriot" interchangeably, as well as "Loyalist" and "Tory." I have also used "American" to denote those who supported the cause of independence unless the context indicates otherwise, although I recognize that Loyalists had just as much right to the claim "American" as the Patriots. See also Merrill Jensen, *The Founding of the Nation* (New York, 1968), Chap. XXIII.

10. Lyman Butterfield, ed., *The Adams Papers: The Diary and Autobiography of John Adams* (Cambridge, Mass., 1961), 2, p. 204.

11. *AA*, 4th ser., 2, p. 620; Edmund C. Burnett, ed., *Letters of Members of the Continental Congress* (Washington, 1921–1936), 1, p. 129.

12. John Adams, *Works*, Charles Francis Adams, ed. (Boston, 1850–1856), 2, pp. 415, 418; Douglas Southall Freeman, *George Washington: A Biography* (New York, 1947–1957), 2, Chaps. XIV and XV for service in the Seven Years' War, Chap. XVII for his selection by Congress; George Washington, *Writings*, John C. Fitzpatrick, ed. (Washington, 1931–1944), 3, pp. 292–93.

13. Washington to John Augustin Washington, July 27, 1775, *WGW*, 3, p. 311; to R. H. Lee, July 11, 1775, ibid., 3, pp. 329–30; *AA*, 4th ser., 2, p. 318; Washington to Lund Washington, August 20, 1775, *WGW*, 3, p. 433; William Emerson to his wife, July 17, 1775, George Washington, *Writings*, Jared Sparks, ed. (Boston, 1834–1837), 3, p. 491.

14. Washington to Congress, Sept. 21, 1775, *WGW*, 3, p. 504; to Joseph Reed, Nov. 28, 1775, ibid., 4, p. 124; Washington to Congress, Dec. 4, 1775, ibid., 4, pp. 142–43; Charles Lee to Benjamin Rush, Dec. 12, 1775, *Lee Papers*, NYHS *Collections*, 5 and 6 (1871–1872).

15. Jonathan Sewall to Thomas Robie, July 5, 1775, MHS *Proceedings*, 2nd ser., 9, p. 414; *Stephen Kemble Papers*, NYHS *Collections*, 16 and 17 (1883 and 1884), 1, pp. 269–70; Washington to Congress, Feb. 18, 1776, *WGW* 4, p. 336.

16. Henry Knox, "Diary," *New England Historical and Geneological Register*, 30, pp. 324–25; North Callahan, *Henry Knox, General Washington's General* (New York, 1958), pp. 33–35.

17. Freeman, *Washington*, 4, Chap. II; James Thacher, *Military Journal of the Revolution . . .* (Hartford, Conn., 1862), pp. 38, 40; Josiah Quincy to James Bowdoin.

March 13, 1776, *The Bowdoin-Temple Papers*, James Bowdoin, ed., MHS *Collections*, 6th ser., 9 (1875–1876), p. 284. The cognomen for the United States for about the first fifty years of its history was "Brother Jonathan" rather than "Uncle Sam."

CHAPTER TWO

1. For Germain see Alan Valentine, *Lord George Germain* (New York and Oxford, 1962). The Minden episode and its political consequences are summarized in Gerald Saxon Brown, *The American Secretary* (Ann Arbor, Mich., 1963), pp. 1–12; relevant documents are in *SS*, 1, pp. 312–22.

2. Brown, *American Secretary*, pp. 14–16, 22, 26; *Parliamentary History of England from the Earliest Period to the Year* 1803, published by T. C. Hansard (London, 1813–1814), 18, p. 192; Germain to the Duke of Suffolk, June [16–17], 1775, *SS*, 2, pp. 2–3; Germain to Gen. Irwin, Sept. 13, 1775, ibid., 1, p. 137.

3. George III to Lord North, Nov. 18, 1774, *Geo, III*, 3, p. 153; Dartmouth to Howe, Sept. 5, 1775, *Parliamentary Register, or History of the Proceedings and Debates of the House of Commons* (London, 1802), 10, pp. 262–64.

4. *SS*, 2, p. 18; Piers Mackesy, *The War for America, 1775–1783* (Cambridge, Mass., 1964), pp. 50–53; Brown, *American Secretary*, p. 38; George III to Lord North, Aug. 18 and 23, 1775, *Geo, III*, 3, p. 248; *Parliamentary History*, 18, pp. 696, 734–35, 789, 795.

5. George III to Lord North, Sept. 11, 1774, *Geo. III*, 3, p. 131; Mackesy, *War for America*, pp. 55, 22–23, 14–18, passim.

6. Gage to Lord Barrington, Nov. 2, 1774, Carter, ed., *Gage Correspondence*, 2, p. 659; Brown, *American Secretary*, pp. 51, 55–57; Mackesy, *War for America*, p. 60; *Parliamentary History*, 18, p. 1180; the treaties are quoted in ibid., 18, pp. 1157–67; Germain to Howe, March 26, 1777, German Papers, CL; Mackesy, *War for America*, pp. 63–64; Ward, *Revolution*, 2, Chap. 58; Edward E. Curtis, *The Organization of the British Army in the American Revolution* (New Haven, Conn., 1926), Chap. IV, and pp. 97–98, 95; Edward J. Lowell, *The Hessians and Other Auxiliaries of Great Britain in the Revolutionary War* (Williamstown, Mass., 1970 [1st printing, 1884]), p. 56; Mackesy, *War for America*, pp. 62–64.

7. Mackesy, *War for America*, pp. 57–58, 69–70; Howe to Germain, June 8, 1776, *SS*, 2, p. 36.

8. There is no satisfactory biography of William Howe or his more distinguished but less famous brother, Lord Richard. See Maldwyn A. Jones, "William Howe: Conventional Strategist," in George A. Billias, ed., *George Washington's Opponents* (New York, 1969), pp. 39–72, and Ira D. Gruber, *The Howe Brothers and the American Revolution* (New York, 1972). Germain to Suffolk, Aug. [16–17], 1775, *SS*, 2, p. 2.

9. Gruber, *Howe Brothers*, pp. 45–48, 51–54, 61–71, passim, 73; Troyer S, Anderson, *The Command of the Howe Brothers During the American Revolution* (New York, 1936), pp. 52–57.

10. Gruber, *Howe Brothers*, pp. 73–79; Richard Howe to Germain, March 26, 1776, *SS*, 2, pp. 25–26; Germain to William Howe, March 28, 1776, quoted in Mackesy, *War for America*, p. 60. In citing correspondence to and from the Howe brothers, the name "Howe" alone indicates General William Howe; since letters to and from Admiral Lord Richard Howe are infrequent I have used either his first name, title, or naval rank to identify him.

11. Howe to Germain, April 25, 1776, quoted in Anderson, *Command of the Howes*, p. 121.

CHAPTER THREE

1. Howe to Germain, April 26, 1776, *SS*, 2, p. 30.

2. Correspondence of Alexander Wedderburn, Lord Richard Howe, and Germain, March 4 to April 24, 1776, ibid., 2, pp. 24–30.

3. French, *First Year of the Revolution*, Chap. XVI; Allen French, *The Taking of Ticonderoga in 1775: The British Story; A Study of Captors and Captives* (Cambridge, Mass., 1928); *The Narrative of Ethan Allen*, intro. by Brooke Hindle (New York, 1961).

4. *AA*, 4th ser., 2, p. 734; *JCC*, 2, p. 110.

5. *AA*, 4th ser., 2, pp. 1702, 1703; Martin H. Bush, *Revolutionary Enigma: A Reappraisal of General Philip Schuyler of New York* (New York, 1967), pp. 28–39; *AA*, 4th ser., 2, pp. 669, 468; Ward, *Revolution*, 1, pp. 160–62.

6. Ward, *Revolution*, 1, Chaps. XII and XIV; Kenneth Roberts, ed., *The March to Quebec* (New York, 1940), especially the journals of Isaac Senter, pp. 193–241, and Abner Stocking, pp. 543–68; Paul H. Smith, "Sir Guy Carleton," in Billias, ed., *George Washington's Opponents*, pp. 117–21.

7. John Sullivan to Congress, June 1, 1776, *Letters and Papers*, Otis G. Hammond, ed., New Hampshire Historical Society *Collections*, (Concord, N. H., 1930–1939), 1, pp. 212–14; *AA*, 5th ser., 1, pp. 253–54; James Haddon, *A Journal Kept in Canada and Upon Burgoyne's Expedition, 1775 and 1776* (Albany, N.Y., 1884), pp. 16–32; Smith, in *George Washington's Opponents*, pp. 122–27; John Lacey, "Memoirs . . ." *PMHB*, 25 (1901), pp. 510–12.

8. Burgoyne to Clinton, Nov. 7, 1776, Clinton, Mss., CL.

9. Smith, in *George Washington's Opponents*, pp. 137, 138, 23n.

10. Daniel McCurtin, "Journal of the Times of the Siege of Boston," *Papers Relating to the Provincial History of Pennsylvania*, Thomas Balch, ed. (Philadelphia, 1855), p. 40; Gruber, *The Howe Brothers*, pp. 89–92.

11. Morris to Horatio Gates, April 6, 1776, *LCC*, 1, p. 416.

12. *AA*, 4th ser., 6, p. 627; Jensen, *Founding of a Nation*, pp. 696–99, 692–93.

13. Knox to his wife, July 15, 1776, Noah Brooks, *Henry Knox, A Soldier of the Revolution* (New York, 1900), p. 58; Thacher, *Journal*, p. 51; Weldon S. Brown, *Empire or Independence: A Study in the Failure of Reconciliation, 1774–1783* (Baton Rouge, La., 1941), pp. 108–14; Gruber, *Howe Brothers*, pp. 93–100.

14. Mackesy, *War for America*, pp. 57–60; Germain to Carleton and Howe, Feb. 17, 1776, quoted in ibid., p. 60; Howe to Germain, April 26, 1776, *SS*, 2, p. 30; Gruber, *Howe Brothers*, pp. 82–85.

15. Howe to Germain, April 10 and 13, 1776, *SS*, 2, pp. 37–39.

16. For Long Island see Freeman, *Washington*, 4, pp. 153–75; Howe's comments are to Germain, Apr. 3, 1776, quoted in Anderson, *The Command of the Howes*, p. 134; Howe, *Narrative*, p. 215, Louis L. Tucker, ed., "'To My Inexpressible Astonishment:' Sir George Collier's Observations on the Battle of Long Island," *New York Historical Society Quarterly*, 48 (1964), p. 304.

17. Freeman, *Washington*, 4, pp. 181ff; *WGW*, 6, pp. 2–6, passim; Baldwin to his wife, June 17, 1776, quoted in Freeman, *Washington*, 4, p. 85.

18. Gruber, *Howe Brothers*, pp. 117–20; Mercy Otis Warren, *History of the Rise*,

Progress and Termination of the American Revolution (Boston, 1805), 1, p. 323; John Adams to Samuel Adams, Sept. 17, 1776, *LCC*, 2, p. 92.

19. *JCC*, 5, p. 733; Freeman, *Washington*, 4, pp. 191–203; George Weedon to John Page, Sept. 20, 1776, Chicago Historical Society Mss., quoted in George F. Scheer and Hugh F. Rankin, *Rebels and Redcoats* (New York, 1957), p. 182; *WGW*, 4, p. 59; William B. Reed, *Life and Correspondence of Joseph Reed* . . . (Philadelphia, 1847), 1, p. 238.

20. Freeman, *Washington*, 4, pp. 217–31; Washington to Lund Washington, Sept. 30, 1776, *WGW*, 6, p. 138. With respect to the junction with Carleton, Howe seems to have intended to make the effort when he discussed with Germain the problem of command when he joined the northern army (June 7, 1777, *SS*, 2, pp. 34–35). By August 10 Howe's tone was less enthusiastic: "I shall not presume we can flatter ourselves much at the present prospect the season being so far advanced. The extent of my expectations are bounded by the possession of New York and Rhode Island, and a junction with the northern army" (ibid., 2, p. 38). By September 25, "From the present appearance of things I look upon farther progress of this army for the campaign to be rather precarious . . . nor have I any dependence upon General Carleton's approach to act with influence this year . . ." (ibid., 2, p. 41). Yet despite his concern about the "season being so far advanced," it took Howe more than eight weeks after Washington's evacuation from Long Island to bring the Americans to battle at White Plains, thirty-five miles away.

21. Freeman, *Washington*, 4, pp. 241–42, 256–58; James McMichael, "Diary . . ." *PMHB*, 15 (1892), p. 202.

22. Lee to Horatio Gates, Dec. 13, 1776, *Lee Papers*, 1, p. 348; Reed to Lee, Nov. 21, 1776, ibid., 1, pp. 293–94; Freeman, *Washington*, 4, pp. 275–76.

23. Germain to William Knox, Dec. 31, 1776, Knox Papers, CL: Gruber, *Howe Brothers*, p. 163. One is reminded of the confident optimism of Sir Douglas Haig after the ghastly blood bath in Flanders in 1917, and of American leaders in Viet Nam who persistently saw "light at the end of the tunnel" in 1967–1968.

24. Some objectives are mentioned more frequently than others. The seizure of New York and the reference to a "decisive action" are in Howe to Germain, April 25, 1776, quoted in Anderson, *Command of the Howes*, p. 121. The occupation of Rhode Island is frequently mentioned, Howe to Germain, June 7, Aug. 10, and Sept. 25, 1776, and Germain to Howe, Oct. 18, 1776 (*SS*, 2, pp. 34, 38, 41, 42–43). The junction with Carleton is in Lord Howe to German, Sept. 25 and William Howe to Germain, May 12, June 7, and August 10 (ibid., 2, pp. 9, 31, 34–35, 38). For the southern expedition see Henry Clinton, *The American Rebellion: Sir Henry Clinton's Narrative of His Campaigns, 1775–1782*, William Willcox, ed. (New Haven, Conn., 1954), pp. 25–38; William B. Willcox, *Portrait of a General: Sir Henry Clinton and the War of Independence* (New York, 1962), pp. 62–93. Howe mentions the occupation of New Jersey to Germain Aug. 10 and Nov. 30 (*SS*, 2, pp. 38, 49), and Germain suggests the "visit to Philadelphia" October 18, 1776 (ibid., 2, p. 43). Howe's confession that he "has not the smallest prospect of finishing the campaign. . . ." is to Germain, Sept. 25 (ibid., 2, p. 41).

CHAPTER FOUR

1. Washington to John Augustine Washington, Dec. 18, 1776, *WGW*, 6, p. 398;

Thacher, *Journal*, p. 67.

2. Howe to Germain, Nov. 30, 1776, *SS*, 2, p. 49.

3. Leonard Lundin, *Cockpit of the Revolution: The War for Independence in New Jersey* (Princeton, N.J., 1940), pp. 52–59; John Pomfret, "West New Jersey: A Quaker Society, 1675–1775," *WMQ*, 3rd ser., 8 (1951), pp. 493–519; James G. Connelly, "Quit Rents in New Jersey as a Contributing Cause to the American Revolution," New Jersey Historical Society *Proceedings*, new ser., 7 (1922), pp. 13–21.

4. Lundin, *Cockpit of the Revolution*, pp. 60–75; 74–78; NJHS *Proceedings*, 2nd ser., pp. 1236, 1242. I have used "Council" to refer to the Governor's Council rather than to the Council of Proprietors.

5. Lundin, *Cockpit of the Revolution*, pp. 87–92, 96–99, 54–55, 103–05; Richard C. Haskett, "William Paterson, Attorney General: Public Office and Private Profit in the American Revolution," *WMQ*, 3rd ser., 7 (1950), pp. 26–38.

6. Lundin, *Cockpit of the Revolution*, p. 110; Catharine Fennelly, "William Franklin of New Jersey," *WMQ*, 3rd ser., 16 (1959), pp. 74–87.

7. Lundin, *Cockpit of the Revolution*, pp. 119ff; *Documents Relating to the Colonial, Revolutionary and Post-Revolutionary History of the State of New Jersey* (Newark, 1880–1917), 10, pp. 699–700, 720–21; 2nd ser., 1, pp. 152, 162–63, 138. Hereafter cited as *New Jersey Archives (NJA)*. *AA*, 5th ser., 1, pp. 2, 37, 17, 18, 37; Margaret Morris, *Private Journal Kept During the Revolutionary War for the Amusement of a Sister* (Philadelphia, 1836), pp. 11–13.

8. Freeman, *Washington*, 4, pp. 146–47; *AA*, 5th ser., 1, p. 834; NJHS *Proceedings*, 52, p. 224; *WGW*, 6, p. 333.

9. Lundin, *Cockpit of the Revolution*, pp. 160–65; *AA*, 5th ser., 3, pp. 601, 1169, 1174; *WGW*, 6, p. 397; McDougall's comment in *AA*, 5th ser., 3, p. 1365.

10. Howe, *Narrative*, p. 9; *Examination of Joseph Galloway . . . before the House of Commons, in a Committee on American Papers* (London, 1780), pp. 43–45; Lundin, *Cockpit of the Revolution*, p. 174; *Kemble Papers*, 1, p. 96; Howe's proclamation is in *AA*, 5th ser., 3, p. 927; Congressional report in Moore, *Diary*, 1, pp. 216–17; Captain Fr. Munchausen, *Journal*, quoted in Lundin, *Cockpit of the Revolution*, pp. 185, 178; William Stryker, *The Battles of Trenton and Princeton* (New York, 1898), pp. 329–35. Note that although British and Tory lootings outraged Americans it did not terrorize them. Reprisals were not sanctioned by the British high command and they did not reach the stage that today would be termed atrocities. A reign of terror might have broken American morale, but even if the Howes or Germain had advocated such a policy it is highly unlikely that Parliament would have stood for it. But see Germain to Howe, March 3, 1777 (note 23 below).

11. Reed to Washington, Dec. 23, 1776, Reed, ed., *Joseph Reed*, 1, 275; cf. Freeman, *Washington*, 4, p. 308n.

12. Washington to Gates, Dec. 14, 1776, to Heath, Dec. 16, 1776, *WGW*, 6, pp. 371–72, 385–86; in the exchange of many letters between Washington and Lee I have quoted from Washington to Lee, Dec. 1, 1776, ibid., 6, p. 318, and Lee to Washington, Dec. 8, 1776, *Lee Papers*, 2, p. 326. Washington to John Augustine Washington, Dec. 18, 1776, *WGW*, 6, p. 398; for troop strength about Dec. 16 see ibid., 6, pp. 352, 420–21; quotation is in ibid., 6, p. 432. Cf. Stryker, *Trenton and Princeton*, pp. 59–60.

13. *WGW*, 6, pp. 360, 632, 407; Freeman, *Washington*, 4, pp. 274, 304 and n. It is here suggested that some of the disasters of military history have been the result of key

decisions made by minds exhausted from fatigue and strain. Even military leaders who are considerate of the physical welfare of their men often fail to take similar care of themselves. Attention is invited to Stonewall Jackson in the Seven Days, 1862, American commanders at Savo Island in 1942, and Erwin Rommel in the latter part of the North African campaign (when he was also ill). The strain on Washington from White Plains to the Delaware (Oct. 28 to Dec. 3) had been severe and continuous.

14. Freeman, *Washington*, 4, pp. 303–04 and n.; Stryker, *Trenton and Princeton*, p. 113; Ward, *Revolution*, 1, pp. 292–93 and Stryker, op. cit., say there was a council of war but cf. Freeman, *Washington*, 4, p. 308 and n.

15. Freeman, *Washington*, 4, pp. 311–24 is an excellent account of Trenton and no specific pages have been cited; Marion V. Brewington, "Washington's Boats at the Delaware Crossing," *American Neptune*, 2, (1942), pp. 161–70; Jac Weller, "The Guns of Destiny: Field Artillery in the Trenton-Princeton Campaign," *Military Affairs*, 20 (1955–1956), pp. 1–15. The normal ratio in the British army was two guns per thousand men (but both Howe and Burgoyne exceeded this). Washington's ratio was more than seven per thousand.

16. Von Jungkenn Mss., William L. Clements Library, Ann Arbor, Mich., 1, p. 31; Weller, *Military Affairs*, 20, pp. 8–9; Ward, *Revolution*, 1, pp. 298–301; Stryker, *Trenton and Princeton*, pp. 153–93. Losses as given by Washington, *WGW*, 6, pp. 443–47, passim; cf. Stryker, *Trenton and Princeton*, pp. 188n., 195.

17. *AA*, 5th ser., 3, pp. 1443, 1445–46; Callahan, *Knox*, pp. 89–90; William A. Slaughter, "The Battle of Iron Works Mill," NJHS *Proceedings*, new ser., 4, pp. 22–30; *WGW*, 6, p. 444; Morris, *Journal*, p. 21.

18. Stryker, *Trenton and Princeton*, p. 364; *AA*, 5th ser., 3, p. 1440; Freeman, *Washington*, 4, p. 327, quoting Cadwalader.

19. Washington to Congress, Jan. 1, 1777, *WGW*, 6, p. 464; Sergeant R——, "The Battle of Princeton," *PMHB*, 20 (1896), pp. 515–16; *Journals of the Continental Congress*, Gaillard Hunt, ed. (Washington, 1904–1937), 6, pp. 1045–46. Congress had finally authorized enlistments for three years or the duration of the war on Sept. 16, 1777. Washington to Congress, Jan. 1, 1777, *WGW*, 6, p. 464.

20. For the second New Jersey campaign see Freeman, *Washington*, 4, pp. 339–59; Alfred Hoyt Bill, *The Campaign of Princeton, 1776–1777* (Princeton, N.J., 1948); Washington to Congress, Dec. 29, 1776, *WGW*, 6, pp. 451–52; Weller, *Military Affairs*, 20, p. 11. Washington had a gun ratio of eight per thousand, Cornwallis less than four per thousand. Both quotations concerning the retreat are in Freeman, *Washington*, 4, pp. 344–48; James Wilkinson, *Memoirs of My Own Times* (Philadelphia, 1816), 1, p. 141.

21. Weller, *Military Affairs*, 20, p. 13; Sergeant R——, *PMHB*, 20, p. 518. Moulder's "long" four-pounders were French guns with unusually long barrels, seventy-eight inches as compared with the standard fifty-eight inch barrel.

22. *SS*, 2, pp. 55–56; Lundin, *Cockpit of the Revolution*, pp. 216–26. The quotations are on pp. 224 and 216.

23. See Gruber, *Howe Brothers*, p. 157; Germain to Howe, March 3, 1777, quoted in part in ibid., p. 179.

24. Nicholas Cresswell, *Journal, . . .* 1775–1777 (New York, 1924), pp. 179–80; Moore, *Diary of the Revolution*, 1, p. 193; ibid., 1, p. 198.

CHAPTER FIVE

1. Howard Peckham, *The War for Independence, A Military History* (Chicago, 1958), pp. 199–200; Don R. Higginbotham, *The War for American Independence* (New York, 1971), pp. 389–90.

2. Harold L. Peterson, *The Book of the Continental Soldier: Being a Compleat Account of the Uniforms, Weapons, and Equipment with Which He Lived and Fought* (Harrisburg, Pa., 1968), p. 205.

3. Curtis, *British Army*, pp. 2–5.

4. Ibid., pp. 4–5; Sir John Fortescue, *A History of the British Army* (London and New York, 1899–1930), 3, p. 4.

5. Peterson, *Continental Soldier*, pp. 24, 26–29, 61–62, 64–69, 24–25.

6. Curtis, *British Army*, p. 6; Harold L. Peterson, *Round Shot and Rammer* (Harrisburg, Pa., 1969), pp. 33–48, passim; Captain George Pausch, *Journal . . .* (Albany, N.Y., 1886), p. 126.

7. Curtis, *British Army*, p. 6; Gruber, *Howe Brothers*, p. 31.

8. Curtis, *British Army*, pp. 52, 54, 55, 67, 70–71, 163, 165.

9. Ibid., pp. 22–24, 55–56, 60, 63, 72, 79; Fortescue, *British Army*, 3, p. 41.

10. Curtis, *British Army*, pp. 11n., 28–29, 30–31; Kemble, *Papers*, 1, p. 386; Hannah Winthrop to Mercy Otis Warren, March 10, 1778, Worthington C. Ford, ed., *The Warren-Adams Letters: Being Chiefly a Correspondence Among John Adams, Samuel Adams, and James Warren*, MHS *Collections*, 72 (1917), 2, pp. 451–52; Curtis, *British Army*, p. 30.

11. Curtis, *British Army*, p. 20, 21 and n.

12. Ibid., pp. 25, 159–60.

13. Ibid., pp. 26–28.

14. French, *First Year of the Revolution*, p. 56; AA, 4th ser., 2, pp. 620–21; *JCC*, 5, p. 855.

15. *WGW*, 4, pp. 317–18; ibid., 5, p. 112; Elbridge Gerry to John Adams, Dec. 13, 1775, AA, 4th ser., 4, pp. 255–56.

16. *JCC*, 5, p. 762; Charles S. Stillé, *Major General Anthony Wayne and the Pennsylvania Line in the Continental Army* (Port Washington, N.Y., 1893), p. 44; AA, 4th ser., 2, p. 1630.

17. *WGW*, 6, pp. 6, 11; *JCC*, 5, pp. 854–55; Arthur J. Alexander, "How Maryland Tried to Raise Her Continental Quotas," MHM, 42 (1947), pp. 184–96; Higginbotham, *War of Independence*, p. 390; *WGW*, 6, pp. 110–11.

18. *WGW*, 10, p. 366.

19. Ibid., 4, p. 194; Benjamin Quarles, *The Negro in the American Revolution* (Chapel Hill, N.C., 1961), pp. 55–57.

20. Quarles, *Negro in the Revolution*, p. 53; "Some Extracts from the Papers of General Persifor Frazer," PMHB, 31 (1907), p. 134; Quarles, *Negro in the Revolution*, pp. ix, 72.

21. Quarles, *Negro in the Revolution*, p. 70; Benjamin Harrison to Thomas Dabney, Oct. 7, 1783, Julian P. Boyd, ed., *Papers of Thomas Jefferson* (Princeton, New Jersey, 1950–00), 6, pp. 430–31 and note; William A. Heming, ed., *Statutes at Large, Being a Collection of All the Laws of Virginia* (Richmond, Va., 1809–1823), 11, pp. 308–09.

22. *WGW*, 3, pp. 309–10, 367, 334, 382.

23. Ibid., 4, p. 202; ibid., 5, pp. 246, 264; ibid., 8, pp. 214, 452; ibid., 7, p. 364; Freeman, *Washington*, 4, pp. 405–06.

24. *WGW*, 3, p. 377; ibid., 6, p. 13; ibid., 6, pp. 107–10.

25. Ibid., 11, p. 237; John S. Pancake, *Samuel Smith and the Politics of Business* (University, Ala., 1972), pp. 24–27.

26. *WGW*, 6, pp. 496–97; ibid., 10, p. 160.

27. *JCC*, 6, 1042–46; Ward, *Revolution*, 1, p. 321; *WGW*, 6, p. 112.

28. Lord Rawdon to the Earl of Huntingdon, Jan. 13, 1776, *Hastings Manuscripts*, 3, p. 167; Christopher Hibbet, *Wolfe at Quebec* (London, 1959), p. 25; *WGW*, 7, p. 33; William Evelyn, *Memoirs and Letters . . . From North America, 1774–1776*, G. D. Schull, ed. (Oxford, 1879), p. 51; *Parliamentary Register*, 14th, 1st sess., 1, p. 135.

29. *AA*, 4th ser., 6, pp. 41–42; *Parliamentary Register*, 14th, 1st sess., 1, p. 421; Hugh Earl Percy to Edward Harvey, April 20, 1775, *The Letters of Hugh, Earl Percy*, Bolton, ed., p. 52; Gage, *Papers*, Carter, ed., 1, pp. 686–87.

30. John Shy, "A New Look at Colonial Militia," *WMQ*, 3rd ser., 20 (1963), pp. 175–85; Wilcomb E. Washburn, *The Governor and the Rebel: A History of Bacon's Rebellion in Virginia* (Chapel Hill, N.C., 1957), p. 31.

31. Shy, *WMQ*, 20, pp. 175–85; French, *First Year of the Revolution*, pp. 38–41, 52–55.

32. Charles J. Hoadly, ed., *The Public Records of the State of Connecticut* (Hartford, Conn., 1894), 1, pp. 94ff.

33. Arthur J. Alexander, "Pennsylvania's Revolutionary Militia," *PMHB*, 49 (1945), pp. 15–25, 18, 53.

34. *WGW*, 6, pp. 110–11.

35. Ibid., 3, p. 490; Peterson, *Continental Soldier*, pp. 42–44.

36. *WGW*, 6, pp. 5–6.

37. For these paragraphs I am indebted to John Shy, "The American Revolution: The Military Conflict Considered as a Revolutionary War," *Essays on the American Revolution*, Stephen G. Kurtz and James Hutson, eds. (Chapel Hill, N.C., 1973), pp. 121–56. Professor Shy and I do not agree on all conclusions, but his is one of the most provocative statements that I have read on the wider significance of the War of Independence.

38. *WGW*, 6, p. 28.

39. Ebenezer Huntington, "Letters," *AHR*, 5 (1900), p. 721; Walter Dorn, *Competition for Empire, 1740–1763* (New York, 1940), pp. 80–94; Alexander Graydon, *Memoirs of His Own Time*, John Littell, ed. (Philadelphia, 1846), p. 135; Adams, *Autobiography*, C. F. Adams, ed., 3, p. 48.

40. Washington to Schuyler, July 28, 1775, *WGW*, 3, p. 374.

CHAPTER SIX

1. Memorandum, "Observations on the War in America," [1776?], Germain Papers, CL, probably not written by Germain; Memorandum, probably 1778, titled "[Germain's?] Own Account of the Campaign of 1777," ibid.

2. Howe to Germain, Nov. 30, 1776, *SS*, 2, pp. 49–51.

3. Same to same, December 20, 1776, ibid., 2, pp. 52–53; same to same, Jan. 20, 1777, *Parliamentary Register*, 10, pp. 377–78.

4. Germain to Howe, January 14 and March 3, 1777, *SS*, 2, pp. 56–59.

5. There is an excellent sketch of Burgoyne by George Athan Billias, "John Burgoyne: Ambitious General," in Billias, ed., *George Washington's Opponents*, pp. 142–92 Francis J. Hudleston, *Gentleman Johnny Burgoyne* (Indianapolis, Ind., 1927) is a popular biography which tends toward the romantic rather than the historical. Edward B. de Fonblanque, *Political and Military Episodes . . . Derived from the Life and Correspondence of the Right Hon. John Burgoyne* (London, 1786), contains many valuable documents. The quotation is on p. 90, quoting an anonymous essayist of the time who wrote under the signature of "Junius." George Coventry, *A Critical Inquiry Regarding the Real Author of the Letters of Junius, Proving Them to Have Been Written by Lord Viscount Sackville* (London, 1825), is not convincing.

6. Howe to Germain, Dec. 31, 1776, *SS*, 2, pp. 53–55; Smith, in *George Washington's Opponents*, pp. 126–28; A. L. Burt, "The Quarrel Between Germain and Carleton: An Inverted Story," *Canadian Historical Review*, 11 (1930), pp. 202–22; Burgoyne's "Thoughts" is conveniently reproduced in Hoffman Nickerson, *Turning Point of the Revolution* (New York, 1928), pp. 83–89.

7. Germain to George III, March 18, 1777, *Geo. III*, 3, nos., 1970, 1971, 1996, 1997, including the King's comments on Burgoyne's plan; Germain to Carleton, March 26, 1777, *SS*, 2, pp. 60–63.

8. Gruber, *Howe Brothers*, pp. 212–13.

9. Freeman, *Washington*, 4, pp. 408–09; Ambrose Serle, *American Journal of Ambrose Serle, Secretary to Lord Howe*, 1775–1778, Edward Tatum, ed. (San Marino, Cal., 1940), p. 226; Nicholas Cresswell, *Journal*, . . . 1774–1777, A. G. Bradley, ed. (New York, 1924), p. 229; Ward, *Revolution*, 1, p. 322; Robert Francis Seybolt, ed., "A Contemporary Account of General Sir William Howe's Military Operations in 1777," American Antiquarian Society *Proceedings*, 40 (1931), p. 4; Charles Francis Adams, "Contemporary Opinion of the Howes," MHS *Proceedings*, 44, pp. 118–20; Freeman, *Washington*, 4, pp. 409–11.

10. Howe to Germain, April 2, 1777, *SS*, II, pp. 63–65; Howe to Carleton, April 5, 1777, ibid., 2, pp. 65–66.

11. Balfour's mission is vague. Gruber, *Howe Brothers*, pp. 210–12; Howe to Germain, June 3, 1777 (two weeks after Balfour arrived), *SS*, 2, p. 68; Germain to Howe, May 18, 1777, ibid., 2, p. 66–67.

12. Freeman, *Washington*, 4, pp. 427–33; Ward, *Revolution*, Chap. 29.

13. Willcox, *Clinton*, p. 160–61; Clinton's notes July 10, 11, 13, and 16, 1777, Clinton Papers, CL; Clinton, *American Rebellion*, pp. 61–65.

After examining the Clinton memoranda I confess that I cannot reconstruct all of the Clinton-Howe conversations. I gratefully accept Professor Willcox's version and confer on him full marks for proficiency in hieroglyphics.

CHAPTER SEVEN

1. [John Spear Smith], "Papers of General [Samuel] Smith," *Historical Magazine*, 17 (1870), pp. 8–10; E. C. Burnett, *The Continental Congress* (New York, 1941), p. 180.

This chapter deals primarily with the time and geographical limits of the study as a whole; that is, it is confined to New England, the middle Atlantic states and Virginia, and to the approximate period 1775 to 1778.

2. Alexander Graydon in *The Library of America*, Edmund C. Stedman, ed. (New York, 1891), 3, p. 461.

3. *AA*, 4th ser., 2, pp. 379–80.

4. Robert M. Calhoon, *Loyalists in Revolutionary America*, 1763–1783 (New York, 1973), pp. 273–74.

5. Leslie F. S. Upton, ed., *Revolutionary Versus Loyalist* (Waltham, Mass., Toronto, and London, 1968), pp. 8–10.

6. Hamilton to John Jay, Nov. 26, 1775, *Papers of Alexander Hamilton*, Harold C. Syrett and associates, eds. (New York, 1961–   ), 1, p. 176.

7. Calhoon, *Loyalists*, pp. 302–03.

8. Larry Bowman, "Virginia Committees of Safety, 1774–1776," *Virginia Magazine of History and Biography*, 79 (1971), pp. 322–23; Isaac S. Harrel, *Loyalism in Virginia* (Durham, N.C., 1926), pp. 41–42; James Madison to James Madison, Sr., March 29, 1777, *Papers of James Madison*, William T. Hutchinson and William M. E. Rachel, eds. (Chicago, 1962–   ), 1, pp. 190–91, 192n.

9. Richard Bauman, *For a Reputation of Truth: Politics, Religion, and Conflict Among Pennsylvania Quakers* (Baltimore, 1971), p. 148; Mack Thompson, *Moses Brown* (Chapel Hill, N.C., 1962), Chap. 4.

10. Calhoon, *Loyalists*, pp. 292–94.

11. *JCC*, 5, pp. 379–80.

12. Laws dealing with test oaths and treason are conveniently summarized by states in Claude H. Van Tyne, *Loyalists in the American Revolution* (New York, 1902), Appendices B and C; Calhoon, *Loyalists*, p. 301.

13. Higginbotham, *The War of Independence*, p. 270.

14. Van Tyne, *Loyalists*, Appendices B and C.

15. Calhoon, *Loyalists*, Chap. 27, passim. The case of John Davis is on p. 308; that of John Cannon on p. 307.

16. John Cuneo, "The Early Days of the Queen's Rangers, August, 1776–February, 1777," *Military Affairs*, 22 (1958), pp. 65–74; Alexander C. Flick, *Loyalism in New York During the American Revolution* (New York, 1901), pp. 121–30.

17. Richard C. Haskett, "Prosecuting the Revolution," *AHR*, 59 (1954), pp. 578–87.

18. Harold B. Hancock, *Delaware Loyalists* (Wilmington, Del., 1940), pp. 11–32; Hancock, "Thomas Robinson: Delaware's Most Prominent Loyalist," *Delaware History*, 4 (1950), pp. 1–36.

19. Calhoon, *Loyalists*, Chap. 34.

20. *Public Papers of George Clinton*, Hugh Hastings, ed. (Albany, N.Y., 1899–1914), 2, p. 251.

CHAPTER EIGHT

1. Nickerson, *The Turning Point of the Revolution*, has conveniently reproduced Burgoyne's regular and auxiliary troop strength from various sources, and a discussion of their interpretation, as well as the losses sustained. See Appendix II. John Burgoyne, *A State of the Expedition from Canada as Laid Before the House of Commons, by Lieutenant-General Burgoyne, and Verified by Evidence; with a Collection of Authentic Documents . . .* (London, 1780), p. 1; for Gen. Fraser see Henry Manners Chichester,

1106–07; Baroness Fredericke von Riedesel, *Letters and Journals relating to the War of the American Revolution, and the Capture of the German Troops at Saratoga*, William L. *Dictionary of National Biography*, Sir Lesley Stephen and Sidney Lee, eds. (London, 1917), 7, pp. 662–63; for Gen. Phillips, see Robert Hamilton Vetch, ibid., 15, pp. Stone, ed. (Albany, N.Y., 1867), p. 120; *State*, p. 13; Friederich Adolphus Riedesel, *Memoirs, Letters and Journals of Major General Riedesel During His Residence in America*, Max von Eelking, ed. (Albany, N.Y., 1868), 2, pp. 28, 63.

2. Edward J. Lowell, *The Hessians and the Other German Auxiliaries of Great Britain in the Revolutionary War* (Williamstown, Mass., 1884), pp. 30, 16–18, 20, 39–40, 138; Pausch, *Journal*, pp. 108, 116.

3. *State*, pp. 10–12, p. iii, John Albert Scott, *Fort Stanwix and Oriskany* (Rome, N.Y., 1927), pp. 35–43; Bush, *Schuyler*, pp. 52–55; *State*, app., p. xxiii; Thomas Anburey, *Travels Through the Interior Parts of North America; in a Series of Letters. By a British Officer* (London, 1791), 1, pp. 283, 285–86; Fonblanque, *Burgoyne*, p. 243.

4. Burgoyne to Carleton, June 7, 1777, *State*, p. lv; Riedesel, *Memoirs*, p. 104; Anburey, *Travels*, I, 305–06; Pausch, *Journal*, p. 65; E. B. O'Callahan, ed., *The Orderly Book of General John Burgoyne*, 1777 (Albany, N.Y., 1870), p. 17.

5. Edward P. Hamilton, *Fort Ticonderoga: Key to a Continent* (Boston, 1964), pp. 40–42, 170; William Henry Smith, *The St. Clair Papers, Life and Public Service of Arthur St. Clair, Soldier of the Revolutionary War* . . . (Cincinnati, O., 1882), 1, pp. 3, 7, 15, 16.

6. James Wilkinson to Horatio Gates, June 25, 1777, Wilkinson, *Memoirs*, 1, p. 178; Smith, *St. Clair Papers*, 1, pp. 407–08; Bush, *Schuyler*, pp. 83–96; Burgoyne to General Harvey, May 19, 1777, *State*, p. lvii; Wilkinson, *Memoirs*, 1, pp. 174–76.

7. Nickerson, *Turning Point of the Revolution*, pp. 140–42; William Digby, *The British Invasion from the North: Digby's Journal of the Campaigns of Generals Carleton and Burgoyne from Canada*, 1776–1777, James Phinney Baxter, ed. (New York, 1887), pp. 202–03; Wilkinson, *Memoirs*, 1, pp. 181–83.

8. Wilkinson, *Memoirs*, 1, p. 184; Digby, *Journal*, pp. 204–09; *State*, pp. xxviii–xxix; Burgoyne to Germain, July 11, 1777, ibid., pp. xxxii–xxxiii; Wilkinson, *Memoirs*, 1, p. 180; Digby, *Journal*, 210–11; Wilkinson, *Memoirs*, 1, pp. 185–88; *State*, pp. xxxiv–xxxvi.

9. Fonblanque, *Burgoyne*, p. 248; John Adams to his wife, Aug. 19, 1777, *LCC* 2, p. 455; Washington to Schuyler, July 11, 1777, *WGW*, 8, pp. 392–93; Schuyler to Washington, July 9, 1777, Schuyler Papers, NYPL; St. Clair to Jay, July 25, 1777, *St. Clair Papers*, 1, p. 433.

10. Bush, *Schuyler*, pp. 125–28; Schuyler to Nixon, Fellows, and St. Clair, July 11, 1777, Schuyler Papers, NYPL; Schuyler to Washington July 9, 1777, ibid.; Wilkinson, *Memoirs*, 1, p. 200.

11. Willard Wallace, *Traitorous Hero: The Life and Fortunes of Benedict Arnold* (New York, 1954), p. 148; *WGW*, 8, p. 459; *State*, p. 15, 54; Digby, *Journal*, pp. 233, 239; *State*, pp. vii, xxxix.

12. Baroness Fredericke von Riedesel, *Baroness von Riedesel and the American Revolution: Journal and Correspondence of a Tour of Duty*, 1776–1783, Marvin L. Brown, ed. (Chapel Hill, N.C., 1964), pp. 55–56; O'Callahan, ed., *Orderly Book*, p. 56; Digby, *Journal*, p. 227.

13. Howe to Burgoyne, July 17, 1777, *State*, p. xlix; *WGW*, 9, p. 77.

CHAPTER NINE

1. *State*, p. 221.

2. Bernard Mason, *The Road to Independence: The Revolutionary Movement in New York*, 1773–1777 (Lexington, Ky., 1966), pp. 26–27, 42. For the evolution and characteristics of parties see ibid., Chap. I, especially pp. 40–41. Cf., Flick, *Loyalism in New York*, pp. 25–36; Mason, *Road to Independence*, pp. 42–43.

3. Flick, *Loyalism in New York*, pp. 40–44; Mason, *Road to Independence*, pp. 8–9, 44–46, 78; Carl Becker, *The History of Political Parties in the Province of New York* (Madison, Wis., 1909), p. 193; William Smith, Jr., *Historical Memoir from 16 March 1763 to 25 July 1778*, William H. W. Sabine, ed. (New York, 1756–1958), I, pp. 212–13; Dartmouth to Colden, Dec. 10, 1774, E. B. O'Callaghan, ed., *Documents Relative to the Colonial History of New York* (Albany, N.Y., 1856), 8, p. 514; Mason, *Road to Independence*, p. 52.

4. Mason, *Road to Independence*, pp. 115–17; Scott, *Fort Stanwix and Oriskany*, pp. 41–43; Mason, *Road to Independence*, pp. 103, 106.

5. Curtis P. Nettles, *George Washington and American Independence* (New York, 1951), Chap. XI; Mason, *Road to Independence*, pp. 131–33, 140, 170–75.

6. Quoted in Mason, *Road to Independence*, pp. 176–77; Livingston to John Rutledge, Sept. 27, 1776, Robert Livingston, *Revolutionary Letters of Importance; The Unpublished Correspondence of Robert R. Livingston* (New York, 1918), no. 95; Flick, *Loyalism in New York*, pp. 95–99; Schuyler to Pierre van Cortlandt, July 27, 1777, Schuyler Papers, NYPL.

7. Digby, *Journal*, p. 248; Baron Frederich von Riedesel, *Letters and Journals*, . . . William L. Stone, ed. (Albany, N.Y., 1868), I, pp. 101, 126–27; "Instructions for Lieutenant Colonel Baum, . . ." in William L. Stone, *The Campaign of Lieut. Gen. John Burgoyne and the Expedition of Lieut. Col. Barry St. Leger* (Albany, N.Y., 1877), pp. 277–85.

8. John Stark, *Memoir and Correspondence*, . . . Caleb Stark, ed. (Concord, N. H., 1877), pp. 46–47; Riedesel, *Memoirs*, I, pp. 128–30; Stark, *Memoir*, pp. 55–58; Riedesel, *Memoirs*, I, p. 131.

9. Ward, *Revolution*, I, p. 426; *State*, p. xiii; —— Glich, "Account of the Battle of Bennington," Vermont Historical Society *Proceedings*, I (1870), pp. 219–23, reprinted in Henry Steele Commager and Richard B. Morris, *The Spirit of 'Seventy-Six: The Story of the American Revolution as Told by the Participants* (New York, 1958), pp. 573–76; Stark's report to Gates, Aug. 23, 1777, Stark, *Memoir*, pp. 129–31; Riedesel, *Memoirs*, I, p. 255; Breymann to Riedesel, Aug. 20, 1777, ibid., I, pp. 256–58.

10. Ray W. Pettingill, ed., *Letters from America, 1776–1779, Being Letters by Brunswick, Hessian and Waldeck Officers* . . . (Albany, N.Y., 1924, p. 92; Burgoyne to Germain, Aug. 20, 1777, *State*, pp. lxxv–lxxvi.

11. A contemporary map is in Scott, *Stanwix and Oriskany*, opp. p. 352; John Jay to Gouverneur Morris, July 21, 1777, quoted in Stone, *Burgoyne and St. Leger*, p. 142; Scott, *Stanwix and Oriskany*, pp. 135, 140–41; Stone, *Burgoyne and St. Leger*, pp. 139, 141.

12. Scott, *Stanwix and Oriskany*, pp. 117–29, 157, 164, 166–72; Stone, *Burgoyne and St. Leger*, p. 140; Marinus Willett, *A Narrative of the Military Actions of Colonel Marinus Willett, Taken Chiefly from His Own Manuscripts*, William M. Willett, ed. (New York, 1831), pp. 49–51; St. Leger to Burgoyne, Aug. 27, 1777, *State*, pp. lxxvii–lxxviii.

13. *State*, p. lxxix; Scott, *Stanwix and Oriskany*, p. 139; Stone, *Burgoyne and St. Leger*, pp. 149–51; the quotation is from Thomas Spencer to Herkimer, July 29, 1777, ibid., p. 150.

14. Scott, *Stanwix and Oriskany*, pp. 204–13; *State*, p. lxxviii; Stone, *Burgoyne and St. Leger*, pp. 176–93; Willett, *Narrative*, p. 51; *State*, pp. lxxix–lxxx; Willett, *Narrative*, pp. 53–58, but see Willett's report of August 11, 1777, for a more believable account of the exchange between him and the British emissary, ibid., p. 134.

15. Bush, *Schuyler*, pp. 132–33; Stone, *Burgoyne and St. Leger*, pp. 212–14; Nickerson, *Turning Point*, pp. 273–75; *State*, p. lxxxi; Burgoyne to Germain, August 20, 1777, ibid., pp. xxv–xxvi.

CHAPTER TEN

1. Samuel White Patterson, *Horatio Gates: Defender of American Liberties* (New York, 1941), pp. 50–51; George Athan Billias, "Horatio Gates: Professional Soldier," in Billias, ed., *George Washington's Generals*, p. 80; Busch, *Schuyler*, pp. 26–27; *JCC*, II, pp. 99, 109–10; Washington to Congress, Aug. 3, 1777, *WGW*, 9, pp. 8–9; Bush, *Schuyler*, pp. 60–63, 95; *JCC*, 5, p. 448.

2. Patterson, *Gates*, pp. 4–9; Billias in *George Washington's Generals*, pp. 80–86, 89; Gates to Hancock, Feb. 26, 1777, Gates Papers, NYHS.

3. Schuyler to Congress, March 8, 1777, Schuyler Papers, NYPL; *JCC*, 8, pp. 180–81; Bush, *Schuyler*, pp. 86–92; *JCC*, 7, pp. 273, 326–27, 375, 364; James Duane to Schuyler, June 19, 1777, *LCC*, 2, p. 383; William Duer to Schuyler, June 19, 1777, ibid., 2, pp. 384–86; Bush, *Schuyler*, p. 129; Samuel Adams to R. H. Lee, July 15, 1777, *LCC*, 2, p. 413.

4. Bush, *Schuyler*, pp. 99–103; Wilkinson, *Memoirs*, 1, p. 217; *JCC*, 8, p. 595; Washington to Congress, Aug. 3, 1777, *WGW*, 9, p. 9; *JCC*, 8, p. 604; Wilkinson, *Memoirs*, 1, p. 222.

5. Burgoyne to Germain, Aug. 20, 1777, *State*, p. xlvi; Wilkinson, *Memoirs*, 1, p. 175; ibid., 1, Appendix A, pp. 155ff.

6. Schuyler to Gens. Nixon, Fellows, and St. Clair, all on July 11, 1777, Schuyler Papers, NYPL; to Washington, July 9, 1777, ibid.; Wilkinson, *Memoirs*, 1, pp. 194–95; Schuyler to Washington, July 14, 1777, *LTGW*, 1, p. 397; Wilkinson, *Memoirs*, 1, Appendix B; Schuyler to the New York Council of Safety, July 24, 1777, ibid., 1, p. 201; ibid., 1, p. 200.

7. Digby, *Journal*, pp. 235–37; Burgoyne to Gates, September 9, 1777, Gates Papers, NYHS; Ward, *Revolution*, 2, pp. 497–98, 898 n. 18; James A. Holden, "The Influence of Jenny McCrae on the Burgoyne Campaign," New York Historical Association *Proceedings*, 12 (1913), pp. 249–310; Seth Warner to John Stark, July 24, 1777, Stark, *Memoirs*, p. 121. Some authorities say Jenny was murdered on July 26.

8. Washington to Schuyler, July 22, 1777, *WGW*, 8, p. 450; Gates to Washington, Aug. 22, 1777, *LTGW*, 2, pp. 427–28; Henry Dearborn, *Revolutionary War Journals*, . . . Howard Peckham, ed. (Chicago, 1939), pp. 103–04; Wilkinson, *Memoirs*, 1, p. 232.

9. Wilkinson, *Memoirs*, 1, p. 232; Benson J. Lossing, *Pictorial Field Book of the American Revolution* (New York, 1850–1852), 1, p. 51; Wilkinson, *Memoirs*, 1, pp. 248–49; Dearborn, *Journal*, p. 105.

10. *State*, p. lxxxiv; Anburey, *Travels*, p. 404; Howe to Burgoyne, July 17, 1777, *State*, pp. xlvi–xlvii; ibid., pp. 22–23.

11. George F. R. Stanley, ed., *For Want of a Horse: Being a Narrative of the British Campaign . . . in* 1776 *and* 1777 *by an Officer Who Served Under Lt. Gen. Burgoyne* (Sackville, N.B., 1961), p. 172; *State*, p. li; Anburey, *Travels*, pp. 373–74; *State*, pp. 130–31; Riedesel, *Memoirs*, 1, p. 144; Anburey, *Travels*, pp. 407–10; *State*, p. 83, pp. lxxxv–lxxxvi.

12. Billias in *George Washington's General*, pp. 93–94; Wilkinson, *Memoirs*, 1, pp. 236–38, 243; Digby, *Journal*, pp. 270–73; *State*, pp. lxxxvi–lxxxvii; Wilkinson, *Memoirs*, 1, pp. 238–40; Dearborn, *Journal*, pp. 105–06; Stanley, ed., *For Want of a Horse*, p. 155; *State*, pp. 103–04; Wilkinson, *Memoirs*, 1, p. 241.

The presence of Arnold on the battlefield is examined in Nickerson, *Turning Point*, Appendix XI, and Ward, *Revolution*, 2, Appendix F. The best evidence seems to be from Arnold's own protest to Gates (September 22, Gates Papers, NYHS), in which he does not mention being on the field. See also Wallace, *Traitorous Hero*, p. 148.

Riedesel, *Memoirs*, 1, pp. 147–50; Wilkinson, *Memoirs*, 1, pp. 249–50, 243–44, Appendix D; Dearborn, *Journal*, pp. 106–07.

13. Burgoyne to Gen. Powell, Sept. 20, 1777, Wilkinson, *Memoirs*, 1, p. 242; *State*, p. lxxxvii; Digby, *Journal*, pp. 266–67; Burgoyne to Clinton, Sept. 23, 1777, Wilkinson, *Memoirs*, 1, p. 251.

14. Anburey, *Travels*, pp. 448, 417; Dearborn, *Journal*, p. 107.

CHAPTER ELEVEN

1. Washington to Gen. Ward, Aug. 11, 1777, *WGW*, 9, pp. 57–58.

2. Howe to Germain, July 16, 1777, *SS*, 2, pp. 72–73; Clinton, *American Rebellion*, p. 63.

3. Mrs. Loring came to Philadelphia after Gen. Howe occupied the city.

W. H. Moomaw, "The Denouement of General Howe's Campaign," *English Historical Review*, 79 (1964), pp. 498–512; Serle, *Journal*, p. 241; Washington to Gates, July 30, 1777, *WGW*, 8, p. 499; same to same, [Aug. __?], 1777, ibid., 8, 503–05; to Putnam, Aug. 22, 1777, ibid., 9, p. 115.

4. Whittemore, *Sullivan*, Chap. IV; Kemble, *Papers*, 1, pp. 127–31; Freeman's evaluation of Washington's lieutenants may be found in *Washington*, 4, pp. 367–83 (Greene), 495–96 (Sullivan), 461–62 (Wayne), 241–42 (Stirling), and 417–18 (Stephen); Washington to Stephen, May 12, 1777, *WGW*, 8, p. 53. See also Billias, ed., *George Washington's Generals*, Theodore Thayer, "Nathanael Greene: Revolutionary War Strategist," pp. 109–36; Charles P. Whittemore, "John Sullivan: Luckless Irishman," pp. 137–62; Hugh Rankin, "Anthony Wayne: Military Romanticist," pp. 260–90.

5. *WGW*, 9, pp. 124–27; Sydney George Fisher, *The Struggle for American Independence* (Philadelphia, 1908), 2, p. 20; Charles Francis Adams, *The Familiar Letters of John Adams and His Wife, Abigail Adams, During the Revolution, with a Memoir of Mrs. Adams* (New York, 1876), p. 298; Walter H. Blumenthal, *Women Camp Followers of the American Revolution* (Philadelphia, 1952), p. 66; for Lafayette see Louis Gottschalk, *Lafayette Joins the American Army* (Chicago, 1937).

6. Washington to Congress, Aug. 29, 1777, *WGW*, 9, p. 146; to Gen. Thomas Nelson, Sept. 2, 1777, ibid., 9, p. 164; Montresor, *PMHB*, 5, pp. 404, 407, 409; Carl Bauermeister, *Revolution in America: Confidential Letters and Journals* 1776–1784 *of Adjutant General Bauermeister of the Hessian Forces*, Bernhard Uhlendorf, ed. (New

Brunswick, N.J., 1957), p. 99; Montresor, *PMHB*, 5, pp. 410–17; Paul H. Smith, *Loyalists and Redcoats* (Chapel Hill, N.C., 1964), pp. 46–47, 51–53; Gruber, *Howe Brothers*, p. 238; Howe to Germain, Aug. 30, 1777, *SS*, 2, p. 75.

7. *WGW*, 9, pp. 131–47, passim; the quotation is to Col. John Thompson, Aug. 28, 1777, p. 141; to Congress, Aug. 27, 1777, ibid., 9, pp. 136–37; to Gen. Maxwell, Aug. 30, 1777, ibid., 9, p. 147.

8. Bauermeister, *Revolution in America*, pp. 106–07; Montresor, *PMHB*, 5, p. 414.

9. Bauermeister, *Revolution in America*, pp. 107–10; Freeman, *Washington*, 4, pp. 471–72; Ward, *Revolution*, 1, p. 342.

10. Washington to Congress, Sept. 11, 1777, *WGW*, 9, p. 206; for accounts of the battle see Freeman, *Washington*, 4, pp. 471–89, and Sullivan to John Hancock, Sept. 27, 1777, *Papers*, 1, pp. 460–65; Bauermeister, *Revolution in America*, p. 108; Freeman, *Washington*, 4, p. 476; Whittemore, *Sullivan*, pp. 56–66, passim; Montresor, *PMHB*, 5, pp. 416–17; Freeman, *Washington*,4, pp. 478–79.

Despite Sullivan's statement that "Colonel Hazen's information must be incorrect," Sullivan wrote to Hancock after the battle, speaking of Hazen's later report on British strength, that "as I know Colo. Hazen to be an old [veteran] officer & a good Judge of Numbers I gave credence to his report."

11. "Papers of General Elias Dayton," NJHS *Proceedings*, 1st ser., 9 (1860–1864), p. 184; Freeman, *Washington*, 4, pp. 480–83; Whittemore, *Sullivan*, pp. 62–64; Bauermeister, *Revolution in America*, pp. 106–12.

12. Ward, *Revolution*, 1, p. 354; Freeman, *Washington*, 4, p. 484; Archibald Robertson, *Archibald Robertson, Lieutenant-General Royal Engineers, His Diaries and Sketches in America, 1762–1780,* Harry M. Lydenberg, ed. (New York, 1930), p. 147; Washington to Congress, Sept. 11, 1777, *WGW*, 9, p. 208; ibid., 9, p. 212; Enoch Anderson is quoted in Ward, *Revolution*, 1, p. 354.

13. Freeman, *Washington*, 4, p. 491–93.

14. Ibid., 9, p. 493; Bauermeister, *Revolution in America*, p. 114; Washington to Congress, Sept. 17, 1777, *WGW*, 9, pp. 230–31; the story of this aborted battle and march can be gleaned from *WGW*, 9, pp. 212–42; Washington to Hamilton, Sept. 15, 1777, *WGW*, 9, pp. 249–50; Hamilton to Washington, Sept. 22, 1777, *Papers*, Syrett et al., eds. 1, pp. 330–34.

15. J. Smith Futhey, "The Massacre at Paoli," *PMHB*, 1 (1877), 291–307.

16. Freeman, *Washington*, 4, p. 498; Bauermeister, *Revolution in America*, p. 117; Washington's call for troops can be found in *WGW*, 9, pp. 216–63, passim; the reprimand to Putnam is Sept. 23, 1777, pp. 253–54; *WGW*, 9, pp. 276, 283–85.

17. Franklin is quoted in John C. Miller, *Triumph of Freedom* (Boston, 1948), p. 220.

18. Moore, *Diary of the Revolution* (abr. ed.), p. 255.

19. Washington to Heath, Sept. 14, 1777, *WGW*, 9, p. 220.

CHAPTER TWELVE

1. Anburey, *Travels*, 1, p. 431.

2. Digby, *Journal*, pp. 276–77; Wilkinson, *Memoirs*, 1, p. 248; *LTGW*, 2, pp. 529–30; Riedesel, *Memoirs*, pp. 151–52.

3. Clinton, *American Rebellion*, p. 63; Willcox, *Clinton*, p. 175; Clinton, *American Rebellion*, pp. 65–72; *State*, p. lxxxviii; Willcox, *Clinton*, pp. 177–79; Wilkinson, *Memoirs*, 1, p. 251.

4. Clinton, *American Rebellion*, pp. 72–77; Clinton to Burgoyne, Oct. 6, 1777, ibid., pp. 379–80; Willcox, *Clinton*, pp. 181–84.

5. Dearborn,*Journal*, p. 107; Wilkinson, *Memoirs*, 1, Appendix E; Arnold to Gates, Sept. 22, 1777, Gates Papers, NYHS; Gates to Arnold, Sept. 23, 1777, ibid.; Wilkinson, *Memoirs*, 1, 253–61.

6. *State*, pp. lxxxviii–lxxxviv; Digby, *Journal*, p. 285; Riedesel, *Memoirs*, 1, pp. 157–62.

7. Anburey, *Travels*, p. 435; *State*, p. 42; Riedesel, *Memoirs*, 1, pp. 162–63; Digby, *Journal*, pp. 286–87; Wilkinson, *Memoirs*, 1, pp. 268–69; *State*, p. lxxxix.

8. Riedesel, *Memoirs*, 1, pp. 163–64; Digby, *Journal*, pp. 287–88; *State*, pp. xc–xci; Pausch,*Journal*, pp. 166–67; Stanley, ed., *For Want of a Horse*, p. 100; Wilkinson, *Memoirs*, 1, pp. 268–72.

9. *State*, p. xci; Riedesel, *Memoirs*, 1, pp. 164–65; Digby,*Journal*, p. 288; Wilkinson, *Memoirs*, 1, pp. 272–73.

There is some disagreement as to the exact time of Morgan's attack and also about the wounding of General Fraser. Since Morgan had the farthest to go to get into position I have concluded that his was the last of the attacks to be made. This agrees with Riedesel and with the unknown author of *For Want of a Horse*. Burgoyne and Digby, who perhaps could not bring themselves to admit that the Germans had given way only after the British left and right exposed their position, barely mention the presence of Riedesel's command. I am also guessing at the time of Arnold's arrival. One account (Samuel Woodruff, in Charles Neilson, *An . . . Account of Burgoyne's Campaign . . .* [Albany, N.Y., 1844], pp. 254–57) credits him with the direction of the shooting of General Fraser. I doubt that Arnold would have bothered with such a detail, i.e., ordering Morgan to direct one of his men to shoot the general. Arnold would have been totally concentrated on gathering troops to deliver a killing attack on the retreating British. My guess is that he arrived after Fraser was down and at the point at which the British were establishing their second line at the redoubts.

10. Baroness Riedesel, *Letters and Journals*, Stone, ed., pp. 119–20; Stanley, ed., *For Want of a Horse*, p. 174; Riedesel, *Memoirs*, 1, p. 166; *State*, p. xci.

11. Clinton, *American Rebellion*, pp. 79–81; Willcox, *Clinton*, pp. 186–89, Howe to Clinton, Oct. 6 and 8, 1777, Clinton Papers, CL; Digby, *Journal*, pp. 300–05; Baroness Riedesel, *Letters and Journals*, Stone, ed., p. 128.

12. Riedesel, *Memoirs*, 1, pp. 170–74; Baroness Riedesel, *Letters and Journals*, Stone, ed., p. 128; Riedesel, *Memoirs*, 1, pp. 170–74.

13. Riedesel, *Memoirs*, 1, pp. 175–78; *State*, app., pp. xcviii–ci; Nickerson, *Turning Point*, p. 386.

14. Stark, *Memoir*, p. 74; Riedesel, *Memoirs*, 1, pp. 179–80; *State*, app., pp. ci–cii; Digby, *Journal*, pp. 306–07; Riedesel, *Memoirs*, 1, pp. 181–86; *State*, app. ciii–civ; Digby, *Journal*, pp. 308–17; Wilkinson, *Memoirs*, 1, pp. 299–320.

15. Riedesel, *Memoirs*, 1, pp. 183–84; Wilkinson, *Memoirs*, 1, pp. 321–22; Pettingill, ed., *Letters from America*, pp. 110–13; passim; Baroness Riedesel, *Letters and Journals*, Stone, ed., p. 135.

16. Germain to Carleton, March 26, 1777, *SS*, 2, p. 62; Burgoyne to Germain, Oct. 20, 1777, *State*, xci; Fonblanque, *Burgoyne*, p. 316.

CHAPTER THIRTEEN

1. *WGW*, 9, p. 279; Washington to Congress, Sept. 23, 1777, ibid., 9, p. 259; to

General William Heath, Sept. 20, 1777, ibid., 9, p. 287.

2. *WGW*, 9, p. 277; Washington to Congress, Oct. 5, 1777, ibid., 9, pp. 308–09; Freeman, *Washington*, 4, p. 501 and n.

3. Washington to Congress, Oct. 5, 1777, *WGW*, 9, 308–09; ibid., 9, pp. 307–08; John Sullivan to Meshech Weare, Oct. 25, 1777, Sullivan, *Papers*, 1, pp. 542–47. The description of the approaches to Germantown are given as actually executed by the various contingents rather than as they are given in the orders.

The orders to Smallwood illustrate the complexity of Washington's plan. Smallwood was to "pass down the road by a mill formerly Danl. Morris and Jacob Edges mill into White Marsh Road at the Sandy run: thence to white marsh Church, where take the left hand road, which leads to Jenkins tavern, on the old york road, below Armitages, beyond the seven mile stone half a mile from which turns off short to the right hand, fenced on both sides, which leads through the enemy encampment to Germantown market houses." *WGW*, 9, p. 307.

4. [Joseph P. Martin], *A Narrative of Some of the Adventures, Dangers and Sufferings of a Revolutionary Soldier* (Hallowel, Me., 1830), p. 75; "Extract from the Diary of General Hunt," *Historical Magazine*, 4 (1830), pp. 346–47; Freeman, *Washington*, 4, p. 509; letter of Timothy Pickering in *North American Review*, 23 (1826), pp. 425–30; Sullivan, *Papers*, 1, p. 545; *HM*, 4, p. 347; Martin, *Narrative*, p. 75.

5. George Weedon to _____, Oct. 8, 1777, Weedon Papers, Chicago Historical Society; Sullivan, *Papers*, 1, p. 546; *WGW*, 9, pp. 309–10; Martin, *Narrative*, p. 76; Thomas Paine to Benjamin Franklin, Oct. 16, 1778, *PMHB*, 2 (1878), p. 298.

6. Washington to Congress, Oct. 5, 1777, *WGW*, 9, p. 310; Peckham, *Toll of Independence*, p. 42; *WGW*, 9, p. 323n.; *WGW*, 10, pp. 89, 138.

7. Worthington Chauncy Ford, ed., *Defences in Philadelphia in 1777* (Brooklyn, N.Y., 1892), p. 292; Washington to Gates, Sept. 27, 1777, *WGW*, 9, pp. 264–65; Gates to Washington, Oct. 5, 1777, *LTGW*, 1, p. 437; *JCC*, 8, p. 668; *WGW*, 9, pp. 387 and n., 391.

8. *WGW*, 9, p. 440; Wilkinson to Washington, Oct. 24, 1777, *LTGW*, 2, p. 13; Freeman, *Washington*, 4, pp. 537, 601, Washington to Col. Lewis Nicola, Sept. 29, 1777, *WGW*, 9, p. 284.

9. Samuel Smith to Washington, Sept. 26, 1777, Smith-Carter Papers, Alderman Library, University of Virginia; same to same, Oct. 14, 1777, Ford, ed., *Defences in Philadelphia*, p. 142; "General Smith," *HM*, 17 (1870), pp. 86–87.

10. *HM*, 17, p. 86; Smith to Washington, Oct. 10, 1777, Smith-Carter Papers, Alderman Library; same to same, Oct. 11, 14, and 15, 1777, ibid.; *HM*, 17, p. 88.

11. Ward, *Revolution*, 2, pp. 375–76; Bauermeister, *Revolution in America*, pp. 125–26; *HM*, 17, p. 88; Martin, *Narrative*, pp. 87–88; Ward, *Revolution*, pp. 373–76; *HM*, 17, p. 89.

12. Gates to Washington, Nov. 2, 1777, *WGW*, 9, p. 466n.; ibid., 9, pp. 466–68; Hamilton to Washington, Nov. —, 1777, *LTGW*, 2, p. 29; same to same, Nov. 10 and 12, 1777, ibid., pp. 32–40.

13. Extracts of Fleury's journal in Ford, ed., *Defences in Philadelphia*, pp. 98–99; reports to Col. Smith and Gen. Varnum, ibid., pp. 98–126; Martin, *Narrative*, p. 90; Smith to Washington, Nov. 9 and 11, 1777, Samuel Smith Papers, Library of Congress; Ford, ed., *Defences in Philadelphia*, p. 88.

14. Ford, ed., *Defences in Philadelphia*, pp. 107, 123; *HM*, 17, p. 90; Smith to Washington, Nov. 15, 1777, Ford, ed., *Defences in Philadelphia*, pp. 135–36; Varnum to Washington, Nov. 16, 1777, ibid., pp. 140–41; same to same, Nov. 21, 1777, ibid.,

p. 157; Greene to Washington, Nov. 24, 1777, ibid., p. 166–67; same to same, Nov. 20, 1777, ibid., pp. 149–54.

15. Germain to Richard Howe, Aug. 2, 1777, *SS*, 2, p. 73; to William Howe, Aug. 6, 1777, quoted in Gruber, *Howe Brothers*, p. 221; William Howe to Germain, Nov. 30, 1777, *SS*, 2, p. 81.

16. Ward, *Revolution*, 2, pp. 379–80; the opinions of the officers are quoted in full in Ford, ed., *Defences in Philadelphia*, pp. 212–96; Sullivan to Washington, Dec. 4, 1777, Sullivan, *Papers*, 1, p. 598.

17. Weedon to Washington, Dec. 4, 1777, Ford, ed., *Defences in Philadelphia*, pp. 278, 279; Washington to Thomas Conway, Nov. 9, 1777, *WGW*, 10, p. 29.

18. Burnett, *The Continental Congress*, p. 281; Freeman, *Washington*, 4, pp. 588–89; Washington to Congress, Jan. 2, 1778, *WGW*, 10, 249–50; see opinions of officers, Ford, ed., *Defences in Philadelphia*, pp. 212–96, and especially, Greene to Washington, Dec. 1, 1777, pp. 219–34.

19. Washington to Gen. James Potter, Nov. 12, 1777, *WGW*, 10, pp. 295–96; to Gov. Thomas Wharton, Jan. 1, 1778, ibid., 10, pp. 317–18; Martin, *Narrative*, pp. 112–14; Greene to Washington, Aug. 24, 1779, George Washington Greene, *Life of Nathanael Greene* (New York, 1867–1871), 2, p. 466.

20. Hatch, *Administration of the Revolutionary Army*, pp. 96–97; Freeman, *Washington*, 4, pp. 529–30, 529n. See also Erna Risch, *Quartermaster Support of the Army: A History of the Corps* (Washington, 1962), Chap. 1; Martin, *Narrative*, p. 110.

21. Dr. Albigence Waldo, "Valley Forge, 1777–1778, Diary of Albigence Waldo, of the Connecticut Line," *PMHB*, 21 (1897), pp. 307, 309; *WGW*, 10, pp. 212–24; passim; Hatch, *Administration of the Revolutionary Army*, p. 89; Sullivan to Washington, Dec. 4, 1777, Ford, ed., *Defences in Philadelphia*, p. 245.

22. *WGW*, 10, pp. 195–96; William Gilmore Simms, *The Army Correspondence of Col. John Laurens in the Year* 1777–78, *with a Memoir* . . . (New York, 1861), p. 136; Greene, *Greene*, 3, 563; Mercy Warren to Mrs. Theoderick Bland, March 10, 1778, Ford, ed., *Warren–Adams Letters*, 2, p. 7.

23. Henry Laurens to Lafayette, Jan. 1, 1778, *LCC*, 3, p. 29; Freeman, *Washington*, 4, pp. 590–92.

24. Gates to Washington, Dec. 8, 1777, Gates Papers, NYHS; Washington to Gates, Jan. 4, 1778, *WGW*, 10, pp. 263–64; same to same, Jan. 9, 1778, ibid., pp. 437–41; Freeman, *Washington*, 4, 594, 604n.

25. Henry Laurens to Isaac Motte, Jan. 26, 1778, *LCC*, 3, p. 52; Thomas Flexner, *George Washington in the American Revolution* (Boston, 1967), pp. 268–69; *WGW*, 10, p. 433; Washington to Gates, Feb. 24, 1778, *WGW*, 10, p. 508.

26. Freeman, Washington, 4, pp. 627–29, and 628n.; Flexner, *Washington and the Revolution*, pp. 268–70.

27. *WGW*, 6, p. 420; ibid., p. 195; Francis Wharton, ed., *Diplomatic Correspondence of the American Revolution* (Washington, 1889), 2, p. 664.

CHAPTER FOURTEEN

1. Hunter Miller, ed., *Treaties and Other International Acts of the United States of America* (Washington, 1931), 2, p. 39.

2. For background on French policy in America and Choiseul's part in it see John F. Ramsey, *Anglo-French Relations*, 1763–1770 (Berkeley, Cal., 1939).

3. Brown, *Empire or Independence*, pp. 174–78; *Secret Journals of the Acts and Proceedings of Congress* (Boston, 1820), 2, p. 5 (Nov. 29, 1775); Benjamin F. Stevens, ed., *Steven's Facsimiles of Manuscripts in European Archives Relating to America*, 1773–1783 (London, 1889–1895), nos. 1310, 1835, 76.

4. Gruber, *Howe Brothers*, p. 264; Samuel Curwen, *Journals and Letters of . . . an American in England from 1775 to 1783*, George A. Ward, ed. (Boston, 1864), p. 188; Gruber, *Howe Brothers*, pp. 260–65; Stevens, ed., *Facsimiles*, n. 1796.

5. Miller, *Triumph of Freedom*, p. 277; Brown, *Empire or Independence*, p. 186; Stevens, *Facsimiles*, nos. 1769, 1835, 1827.

6. Stevens, ed., *Facsimiles*, nos. 1775, 1805.

7. Brown, *Empire or Independence*, p. 190; Stevens, *Facsimiles*, nos. 1774, 1829, 1831.

8. Stevens, *Facsimilies*, nos. 1811, 1823, 1857; Gruber, *Howe Brothers*, pp. 272, 276; Germain to Howe, Feb. 4, 1778, *SS*, 2, p. 92; Germain to Clinton, March 8, 1778, *SS*, II, pp. 94–99.

9. Brown, *Empire or Independence*, pp. 6, 197–99, 216; *Parliamentary Register*, 21, pp. 133–34.

10. *JCC*, 5, p. 827; John Adams to James Warren, May 3, 1777, *LCC*, 2, p. 355; Brown, *Empire or Independence*, p. 176.
Perhaps the most unusual aspect of the whole negotiation between the United States and France was the fact that French motivation was purely and simply to weaken Great Britain. It is hard to believe that France, once a great colonial power in North America, entertained no territorial designs in America (other than the protection of her West Indian possessions). But such, in fact, was the case. The inquisitive reader is invited to examine the following correspondence: the American ministers (Franklin, Deane and Lee) to the Committee on Foreign Affairs, Sept. 8, 1777, Francis Wharton, ed., *The Revolutionary Diplomatic Correspondence of the United States* (Washington, 1889), 2, pp. 388–91; same to same, Oct. 7, 1777, ibid., 2, pp. 404–06; Lee to the Committee on Foreign Affairs, Nov. 27, 1777, ibid., 2, pp. 429–31; the ministers to the Committee on Foreign Affairs, Dec. 18 (ten days after the first conversations between the American ministers and the French representatives), ibid., 2, pp. 452–54; Franklin and Dean to Congress, Feb. 8, 1777 (two days after the signing of the treaties), ibid., 2, pp. 490–91; same to same, Feb. 28, 1777, ibid., 2, pp. 507–09.

11. Carl Van Doren, *Secret History of the American Revolution* (New York, 1941), pp. 61–63; *JCC*, 10, pp. 374–80; Brown, *Empire or Independence*, p. 258; Miller, ed., *Treaties of the United States*, 2, pp. 38–39.

12. Brown, *Empire or Independence*, pp. 260–66; Stevens, ed., *Facsimiles*, nos. 1059, 509; George III to Lord North, March 23, and March 26, 1778, *Geo. III*, 4, pp. 74, 80.

CHAPTER FIFTEEN

1. Higginbotham, *War of Independence*, pp. 177–78, citing Alexander Hamilton, *Papers*, Syrett, et al., eds., 1, pp. 200–21.

2. The reference here is, of course, to the studies of Troyer S. Anderson and Ira Gruber previously cited.

3. Ayling, *George III*, pp. 260–61; cf., George III to Lord North, Jan. 13, 15, 1778, *Geo. III*, 4, pp. 14–15; same to same, March 27, 1778, ibid., 4, pp. 82–83.

4. Wilkinson exaggerated his return in order to convince Burgoyne (who received

a copy) that his situation was hopeless. Charles K. Lesser, *The Sinews of Independence* (Chicago, 1976), p. 50, gives Gates' army 13,216 rank and file, present and fit for duty.

For the effect of the Saratoga victory on Gates' self-esteem, see Gates to his wife, Sept. 19, Oct. 20, and Nov. 17, 1777. Gates Papers, NYHS.

A Bibliographical Essay

In any research project the writer always has at hand a few basic works that provide handy reference and enable him to preserve a properly broad perspective. Yet these volumes are usually cited infrequently or not at all in the notes on sources. Let it therefore be herewith gratefully acknowledged that the following volumes were always within arm's reach while this study was being prepared: Mark W. Boatner, III, *Encyclopedia of the American Revolution* (1966); Douglas Freeman's fourth volume of his magnificent biography of George Washington, *Leader of the Revolution* (1951); Christopher Ward, *The War of the Revolution* (2 vols., 1952); Hoffman Nickerson, *Turning Point of the Revolution* (1926); Henry Steele Commager and Richard Morris, eds., *Spirit of 'Seventy-Six* (1967), with its splendid guide to source materials, and the equally valuable *Rebels and Redcoats* edited by George F. Scheer and Hugh F. Rankin (1948); John C. Miller, *The Triumph of Freedom* (1948), and Don R. Higginbotham, *The War of American Independence* (1971), which will guide the reader to the bibliographical tools of the history of the war.

Few periods in United States history have produced such a deluge of source materials that have found their way into print. John C. Fitzpatrick has edited the *Writings of George Washington* (39 vols, 1931–44), which is, of course, basic to any study of the War of Independence. Peter Force's monumental *Archives of American History . . .* (4th ser., 6 vols, 1837–46 and 5th ser., 3 vols., 1848–53) contains a mass of material on all phases of the war, as does Edmund C. Burnett's *Letters of Members of the Continental Congress* (8 vols, 1921–36).

On the British side the most important printed sources are Sir John Fortescue, *The Correspondence of George the Third . . .* (6 vols., 1927–28), and the Historical Manuscripts Commission *Report on the Manuscripts of Mrs. Stopford-Sackville* (2 vols, 1904), the latter containing much of the correspondence between Lord Germain and the Howes.

But it is in the area of personal journals and memoirs of people from generals to privates to Mrs. Mercy Otis Warren that one encounters a nearly inexhaustible mine of materials (Professors Commager and Morris list more than one hundred and fifty) ranging all the way from single letters in historical journals to James Wilkinson's three-volume *Memoirs*.

The brief listing here will contain only those which the author found especially valuable. On the American side *Private Yankee Doodle*, edited by George F. Scheer (1962), provides an incomparable story of the unflappable Joseph Plumb Martin. James Wilkinson's *Memoirs of My Own Times* (3 vols., 1818) is indispensable although one must proceed with caution when the "Admirable Trumpeter" is recounting his own exploits. Similar care must be used in William Stone's *The Campaign of . . . Burgoyne and . . . St. Leger* (1877) and John Morin Scott, *Fort Stanwix and Oriskany* (1927) since much of the narratives are shot through with "well known" regional or family legends, but both contain important documentary material. There are innumerable other letters, memoirs and diaries which are valuable for specific episodes connected with the campaigns.

On the British side Sir Henry Clinton tells his story in *The American Rebellion*, edited by William Willcox (1954). John Burgoyne, *A State of the Expedition from Canada . . .* (1780) is obviously self-serving in places but contains many indispensable documents as well as testimony of the participants in the hearings before Parliament. William Howe's *Narrative . . . in a Committee of the House of Commons* (1780) is perhaps more revealing of Howe himself than of the events of his campaigns. William Digby's *Journal . . . 1776–1777*, edited by James Phinney Baxter (1887) is a junior officer's view, as is G. B. Stanley, ed., *For Want of a Horse* (1961). The latter is especially valuable for the summary of Burgoyne's troop strengths and losses at various stages of the campaign, obviously compiled from a variety of sources including Digby, Burgoyne, and Wilkinson.

For the German auxiliaries both Baron Riedesel, *Memoirs*, edited by William L. Stone (2 vols., 1868) and *Baroness Riedesel and the American Revolution*, Marvin L. Brown, ed., give valuable and lively accounts of the northern expedition, and that hard-bitten gunner of the Hesse-Hanau artillery, Captain George Pausch, in his *Journal . . .* gives us splendid scenes from the battlefield but also from the bivouac where his German gunners frequently battled their British allies. Edward J. Lowell, *The Hessians* (1884) adds valuable material as does Ray W. Pettingill, ed., *Letters from America* (1924). One of the best sources for Howe's Pennsylvania campaign is Major Carl Bauermeister, *Revolution in America*, Bernard Uhlendorf, ed. (1957).

The principal government documents were Gaillard Hunt, ed., *Journals of the Continental Congress* (34 vols., 1904–1937), John Almon, ed., *The Parliamentary Register . . .* (17 vols., 1775–80), William Cobbett, ed., *The Parliamentary History of England . . . to the Year 1803* (36 vols., 1806–1820), and Frances Wharton, ed., *The Diplomatic Correspondence of the American Revolution* (1889).

The major manuscript collections that were utilized in this study were the Horatio Gates Papers in the library of the New York Historical Society, the Philip Schuyler Papers in the New York Public Library, and the Germain and Clinton Papers in the William L. Clements Library at the University of Michigan.

Almost all of the major figures on both sides have attracted biographers. Handy references are George A. Billias, ed., *George Washington's Generals* (1964) and his *George Washington's Opponents* (1969). Biographies of Horatio Gates by Paul D. Nelson, and John Burgoyne by James Lunt appeared too late to be included in this study.

The following biographies were especially useful not only for their fine character portrayal but for the depth and range of the setting in which their respective subjects lived and moved: William Willcox's, *Portrait of a General: Sir Henry Clinton and the War of Independence* (1962) is especially valuable when used with Clinton's *American Rebellion;* Louis Gottschalk's three volumes on Lafayette, *Lafayette Comes to America* (1935), *Lafayette Joins the American Army* (1937), and *Lafayette and the Close of the American Revolution* (1942); Thomas Flexner, *George Washington and the American Revolution* (2nd of 3 vols., 1967), Martin Bush, *Revolutionary Enigma: A Reappraisal of Phillip*

Schuyler of New York (1967); Don Gerlach, *Philip Schuyler and the American Revolution* (1964), especially good on the political background in New York to 1776.

There is no good biography of either of the Howes, but Ira Gruber, *The Howe Brothers and the American Revolution* (1972) and Troyer S. Anderson, *The Command of the Howe Brothers in the American Revolution* (1935), have thoroughly explored the participation of the Howes in the war. Alan Valentine has written a fine biography of *Lord George Germain* (1962), but this needs to be supplemented by Gerald S. Brown, *The American Secretary* (1963) and Piers Mackesy, *The War for America, 1775–1783* (1964), both of whom have done much to refurbish Germain's tarnished character. Mackesy is especially valuable on the British government's conduct of the war. Of the several biographies of George III I found Stanley Ayling's *George the Third* (1972) to be the most useful.

For the two armies Edward E. Curtis, *The Organization of the British Army in the American Revolution* (1926), Charles K. Bolton, *The Private Soldier Under Washington* (1902), and Louis C. Hatch, *The Administration of the American Revolutionary Army* (1904) are required reading. For weapons and accoutrements of the soldiers see Harold Peterson, *The Book of the Continental Soldier* (1968) and his *Round Shot and Rammer* (1969). The increasing use—and effectiveness—of artillery in both arimes is discussed in Jac Weller, "The Guns of Destiny: Field Artillery in the Trenton-Princeton Campaign," *Military Affairs*, 20 (1955–56). The role of black Americans is ably treated in Benjamin Quarles, *The Negro in the American Revolution* (1961). The full story of the militia has yet to be told, but when it is, the man who will probably do so is John Shy who has already raised some provocative questions in "A New Look at Colonial Militia," *WMQ*, 3rd ser., 20 (1963) and in "The American Revolution: The Military Conflict Considered as a Revolutionary War," in *Essays on the American Revolution*, Stephen B. Kurtz and James Hutson, eds. (1973).

There have been several recent studies on the Loyalists that finally pick up a story first told by Claude H. Van Tyne in *Loyalists in the American Revolution* (1929). An excellent recent work is Robert M. Calhoon, *Loyalists in Revolutionary America, 1760–1781* (1973). Another essential work is Paul H. Smith, *Loyalists and Redcoats* (1964). William Allen Benton, *Whig-Loyalists in the American Revolution* (1969), deals effectively with the puzzling question of divided loyalties. There have been a number of studies of Loyalism in individual states. Among these are Alexander Flick, *The Loyalists in New York in the American Revolution* (1901), Isaac Harrel, *Loyalism in Virginia* (1926), Robert O. DeMond, *The Loyalists in North Caroline During the Revolution* (1940), and William H. Siebert, *Loyalists in Pennsylvania* (1920).

In reviewing my notes I am appalled to find that nowhere do I cite Samuel Flagg Bemis' *Diplomacy of the American Revolution* (1935). It was, of course, essential to my understanding of the French Alliance. A more detailed treatment of the circumstances surrounding the negotiations is Weldon Brown, *Empire or Independence: A Study of the Failure of Reconciliation* (1941).

This essay deals only with those works that were most useful in preparing this particular study. It does not cover many of the sources cited in the notes nor could it conceivably include the many works read over a period of years that conveyed impressions and generated ideas thereby conditioning the attitudes and conclusions herein expressed.

Index

Praise for
THE COPERNICUS LEGACY
SERIES

"I had to keep reminding myself *The Copernicus Legacy*
was intended for a young audience. Full of mystery and
intrigue, this book had me completely transfixed."

—Ridley Pearson, *New York Times* bestselling author
of the Kingdom Keepers series

"*The Copernicus Legacy* takes you on a fantastical journey that
is as eye-opening as it is page-turning. With mysteries hiding
behind secrets coded in riddle, this book is like a Dan
Brown thriller for young readers. The further
you get, the more you must read!"

—Angie Sage, *New York Times* bestselling author
of the Septimus Heap series

"*The Copernicus Legacy* has it all: A secret code, priceless relics,
murderous knights, a five-hundred-year-old mystery, and
a story full of friendship, family, humor, and intelligence."

—Wendy Mass, *New York Times* bestselling author
of *The Candymakers* and *Every Soul a Star*

"With engaging characters, a globe-trotting plot, and dangerous villains,
it is hard to find something not to like. Equal parts edge-of-your-seat
suspense and heartfelt coming-of-age."
—*Kirkus Reviews* (starred review)

"Fast-paced and clever, the novel reads like a mash-up of the National
Treasure films and *The Da Vinci Code*."
—*Publishers Weekly*

ALSO BY TONY ABBOTT

The Copernicus Legacy: The Forbidden Stone
The Copernicus Archives #1: Wade and the Scorpion's Claw

TONY ABBOTT

★BOOK 2★

THE SERPENT'S CURSE

ILLUSTRATIONS BY BILL PERKINS

KATHERINE TEGEN BOOKS
An Imprint of HarperCollins Publishers

Katherine Tegen Books is an imprint of HarperCollins Publishers.

The Copernicus Legacy: The Serpent's Curse
Text copyright © 2014 by HarperCollins Publishers
Illustrations copyright © 2014 by Bill Perkins
www.harpercollinschildrens.com

Library of Congress Control Number: 2014937634
ISBN 978-0-06-219448-0 (pbk.)

Typography by Michelle Gengaro-Kokmen
17 18 19   BVG   10 9 8 7 6 5 4 3 2
❖
First paperback edition, 2015

To Guardians everywhere

CHAPTER ONE

Twelve hidden relics.
One ancient time machine.
A mother, lost.

Seven minutes before the nasty, pumped-up SUV appeared, Wade Kaplan slumped against his seat in the limousine and scowled silently.

None of his weary co-passengers had spoken a word since the airport. They needed to. They needed to talk, and then they needed to act, together, all of them—his

1

father, astrophysicist Dr. Roald Kaplan; his whip-sharp cousin Lily; her seriously awesome friend Becca Moore; and his stepbrother—no, his brother—Darrell.

"Ten minutes, we'll be in Manhattan," the driver said, his eyes constantly scanning the road, the mirrors, the side windows. "There are sandwiches in the side compartments. You must be hungry, no?"

Wade felt someone should respond to the older gentleman who'd met them at the airport, but no one did. They looked at the floor, at their hands, at their reflections in the windows, anywhere but eye to eye. After what seemed like an eternity, when even Wade couldn't make himself answer, the question faded in the air and died.

For the last three days, he and his family had come to grips with a terrifying truth. His stepmother, Sara, had been kidnapped by the vicious agents of the Teutonic Order of Ancient Prussia.

"You can see the skyline coming up," the driver said, as if it were perfectly all right that no one was speaking.

Ever since Wade's uncle Henry had sent a coded message to his father and was then found murdered, Wade and the others had been swept into a hunt for twelve priceless artifacts hidden around the world by the friends of the sixteenth-century astronomer Nicolaus

Copernicus—the Guardians.

The relics were originally part of a *machina tempore*—an ancient time machine that Copernicus had discovered, rebuilt, journeyed in, and then disassembled when he realized the evil Teutonic Order was after it.

What did an old time machine have to do with Sara Kaplan?

The mysterious young leader of the present-day Teutonic Knights, Galina Krause, *burned* to possess the twelve Copernicus relics and rebuild his machine. No sooner had the children outwitted the Order and discovered Vela—the blue stone now safely tucked into the breast pocket of Wade's father's tweed jacket—than the news came to them.

Sara had vanished.

Galina's cryptic words in Guam suddenly made sense. Because the Copernicus legend hinted that Vela would lead to the next relic, Sara would be brought to wherever the second relic was likely to be—to serve as the ultimate ransom.

Wade glanced at the dark buildings flashing past. Their windows stared back like sinister eyes. The hope that had sustained his family on their recent layover in San Francisco—that Sara would soon be freed—had proved utterly false.

They were crushed.

Yet if they were crushed, they were also learning that what didn't kill them might make them stronger—and smarter. Since their quest began, Wade had grown certain that nothing in the world was coincidental. Events and people were connected across time and place in a way he'd never understood before. He also knew that Galina's minions were everywhere. Right now, sitting in that car, he and his family were more determined than ever to discover the next relic, overcome the ruthless Order, and bring Sara home safe.

But they couldn't sulk anymore, they couldn't brood; they had to talk.

Anxious to break the silence, Wade cleared his throat.

Then Lily spoke. "Someone's following us. It looks like a tank."

His father, suddenly alert, twisted in his seat. "A Hummer. Dark gray."

"I see it," the driver said, instantly speeding up. "I'm calling Mr. Ackroyd."

The oversize armored box thundering behind them did indeed look like a military vehicle, weaving swiftly between the cars and gaining ground.

"The stinking Order," Lily said, more than a flutter of fear in her voice.

"Galina knew our plans from San Francisco," Wade said. "She knows every single thing about us."

"Not how much we hate her," said Darrell, his first words in two hours.

That was the other thing. If their global search for the Copernicus relics—Texas to Berlin to Italy to Guam to San Francisco—had made them stronger, it had made them darker, too. For one thing, they were armed. Two dueling daggers, one owned by Copernicus, the other by the explorer Ferdinand Magellan, had come into their hands. Wade was pretty sure they'd never actually use them, but having weapons and being a little more ruthless might be the only way to get Sara back.

"Galina Krause will kill to get Vela," Becca said, gripping Lily's hand as the limo bounced faster up the street. "She doesn't care about hurting people. She wants Vela and the next relic, and the next, until she has them all."

"That's precisely what I'm here to avoid," the driver said, tearing past signs for the Midtown Tunnel. He appeared to accelerate straight for the tunnel, but veered abruptly off the exit. "Sorry about that. We're in escape mode."

Roald sat forward. "But the tunnel's the fastest way, isn't it?"

"No options in tunnels," the driver said. "Can't turn or pass. Never enter a dark room if there's another way."

He powered to the end of the exit ramp, then took a sharp left under the expressway and accelerated onto Van Dam Street. The back tires let loose for a second, and they drifted through the turn, which, luckily, wasn't crowded. Less than a minute later, they were racing down Greenpoint Boulevard, took a sharp left onto Henry, a zig onto Norman, a zag onto Monitor, then shot past a park onto a street called Driggs.

Why Wade even noticed the street names in the middle of a chase, he didn't know, but observing details had also become a habit over the last days. Clues, he realized, were everywhere, not merely to what was going on now, but to the past and the future as well.

Becca searched out the tinted back window. "Did we lose them?"

"Three cars behind," the driver said. "Hold tight. This will be a little tricky—"

Wade's father braced himself in front of the two girls. *Dad!* Wade wanted to say, but the driver wrenched the wheel sharply to the right, the girls lurched forward, and he himself slid off his seat. The driver might have been hoping that last little maneuver would lose the Hummer. It didn't. The driver sped through the intersection on Union Avenue and swerved left at the final second, sending two slow-moving cars nearly into each other. That also didn't work. The Hummer was on their tail like a stock car slipstreaming the tail of the one before it.

Lily went white with fear. "Why don't they just—"

"Williamsburg Bridge," the driver announced into a receiver that buzzed on the dashboard, as if he were driving a taxi. "Gray Hummer, obscured license. Will try to lose it in lower Manhat—"

They were on the bridge before he finished his sentence. So was the Hummer, closing in fast. Then it flicked out its lights.

Becca cried, "Get down!"

There were two flashes from its front passenger window and two simultaneous explosions, one on either side of the car. The limo's rear tires blew out. The driver punched the brakes, but the car slid sideways across two lanes at high speed, struck the barrier on the water side, and threw the kids hard against one another. Shots thudded into the side panels.

"Omigod!" Lily shrieked. "They're murdering us—"

As the limo careened toward the inner lane, the

Hummer roared past and clipped the limo hard, ramming it into the inside wall. The limo spun back across the road, then flew up the concrete road partition. Its undercarriage shrieked as it slid onto the railing and then stopped sharply, pivoting across the barrier and the outside railing like a seesaw.

The driver slammed forward into the exploding air bag. Lily, Becca, Wade, and Roald were thrown to the floor. Darrell bounced to the ceiling and was back down on the seat, clutching his head with both hands.

Then there was silence. A different kind of silence from before. The quiet you hear before the world goes dark.

Looking out the front, Wade saw a field of black water and glittering lights beyond.

The limo was dangling on the bridge railing, inches from plunging into the East River.

CHAPTER TWO

"Is everyone . . . ," somebody was saying when Wade lifted his throbbing head. The Hummer had spun around fifty yards up the bridge, pulled into the outside lane, and was now aimed at the damaged limo, revving its engine.

Wade yanked up on the door handle. "Get out of the car!" The door wouldn't open. He kicked it. Pain spiked his leg. "Darrell—"

A thin stream of blood trickling down his cheek, Darrell kicked too. The door squealed open a crack. Lily and Becca threw themselves at it. The hinges groaned and the door fell to the roadway. The sudden loss of weight in the back sent the limo teetering forward. There was a moan from behind the wheel.

"The driver!" Wade's father said. He shattered the divider to the front compartment, then grabbed the man's shoulder and squirmed carefully over the seat to him. First puncturing the air bag, he jerked open the passenger door to his right and dragged the driver through it onto the pavement, just as the Hummer pulled up. Four black doors flew open and four oak-sized men emerged.

One of the men walked out into the road and gestured for the oncoming cars to go past. Was he smiling?

Yes, he was.

Wade's frantic thoughts drew to a point: stay close, physically close, to Darrell and the girls. He huddled them together, himself in front. His father staggered over with the driver leaning on his shoulder.

One thick-necked thug, somewhere between seven and ten feet tall, glared down at them with eyes the color of iron. His face was dented and garbage-can ugly.

"Make no movements," he said in a voice like a truck shifting gears. Then he must have thought better of his words, because he added, "One movement.

Give us relic and daggers."

Seriously? Wade thought. *He's clarifying his threat? Who does that?*

But there was nothing funny in the guy's features. There were lumps all over his face as if *he'd* been the one in the accident, but they were neither recent nor red. He'd grown up a monstrosity, Wade guessed, so what choice did he have but to become a thug?

No, that wasn't right. Everyone had a choice.

"Now," the man grunted, drawing an automatic weapon from inside his tight-fitting jacket. He stood with his big boots planted flat on the pavement like one of the bridge girders.

Sirens sounded from the streets they had just come from.

"Or we could wait for the cops," Wade said, stepping forward as if his new toughness meant being aggressive and blurting stuff at bad guys. His father, still holding up the driver, yanked him back.

In a move Wade didn't quite understand, one of the thugs splayed his thick fingers and grabbed Lily by the arm. Then he lifted her off the ground like a rag doll— probably because she was the smallest—and strode with her to the railing. "She goes over."

Before Wade could react, before he could *think* of moving, his father slid the driver onto him and jumped at the thug, wrenching his arm to let Lily go, which the man didn't—until there was a sudden flash of silver, and the goon screamed.

Shouting incomprehensibly, Becca had thrust Magellan's priceless dagger into the man's arm. Its ivory hilt cracked off in her hand, while the blade stayed in him. She pulled Lily from him and staggered back, stunned at what she had done.

Wade whipped out his own dagger, ready to fight, when a sleek white town car raced up the bridge from the Manhattan side, a blue light flashing from its dashboard.

The other goons dragged their wounded comrade into the Hummer, Becca's hiltless blade still in his arm.

"Ve get you all, dead and dead—" one goon was muttering idiotically.

Not this time, Wade thought, staring at Becca. *Because of you . . .*

The town car shrieked to a stop, and the passenger door flew open. "I'm Terence Ackroyd," the driver said. "Everybody in!" Then he helped Wade's father slide the limo driver inside. As the Hummer tore back to

Brooklyn, the others piled into the town car, and they roared away, shaken but alive and mostly unhurt.

Wade couldn't breathe, couldn't speak. *Becca was amazing*, he thought. *She saved us. She . . .* He quaked like an old man, his hands trembling uncontrollably as they sped across the bridge into the winding streets of lower Manhattan.

CHAPTER THREE

Madrid, Spain
March 18
2:06 a.m.

Thin, pale, and slightly bent, the brilliant physicist Ebner von Braun stepped wearily inside a nondescript building buried in a warren of backstreets off the Plaza Conde de Barajas in old Madrid.

Madrid may well be one of the most beautiful cities in the world, Ebner thought, but that entry hall was disgusting. It was dismal and dark, its floor was uneven, and its grotesquely peeling walls were sodden with the odor of rancid olive oil, scorched garlic, and, surprisingly, turpentine.

Breathing through a handkerchief, he pressed a button on the wall. The elevator doors jerked noisily aside. He stepped in, and the racket of the ancient cables began. A long minute and several subbasements later, he found himself strolling the length of a bank of large, high-definition computer monitors.

Here, the smell was of nothing at all, the pristine, climate-controlled cleanliness of modern science. Ebner gazed over the backs of three hundred men and women, their fingers clacking endlessly on multiple keyboards, text scrolling up and down, screen images shifting and alive with video, and he smiled.

Such busy little bees they are!

Except they are not little bees, are they? he thought. *They are devils. Demons—Orcs!—all recruited, mostly by me, for the vast army of Galina Krause and the Knights of the Teutonic Order.*

The round chamber, one hundred forty feet side to side, with multiple tiers of bookcases rising to a star-painted ceiling, reminded him of the main reading room in the British Museum.

Except ours is better.

In addition to the NSA-level computing resources collected here, the bookshelves and glass-fronted cases alone were laden with over seven million reference books in every conceivable language, hundreds of thousands of manuscripts, many more thousands of early printed works, geographical and topographical maps, marine charts, celestial diagrams, paintings, drawings, engravings, ledgers, letters, tracts, notebooks, and assorted rare or secret documents, all collected from the last five and a half centuries of human history for one purpose: to document every single event in the life of Nicolaus Copernicus.

Behold, the Copernicus Room.

After four years, the massive servers had at last come online, and this army of frowning scientists, burrowing historians, scurrying archivists, and bleary-eyed programmers was now assembled to collect, collate, and cross-reference every conceivable atom of available knowledge to track Copernicus's slightest movement from the day of his birth, on 19 February 1473, to his fateful journey from Frombork, Poland, in 1514, with his assistant, Hans Novak, to his discovery of the time-traveling, relic-bejeweled astrolabe in a location still unknown, and every moment else, all the way to his death in Frombork Castle, on 24 May 1543.

All to determine the identity of the twelve first Guardians.

Now that the modern-day Guardians had invoked the

infamous Frombork Protocol, which decreed that the relics be gathered from their hiding places around the world to be destroyed, Ebner found himself wondering for the millionth time: Who were these original protectors, the good men and women whom Copernicus asked to guard his precious relics? One was Magellan, yes. They knew how his relic was secreted in a cave on the island of Guam. Another was the Portuguese trader Tomé Pires, who brought the poisonous Scorpio relic to China, a relic nearly recovered in San Francisco two days ago. But who were the other ten? And what of the mysterious twelfth relic?

If it was possible to know, the Copernicus Room would tell them.

And yet, Ebner mused as he strolled among the Orcs, *at such a cost.*

The rush of the Order's recent renaissance, their rebirth at light speed over the last four years under Galina's leadership, had not been without blunders. The unprecedented and impatient Kronos program, the Order's secret mission to create its own time machine, had resulted in catastrophically botched incidents:

The ridiculous Florida experiment, an ultimately insignificant test that was still trailing its rags publicly. The spontaneous crumbling of a building in the bustling heart of Rio de Janeiro. And, perhaps worst of all, the strange, half-promising, half-calamitous episode at the Somosierra Tunnel, a mere hour's drive from where he stood right now.

Somosierra was particularly troublesome.

Ebner drew the newspaper clipping from his jacket.

The incident remains under investigation by local and federal crime units.

Of course it does! A school bus vanishes in a tunnel and reappears days later, bearing evidence of an attack by Napoleonic soldiers from 1808? To say nothing of the disappearance of two of its passengers or the subsequent deadly illness of the survivors?

To Ebner, these mistakes meant one thing: only Copernicus's original device—his Eternity Machine, as a recently discovered document referred to it—could ever travel through time successfully.

Every effort otherwise seemed doomed to failure. That was why he had issued a moratorium. No more experiments until further data was amassed and analyzed.

Meanwhile, the workers worked, the researchers researched, and the Copernicus Room, Ebner's beloved brainchild, hummed on.

For example . . . him . . . there . . . Helmut Bern.

The young Swiss hipster sat hunched over his station as if over a platter of hot cheese and sausages. With an improbably constant three days' stubble, an artfully shaved head, and a gold ear stud, Bern had just been relocated from Berlin. The man was now dedicated to uncovering the errors in the Kronos program, and especially Kronos III, the time gun used in the Somosierra mess.

Ebner was strolling over to question him on his progress when the thousands of fingers stopped clacking at once. There was a sudden hush in the room, and Ebner swung around, his heart thudding wildly.

It was she, entering.

Galina Krause—the not-yet-twenty-year-old Grand Mistress of the Knights of the Teutonic Order—slid liquidly between the elevator doors and strode into the Copernicus Room.

As always, she was dressed in black as severe as raven feathers. A silver-studded belt was nearly the only color. But then, who needed color when the different hues of her irises—one silver, one diamond blue, a phenomenon known as heterochromia iridis—took all one's breath away, made her so forbidding, so strangely and mysteriously hypnotic? The very definition, Ebner mused, of dangerous beauty. *Femme fatale.*

Draped around her neck was a half-dollar-sized ruby carved into the shape of a kraken, a jewel once owned by the sixteenth-century Grand Master Albrecht von Hohenzollern. Galina's personal archaeologist, Markus Wolff, had found that particular item, though he, Ebner, had been the one to present it to her last week.

Ebner bowed instinctively. Anyone standing did the same.

Observing the attention, Galina waved it off with her hand. "Vela will inform the Kaplans where the next relic is," she said, her voice slithering toward him as she approached. "If they are intelligent enough to decipher its message. Where are they at this moment?"

"Newly arrived in New York City," Ebner said. "Alas, after Markus Wolff left them in California, they are once again safe and sound. Our New York agents got nothing from them but the blade of Magellan's dagger. We have dispatched a more seasoned squad from Marseille."

"The Kaplan brood is learning to defend itself," Galina said. "Continue to have them watched closely and every movement entered into these databases. Assign one unit specifically to monitor them, but do not stall them. We may need their lead, if all of this"—she flicked her fingers almost dismissively around the vast chamber—"does not offer up the names of the original Guardians."

"It shall," Ebner said proudly. "No expense has been spared. One hundred interconnected databases are now online."

"Alert our agents in Texas to watch their families, too, and ensure that they know they are being watched."

"Ah, an added element of fear, good," said Ebner. "On another matter, we have traced a courier working with the present-day Guardians."

"Where?" she asked.

"Prague. He recently returned there from somewhere in Italy. We do not have his Italian contact yet, but the courier's identity is known to us."

"Curious," she said softly. "I have business in Prague. I will . . ." Galina suddenly looked past Ebner at a tall, broad-shouldered man with a deep tan stepping off the elevator. He wore wraparound dark glasses.

Who the devil is this, thought Ebner, *a film star?*

The man approached. Ebner raised his hand. "You are?"

"Bartolo Cassa," he said. "Miss Krause, the cargo from Rio is now on Spanish soil."

Galina studied him. "The cargo from South America. Yes. Sara Kaplan. Have it transferred to my hangar at the airport."

"Yes, Miss Krause." He bowed, turned, and left the room the way he had come.

Good. The fewer minutes this "Bartolo Cassa" is around, the better. Something about him is simply not quite right. Not . . . normal. And those sunglasses? Is he blind?

Galina gazed across the sea of workers. Her voice was low. "Despite all this data gathering, Ebner, there are holes in the Magister's biography. We require someone on the ground."

"On the ground? But where?" he asked, gesturing to the tiny lights glowing on one of two giant wall maps. "From Tokyo to Helsinki, to London, Cape Town, Vancouver, and everywhere in between, our agents span the entire globe—"

"Not here. Not now," Galina said. "Then. There. We need someone in Copernicus's time to follow him. One hundred databases, and yet there are far too many gaps in our knowledge of the Magister. We must send someone back."

"Back?" Ebner felt his spine shudder. "You do not mean another experiment?"

"One that will succeed," she said, her eyes piercing his.

"With a human subject?" he said. "A subject who can report to us? From the sixteenth century?" Ebner found himself shaking his head, then stopped. It was unwise to deny one so powerful. "Kronos Three is by far the most successful temporal device we have constructed, yet you see the untidy result at Somosierra. Two souls were left behind in 1808! These experiments are far too risky for a person. The possibility of simply *losing* a traveler is too great. You must realize, Galina, that only the"—he barely whispered the next words— "only Copernicus's original Eternity Machine has been proved to navigate time and place accurately. The Kronos experiments are far from foolproof—"

A desk chair squeaked, and Helmut Bern hustled over, breathing oddly. "Miss Krause!"

Helmut Bern! Always Johnny-on-the-spot, lobbying for Galina's blessing.

"What is it?" Ebner snapped.

"Two things. Forgive me, I heard you discussing the Kronos program. I believe I have just pinpointed the central error of the devices. A rather long and twisted string of programming. A difficult fix, but I can manage

23

it. Three days, perhaps four."

"And the second thing?" Galina asked.

"A bit we've just picked up," Bern said, grinning like an idiot. "Copernicus sent a letter from Cádiz in May of 1517. It mentions a journey by sea. Much of it is coded, but we have begun to decrypt it."

"Cádiz," Galina said, studying the other large map in the room, one illustrating the sixteenth-century world of the astronomer. "Fascinating. The Magister sails the Mediterranean. Good work, Bern. Continue with all due haste."

"Yes, Miss Krause!" Bern returned gleefully to his terminal.

"There. You see, Galina," Ebner said. "There is no need for another Kronos experiment. This information will help us track—"

"Send her."

His eyes widened. "Send . . ."

"You told me our recent experiments were too risky," Galina responded. "A trial, then. A minor experiment. With someone expendable. Send Sara Kaplan."

"No experiment in the physics of time is minor!" he blurted, then caught himself. "Forgive me, Galina, but that woman was to have been our insurance that the Kaplans would give us the relics."

"All the family needs to know is that we have her," she said. "Fear will do the rest. What actually happens to the woman is of little consequence."

"But, but . . ." Ebner was sputtering now. "Galina, even assuming we manage to get the woman to *report* to us, *how* would she do it? By what mechanism? To say nothing of the havoc she might create five centuries ago. Any tiny misstep of hers could shudder down through the years to the present. Her mere presence could cause a greater rupture—"

"Ready Kronos Three for her journey. In the meantime, I go to Prague to persuade this courier to reveal his Italian contact. A message was delivered. I want to know to whom." Galina turned her face away. It was a face, Ebner knew, from which all expression had just died. She was done listening. She had issued her command.

So.

Sara Kaplan would go on a journey.

A journey likely to result in her death.

Or worse.

CHAPTER FOUR

New York

"That didn't just happen," Becca heard someone saying.

She turned. It was Darrell.

"Oh, it happened," someone else said. That was Wade, who was looking at her when he said it. There was a hand on her arm, urging her gently out of the town car and onto the street. Even at night, New York City was noisy. And cold, bitter cold for the middle of March. But she hardly registered those things. Her head buzzed. Her eyes could barely focus enough to keep her from smashing into stuff.

She had just attacked a man.

Stabbed a man.

No matter that he was a thickheaded creepy goon, or that he had mauled poor Lily and threatened to toss her off a bridge, or that three days ago his boss, Galina, had shot Becca herself with a gas-powered crossbow, giving her a wound that still hadn't healed. Forget all that. Becca was a girl who read books, a girl with a loving family, a girl who was just a girl. The Hummer goon was maybe a goon, but he was also a human being, and she had *stabbed* him. With a *dagger*.

She glanced at her hands. One was shaking like a leaf in a storm, but at least there was no blood on it. She would have freaked if there'd been blood on it. The other hand? Lily was holding it. Tightly. Comfortingly.

"It's okay, Bec," Lily said, pulling her along the sidewalk by her unhurt arm. "You saved my life. You were awesome. Really. *Thank you* doesn't begin to cover it. I was so scared and . . . well . . . I guess you knew that and that's why you . . ."

Becca's cell phone vibrated suddenly, and she didn't hear the rest. She pulled it out and glanced at the screen. She saw who was calling her. She let it vibrate.

Before they had departed the San Francisco airport that morning, Uncle Roald had picked up new phones for each of them. Despite the danger of their phones being tracked, he said it was unrealistic to think that the five of them would always be in the same place at the same time. They needed to be able to communicate with one another at a moment's notice. Though Lily had immediately cross-programmed the phones with all their numbers as well as family numbers, they all kept their batteries out most of the time. The first thing Becca herself had done was to call her mother to say she was safe. Her mother hadn't answered. No one had answered. So she'd left a voice mail. She realized now that she must have forgotten to remove the battery, because someone was calling back.

The dark screen was lit with four large white letters. *Home.*

But how could she answer it? She had just . . . she had just . . .

The phone stopped vibrating, and Becca watched the number 1 appear next to the voice mail icon. She slipped it back into her pocket. Lily was still talking.

". . . are definitely my hero, and I *so* owe you one, or probably way more than one, but we'll round it off to one big one . . ."

"Uh-huh," Becca said. "Uh-huh."

What would Maggie say if she knew what I just did? Becca's younger sister was the reason for so many things

28

in her life. After nearly dying two years ago, Maggie was always on her mind, and when that creep grabbed Lily on the bridge, Becca saw Maggie in the thug's powerful grip. How could she not jump at him? And if her hand went to Magellan's dagger first, well, she couldn't stop herself. But no way could she talk to anyone at home. Not yet.

The doors of the Gramercy Park Hotel whisked open, and warm air engulfed them. After raising his hand to the man and woman behind the check-in desk, who smiled warmly, Terence Ackroyd led the Kaplans into the elevator, pressing the button for the seventh floor.

It was Mr. Ackroyd who'd originally told them that Sara had disappeared. Sara was supposed to fly from Bolivia to New York to meet him, but her luggage arrived without her. His rescuing them in the car, not an instant too soon, was their first actual meeting with the famous writer, though Becca had started reading one of his books, *The Prometheus Riddle*. The spy thriller she'd picked up in Honolulu was like their lives now. Full of death and near death. She wondered where the novelist got his ideas. He didn't look like a spy as much as a rich man. He was tall, casually dressed, with longish dark hair, graying at the temples. He moved easily among all the glitter and obvious wealth in the lobby, as if he owned the place.

Maybe he did.

She was coming back to herself now. Observing things. Beginning to remember stuff and hear things in real time. Happily, their limo driver was all right, just shaken up, and had already retired to his own room on a lower floor. Darrell's forehead was gashed slightly from the limo's ceiling light and had been bandaged using the first aid kit in Mr. Ackroyd's car. There was talk about getting a doctor to look at her arrow wound, which she hardly felt at the moment.

They entered the elevator. It was warm. Her breathing was slowing down, her breaths becoming deeper. She took her place between Lily and Wade at the back of the glass-and-wood-paneled car and clamped her elbow tightly on her shoulder bag. The bag held not only the cracked hilt of the Magellan dagger, but something even more priceless. The secret diary of Nicolaus Copernicus.

Written by the astronomer and his young assistant, Hans Novak, from 1514 to about a decade later, the diary was the main source of what they knew about the time-traveling astrolabe. The book was composed in several languages and was heavily coded. Thanks to her maternal grandparents, Becca had a gift for foreign languages, and with the help of Wade's science and math smarts she had already translated pretty good-size chunks of the diary into her red notebook. In fact, it was on the jet here from San Francisco that they'd discovered what Copernicus had come to call his time-traveling device.

Die Ewigkeitsmaschine.

The Eternity Machine.

It seemed the perfect name for something so mysterious, and so deadly.

"Here we are," Terence Ackroyd said as the elevator opened directly into his suite.

Whoa. The suite was huge, a multiroom apartment with broad windows looking out over lower Manhattan. It was furnished like a billionaire's home, with a combination of antique chairs painted gold and white and modern leather sofas, two of which shared a lacquered Japanese coffee table that Mr. Ackroyd went straight to. He motioned for them to sit. "Please, rest, while we brew some fresh tea."

We?

"I have it, Dad."

A boy entered the room, carrying a tray with a steaming teapot and several cups on it. He seemed a couple of years older than the kids, and had long, sandy-colored hair and very blue eyes. He set the tray on the table between the couches.

"I'm Julian," he said.

Terence smiled. "My son. Excuse me for a moment." Then he slipped off into a room with double doors, leaving them open. It was a study, from which a keyboard suite by Handel was playing softly from hidden speakers.

Is that where he writes his thrillers?

"I have to apologize for your welcome to New York," Julian said with as pleasant a smile as his father's, which he kept while they introduced themselves. "The Knights of the Teutonic Order have been violent since their first appearance in Jerusalem in 1198. Lawless in Poland and other northern European cities after the Crusades. Copernicus himself fought them several times. They were finally abolished by Napoleon in 1809, but a sect related to Albrecht von Hohenzollern has continued underground since then, hanging on through bloodlines, mostly, and has grown suddenly very wealthy."

His way of speaking was a bit PBS, Becca thought, but he went straight to business, which was what they needed right now.

"But Mr. Kaplan, I'm sorry," he said, suddenly bouncing to his feet. "Of course you want to know about Mrs.

Kaplan. Let me bring her luggage."

"Thank you. And call me Roald, please."

Julian trotted down a hall as his father returned from his workroom. "Becca, the hotel doctor is on his way up to take a look at your arm," Terence said. "In the meantime, Dennis, our driver, sends his heartfelt regards." He breathed out. "Now . . . you've been through—are *going* through—a terrible shock, and I'm very sorry."

"We appreciate anything you can tell us about Sara," Wade said, with a look at Darrell. "About Mom."

Terence nodded and sat among them. "First, let me say this. I have sources on the ground all over the world. For my writing, you understand. This apartment is one of a few research stations I have that's fully equipped: a workroom, communications study, and so on. I'm trying to say that my research team and I are fully at your disposal."

"And why are you helping us exactly?" Darrell broke in. "I mean, sorry, but you don't really know us, and we've learned we can't trust new people."

"Whoa, Darrell," Lily said. "That's rude."

"No, no. Fair question," Terence said. "It's simple. The moment I received Sara's things, I knew something was off, you see. Something was dreadfully wrong. Since I'm a mystery writer, my antennae shot up. More

33

than that, I've just started, well, a foundation for causes that are actively fighting injustice here and around the globe. The Teutonic Order is far more powerful than you. More powerful, actually, than any international organization I've come across. And they've become that mainly in the last four years. I've asked myself, what exactly is going on here?"

"War," said Darrell gloomily. "That's what's going on. Galina Krause and the Teutonic Order have declared war on us."

"I completely agree," Terence said. "And on the world, too, which is why my foundation and I want to help you however we can . . . but there will be time later for that. Here's Sara's suitcase."

The moment Julian entered the room with Sara's main bag and set it down on the coffee table, Becca watched Uncle Roald and Darrell. Roald practically leaped on the suitcase. But his fingers shook, and she saw the blood drain visibly from his cheeks. Darrell hovered over the suitcase next to his stepfather, his fingers poised but apparently unable to touch anything. Becca wanted to help, but stupidly couldn't think of how. It took Roald a full minute to open the clasp and unzip the case, and by the time he lifted the top, he had to wipe away tears.

Sara's clothes, toiletries, books, shoes—everything was stowed neatly in its place, just as Sara must have packed it for the return flight from South America, the flight she never made. A lump forced its way into Becca's throat, and she teared up, too. On the table in front of them was the clearest evidence so far that Sara was lost, and that no one knew where.

Darrell put both hands over his eyes. "Oh, Mom . . . Mom . . ."

Becca looked at the floor. Her heart thundered as loudly as it had when she'd thought of Lily and Maggie on the bridge.

CHAPTER FIVE

" **I** hasten to say that I have every reason to believe that right now your mother is safe," Terence said earnestly to Darrell. "Step by step, here's what we think. . . ."

The voice blurred in Darrell's ears, then faded away.

Something had cracked inside him when his mother's suitcase was opened, and it was still cracking. Seeing her clothes like that was like looking at stuff belonging to somebody who was dead. His throat tightened. He threw himself back on the sofa to be able to breathe, but just as quickly bent over the suitcase again. His ears were hot, like something was screaming into them. His stepfather was on his feet now, looking away.

When Lily patted him awkwardly on the arm,

Darrell realized that the room was quiet and everyone was waiting for him. To do what? He glanced up to see them all staring at him; then he brushed his hand over his face. *Oh, right. To stop crying.* He wiped his cheeks. "Sorry. Go on, Mr. Ackroyd."

"No need to be sorry," the man said, glancing searchingly at Julian.

Uh-huh, and what was that look?

"To continue, when I realized that Sara's luggage had arrived here without her, I immediately examined it, without actually *moving* too much. All of her belongings, including her phone and wallet, everything seemed to be here and intact."

"As my dad told you on the phone in Guam, we didn't contact the police because of what else we found," Julian said. He was now sitting in a chair across the room, alternately looking down from behind the curtain, as if he was surveilling the street, and tapping the keys on a laptop.

"Exactly," said Terence. "We've discovered two things. The first is what I take to be a warning, hidden cleverly in the inner lining." Terence carefully peeled back a portion of the patterned lining. It had been pried open and reclosed with a safety pin. Tucked into the space behind the lining was a charm bracelet.

Roald lifted it out. "I know this bracelet. Sara's had it for a long time, but . . ."

One of its charms was wrapped inside a self-adhesive Forever postage stamp depicting the American flag.

"May I?" Carefully unpeeling the stamp, Terence revealed the charm inside. It was a silver skull.

"I don't like the way this looks," Darrell said. "Dad, a skull? Mom's not a skull kind of person. And I don't remember this charm. When did she get it?"

Terence was about to speak when Roald said, "I think she got it last year at a conference in Mexico. It's a standard icon there. 'Day of the Dead' and all that."

"But wrapped inside a picture of the American flag," said Lily. "Is that like something against our country?"

"No, no." Terence shook his head vigorously. "Not at all. I attended that same conference. It was, in fact, where I met Sara for the first time and decided to donate my manuscripts to her archive in Austin. I believe this part of the clue was actually meant for me. It is a direct reference to a silly thing I wrote about in my first novel—"

"*The Zanzibar Cryptex*," Julian said from across the room. "Not one of your best, Dad. The ending on the ocean liner?"

Terence smirked. "Everyone's a critic. But seriously,

in that book there was a similar clue, an item wrapped in a stamp. And it meant something very specific, which Sara well knew. You see, the skull represents, well, death, or at the very least danger. The flag quite simply means the authorities. The message in the novel—and here—is plain: contacting the authorities will put Sara in more danger. At least she thought so. She must have been threatened or somehow understood that bringing the police in—"

"Or the CIA or FBI," Julian added.

"—would not help," Terence said. "For the moment, then, finding her should remain a private matter. But not without resources."

"Sara's in danger but she's sending us codes and clues?" Lily said. "What a mom."

"You better believe it," Wade whispered.

The elevator chime rang behind them, and Terence hopped up. "Ah, Becca. Your doctor." A middle-aged woman entered, smiling, and Becca went with her to the dining-room table, where they chatted softly, so Becca could also listen.

Roald stood anxiously. "All right, so Sara is telling us to be cautious. Terence, you said you found two things."

"That's my cue," Julian said, leaving his chair by the window after one last look at the street and setting his laptop on the coffee table. "Three hours ago we received a heavily encrypted video from our investigators in Brazil. I've just been decoding it and cleaning up some of the images." He adjusted the screen, and hit the Play button.

A fuzzy nighttime video image appeared, showing an old station wagon creeping slowly along what appeared to be a utility road behind a large building. There were words on the side of the building: *Reparação Hangar 4*.

"Hmm. An airline-repair hangar," Terence whispered, shooting a glance at his son. "In Rio de Janeiro."

In the video the car stopped abruptly. Behind it, a set of double doors slid aside on the hangar, and two shapes emerged from it. The driver and a passenger climbed from the car, opened the back of the station wagon, and began to tug something out, while the two men from the hangar assisted. It was a coffin. The four men carried it like pallbearers into the hangar. A few minutes later, the two from the station wagon reappeared, closed the rear door, and drove off. The video ended.

Darrell stared at his stepfather, not wanting to believe what he saw, but his lips formed the words. "Mom is dead?"

"No, no," said Terence, rising and putting his hand on Darrell's shoulder. "What we have just witnessed means precisely the opposite. The shipment of coffins is a well-known but poorly policed method of moving people from country to country without documents. The time stamp tells us that this occurred at two twenty-seven a.m. last night, Rio time. Precisely thirty-six minutes later, two small private jets took off, both heading east on different routes, possibly to Europe or Africa. By tomorrow, we will know where each landed. If your mother is indeed in that coffin, it means that the Order is flying her somewhere, *smuggling* her to another country. Excuse me for being blunt, but if Sara were . . . dead, the Order would not go to such lengths. This video not only means that she is alive, but that precautions are being taken to ensure her safety."

It didn't sound right to Darrell, but Terence's face—and Julian's—betrayed no sense of hiding the truth. "She's alive? You're sure?"

"I quite believe so," Terence said, nodding heartily. "It is a matter now of tracking down both jets to see where they may be moving her."

"We had heard something about Madrid," said Becca from the dining room. "In San Francisco, we discovered that the Order has some servers, big computers, there, and Galina might have been there, too."

"Good. I'll alert my people. This may be a solid lead."

"We've been tricked before," said Lily.

"I understand your disappointment in San Francisco," Terence said. "But my network is largest in Europe. I've taken the liberty of arranging a meeting between Dr. Kaplan and myself and Paul Ferrere, the head of my Paris bureau, tomorrow morning, here in the city. Ferrere is ex–Foreign Legion and has a team of detectives spread across the length and breadth of Europe. We have hopes of finding Sara Kaplan before very long."

"Hopes?" Darrell grunted.

Roald patted him on the arm. "Not false hopes. Never again. But we can inch ahead. Keep moving forward."

Darrell wanted to believe him. "Okay . . ."

His stepfather took one more look at the paused video on Julian's laptop and began to pace the living room. "Here's the way I see it. Galina Krause may be waiting for us to lead her somewhere, and we'll be in danger the moment we make a move. I get that, but while we're waiting for a solid lead about Sara, we have to continue our search for the second relic, the one Vela is supposed to lead us to. Wade, you have my notebook; Becca, you have the diary. Lily, you're the electronic brains. Darrell, you cracked some riddles in San Francisco that baffled the rest of us. Together, we *will* find the second relic, and we *will* find Sara."

Darrell got it. He understood. It made sense, and having Terence and his detectives on the case gave them a way forward. His lungs were gasping for a deep breath, and his heart pounded like pistons in his chest, but being scattered or afraid wouldn't help them or his mother. He wiped his cheeks. "Okay. Good."

The doctor left, with a silent smile and thumbs-up to the family, and Becca rejoined them, a clean bandage on her arm.

"All set," she said. "It feels great. Thank you, Mr. Ackroyd . . . Terence."

"Not at all," he said.

"And now . . . Vela," said Roald.

Still worrying about his mother, Darrell watched his stepfather move his hand inside the breast pocket of his jacket. When he drew it out, he was holding the brilliant blue stone.

CHAPTER SIX

"I'm Sara Kaplan," she told herself for the thousandth time. "I'm an American. I've been kidnapped. I don't know by whom, and I don't know why. I had no time—almost no time—to alert anyone. It happened too fast."

She had rehearsed these words over and over so she could tell the first person she saw in as short a time as possible. But she hadn't seen anyone at all since . . . since when? Since the hotel on the morning of her flight from La Paz, Bolivia, to meet Terence Ackroyd in New York City. She'd rehearsed *that* scene over and over, too.

A bright tap on the hotel room door.

"Just a minute!" she'd said.

Thinking it a hotel employee come for her luggage, she opened the door.

The man—broad shouldered, mean faced, in sunglasses—was on her in a flash. Hand over mouth, pushing her back into the room, kicking the door shut behind him. "Resist and your family will be killed. If they notify the authorities, you will be killed. Silence. Silence—"

She twisted away from him, threw herself at the bathroom door, and locked herself in. "Do not panic!" she'd told herself. Look around, look around. Her suitcase was in there. She'd been packing to return home. Her phone, her pocketbook, everything was there. No time to make a call. Futile to scrawl a message on the mirror—he would smear any message to illegibility.

Then, inspiration. The silliest thing in the world, but it made sense. Her charm bracelet. She slid it off, wrapped the skull in a stamp. It seemed idiotic, but Terence would recognize it. From his novel. The Madagascar Codex. No, The Zambian Crypt? The Zimbabwe—

The door split open on its hinges as she stuffed the bracelet into the lining of her suitcase and pinned it closed. The face above her was flat and brutal. The eyes . . . the eyes were invisible behind those black-lensed sunglasses. She was screaming now at the top of her lungs, and couldn't imagine how she could not be rescued, when there came another thought: she

45

was not screaming at all, but falling silently to the floor of the bathroom. There was a stabbing pain in her neck, and her cries, if they ever came out at all, were choked to silence. She stared up at the ceiling as she slipped to the floor, wondering if she would crack her head on the tiles.

Seconds passed. Minutes? Then there was the sound of a zipper coming from somewhere at her feet, and then flaps of black plastic were being folded over her face, and all the light was gone.

Darrell's face came to her then, in a swift sequence of his ages from birth up to when she saw him that last morning in Austin. And Wade. And Roald. What would they . . . what would . . .

Then all her thoughts faded, and she fell away to a place of no dreams.

Nothing for hours and days until today. She was unable to move. There was a freshness to the air in the . . . what *was* she in, anyway? A bag? A box? There were tubes in her arm. She couldn't raise herself or move her hands to find out. *I'm in restraints.* But there was air in there, so he wanted her alive, whoever he was. The man in the sunglasses . . . Zanzibar! That was it!

The Zanzibar Cryptex.

She wanted to scream that she was alive and being

taken somewhere, but . . . The waves that had been falling over her became more rhythmic, and sleep took her, or what she thought might be sleep, but she wasn't very sure of that.

CHAPTER SEVEN

New York

Even under the Ackroyd living room's subtle lamp-light, Vela shone as if it were its own star. Like a heavenly body not of this earth. *Which it might actually be*, thought Lily. What did any of them really know about the shadowy origins of the relics? Copernicus had supposedly found an old astrolabe built by the Greek astronomer Ptolemy. But that was all pretty hazy.

"Let's bring it into the study," said Julian.

Julian seemed to be really bright. His father was kind of brilliant, too. How many books had he written? Ten? A hundred? She and the others were surrounded by smart people, so you had to think they really would get Sara back *and* find the relics.

The study off the living room was large and lined with thousands of books—not all of them written by Terence Ackroyd, thank goodness. It was traditional in a way, sleepy almost, but also equipped with a really high level of computer gear.

There was a long worktable with a wide-lens magnifying device perched on it. Several shelves of cameras, printers, and scanners were next to the worktable along with stacks of servers. On the wall behind them was a range of twenty-four clocks showing the current time in each of the world's major time zones. Except for a gnarly old typewriter on a stand by itself like a museum piece from another century, the room was like she imagined a secret CIA lair would be.

The only other thing I'd need would be . . . nothing.

"First things first," Julian said, opening a small tablet computer that lay on the worktable next to five sparkling new cell phones. "These are for you. We've loaded this tablet with tons of texts and image databases that can help with the relic hunt."

"Wow, thanks," Lily said, practically snatching it from his hands. "I'm kind of the digital person here."

Julian laughed. "Ooh, the tech master of the group. The intelligence officer. Very cool. I've modified each phone's GPS function with a software app I invented. The tablet likewise. Except to one another, and mine and Dad's, these units will emit random location coordinates, making them essentially blind to most conventional GPS locators." He passed a phone to each of them, and turned to Roald. "Now . . . the relic . . ."

Roald set Vela gently on the worktable. When he did, Lily realized they'd been so completely focused on hiding and protecting Vela over the last few days that this was only the second time since Wade and Becca discovered it that they'd been able to bring it safely out into the open.

Wade and Becca, she thought.

Wade had been giving Becca goo-goo eyes ever since Mission Dolores in San Francisco, where they'd discovered that the Scorpio relic was a fake. Maybe it was because of the stare the Order's assassin, Markus Wolff, had given Becca in the Mission. Or maybe Wade realized something about the twelfth relic that Wolff had been all cryptic about. Either way, something was up, those weird looks meant something, and Lily would find out. She could read Darrell. He was hot or cold. Not so much in between. And by hot or cold she meant either hilarious or ready to explode. Wade was a differ-ent story. Becca, too, for that matter, and . . . *Wait, where was I? Oh. Right. Vela.*

Triangular in shape, about four inches from base to upper point, with one short side and two of roughly equal length, Vela was something Roald called "techni-cally an isosceles triangle." Except that one of its long sides curved in slightly toward the center like a sail in the wind. Which made sense, since Vela was supposed to represent the sail in the constellation Argo Navis. It also had a slew of curved lines etched into it.

When they examined the stone closely they saw that even though it was about the same thickness from the front side to the back—about a quarter of an inch—Vela was undoubtedly heavier in the middle than in any of the corners, a fact that she was the first to voice. "Look." She placed it flat across her finger and it balanced. "Something's in there."

"Maybe an inner mechanism," Roald said. "Some-thing hidden inside its heart."

"Yes, yes," Terence said, taking it now from Lily. "I can see the faint design on both sides of the stone and a series of very tiny, even infinitesimal, separations that could mean that the stone somehow opens up. It is far too heavy to be a normal stone."

Passing it around, they gently tried to coax the stone to reveal its secret, but short of prying it open and maybe busting it, they couldn't find a way. Vela told them nothing.

"Have you considered that it's fairly dangerous to be lugging this around with you?" Julian said. "There are vaults in the city that are pretty near uncrackable, even by the Order."

Roald nodded. "A good idea, I agree. But the legend says 'the first will circle to the last,' meaning that something about Vela is a clue to the next relic or maybe its Guardian. We need to discover something soon or we won't know where to look."

"There's also this." Becca slid her hand into her shoulder bag and tugged out the cracked hilt of the Magellan dagger. "The handle cracked when I . . . you know. I'm sorry . . ."

"I'm so glad you did," Lily said, shuddering to see the hilt again. "It was, well . . ." She was going to say that what Becca had done—stabbing the goon on the bridge and saving her life—was something so *beyond* amazing, but she felt suddenly on the verge of tears, which she never was, so instead she just closed her mouth, which was also pretty rare, and smiled like a dope at whoever, which turned out to be Wade, who, as usual, was staring at Becca with his googly eyes.

"That's quite something," Julian said, drawing in a quiet breath when Becca set the hilt on the table. "Italian, by any chance?"

"Bolognese," said Wade, finally tearing his eyes from Becca.

"Yes, yes." Julian picked it up gently, but it suddenly separated into two pieces of carved ivory and fell back on the table. "Ack! I'm sorry!"

"Hold on . . ." Lily used her slender fingers to tug something out from inside the hilt. It was a long, narrow ribbon. "What is this?"

Terence stood. "Oh, ho!" He pinched one end of the ribbon and held it up. It dangled about three feet.

"Microscope!" said Julian. He snatched the ribbon from his father, then jerked away from the table to the far end of the room, where he sat at a small table. Not ten seconds later, he said, "Dad, we've seen this kind of thing before."

They all rushed over to Julian in a flash, but Lily pushed her way through the crowd to be the first one leaning over the lens. "Letters," she said. "I see letters. They're pretty faded, but they're there, written one under the other the whole length of the ribbon."

Darrell moved in next. "*T-O-E-G-S-K*, and a bunch

more. We've done word scrambles and substitution codes. Is this one of those? They look random."

Terence took his own look and smiled. "Not random at all, actually. These letters are one half of a cipher called a *scytale*." He pronounced the word as if it rhymed with *Italy*.

"Invented by the ancient Spartans, the cipher consists of two parts: a ribbon made of cloth or leather with letters on it, and a wooden staff," he continued. "The staff has a number of flat sides on it, rather like a pencil. You wrap the ribbon around the staff like a candy cane stripe, and if the staff is the right size, the letters line up in words."

Julian grinned. "The trick is that you always have to keep the ribbon separate from the staff until it's time to decode the message." He paused and looked at his father. "Dad, are you thinking what I'm thinking? Two birds?"

"Two birds?" said Wade. "Is that code for something?"

Julian laughed. "It's a saying. Kill two birds with one stone. The Morgan Library up the street has an awesome vault for Vela. It also happens to have probably the best—and least known—collection of scytale staffs on the East Coast. I'll bet we can find one that works with this ribbon."

"I suggest we hit the Morgan Library at eight tomorrow morning," Terence said.

"Don't museums usually open later than that?" said Becca.

"Yes, but for Dad and me, the Morgan is never closed," said Julian with a smile that seemed to Lily like the sun breaking out after a long darkness.

CHAPTER EIGHT

Prague, Czech Republic
March 18
9:13 a.m.

Galina Krause kept her hand inside her coat, where a compact Beretta Storm lay holstered against her ribs. Its barrel, specially filed to obscure its ballistics, was still warm. She would be gone long before the police discovered the body of the Guardian's courier, Jaroslav Hájek, or the single untraceable bullet in his head.

She disliked killing old men, but the courier had refused to reveal his Italian contact, although his flat did contain a collection of antique hand clocks, which was likely a clue to how the message had been transferred.

In any case, a dead courier working with the Guardians was never a bad thing, and one obstacle less in her overall journey.

As Galina walked the winding, snow-dusted streets of Prague's Old Town, she passed through deserted alleys and passages barely wider than a sidewalk. Finally, she entered into the somber "antiquarian district." This section of Prague deserved its designation. A neighborhood forlorn, yet rich in history and the smell of a past carelessly abandoned by modernity. For that reason alone, she adored it.

She halted three doors down from a tiny low-awninged shopfront on Bělehradská Street. Antikvariát Gerrenhausen appeared as it must have generations ago: crumbling, forever in shadow, hauntingly like those sad, cluttered storefronts in old photographs of a forgotten, bygone era.

A man entered the street from the far end. He was tall. His close-cropped white hair cut a severe contrast with the stark black of his knee-length leather coat.

Markus Wolff had recently returned from the United States.

She moved toward him, though their eyes would not meet until the standard subterfuge was completed. Wolff approached her, passed by, and then, after scanning the street and its neighboring windows for prying eyes, doubled back to her.

"Miss Krause." He greeted her in a deep baritone, a voice that was, if possible, icier than her own. He unslung a black leather satchel from his shoulder and set it on the sidewalk at her feet. "The remains of the shattered jade scorpion from Mission Dolores. The Madrid servers can perhaps make sense of them."

"Excellent," she replied. "Do you have the video I asked you to take in San Francisco?"

"I do." He pressed the screen of his phone.

A moment later, a file appeared on hers. She opened it. A boy, seven and three-quarters years of age, ran awkwardly across a field of green grass, kicking a soccer ball. The camera zoomed in on his face. The tender smile, the pink cheeks, the lazy blond curls flying in the wind. She paused it. The boy was oblivious to his own mortality.

"Splendid," she said sullenly. "Wolff, take note of this street. This shop."

"I have."

"You may be asked to return here in the weeks to come," she said. "For now, I want you to look into the Somosierra incident. Ease my mind."

"The stranded bus driver and student," he said. "I

will search for physical evidence."

She felt suddenly nauseated and wanted the conversation to end. "In six days' time I will be in Istanbul. We will meet there."

Markus Wolff nodded once and left.

Man of few words, Galina thought. *How refreshing.* Shouldering the leather satchel and drawing a cold breath, she entered the shop. A cadaverous gentleman, the seventh generation of Gerrenhausens, stood hunched and motionless behind a counter cluttered with books and rolled maps, yellowed file folders, and an assortment of wooden boxes. He listened as a gramophone on the shelf behind him emitted a scratchy yet plaintive string quartet movement. She recognized it as Haydn. The D-minor andante.

"You have the item I requested?" she asked. The sound of her voice was nearly swallowed by the yearning violins and the thick, paper-muffled air in the old shop.

The slender hands of the emaciated proprietor twitched, while his lips formed a smile as thin as a razor blade. "It has just arrived, miss." He reached under the counter and withdrew a small oak box, burnished nearly black with age. He opened the lid.

Nestled deeply in maroon velvet was a delicate

miniature portrait of a kind common in the sixteenth century.

The framed circular painting, two inches in diameter, was a product of Hans Holbein the Younger. "Incorrectly dated 1541, it was created actually between 1533 and 1535, during the painter's years in England at the court of King Henry the Eighth, as you know," the proprietor said.

The portrait featured the face and shoulders of its sitter, a brilliant bloom of flesh in a setting of velvety black and midnight blue. It was a three-quarter view, in which the sitter, aged somewhere between seventeen and nineteen, gazed off, a sorrowful expression on the face, eyes dark, lips pursed, almost trembling. It was not a peaceful portrait, and Galina found herself shuddering at the sight of it. She closed the box.

"The fee is one hundred seventy-five thousand euros," the proprietor said softly, as if only slightly embarrassed by the number. "Its former home, a boutique museum in Edinburgh, will not soon realize it is displaying a forgery. Such workmanship is costly."

To Galina the miniature was worth ten times as much, a hundred times. It was not the money that mattered in this instance. She had become aware over the last years that she required the strictest loyalty and silence from an antiquarian such as Herr Gerrenhausen and knew how pitifully easy it was to gain such loyalty and silence when a loved one was threatened. Smiling at the old proprietor, she swiped her phone open to the frozen video. "Do you recognize this young boy?"

The man squinted at the phone and beamed. "Why, yes! That is my grandson, Adrian. He lives with my youngest daughter and her husband in California. But why . . . how . . . why do you have a video of Adrian . . . ?" He trailed off. His face turned the color of white wax.

Galina slid a list of several items across the counter to him. "This is what I need. You will acquire the items for me. There will be no end to our relationship until I say there is. Currently the boy is safe. But he is within our grasp at any moment. You do understand me."

Rapid nodding preceded a long string of garbled words, which the man punctuated finally with "I understand."

She felt her expression ease. "I am wiring the purchase fee for the miniature to your Munich account. The first item on the list is to be auctioned at the Carlton Hotel in Cannes in June. You will acquire it anonymously."

"Of course! I will. Yes, everything."

The Haydn andante ended morosely behind him.

Galina swiped the image of the boy from her phone, then inserted the blackened oak box into her leather satchel and left the shop, short of breath and shivering, but not from the cold.

CHAPTER NINE

New York

The morning after the discovery of the ribbon in the dagger's hilt, Darrell woke early from somber dreams about his mother to hear his stepfather and Terence Ackroyd working out an elaborate plan for that morning, a ruse intended to throw off any agents of the Teutonic Order who might be watching the hotel.

"The first of many new plans," Roald had told him.

"I hope they work," Darrell grumbled to himself.

The plan involved three cars, the family of the Gramercy Park Hotel's assistant manager, two retired New York City policemen, a traffic officer, and a crew of window cleaners—all creating multiple distractions while the kids zigzagged uptown with Julian, and Roald and Terence headed on foot to the West Side to meet the detective Paul Ferrere.

A half hour later, Darrell and the others were streaming up Madison Avenue, shielded by crowds of commuters and early shoppers. Since he had no sense whatsoever of anyone watching them, Darrell accepted that their plan had actually succeeded.

Despite the latest storm having dumped nine heavy inches of snow that was now aging into black and crusty walls, narrowing the streets and the sidewalks to half their width, their walk uptown was brisk but still not fast enough for him.

As soon as Darrell pictured his mother tied to a chair or pounding on a door or lying bound up in a locked closet, his mind went red, and blood rushed like waves inside his head until he couldn't see straight.

But he had to hope, right? He had to put his mother's situation in a pocket and get on with what he knew he had to get on with. *We're doing everything possible. We have detectives. We have Terence's assistance. Sooner or later, Mom will be where the next relic is, because that's where Galina will take her.*

So fine. Get your head in the game.

He managed to refocus himself in time to hear Julian

saying to Wade, who was five steps behind him, "I was born in Mandalay, actually. Myanmar. What they used to call Burma. It's where my mom died. I was four. I never had much time with her."

So. That was why Terence had given his son that look last night. Julian had lost his mother, too. How do you even deal with not growing up with your mom, having so little time to be with her? And Myanmar? Myanmar was right next to Thailand, where Darrell's father had grown up.

They came to the southwest corner of the intersection of Madison Avenue and Thirty-Sixth Street and waited for the light. Lily nudged him and nodded at two low-roofed Renaissance-style mansions—one of brown stone blocks, the other white—with a modern glass-and-steel atrium joining them.

"We are going to get so much help here," she said. "I have a feeling."

Becca nodded. "Like Wade said in San Francisco, the more relics we find, the more leverage we have."

"I know," Darrel said, mustering up a smile. "I get it."

The truth was that he *wanted* to go after the next relic. Not as much as he *needed* to find his mother, of course, but a real close second. This was important.

The Copernicus Legacy was life-alteringly amazing. It was cosmic. Time travel blew his mind, and if Galina wanted to reassemble the astrolabe, that was enough to make him vow she never would. He needed to be a part of what they were doing, no matter how dangerous or scary.

We have to stop Galina. At all costs.

Lily was very impressed. And, seriously, not a lot of stuff impressed her. But exactly as Julian had promised the night before, even though the Morgan Library and Museum was still closed to the public, its doors whisked open for them and sealed solidly after they entered.

Wow.

"You'll be rather astounded at their collection," Julian told them when they filed into the tall, glass-walled atrium. "And their security." He nodded at a pair of hefty guards by the doors who looked more than a match for the oak-headed thugs from last night.

"I should also tell you that your new tablet contains a slew of one-of-a-kind documents from the Morgan's private holdings," he added. "Sixteenth-century biographies. Maps. Astronomical treatises. Code books. It'll take you months to go through it all."

"I could do it in a few days," Lily said, shrugging.

"I'm sure you could," he said with a smile.

Lily had felt special last night when the Ackroyds, both father and son, had recognized that she was, in Julian's words, "the tech master of the group. The intelligence officer."

I so like that! Intelligence officer. That's exactly what I am.

"Good morning." A slender man in a dark blue suit with soft-heeled shoes, who Julian whispered was one of the two chief curators, met them in the atrium. The kids took turns explaining why they were there.

"Scytales and the vault," the curator said, tapping his fingers on his chin. "Got it. Vault first. Please follow me." He spun around and led them through several still-darkened galleries to a bank of elevators. They took one down into the library's underground level. "Perhaps Julian has told you, but the lowest level runs beneath the entire length of both the library and Pierpont Morgan's original residence."

"This is where my dad is suggesting you keep . . . the object," Julian said. "For the time being at least. We have extensive vault privileges here."

After leading them through several passages, the curator paused at a large steel door. "When Mr. Morgan had the house built, he constantly rotated his collection between what he displayed upstairs and what was stored in the vault. In the century since then, security has been updated countless times. The vault is now virtually invulnerable. Even in the case of nuclear attack, which, surprisingly, is a factor . . . no matter how slight."

For instance, what if the Order . . . never mind.

He opened the door with a pass code and a fingerprint scan. Inside stood a narrow entry hall leading to a second door. "Built into the side walls is a kind of electronic gauntlet," the curator said. "You have to pass through it to reach the vault."

"You'll like this," Julian said to them as they entered. "Gates trip and floor tiles sink if you take the wrong route to the inner chamber. Any intruder would be trapped between the walls long before any theft or damage could occur."

The curator nodded. "For example, several infrared sensors are scanning us as we're passing through right now—"

Beeep!

The curator turned to Wade. "Er . . . you appear to have something on you . . ."

Even in its unique protective holster, one that had fooled various airport security scanners, Wade's antique dagger now set off the Morgan's sensors. "It's the first time that's happened," he said. "You have the best security I've seen."

"About the dagger," Julian said. "Your dad wanted it in the vault, too, didn't he?"

Wade nodded reluctantly. "He told me this morning. He's right, I guess." He slipped off the holster with Copernicus's dagger housed invisibly inside and handed it to the curator.

Lily hated weapons of any kind, but Wade giving up the dagger? Wouldn't they need it? He'd carried it since Berlin last week, and the Magellan dagger had saved her life just yesterday. They were, after all, at war with the Teutonic Knights. On the other hand, Copernicus's own private weapon was far too precious—and, she supposed, too dangerous—to carry around. *So, yeah. Good idea*.

The large steel door opened on a staggeringly wide, deep, and high-ceilinged room.

Becca started to wheeze.

"Indeed," said the curator, grinning for the first time since they'd met him.

One side of the room was lined with numerous three-tiered display compartments and multishelf bookcases. On the far end was a honeycomb of hundreds of narrow slots built up to the ceiling. Paintings were shelved upright in these spaces. Classical sculptures of people and animals—some realistic, some fantastical—were clustered here and there the entire length of the vault.

The curator set the dagger and its holster reverently on a worktable, then stepped over to a portion of the wall containing built-in safe-deposit-type boxes.

"What is your birth date, Wade?" he asked.

"Me?"

Lily remembered how the deciphering of Uncle Henry's original coded message had involved a reference to Wade's birthday. That was what had started their quest.

"October sixth."

"So . . ." The curator selected and removed one of the boxes, which he said was "made of a titanium alloy," and brought it to the table. He placed the holster and dagger inside the box, sealed it, tapped in a key-code combination, and returned the box to its slot in the wall. He then withdrew the box directly below it. "The, ah, object you wish to store here?"

Darrell drew Vela from an inside pocket.

Raising his eyebrows very high, the curator took the heavy blue stone—the relic with something buried in its interior—and swaddled it carefully in new velvet.

"It's priceless," Lily said.

"I believe it," the curator responded. He set the velvet-wrapped stone in a wooden box. Then he placed that box inside a second titanium container, which he inserted below the one with the dagger inside. When he pushed it all the way in, there was a low whump followed by the clicking and rolling of tumblers that stopped with a hush.

"Now you'll want to see our head of antiquities," the curator said, leading them all briskly out of the vault and security corridor. "I'll ask her to meet you upstairs in the atrium. If anyone can help you decode your message, she's the one."

Taking one last look at the sealed vault door, Lily breathed easily. Vela, the first of the Copernicus relics, was now hidden safely underneath New York City.

CHAPTER TEN

The curator led them back up to the atrium.

As Wade watched the man disappear, Darrell's hip pocket began to ring. "It's Dad," he said, and stepped away, listening, Lily along with him. Becca turned to follow them when Wade stopped her.

"How's your arm?" he asked.

She smiled. "Okay. Better all the time."

"Good." He was still deciding if he should tell Becca about *the dream*. The one he'd had leaving Guam in which Becca had seemed to be, well, dead. He'd so far been unable to say it out loud. It was too upsetting, even for him. Naturally, he worried that his dream had something to do with Markus Wolff's intense look at her in the Mission in San Francisco, although that was clearly impossible, since his dream had been earlier.

"What about the Mission?" Becca asked.

"What?"

"You said *Mission*, just now."

His face went hot. "I did? Well . . . it's just . . . I wonder what Markus Wolff meant about the twelfth relic. That we should ask ourselves what it was."

"Me, too. Strange, huh?"

"Yeah."

That went nowhere.

Darrell was off the phone now. "Good news. Investigators are spreading across Europe."

"He said we have to be prepared that they won't find your mom today or probably tomorrow," Lily added. "That it'll take some time, but everybody feels good about it."

"Excellent," said Julian. "It may not be long now before we know what the ribbon says and where it points."

"Find the relic, find Sara," Becca said.

"That's the idea," said Wade.

There was a slow click of heels on tile, and a tiny,

very old woman hobbled into the open atrium as if wandering in from the long past. She wore a dark beige pantsuit with a bright pink scarf flowing up out of her vest like a fountain. Her eyes flickered like a pair of tiny flashlights low on battery, and she bleated, "I'm . . . ancient . . ."

Wade glanced at the others, then back to the woman. "Oh, not so much—"

". . . curator here at the . . . Morgan," she said, scowling at him. She huffed several more breaths as if each could be her last. "Dr. Rosemary Billing . . ."

"Pleased to meet you, Dr. Billing," Becca said.

"Ham," the woman said.

"Excuse me?" said Lily.

"Ham," the woman repeated. "Billing*ham*. My name is Bill . . . ingham. Why won't you let me . . ." Three, four breaths. ". . . finish? Now . . . who are . . . you all . . . and how . . . may I help you?"

One by one they told her their names. She frowned severely at each one until Julian's. "Julian?" she gasped, adjusting her glasses. "There you are! Well, if you're . . . here then it's quite all right. Fol . . . low me."

Stopping and starting several times, like a car backing up in a tight space, Dr. Billingham turned around and toddled down the hallway she had just come from, wheezing the whole time. What seemed a day and a half later, they arrived at a small, windowless room. Rosemary flicked on the lights and, after much finger motion, unlocked a glass-topped display case.

"Despite these . . . scytale staffs being, in many cases, also used as . . . weapons, they're old, and . . . we must consider them extremely fragile. Rather . . . like me . . ."

Wade didn't know whether to laugh or not, but he knew to wait.

Five breaths later, she added, ". . . dieval manuscripts."

Then Rosemary waved her hand over the contents of the case like a game-show hostess. She was right to do so. As Julian had promised, the library's collection of scytale staffs was special. They were obviously ancient, and all were roughly between five and ten inches long. Two were carved in thick ebony, one appeared to be cast in bronze, and the others were shaped of ivory or wood. Each was nestled in its own formfitting compartment and labeled by date. The earliest was from the sixth century BCE—"Before the Common . . . Era," Rosemary explained—the most recent from Germany in the eleventh century. The smallest staff was little bigger around than a pencil, while the largest bore a circumference similar to the handle on a tennis racket.

"Now show me your rib . . . ," Rosemary asked Becca alarmingly, then finished with ". . . bon."

Becca removed the ribbon carefully from her pocket, unrolled it, and laid it flat on the table.

The curator frowned through her spectacles as she examined the ribbon. "About a . . . hundred letters?"

"Ninety," Becca said, glancing at Julian, who nodded.

"Ah, just . . . like . . . me . . ."

Wade waited six, seven breaths, but that turned out to be the end of her sentence.

Rosemary tugged either end of the ribbon lightly. "The fabric is silk. Without . . . running tests, I would guess it was woven sometime in the fifteenth or six-teenth century."

"That fits our date," Darrell said.

The curator raised a finger as if to shush him. "Also, it doesn't . . . stretch very much. This is good. It means we'll have better luck finding an exact fit. Let's start small . . . and go up from there." Then, chuckling to herself, she added, "The narrower the staff, the larger the mess . . ."

Two breaths.

". . . age."

Rosemary took up the narrowest of the staffs, more of a dowel than anything else, with five equal sides. Pinching the top end of the ribbon against one of the sides, she gently spiraled it around the dowel like the stripe of a candy cane, making sure that the letters sat next to one another. The first line of the message read:

TGOSNOTSTPHID

Which, because of the peculiar wiring of his brain, Darrell said aloud before anyone could stop him. "'To go snot stupid.' No, wait. 'Togo's not stupid.' Is that the dog from *The Wizard of Oz*? Who's Togo?"

"You are," said Wade, glaring at his stepbrother. "And we're not sure what language it's in, remember that. Copernicus knew several. Either way, that's obviously not the right staff. Can we try a bigger one, to spread out the letters—"

"Keep your pant . . . s on, young man," Rosemary growled at Wade, who she suddenly seemed to like less than she liked Darrell. "I shall choo . . . se what we do next. And I choose . . . a bigger one, to spread out the letters more." She returned the first dowel to the case, then selected a thicker one and carefully wrapped the ribbon around it. It produced the following sequence of letters:

TOSMNHTTHLDE

"That's not a word," said Lily. "Another one?"

The curator's wobbly cheeks turned red, and Wade wondered if she would explode and what that might look like. He stepped back. Rose . . . mary waved a hand in front of her face as if to cool off, then pulled out a staff with ten sides and a diameter of about one and a half inches. Wrapping the ribbon around it produced the following first three lines in English:

TOTHELAND
OFENDLESS
SNOWTOBEG

"To the land of endless snow . . ." Becca gasped. "That's it! Yay, we found it!"

Rosemary's face was purple when she whirled it around to Becca's. "*Who* found it, dear? Did *we* . . . find it? Because I rather th . . . ink *I* found it."

"You did, Rosemary," said Julian. "As usual, you

are being tremendously awesome. My friends here, as grateful as they are, are simply super anxious to know what the rest of the message says. Forgive them, please."

"Dear . . . boy!" Rosemary said, pausing to pinch Julian's cheeks a few times. "Here then . . . is the whole th . . . ing."

TOTHELAND

OFENDLESS

SNOWTOBEG

THEATHOSG

REEKCONCE

ALTHEUNBO

UNDDOUBLE

EYEDBEAST

FROMDEMON

MASTERAVH

Wade drew out the notebook containing the major clues they'd discovered so far and, after much scribbling, broke down the text into individual words.

TO THE LAND OF ENDLESS SNOW TO BEG THE ATHOS GREEK CONCEAL THE UNBOUND DOUBLE EYED BEAST FROM DEMON MASTER AVH

And there it was, a riddle to the location of the second Guardian and the second relic.

"We're all thinking it, right?" said Becca. "'Demon Master AVH'?"

"Albrecht von Hohenzollern, Grand Master of the Teutonic Order in the fifteen hundreds," said Darrell. "I like that Copernicus finally called him what he was."

Wade set his father's college notebook on the table, closed his eyes, and tried to think. *Land of endless snow, Athos Greek, conceal the unbound . . . double-eyed beast . . . double-eyed . . .*

"If I close my eyes . . . for that long . . . people think I'm dead!" Rosemary cackled.

"No, no," Wade said, opening his eyes. "It's just that . . . *double-eyed beast* describes the object we're looking for, and it's based on a constellation." From his backpack, he took out and unfolded the celestial map his uncle Henry had given him.

"Oh, there are several star charts in our collection," Rosemary said, "but that's a very nice one."

"Thanks." Carefully running his fingers over the constellations, Wade searched the chart's colorful illustrations, hoping something would pop out at him. His mind flashed with the idea of the twelfth relic, but he waved it away. Right now there were at least a dozen candidates for *double-eyed beast*—constellations named for dogs, wolves, dragons, monsters—but not one of them suggested that it and it alone was the one Copernicus referred to on the ribbon. "If I study this long enough, I bet I can figure it out."

"Then my work here is done," Dr. Billingham said. She slid the ribbon from the staff, pressed it into Becca's palm, replaced the staff in the display case, snapped the case shut, and locked it away. "For the further meaning of your message, I suggest you all trot off to Hell . . ."

CHAPTER ELEVEN

" ...**E**nistic archives," Rosemary finished. "The phrase *the Athos Greek* undoubtedly points to Hellenistic culture. You should start with section five in the reading room. Good-bye."

The curator brusquely shooed them from the room by flicking her fingers toward the door, and they headed back to the atrium.

"That took a week," Lily said, blinking her eyes as if coming out of a cave.

"But we have the message," said Becca. "Now we just need to know what it means." The truth was, the instant Becca had heard the words *reading room*, her pulse had sped up. As always, she had the Copernicus diary in her bag and knew it was as precious as just about any rare book anywhere. But the Morgan's collection was world famous for a reason. Gutenberg Bibles, Dickens manuscripts, diaries, biographies, histories, artwork, political documents. The Morgan had them all.

"The Athos Greek," she said. "Land of endless snow. Those are awesomely definite clues to who the Guardian might be. Greece is in the south of Europe, but endless snow sounds like the north. I'm sure the diary will tell us even more."

"And I can't stop thinking about the double-eyed beast," Wade added, looking back at her as he had *so* many times since San Francisco. What *that* was all about, Becca didn't know. "If I keep studying the star map, I might be able to narrow it down." Then he started chewing his lip, that little thing he did when he was thinking.

Before entering the Morgan's upstairs reading room, they were asked to stow their belongings—except for notebooks and computers—in special lockers outside the room and, interestingly, to wash their hands.

"Because of the oils," Darrell said, wiggling his fingers. "The oils in our skin can damage original materials. Mom knows stuff like that."

"And now so do you," said Lily.

After they explained the basic reason for their visit—
"Greek monasteries and monks of the early sixteenth
century"—the young man who'd let them in gave them
a brief tour of the holdings, and they each decided to
take on a different aspect of the research. Wade unfolded
his celestial map and sat his notebook by its side. Julian
pulled down from the shelves a large photographic book
on Mediterranean monasteries as well as several maps
of the world and Greece for the exact location of Athos.
Lily gave herself the task of scanning the five Copernicus biographies loaded on the new tablet, while Darrell
hunted down a handful of books on sixteenth-century
Greek history.

As they got to work, Becca stood staring at the filled
bookshelves and glass bookcases, at the dozens of reference stacks, and at the lone, lucky, lucky librarian
behind the counter, and she wondered how in the world
she could ever get his job.

*Imagine being the master of this room! I would totally live
here.*

"Becca, are you with us?" asked Lily. "Or lost in your
own head?"

"Yes, yes," she said. "I mean, no. I'm fine."

She set down on the table in front of her a book disguised in a wrinkled copy of the London *Times*, knowing

that the librarian would envy *her* if he only knew that, ten feet away, was the five-hundred-year-old diary of Copernicus.

Before running for their lives in San Francisco, Becca had discovered in the diary's final pages a sequence of heavily coded passages along with a *tabula recta*, a square block of letters. When she'd discovered the right key word, the square had allowed her to decode a particularly difficult passage. That passage, among other things, had confirmed that the original Guardian of the Scorpio relic was a Portuguese trader named Tomé Pires. The clue had eventually led to them locating not the original relic, but a centuries-old decoy.

Then, just this morning, when the pain in her arm had woken her, she'd distracted herself by studying the other coded pages. As in San Francisco, where she'd come across a tiny sketch of a scorpion in the margin of a page, Becca had discovered a date written in tiny letters—*xiii February 1517*—and another drawing. It was so faint as to be nearly invisible.

At first, she'd thought

the image—almost certainly sketched by Copernicus himself—was meant to be two diamonds touching end to end. But now the "double-eyed beast" of the scytale message suggested that the drawing was really of two eyes, and that the passage next to the drawing might tell the story of the Guardian whose name they were searching for. Either way, the first line of the double-eyed passage was impenetrable.

Ourn ao froa lfa atsiu vlali am sa tlrlau dsa . . .

Without the right key word, it might prove fruitless to try to decode it, but maybe she had to try anyway. Still, where to start? *Ourn ao froa . . . ?*

"Becca, can you read Greek?" asked Darrell, holding an old volume bound in red leather. "This one's about the lives of monks in the time period we want."

"Sorry," she grumbled. "I feel like I'm doing it now."

"I can help," the librarian whispered at the counter. He then showed Darrell to a scanner whose output was linked to a translation program. "I suggest you scan the book's table of contents first, find the pages you think you want, then scan *them*. The translation will appear on this computer."

"Perfect," said Darrell.

After some minutes of quiet work, in which they all searched for anything that might connect to the scytale message, Julian sat back from the table. "First of all, there are over twenty monasteries in Athos. Some are like fortresses built on cliffs over the ocean. You have to climb these endless narrow stairs cut into the rocks. But it makes me wonder if Copernicus ever visited Greece. I mean, how did he meet the Athos Greek?"

Lily did quick word searches through the several biographies on the tablet. "Copernicus traveled, but it doesn't look like he ever visited Greece. At least I can't find any journey recorded in these books. So we're back to square zero."

"I think you mean square one," said Wade. "But they're pretty close together."

"Um, yeah, until me," said Darrell inexplicably. "It scrambles my brain, but I think I found something. It's from a Greek book called something like *Holy Monks of Athos*. The translation is rough, but listen to this."

He cleared his throat and read the words on the computer. "'One big monks Athos be Maximus, living 1475 until 1556 when he became no longer."

Wade stared at him. "Which I think means . . . the same time as Copernicus."

"I think so, too," Darrell said. "Now . . . 'unlike monk

brothers of his, Maximus studied far Italy, Padua, when 1502 came round.'" He grinned. "Nice style, huh?"

"Padua," said Becca. "We know Copernicus was in Bologna . . . Lily?"

Lily scanned the indexes again. "Yep. He was a student at the University of Padua from 1501 to 1502."

Becca looked up from the diary and grinned. "Darrell, it proves what you said."

"Probably. What are we talking about?"

"That everybody knew everybody back then. The world had lots fewer people, and they all gathered in the same places."

Darrell nodded. "I did say that. So, yes, I am right. Plus, Italy, right? Everybody went there because of the weather."

"Well, that's just it, isn't it?" said Julian. "*The land of snow and endless night* doesn't sound like either Italy or Greece. Something more northern, maybe . . ."

Darrell squinted at the screen. "'Maximus can be known as Greek Maxim or Maxim Grek or Maximus Grekus or Grekus Maximus.'"

"Huh," said Lily. "Greek Maxim. I get it."

"You do?" asked Wade.

"Sure, I mean, I ask myself why they would call him Greek Maxim, right?" They shook their heads. "Well, think about it. Would you call a Greek a Greek when he's in Greece? No, you wouldn't, because they're *all* Greek in Greece. So . . . anyone—"

"Ooh!" Becca said. "They called him 'the Greek' when he lived in another country!"

"A country with snow?" asked Julian. "Darrell, what does the book say?"

Darrell squinted at the screen. "Um, yeah. Lots of snow. The endless kind . . ."

"Norway!" said Wade. "No! Iceland!"

"Russia, my friends," Darrell said, pleased with himself. "At least I think that's what this says. Listen. 'Come later Maxim was by Russia Duke Vasily the Three invited Moscow to. There he Russian make of Greek into Russian word pages.'"

"That makes sense," said Becca. "They wanted Maxim to translate Greek stuff into Russian because the Greeks probably had all kinds of books they didn't have in Russia."

Darrell grumbled. "Which is exactly what I said."

"When did Maxim go to Russia?" asked Wade.

"*If* you'll let me continue—"

"It's hard to listen to," said Wade.

"So are you." Darrell cleared his throat and started up. "It says . . . 1515. Exactly when we need him to be

89

in the land of endless snow. I totally bet Maxim Grek is the second Guardian."

Becca stood. "Darrell, this is huge. I think maybe you did it—"

"Russia is huge, too." Lily pushed a map to the middle of the table. "Look at it. Where do we even begin?"

"Wait. There's more." Darrell scanned another page of the book. "'His life problems came big in Russia. Duke Vasily make him prison for Maxim when Maxim say Duke no marry.' Which means that after going to Russia things turned pretty rough for Maxim. Vasily threw him in jail because Maxim didn't like him marrying some lady."

"As opposed to who?" asked Becca.

Darrell scanned the text. "His wife."

"Oh."

Julian stood and paced the length of the table. "Did Maxim die in Russia? If he did, the relic may still be there. Besides that, sometimes people do important things on their deathbeds. Like the Frombork Protocol, right? Maybe before he died, Maxim left a clue about where he hid the relic."

Darrell stood away from the computer. "I anymore read cannot. Eyes of me blur big. Anyone . . . ?"

"I'll do it," said Lily. She slid over to the computer

and read the screen for a few seconds. "Oh, and double oh. It says . . . 'Duke Vasily many had of alliances. One of with' . . . ack! Guess who?"

"The pope," said Darrell. "Napoleon. Dracula! Final answer!"

She shook her head. "The Demon Master, AVH himself!"

"Seriously?" said Wade. "Duke Vasily's ally was Albrecht von Hohenzollern?"

"'Albrecht of Hohenzollern Prussia,'" Lily read. "The one and only Grand Master of the creepy Knights of the Teutonic Order, and the creepy nemesis of Copernicus!"

The reading room went quiet.

Becca closed the diary, unable to read anymore. "So . . . Copernicus meets Maxim Grek in Padua when they're students. Later, when he has to hide the relics, he remembers his college friend, who is now in Russia, where Maxim quickly becomes the enemy of Vasily *and* Albrecht at the same time. Maxim Grek is very possibly our Guardian!"

Lily smiled. "And because the first will circle to the last, Copernicus leaves the clue in Magellan's dagger, which we only found when Becca cracked it—saving *my* life. In other words, you're welcome."

Darrell eased back to the computer. "It goes on . . .

'War plenty. Maxim prison was after and after for his life. Last years in Saint Sergius monastery inside out of Muscovy. Only after Maxim die is he buried. This can be 1556!'" Darrell blinked. "To translate the translation, Maxim was jailed in one monastery after another and finally spent his last years in a place called Saint Sergius, a monastery 'inside out of Muscovy.' He never made it back to Greece. They buried him in the monastery after he died."

"Here's Saint Sergius." Julian turned a large photographic book around. Spread across two pages was a picture of the massive Saint Sergius monastery. It was an enormous and opulent fortress. Towering over its high white stone walls were dozens of plump domes painted brilliant gold or deep blue and flecked all over with silver stars.

"Can you imagine how many places you could hide a relic there?" asked Lily. "Seriously, it makes sense to start at the end of his life and work backward. It's how we zeroed in on Magellan."

Which Becca realized for the first time was true, as it had been for Uncle Henry, too. It was at the end of *his* life that he had passed the secret on to them.

"Man, I wish I was going with you," said Julian.

"Going with us?" Wade asked. "To Russia? Are we

seriously thinking the relic is in Russia?"

"Go to where he died. That's where I would begin," Darrell said. "Russia. The monastery at Saint Sergius. For which, by the way, *you're* welcome."

"All right, then," said Wade. "It would be totally amazing if we think we've already figured out who the Guardian might be. But I'm getting nowhere on what the double-eyed relic is—"

Julian's cell phone buzzed. He swiped it on and answered it. He nodded once, ended the call, and stood up. "We have to go right now."

"Did the Order find us?" said Darrell. "Are they here? Why do we have to leave?"

"For brunch," Julian said. "Our dads are meeting us in half an hour!"

CHAPTER TWELVE

A s a precaution, Lily, Julian, and a guard left the Morgan from the old entrance on Thirty-Sixth Street, while Wade, Becca, Darrell, and another guard exited the brownstone through a pair of glass doors at 24 East Thirty-Seventh Street. They met one another a block east of the museum, on Park Avenue, where a brown four-door Honda sedan was idling at the curb. Dennis, the Ackroyds' driver, sat behind the wheel. He smiled and unlocked the doors, the kids climbed in, and the two guards trotted back to the museum.

"Dennis, how are you feeling this morning?" Julian asked.

"Fine today," he said. "Where to?"

"The Water Club."

"I hope they have food, too," said Darrell.

Wade laughed. Darrell was feeling good. They all were. In a couple of short hours, they had gained a solid idea of who the second Guardian was. That was real progress.

Ten minutes later, after zigzagging from block to block across streets and down avenues, they arrived at a broad, low restaurant overlooking the river. Julian thanked Dennis, who drove off to park nearby.

"Your father will arrive in . . . seventeen minutes," said a man at the desk, checking his watch. "Your table is ready for you now."

The dining room smelled deliciously of hot coffee, fried eggs, bacon, and pastries, and Wade's stomach wanted all of them. They crossed the floor to a large round table by a wide bank of windows. Snowflakes, heavier now, were falling gently and dissolving into the river outside.

Becca took a seat next to him. "What's this river?"

"The East River," said Julian. "You can just make out the Williamsburg Bridge."

"Oh." She shivered. "Better to look at it than be on it."

As soon as they were all seated, Wade drew the star

chart from his backpack and unfolded it. "The constellation is here, somewhere," he murmured. "The double-eyed beast has got to be one of Ptolemy's original forty-eight constellations. But which one?"

"There are a dozen or so 'beasts,'" Lily said, making air quotes around the last word. "And I'm including dogs, birds, Hydras, dragons, and bears."

Wade nodded. "But some are profiles. Not all of them have both eyes visible." As he looked at his antique sky map, Wade imagined Uncle Henry's kind, old face, and he felt something shut off in his brain. The table, the windows, the snow vanishing into the river, even Becca and the others around him, seemed to fade into the background. His talent for blocking out noises and distractions—so tested lately—came forward.

He mentally ticked off the constellations that couldn't for an instant be considered "double-eyed." That still left a number of water creatures, centaurs, a lion, bears, a dragon, a horse, and more. Studying the golden and silver constellations, he remembered what his father had taught him about stars, and a small thought entered his mind.

Could *double-eyed* refer to the astronomical phenomenon known as a double star? "Huh . . ."

"Huh, what?" asked Lily.

"Well, maybe Copernicus meant that there's a double star in the constellation's head."

"What's a double star?" Darrell asked. "And don't say two stars."

Wade laughed. "Well, they kind of *are* two stars—"

"I asked you not to—"

"Which is why I did. A double star is really where two stars are so close together that they sometimes appear like one really bright star. It's only when you observe them for a long time that you discover that there are two of them. Lily, can you cross-check double stars against Ptolemy's forty-eight constellations?"

"Smart," she said, her fingers already moving over the tablet's screen, "for a non–intelligence officer, that is. I'm searching, searching, and . . . oh."

"You found something already?" asked Julian.

"Actually, no. There are a ton of double stars in the constellations and a bunch where the eyes could be."

Darrell leaned over Wade's notebook. "Well, then, what about this 'unbound' beast? What does that even mean? A wild beast? A beast out of control?"

"Right," said Julian. "Or maybe it's loose somehow? Not together—"

"You mean like Wade?" said Darrell.

"Good one," said Julian. "I mean like in a bunch of

different parts? Is there a constellation, *one* constellation, in more than one part? That *also* has a double star in its head?"

Wade studied the star chart carefully before ruling out one constellation after another. Then he stopped, shaking his head. He ran through the constellations a second time. He felt a smile coming on that he couldn't hide. "You got it, Julian. There *is* one constellation that has two stars in its head, and it *is* in two separate parts," he said. "Just one . . ."

They waited.

"Wade. Seriously," said Becca.

"And they call the name of that constellation . . ."

Lily narrowed her eyes at him. "Tell. Us."

"Serpens," he said, tapping the chart directly on the constellation appearing in the northern sky. "Serpens. Which stands for—"

"The Serpent, yeah," Darrell said. "We figured it out. Let's go find it."

"Except . . . look at it," said Wade. "The Serpens constellation really *is* in two parts. In the west is the serpent head and in the east is the body. In between is the figure of the guy who's wrestling it—Ophiuchus—and he's got his own other constellation. Serpens is actually divided into two parts. It's odd that way."

"You're odd that way," Darrell said, squinting over the chart.

"I get it from you," Wade said. "I'm just hoping the relic isn't in two pieces, each one hidden in a different place."

"We'll still find it," Darrell said. "Both of it."

Wade was wondering what it might really mean if the relic was split and hidden in two places when his father and Terence Ackroyd entered the restaurant. They both wore cautious smiles.

"Paul Ferrere is already on his way back to Paris, certain that Sara is in Europe, probably southern Europe," said Terence. "All other destinations for the two jets have been ruled out, and the detectives are paying particular attention to Madrid's several municipal and private airfields."

"Which is very good," Wade's father added. "Their extensive team of investigators is fanning out across the continent."

"Really good!" said Darrell. "This is soooo good!"

"From this moment on, I will be the go-between for the detectives and you," Terence said. "Now, what did you learn at the Morgan?"

"Maxim Grek."

"Serpens."

"Russia."

That's what Wade and the others told his father and Terence. Both men countered their arguments here and there, and the kids countered back. This went on during their three-course brunch, until both men agreed that, given the evidence, they were very likely on the right track.

"Russia," Roald said finally. "As soon as Galina finds out, and she *will* find out, she'll bring Sara to Russia, too. If we have no other leads, then Russia is a start. Don't travel visas take several days to get?"

Julian glanced at his father. "Are you thinking what I'm thinking? Comrade Boris?"

Terence seemed strangely reluctant, then nodded. "I think so, yes. There is a man. A Russian fellow. His name is Boris Volkov. He's lived in London for the past few years. I think you should fly there first and see him. He can likely be of help to you."

"Likely?" said Becca.

"Volkov is a scholar of languages and a historian of Russia's medieval period," Terence said. "I met him when I was writing a book about the treasure the Crusaders brought back from the Middle East. He knows a lot about the Order, perhaps the Guardians, too. Whether he is an agent of one or the other, I can't say.

He's quite cagey about what he reveals. But he may be able to help you get into Russia quickly and aid you while you're there. Boris Volkov seems to have . . . connections."

"Well, we can't afford—" Wade's father began.

Terence waved his hand to stop him. "Think no more about that. I told you, my resources are yours. Since you don't have the authorities on your side, the Ackroyd Foundation will bankroll your continued travels. I'll do everything in my power to help you get Sara back safely and find the relic."

"Awesome," said Lily, smiling at both Ackroyds. "Thank you, again."

Wade's father took a breath, then raised his eyes to the two girls. "There's . . . something else," he said. "Becca, I called your mother this morning, and Lily, your dad, about you going home or going on. You both need to call your parents, not at home, but on their cell phones."

Becca's face fell. "What is it? Oh, I should have answered when I got the call last night. I didn't want to. What's happening—"

Roald held up his hands. "Everyone is fine, they're fine, and in fact Paul Ferrere has already alerted his people in Austin. But there was an incident at Maggie's school the other day, and Lily, your father was followed home from work. Nothing happened, nothing at all, but as of this morning, both of your families have been relocated temporarily."

Lily held one hand over her mouth as she dug furiously for her phone.

Becca did the same. "Maggie, Maggie, I should have answered!"

For the next few minutes, both girls were sitting at different tables, glued to their cell phones, deep in conversation with their parents, while Terence filled in the details.

"The stinking Order," Darrell grumbled.

"Dad—" Wade started.

"I already talked to your mother," his father said, assuring him. "She's fine and traveling in Mexico. She doesn't appear to be on their radar at all."

A weight had been lifted, but Wade realized it had been days since he had spoken with her. "I'll call her right after this."

"Basically," Terence said, "it's best for none of you to return to Austin until we're sure of what we are dealing with. The Order could simply be flexing its muscles. I have no doubt that whatever they are doing comes from Galina herself, but my feeling is that she won't want to spread herself too thin with actions as intimidating as doing anything to the girls' families. Her empire is huge. She will need to focus it."

Wade shared a look with Darrell, who muttered something about Galina that Wade knew he probably shouldn't repeat. That was when his father produced a narrow silver tube from his pocket. It was the size of a fat ballpoint.

"It's a stun gun," he said. "A miniature Taser. Totally legal. The investigators gave one to me."

"Do we each get one?" asked Darrell.

"Absolutely not. And it's for defense only."

"A little something," said Terence. "It can be handy in tight quarters, without being a dangerous weapon."

Minutes later, Lily returned, wiping her cheeks. "They're all right. Way upset, with, like, a million questions, but they don't think I should be there right now." She started crying again behind her hands. "I'm sorry." Darrell put his arm around her shoulders, and she leaned into him.

Becca came back to the table looking like a zombie, blinking tears away from her eyes, unable to sit down. "Maggie's okay, worried like crazy. My parents, too, but they said I should stay with you. I never even thought of going home, and now I really want to, but I guess I should stay. I don't know."

Lily pulled away from Darrell and put her hand on Becca's wrist, and Becca sat. It was like that for a long while, everyone quiet, eyes down, not knowing what to say.

Wade once more remembered his dream of the cave: Becca lying lifeless on the floor. Then the way Markus Wolff had stared at her in San Francisco. He suddenly feared that Becca might be in some particular kind of danger, but he still didn't know how to express it. He just gazed at her, then at Lily, then at Becca again.

Finally, dishes were removed and dessert came, and that seemed to reset things.

"Is Boris Volkov a friend of yours?" Roald asked over a final coffee.

"No, not a friend," Terence said, waving a waiter over and asking for the check. "But he's useful. Listen to what he has to say. He knows many people in Russia who may be able to help you. However, I wouldn't entirely trust him. Boris doesn't do anything for nothing."

Wade felt uneasy to hear those words. But he hoped that the mysterious Russian would shed light on the relic's whereabouts. At the very least, the family was, as his father had hoped, moving forward.

To Russia. To the second relic . . . and Sara.

"In the meantime," Julian said, "Dad and I will focus on finding out what we can from our side. The instant we discover anything, we'll call you."

"Night or day," Roald said, looking around at the children.

With a final firm pledge of assistance, Terence made a call. Seven minutes later, Dennis pulled up outside the Water Club in yet another limo. Their luggage packed and safely in the trunk, the kids and Roald began their roundabout journey to JFK, to await their evening flight to London.

CHAPTER THIRTEEN

Madrid; London
March 19

Ebner von Braun woke to the tinny ascending scale
of a digital marimba that suddenly sounded like
a skeleton drumming a piano with its own bones. It
was a ringtone he was determined to change at his first
opportunity.

He blinked his eyes onto a black room.

Where am I?

More marimba.

Right.

Madrid.

He slid open the phone. *"¿Hola?"*

It was an Orc from the Copernicus Room. He listened. *"¿Londres?"* he said. *"¿Cuándo?"* The voice replied. Ebner pulled the phone away from his face. *"¿Quién es el jefe del Grupo de los Seis?"*

"Señor Doyle."

"Then send Señor Doyle."

Click.

The aroma of grilled tomatoes greeted Archie Doyle when he woke up. He gazed through sleepy eyes at the bedroom of his three-room flat at 36B Foulden Road in the Borough of Hackney in London. He yawned.

It was 5:51 a.m., and his wife, Sheila, and his son, Paulie, were already awake.

Ah, family.

He flapped his lips and blew out the stale breath of sleep. "Bbbbbbbbbb!" This habit, and other exercises of the face and vocal cords, were ones he had learned in his unsuccessful years as an actor, which, alas, were all of them. As an actor, a mimic, a stand-up comedian, and the sad clown Tristophanes, in whose guise he appeared at birthday parties and bar mitzvahs, Archie Doyle had struggled.

He was far better at his other calling.

He liked to kill people.

And he'd be getting to do more of it soon. A recent and bizarre auto accident involving no less than three operatives had left Archie next in line to head Group 6 of the East London section of the Teutonic Order, a post he held while Berlin made up its corporate mind about more permanent arrangements.

Archie was determined to make a good impression.

"The rrrrrain in Spppppain stays mmmmmainly on the pppplain!"

"That you, dear?" came the call from the kitchen. "Breakfast in five minutes."

"Coming, luv," Archie responded happily. Sitting up, he slid his laptop from the end table onto the bed and opened it. He then typed in seven distinct passwords, and the screen he wanted came up. On it was a photograph of five rather downcast people, a man and four young teenagers, at a departure gate in what his trained eye told him was JFK airport in New York. Did they know they were being tracked? Their expressions suggested they might. It was next to impossible to avoid detection in such places when the Order was after you. On the other hand, a father and four children? Where was Mum?

Mine not to reason why.

Beneath the photograph were the names of the five persons, and these words:

Guardian alert: 19 March. NY flight Virgin Atlantic 004. Arrival 7:25 a.m. Heathrow Terminal 3.

"Oh, brilliant!" he whispered with a smile. There was a standing order to terminate all Guardians when identified as such. Five kills in one day. This would be a rather lovely way to convince his superiors that Archie was the man for the top job.

When he scrolled down a little farther, however, his smile crinkled to disappointment. Beneath the names and destination of the people in the photograph was a series of items with little boxes to be checkmarked as to Archie's course of action.

☐ *Terminate immediately*
☐ *Terminate off site*
☐ *Kidnap and report*
☑ *Follow only and report*

"Blast it all!" he breathed softly. "I am a termination machine!"

Still, a job was a job, and pleasing the Order was far preferable to displeasing them. And by *them* he meant *her*, and by *her* he meant Galina Krause. He'd seen her angry once. He hoped never to see it again.

Pulling up the train schedule, Archie calculated that the journey from his local railway station of Rectory Road to Heathrow would take a total of ninety-four minutes. Just before 6:30, he would snag a seat on the excruciatingly slow one-hour service west to central London, disembark at Paddington Station, dash over to Platform 6 for the 7:30 Heathrow Express to Terminal 3, and arrive twenty minutes later. Given another twenty or so minutes spent deplaning, collecting bags, if any, passport control, bathroom time, etc., the gloomy family couldn't be expected to be out of the arrivals hall until eight a.m. at the earliest, anyway. He checked the time again. Six o'clock.

I do have to get a move on.

Archie Doyle was of normal height and build with features that were, in the best tradition of foreign agents, nondescript. He leaped from bed, cleaned himself up, dressed in a smart wool suit of dark blue and a white shirt with muted tie, and topped it all off with a crisp bowler hat. He then slipped his briefcase onto his dresser and flipped up the lid.

Inside were the tools of his trade: several thicknesses and shades of adhesive mustaches and matching eyebrows, a range of eyeglasses, a tube of rub-on tanner, two false noses, three slender vials of poison, a small pistol and silencer, a stiletto, and assorted untraceable cell phones. It amazed him how many of these items he also used for his party activities. He placed his computer inside and clamped the briefcase shut. Then he slid his brolly—umbrella—from the closet, opened and closed it once, then tapped one of two small buttons inside its handle. With barely a breath, a hollow two-inch needle emerged from the umbrella's tip. Such a weapon could inflict a range of wounds, from a simple annoying scratch to a deadly puncture, if the needle was infused with poison. That was what the second button was for.

Archie wondered for an instant: Who *were* the Kaplans, anyway? Why "follow only and report"? Why not terminate? With no answers coming, he carefully retracted the umbrella's needle, gave his bowler a slap, and was in the kitchen—all in less than ten minutes from the time he woke.

His lovely wife, Sheila, turned to him, her smile like sunshine on the lawn of Hyde Park. In the tiny room with her, and taking up much of the floor space, was a portable crib. Fingers in mouth, sippy cup wedged between his plump legs, sat Paulie Doyle, fourteen months of pudge and drool and grins.

"I'm nearly plating the tomatoes, dear," Sheila said. "Kippers this morning?"

Archie Doyle sighed. "Sorry, dear. Must leap to the office immediately. I'll grab an egg and bacon on the way to the train. Save the tomatoes, though. Should be home for lunch."

"All right, dear," she said. "You have a wunnyful day."

"Thanks, luv," Archie said, kissing her ample cheek. "And bye-bye, Little Prince Paulie." He ruffled the wispy hair on the head of his son on his way to the door.

Archie was out, down the stairs, and on the sidewalk in a flash. Brisk day. Gray but pleasant. A perfect day for a termination—or five—he thought, but good enough to follow only and report.

"We shall see," he murmured, fingering the second button on his umbrella, "what we shall see."

CHAPTER FOURTEEN

London

Knowing there was little escape from airport cameras, Becca emerged head down from the Jetway in the arrivals terminal at London's Heathrow Airport. She trailed Lily, who as usual was acting as a sort of guide through the crowded world of crowds. It was the morning after the flight, and early, only a few minutes after eight a.m. But already the gates and concourses were busy, and Becca couldn't look up without feeling nauseous.

A really annoying personality trait.

It was like shouting, *Hey, everybody, look at me! I'm not looking at you!*

"You'll have to learn to do this one day, you know," Lily said over her shoulder.

"Not if you're always here."

"I just might be!"

Before the flight had left New York the previous evening, both girls had received a second and third round of phone calls from their parents, and Becca had had a very long talk with Maggie, which had managed to settle them both so that by the end they'd been laughing through their tears and whispering promises to each other to be good and safe. Becca felt that for her and Lily, hearing from their families was like Roald, Darrell, and Wade hearing from the investigators: all of them were now more or less assured that things were as okay as they could be for the moment and moving in the right direction. Without that, Becca didn't know how they could possibly focus on the relic and Russia and whatever else was to come. But here they were, on their first leg of the Serpens quest, and they were doing it.

"Oh, brother, now it begins," Lily grumbled as an airport official waved them and a hundred thousand other international passengers into the same skinny line.

There was no hiding here, Becca thought. No possibility of evasive action. Everyone had to go through passport control. And they were undoubtedly being filmed. In San Francisco they'd learned about the Order's awesome "Copernicus servers," with a computer power most first-world countries would envy. The family had probably been spotted at Kennedy airport, back in New York, so the Order *had* to know they were already in London. Eyes were on them. Of course they were.

Nearly an hour of blurring movement and bouncing from one line into another and opening bags and zipping them up and showing documents and squeezing into another line finally ended, and they were out of the terminal, and it was great, but not that great.

London might have been the home of Oliver Twist and Sherlock Holmes, but Becca's first experience outside the terminal was a stabbing downpour of cold, heavy, exhaust-filled, vertical rain.

"Absolutely fabulous, it's not," Lily grumbled. "Who knew it rained in England?"

"Uck, okay. Stay together," Roald urged, and they did, sticking close as he moved them quickly across the lanes of bus and shuttle traffic to the taxi stand, where they piled into a bulbous black cab that looked very much like the old one they'd seen in San Francisco last week. The sight of it started a superfast stream of memories in Becca's mind, culminating with a gun at her head at Mission Dolores, which, thankfully, hadn't gone off. Best not to live those days again. These days were bound to be scary enough.

"We'll be stopping at various places," Roald told the driver from the backseat. "First destination, Covent Garden."

"Certainly."

The taxi, piloted by a very quiet driver who wore a Sikh turban, was soon grinding its way from the airport and up onto a broad highway known as the M4. One of the things both Terence Ackroyd and the investigator had advised, to confuse would-be followers, was to take a roundabout route wherever they went. Terence Ackroyd's private apartment—or "safe flat," as he called it—was near the British Museum, but it would likely be a couple of hours before they actually reached it.

"Evasive maneuvers," Roald called them.

In the same spirit, Darrell and Wade had worked out a set of secret finger gestures on the plane. "To use if something bad is happening but you can't tell anyone," Darrell had said.

Lily gave them a blank look. "Um . . . what?"

"The complete range of bad things can be said with only five fingers," Wade insisted. "You raise them to your face in a casual way, and the rest of us know what to do."

"What?" she said again.

They explained it this way:

One finger: The Order is near—run.

Two fingers: Meet me at (location to be determined).

Three fingers: Create a diversion.

Four fingers: Help.

Five fingers: Just get away from me.

The last one was added by Darrell specifically, he said, for use between the brothers. Becca and Lily spent a long time rolling their eyes, then shrugged and practiced the gestures. Roald woke from a brief nap as the plane was descending and learned them as well, but he thought he might be able to come up with a better set of commands.

"I dare you, Dad," Darrell quipped.

Becca watched out the cab window as they motored swiftly past brick and brownstone neighborhoods with names that exuded Englishness: Cranford and Osterley, Brentford and Shepherd's Bush. She could practically see the sheep grazing in pastures, though that was a scene from old novels and, by now, there weren't many pastures that hadn't been developed and built on.

Still, the slower the taxi went, the more clogged the streets were, and the more Becca began to feel the aura of "London, England" breathing from the sights around her. It came powerfully. All those English novels by English writers! They were written here, about here, and they were everywhere, as if those books had spilled their pages out into the living city. Even the presence of the Sikh driver spoke of the once-great colonial empire that was Great Britain, and how London gathered in its vast geography everyone from everywhere it had ever ruled.

"My first time to London in ten years," said Roald, his neck craning around here and there to catch every moment, just as she was doing. "There was a conference at the University of London. I presented a paper on Europa, one of Jupiter's moons. It was my first international paper."

"So cool," Becca breathed, aware that there was little volume in what she said.

"Only if you don't read the paper," he said with a laugh. "Pretty dull stuff."

"Still," she said. "London."

Trying not to annoy or alarm the driver, Roald gave him several addresses to drive to—as if they were sightseeing—before the final one. After Covent Garden, a bustling market in the heart of the city, they drove through the madly snarled traffic of Piccadilly Circus, around to Selfridges department store, across a bridge to Southwark, and back over another bridge to Saint Paul's Cathedral. When, finally, they motored toward their final stop, Darrell suggested they call the telephone number Terence had given them, "to get things started." Roald tapped a number on the cell phone installed with Julian's homemade alert software.

"Galina probably knows we're in London," Wade whispered; then he frowned. "There's no probably about it. She knows. We have to be supersmart."

Becca shared a grim look with the others. Despite their hopped-up phones, if for some reason Galina Krause *didn't* already know their exact location, she would soon.

"I've never been not smart," said Lily. "An intelligence officer can't afford to be. That witch is out there. Her and her thugs. I'm sure of it."

The Sikh driver half turned. "*Thugs*, miss. This is a word coming from the Hindi term *thuggees*, the name given to some fanatic followers of Kali. The goddess of destruction."

"Thank you," Lily said, her eyes widening. "How weirdly . . . accurate. . . ."

Becca's blood tingled in her veins. The quest was on, and she believed, as they all did, that if Maxim *was* the Guardian, and Serpens *was* the second relic, then Russia was the place, and she hoped Boris Volkov would help confirm it.

"Hallo? Who is?" The voice crackled loudly from Roald's phone.

"Hello. Is this Boris Volkov?"

"Ya. Hallo. Who is?"

"Excuse me," Roald said as they eased deeper into the streets. "This is a friend of Terence Ackroyd's. He told us—"

"Ah, yes, Terry! Dear friend, Terry. Yes, yes. Family Keplen. Come see me. Is Boris. Boris Volkov." There was the sound of ice clinking into a glass on the other end. "You come Promenade. Ten thirty this morning. Dorchester Hotel."

"Uh . . . we would prefer somewhere more private," Roald said.

"No. Public is safe. Witnesses be there. Public only. Bring item with you, yes?"

"Item?" said Roald. "I'm not sure I know exactly—"

"Park Lane. You find? Yes? Good. You come."

Click.

"Dad, what does he want?" Wade asked. "We don't have any *item* for him."

Roald tapped the phone and returned it to his jacket pocket. "I think we'll find out soon enough. Hotel Cavendish, Gower Street," he told the driver.

"Certainly."

CHAPTER FIFTEEN

The Hotel Cavendish was a small boutique hotel near the corner of Gower Street and Torrington Place in the neighborhood surrounding the British Museum. Wade wondered what their rooms were like. He would continue to wonder. When their taxi wove through a series of narrow streets and passages and finally stopped outside, his father paid their driver handsomely. They entered the hotel, where they booked two rooms, made sure the taxi was gone, then turned and walked right back outside, to the bewilderment of the desk clerk, who was dangling two sets of room keys for no one.

"That looked kind of comfy," said Lily. "And expensive."

"Paul Ferrere always books a room he never stays in," Wade's father said. "This is the kind of life we're living right now. Our flat is a few short blocks away."

He then led the kids up Gower Street, took a left onto Torrington Place, and hung a right into the narrow Chenies Mews, an L-shaped passage whose long side ran parallel to Gower. They walked along the Mews to the corner of the L, where Roald paused in front of a nondescript and, Wade thought, seedy-looking brick building. But the narrow street was quiet and the building more warehouse-like than domestic, both precautions Wade appreciated as Terence's way of keeping them under the radar.

"Just for a day or two," said Roald. "And just so we're all clear: this is our 'location to be determined.' Memorize where we are in relation to the neighborhood."

"Got it," said Becca.

Wade and Darrell quickly left their bags in their ample rooms inside. It was 10:03 a.m. On their return to the Hotel Cavendish by a different route, Wade kept scanning the neighborhood. He noticed no slowing cars or anyone loitering suspiciously. He saw only a young couple in running gear heading to breakfast and a businessman in a blue suit and bowler hat, shaking out his umbrella under a bus stop shelter. But then, according to Darrell, he wouldn't see an agent of the Order until it was too late.

They assembled on the sidewalk in front of the Cavendish while the desk clerk gawked from the lobby. Roald hailed a black cab. The roundabout twenty-minute drive took them past the massive and imposing British Museum, which drew an extended gasp from Becca.

"Next time," she said. "Next time, all the sights."

"Maybe the Ackroyds have special privileges there, too," said Darrell.

Becca's jaw dropped playfully. "Don't kid me."

The cold rain continued to fall on the street, on the cars, on the gray buildings. Wade thought it made the city look sadder than it probably was, but they likely wouldn't get to see much of London anyway. Not if Boris Volkov told them what Wade hoped he would. By this afternoon, they'd be flying to Russia, to find both the relic and Sara.

"We should buy winter coats in London before we leave," Lily said out of nowhere. "*If* we leave. For Russia,

I mean. We should go back to Selfridges. For parkas and scarves and gloves. And Uggs."

For what seemed like a day and a half, they drove past the famous and huge expanse of lawn known as Hyde Park before coiling into an area congested by expensive cars, where the cab left them off. A five-minute evasive walk brought them finally to the graceful Dorchester Hotel. Under its broad awning a top-hatted doorman directed them through the revolving doors into the marble lobby. With a quick look around them, they wove their way into the bustling Promenade room.

CHAPTER SIXTEEN

A tuxedoed man stood behind a tall desk at the entrance to the restaurant.

He nodded politely when they told him who they were there to meet. "Yes, yes. Mr. Volkov has been waiting. One moment." He stepped out and cast a glance over the restaurant.

The Promenade was a deep, busy room lined with elegant tables and chairs on either side, with a central bank of velvet-cushioned sofas. Short potted palm trees were placed every few feet, and gold-topped columns rose to a tiered ceiling. There was also a lot of gold in the other fixtures and hangings, and a jungle of enormous flower arrangements on tables.

The place boomed with the sound of clinking cutlery and tinkling glass and the bubbling murmurs of dozens of breakfast conversations. It was also filled with the smell of toast and coffee, which was fine, but Wade wondered if they'd ever heard of the basic bacon, egg, and cheese on a hard roll.

The maître d' adjusted his glasses and pointed. "Mr. Volkov is right over . . ."

He didn't have to go on. A very big man wearing a very big suit waved both arms from the end of the room as if he were trying to stop traffic.

"You must be Keplens!" he bellowed.

"Great," Darrell whispered. "Three seconds in a public place and already we've been outed."

By a really enormous guy.

Wade's antennae went up instantly. "Dad, I don't get it. Why did he want to meet here?" he whispered. "The whole world sees us."

"Unless it's a trap," Darrell said.

"Maybe," Wade's father said. "He *is* right that being in public might protect us from outright attack. Remember, the Order doesn't want to get caught, either. Maybe he knows something about being careful that we don't."

Boris Volkov was completely huge, and seemed to grow more huge the closer they came. He appeared to

Wade every bit as cagey and suspicious as Terence Ackroyd had suggested. Weaving around the tables toward him, Wade kept a lookout for anyone paying special attention to them, but after turning to see who the "Keplens!" were, the other patrons seemed to have gone back to their private conversations. *Good,* he thought. *I'd rather eat than run.*

The large Russian bounced up awkwardly when they came over, nearly taking the tablecloth with him, and wrapped his arms around them in a weird group hug.

Wade wanted to trust him, but he didn't care for the heavy, fumy smell that blossomed from him. Alcohol in the morning? What sort of person had Terence hooked them up with? Everyone, he told himself, every single person was under suspicion until proved otherwise. That was a lesson they'd learned in San Francisco, with the killer Feng Yi, who had betrayed the kids *and* the Teutonic Order.

His father introduced them all, and Volkov forced them into a very precise arrangement at the table. He asked Becca and Lily, who he called by each other's name—*Lee-lee* and *Bake-ahh*—to squeeze in alongside him, while he gestured Wade, his father, and Darrell to take seats on the other side. Settling in, Wade tugged out his notebook and turned to the first clean page, ready for whatever the strange man told them.

In the few moments that followed, during which they ordered, Wade eyed Boris Volkov as best he could without staring. First off, everything on the guy was sweating. His jowly cheeks, his forehead, the ridge above his chin, his levels of neck. The front of his shirt was soaked through. There was a drop of sweat dangling from the tip of his nose, which he didn't wipe away, but which never appeared to fall, either.

It was when the man's eyes turned on Wade that he noticed Boris Volkov's real distinguishing feature. It was neither his plump lobster face nor his short chubby fingers, but the two large dark eyes that were severely misaligned. The left one slanted to the left, while the right one stared straight ahead.

Which one do you look at?

And did it mean anything that this guy *and* Galina Krause both had eye things going on? Hers, two colors; his, wandering around?

"So, so," the man said, turning his head completely to Wade's father, which didn't help answer the question of which eye to address. "Promenade safe place. Over there, deputy head of MI6, British Secret Intelligence Service. At table alone, British foreign secretary. Safest place in all of London, right here!"

"Thank you for meeting us," Wade's father said. "And yes, I agree, a good location."

The Russian arched up in his seat. "You want to know who is Boris Volkov, yes? Why is Russian in the country of Wimbledon and Big Ben?" He shrugged and breathed out a flammable gust. Wade was glad there were no candles on the breakfast table.

"I graduate Moscow State University," he said. "Scholar for many years. Dead languages. Boris love dead languages. Russia is land of the dead, no? But, I say wrong things at wrong time. Government not like so much. I spend time in famous Lubyanka prison, yes? Not serious. Just questions, you see? I notice there the wood floor. Oak. Very nice. Like this, yes?" He paused, flattening his big hands and angling them, one to the other.

"Parquet," Darrell said.

"Yes!" Boris boomed, patting Darrell's hand on the table. "You very smart American boy. How you know parquet?"

"My mom's office in the archives at the University of Texas has parquet floors," he said.

"Ah, yes. Mother. She in this, too. Terry tell me. Sad, sad."

Wade didn't know what Boris knew, but wondered

130

once again what exactly Terence had told him.

"So, future of Boris is not in Russia. Zoom-boom! I come London, yes?" He slapped his chubby palms on the table. "I perch now in small flat owned by friend. Is beautiful little birdcage. Tiny. Top floor. Five stairway. No elevator. Is hard for old legs, but this is way I live now. Boris walk everywhere. He never take car. Car take you to Lubyanka, yes?"

I don't know, does it?

Boris paused a moment to move the sugar bowl from one side of his place setting to the other. "But enough. You call me Uncle Boris now, yes?"

No, thought Wade, *we don't. You're not our uncle. I had an uncle, Uncle Henry, and he was murdered by the Teutonic Order, and so was nice Mr. Chen on the plane to San Francisco, and we don't know if you're with the Order or not.*

It wasn't that Wade wanted his mind to go there, accusing everyone, suspicious of everyone, but how could he do anything else? Heinrich Vogel's death had been sudden and brutal—an old man murdered in his home. It was fresh, barely a week and half in the past, and, like Sara's kidnapping, Wade realized it was hovering like a shroud over everything they thought and did. It was Uncle Henry's murder that had sent them on the relic hunt in the first place, the quest that had quickly become their urgent mission. The quest that was changing them in ways he didn't fully understand.

After a few pleasant remarks with Roald about the weather and hotels and so on, Boris Volkov tapped his meaty fingers on the tabletop. His smile dropped away.

"You see, it is this. History of Russia is history of pain. Invasions? Countless invasions. Poland. Napoleon. Hitler. Then invasions from inside—Lenin, Stalin, demon masters buried now with honors in Red Square. Horrible history. Still Russia survives."

"We know that the Teutonic Order was friends with the Duke of Moscow," Becca said. "Vasily the Third had an alliance with Albrecht."

"Teutonic Order of Ancient Prussia." Boris's face reddened. "This is the way of the Order. They seep everywhere, like poison." He lowered his voice. "In Russia, you see, the Order is known as Red Brotherhood. Keplens, you do not know this, but Teutonic Order kill Boris's brother. Galina Krause murder him while she in Russia. Yes, is true! Dental records prove it. I see his teeth. I *have* his teeth." And he raised a finger behind his open collar and tugged out a chain on which hung a blackened molar. "It belonged to Aleksandr in his mouth. Alek was doctor, very fine doctor. His tooth is all I carry. No money. No wallet. No key. See, I have nothing." Boris tugged at his pants pockets to show they were empty. "Of course, Alek's name not really Volkov. Nor he, nor me."

Meaning what, exactly?

"I'm so sorry to hear that," Roald said. "We didn't know. Terence did tell us about your knowledge of the Order in Russia. It's part of the reason we've come here today. We need to do research there. In Russia. Terence said you might be able to help us."

"Yes, yes." Boris tucked the tooth back behind his collar. Then he slid his hand inside his voluminous jacket and produced a narrow manila envelope. He set it on the table and pressed a stubby finger on it. "Documents necessary to get into Russia this very day. Terry phone me with names, so these ready to use. Russian tourist visas. Completely genuine. Notarized by Russian embassy. Smuggled, of course, but what is little smuggling among friends, yes? After you are settled there, I must take side trip, but is not for some days. All us go tonight, yes? You pay? I tell you I have no money."

They went quiet.

"All of us?" said Wade finally. "I didn't think we *all* had to go."

"Perhaps Mr. Ackroyd didn't explain our journey to you," his father added. "It's, well, rather a private family project. We actually don't need—"

"You must have me," Volkov said. His face darkened and his misaligned eyes flashed with anger. "You need Boris. Boris has urgent journey. Boris have friends you require. I did not suffer Lubyanka prison for nothing. I go. I help. For price."

Here it is, Wade thought. *He doesn't do anything for nothing.*

Volkov leaned over the teacups toward them, fixing his eyes on both Darrell and Wade at the same time. "I am collector of unique objects. I want Copernicus dagger."

Wade's blood froze.

How does Boris Volkov—or whatever his real name is— know about the dagger? Is he a Teutonic Knight? Is this a trap?

"I . . . don't know exactly what you mean," Roald said, lying. "A dagger?"

Boris Volkov snorted angrily. "Then go back to Texas, USA. No tea. Good-bye. You are liars, try to trick Boris. Like all the rest. You have nothing!" He slumped back into his chair with such force the table shook. Again, the room hushed.

Texas? How much does he know about us?

"No. Wait," his father said. "We don't actually have . . . what you want."

"But you can get it? As sign of good faith?"

"Let me call Terence." Roald rose and pulled away from the table. "I'll get in touch with him right now."

"More like it," Volkov said, mopping his brow with his napkin, then bouncing right back with a big grin. "Take moments, Dr. Roald Keplen. Time, she does not matter, does she?"

At the word *she*, Darrell fidgeted in his chair, and his face darkened even more than the Russian's had a moment before. "Oh, yeah?" he said. "Yeah?"

"Darrell," Becca whispered. "Not here."

Surprisingly, he calmed down, but Wade could feel his legs pumping under the table.

Right. The real point of meeting this guy is to get Sara back. Time, she does not matter? Time matters more than anything.

His father disappeared into the lobby with his phone at his ear. Volkov stood to massage his right leg as if he weren't in public. It was hard to look at. "Old body hurts, yes?" He thundered back into his chair and pressed his giant bulk across the cups and plates, gesturing the four of them closer. Given how he took up so much table space, there was hardly any room to *be* closer.

"You," Boris said, apparently looking at Wade. "You are Vade, yes? Vade Keplen?"

"Yes."

"Good. You are scientist, yes? I hear it from Terry in New York. And Darrell, you are brother of Vade. I tell you story about scientist and his brother." He set his wandering eyes on the kids, one after the other. "I amuse American children with little story."

The words were sinister enough, but they were nothing compared to the way his wild eyes beckoned them. When he began to speak, slowly and almost in a whisper, the sounds of clacking cutlery and plates, the tinkle of glassware, the murmuring of voices around them—all seemed to fade away.

Even with his seriously broken English, Boris Volkov became suddenly—and inexplicably—a master of words, losing the trappings of the blustery, moody exile. Right there in the middle of a bustling London restaurant, amid the whirl of modern life, he conjured up another time, a forgotten world.

"Listen. Listen to words. Listen to Boris. . . ."

CHAPTER SEVENTEEN

Perhaps you know this already, but long ago there was a man and his brother. Nicolaus and Andreas Copernicus. A scientist and his brother. Andreas was, alas, dying. Illness took people young in those days.

Wade and the others had learned the story of Andreas Copernicus in San Francisco. In fact, it was precisely *because* Andreas had become ill from handling the deadly Scorpio relic that Copernicus had asked his friend Tomé Pires to hide it inside a jade figurine. Wade and later his father believed Andreas might have died from radium poisoning.

"We know a bit about that," said Lily, shooting Wade

and Darrell a glance.

Ah, yes, the bond of brothers is strong. My own brother, Alek, was very skilled doctor. We grew up together in coal mine. A strange place to grow up, is it not?

You see, after Russia's Great Patriotic War, in 1945, our father was sent to labor camp to dig coal day and night in a mine in the gulag. Forced labor, for what they said was his defiance of the government. Camp is far away in Siberia, north of Arctic Circle. You do not know cold like this. Pray you never do.

Two years later, we are born. Twins. Mother dies in childbirth, so Father names us. Alek born first, so he A, for Aleksandr. Me. I am B, for Boris. Is humor. You get?

His eyes bounced back between Wade and Darrell. Did this old Russian see something in them, a kinship that proved they were all Guardians in this together? Or was he weaving a story like a spider weaves a web, drawing them in and snaring them before they realized it was too late? Words mattered, Wade knew. Words had power.

As boys we send message to each other, even in . . .

Boris said something then that Wade wrote in his notebook as *log punked*.

World-famous code is solved when we are boys. Is joke to

138

us, yes? A and B? He send code to me, me send to he. Even when we grow up and go our ways, we send messages. Oh, the vastness of Russia. Me to Moscow, then here, never to return to dark circle of Mother Russia. He to Saint Petersburg, jewel on the Gulf of Finland.

Then the real horror begins.

Four years ago, Galina Krause appears out of the night. Alek works for her. What he does for the Order no one knows; he is doctor! But there is fire. Alek vanishes, is never heard from. Messages stop. I ask friends in Russia, what happen to my brother? They say the girl, Galina. His teeth are sent to me to prove he is dead. Me? I feel something break inside my heart. I cry—"Alek is dead! Galina has killed him!"

The restaurant hushed momentarily, then resumed its noise.

Galina Krause has murdered my brother, Aleksandr. In my heart, all is gone. Father, mother, Alek, even log punked is gone. But from London, I can do nothing. Until now today with you Keplens. We shield each other, yes? I have traced Red Brotherhood. I arrange gift for Galina. We go together in group, me to avenge my poor brother, Andreas . . . I mean Aleksandr . . .

The large Russian paused to wipe his eyes and his cheeks, then slumped back into his chair, making the table quake. "Me, I am nothing. I am like brother with disease. Leper. I am like dead languages that I study. My brother, he is the real one. He had pain. Much, much pain. He was the great one of these two brothers. Then Galina kill him."

CHAPTER EIGHTEEN

In the silence that followed, even through her own misty vision Lily couldn't help staring across the table into the Russian's jiggling left pupil. Not that she wanted to.

Look away! she told herself. *You really have to be more accepting of other people's different little things.*

Boris vacuumed in a long breath. "Russia is a grave, you see? Not only of fathers, not only of brothers. But of the past. But perhaps *you* tell Boris now what *you* know?"

Um, sure, Lily said in her head. *We found out from the coded ribbon in the Magellan dagger that Copernicus wanted to give Serpens to a monk named Maxim Grek, who was invited*

141

to Russia, then thrown in jail. Serpens is maybe a two-part serpent-shaped relic representing the northern constellation of the same name. It fits into the big wheel of Copernicus's astrolabe.

Lily didn't say any of those words. Boris Volkov—which he said was not even his real name!—could simply be trying to trick them into telling what they knew.

I'll try to be okay with the eye, but I'm not going to spill the beans to any old person. Or young person. Or anybody.

"We'll let Uncle Roald tell you what we know," Becca finally said.

"Ah? Yes, of course. Caution. This is wise."

Lily surprised herself that she'd become as wary of others as Wade and Darrell had. Generally, she liked people, even if she made fun of some of them, like Darrell and Wade, but that was so easy to do, and anyway it was friendly, and sometimes they didn't even get it until she explained it to them. This was new to her, meeting these kinds of people she'd never met before except in a movie or a book, but those were fake and this was real. Except maybe for one of his eyes.

"Well, thanks for the story," she said, and Becca nodded with her.

"Is but story. A tale of long time past. Four years ago,

sixty years ago, five hundred years ago, all same. The clock ticks many hours. The journey to the end of the sea is long, yes? Copernicus himself wrote these words. But what do *we* know? Who can say what is true, yes?"

You're right about that, Lily thought. There were so many names and dates in his story that she wished she'd recorded it. *The journey to the end of the sea is long?* It sure is. *Wade's jotting things down, but somebody should be taping the whole thing. Wearing a wire. Like a real spy.*

Roald finally wove his way back through the tables, off the phone now. "The dagger is secure, out of the country, but I think we can make some sort of deal, once we get into—and safely out of—Russia."

Lily tried to read her uncle's face. He was fibbing, right? She hoped he was. They should *never* give up the Copernicus dagger. *Ever.*

"Yes!" Volkov lifted his teacup as if it were a beer mug, chugged it down, then "cheered" the cup into the air. "To our journey, then. I shall close up my flat, then to Russia we go—"

He sucked in an enormous groan and lurched to his feet, like a sea monster rising from the deep. Silverware clattered to the floor because he had stuffed the table-cloth into his belt. His teacup hung out in the air, his sausage-like fingers dwarfing its tiny size, when it fell from his hand and crashed on the table.

"Kkkk—kkk!" Boris's face twisted and bulged as if he were turning into a werewolf.

"Doctor!" Roald yelled. "Is there a doctor—"

The man's cheeks went deep purple. He pawed his leg mercilessly. Roald struggled to wrap his arms around Boris from behind to give him the Heimlich maneuver while both Darrell and Wade held him up, but the Russian was too big, and now his arms were flapping straight out. Suddenly, his eyes ballooned, and he clutched his neck with both hands, gasping for air that wouldn't come.

Customers at other tables were jumping to their feet, some rushing over to help. A waiter dropped his tray and raced back to the desk for the phone.

Boris spat out breaths, trying to form a word, but nothing would come. Roald held him up. "Boris, do you have any medication with you? Someone you want us to call? Anything I can get you?"

The huge man stared down at Lily. Right at her! *Why?* He suddenly blurted "Bird!" right into her face.

"Excuse me? What?" she said, backing up.

"Cage!" He seemed to want to fall on top of her. She stepped back again, saw a bloodstain on his pant leg where he had been rubbing it. She frantically scanned the chaotic room for someone who might be a doctor. On the far side of the restaurant, a calm-looking middle-aged man in a dark blue suit rose from his table. She beelined between the tables to him. "Are you a doctor?" she said. "Sir, can you help him?"

Boris bellowed, then slammed facedown on the table like a whale free-falling from the top of a building. The whole table went over, everything splattered, and Boris slumped to the floor, clutching at Wade for a moment, then slid away, motionless.

Lily screamed, grabbing the sleeve of the man in the dark suit. "Help him!"

"Alas, child," the man said, gently removing her hand, then patting her arm. "I am not a doctor." Tipping his bowler, he swung his umbrella toward the lobby and wove through the tables to the sound of sirens howling up the street.

CHAPTER NINETEEN

Madrid

Galina Krause watched two men in overalls roll a shiny brown coffin across the floor of her private hangar at the Madrid-Barajas Airport. Her mind ticked with a hundred possible scenarios for what might happen over the next hours and days.

Ebner leaned toward her. "We will be in Berlin in three hours' time," he said. "We can take the coffin to Station Two, if you are still intent on sending the woman, which I would not—"

"Yes, Berlin," Galina said.

But is Berlin the best destination after all? she wondered. She didn't like that the Copernicus Room had come up with nothing useful so far except, perhaps, the astronomer's supposed 1517 voyage south from Cádiz, a coastal city less than an hour's flight away. The Kaplans were in London now, but what if they suddenly jetted off to Spain or other parts south? Berlin would put her that much farther away.

"*¿Señorita? ¿A dónde?*" one of the men ferrying the coffin questioned. He pointed from one to the other of two small jets in the hangar.

"*En el avión negro, por favor,*" she replied.

They pushed the coffin to her dark, gunmetal-gray Mystère-Falcon and up a short ramp into its cargo hold. They collapsed the legs of the coffin stand like one would with a hospital gurney, secured the coffin in place, and left the hangar.

Ebner paced annoyingly. "Is *he* to be with us the entire time?"

Galina turned to see Bartolo Cassa stride into the hangar from the sunny tarmac. "You object? Do you think he cannot be trusted? He brought the cargo undamaged from South America. He removed three . . . obstacles to bring the coffin to us. Can he not be trusted?"

Ebner seemed to be debating his answer to that question when the breast pocket of his coat sounded with the tinkling scale of a frantic marimba. He reached for his phone, slid his thumb across the screen, and held it to his ear. "Speak."

Hitching a long, box-shaped canvas bag over his shoulder, Cassa strode easily to the Falcon, walked up its stairs, vanished for a moment, then reappeared in the cockpit.

Galina fixed her eyes on Ebner. "Who is it?"

"Mr. Doyle with his report." Ebner flicked his phone to speaker.

". . . early this morning," Mr. Doyle was saying in a clipped British accent. "The Kaplan family, all of them, met a gentleman, a native Russian known currently as Boris Volkov, for breakfast at the Dorchester Hotel. Papers were passed between them. As directed, I have not interfered with the family, but per protocol, Volkov has been removed. He suffered a leg wound laced with ricin."

"Volkov? You mean the dissident scholar?" asked Ebner.

"Indeed," chirped the Londoner, "although Volkov is not his real name. Up until he was expelled from Russia, he was known as Rubashov. Boris Rubashov."

Galina breathed in suddenly, her eyes flashing. "Rubashov?" Her limbs stiffened for what seemed like an eternity before she said, "They are going to Russia."

"Ah, that explains the papers," said Mr. Doyle from the phone. "They had the look of tourist visas. In a rather curious turn, the smaller girl came up to me, thinking I was a doctor. The bowler, perhaps. I am tracking them, in case he gave them something I didn't see. I am also monitoring the stages of poor Boris's demise. Group Six has an agent in the hospital system."

Ebner seemed to want Galina to speak, but she could not find the words. "Very efficient, Doyle," he said. "This bodes well for your promotion in Group Six. Keep close to the family. Request backup if you need it."

"I shall. Cheerio!"

The fingers of Galina's right hand rose to the three-inch scar on her neck, then fell to her side. "The Kaplans," she said, "have met this Russian for one reason only. Ebner—"

"Galina." Ebner shuddered as if freezing. "Galina, the name Rubashov could simply be a coincidence."

"—the Kaplans are going after the Serpens relic."

Silver, diamonds, and hinges of sparkling wire swam in her vision.

"But surely they know nothing of the full story of Serpens," Ebner said softly. "They could not. The two parts, where they may have ended up—and why. I am certain it is but a stab in the dark, consistent with all of

149

their . . . advances in the quest." He took a breath. "Still, I will inform the Copernicus Room to direct all their research on it now. But any more than that would be premature—"

"Alert the Red Brotherhood to follow the Kaplans wherever they go."

Ebner now appeared to swallow with difficulty. "Galina, the Red Brotherhood are hooligans, gangsters, thugs. They cannot *follow*. They maim; they kill. That's all they know. Let me bring in the Austrians."

"There is no time. Alert the Brotherhood. Naturally, you and I must fly directly . . . there."

"Not the castle—" The word escaped Ebner's lips before he could unsay it.

"Have the Italian brought to the castle, too. And Helmut Bern, as well."

"Tell me you do not mean . . ."

She turned her eyes on him. "I had hoped to wait, but there is no waiting. Ebner, we return to Greywolf immediately."

Greywolf—the Order's Station One—was an estate three hundred kilometers east of Saint Petersburg. It was a huge property: fifty square kilometers of steep, forest-thickened hills, at the summit of which stood a sixteenth-century fortress that the Order had abandoned to a destructive fire four years before.

"Galina, no. I beg you, another place. Kronos One lies in ruins after all this time. Lord knows if the main tower even exists any longer. If you are set on experimenting with Sara Kaplan, I beg you let me send for a newer device."

She laid her hand gently on his and then began to squeeze it under her iron fist. "Greywolf. Kronos One. We go now."

"All because of Rubashov," Ebner muttered, sulking away to the jet.

At the mention of the poisoned Russian's true name, and at the memory of Greywolf, the aircraft hangar around Galina began to vanish, and she soon saw herself laid out, comatose, on a vast slab of undifferentiated white, a wasteland of permafrost and tundra. She had hoped and prayed—bled, even—never to return to the monster country, and certainly not to the fortress. Serpens was in that bleak wilderness somewhere, or half of it, at least. But she was hoping to avoid ever entering that poisoned land to dig for it.

As she climbed the stairs to the Falcon, Galina realized that this flight to Russia was very nearly superfluous. In her mind, ticking like a geared clock-work, like a sequence of tumblers in a combination lock, she had never left.

Wherever she was, there would always be Russia.

CHAPTER TWENTY

I am moving.
Again.

Sara knew this as the cushioned walls so tight around her tilted side to side, inclined up, then leveled out, and stopped. Her moment of clarity wouldn't last long. *They'll soon drug me again*, she thought, *and I'll be out another I-don't-know-how-many days.* She tried to think, to process. She'd read Terence's spy novels, his international thrillers. What could a kidnap victim do? What could a victim learn from her surroundings?

One thing was the conditions of the kidnapping. Here, there were elaborate measures taken, not only for her restraint but also for a kind of comfort. Her hands and feet were bound, and there was some kind of thick belt across her forehead, in addition to an impenetrable blindfold. She was gagged. But she also knew a tube was attached to a needle in her right arm. There was oxygen, pure and cool, being pumped into her nostrils. She was cushioned like an artifact in a box.

She was being cared for, if *cared for* could ever be the proper term.

Though the low pulse of an oxygen pump somewhere near her feet obscured most sound, her ears were open. *Listen!* She made herself still. Unless it was her own mind, she detected a murmur of voices nearby. Faint, almost like whispering. Then a whirring sound around her. And . . . bolts? One, two, three, four. Then the box jostled. Air—real air—swept over her face, her arms. The lid of her prison was open. Was it her keeper? The man with sunglasses, her handler from Bolivia? *Handle me, and I'll bite your arm—no, scream—no, both!* She couldn't, of course, do either.

"*¿Está viva?*" a voice said.

Yes, I'm viva! Sara snapped. Then she thought: *Spanish. Spanish, yes, but not the accent of Bolivia or even of New York. Spain? Am I in Spain?*

A sharp poke in the arm. Sara screamed—tried to scream—but the pressure went straight into her brain like a magician's sword through his assistant in the box, and she was falling again. Quick. Remember. *Spain.*

Roald! Darrell! I'm in Spain! RoaldDarrellRoaldDarrell-WadeDarrell . . .

The lid of her prison crashed shut, and the roar of an engine thundered through the cushioned walls so tight around her, and . . . and . . .

CHAPTER TWENTY-ONE

London

Seemingly within moments of Boris Volkov's thundering fall to the floor, the Promenade was invaded by squads of police and scurrying medical technicians.

In the chaos, Becca saw Uncle Roald sweep the envelope of documents from the table and subtly tuck it into his jacket pocket just before he was called away for questioning by several plainclothes policemen. Lily simply stood there, shaking her head, hands poised in the air as if not knowing what to do with them, her mouth gaping open, nothing coming out.

She's terrified to death! Boris spoke to her. Why?

Becca wrapped her fingers around Lily's wrist and pulled her gently to the far side of the room with the others. "Boris was telling us a lot. Too much," she whispered. "Someone wanted him to stop talking, and stop him going with us."

"That was no heart attack," Darrell growled. "No way."

Wade shoved his hands deep into his pockets. "Do you think we should try to find his flat? He practically told us where it was. Five floors, no elevator."

Two police officers were standing in front of Roald now.

"Either Dad's waving to us or he's doing the code," Darrell whispered. "Look. Five fingers. What's five fingers? Create a diversion? Like a food fight?"

"No, that's three fingers. Five fingers means get away from me," said Wade. "Which I thought was just for us."

"Apparently not," said Becca. "He keeps doing it. We should leave." Bowing her head, she urged them with the other guests toward the lobby just as the medical personnel loaded the giant man onto the gurney. It took three technicians plus two policemen, hissing at one another to make sure he didn't fall off it. It was horrifying to see the once-animated Russian hanging limply over the sides of the gurney. Tables and chairs squeaked and knocked as a handful of remaining customers pulled them aside to make way for Boris to be wheeled to the ambulance.

"Where are we going to go?" asked Lily, still shaking. "What are we even doing?"

"Look, Uncle Roald wants us out of here, and Wade's right," said Becca. "Boris told us he only walks. So his flat is walking distance from the Dorchester. Lily, maybe we should check maps. Can you?"

"Maps?" she said, turning to her. "Are you thinking we should find his place? How are you thinking about anything?"

"I don't know, but he said his flat is on the fifth floor," Becca said as they gathered under the hotel awning. "There's no elevator, remember? Plus, he said he never takes a car or a cab. He walked here. Boris was way out of shape, so it can't be far away."

"His last words were *bird* and *cage*," Darrell added.

"To me," Lily said. "He was talking to me."

"Plus, he gave me this," Wade said, digging into his pocket. "I don't think it's a clue, though. I think . . . he just wanted us to have it?" He opened his palm. In it lay the blackened tooth of Boris's brother.

"Seriously?" said Darrell. "He gave you the tooth?

Why did he give you the tooth?"

Wade shrugged nervously, then said, "I don't know, to keep us moving? To remind us of what the Order and Galina are capable of?"

Becca glanced through the doors and saw Roald sitting in the lobby now with one of the policemen, who was writing in a pad. "Your dad always does the dirty work," she said. "Lily, the maps."

"All right, already," Lily said, finally coming back online. She flipped out her tablet and keyed in several words as she spoke them. "London. Five-floor building. Near Dorchester Hotel. Bird. Cage. No elevator." After a few moments, she perked up in surprise. "That was easy, even for me. I guess the reason Boris was saying stuff to me was because I'm the tech brain of the family. A real estate site just gave me a couple of addresses on a street called"—she turned her tablet around for them to see the map—"Birdcage Walk. Twenty-four minutes from here on foot."

Becca nodded. "Boris was telling us to go to his flat to find another clue. We can swing by his place before we head to our safe flat. Wade?"

They peeked in as Roald's face grew exasperated, one more policeman came over, and they all sat at another table. Roald caught the kids watching him and seemed to deliberately raise a single finger. *The Order is near—run.*

"Whoa," Wade said. "We'll text him later. Let's beat it!"

Following Lily's map, they doglegged quickly to Stanhope Gate, South Audley, Curzon Street, then to the quaintly named Half Moon Street and across a large park that practically connected to another park. Twenty minutes later, they arrived at the short, classy street known as Birdcage Walk.

Trying to determine which building might hold Boris's flat, they dismissed those that were offices or complexes that undoubtedly had elevators. That left a brief half block of older buildings. Each had a stately, crisp exterior, and all of them were set deep on bright green lawns closed in by tall wrought-iron fencing. The neighborhood appeared very exclusive. It was hard for Becca to think of rumpled, maybe-dead Boris living there, but then she remembered that he was staying in a flat owned by someone else.

"You know how I know when we're being followed?" Darrell said. "It's a gift, I understand, but someone's after us now. Whoever Dad warned us against must have followed us."

They looked down the street in both directions and across to the park.

"No one," said Lily. "Which to you only proves that someone is there."

"You bet it does," Darrell said. "We should definitely hurry this up and get back to the safe flat."

"Right. So some of the buildings only have four floors," Becca said. "That leaves seven houses old enough not to have elevators, and where the fifth floor is the top floor."

They were the narrow-fronted row houses of the charming sort she had seen on the way from the airport, though now they were shrouded with the aura of a possible death. She didn't want to think about it, but Boris's fall, his great booming crash onto the table, kept playing in her head.

They spread out across the housefronts and knocked on the doors. What could have been a lengthy process of elimination was made unnecessary by a middle-aged woman who came to the door for Wade, the third door they'd tried. He called them over.

"The *Russian* fellow?" the woman said, a tiny dog nestled in her arms. She narrowed her eyes at them. "I don't *know*. I mean, I *know* him, of course. *Borrrris.*

So does Benjy here, don't you, *Benjy*? You remember *Borrrris*."

The dog started yapping and didn't stop for a full minute.

"Can you tell us where he lives?" asked Lily.

"Where he *lives*?" she said, her eyes squinting even more, if that was possible, and stepping back from the door. "Oh, I *could* tell you, dear. Certainly I *could*, but why, my dear, *that's* the question, *why*? He's not there, no, I *seen* him walk out of his flat just this *morning*. Cross the park. But I don't know as I should tell *you* where he lives, no, because, as I say, *why*?"

That stumped them. There was no reason why the woman should volunteer such information to random people who came looking for a neighbor. Until Darrell said the obvious.

"We know he's not here," he said. "We were just with him across the park at the Dorchester Hotel for breakfast. And . . . but . . ."

He started to falter when Wade jumped in. "He left something behind that we need to return to him."

"*Oh?* And what did Boris leave behind?" she asked, edging even farther back into the hallway.

"Show the lady," said Lily, apparently guessing right away and nodding at his pocket.

Wade held up the black tooth. "This."

"Oh, *goodness*!" the woman screamed, and Benjy growled. "That *awful* thing. He shows everyone. He'll be wanting *that* back for certain. Number Five, two doors over," she said. "Top floor. *Mind* you don't trip on Boris's *bottles*!"

Two minutes after thanking her and petting Benjy to calm him down, they stood in front of Number Five Birdcage Walk. The building door was, happily, unlocked. They entered. The lobby was quiet. They ascended the stairs quickly. The top-floor landing was small, half the size of the others. The flat's door was closed. Wade tried the knob. That door was, unhappily, locked.

Wade and Darrell put their ears to the door as if it were a thing brothers normally do.

"We should just break it open before the cops come and seal it up," said Darrell. "Cops always do that when there's a crime. Everywhere becomes a crime scene." He stepped back and lifted his foot.

"So we're sure it's a crime?" said Lily. "Because I'm not a hundred percent sure. It could be a heart attack."

"You should be sure. The restaurant was the scene of the crime," Darrell said. "Now, stand back. . . ."

"Stop!" Becca said. "Boris said he carried no money,

no wallet, no keys, remember? Well, if the door is locked, but he didn't have the door key, how did he get in? He must have left the key somewhere—"

"I can still kick it open," said Darrell.

"Will you wait!" Lily snapped. "Becca's thinking."

Becca scanned the landing. The only other door in sight was narrow, as if to a utility closet. She tried it. It was unlocked. Looking all around, she reached to the top of the closet's door frame and felt along the outside first. Nothing. Then the inside. She stopped. "Yes!" She pulled her hand away. She was holding a key.

Lily grinned. "Well, aren't you the genius."

"I try."

Becca inserted the key in Boris's door and turned it. The door inched open. It was small and cold inside. And dark. A petite table lamp sat on a desk inside the door. Lily tried the switch several times. There was no power.

"Maybe there's a coin box here," Becca said. "I've read about them in novels. If the electricity is coin-operated, you can only use it if you pay for it. Boris was frugal. Or maybe he wasn't planning to stay very long. Anyone have change?"

Wade cast a quick look around and found a dish of coins sitting on the counter in the kitchenette, near the electric box. He pushed some coins into the slot, and several dim lights turned on.

The furniture in the three spare rooms was plain. The bed was unmade. The kitchen, such as it was, was a small nook off the living room. There was next to nothing of any personality about the place, except for one whole wall of Russian books.

"Boris was a scholar, right?" said Darrell. "So maybe one of the books is a clue?"

Becca found herself drawn to the shelves, even though she couldn't read any of the titles. "I don't know any Cyrillic. I should learn. I'll buy a phrase book before we leave." She suddenly hoped they had interpreted Roald's signal correctly. *Was* the Order near? How did he know? Was he in danger? Should they really be helping him? Did he mean to raise four fingers instead of five? She was finally only certain of one thing: that she felt afraid in Boris's dark apartment. Boris, who might already be dead.

"Come on, everybody," said Wade. "It's here, and we're not seeing it. Boris *wanted* us here. I think we're all pretty sure of that. So what did he want us to find?"

"Maybe it's not here," said Lily. "Maybe we should get back to your dad. Or the safe flat. Or somewhere else. This place is kind of sad. If Boris is, you know . . ."

"Dad would call," said Darrell. "And if he doesn't

call, it means he's tied up. If he's tied up, it means *we* have to move forward. His words. He told us to."

"Okay, you're all witnesses," Lily said. "Whatever happens, it's Darrell's fault."

"Fine," he said. "But if there's something here Boris wanted to give us, it'll take us closer to my mom, so yeah, bring it on."

Wade and Lily started opening every drawer they could find, while Darrell looked into and under every piece of furniture in all three rooms. For her part, Becca found herself unable to leave the books. She fingered them one after another, as if they would somehow make sense to her the closer she was to them. Rows and rows of old bindings, some with dust jackets with faded colors, others with dented spines, wrinkled boards, and vanished titles. Then she stopped. She tugged a book bound in black cloth from the shelf. She read its title aloud. *"The Teeth, in Relation to Beauty, Voice, and Health."*

"You *can* read Russian," said Darrell. "That didn't take long."

"No," she said. "It's in English. It's the only book in English out of all of them." She turned. "Wade? It's about teeth. Do you think—"

He moved next to her, and she handed it to him. He opened the cover, only to find that a rectangular area

166

had been cut out of the pages to a depth of about one and a half inches. Inside the hole was a black plastic box.

"A videotape," he said. "Do you think he wanted us to see the tape?"

"How can we play that?" said Lily. "That's like 1970 or something, isn't it?"

Becca whirled around. There was a low cabinet against the opposite wall. She knelt to it. A small television was inside. On top of the television was a tape player. "Oh, man. This is it. This is what Boris wanted us to find."

She turned on the television, popped the tape into the player, and hit Play.

The screen slowly came alive with gray snow, then went black with a flicker of color, and there was Boris, reaching his hand away from the screen and plopping his bulk down on a couch that was not the same as the couch in the room with them.

Boris was as large as he had been in the restaurant, but younger, as if the video had been made some years ago and somewhere else.

"So . . . ," he began. "Is Boris here. If you find this, you know. My little time here is over. Your time has just begun. Your journey? Miles, miles, and more miles.

The clock ticks many hours, and still you may not find what you wish to find. But as last final thing, Boris tell what *he* knows."

He had said some of those words at the restaurant, Becca recalled. It was strange and sad to see his large face staring at them from beyond the television, maybe from beyond the grave. *Was* Boris dead? They might have resuscitated him in the ambulance, or at the hospital. Maybe . . .

"We all want to know secret, yes?" Boris went on. "This is why we are here on this earth. Starting with great astronomer Nicolaus Copernicus, then with Guardians, secret is hidden inside secret!" His face, even on the video, grew dark, and the gleam of perspiration was already on his forehead. "Secret is hidden, and is hidden, and is hidden like layers of onion. In the center . . . is relic."

"This is meant for the Guardians," Darrell said. "He's going to tell us—"

"Once comes powerful man," Boris said urgently. He twisted his body this way and that, apparently unable to settle into his surroundings, until his own story took him, and he looked away from the camera. "He is ruler of men. Of nation. Many nation. His name, Albrecht von Hohenzollern. Grand Master of Teutonic Order. He

168

live in castle far away. Today it is in Mother Russia. Not so then. Not so in 1517 . . ."

And just like at the restaurant, his tortured English dissolved, and, despite themselves, the four of them fell under his heavy spell.

CHAPTER TWENTY-TWO

*M*oonlight falls over the frosted ramparts of a castle on the banks of a black river.

It is Schloss Königsberg, crowning fortress of the Teutonic Knights.

The year is 1517, the month February, the day the eighteenth.

A figure wrapped in long robes stalks the snowy walls silently. It is he, the Grand Master, Albrecht von Hohenzollern. His face is a mask of sorrow, wet with tears he futilely attempts to wipe away. Bitter howling coils up from the rooms below, a tender voice in agony. Albrecht slaps his hands over his frozen ears, yet louder, louder come the shrieks. Then—clack-clack!

It is the clatter of hobnail boots.

"What is it?" Albrecht growls.

Two knights appear: his nephews, sons of his sister. "Grand Master, we have returned from the wastes of Muscovy with words from Duke Vasily—"

"Words? Only words? What of the astronomer? His machine? I sent thirty knights after one man! Where are the others?"

"Dead," says one nephew. "We two alone have returned."

"The others were slain by the astronomer's sword," says the other. "Their bodies prayed over by a monk. But we managed to steal part of the relic."

"Part of it? Part of it! What part?"

"The head, Grand Master. The double-eyed serpent's head."

Suddenly in Albrecht's palm sits a jeweled device, glittering in the moonlight. The twin diamond eyes of the serpent are surrounded by a complex fixture of filigreed silver and more diamonds.

"Duke Vasily sends a hundred knights in pursuit of the astronomer and the traitor monk," says one nephew.

"To honor his alliance with you," says the other.

Albrecht breathes more calmly, or so his nephews think. "You have accomplished half your mission. Kneel before me."

Without a word, they do.

He draws his sword and swings it once, and the head of one

nephew rolls across the stone to his feet, where he kicks it over the wall into the snow.

To the other, Albrecht says, "I have another task for you. The child below . . . the child must leave here with its nurse. There is a ship departing Königsberg in three days' time—"

A deafening shriek freezes his voice, his blood.

The Grand Master turns away, all too aware that the journey to the end of the sea is long, so very long.

"Child!" he cries. "Child, cease your cries! Your mother is lost . . . lost . . ."

Alone once more, Albrecht stalks the walls over and over, night after night, lamenting, pondering, waiting . . .

And that was all. Boris slumped back into himself and said no more.

"Boris, where is Serpens now?" Becca asked, staring at the face on the screen as if it could answer her, until the screen went black again.

Darrell switched off the player and the television. "So Albrecht had his goons steal the head of Serpens when Copernicus was in Russia, and after that Albrecht had it. But . . . is Boris also saying that Albrecht had a baby, and that his wife died?"

"I think so," Lily said. "At least maybe. But did everyone hear that? He said 'the journey to the end of the

172

sea is long.' He said at the restaurant that it's a quote from Copernicus. What did he mean? What sea? Whose journey? Ours? Albrecht's? And 'the clock ticks many hours.' Boris talks like a fortune-teller."

"One thing is sure," said Wade. "And it's kind of what I suspected. That Serpens was, and may still be, in two parts. The head that Albrecht stole, and the body that Copernicus still had."

As they sat in the cold room, staring at the blank television screen, the fence gate outside squealed on its hinges, the front door down below edged open, and someone stepped inside the building.

CHAPTER TWENTY-THREE

Wade rose to his feet. "Don't anyone move."

"You just did," said Darrell.

"Shhh!"

The buzzer on the wall next to the flat door sounded. Wade shot his finger to his lips. The buzzer sounded again. After a few moments of silence, slow footsteps echoed up the staircase.

"What do we do?" Lily whispered.

Wade listened. The footsteps were closer, louder, but slow, like those of an elderly person. And . . . what was that? . . . The clacking of a cane up the stairs. "Maybe it's . . . let's just be cool." He went to the door and pulled it open casually as if they had not just entered a possibly dead man's apartment and weren't being hunted by international assassins.

A man with a mop of gray hair and a beard made his last slow steps up to the fifth-floor landing. He wore thick spectacles and a bulky buttoned sweater, and he used a slender umbrella as a cane. He wheezed for breath, adjusted his glasses, and gazed blinkingly at the children. "You . . ." His voice was hoarse. "But you are not Boris Rubashov. Where is my dear friend Boris?"

Rubashov, Wade thought. *Is that Boris's real last name?*

"No. We were just looking in his flat. He . . . asked us to come over. But he's not here . . . yet."

"Ah," the man said, scratching his chin and leaning inside. "He asked you to pick up the, er, thing, did he?"

Darrell stepped forward next to Wade. "What thing?"

The old man blinked quizzically through his glasses. "You know, the, er, thing. You know." He cupped his free hand on the side of his mouth and whispered, "The relic!"

Suddenly, Lily pushed her way between the boys. "You're *him*," she said, pointing to the umbrella. "The man . . ."

"Man? Me? No, no. I'm not him. Him who?"

"The man at the Dorchester Hotel. You wore a suit. You pretended to be a doctor."

"No, I didn't. You *thought* I was a doctor because I am such a good actor!"

"You poisoned Boris!" she screamed. "It *is* murder! You killed him. That umbrella. And this . . . beard . . ." She grabbed it and pulled hard.

"Owww!" the man cried as his beard peeled halfway off his cheeks. "Bloody rude, that was! Now you've changed the game. Ex-ter-min-ate! Ex-ter-min-ate!" He swept his umbrella up like a sword. There was the sound of a spring letting loose, a slender silver point thrust itself from the tip of the umbrella, and he stabbed the air in front of Wade. "You—die—now!"

"Murderer!" Becca shouted, tugging Lily past the boys and back into the room.

Wade felt his hand move instinctively to his left side, but the dagger was in a vault in New York. Instead he grabbed the nearest unattached thing—the small table lamp by the door. He yanked its cord from the wall and knocked the end of the umbrella down. But the guy, with his fake beard still dangling from his chin, swung the weapon around in a neat O and jabbed. Its needle point gleamed in the half-light and pierced the lampshade. The man danced back like a stage actor in a duel.

"She forbade me terminate you, but I have a duty to defend myself!" the man said. "For the Order!" He slashed away madly in the air, while Becca spun around in the flat and grabbed a handful of fat Russian novels from the shelf and threw them at the weird little man.

He batted them away one by one. "I also play cricket!"

Wade's cell phone began to ring. He couldn't answer it, but he managed to pull it out and throw it to Lily, as Becca and now Darrell both heaved things at the man. Wade sliced down and brought the umbrella close enough to grab the shaft of it. Dropping the lamp, he yanked the umbrella hard to get it away from the man, who growled and held on with both hands, pumping it at Wade.

"Your dad is on the phone, screaming to know where we are!" Lily said.

"Tell—him—the—morgue!" the man said, his face a gnarled grimace, until Becca heaved the videotape player, trailing cords and all, at his head. He groaned once and fell backward. The umbrella dropped to the floor, and Wade kicked it off the landing. It clattered between the stairs for five floors before crashing to the lobby below.

"We shall meet again!" the man coughed at them. "Oh, yes, we shall!"

"Can it!" Darrell snapped. He had Wade by the forearm and dragged him from the landing and down the stairs behind Lily and Becca. They all hurried down two flights when Darrell stopped suddenly and spun on his heels. "You know what? Tell Galina," he yelled, his chest heaving, "tell Galina that we're coming for my mother. And then we're coming for her!"

Out on the street, the rain had begun again.

Lily paused for a second. "Wade, your dad wants us at Victoria Station right now. He's already got our stuff from the safe house. We're flying to Moscow on the next flight." She handed him the phone. "Everybody, Boris is . . . Boris died."

Chapter Twenty-Four

Northern Europe

Galina Krause's jet droned low over the Baltic Sea, skirting the northern shores of Poland. In her mind, she conjured the burning tower in Frombork. How Nicolaus Copernicus, sword in hand, had rushed down the stairs outside the tower to save Hans Novak from Albrecht's knights. The flames, the snow, the furious attack on the tower were sights and sounds she imagined often.

And now, if she turned just so in her seat, she could see that other momentous location, the spot where Albrecht's castle at Königsberg had stood so long ago.

These two places—the Magister's tower and

Albrecht's castle, barely one hundred fifty kilometers from each other—were deeply and inextricably linked.

And the words came back to her.

Eine Legende besagt . . .

One legend says . . .

Four years ago, Galina first entered the ruins of Schloss Königsberg. She was barely sixteen years old and as near death as a human can be and still breathe, yet even then her mind was filled with tales of that burning Frombork tower.

Buried under the monstrous Cold War architecture known as the House of Soviets in the renamed city of Kaliningrad, the ruined foundations of Albrecht's castle concealed a history as grand as it was bleak. Among the fallen stones and crumbled walls she squirmed her way, snakelike, to the undercrypt. There she had located the legendary Serpens relic she had heard stories about, but which only she had known was there.

"Why did Albrecht not hide *both* parts of the relic in the same place?"

Ebner von Braun, sitting against the windows on the opposite side of the jet, raised his head from a pristine second edition of *Faust*, part one, from 1828. "Excuse me? I didn't catch that."

"The legend," Galina said. "If it was true, as one

legend says, that Albrecht had *both* parts of Serpens, why were they not both at Schloss Königsberg?"

Ebner gazed at the sea below, a finger marking his place in the book. "The legend. Yes. Perhaps it is false. Perhaps Albrecht did hide both parts there. After all these centuries, we do not know. If he did, possibly the other part was stolen before you got there. We know only that you discovered the head before it was lost again."

Galina knew it was still a puzzle to Ebner—and to the entire ruling circle of Teutonic Knights—how a young dying girl could possibly have known what the great Albrecht von Hohenzollern had possessed five centuries before, let alone where to find it so long after the Grand Master's death. The answer was trivially simple, but letting the puzzle fester kept them convinced of her brilliance.

"It must have been the war," she mused. "When the Soviets invaded East Prussia in April 1945, they sought to retrieve Russian treasures looted by the Nazis. One nameless soldier likely discovered the body of Serpens. Bedazzled by it, he took it home with him in his rucksack. He kept it for years on the shelf between his bottle of vodka and his jar of borscht. There is only the legend, Ebner, but I believe both body and head of Serpens remain in Russia to this day. In fact, I am certain of it. As I am certain that we shall find them both."

Ebner returned to his reading, silently turning a page as the jet droned.

She watched the slender wrist of the Baltic Sea widen into the Gulf of Finland. In the farther distance, she could just make out that glittering and audacious jewel dredged from an abysmal swamp, the czarist refuge of incomparable wealth and the source of so much beauty and pain: Saint Petersburg.

Take me to the clinic, she had told Ebner at Schloss Königsberg that stormy night four years ago, nearer death than when she had entered the ruins, but with the head of Serpens clutched in her shivering hands. *Take me now.*

More than three hundred kilometers east of Saint Petersburg lay the dark den of Greywolf. As horrifying as crawling through the ruins of Königsberg had been, as near a nightmare as one could possibly conceive, she would soon be in a worse place.

All because both parts of Serpens might still be on Russian soil, as one legend said.

Eine Legende besagt . . .

CHAPTER TWENTY-FIVE

Moscow
March 21

"Come sroo. Sroo!"

In a species of English, a stout middle-aged woman in a vaguely official outfit shooed Wade and the others through passport control at Moscow's Sheremetyevo airport.

"Thank you," he said, not really knowing why. She didn't acknowledge him anyway.

The cramped, airless arrivals hall smelled of too many people jammed into too small a space, but to Wade it was a kind of progress. They had not, as it turned out, been able to take the next flight to Moscow. They'd been on their way to Victoria Station for the train to Heathrow when the police had stopped them. Their renewed investigation of the sudden collapse and death of Boris Volkov—officially revealed as Boris Rubashov—had taken nearly the full day. After spending the evening at their safe flat in Chenies Mews, the children had finally been interviewed by the police the following morning. They'd replied to questions they had no answers to, then languished back at the flat for several more hours, until the ruling came down—false, they knew—that, awaiting toxicology results, there were no immediate signs of foul play.

While the medical examiners waited for the findings, the authorities had no reason to hold the Kaplans, so Roald had booked seats on the earliest possible flight to Moscow. They were finally off the ground by the very late evening of the day of the interview, but not before Wade's father had blown up—several times—about actually fighting with an agent of the Order, as they'd done at Boris's flat.

"An assassin!" his father called the umbrella man. "You totally went off script! I clearly raised five fingers!"

"Which means get away from me," said Darrell.

"No, it means meet me at the safe house."

"No, meet at the safe house is two fingers," said Becca.

"No, two fingers is wait for me!" Roald said.

"Dad, wait for me is not any of the fingers," said Wade, flipping open the notebook. "See?" His father grabbed the notebook, read the finger gestures of the family code, and grunted. "Oh."

"Dad, maybe it looks like we were careless—" Darrell started.

"You *were* careless!"

"Excuse me, Uncle Roald, but not really so much," Lily added boldly, but also sweetly. "I mean, it might seem like we got away with something, but we thought you gave us a message, and we used our instincts. Plus we were smart, never splitting up from one another, and the thing we got away with was . . . a clue. A pretty big clue."

Wade's father stared at them for a full two minutes; then, just as it appeared as if he was going to go on another tirade, he got a call from Paris. "Paul Ferrere, the investigator." Listening for a few moments, his father nodded, then said, *"Merci."* He pushed End Call. "Sara left Madrid, flying northeast. To Russia."

"That settles it," said Darrell, jumping up. "We're going to Russia."

And now they were. Slowly. Even after catching the

plane, a four-hour time difference, plus a Siberian snow front that delayed by nearly three hours a normally four-hour flight, it was now three days since they'd left New York City. But they were on Russian soil at last and were ready to move forward once more.

"Hurry sroo!" the official repeated, waving the line ahead.

Darrell piled into Wade. "Even the lady with the bun thinks this is going way too slow."

"Poor Boris," Lily whispered, zipping and unzipping her bag nervously. "He should be coming sroo with us."

"Wade," said Becca, "I hope you wrote down what he said at the restaurant."

"The key words."

"Well, I made a video of the videotape at his flat, which may be against copyright, but I don't think so," Lily said as Roald ushered them gently along the line, then positioned himself at the head to speak with the passport-control officials.

"Whatever you do, bro, don't look guilty." Darrell nodded toward the officers.

"Of what? I haven't done anything."

"Doesn't matter. Did you know that when your adrenaline spikes, you suddenly need the bathroom?"

"Eww, Darrell, gross!" said Lily. "Get away from me."

"You have to do five fingers if you're going to say that," said Darrell. "But most of all, bro, don't sweat. Fear is all about stuff coming out of your body. They'll know you're lying if you sweat, plus you'll need the bathroom, but you won't get to go because they'll send you straight to Sumeria without a key."

"Siberia," said Becca.

Darrell smirked. "Sure, if you're lucky."

"Bags be open. Computers be in themselves bins. Passports and visas be out."

Wade pushed his stuffed backpack between Becca's and Lily's bags on the conveyor and suddenly wanted to thank Boris for everything he'd given them. The visas were one thing, but there was also the tooth. Why Wade hadn't gotten rid of it, he wasn't sure, except that it was like a voice urging him on to do whatever he had to do. His father had said they should keep it in case it turned out to be another clue, so he'd stowed it in his backpack among his socks.

Oddly, or maybe not so oddly, since Boris had made a point of his possible "side trip," they'd also found a ticket to a theater performance among the documents.

The ticket was for an opera performance in Venice, Italy, the following evening.

"Mozart's *The Magic Flute*," Becca said. "The last line of the ticket says, 'The bearers are allowed entry to Box Three-Seventeen.' *Scatola del teatro* means 'theater box.'"

What was so necessary about Boris attending an opera eluded Wade, and he wondered what would happen if the Russian didn't show up, but he lodged the question in the back of his brain anyway. *Everything is a clue. Everyone is suspicious. Nothing is coincidental.*

"You first. Others stay," a stern-looking immigration official barked at his father, who had been successfully keeping them together as a group. Glancing back, his dad went to the counter and spoke with the official, who looked past him at the kids. Finally the official nodded and let him through.

"Cool. We're in," Lily said. "Saint Sergius monastery,

here we come." She was next with her documents, then Darrell, then Becca, and finally Wade.

As the others had done, Wade handed over his passport and the tourist visa that Boris had filled out in his name. His chest spiked with a sudden fear. Was there any way the officials could tell just by looking at them that the visas were "smuggled," whatever that actually meant? And if not here, how long *would* it be before they were stopped, pulled off into a small room, and interrogated?

Or worse. You could be arrested, right? Jailed like Maxim? What was Boris's prison with the parquet floors? Kremlin? Red Square? No. Lubyanka. A somber word.

The official nodded him forward, and he breathed with relief, when a male guard with one hand on a holstered handgun stopped him abruptly. "No, no," he said, planting his feet in front of Wade. "No, no. Step aside. Here."

For a half second Wade imagined they had discovered the dagger, but he didn't have the dagger. Certainly not the tooth?

"Excuse me," his father said, "this is my son—"

"Stand back, sir," the guard snapped, shooting his father a look. Then, fingering Wade's passport and visa, he nodded at the officers tending the security gate. "Vade Keplen of America, step aside. Others go through."

When they didn't move, the guard repeated, "Go through!"

Wade's heart misfired. The back of his neck froze. He watched blurrily as his father and the others stepped down the narrow hallway toward the terminal, staring back at him, He fought an icy stream of nausea coming up his throat.

Don't sweat, bro.

Yeah, that ship had sailed. His armpits were soggy; his forehead was beading up.

"I really didn't do anything . . ."

A heavyset woman with gray hair waddled through the mass of officers surrounding him. She smelled of boiled food. Her name tag read *I. LYUBOV*. She snatched his documents from the guard and flicked her eyes from them to Wade without raising her head. "You are Vade Keplen from Texes."

If it was a question, it didn't sound like one, but he answered anyway. "Yes, ma'am. Wade Kaplan. From Texas." A moment later he thought to add, "America."

Another long minute of nothing. No movement or sign from the stony face. He wiped the sweat under his eyes, careful to raise his hand slowly in case they thought he was going for a weapon. His insides were turning to water. How had Darrell known? He glanced down the hall. His family was nearly invisible now among the crush of approved passengers. *Becca, is that you?* The woman shifted heavily from foot to foot. Her eyes told him nothing. Steel hatches bolted closed. *She's trying to get me to crack. That's what she's doing. She expects me to blurt out the name of the relic and its original Guardian and the monastery we're going to—*

"Yes. Fine. Go now vis femily. Enjoy stay." The woman handed him back his documents, spun on her low heels more lightly than he'd imagined she would, and slid into a glass booth, where she picked up a telephone.

Startled, he emerged into the hallway and into the arms of his father.

"What did she ask you?" his father asked him.

"Nothing. Nothing at all."

"Russia," Lily said. "Our grandparents have stories."

Wade swallowed hard. "I need to go to the bathroom."

Becca wanted nothing other than to yank Wade away from the plump woman with the bun and the constant scowl. She saw his eyes find hers out of the crowd and tried to lock on to him, but things moved too quickly from that point on and didn't stop until they were out in the stale air of the main terminal, and the noise crashed in on her again.

"What was that all about?" she asked when they piled on an escalator down to ground level.

"I don't know." He was shaking all over. His voice was hoarse. "I don't even know."

"Maybe now we're tagged," Lily whispered. "They tagged us."

"Tagged?" said Darrell.

"Like when you take clothes into a dressing room," she said. "Some stores scan the tags to make sure they know exactly what you went in with. There might have been something about your tourist visa. I saw Bun Lady make a phone call after she let you go. Maybe we're being followed by the Russian police right this minute."

"Or KGB agents," Darrell said. He glanced quickly around them. "They're in disguise, of course. Much better than Lily's umbrella killer. You never see them until they pounce on you; then it's too late. James Bond could tell you."

"The KGB is called the FSB now," Becca said, "and anyway, we should totally expect it. Duke Vasily was a friend of Albrecht's, remember. Maybe they're still working together. The Order and the FSB. As scary as

Berlin was, or London, this is worse. So much worse."

It was a lot of words for Becca, she knew that. But she felt she had to get it out there.

Because when you think about it . . . what just happened with Wade almost certainly means that the Order knows exactly where we are and what we're doing. The Russian safe house, she thought. *How will we get there without the Order's agents tracking us? Even with Julian's untraceable phones, going to an airport tells everyone where you are.*

They walked unhindered through the terminal and outside into the icy, smoke-thick, and diesel-clogged air. It was frigid, a new kind of iron cold that froze your bones.

"Even though we pretty much know that Umbrella Man killed Boris," Lily said as Roald led them to the platform for the shuttle that was supposed to take them to the rental car center, "does it mean we automatically believe everything Boris told us? He did hide his real name from us. Could our trip to Russia be a setup?"

Darrell stomped his feet to keep warm. "Yeah, we have to think of that. Even though his visas got us in here safely. All except Wade, I mean. He's on borrowed time. Lubyanky, here you come."

"Funny," said Wade, splaying five fingers in Darrell's face.

"Calm down, everyone," Roald said. "We'll talk when we get into our car." He waved down the rental car shuttle bus like a soccer dad on the sidelines. The driver seemed to make the stop grudgingly, as if picking up passengers were voluntary. Scowling, he whisked the door open but didn't leave his seat or help them stow their bags.

"Let's keep focused," Roald whispered as they mounted the steps to their seats. "The car ride to Saint Sergius will take us a couple of hours. But we have to remember, it's a holy place and a shrine, where Maxim and thousands of monks lived, all the way up to now. We are polite, we're tourists, we're Texans, but we watch our backs, stay together, and if we find ourselves against a wall, we *don't fight anyone.*" His voice grew louder with the last three words, but he lowered it again. "There's always another way to solve things. After Saint Sergius, we'll drive back to Moscow. We'll be here again before it gets dark."

"If you ask me, it's already dark," Darrell grumbled. "Let's go already."

CHAPTER TWENTY-SIX

It was just after two o'clock in the afternoon when Lily and the others emerged from the rental car center under a grim sky swirling with gray clouds. Uncle Roald squeezed behind the wheel of a boxy blue Aleko sedan like a giant on a tricycle. The rest of them squished in wherever they could. The car stank of diesel fuel inside and out, but it drove perkily enough to push Lily back in her seat when Roald hit the accelerator.

"Finally, we're moving," Darrell said with a sigh.

"Agreed," said Wade. "Thank you, Boris."

"And Terence Ackroyd," Roald reminded them. "This car will free up our movements. Public transportation here is too public. There are CCTV cameras everywhere.

After the monastery, we'll hole up in the Moscow safe house, but until then we have no footprint. We spend as little money as we can. We slip in and out of wherever we are like ghosts."

Lily wasn't sure he expected or wanted a response from anyone, but she gave one anyway. "I'm totally into that." She liked their new secrecy and felt safer because of the precautions, even the troublesome finger gestures. *But ghosts? I really like that.*

The roads out of the airport were surprisingly simple. But the weather was turning grayer by the minute, more bitterly cold, and the clouds announced that serious snow was on its way. The Aleko's heating system was loud and ineffective.

"If, as we all pretty much hope, Maxim Grek *does* prove to be the second Guardian," Becca said, turning to the double-eyed figure sketched in the diary's margin, "the monastery where he lived his last years might actually give me something to decode these pages, which I am now calling 'the Guardian Files.'"

Darrell nodded, smiling. "Nice. I think we should name everything. It makes it seem more important that way."

Wade turned. "I name you . . . Darrell."

Darrell grinned. "I already feel important."

For the next hour, Lily searched online encyclopedia entries about Saint Sergius on the tablet, covering as much history as she could. "Sergiev Posad," she told them, "is the first stop on the western side of what is called 'the Golden Ring,' a four-hundred-mile drive through a bunch of ancient monastic towns stretching northeast of Moscow. The monastery of Saint Sergius was founded in 1345 and is still the most important monastery in the country. It's also the center of the Russian Orthodox Church. It's called a *lavra*, which is a monastery including a bunch of cells for hermits. There are over three hundred monks there now."

"An army, if they're all working for the Order," Darrell said.

"Darrell, they're not," his stepfather said.

There was little information about Maxim's stay there, except to say that cells from around the time of his death might still exist. "Which is good," she said. "But the monastery's also under renovation, which could be a problem. The original cells were built inside the walls. We should start there and see where it takes us."

After a good stretch of highway driving, Wade

arched up in his seat. "I think I see it. The monastery."

They were still miles from the city proper, but a cluster of towers rose over the landscape like beacons. The monastery seemed enormous, perched on a hill and surrounded by tall, powerful, whitewashed stone walls set at irregular angles. Some portions of the walls were fitted with scaffolding, while dozens of domed towers loomed over the walls, some dazzlingly blue and spangled with stars like the night sky, others brilliant gold, and every one of them dusted with a ring of fresh snow.

All told, the drive to Sergiev Posad had taken a little over two hours, putting them there at roughly half past four. The large parking area had only a few cars in it, a smattering of work trucks, and one police vehicle, idling at an angle to the front gate. Roald parked at the far end of the lot, and they got out. They walked quietly through the mounting wind toward the entrance gate in the shadow of the walls.

Then Roald paused and checked his watch. "Kids . . ." His voice was low, almost hoarse from not speaking. "This is a different land, one with centuries of history that Western visitors might not understand. Be on your guard, all of you. And I'll say it again. Absolutely *do not* confront anyone. This is serious. More serious than serious."

As if the few birds and the roaring of traffic and even the movement of the air understood his words, the instant they passed through the massive monastery gate, quiet fell over them like a low, gray, heavy, ominous shadow.

CHAPTER TWENTY-SEVEN

Greywolf, Republic of Karelia, Northwest Russia

When her silver Range Rover stopped three hundred kilometers northeast of Saint Petersburg, Galina Krause's stomach twisted like a cloth being wrung out.

In one sense, Greywolf, the secret sixteenth-century fortress of Duke Vasily III, seemed like any private lair built outside any city the size of Saint Petersburg: a summertime resort used by those in favor with the current political regime.

Except that in 1515, there *was* no Saint Petersburg, and Greywolf was hundreds of miles from any shadow of civilized life. It was constructed in a time of blood law, betrayal, and murder, the menacing fortress of a powerful and quite paranoid ruler.

Vasily III had built the blocklike main structure using an army of slave labor—who he'd then had slain because they knew far too much. Greywolf—or *Seriyvolk*—was, in fact, where Vasily and Albrecht had cemented their mysterious and violent alliance. The building was born, existed, and aged nearly two centuries before Saint Petersburg existed. By that time, Greywolf was already buried deep in the wolf-ridden wastelands, far from the prying eyes of any human being, let alone an intrigue-besotted royal court.

To Galina Krause, Greywolf represented the deepest circle of torment she had ever endured in her young life.

"Open the doors," she said.

Ebner tore himself from his heated seat in the Range Rover, slogged past the burned-out husk of the east wing, whose beams had been blackened four years earlier by a violent inferno, and trod up the wide stairs to unlock and unbolt the heavy front doors.

Glancing up at the fortified tower that protruded from the castle's heart like the hilt of a dagger, Galina ascended the steps behind him. He shifted aside. She entered, intent on ignoring the shadow passing over her, although—inauspiciously—the Madrid coffin followed her in.

Two faceless men from the Red Brotherhood rolled the box through room after spacious room and into a windowless chamber in the center of the ground floor. From there they moved into an elevator installed in Stalin's time. A half minute later, they reached the summit of the tower, and the box was wheeled out. The room was a broad, circular, and high-ceilinged laboratory with a gallery running around the upper level. Save for a very large object in wraps, the room was bare.

"Galina," Ebner began, "there is still time to rethink—"

"We have different concepts of time, Ebner. Remove the cover."

He sighed and walked to the center of the room. He tugged at the heavy black cloth. It fell away from a construction of gears and rods and barrels that vaguely resembled an alien weapon.

Kronos I.

Despite the airy promises of the Copernicus Room, or the chance of overtaking the Kaplans in their freakishly successful run for the relics, to Galina it was Kronos I that held out the most hope.

"Miss Krause . . ." Ebner cleared his throat. "This prototype was a failure. Built before I could conduct the necessary and exhaustive tests. Built, Galina, you must recall, in the horrifying days of your recovery four years ago. The poor creatures we sent God-knows-where never had a chance of survival. Kronos One was born of impatience, constructed years before I could assemble the data needed to—"

"You built it."

He paused. "I did. I did build it. I built Kronos to your specifications. And the concept was brilliant. To mimic the Copernicus astrolabe in such a manner, with such inconceivable detail, was a lofty goal. But after four years of improvements, even Kronos Three, our most effective model, is fatally flawed. Our goal of a faultless time journey has proved unattainable. Heaven knows how you ever conceived of something so devilishly . . . magnificent, particularly in your weakened state. But your—our—ideas were frighteningly incomplete."

"Helmut Bern will complete them."

"Galina, please—"

She raised her hand with such suddenness it must have taken his breath away. He coughed and stifled himself.

She approached the ten-foot spoked wheel of platinum. The barrel protruding from its center was winged with a series of angled flanges, large at the body of the gun and narrowing to a point at the tip. There was no helical coil of superconducting fiber, which they had implemented on later models, and little finesse to the targeting mechanism.

On the other hand, no machine, not even Kronos III, had ever attempted to send a living thing back half a millennium. Their only real success, the botched Somosierra test, had been a mere two hundred years. Kronos I, unlike any subsequent version of the machine, contained a seat of sorts, a kind of cage, which held the passenger, though the controls were set wisely out of reach.

"Kronos One was both crude and audacious," Galina said softly, running her fingers along the machine's razor-sharp angles. "And therein lies its beauty, Ebner. Open the coffin."

With an even sadder breath, Ebner undid the four latches around the perimeter of the death box. His face grimacing like a weightlifter's, he lifted the upper half of the lid to reveal the blindfolded, unmoving body of Sara Kaplan.

Her unkempt brown hair had twisted across her face during the flight from Madrid. Her clothes, a summer-weight linen camping suit, were wrinkled, stained, sunken. Her face was pale white but bore a surprising rosy tinge in its cheeks.

Galina turned to the two silent men. "Move her into the cage."

The two men undid the restraints and removed Sara from the coffin. They carried her dead weight to Kronos I and inserted her in the cage's reclining seat. They closed the cage door and chained and bolted it shut.

"Leave us," Galina said to the men. They bowed wordlessly and left.

She untied the woman's blindfold, then removed a small black case from her belt. From it she withdrew a syringe and a bottle of clear liquid. She tapped the syringe's glass barrel. Pressing her thumb on the plunger, she watched the needle release a tiny bubble of air, then a narrow fountain of the liquid.

How often Galina had seen the same thing done by doctors over the last four years. First here in Greywolf, then in Argentina, then in Sydney, Oslo, Myanmar, and most recently Budapest. A seemingly endless series of injections, endured for but one end.

She sank the needle into the woman's arm.

I know exactly how this feels, my dear. The cold pinch. The pressure on the skin. The heat in your arm as the chemical swims into your bloodstream.

The body in the cage jerked violently, ripping its worn camping suit. Her legs stiffened against the iron bars, her head convulsed, the jaws ground each other, her eyes shuddered open, and she screamed, her first words for days.

"You insane crazy *freak*—"

Sara Kaplan screamed and screamed, then coughed and gagged until her lungs gave out and her head fell back.

"Perhaps I am such a thing," Galina said, stroking the scar on her neck. "On the other hand, you are, thus far, unhurt. You will remain alive as long as you help us locate some stolen property."

"In your dreams, witch—"

"You will help us," Galina repeated in a dry, unemotional tone. "Or not only you, but Roald Kaplan and your two sons will die. Then we shall simply close this house and walk away. No one will think to look for you here. No one comes to Greywolf."

"Except maniacs like you," Sara gasped, looking around at the cage and the machine. "Did you invent this nightmare? Is this, like, the inside of your sick head?"

"You, my dear, are ransom," Galina said, suddenly smiling. "And your future is controlled by this nightmare. Think of Darrell and of Wade. Think of your husband. Soon, your family will discover that you can be saved in only one way. By giving me the Copernicus relics."

"I have no idea what you're talking about."

"If they do not give them to me, well . . ."

Sara started yelling at the top of her lungs.

"Shall I?" Ebner asked.

With a nod from her, Ebner roughly gagged Sara with a cloth soaked with sedatives. He strapped the gag to her face with a band stretching around her head and retied her blindfold. He retested the cage's locks and bolts and stepped away.

Helmut Bern entered the chamber, dusting snow from the shoulders of his Prada overcoat and gawking like an idiot. "What *is* this place? It looks like the set of a Frankenstein movie. . . ." He trailed off when he saw the machine. Puzzled, he looked to Ebner, then to Galina, then back at the machine. "There's a woman in that thing."

"Which is no concern of yours," Galina said impassively. "Bern, I want you to reprogram Kronos with what you discovered in Madrid. You will also incorporate at the moment of transport a particle injection into its passenger."

"A *particle* injection?" Bern said. "What sort of particle?"

"A radioisotope," she said. "For tracking purposes."

"But that will poison the passen . . . *her*. It will poison *her*."

"Once more, this does not concern you. Finally, I wish you to decrypt the Magister's Cádiz code and enter its coordinates into the computer. You have until"—she glanced at her phone—"the end of the day on Sunday. Let us say midnight."

"Midnight on Sunday?" Bern said. "That's barely two days!"

Galina leaned over to a clockwork mechanism that was mounted outside the cage near the spoked wheel. She touched a number of minute levers sequentially, and the sound of clicking began. "The timer is set at fifty-six hours, eleven minutes, twenty-two seconds . . . twenty-one . . . twenty. . . . No delay, Bern."

"But, how can I work with such a deadline?" he said, his voice gaining pitch with each word. "Miss Krause, please. I will certainly labor as hard as I can, but by midnight Sunday? What the devil will happen then?"

"Kronos will do what it was meant to do."

"With unfinished programming?" Bern's voice was

at toddler pitch now. "What if I need ten minutes more? Three seconds more?"

"I have an appointment in Istanbul Monday morning that cannot be missed. No delay, Bern. Please do not make me say this a third time." Galina turned away from the incredulous expression on his face, her lips warming into a smile as Bartolo Cassa entered the chamber, pushing in a second coffin.

"Ah, the Italian shipment," she said.

"Leave it against the wall," Ebner said sharply. "Is there anything else?"

"A message from the Copernicus Room," Cassa said. "They have just traced the Prague courier's contact in Italy, the agent who was to pass a message to Boris Rubashov tomorrow night, and where." He handed Galina his phone.

On it was a single image.

She felt a shiver run up her spine to the base of her skull. "Is this all? No other word?"

"None."

Ebner stole a look at the image, then lifted his eyes to her. "I shall join you—"

"We shall both," Cassa said.

"No. See that Bern does not leave the machine. I will

return by Sunday at dawn." She breathed in the frigid air of the tower, then moved to the elevator, managing only in the final seconds to shake off her sense of imminent doom.

"Der Hölle Rache," she sang, *"kocht in meinem Herzen!"*

CHAPTER TWENTY-EIGHT

Sergiev Posad

Wade felt his guard go up the instant a tall bearded man in a stiff black hat and long robe strode over the monastery's cobblestone court toward them. The Teutonic Knights began as a religious order. He knew enough of their history, and Boris's story, to be cautious.

"Ah, English," the young man said with very little accent. "I can tell by your clothing. Welcome."

"American," Roald said pleasantly. "But you're right. We just arrived from London, where we bought these winter coats."

"So, I am a detective," the man said with a bright

laugh. "I am Brother Semyon. You wish a tour of Trinity Saint Sergius monastery? The last of today's English-language tours will begin in approximately fifteen minutes. I will deliver it myself." He spoke English easily and well. He handed them a map, which Darrell took.

"Perfect. And are the old fifteenth- and sixteenth-century monks' cells on the tour?" Wade asked, trying to sound as casual as his father.

"We read online that you still have some of the old monks' cells here," Lily added. "We'd love to see them if we could."

The young monk's smile began to fade. He looked them over, studying their faces methodically, lingering on Wade's the longest, as if his brain were doing a quick calculation. "Unfortunately not . . . ," he said.

A man in civilian clothes strode across the cobblestones toward them. The young monk turned. "One moment, please," he said softly to Roald. He went directly to the approaching man and stopped him with a raised hand. They spoke quietly to each other while the second man glanced over the monk's shoulder at them.

"Uh-oh," Becca whispered as Wade turned his face away. "We've been outed again. Do you think they already know the relic we're after?"

Wade's father put on a false smile. "Let's not panic. Not yet. It may be nothing."

The young monk returned to them. "I am sorry, but foreign visitors must sign waivers first. This is policy, I'm afraid. We are a monastery of meditation and prayer."

"And the gentleman you spoke with?" said Roald, smiling. "He is . . . ?"

"Alas, there exists a complex relationship between the monastery, the government, and their security at public sites," the monk said. "Besides, it is perfectly true that some areas are not on view this time of day. There is no way otherwise, and it would be better to comply than to leave at this point. Please, sir," he said to Roald directly, "I hope you understand and come with me. Children, remain here, won't you? Sir, please do come with me." Gesturing firmly ahead of him, he took hold of Roald's elbow and directed him toward what appeared to be an administration building. The other man followed on their heels, leaving the children by themselves.

"Oh, man," said Darrell. "Now we've done it. Or, more accurately, Wade's done it."

"I have not—"

"Tagged," Lily whispered. "I knew we were."

213

"Well, something's up," Becca said softly. "Monk or no monk, praying or not, this isn't right. Why is some guy in a suit telling the monks how to run their place?"

"Did you see the way his smile just died when we asked to see the old cells?" said Wade. "He knows exactly why we're here. We can't be this open with people, even religious people. I know that doesn't sound right, but we can't trust anyone."

He saw his father briefly in the doorway of the building, looking out at them. He did not use any finger signals, and Wade couldn't be sure he had memorized the family code correctly anyway. Then a third man, an older monk, drew his father gently back inside.

"Not again," said Lily. "They're taking your dad away?"

No. Not again. Wade's father was out a moment later, his forehead furrowed in a frown. "Sorry, kids, not today," he said loudly.

"Dad—" Wade started.

"Shhh," his father said. "We're to go to the Saint John gate. Brother Semyon will meet us there. Darrell, do you still have the map?"

Darrell flipped it open. "Back the way we came in from the parking lot. The Gateway Church of Saint John the Baptist."

"He's helping us?" Wade asked as they headed back across the cobblestone court.

"As much as he can. The security man is with the government. He doesn't appear to suspect us, but he may have ties to the Red Brotherhood. Brother Semyon will try to get us to the oldest cells. He's really risking a lot."

By the time they had crossed the courtyard, a bank of heavy gray clouds had moved in from the west. It was going to snow. *Soon and hard,* Wade thought. He pulled his cap low.

They were only halfway through a thick arched doorway, which was more like a tunnel, when Brother Semyon appeared from the shadows. "We must hurry," he whispered. "Our government friend is a bit thick-headed, but even he will check up if I do not return soon."

Wade's father nodded. "Thank you for what you are doing."

"How did you know about us?" Becca asked.

Brother Semyon turned to a door inside the tunnel. "The Guardians in Russia are known as the Circle of Athos. Surely you have heard the name Hans Novak?"

"Of course. He was Nicolaus's assistant," said Lily.

"Hans Novak was young, yet he spent his life

protecting the Legacy. You—you four children—because you are young, have been called *Novizhny*, the new followers of Hans Novak." He pronounced the word "no-VIHSH-nee."

"Cool," said Darrell. "*Novizhny*. I told you things need to have names. Wade, write it down."

Brother Semyon smiled. "A friend of the Circle of Athos told me to expect you. I have been waiting for days."

"A friend?" said Wade's father. "Do you mean Boris Volkov, from London?"

"I do not know him. We have little time. This way. Come."

Brother Semyon led them through the door into a high-ceilinged room. Every inch of wall space was fixed with religious icons, frescos, and beaded and jeweled paintings.

"These are the prizes of Russia," he said, moving quickly. "But Saint Sergius chapels and ancient art are not important to you just now." They entered a narrow stone corridor that was lit by fat candles set into niches in the wall at eye level. Because they had to walk in single file, Wade couldn't see what they were approaching. It was a blank wall. The young monk turned to face them.

Wade's sense of alarm went up. "What's going on?"

The monk bowed his head. "The cells the tourists see are reconstructions. Back when there were many more of us in the Circle of Athos, we hid Maxim's true cell behind a false wall."

He turned to the blank wall and pushed firmly at five blocks on it. They seemed five random blocks, until he stepped away and Wade saw that the blocks formed the shape of a large letter.

M

A moment later, the entire wall shifted backward into darkness.

"Silence, please, from here on," Brother Semyon said. Gathering the folds of his robe in one hand, he led them up a set of steep stairs that ran inside the monastery wall.

Wade counted forty steps until they reached a level stone passage. It was narrow, although dim light from the end of the passage gave enough visibility to see that it ran forward twenty or thirty feet. A single wooden door was set into the wall on the left, the outer side of the monastery wall.

"Maxim's cell," the monk said. He led them past a wrought-iron panel set against the passage wall. "It is

nearly bare, as it was in the time when he occupied it."
Brother Semyon paused and stepped closer to them.
"We members of the Circle are now very few in number.
The Order and its Russian allies, the Red Brotherhood,
have diminished our forces to a piteous handful. I have
only become aware of the invocation of the Frombork
Protocol, but my duty is to keep the great legacy of
Copernicus from being reassembled. I leave you here to
discover what you can."

"Don't you know what the relic is or where it is?"
Wade's father asked.

Brother Semyon shook his head firmly. "I am a
Guardian of Guardians. My role here and now is to
keep the *Novizhny*, and their father, safe. You are the
hunters; I am your servant. The only thing I can say is
that other than his bones, nothing belonging to Maxim
exists here anymore, except for seven religious icons he
is said to have painted in his last months."

He then pointed to a switch box on the wall. "Ring
this when you wish to be released. Please do your work
quickly."

"Released?" Wade's father said. "What do you
mean?"

Reaching to his right, Brother Semyon pulled the
iron panel closed and locked it on them. "I am obliged

by the Circle of Athos to protect you. I alone will hear the bell. It rings in my cell. Hurry and do your work." Moments later, he was gone.

Breathing in slowly, Wade turned toward the single cell in the passage.

Lily went up and tried the gate. "Okay, this is way against every rule. This is locked solid. The Circle of Athos is part of the Guardians. Brother Semyon says he is a Guardian. Do we believe him? Do we believe anyone? I'm kind of freaking out now."

"Calm down, Lily," said Darrell, tapping the monastery map. "I'm already planning our way out of here."

Then Wade stepped down the hall and entered Maxim Grek's tiny cell. "Everybody, get in here!"

CHAPTER TWENTY-NINE

Lily stepped into Maxim Grek's square cell, a tiny, cold, stone space that barely held the five of them.

The room was completely featureless except for a high horizontal upper window, from which they could see the storm-clouded sky, and seven small icons, paintings on wood panels hanging on the inside wall.

The images were plain, flat, and almost crudely painted, though the colors were brilliant and rich— red, gold, and green, with strokes of blue as deep as on the domes outside. The five men and two women wore halos—plain gold circles—behind their heads, and were shown in a variety of poses, some at labor and others at prayer.

"Saints," said Becca.

"The backgrounds of all seven pictures seem to be the Saint Sergius monastery," said Roald. "There's the Red (Holy) Gate, the courtyard, and the older towers. The saints are identified in Greek."

"Oh, boy," said Becca. "Lily, can I borrow your tablet?"

While Becca searched the tablet for a Greek dictionary, Lily examined the images for clues. There were either hundreds or none at all. She felt a little helpless. Wade and Darrell were standing around looking bewildered, too.

Becca had better luck, soon identifying one of the women, kneeling in prayer in a kind of chapel, as Saint Matrona. One of the men, who was holding two books with crosses on their covers, was Saint John Chrysostom.

"This one here is Saint Anysia," Becca said. "She's often shown standing on a mountain of gold because she gave away her money. Next to them is Saint Joachim of Ithaca. He's holding a tiny church. Saint Achillius of Larissa and Saint Nikon are praying. The last one is Saint Dominic, who is tending his garden."

"Wade, my notebook," his father said. "I remember Uncle Henry lecturing once and mentioning something about saints."

"Do you think there's a clue in there about who the saints are?" asked Lily.

"Maybe," Roald said, flipping the pages slowly.

"If all the saints are Greek," Wade said, "Maxim was probably remembering his home. He painted them at the end of his life—"

"No," said Roald. "Not all of them. Six are Greek, but Saint Dominic is Italian. That's what I was remembering. Here it is, from Uncle Henry's first lectures about cosmology. He told us that Saint Dominic was the patron saint of . . . guess what?"

"Uncle Roald, that's my line," said Lily.

"Astronomy!" he said. "Uncle Henry told us at the beginning of his survey course. Of all the seven icons, this one might be the real clue."

Lily stood in front of the painting and snapped a picture of it on the tablet. "There aren't any astronomy things in the picture," she said. "Dominic's right hand is pointing to a tall tower, while his left is holding some kind of stalky plant with a white bulb dangling from it."

"That's an onion," Becca said.

"An onion," Wade mumbled, taking the notebook back from his father. "Boris said 'onion' on the videotape . . . 'secret is hidden,' he said, 'like layers of onion.'

222

Does everyone remember that? Then he said 'In the center . . . is relic.'"

The cell went quiet. Lily suspected it was because they were all remembering Boris Volkov, or Rubashov, as they found out his real name was. Boris was the first victim of the hunt for the second relic. "Maybe Maxim is saying he *planted* the secret," she said. "Or he hid it in the ground somewhere, like an onion."

"The domes in the monastery are called onion domes," said Roald.

Lily recalled that from her reading. Was that a clue, too?

Darrell looked up from the map and tried to listen to the crisscrossing voices, even his stepfather's, but all he could see was the tiny prison cell, and he couldn't *not* think of his mother. Her cell might be like this, clean and white. Or more probably it was filthy and dark and cold and horrible. . . .

Don't go there.

Dad said it isn't healthy and it doesn't help. Be useful. Back to the map. My job is just to plan a way out of here.

He rubbed his face with one hand, then tried to match up the nearly sixty numbers on the map with the list of names on the facing page, to pinpoint their current position in the vast monastery. If they had to escape, how would they do it? Which route would they take, leading to where? *Here's the wall above the Gateway Church of Saint John the Baptist* . . .

There was the sound of an engine stuttering in the parking lot below the window, and Roald instantly looked out. "Two cars just pulled in. And it's snowing harder now."

. . . and there's the Good Friday Tower . . .

"Saint Dominic was also the patron saint of people who have been falsely accused," Becca said, still reading Lily's tablet. "Like you, Wade."

"Thanks for reminding me—"

"Darrell, you look at art all the time," Lily said. "Your mom and everything. What do you see when you look at the painting?"

He lifted his head from the map and stared squarely at the icon. "A saint. He's pointing to a tower with one hand. In the other he's holding . . . he's holding an onion. . . . Holy cow. Could it be that simple?"

"What's simple?" asked Wade.

Darrell flipped the map around. "Look at this right here. Two towers away. This one on the corner is called the Good Friday Tower, right? The next one is called the

Onion Tower. Right here on the south wall of the monastery. In the painting, Dominic is holding an onion and pointing to a tower. He's saying Onion Tower. The relic is in the Onion Tower—"

There came the sudden sound of footsteps from the bottom of the stairway outside.

"Dr. Kaplan! Children!" someone called. "We know you are up there!" The voice was unfamiliar.

Roald peeked out of the cell, then quickly jerked back in. "The government man from before. He must be with the Brotherhood. He's not alone."

The stairway groaned with several sets of feet. "Dr. Kaplan, come out this instant," another voice shouted. "You are all in violation of the laws of Holy Trinity—Saint Sergius Lavra and the Russian Federation!"

CHAPTER THIRTY

Becca held her breath as at least two, maybe three or even four people stomped up the stairs and into the passage outside Maxim's cell, only to find the gate at the far end of the passage padlocked. The urgency of the raised voices and the rattling of the gate told her they didn't have the key with them.

There was a good deal more yelling before the men hurried back down the steps. One of them yelled over and over, *"Poluchit' klyuchi!"* The final word sounded enough like *key* in both French and Italian for Becca to know that the men would soon be back.

"I hope Brother Semyon is okay," said Lily.

"We'll have to hope he can take care of himself." Roald peeked out again. The hall was empty. "Darrell, how do we get to the Onion Tower?"

"Without going back down the stairs? Only one way. Over the roof on the outside wall. But I don't see how to get up there."

"There's scaffolding along parts of the outside wall," said Wade.

Roald shook his head. "Let's see what's at the other end of the passage."

They scurried out of the cell and down the narrow hallway to where it ended in a brief L, a dead end that led nowhere except for a small window set high in the wall. Becca suspected it might offer the only way to go, besides back down the stairs and into the hands of men who were most certainly from the Red Brotherhood.

"The window is our only way out," she said softly.

"Like you know," said Darrell.

"Do you have a better idea, smarty?" asked Lily. "As the intelligence officer around here, I'm siding with Becca. Which is like her getting an A and you getting . . ."

"Yes?"

"Not an A," she said. "But can we even get it open?"

Roald reached to the sill and pulled himself up high enough to see out. "There's scaffolding right outside. I guess we'll have to go this way."

More shouting from the hall, then the clank of chains hitting the floor. There was only the bolt now that kept the men from getting to them. Together, Wade and his father pushed out on the window. It groaned. "Careful, Dad. You're pushing too hard—"

More groaning; then the window fell away. Snowflakes flew in on them. Becca expected to hear the glass shatter down the side of the wall to the courtyard below, but it clanked to a stop just under the window.

"Let me test the scaffold," Roald said.

"It's probably slippery. Be careful," said Lily.

Roald clambered up to the sill, reached his arms through, and pulled himself outside. "It's slippery as anything, but strong enough to hold us. Come on, who's next?"

Wade and Darrell both boosted Becca up; she took Roald's hand and slid forward through the window, scraping her wounded arm, though she tried to ignore the sudden pain. When she was out, she found herself standing on a slightly slanted scaffold running along the inside walls, with cold snowflakes whirling in her face.

An iron framework supported the narrow planks all the way to the corner. Lily crawled out next. Wade went after her, then Darrell, who immediately pointed to a green-topped tower midway between the nearest corner and the one next to it. "That's Maxim's Onion Tower."

A rough voice yelled out suddenly from the courtyard below. "Do not go any farther. You have nowhere to run!" It was the rumpled-suited man from before. He was with three other men wearing lousy suits. One of the men held two phones and yelled into both. The men were soon joined by a half-dozen others, who started up the scaffold from the ground. Brother Semyon stood by helplessly.

"Never mind them," Darrell snapped. "To the corner." They made their way quickly along the planks as far as they could. Another stretch of boards ran along the outside walls from the corner to the Onion Tower.

"Dad, we can make it over the roof to the other scaffold," Wade said. He didn't wait for a response from his father, just crawled over the roof. Minutes later, they were all standing on the boards running along the outside walls.

Becca pointed to the parking lot. "Look. Our car.

Uncle Roald, what if you got the car and drove it down the outside wall under the tower? We can get to the tower, find the relic, and get down from there. We won't have to run into the guys climbing up."

Roald looked both ways, down the scaffolding to the ground and back at the men slowly climbing up. He wagged his head. "All right. Five minutes. I'll try to draw the men away. You be down there right below the Onion Tower. I'll meet you. Go!"

As Roald carefully worked his way to the ground outside the monastery, Wade led the others to where the scaffolding intersected with the Onion Tower's top floor, just below a set of high-arched windows. "I'm going to slide down to the gutter to get a foothold and open a window. Break it, if I have to."

Once down there, he found one of the three windows unlocked. He pushed it in easily. Darrell was right behind him. They dropped down onto a wide-planked wooden floor. Lily and Becca slid in next.

They were in the Onion Tower.

It was empty; the walls were simple and bare. It had a wooden floor that looked, at most, a hundred years old—a bad sign, if Maxim hid something in 1556. Walls of plain gray stone led up to a wooden ceiling that was nothing more than the inside of the cupola.

"Not a lot of hiding places," said Darrell.

Wade quietly lowered two planks that barred the doors. They were sealed in. "So now what?" he asked.

"Back to the picture," Lily said, bringing it up on her tablet. "Maxim is pointing—I mean, Saint Dominic is—to the base of the middle window."

"Do you think he was being that exact?" asked Darrell.

Becca looked around the small space. "Each side of the tower has three windows, but he's standing on the ground in front of it, which eliminates the sides where the walls meet the tower. So there are only two walls where it could be—"

"Actually, one," Lily said. "Dominic is obviously standing inside the monastery, because he was a prisoner like Maxim was. So it's got to be on the inside wall."

"It," said Darrell. "I sure hope we're talking about the relic. Either way, Maxim can't have known how long his secret would need to be hidden, so he probably hid it in something made of stone."

Wade peeked out the window. "Dad's in the car. There's a van in the parking lot now. Hurry this up."

As quickly as they could, they went over the entire inside wall, and especially the window area, but saw nothing, until Becca, brushing away stone dust accumulated over the years, ran her fingers over the shelf at the bottom of the middle north window.

At the base of the mullion, the pillar between the windows, two small figures were scratched into the surface of the stone, deeply enough to have endured for a long time.

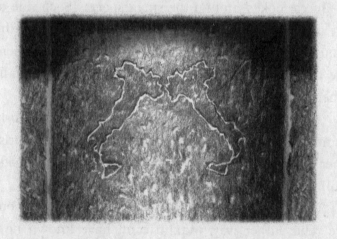

"Boots?" said Darrell. "A pretty gnarly pair of boots, if you ask me."

"Or the gnarly outline of Italy," said Becca. "Which makes perfect sense. Dominic was Italian. Maxim and Copernicus were in Italy at the same time."

"But why *two* Italys, and why is one of them backward?" Darrell asked. "Italy against Italy?"

"Or . . ." Becca dug Copernicus's diary from her bag and quickly leafed to the final pages—the Guardian Files—she had isolated. "Or . . . Italian against Italian?"

"Meaning what?" asked Wade.

"The coded passage," she said. "Maybe it's coded in the same language, only one of them is used backward."

"I am so not understanding you," said Wade. "Plus we need to hurry."

Snow flew in the open window behind Becca. The storm was getting worse. She had to block it out. "What I mean is that two Italys, one facing the other, might mean that there aren't two code languages, only one, and part of the message is backward."

"Up there!" said Lily, searching the wall above the Italy drawing. "The boots are pointing to something. I'm not . . . tall enough to see what it is."

Wade almost smiled. "The oldest cryptogram in the book. You point to the answer." He reached up and slipped his fingers into a small gap between two stones. He carefully drew out a rolled-up strip of parchment. It was nearly black with dense writing. There was a date—xvii January 1556—followed by a brief passage in a language that seemed like gibberish. "Becca, can you read—"

Footsteps scraped the floor heavily in the passage outside the tower. Something slammed roughly against the door. A similar sound fell against the opposite door.

"They're breaking in," Darrell whispered. He moved to the far window. "We need to get down the scaffold to the car."

More footsteps stomped down the halls outside the tower. The doors thundered. A hinge tore off one door frame and clanked to the floor.

"Out the window!" Lily said. "Now!"

CHAPTER THIRTY-ONE

Wade crawled first out the window and onto the ledge along the wall. At that point, the scaffold was a single slippery board. He hated this, hated heights, and the snow didn't make any of what they were doing smart or easy.

"Where's Dad?" Darrell asked, sliding out next to him.

Lily was next. "They got him," she said. "They got him, and they arrested him, and now they're coming for us—"

Then there he was, his tiny car sliding around the corner too quickly for the snow, nearly crashing into the trees that edged the wall, but he managed to right it and skidded to a stop beneath the tower. They climbed down the scaffolding as quickly as they could, jumping the last five feet, where there were no more boards. Then the van appeared, roaring from the parking lot onto the snowy ground, until its driver realized it was too large to fit between the trees and the outer wall. The van slid to a stop. The doors opened, and several men bolted out.

"The Brotherhood!" Roald said from the open window of the car. "Get in!"

As soon as they were safely inside, Roald gunned the engine. The Aleko spun down the narrow strip of ground and around the walls, losing their pursuers as they slid and careened over the property. They finally thudded onto an actual road and bounded up the entrance ramp of the highway. Roald swerved abruptly into traffic and crossed like a crazy man to the fast lane, gaining as much speed as the rattletrap could handle. It was approaching seven o'clock, the traffic was still heavy, but they were on their way back to Moscow.

"Good work, Dad," said Darrell. "You were awesome."

Roald grumbled under his breath. "I feel like a teenager," he said. "And not in a good way. What did you discover in the tower? Not Serpens?"

"No. A small document," said Becca. "And a decryption key. I think it's a decryption key, maybe to the passage in the diary. I hope it is . . ."

"It's a start, anyway," his father said.

Which only reminded Wade of that line Boris had told them twice. *The journey to the end of the sea is long.* Well, their long day was ending, they had all risked their lives, and they had no relic, only a tiny scroll of paper that they *hoped* would be a part of the puzzle, but they weren't even sure of that. Sara was still lost, somewhere in Russia. But Russia was enormous. Maxim Grek was looking like just the beginning of a very long journey. But they wouldn't know for certain until they deciphered the scroll. Even if they did find something, it might be just one clue leading to another and another . . .

Is hidden, and is hidden, and is hidden like layers of onion.

Roald switched lanes suddenly, then switched again, just as abruptly.

"Dad?" Darrell said. "What is it?"

"They found us. The van parked outside the monastery. Hold on—"

He swerved boldly across the highway and took the nearest exit ramp onto a side road. They bounced onto the street at the bottom of the ramp and headed for the highway underpass, where Roald spun the car around. He switched off the headlights.

The large gray van screeched down the exit ramp after them, then paused when it spotted them hiding under the highway. It motored slowly toward them. A moment later, a black car appeared. They could see the man in the rumpled suit from the monastery behind the wheel.

"This is not good," said Lily. "Should we get out and take cover?"

"We can take the little guy," said Darrell.

"No way," said his father, staring in each direction as if memorizing what he saw.

Suddenly the driver of the black car jumped out and approached them, his gun drawn. Wade's father glared at him intently. "Wade, get in the driver's seat, foot on the brake, put it in gear, and don't take your eyes off me."

"Dad, I can't drive!"

"You might have to. The rest of you stay put." His father jumped out of the car, leaving the engine running, and started talking, babbling really, as Wade warily shifted behind the wheel.

"I have what you're looking for!" his father yelled. "We found it at the monastery. The monk tried to stop us, but we found it. You can take it. We don't even know what it is, but you can take it. Just leave us alone. Let us leave in peace, and that's it. We'll go home."

Wade knew his father was bluffing, but what else he was planning he had no idea, until he saw his father reach into his hip pocket and palm the little silver device the detectives had given him in New York. The stun gun.

"You are being smart," said the man in a thick voice. He waved his gun casually, not at anyone.

Keeping the thick-voiced man between himself and the van, Wade's father marched right up to him, still jabbering like a lunatic, waving his arms. All at once, he crouched and jerked the Taser into the guy's chest. The man went spasmodic. He cried out and arched backward, dropping his gun. He fell in a quivering heap onto the snowy pavement. The goons from the van bolted over on foot.

"Wade! Now!"

He couldn't believe his father actually wanted him to drive the car, but his father was obviously trapped. The only way he could escape was if Wade jammed his foot on the accelerator and plowed the car between the charging men and his father.

"Omigod, Wade!" Becca cried. "Do it!"

"I—ahhh!"

The squeal of tires and the groaning of the engine weren't the worst things. Becca and Darrell both shrieked when he nearly ran his father down. At the last second, Wade stomped his foot on the brake. The car skidded ten feet toward the goons. They scattered. Lily reached over the seat and swung the front passenger door open. Wade's father dived into the car.

"Heads down! Gas!" his father yelled. Wade pressed the pedal to the floor.

His father grabbed the wheel, and together they swerved at the men again. The air exploded with shots. The car skidded between the van and the black car, then back up the wrong way onto the exit ramp. Bullets thudded into the side panels and blew out the rear window. With a crazy turn of the wheel, they spun into traffic and righted seconds before they would have smashed into a tractor trailer.

"Good . . . good . . . ," his father said, finally lifting himself over Wade and switching places with him. Under cover of quickly thickening snowfall, they tore back down the highway to Moscow.

Chapter Thirty-Two

Greywolf

Sara Kaplan woke up to ticking.

It sounded like the teeth of one gear joining with another's. Or the rhythmical oscillations of a giant clockwork. Either way, it wasn't normal.

"Where am I?" she mumbled through gagged lips. No answer. Blindfolded, she listened with every atom she could muster. No sound but the strange, loud ticking behind her head. The man who always seemed to be humming wasn't nearby. She was alone, still caged in that horrifying machine.

It had been hours since the troll and the supermodel had had her removed from the coffin. While her brain was still oozing forward like sludge, making only the most obvious connections, Sara deduced that the coffin had been used to keep prying eyes away as they smuggled her from place to place. She also reasoned that she had taken a series of airplane flights since she was first drugged in La Paz and could be just about anywhere now.

It was cold here. What did that crazy witch call it? Greywolf? What in the world were the Copernicus relics, and what did her family have to do with them? And of all things, a coffin! What sort of people . . .

But Sara guessed what sort of people they were. Not what they were all about, of course, but the kinds of things they did. Evil things. Very expensive evil things.

This wasn't your ordinary kidnapping for ransom.

At the thought of ransom and the image of her family around the living-room table waiting for a call, her eyes welled up. Then her brain sparked again. No. Not the living-room table. Roald had taken the children to Europe. Berlin. She'd received that message on her phone before she landed in Bolivia. A series of messages, even a couple from Darrell a few days later, put them somewhere—Italy?—with Roald's niece and her friend. Seriously? What was going on? What in the world was her family doing, traveling across the globe while she was transferred from a coffin to a horrible ticking engine? At least there didn't seem to be any more flights for her. She was where her kidnappers wanted her.

Greywolf.

Wherever that was . . .

Footsteps approached.

"Please tell me where I am," she gasped, scarcely more clearly. The footsteps came closer. She took in a breath and tried again. "Where—"

"Hush, my dear. Quiet!" A woman's voice, her breath hot and stale.

"Who's there?" All at once, Sara's blindfold was lifted and her gag removed. She blinked in the light, and the face before her clarified. The woman was her age, maybe a few years older. Her dark hair was limp, dangling over her face, her clothes filthy, stained. In one hand she held . . . a kitchen knife? Was there blood on it?

"Don't hurt me, please," Sara said. "I've been kidnapped."

"What? No," said the woman. She placed the knife carefully on the floor at her feet, then set about struggling with the chains that bound Sara into the machine, but her weak, bruised fingers could do nothing. "I must get you out of here," she said. An accent. Italian?

"Who are you?" Sara asked the woman.

"You have . . . I heard them saying . . . two days only."

"Two days? Before what? Who are you?"

The woman seemed half delirious, her thin fingers shaking, her eyes darting back and forth over the clockwork mechanism whose ticking had woken Sara. "Two days before the machine does what it does! The clockwork. Look. It counts down!"

"Who are you?" Sara repeated. "And these people? Where is Greywolf? Please, you have to get a message to my husband. His name is Roald Kaplan. His cell number is—"

The woman's fingers froze. She stared at Sara. "Roald Kaplan . . . you said Roald Kaplan? You are Sara Kaplan! They took you, too! Because of the relics!"

"Wait, how do you know Roald—"

"I will try to find him. I have a friend at Moscow State University."

"Moscow? We're in Russia?"

Something clanked from outside the room. The door to the upper gallery swung open, and the humming man in the lab coat entered in a rush, holding a tray and focused on keeping whatever was on it from spilling. The woman quickly replaced Sara's gag and the blindfold. Sara heard her pick up the knife and duck around behind the machine. *Who are you?* she wanted to scream, but she let her head drop to her chest as if she were still drugged. She'd read enough Terence Ackroyd stories to know to do that. When she heard the man in the lab coat humming as he trotted down the stairs to her, and smelled the hot coffee, she realized he hadn't seen the woman. She had escaped.

Whoever she is, she knows Roald! She'll find him. She'll tell him where I am. He'll come for me. Darrell and Wade, too. Soon they'll come for me!

CHAPTER THIRTY-THREE

Moscow

Strangely, to herself at least, Becca didn't freak out after the insanity of the car chase. Even racing to Moscow in a smoking, sputtering, nearly windowless rental car with a bullet-riddled engine didn't faze her. And while everyone else was either breathless (Lily) or crazy anxious (Wade) or jabbering his head off (Darrell) or staring zombielike down the road ahead (Uncle Roald), Becca was calm.

More than calm, she was serene.

Something had clicked, and her mind was blocking everything out and holding a single image. The mirrored outlines of Italy.

She was certain they were the key to decrypting the Maxim passage in Copernicus's diary, the one marked with the date "xiii February 1517."

If they were *also* the key to the tiny scroll from the Onion Tower, she would translate both texts here and now. She would do it in that freezing, smoking, cramped Aleko, and she would conjure the astronomer's words and Maxim's five-hundred-year-old message.

Badgering Wade and Darrell to shield the diary from the wind, Lily focused the tablet in flashlight mode overhead so Becca could work out the double-eyed code.

Like a television chef preparing a delicious dish, she ran her finger along the diary page and narrated everything.

"First, we have the coded passage. Here is the beginning line."

Ourn ao froa lfa atsiu vlali am sa tlrlau dsa . . .

"If I'm right about the two facing Italys, the double-eyed passage is created by sort of *braiding* the words from the beginning *and* the end. To decode it, we have to separate every other letter into the two halves of the message. So the first, third, fifth, and so on give us *this* line." She wrote the letters carefully in her notebook, hoping she could hold on to the slender thread of how she thought the code worked.

orafolativaimallus

"And the second, fourth, sixth, and so on, give us *this* line."

unorafasullastrada

She wrote those letters down beneath the first. She recognized a word in that line—*strada*, for "street"—but it could be meaningless if the backward half of the code didn't work too.

"Will there be a quiz on this?" asked Darrell. "Or do you want us to know this because you are planning to leave us?"

"Neither," she said.

"Good," said Lily.

"I just think you should know this stuff," she added.

"We should," said Wade, leaning over her and her notebook.

The snow had let up a bit, and traffic was faster now. She spied the dim lights from skyscrapers in northern Moscow in the distance. Somehow that comforted her.

"So . . . since the backward shape of Italy was on the *left*, or *first*, if we're reading left to right, the code actually starts at the *end* of the message. This means that *o-r-a-f-o-l-a-t-i-v-a-i-m-a-l-l-u-s* is backward. Turned around it becomes *s-u-l-l-a-m-i-a-v-i-t-a-l-o-f-a-r-o*."

She wrote that down as neatly as she could, bouncing along in a wrecked car at eighty miles an hour. She saw a word there, too. "Now, because the passage *starts* with the end of the message, I'm going to guess that the *lengths* of the coded words—*O-u-r-n a-o f-r-o-a l-f-a a-t-s-i-u*—correspond to the length of the words of the final words of the message, starting from the end. In other words, four letters, then two letters, four, three, five, and so on."

Becca doubted whether they could follow this, but she felt she needed to explain it as thoroughly as possible, praying it actually did what she hoped it would.

"So, assuming it means something real, we break up *s-u-l-l-a-m-i-a-v-i-t-a-l-o-f-a-r-o* into words, starting from the end, of four letters, two, four, three, five, et cetera. The letters form the words like this . . ."

sulla mia vita lo faro

Becca had to pause. She read the separated words over and over, stunned to realize that her method actually *had* worked. She had deciphered the code.

"What is it? What does it mean?" asked Lily, still holding the light over the notebook. "Anything?"

Becca could barely bring herself to speak it. "It's the last line of the passage. It means, 'Upon my life I will.'"

"Astounding," Roald said from the front.

"Oh, man." Darrell breathed out a cloud of cold air. "You did it. You totally cracked the cipher."

After that, it was short but brain-heated work to translate the first half of the diary passage, though a bit tougher to discover exactly where the forward and backward messages met. She tugged her woolen hat down low and finally finished. Shivering between Lily and Wade, she read the deciphered passage aloud, even as the Aleko slowed in the approach to Moscow's center.

xiii February 1517.

One hour ago on the frozen road to Muscovy, Maxim Grek and I were ambushed by the knights of East Prussia.

The battle was brief but fierce. Sword in hand, I flew and struck like a Persian dervish. Thirty men came at us. Many will not return to their homes this night, but two escaped with a treasure beyond belief.

"Half of Serpens is in their hands," I tell Maxim. "I need a strong man to guard its other half, to keep it hidden

from men's eyes. From Albrecht's, from Vasily's as well."

"Friend, why me?" he asks.

"Sir," I say, "I have sailed with ancient Caesar. This cut above my brow was gained when I fought side by side with the great Alexander. These bruises on my hands? From crawling through a trench battling iron monsters!"

"Holy cow," Wade interrupted. "Dad? It sounds like World War One."

"What do you speak of?" he asks me.

"The past, the future, all times between. Maxim, three years ago I discovered a device that, used by the wrong men, can be a terrible weapon. This is why I have disassembled it. This is why, my friend, I am asking you to hide a piece of it."

He bows his head. "Tell me, Nicolaus, what would you have me do?"

I loosen the straps of the bag. The relic falls into my palm. Maxim's eyes widen. "It glitters like Vasily's jewels!"

"All told," I say, "this relic is a construct of nine diamonds, one for each star in the Serpens constellation, set in a hinged device of silver. The artifact, when whole, breathes like a living thing. It now lies lifeless

in my hand because its head, three diamonds circling twin eyes of such blue splendor, was stolen this night by Albrecht's men. It is the head that makes the body move. It is the head that gives it life. Many have died because of it."

"Boris's story about Albrecht and the crying baby was on February eighteenth, five days later than this," said Lily. "Sorry. Go on."

"Serpens, indeed, sounds cursed," Maxim says.

"Pain. Loss. Greed," I say. "These are the serpent's curse. I am asking you to take it with you wherever you go. Where would you like to be?"

Maxim smiles. "Italy, without a doubt. My days with you and your brother, Andreas, in Padua were the happiest of my life. I dream of Italy."

"Then bring Serpens with you. And devise a code to speak with future friends. You will need it."

He nods slowly. "I think backward to what I have said to you, and there is my code."

"Good," I say. "Now, Maxim of Athos, will you guard the relic, keep it safe from Albrecht and the eyes of sinful men?"

He blesses me and whispers the words that the first

Guardian himself spoke.

"Upon my life I will."

Uncle Roald made a sound through his lips. "This is one of the first times Copernicus has talked about his journeys. He met Caesar? And Alexander the Great? Excellent work, Becca. It's extraordinary." He was forced to slow the car several streets away from the rental agency.

"Does the same decryption key work for the scroll, too?" asked Lily. "We need to hear from Maxim."

Becca studied the first words of the scroll that appeared under the date. *Laonmd brrea sdmeo lrliar moonro . . . .* "I think so. Give me a few minutes."

The traffic eased a bit, and Roald pulled the damaged car into the rental center garage to the astonished stares of the desk agents. While he endured the agents' screaming and arguing, and a mountain of paperwork, Becca kept going. Wade held the diary and Darrell her notebook as she used the same system—two sets of words folded into each other back to front—to translate the scroll Maxim hid in the Onion Tower.

xvii January 1556

Andreas died one brief year after I took the Serpens

body from Nicolaus.

Nicolaus himself has been gone more than a decade.

I never saw Italy again. Saint Sergius has become my tomb. I prepare for death. Then, one day, I have a visitor.

"I am Rheticus," he says. "I was the Magister's friend. Trust me with Serpens now."

I can tell from his eyes that Rheticus is a good man, but the serpent has cursed me. I do not want to give it up. To save my soul, I hand the relic to this good man. "Take it."

To find the body of the serpent now, follow the man named Rheticus.

I have done my duty to Nicolaus.

The shadow of death comes soon.

Uncle Roald led them from the rental car center into the bitter Moscow night, listening while Becca read over the coded scroll. "I remember Rheticus," he said.

"You took good notes at Uncle Henry's lectures," Wade said. "It's all in the notebook. Rheticus came to Copernicus at the end of his life and convinced him to publish his proof that the earth revolves around the sun."

"So we have to follow him now?" asked Darrell. "Does this mean the quest will take us somewhere else?"

Becca frowned. "It might, if all this is just another layer of the onion."

"Possibly," Roald said. "Rheticus was the one who really made the world aware of Copernicus's brilliance. Interestingly, he came into Nicolaus's life at least twenty years *after* the relics were hidden. I guess what Maxim is saying is that Rheticus knew about the time machine, the relics, everything. We can talk this over in the safe house."

CHAPTER THIRTY-FOUR

Terence Ackroyd had booked the Kaplan family into a tiny flat of three rooms. It was located on the fourth floor of a building operated as part student hostel, part long-term hotel, run by an expatriate Austrian couple in their sixties. Just two streets off the broad-laned Teatral'ny Proyezd, the flat was not too far from Red Square and the Kremlin, the centuries-old seat of the Russian government. Wade tried to imagine a warm room, food, and rest, but he couldn't.

In the center is a relic, he thought as he marched through the stinging, almost horizontal snow. *Copernicus to Maxim to Rheticus to who? One clue to another and another, but how far away from the center are we?* It seemed to Wade that the layers of the onion were all they'd seen so far. What he was certain of, as they stomped block after frozen block toward their rooms, was that another day was gone, Sara was still missing, and they had a clue or two, but no relic.

"A few more intersections," his father called over his shoulder. "Stay together."

The flat was still a half-dozen snowbound blocks away when, as they tried to turn onto Teatral'ny, they found several police vans parked end to end across the avenue. A brigade of policemen with automatic rifles was busy cordoning off the street at the corner.

Becca dug into her bag for her phrase book. She sidled up to a group of spectators. "What's going on?" she whispered in halting Russian. The man she'd asked said nothing or something unintelligible, then snapped his fingers at a uniformed policeman, who trotted over.

Wade's first thought: *What if the police are looking for us?*

But the officer took only a brief glance at them and jetted off some harsh-sounding words, one of which Wade recognized: Lubyanka. The Soviet prison Boris said he had spent time in. It was just up the hill from them right now.

"Lubyanka Square is the scene of some kind of

protest against the government," Becca told them. They now heard yelling and raucous singing from up the street. "He said it's none of our concern, and we should go away."

"But our flat," Lily said. "And I'm frozen, and my poor feet. The ground is cold—"

"*Nyet!* No go here!" The policeman scowled, making a show of regripping his rifle for effect. "All you, go away!"

Roald pulled them back, smiling to the officer as he did. "If we can't get there this way, we can't," he said under his breath. "We don't want to get tangled up with the authorities. All they have to do is check with passport control, and who knows what the flak is from our performance at the monastery? Let's backtrack until we find an open street. I'm sure they're not just closing off a big part of the city where people live. I have a street map. Let's try another way."

They slid back among the streams of people moving down Teatral'ny Proyezd from Lubyanka Square. Wade's father studied the map to find a side street that might swing them back around to their flat. The sidewalks were iced over, narrowed by mounds of shoveled snow. When they reached the end of the street, police vans were parked end to end one way across that road, too, while on the far side of the street another crowd was assembling.

"Is this the same demonstration or another one?" Lily asked. "What now?"

Someone barked out loudly on a bullhorn. A banner unfurling awkwardly among the protestors seemed to galvanize the growing crowd into movement. The thump of footsteps, a roar at first, quickly became a kind of rhythmic thunder. A flag appeared suddenly.

"What is this, *Les Miz*?" said Becca. "We shouldn't be here, Uncle Roald."

"Let's make our way around the crowd to the far end of the block," he said firmly. "Don't get separated. Always have one another in eyeshot. Yell out if something happens. Look for signs for Teatral'ny Proyezd. That's the street our flat is off of. Teatral'ny. Ask if you need help. Use your phones if we get separated, but *don't* get separated, but here's cash and change in case," he said, dividing up the currency he had in his pockets. "The demonstration can't last all night. Stay close. Come on."

Wade's father began weaving along the sidewalk, his hand up for them to focus on. But the crowd was large, spilling beyond its original shape and rolling like a wave now.

Darrell nudged Wade's arm. "Look." A group of men in black parkas and wool caps emerged from the crowd. They were moving slowly toward them. "I don't like this."

Following Wade's father, the kids pushed through the stragglers on the fringes, when the police abruptly moved into position behind the vans, like soldiers defending a wall.

Wade expected to hear the crack of gunfire any second. "Dad, maybe we should—"

The men in parkas weren't visible now. Wade's attention was taken by a tall flat-faced man in a long overcoat who snapped orders to the officers crouched behind the cars. He was bald and had a bushy black mustache. The police shifted not only behind their cars but on both sides of the avenue. A second bullhorn squealed angrily. The front of the crowd stopped, but the back kept pushing forward. The shouting was punctuated by screaming now.

"Wade, get over here!" his father yelled, and Wade saw the mustached policeman spin around on his heels as if he'd heard Wade's name—seemingly impossible in all the noise. The man stared in their direction until he fixed on Wade. The men in parkas were there again, too, striding toward Wade. *Oh, no. No.*

Lily threaded her way through the crowd. Wade saw Becca's ponytail swinging. They were together, at least. Where was Darrell? The protestors were moving again in waves. He swam against the tide of bodies, trying to reach the girls, while Darrell was suddenly deep in the crowd, abreast of their father. The demonstration was all around him now and frightening. Strange faces yelled angrily. He felt a punch in his side. Spittle sprayed his cheek. He looked up. The men in parkas were closer. But his father wasn't where he'd last seen him.

Jumping to see over the crowd, he yelled, "Dad!" then heard a sudden loud pop. Becca whirled around toward him, cringing, while Lily slid past a cluster of protesters to Darrell. There was his father again, reaching backward for them but being dragged farther away. Wade muscled through the crowd and snagged Becca's sleeve. "Bec, let's get out of this. There's a subway over there somewhere."

"You want to eat? *Now*?"

"No, a metro!" Wade said. "We can ride it back to the flat—"

They broke free of the jostling bodies and ducked between close-set stone buildings, hurrying to where the subway arrows pointed. He searched the crowd. His father, Darrell, and Lily were already across the street, looking back to find him and Becca. Wade waved his arms, but they didn't see him. There was another pop, then a shout. He couldn't see the men in parkas. Groups of demonstrators were spilling around quickly as if they would start running. Then Wade spied the stairs. Together he and Becca entered the heated subway. He held her by the hand, afraid without his father and the others, but responsible for himself and Becca. When they reached the bottom of the stairs, heat washed over them, and being underground had never felt so good.

"This is like Boston a little," Becca said nervously. "They call their subway the T."

"Good. Then you lead."

She cracked a smile. "I think we follow the noise down the stairs."

After paying for tickets with pocket change, and snatching a color-coded map of the subway system, they jumped down the nearest steps to the platform. They huddled behind a vending machine for minutes before boarding the first train that came screeching to a stop. It was immaculate and filled with passengers.

"If this station is called Okhotny Ryad, we'd better get off at the next station, wherever that is," said Becca, reading the map on the subway wall. "It's pretty far anyway. We'll either walk back or take a cab to the flat.

Maybe the demonstration will have moved on by then."

"That was crazy, huh?" Wade said. "Those guys were chasing us, weren't they?"

"I didn't see them, but Darrell seemed to. There were so many people."

They were crammed together face-to-face in the standing-room-only car. It was a sea of thick coats, knit caps, shopping bags, and teetering bodies as the train lurched forward. Wade wasn't sure exactly why, but he suddenly wanted to say something comforting to Becca. All he came up with was "How's your arm?"

She cradled an area between the elbow and shoulder of her left arm. "It itches, so that's a good sign, right? Like it's beginning to heal?"

"Good," he said, trying to smile. The truth was that her bandages, when he'd glimpsed them under her coat, were dark, as if she had bled some. "We need to find another clinic to have it looked at. The Austrian couple who run the hostel will know where to go."

She shook her head. "I don't want to slow us down—"

"Becca. You won't. We need to protect you." Was that comforting? He didn't know. He tried to follow up with something more promising than what he was thinking when the tunnel outside the windows brightened, and the train began to slow.

"We'd better get off," she said, rummaging through her bag. "The next stop is way beyond Red Square, and too far to walk back. And I actually don't think we can hail a cab. I must have lost my phrase book in the crowd, and I didn't get to the taxicab page. We don't want to end up even farther away."

Wade snorted a laugh. "Agreed."

He eased through the passengers to be ready to jump off when the train stopped. Before it did, the door from the next compartment opened with a breath of air, and Wade's heart thumped. The tall policeman with the bushy mustache pushed in. His gray overcoat flapped open to reveal a thick leather strap across his chest. He gripped something like a phone in his hand, reading it and then staring into the crowd.

"Becca . . ."

"I see him. Did he follow us down here? He's either with the police . . . or he's part of the Red Brotherhood."

"Or both. Watch out for guys in black parkas."

The train screeched to a stop. The doors groaned aside. Wade instinctively took her arm, but it was the wrong one. She winced, and he let go. He jumped onto the platform and turned for her, but a block of people pushed past him into the car, and Becca was forced away from the doors.

"Becca—" He tried to push his way back onto the car, but she was crowded even farther from the doors. He couldn't get on. She couldn't get off. The whistle sounded. The doors began to close. "Becca!" Then the mustached man jumped from the rear door of the car onto the platform. With a single look at Becca, Wade charged away into a warren of tunnels as the subway roared off into the dark.

CHAPTER THIRTY-FIVE

Snow was falling heavily when Wade stumbled up the metro stairs to the street. The flakes were large and wet and flying in his face and down his neck. He pulled his woolen cap low and ran up the sidewalk to the nearest corner. His shirt was soaked through. Everything was soaked, though his chest was a block of ice. He looked back. No one else came out of the subway. He searched the intersection.

"Wait!" someone yelled in English. Or was it "Wade"? He didn't look back. Panicking, he hurried down the sidewalk, slipping, nearly falling. He reached the next intersection. Footsteps thudded behind him. Several sets. Running this time.

At the first break in traffic, he tore across the wide avenue to a park on the other side. He ducked behind a shuttered kiosk. The mustached man paced the far corner, his overcoat flapping and flapping, scanning the intersection. Was *he* the one who had called to him? Why would anyone "wait" for someone pursuing him?

Trying to keep the kiosk directly between him and the tall man, he made himself small and ran as quietly as he could in the opposite direction. He soon found himself in a maze of grim gray buildings that resembled a movie set for the apocalypse.

He ducked into the first side alley he saw. Narrow, barren. Cold.

He'd lost his breath and couldn't get it back. Not from running so much, but deep inside. As if his lungs were failing him.

"Wait!" the voice called.

He stormed deeper into a cement quadrangle and glanced back, and something told him to turn at the first corner. He slipped on the ice, smashing his knee on the pavement. The pain speared up his side. On his feet again, turn, and down the passage, then turn again. His legs were lead. The snow was heavier, wetter. He started to remember the warmth of Rome, that night outside the Museo Copernicano, when they'd slept under the stars. Of being together with Darrell and Becca and Lily. But there wasn't enough of his brain to do anything but run.

He was running on bone. He stumbled to the end of the alley, hoping for an outlet. There was none. It ended in gray stone, a coffin of concrete. Heavy footsteps crashed behind him. Many more than before. Twenty paces behind him. Ten. Five. Three.

Wade rested his head on the cold cement wall, then spun around with a cry—"Help me!"—as a group of men in hooded coats closed over him.

CHAPTER THIRTY-SIX

Becca raced through the slushy streets. The demonstration had broken up as quickly as it had formed. She found the safe house, but Wade hadn't returned.

Roald was on the phone to the police, getting nowhere.

"They have him," she gasped. "The police or the FSB or the Brotherhood. They took him!" She told them everything, and Darrell started doing his caged-animal thing. He eyed the tiny window of their room as if he was going to jump out of it. Then he shot her a look as if it was somehow *her* fault that Wade wasn't there. As if *she* should be lost, instead.

She understood. Brothers. She was nearly as close to

Lily as she was to her own sister, Maggie. If anything happened to her . . .

"I couldn't get off the train," she said. "The crowd was pushy, and I—"

"We know, Bec," Lily said, patting her hand. "It's not that—"

"Of course it's not that!" Darrell practically shouted, then breathed out sharply. "It's this dumb freezing place. Wade could be anywhere—"

The door swung in. Becca jumped for it, but it was a man in a parka and black combat fatigues and boots. Behind him were several other men dressed the same. "Put down the phone," the first one said to Roald. "Gather things. Come with us. No time."

"But—" Roald began, the phone halfway to its cradle.

Darrell shook his head crazily. "No! I'm not leaving! I'm not going anywhere without Wade!"

The lead man pulled his pistol out of its holster. "No words. Put down phone. Chief Inspector Yazinsky has ordered us to bring you to station." Becca then watched as the man did an odd thing. He put a finger to his lips, and whispered, "Red Brotherhood are entering lobby downstairs. They are coming. We do not want firefight in building. Please. Hurry."

And that was it. She went electric and so did everyone

else. They threw their things together. The men—were they even real police?—shut off all the lights but one and hovered at the windows and doors, guns drawn.

The man made a hissing noise. There was a shout from outside their room. The men at the door crouched. A shot exploded through the door frame and crashed back out the window. The men at the door returned fire.

"Stair escape through bathroom," the lead man said. He pushed them efficiently through the room and into the bathroom, where he slammed the bottom sash up as far as it would go. Eight inches. Not enough. He raised a jackboot and kicked it out entirely. Glass splattered onto an iron landing. "Mister first," he said, "then others."

Roald slipped through the opening into the whirling snow and waited on the landing for Becca and Lily. They took the iron steps down to the next landing and the next, while Darrell followed with the officer. An unmarked car was waiting at the bottom. The gunfight above had stopped and been replaced with yelling and the sound of multiple sirens approaching through the snowy streets.

"Who are you?" Roald said as they were hustled into the back of the cruiser. There was no answer. The driver started up, the electronic door locks engaged, and the car slid away, leaving the officer who had helped them on the street, trotting into the hotel, his weapon raised. The cruiser was nearly around the corner when Becca felt the air shudder. Glass and wood and fire blew like a rocket's ignition out of their room, showering the street with flaming debris.

Darrell screamed, "They bombed our room! Those freaks bombed our room!"

A second blast blew fire out everywhere. The cruiser picked up speed and they were on another street and another. More sirens. The driver tore through several blocks north from the safe house, down the hill from Lubyanka Square, whizzing past the ragged remains of the demonstration, slowing only as they entered a wide plaza. In the center of the plaza was a big box of a building. There was a range of brightly lit double-arched windows across the front and a heavy square tower sprouting from the roof. The area in front of it was filled with taxicabs.

"This is . . . I thought we were going to the police station," Roald said.

Becca read the sign: ЛЕНИНГРАДСКИЙ ВОКЗАЛ. "What is this place?"

"Leningradskiy train station," the man said in English. "You leave on next train."

"Dad, what is this?" Darrell cried.

"No talking now," the officer said. He pulled the cruiser to the front of the building and, without looking at them, electronically unlocked the doors. "Inside. Officer will find you. Go. Now!"

They stumbled out into a tumult of circling cars and still heavier snow.

CHAPTER THIRTY-SEVEN

The bag over his head had been the worst. Wade could barely stomach the smell of someone else's face and hair and breath so close to his own.

Even now he spat out a greasy thread. "Gross . . ."

The room was tiny, a small box, four feet by nine feet—he'd paced it out—with only a padded bench in it. It was a cell smaller than Maxim's. They'd thrust him inside and slammed the door behind him. He'd torn off the bag immediately and thrown it on the floor. That was—what—two hours ago? Longer? Was it the middle of the night?

The stained bag sat on the floorboards, a lump of gray canvas. Floorboards. Not a concrete floor. In the dim light of the hanging bulb he studied the narrow oak boards set in an angled pattern, one next to another, like the weave of a fancy overcoat.

His breath left him.

Parquet.

"I'm in Lubyanka prison."

His heart sank, then squeezed tight, and something wrenched up his throat. He wanted to cry. He pounded on the door with his fists. "Let me out. I'm an American! You hear me? You can't do this! I'm an American citizen!"

No answer. But the mustached man knew who Wade was anyway. Of course he did. He and a handful of large, hard men had cornered him, bagged him, and pulled him into a car. Boris's words came back to him. *Car take you to Lubyanka.*

He remembered Lily telling them how Saint Dominic was the patron saint of those who were falsely accused. Like Sara? Yes, like Sara. Thinking that actually gave him hope. He was locked up, but alive. And Sara was, too. She had to be.

Wiping his face, Wade paced the cell front to back, door to bench, three and a half steps, turn, then three and a half steps back. He tried to find a place of calm inside him. If there was silence, if he was alone, he could make use of it.

So far, they had nothing. They didn't have a relic yet. They had nothing but words. But it wasn't just a mess of unrelated words. It wasn't random. It was a kind of history, where things from here and there were connected and made a picture.

It was like . . . what?

A constellation, his astronomical brain told him.

Isolate the things I see. Put them in order. Make the connections. Bring all the stories down to points of light.

He stooped to the floor and ran his fingers along the floorboards where they met the wall, looking for a nail or something sharp. Nothing. Then he remembered. The tooth. He slipped his hand into his pocket and pulled it out. Black, chipped, dead. The tooth of a martyred Guardian, perhaps. A victim of Galina Krause. It was the perfect thing to use against her.

With the tooth pinched between his fingers, Wade scratched a letter into the wall.

C

That was for Copernicus. In 1517 he gave the body of Serpens to Maxim—*M*—who at his death, in 1556, gave it to Rheticus—*R*—who died in 1574. But the other thing that happened in 1517 was that the nephews of Albrecht—*A*—stole the head of Serpens. Albrecht himself died in 1568, a generation after Copernicus's own death in 1543.

So what did that look like? It looked like this:

Strangely, reducing the confusion of his thoughts to a clear drawing calmed him. It really did look like a constellation, the shorthand for a long story. A story reduced to glowing points of light, which then became the story again.

His breath slowed. His panic ebbed. Moving from there to there to there was progress. It gave him a direction.

"So now we have two questions," Wade said to himself, pocketing the tooth. "Where did the head go after Albrecht, and where did the body go after Rheticus?"

Keys jangled outside the door. It burst wide, nearly smacking him in the face. Before he could see anyone, he was spun around and his wrists were shackled behind his back. The canvas bag, wet now and smelling of mice, was dropped over his head again.

CHAPTER THIRTY-EIGHT

Darrell was stone. He refused to move or set foot in the Leningradskiy train station. "We're not leaving without Wade. First Mom, now Wade? We're not leaving."

"We're not going anywhere," his stepfather said. "I'm calling the embassy right now. I don't know who Chief Inspector Yazinsky is, but authorities or no, we need help here."

Before Roald could locate the number, a short older man in a gray overcoat hanging loose over a suit and tie—obviously a policeman or secret service officer—pushed out the station doors into the parking lot. "Please close the phone, sir. The inspector wishes no calls. Not from your phone. We cannot take chances. Please . . ." Roald looked shocked but didn't resist. The man pulled the cell from his hand, swiped it off, removed its battery, and pocketed it. "Follow me, please." His grip on Roald's arm was apparently strong, as he tugged him forcefully to the door.

"Uncle Roald—" Lily started.

"Do as he says."

Cursing to himself, Darrell reluctantly followed him into the station.

It was an enormous open room with a lighted arcade running down each of the long sides. Hundreds of people wove across the floor from end to end, even at that time of night. The air was filled with the din of voices and footsteps, the rumbling of wheeled suitcases, and overlapping announcements in Russian, English, and French. The incessant clink and clatter from late-night restaurants and snack bars added its own kind of roar in his ears. Beneath it all rolled the thunder of the rails running from the station out into the countryside beyond Moscow.

"Wait here one minute," the officer commanded, and strode several feet away.

Becca huddled together with Lily and Darrell. All of

them were mumbling, afraid, trying to be logical, but everything they said came down to some crazy version of "What in the world is going on?"

Then Lily's cell phone rang. "Who's calling me?" she answered. "May I help you?"

The voice on the other end was slow and faraway. "I'm calling from the morgue."

"Ahhhh!" Lily screamed, and dropped the phone.

"What!" Becca cried.

"It's the morgue! Someone's dead!" Lily scrambled for the cell phone, but Darrell tore it from her fingers and punched the speaker button.

"Hello? Hello? Are you there? Is it Wade? Is it my brother? Is he . . . dead?"

"Dea . . . I . . . not . . ." The voice was faint, crackly.

"Can you please speak up," Roald said into the phone. "Is this the morgue? Are you calling from the morgue?"

". . . an Library," said the suddenly familiar voice. "The Morg . . . an Library. In New York City. Is this the Kaplan family?"

Darrell buried his head in his hands, practically sobbing. "Good God."

Roald said, "Hello, you are Dr. Billingham, I presume? This is Roald Kaplan. We're just . . . never mind.

Do you have some news for us?"

"I am a mess . . . ," Rosemary said, " . . . enger for Julian Ackroyd. He says his fa . . . ther has business in London, but will arrive in Mos . . . cow on Sun . . . day morning. There is news, he says. Are you under . . . standing me?"

"Thank you," said Roald. "Thank you so much!"

"That's not . . . all," Rosemary said. "Last night there was a robbery . . . "

"Oh, my gosh, Vela!" Lily said.

". . . attempt at the library. Of course, nothing was taken. The police are hunting for a Germ . . ." There was a long few seconds before ". . . an man and three French ass . . . ociates. That's . . . all. Good day."

The short officer returned and drew them swiftly down the perimeter of the room toward the far inside corner. He scanned the crowd like a hawk, but gave no answer to Darrell's—or anyone else's—urgent questions.

At the same time an unmarked automobile motored swiftly from one snowbound street to the next. The car made constant turns, approaching a yellow-towered public building three times before turning away to begin another series of zigzags and cutbacks.

Chief Inspector Simon Yazinsky sat in the rear seat. He tugged one end of his bushy mustache and turned to the passenger sitting next to him.

"Truly, Wade," he said in lightly accented English, "my sincerest apologies for the filthy bag. A bit dramatic, I know. Lubyanka, as well. All of it. It was for your own safety that you remained anonymous. You see, in Russia the Teutonic Order and its allies here, the Red Brotherhood, are everywhere and powerful. Your visit to Saint Sergius alerted the Brotherhood. They planned to use the demonstration as a cover to kidnap you. I had to intervene. For your own safety, you must leave the city."

Wade nodded slowly, desperately trying to take it all in with the fraction of a brain he had left. "So you arrested me because the Brotherhood was after us? The men in black parkas at the demonstration?"

He nodded. "Although I have a distinguished rank in the FSB, even after I scooped you up, I wanted no one to see you. I can trust my friend here behind the wheel, but few others on my staff. I must also inform you that there has just been an attempt on the safety of your family. An attack and explosion in your rooms."

"Oh, my gosh, are they—"

"They are fine, and waiting nearby."

The car drove smoothly from street to street.

"You were following us, tracking me from the beginning," Wade said, feeling more and more brain coming back to him. "How did you know to do that?"

Chief Inspector Yazinsky cleared his throat. "The Circle of Athos has been aware of you since your arrival at Sheremetyevo airport."

Wade thought back. "The guard who stopped me at the passport control? What was her name . . . I. Lyubov?"

"Cousin Irina," he said, smiling under his mustache. "Carlo Nuovenuto—you know him—sent encrypted pictures to the Guardians in Europe and elsewhere. The clearest image from the fencing school in Bologna was of you. We have eluded our pursuers, and here we are."

The building with the tower reappeared once again, and this time Wade saw its blazing letters.

ЛЕНИНГРАДСКИЙ ВОКЗАЛ

The driver pulled up to it. "The train to Saint Petersburg," Inspector Yazinsky said. "The station is quaintly still named Leningradskiy." He leaned across the seat to Wade, and his voice went low. "The Circle of Athos comprises a handful only, while the Order is a kraken of great size, a monster. Even with our precautions, we must be careful when we enter." The inspector reached across Wade and opened his door. It swung out into the cold. Wade stumbled out, then followed the man into the station.

CHAPTER THIRTY-NINE

Wade was bewildered by the massive, brilliantly lit hall. It was elegant and insufferably loud. His father was not visible; neither were Becca, Darrell, and Lily. He didn't like it. The roar of noise and movement could drown out any number of dangers.

"Be careful," the inspector repeated. "This way."

His senses on high alert, Wade followed the inspector, hugging close to the side of the huge open room. They went under one of the two large arches to an office door. "Railroad security," the inspector whispered.

"Are they Guardians, too?" he asked.

"Guardians? No. But they are friends, even if they do not know exactly why we're here." The inspector knocked three times, paused a moment, and then knocked twice more. The door opened, Wade entered, and his shoulder thudded with a series of blows from behind. He went into an immediate crouch, but hands were suddenly all over him, spinning him around.

"Wade, Wade, Wade!"

Darrell, Becca, and Lily wouldn't let go of him, as if he'd been missing for a year. He coughed out, "I'm okay, I'm okay," a hundred times, but they barely let him breathe.

When he finally pulled away, his father wrapped him in his arms. "Wade, we were worried sick about you!"

"Really, I'm okay," he said. "I heard there was a bomb."

They told him about their last-second rescue from the safe house, then that Terence was on a jet flying to them right now. It was several minutes before Wade could properly introduce them to Chief Inspector Yazinsky.

"I apologize for all the secrecy," the inspector said to them, nodding at a short, smiling security officer. "The reason you are here is twofold. As I told young Wade on the way over, the Red Brotherhood has closed in, and you must leave Moscow. But this is what you might wish to do anyway. Dmitri?"

The short officer stepped forward. "One hour ago, we arrested someone at the station, coming in on the train from Saint Petersburg. No identification, no story. A vagrant, we thought. Or worse. She was armed—"

"She?" said Darrell. "A woman?"

"Not your mother," said Inspector Yazinsky. "We are certain. Continue, Dmitri."

"She was armed," the officer continued. "And she bears bruises on her face and hands. She is dehydrated, weak. She is being treated right now for shock, exposure to extreme cold, exhaustion, cuts, bruises, frostbite—"

"Oh, my gosh," said Becca.

"Who is she?" Roald asked.

Dmitri lowered his head. "The woman will not speak to us. She will say nothing."

Roald looked at the inspector, then back at the short officer. "Then, I'm sorry, but what does this have to do with us?"

"She will say nothing, sir," the officer continued, "but your name. Roald Kaplan."

"Dad!" said Wade. "Who is it?"

"Allow me to bring you to her," the officer said. "The station clinic is this way."

The inspector motioned them through the door, and

they hurried down a very narrow corridor toward a white circular sign beaming with a flickering neon red cross. The short officer turned the knob, then bowed at the doorway.

"I take my leave of you here. She has been sedated, but is awake."

The clinic inside was clean and spacious for a railway station. It smelled of chemicals and food. In a cubicle surrounded by thin curtains sat a low hospital cot. A woman lay on it, her arms connected to tubes, her hands and feet and cheeks bandaged. No, it was not Sara. It was, in fact, no one Wade recognized, but his father let out a gasp.

"Isabella! Isabella Mercanti!" He knelt to the cot and gently took her hand. Her eyes flicked open, then closed again. "Isabella," he said, "it's Roald. . . ."

The children watched as the woman slowly turned her face to him. "Roald? Roald!" She reached for him, but the tubes held her back. She started to cry.

Isabella Mercanti was the Italian professor Wade's father had told the children to meet in Bologna last week. She was the widow of Silvio Mercanti, a member of his father's old college circle, Asterias. When she had gone missing, and even her university hadn't heard from her, they had all presumed the worst.

Wade felt his knees give way. He plopped into a chair next to a rolling cart. On the cart were instruments, bloodied gauze bandages, and, strangely, a kitchen knife. Why was Isabella Mercanti in Russia, of all places? And on a train originating in Saint Petersburg, four hundred miles from here?

Was this anything but another weird layer of the onion?

"Some water, please," his father said, and the inspector stepped into the next room. "Isabella, tell me what happened to you? Why are you in Moscow?"

"I saw her," she whispered. "I saw Sara . . ."

Darrell knelt to the cot. "My mother? Where is she? Is she okay?"

"She did not escape, not like me," she said, taking a sip of water. "But yes. Alive. In a horrifying castle many kilometers outside Saint Petersburg."

"When did you see her?" Becca asked.

"It is after midnight now? Then yesterday," she said. "Yes, yesterday. She was captive. In a tower. I could not get her out of the thing. I wounded a soldier. No, not a soldier. A brute, an animal. Maybe he died. I do not know. I stab him and escape."

Wade glanced back at the knife on the cart, then at Becca. She was staring at it, too, wiping her cheeks.

"I run barefoot to a small city. Far, many hours away. People pity me, get me to train in Saint Petersburg, pay for me. I come here. I have friend in Moscow. Sara"— she paused, looked at Darrell—"your mother is in a . . . device. Horrible. Big device."

Darrell stood and pounded the nearest wall. "What kind of device? Tell us!"

"Let her speak," Roald said softly, cradling Isabella by her shoulders.

She sat up, her eyes wild. "I only caught a glimpse of the machine. Then a man comes in. I have to run. Sara is a prisoner of clockwork. Something happens at midnight some days from now. No, not some days. Sooner. It is Saturday in the early morning, yes? Then tomorrow. Sunday at midnight. That is what I heard them say."

"Mom is being tortured?" Darrell slammed his fist once more on the wall.

"No, not tortured. It is clockwork. Gears and wheels."

"What does the machine do?" asked Lily.

"I don't know!" Isabella answered.

"Do you know where the place is exactly?" Roald asked.

Isabella shook her head. "I hear some things. A German woman. Young."

"Galina Krause," muttered Wade.

She nodded. "I hear her voice. She say, *'Der Hölle Rache'*? It is German, but what is this?"

No one knew. Becca asked for Lily's computer.

"And I hear one word. The name of the horrible place where we are held. A fortress. It is called . . . Greywolf."

"Greywolf." Roald rose to his feet and began to pace around the cot. "Inspector?"

"I do not know of it," he murmured, dragging his phone from his pocket. "I will find out."

"Dad, we're going to get Mom right now," Darrell said slowly and in a whisper. "It's nearly three a.m. Saturday morning. Only forty-something hours to Sunday midnight. We have to go get Mom before that machine does anything to her."

"We will," Roald said firmly, looking deeply into Darrell's eyes. "We will. We'll find out where this Greywolf is, and we'll go for her. I'll phone Terence to change his flight plans and meet us in Saint Petersburg."

Isabella was breathing more easily now. "I cannot go back there and I do not know the way. Roald, I am sorry. But I must return to Italy as soon as possible. My husband discovered a secret before he was murdered. That is why the Order took me. The clue is in our apartment in Bologna. I must go there as soon as possible to protect it."

"Oh, man . . ." Becca stood, Lily's computer tablet quivering in her hands. "Boris's ticket . . ."

Wade turned to her. "Ticket? You mean to the opera in Italy? What about it?"

"*Der Hölle Rache kocht in meinem Herzen,*" she said. "What Galina said. It means 'Hell's vengeance boils in my heart.' It's a line from *The Magic Flute*. The opera in Venice that Boris had a ticket to see. He was going there Saturday night. Tonight! Galina is going there, too! That's what she meant when she said those words. She must have heard that Boris was going to meet someone, and now she's going! We have to go to Venice!"

Wade felt the tooth in his pocket. Aleksandr. Boris. Andreas. Nicolaus. The connection between brothers. "A message for Boris. It was about the relic. A message about Serpens, maybe. We need to know what someone wanted to tell Boris—"

Darrell shook his head vehemently. "No we don't. We're going to Greywolf. Dad, I don't care where Galina's going. Mom is tied up in some death machine, and we're going to save her. We're not leaving Russia!"

"Darrell, calm down," his stepfather said. "We're not going anywhere. We're not."

"Dr. Kaplan." The inspector cleared his throat. "May I make a suggestion? I feel responsible and will make the trip to Italy to escort Dr. Mercanti home. If you approve, I will also escort anyone who wishes to go to Venice for the rendezvous. I will protect them as if they are my own. Clearly the Circle of Athos cannot keep you safe against the Order here. I suggest you continue to Saint Petersburg. I will personally provide all assistance to ensure Dr. Mercanti's safety. Perhaps Wade and another of the children should accompany us, to follow through on the meeting at the opera house. We will then return together. I leave it to you."

Wade knew the gears were moving in his father's head. His dad would never want to split the family apart. But now that there was a deadline in one place and a clue in another, they might have to. "Dad," he said, "the inspector might be right."

His father looked at him, then at the others, and finally at Isabella. "What do we think?" he asked softly. "Isabella, I know it's a lot to ask, but what do you think about stopping in Venice before you go home to Bologna? With some of us. I think we need to know what will happen in Venice tonight. Can you—"

"Yes," Isabella said quietly. She sat up more firmly, her bandaged feet resting on the floor. She teetered a little, but took a deep breath and steadied herself. "Yes, Roald, of course. Thank you, Inspector. I will help as much as I can. It is my place to do so. My husband was a Guardian. This makes me one, too."

"Wade, girls?" his father asked.

"Venice," said Lily.

Becca nodded. "Venice."

Darrell looked at Wade. "Dude, go. We'll have Terence. Plus, you're kind of klutzy and will probably slow us down."

Wade knew it was Darrell's attempt—a weak one—at humor. But it allowed him to say what he felt he should say. "All right, then. Venice."

Becca passed the tablet back to Lily. "Airlines . . ."

"Oh, I know," she said, smiling over the screen. "Five tickets to Venice. Trust me. We'll be there in plenty of time for the opera."

"Darrell and I will go to Saint Petersburg," Roald said. "We'll find out where Greywolf is. And we'll find Sara. We will."

CHAPTER FORTY

Saint Petersburg; Venice

L ater that morning, following the appearance of Isabella Mercanti, Darrell and his stepfather sleeplessly
took the train to Saint Petersburg.

After Chief Inspector Yazinsky had seen to it that
Roald's cell phone was returned to him, the first call he
made was to Terence Ackroyd, who said he would meet
them in Saint Petersburg. The investigator Paul Ferrere
and a colleague from Paris were on their way there, too.

For his part, Chief Inspector Yazinsky searched but
could discover nothing about Greywolf from official
sources. Neither could he promise much Guardian help

in the northern city, beyond the offer of the name of a low-level aide at the seldom-visited Railway Museum, "because of their extensive maps of the Russian frontier. Pray you find Greywolf listed on one of them."

Because of Isabella's condition, it was several hours before she felt well enough to fly. Once she gave the go-ahead, Lily booked them all—the inspector, Isabella, Becca, Wade, and herself—on the earliest nonstop to Venice. It would leave at two p.m. Given the time difference, Venice being three hours earlier than Moscow, the three-and-a-half-hour flight was scheduled to arrive midafternoon. That would leave them five solid hours before the opera performance on Saturday evening.

"Venice is quite different from Rome or Bologna," Isabella said as they took their seats on the flight. "But I have always loved it there. So will you."

Lily felt they could trust Isabella. One of the marks of Guardians seemed to be that they didn't press, they didn't force, they didn't make you feel as if you had to *do* or *feel* or *tell them* something. That was plain in Copernicus's conversation with Maxim. He asked; he didn't force. Maxim agreed anyway.

Upon my life I will.

"The relic we're searching for in Russia is called

Serpens," she told Isabella. Remembering that Isabella's husband, Silvio, was a friend of Uncle Roald's, she added, "I'm so sorry your husband passed away."

Isabella shook her head. "Silvio's murder was disguised as a skiing mishap. He was murdered by an agent named Markus Wolff. I know you know him. It was Silvio's obsession with what he called 'number twelve' that got him killed. There is a mystery about the twelfth—the final—relic. It is somehow odd and unlike the others."

"Wolff hinted at the same thing in San Francisco," Lily said. "He said that what the twelfth relic is, is the answer to everything. What did Mr. Mercanti find out?"

Isabella frowned. "I know little, but he was close to discovering something. The Order thinks I know what it is. The answer lies hidden in our apartment in Bologna. I will find it. For Silvio, I will find it."

"We know how terrible the Order is," said Wade. "The death of my uncle Henry—Heinrich Vogel—pulled us into the relic hunt in the first place."

"Heinrich was a good man," she said. "I was calling him when I was kidnapped."

"Thanks to him, we have one relic so far," said Becca. "But Serpens is in two parts, and we have neither, which isn't good."

"But neither does Galina, yes?" said the inspector.

"Right," said Lily. "And that *is* good. Really good."

"Maybe having lots of layers to the onion are all right, after all," Becca said.

It was warm and sunny when they arrived at Marco Polo Airport, a small and clean affair built out over the water six and a half miles north of the city. Lily shed her coat at the earliest opportunity. Though brisk in late March, Italy was already showing signs of spring, and after so much cold Lily began to feel, as they all did, thawed out, rejuvenated, alive. "No more hunching against the cold," she said. "I can stand straight up for the first time in days. No more windburn, either. Or frozen fingers."

Maybe best of all, they weren't being followed yet. Galina might already be there, but likely didn't know that they were.

Becca seemed to be beaming. The attention to her wound by an intern at the railway clinic where they first saw Isabella, and a set of fresh bandages, had obviously made her feel better. And hopeful. They all felt that, too.

"The south," Becca said. "The sun feels so amazing."

Isabella was feeling better, too. She had eaten two large meals since they'd found her in the clinic, had called her friends in Bologna, had slept like a stone, and was anxious to return home as soon as possible. Chief Inspector Yazinsky tried to persuade her to take a police escort back to Bologna, but two friends from her university met her at the airport. After a long round of good-byes and tears and hugs, Wade said, "Thank you for everything you are doing. You are the most amazing person. . . ."

"So are you," Isabella said. "So are you all. I will call your father, Wade, when I reach Bologna. You will all see me again."

They left Isabella with her friends to await a connecting flight.

Then, at a little after three o'clock, after using Terence's Ackroyd's credit card to withdraw euros from an airport ATM, the kids and Inspector Yazinsky climbed aboard a launch called a vaporetto for the hour-long water ride into Venice. They settled into seats by the windows facing east and were soon motoring past long strips of land that Lily's maps told them surrounded and formed the giant Venice lagoon.

"This is great," Becca said. "We can almost pretend we're tourists."

"Almost," said Wade. "We should blend in, but be alert to everything."

Lily knew this was true. They were seriously the furthest thing from being tourists. None of what they saw, heard, or thought about was what a tourist saw or heard or thought about. Everything meant something on their quest for the relic. After all, would this strange place, so far from everything they were learning in Russia, give them the vital information they sought?

She hoped so.

The vaporetto slowed and sidled into the dock. They emerged by a series of walkways and ramps into the Piazza San Marco—Saint Mark's Square.

Now that it was midafternoon on a warm day, the area was thronged with tourists. It was almost too much for Lily not to run over and talk to fellow Americans, but it was out of the question, as the inspector kept telling them.

"We are undercover," he said, "as much as a Russian inspector and three American teenagers can be undercover."

The immense domed Basilica di San Marco loomed over the square on one end. Adjacent to it was the Doge's Palace, a colonnaded structure with rose-shaped cutouts and a long gallery of pointed arches. Everywhere else were outdoor cafés and stalls selling postcards and scarves and every kind of souvenir. Pigeons constantly fluttered up and settled here and there across the stones. And then there were the canals: wide avenues of water between blocks of buildings, and narrower inlets down the side streets, alleys, and passages.

"So beautiful and warm," said Wade, making notes about the sites in his notebook. "Strange sensation. My fingers don't actually ache."

"Going back will be hard," said Lily. "Mostly on my toes."

When they entered the plaza between the twin pillars of San Marco and San Teodoro, Becca stopped dead. Against one side of the piazza stood a tower whose main feature was a giant twenty-four-hour astronomical clock. The face of the clock was brilliant blue, the numbers around its face—Roman numerals, of course—were gold, and at the center stood an unmoving, dull-colored globe representing the earth.

"It is pre-Copernican, is it not?" asked the inspector.

"It is," said Becca. "The earth is in the center of the clock, as if the sun were revolving around it."

"Kind of my line," said Wade, nudging her. "But exactly right."

"The tower is called the Torre dell'Orologio. Saint Mark's Clock Tower," Lily said. "Built in 1497."

The fiery, smiling face of the sun was mounted on the

hour hand. The face was divided into several concentric discs, which, they guessed, turned at different speeds to reflect the movement of the sun and the moon around the earth. The moon was an orb sunk halfway into its circling disc, and turned on its own axis. Half the orb was blue, the other half gold, and when it revolved, the golden half illustrated the phases, from new moon to full and back again.

"It's so beautiful," Becca said. "It makes you think that astronomy—and Copernicus—are everywhere."

"They are everywhere," the inspector whispered as he scanned the piazza. "But Galina is here as well. Let us lay low until the opera."

That brought Lily and the rest of them back to reality. They weren't tourists. They had never been tourists.

After finding reasonably priced clothing shops, where they bought a few scarves and a necktie each for Wade and Inspector Yazinsky, they hid out the rest of the day.

At twenty minutes before nine, under stars glittering like jewels against the blue Venetian sky, they arrived at the old opera house, hoping to peel away yet another layer of the onion.

CHAPTER FORTY-ONE

Saint Petersburg

Near the intersection of Rimskogo-Korsakova and Sadovaya Streets stood Saint Petersburg's Central Railway Museum.

To Darrell it was a world of dust. A bright young man who looked like he did everything from cataloging ancient maps to mopping the floors ushered them into a large, frigid room known as the Cherepanov Archives. The collection included virtually untouched and unexamined historical and topographical maps from the last one hundred sixty years of railway exploration.

Narrowing their search was Isabella Mercanti's vague but vital clue—"Greywolf"—along with a surprise lead the detective Paul Ferrere had brought from Paris: an unidentified private jet had been tracked into the wastelands north and east of the city.

One hour earlier, Paul had met them at the train station and introduced his colleague. "My right-hand operative, Marceline Dufort," he said.

"Dufort?" said Roald as they headed for a taxicab. "Are you related at all to—"

"I am Bernard's sister," she said.

Like Isabella's husband, Bernard Dufort was another original member of Asterias, and a Guardian. His murder in Paris had led directly to the death of Heinrich Vogel—Uncle Henry—which had then led the Kaplans to become involved in the relic hunt.

"Wow, we're pleased to have you with us," said Darrell. "Thanks for helping."

At the museum, Marceline located a large map from 1852 and spread it out on one of the many worktables in the main map room. "Let us begin with this."

Paul traced his finger across it, north from Madrid. "The jet that Galina Krause flies is a Mystère-Falcon," he said. "On a full tank, the Falcon has a flying range of two thousand kilometers. If she flew from Madrid to here, she would have to refuel, most likely in Berlin, where we know she has a private airstrip. Assuming that she did not refuel again, a straight flight from Berlin to the Saint Petersburg area would have landed her no farther than this area."

He circled a two-hundred-mile region of forests and hills to the northeast of the city. "Because we believe the fortress was a former headquarters of the KGB, and thus within heavily monitored airspace, no present-day satellite map we could find shows its exact location. That is why our search of old maps may provide our only real evidence of Greywolf's existence."

Darrell felt upbeat for the first time in days. "We're getting closer, Dad."

"I think so, too."

They each took a different group of maps and scoured the region, with, at first, little luck. Then Darrell found something. He *thought* he found something. While searching a crusty French map from 1848 of the forests of the Republic of Karelia—in the center of Galina's flight zone—Darrell found himself squinting at the tiniest inked writing he had ever seen. Inside a series of concentric circles meant to designate a hill were six almost invisible letters.

Chât. L.G.

"What does *chat* mean in French?" he asked.

Marceline smiled. "It means 'cat.' Where do you see this?"

He pressed his finger on the map. Marceline saw what he was pointing at, and her smile dropped. "No, no. *Chat* means 'cat,' but *chât* with a period and an accent like this means it is an abbreviation. It could mean *château*. 'Castle.'"

Roald was by his side now, bending over the map. "What could the initials *LG* mean?"

"Ah!" said Paul, sharing a look with his colleague. "Your son has found something. *LG* are not the initials for a person. *LG* very probably means *loup gris*."

"Dad?" said Darrell.

Roald instantly put his arms around him. "*Loup gris* is 'grey wolf.' You found your mother, Darrell. You found her!"

CHAPTER FORTY-TWO

Venice

The Gran Teatro opera house was a simple stone box with four columns separating large, dark-paneled entry portals.

Now that they were hiding behind the base of a large statue of a man in armor, knowing that Galina would soon be there, Wade was a mess of nerves. His senses were raw. Everything meant something. Nothing meant nothing, and he needed to take in every detail.

"Let us wait and watch," the inspector whispered. "Once everyone enters, we will lose ourselves in the crowd."

"I feel so out of place," Becca said.

"No way," said Lily. "We're as important as anybody. More important, I'd say. Just think about what we're doing. Who else in this crowd is after an ancient relic *and* a murderer *and* is a Guardian *and* is going to see a famous opera? Nobody but us. Not that anyone will ever know, because real heroes don't seek the spotlight, but we'll know."

"You're starting to talk like Darrell now," Wade said.

"He must have infected me," she said.

At ten minutes before nine, four boys in feathered costumes descended the stairs, ringing hand bells. This was the signal that it was time to enter the opera house.

"That is our invitation," the inspector said. "Let's find our box. Be alert."

Weaving into the crowd, the four ascended the stairs and were greeted by two smiling attendants in muted uniforms. Presenting their ticket, which was apparently good for up to eight people, they entered the lobby. A wide and tall flight of carpeted stairs stood ahead of them. It led to the upper seats.

"Box Three-Seventeen is on the third tier, halfway up," Becca said, holding Boris's ticket. "I feel like we're approaching the scene of a crime now that Boris is . . . you know."

Wade nodded. "Me, too. Everybody, keep your eyes open."

"And ears," said Lily. "This is an opera, after all."

"Well said," added the inspector.

They were finally shown to *scatola del teatro* 317 by a woman in a maroon suit. She unlocked the door and let them into a narrow room opening up to the inside of the theater. A heavy velvet curtain hung from the ceiling of the box, separating the hallway door from the seats.

When Wade gently pulled the curtain aside, he gasped. "Are you kidding me?"

From the square outside, the plain facade of Gran Teatro La Fenice gave little hint of the opulent and enormous theater inside. The walls were painted gold. Sconces of spherical lights outside each box shone like fairy bulbs on the orchestra-level seats below. Dozens of boxes on five levels were filling up, while hundreds of people moved about in the aisles below. The orchestra pit was peopled by black-suited musicians, tuning, playing scales and melodies, chatting, or calmly waiting for everyone to sit.

Their box opened onto the hall like its own stage, while the box itself was luxury Wade had never experienced before. Beside the velvet-covered railing were eight tufted armchairs aimed at a precise angle to the stage. The chairs were gold and white and reminded him of the furniture in Terence's apartment in New York. As if the theater weren't showy enough, a heavy crystal chandelier hung from the center of the ceiling, bathing the hall in brilliant, warm light. It blinked once, twice, and they sat down in the shadows of the box and waited.

Wade knew Mozart, of course, though Bach, being so mathematical, was his favorite composer. Still, he was eager to hear *The Magic Flute* and wished Darrell were there with him to appreciate it. On the other hand, he wanted to be discovering the location of Greywolf with Darrell and his father in Saint Petersburg, too. He decided to phone his father. It went to voice mail. He tried Darrell and that too went to voice mail.

Five minutes passed. No one entered the box from the hall. The lights dimmed. The last remaining guests took their seats; everyone quieted.

"I hope they find where Greywolf is," Wade whispered.

"They will," said Becca.

"I believe so, too," said the inspector. "Let me tell you, I will be happy to get you back together with them as soon as I can. I am far out of my comfort here. But hush now. It begins. Eyes open."

The conductor waved his baton several times, and the audience's quiet turned to utter silence. It was an amazing moment, but nothing like the one that followed, when the conductor flicked his baton up.

Coming from such profound silence, the initial chord of the overture was thunderous and deep, a call to attention and an invitation to the mystery to follow, as if to say, *Wake up! Listen, and you'll hear a fantastic story . . . !*

From that instant on, Wade was hooked.

Whenever Becca heard a piece of music that touched her somehow—and *The Magic Flute*'s overture was exhilarating and deeply moving—she wanted to share it right away with her sister. Maggie was far more musical than she was. As soon as she made it back to Austin, and everyone was safe again, Becca would share this, too.

The overture ended with booming chords, kettle drums, and bright strings, and the audience applauded wildly. This lasted several seconds, until the conductor raised his baton high once more, and the hall quieted again.

With intimations of danger, the stage curtain lifted on a scene of stylized rocks in a wilderness of mountains.

A man named Tamino came in singing urgently. The insistent strains of violins rose and fell behind him. Still singing, he pulled an arrow out of a quiver and shot it offstage.

The arrow reminded Becca that they were looking for Galina. She scanned the rows of spectators below. But would the leader of the Teutonic Order be sitting among them? No, she'd be moving around like a cat, in the halls, maybe in the high seats, searching.

The children in the audience shrieked with delight. A green, scaly, outrageously horned, and slightly comical serpent appeared. A serpent, of all things!

With human feet obviously visible below the scaly hide, the serpent opened its mechanical jaws. It belched out a cloud of red smoke, as if it were breathing fire. It lunged awkwardly at the man, who shot more arrows. Then the serpent wounded the man. He fell. At the same time, three cloaked figures emerged from behind one of the strange rock formations. They carried spears, and—singing, of course—they stabbed the serpent, who fell over in a heap, which set the children cheering once more.

Despite the opera's comedic elements, Becca saw another story unfolding. The evil serpent was Albrecht. Copernicus was the archer, and the three mysterious helpers who slayed the serpent were none other than the Guardians.

Becca glanced over at Lily and Wade. Their mouths were open, their eyes fixed on the stage. She tapped Lily's hand.

Lily turned to her. Her cheeks were wet. "It's so . . ."

"It is!" Becca whispered.

The opera was performed in German, but the super-titles were in Italian. Either way, only Becca and, from the look of it, Inspector Yazinsky understood the story, though it was easy enough to grasp the action. After the serpent-slaying scene, there appeared a comical friend of the archer. This was the bird catcher Papageno, a scruffy-looking guy laden with birdcages. *Birdcages!* She thought of Boris again and grew sad. Though parts of the story were funny, it was hard not to see it as deadly serious. The story centered on a flute with magical pow-ers, but its true meaning was in the trials of the young archer and a young woman who was the captive of a bunch of evil people. That, too, was like their life right now.

Sara was the captive.

After what seemed like a short while but was nearly an hour, Wade leaned over to her and Lily. He was frowning. "If no one's going to show, maybe the message for Boris is hidden in the box somewhere. Or maybe we've been fooled—"

The hall door whooshed open behind them and the velvet curtain twisted aside. An older woman in a gown stood there, clutching the curtain, her face as pale as ice. Inspector Yazinsky rose instantly. "Madam, you are hurt?"

"Where is Boris?" she gasped. "Galina Krause . . ."

"Boris is dead," Wade said, rising from his chair. "Galina killed him. Is she *here*—?"

The woman stumbled forward, tearing the curtain from its rings. She fell awkwardly toward the inspector, then slid to the floor among the chairs. The black handle of a knife protruded from her side.

"She . . . took . . . it . . . ," the woman gasped.

"It? Boris's message?" asked Wade.

The inspector bolted out the door into the hall. "I'll follow Galina."

"I'll get a doctor!" said Wade, and he ran out of the box with the inspector.

"Help is coming," Lily said to the woman as she and Becca knelt next to her.

"I never knew what the message meant," the woman mumbled. "Only Boris . . . the clock . . ." Her voice faded as the music continued.

"What clock?" asked Lily. "Did you have a clock for Boris?"

"Midnight . . ." The woman's eyes glazed, and breath rushed out of her mouth.

"Oh no. Oh no." Becca leaned over the railing. "Doctor!" she cried. "We need a doctor!" People in the neighboring boxes tried at first to shush her. *"Medico!"* she shouted. *"Abbiamo bisogno di un medico!"*

The music stopped raggedly. Faces stared up from the orchestra and the stage. The rear door of the box opened. Wade rushed in with a handful of medical personnel.

"Galina stole the message, a clock," Lily said. "Where's the inspector?"

"Following her. Come on!" Wade took Becca and Lily by the wrists and pulled them after him. "She's escaping, but we can catch her." They pushed against the crushing flow of people running to box 317.

CHAPTER FORTY-THREE

Wade was out quickly enough to see Inspector Yazinsky racing after Galina down a set of stone steps leading to the water. Galina flew like a shadow around a corner and vanished. Wade panicked. She reappeared on the stone landing.

"Is she alone?" asked Becca "I don't see—"

"Not likely," said Lily. "Not if there's a relic at stake."

But is the relic here? Wade wondered as they tore down the steps to the inspector. Or was Galina in Venice only to intercept the message meant for Boris? And a message about what? From whom? Galina wouldn't take this side trip from Russia by herself. Then where were the others?

The Italian faction of the Order they hadn't seen yet?

They reached the water just as Galina hopped into a waiting motorboat. The man at the helm didn't look like an agent of the Order, but he gunned the engine loudly, and the boat roared away. The inspector waved to the boats, calling in Russian. They didn't move.

Becca pushed down the steps in front of him. *"Un motoscafo! Presto!"*

One started up his motor and whirred quietly toward the landing. *"Sì? Per dove?"*

Becca pointed down the canal. *"Seguire quella barca!"*

The pilot wagged his head from side to side when the inspector drew out his badge. Then Lily waved a ten-euro note at him. *"Sì! Sì!"* he said. They jumped in. He threw the boat into gear.

What Wade hoped would be a high-speed chase was anything but. The canal outside the theater, Rio delle Veste, was narrow and clogged with scores of black gondolas moored along the sides. Slicing past them, Galina's boat nearly tore one of them in half.

"Faster!" said Wade.

"Is electric motor," the pilot said. "For eco, yes?"

"That woman stole something from us!" Becca snapped. "Chase her!"

"*Sì*, but, *la polizia*," said the pilot.

"I *am* the *polizia*!" boomed the inspector, slapping his badge again.

"Not here you not," the driver said.

Lily pushed two more bills into his hand. "Go!"

The pilot shrugged and hit the accelerator. They made up some of the distance, but Galina's gas-powered boat was pulling away. Then, seconds before it vanished around the corner, she turned back, her hair flying around her face. There was a silent flash of light from the vicinity of her hip, a splash, and the sound of a thud striking their motorboat below the waterline.

The inspector tugged out a small pistol. "Keep your heads down!"

"*Che cosa?*" the driver cried out. "*No, no—*"

When Galina's own driver realized she was firing a gun, he cut the engine and began shouting at her. So, he wasn't one of her agents. She whipped her gun at him, and he splashed noisily into the canal. She took the wheel herself.

"Please!" Becca urged. "It's life and death!"

"Death of motor license!" the pilot said, even as he jammed down the accelerator.

They trailed Galina left onto the curving Rio dei Barcaroli. Pedestrians on the bridges overhead shouted in punctuated phrases—curses, Wade was certain—but their boat sped underneath, barely squeezing past gondolas that looked suddenly like bobbing coffins. Galina yelled out something in Italian, and dark figures swarmed out of the shadows on the sides of the canal and darted across the bridges, taking aim with pistols.

Shots slapped dully into the water in front of their boat. The pilot swerved once, twice, eluding them, and made it past the bridge. Galina's boat thundered north onto the Rio di San Luca. Wade saw an approaching marker leaning over the canal like a dented street sign. Rio Fuseri. "She's heading for the Grand Canal. We can cut her off if we go right."

"Please," the driver said. "Too much traffic. Too much police launches. Is forbidden."

"I'll deal with them," said Yazinsky. "Do as Wade says!"

Another ten euros from Lily and the driver roared into the Rio Fuseri, picking up speed as they lost sight of her.

"This better be the right move," Lily growled. "We could lose her altogether."

"We won't," Wade said, hoping he was right. Galina had stolen what they needed desperately—without leverage, his stepmother was in more danger. He wasn't going to leave Venice without it. The canal was blocked at the next intersection with a mangle of gondolas. The driver sped right, then turned left behind the great piazza. They could see the domes of the basilica lit up like giant festive balloons.

They zigzagged right, then left and left again, away from the piazza, and burst suddenly out onto the Grand Canal in a wide sweep of spray. The famous Rialto Bridge arched over the water straight ahead. And there was Galina, headlights glaring, speeding toward them from the opposite direction. Her face was pale, angry, startled.

She cut her engine suddenly. Wade studied her face, her strange, hypnotic eyes glinting in the canal lights, the hanging lamps, the lacquered hulls of the gondolas, the lights from the houses looming over the water. Time seemed to pause for a second. He saw in her eyes that she would do anything to avoid being caught.

Shoot them all dead, if she had to.

Then it was over. She gunned the engine and aimed toward them.

Inspector Yazinsky aimed his pistol. "Full speed ahead!"

"Sul serio?" their driver spat. He matched Galina's speed, his motor whirring like a top, then tried to steer

away when he realized she wasn't going to stop. Too late. The boats scraped each other horribly, and Wade found himself a bare two feet away from Galina. His legs took over, and he leaped from their boat right onto the deck of hers.

An instantaneously stupid move. He crashed to his knees, then staggered to his feet, pain knifing up his legs. Galina whipped him across the face with the side of her hand. Her hand!

It was ice-cold and strong as steel. It flattened him. He tried to climb to his feet, but she had the engine at full throttle. He thudded awkwardly onto the deck, half on and half off the boat, water spitting into his face. He arched up again. "You! Always you!" she cried, kicking his legs out from under him.

He slammed back to the deck but managed to swing his arm around, clamping onto her leg. He pulled with all his strength. She fell to the planks. The engine idled while the wheel was locked in an ever-widening turn.

"Wade!" Becca yelled from somewhere. "You—"

"Stop at once!" the inspector bellowed at Galina.

Wade couldn't hear the rest. He grasped at Galina's hand, trying to force the gun away from her, when he saw a shiny disc on the deck. The clock! She had dropped it! Releasing Galina, risking that she would turn the gun back on him, he dived for the clock with both hands, when she swung her gun at his head. It was like being struck by a baseball bat. He was up and over the side, half falling, half jumping, and fell headfirst into the canal.

CHAPTER FORTY-FOUR

"**W**ade! Omigod, Wade!"

Becca was half out of their boat as it drew alongside, grasping at the water with the inspector. Wade flailed and splashed like a drowning man. Together they lifted him out.

"I have it," he gasped, spitting out a mouthful of canal water. "I . . ."

"Here come the police launches," said Yazinsky.

"Galina took off," Lily added. "She's gone. We can't get stuck here. Come on."

Becca draped her jacket over Wade's shivering shoulders, and she and Lily squashed him between them. Their awesome driver, to whom Lily gave another twenty euros, motored them quickly to the nearest landing. Hurried away by the inspector, the kids disappeared into the crowded streets just as the Venice traffic police arrived with sirens blaring.

At the first corner, Wade stopped hobbling along. "Wait," he said. "Look."

When he showed them what he had stolen from Galina, Becca recognized it instantly. "That's a souvenir of the Saint Mark's clock. The astronomical clock in Piazza San Marco. The messenger said it was a clue for Boris that only he would understand."

"She also said 'midnight,'" Lily added.

"It's nearly midnight now," Yazinsky said. "Do you think that Boris was to go to the clock in the piazza?"

Wade shivered in Becca's jacket. "I don't know. But there's probably something with the clock that we need to see. There are bells, right? Chimes? Maybe something will happen when they ring at midnight, something that Boris was supposed to see."

"Quickly, then," the inspector urged.

They zigzagged through the streets, the inspector leading them along the fringes of any piazzas they had to cross, joining bunches of tourists as a shield. They saw neither Galina nor any agents she might have in Venice. Four minutes before midnight, they emerged from the Salita San Moise, through the colonnade, and into Piazza San Marco. Even at that late hour, the crowds were heavy and noisy. Soon the bell atop the tower began to chime, struck by two monumental bronze figures with hammers. Twenty-four slow, momentous peals that seemed to roll beneath the stones under their feet and out into the lagoon.

At the fading of the last of the echoes, everyone resumed their strolling and talking. Becca, Wade, Lily, and Inspector Yazinsky just stared at the clock. A minute passed, another minute, five minutes.

"Nothing's happening," said Lily. "What did the messenger mean? 'Midnight'? Are we supposed to go up there and find something behind the clock or in the mechanism or something? What's the message? Don't tell me we have to climb up there. . . ."

"I can get us in, if it comes to that," Yazinsky said.

On a whim, Becca hurried over to a vendor's stall just closing up. She quickly found souvenir clocks similar to the one meant for Boris. But they were not identical. She called them over. "These souvenirs are trinkets, not nearly as detailed as ours is. Ours is metal, not plastic, with movable faces and all. It's much more like the real one."

Wade took Boris's clock from her. Even before being

aware of it, his fingers started working the miniature like a Rubik's Cube, twisting and turning its various faces and dials, trying to match its faces to the one on the tower, setting the time to midnight.

A shrill whistle sounded from the motor launch landing along the water's edge. It would soon make its final run to the airport.

"We should go," said Lily.

"Hold on," he said, still working the miniature clock, shifting its movable parts to show the exact moment of midnight. Nothing happened. It was a dead metal toy in his hands, until he twisted the tiny moon's face a fraction backward, so less gold peered out of its face. Then—*click*—the back of the clock sprang open in his palm.

CHAPTER FORTY-FIVE

Under the warm blue-black sky, her heart thumping at this new discovery, Becca studied the device in Wade's palm. Inside its open cover were four unusual characters—not inscribed, but scratched, roughly, as if in haste.

"They are not Cyrillic," Yazinsky said. "I have never seen such marks."

Wade moved the clock closer to the nearest lamp-light and turned to Becca.

"Don't ask me," she said. "I was going to ask if they're math symbols or something from physics maybe."

He shook his head. "I don't know all the symbols in trigonometry—my dad does—but these aren't any astronomical or mathematical symbols I've ever seen. Hieroglyphics, maybe?"

Becca didn't think so.

"If Darrell were here," Lily said, "he'd go, 'Aaatheee.' Because if you squint, the letters almost look like they could be *A-T-H-E*—"

Becca breathed in sharply. "Boris was a scholar of dead languages. This message was meant for him. A dead language from some old civilization. Oh, what did Boris say at the restaurant about it . . . ? Wade, your notebook."

His cell phone buzzed. "Here." He gave her the notebook. "It's Darrell. It's three in the morning there!" He switched the phone on speaker. "Darrell, what's going on—"

"Greywolf is a creepy old castle," Darrell interrupted, his voice hoarse, faraway, gloomy. "We checked it a dozen different ways on lots of crumbly old maps, and we're sure. It's two hundred miles from anywhere.

Plus it's, well, never mind. You have to meet us in Saint Petersburg. Pulkovo Airport it's called. We'll fly from here. What's happening down there?"

"We got a little wet," Becca said. "Mostly Wade. Galina stole the message meant for Boris, but Wade fought her and stole it back. We don't know what it says yet."

"Don't tell Dad about me fighting her," Wade said. He took a breath. "Boris's contact in Venice was attacked by Galina. We had to leave her. I don't know . . ."

"The Order is taking out the Guardians, one by one," the inspector said, leaning in to the phone.

"Is there any word about Mom?" asked Wade.

"Just get here as soon as you can, that's all."

The call ended with that grim statement. The launch blasted its horn once more for passengers.

"Come, come," Yazinsky said. "There's no reason anymore to remain in Venice. We must return to Russia."

An hour later, the four of them were in their seats on a small jet ascending from the Marco Polo Airport. After a brief layover in Moscow, they would arrive in Saint Petersburg at dawn on Sunday. The day of the midnight deadline.

At which time a weird machine would do something horrible to Sara.

"Listen to this," Becca said, studying Wade's notebook. "Boris said that a world-famous code was solved when he and his brother were young and living in Siberia. That must have been in the 1950s. He said that *A* and *B* was a kind of joke to them. And they sent coded messages 'even when we grow up.' What do you think that means? That *A* and *B* was a joke?"

Lily nodded. "I'm typing it all in—Boris, Aleksandr, *A, B*, dead languages, Siberia, the whole business."

Wade stared out the window down at the receding lights of Venice. Only from up there could he truly see the serpentine shape of the Grand Canal that he had fallen into, winding away through the narrow streets of the city. "Aleksandr is dead, so someone else sent Boris this message in their old code."

Lily let out a long slow breath, her fingers poised over the tablet's screen. "Well . . . there was something called Linear A and Linear B, ancient languages discovered in the early twentieth century. No one has cracked A, but Linear B was decrypted in the 1950s."

"When Boris and Aleksandr were boys," said Becca.

"It is a wonder to watch you work," the inspector said. "You are rather amazing."

"Thanks," said Lily. "We're learning." She hit another link, then another, started scrolling and scrolling, then stopped. "Yes, oh, yes! This is it. The message inside the clock is written in Linear B. Look."

She flipped the tablet around for everyone to see.

"The note for Boris uses the symbols of Linear B," she said. "Each symbol translates to the sound shown

underneath each character."

The four characters of the message . . . translated to . . . *wo ro ku ta*.

"What's *worokuta*?" Becca asked. "Lil, again, please?"

She typed that in. "There's 'Wirikuta.' It's a site sacred to the Wixárika Nation, Indians in Mexico. It's supposed to be the place the world was created—"

"No," Becca said.

"It's *not* where the world was created?" asked Wade.

"No, *worokuta* is not *Wirikuta*," she said, "because there are actual Linear B symbols for 'wi' and 'ri,' but the message uses the ones for 'wo' and 'ro,' which means that whoever sent it was saying something else to Boris."

They looked to the inspector. "I am sorry. I wish I could tell you what *worokuta* means, but I studied criminal justice, not dead languages. It means nothing to me."

They all went quiet. Their most recent rest had been on the flight to Venice, many long hours before. Since then, the attack on the Guardian messenger at the opera, the canal chase, the enigma of the clock's strange code, and Darrell's gloomy message had left them drained and exhausted.

They really needed to rest.

But Wade knew they never would.

CHAPTER FORTY-SIX

Saint Petersburg
March 24

Darrell stared from the windows of the arrivals hall at Saint Petersburg's Pulkovo Airport as he had without pause for nearly three hours, hoping every incoming flight would be his brother's jet from Venice by way of Moscow.

His stepfather was pacing as usual, but Darrell found himself frozen to the spot, unable to do anything but scan the sky for incoming aircraft. He feared that the moment he left his post, or moved a single atom of air, the last three hours of fruitless waiting would reset and begin again.

Greywolf was a centuries-old fortress buried in ever-green forests and rocky terrain more than two hundred miles from where he was standing. His mother was a prisoner there, trapped inside a device that was ticking down to midnight that night, a mere fifteen hours away.

But if Galina Krause had kidnapped his mother as ransom to force them to give her Vela—and Serpens, if they had it—why, Darrell asked himself, why was his mother in a machine ticking down to something horrible?

Why kill my mother?

What does the machine do?

A flurry of people broke into the baggage area. Looking exhausted, dragging luggage, they swarmed across the floor. Then he saw three people weaving through the crowd, running when they could, followed by a tall mustached man. There was Lily's worried face. Then Wade's. Finally Becca's. There was no reunion, no time for one.

"Terence will be here soon," Darrell said, hurrying to meet them. "Flying one of those NetJet thingies, a private plane from London. He's a pilot. A good one, they say. Anyway, Greywolf is an old castle, two hundred miles outside the city. An hour's flight. Once we get started."

"Darrell found the fortress," Roald told them. "We confirmed and double confirmed it, but he found it first."

"It's that brain." Wade gave Darrell a soft punch in the arm. "Every once in a while, he blows out the cobwebs, and it works. It even surprises him. Not us, though."

Darrell wanted to laugh, but he couldn't make himself. All he saw was his mother's face and *it*—a giant clockwork machine . . . gears and wheels . . . "Greywolf is a horrible place. But we have help." He nodded toward the two investigators, who were busily checking their computers. "They're coming with us."

Terence landed at noon, two hours later than expected. He'd had to switch jets at the last moment, for one with a greater flight range.

"So sorry," he said. "But the delay gave me time to consult with the archivist at the Ministry of Defence in London. She discovered a rare aerial snapshot of the area taken in 1941. It's apparently the last clear photo of the place before the Soviets completed camouflaging the grounds. The image indicates a private landing strip on the Greywolf property." He enlarged it on his phone. "Pray that the strip is still functional."

As soon as his jet had refueled, the Kaplans, Paul, and Marceline took their seats in the cabin and Terence in the cockpit. The jet was a sleek winged missile with a single large cabin, and a half-dozen swivel chairs and low tables. According to Terence, it was quite fast and nimble.

"There's an arctic blast roaring down from Finland," he said from the cockpit. "We've no time to lose if we're to stay ahead of it."

Within minutes, the jet was speeding down the tarmac. It lifted off into a bleak gray sky, even as the first wave of snow moved in from the west. Darrell checked his watch. It was 1:07 p.m. Ten hours and fifty-three minutes to midnight.

CHAPTER FORTY-SEVEN

Republic of Karelia, Northwest Russia

Now that they were on their way to Greywolf—all eight of them—Lily wondered if they would bust into Galina's creepy lair with guns blazing and bombs booming. Well, guns, anyway. The two private investigators were huddled together, checking and rechecking their weapons.

"The Red Brotherhood will be in force," Paul Ferrere said. "We must expect a battle."

"We will shield you to do your work," said Marceline.

Our work, Lily thought. *We know that Sara's there, caged up in a machine with gears and wheels and junk—whatever that is. But is the relic there, too? And what about* worokuta?

Becca and Wade were furiously consulting their notebooks to put that latest clue into place. Lily knew that soon her digital fiddling wouldn't cut it anymore. The relic hunt, the *Sara* hunt, would soon become physical. Analog. Trekking through the trees and rocks and snow. Not Lily's area of intelligence officering.

But right now she was ready for the next digital problem they might throw at her.

"Anything?" she asked.

Wade tapped a page in his notebook. "There are words I must have gotten wrong when Boris was talking. He said 'log punked.' Remember that?"

"I do," said Darrell. "He and Alek sent messages to each other 'even in log punked.'"

"Well, I know I got it wrong," said Wade, "but does anyone remember it better?"

Lily had forgotten *log punked*. Probably because she'd been too busy deciding which of Boris's eyes to respond to.

But Uncle Roald tilted his head as if searching the air between their seats. "You told me Boris said he grew up in a labor camp, because that's where his father was sent after the Second World War, right? Well, the Soviet system of labor camps was called the gulag. It's an anagram of some kind, but the 'ag' in Russian is a common thing. Maybe Boris was saying *l-a-g* something, not *l-o-g* something. Whatever that might mean."

"Is that enough to start?" Becca asked Lily.

"Since you asked so nicely . . ." But no sooner had Lily keyed in the letters *l-a-g-p-u* than the search window filled in the remaining letters.

l-a-g-p-u-n-k-t

Holding her fingers up to get everyone's attention, she hit Enter.

The plane bucked once, and her screen froze. The connection was severed.

Terence came on the address system. "Sorry about that. The storm is moving down really fast—" Another slight loss of altitude shook the cabin. "I'm trying to fly south of it. It'll increase our flying time, but maybe we can gain time later. Hold on."

A few rough minutes passed before they were cruising more steadily. Lily tried again. The connection was restored. She rekeyed the search on *lagpunkt* and hit Enter for the second time. The screen refreshed.

"'A *lagpunkt* is a subsection of a forced labor camp,'" she read. "Which is helpful but not too specific." She hit a second link, which featured an excerpt from a book about the history of Siberian labor camps. She silently scanned a paragraph about the day the inmates received the news of Josef Stalin's death in 1953—Stalin being the guy who'd exiled many of them to the labor camps in the first place. It said that Stalin would be buried with honors in Red Square. Boris had told them that, too. Lily quickly read the rest of the piece, then nearly jumped out of her seat.

In a very slow voice, she said, "There is a reference here to . . . to . . . Hey, are you all listening? There is a reference here to a . . . 'Vorkuta *lagpunkt*.'"

Becca gasped. "Vorkuta! *Worokuta!* Lily, you—are—brilliant!"

"I know, right?" Lily said. "There's got to be more." Which there was. Again, thanks to the nifty feature that filled in the letters of a possible search even before you keyed it all in, she typed *v-o-r-k* and, boom, the term was identified.

"Vorkuta is a Russian industrial city in Siberia, about eleven hundred miles from Saint Petersburg. We're actually flying in the same direction right now. It was a big coal mining area from the nineteen thirties. There was a prison camp there until the nineteen seventies. Now it's a giant city with a shrinking population and not much coal. . . ."

"So what are we saying?" asked Darrell. "That's where the relic is? Or part of it?"

"Maybe," said Roald. "But if there were any records, we *might* find that Vorkuta is where Boris and his brother grew up, and where they sent coded messages to each other."

"Whoa." Becca's eyes widened. "Someone sent a coded message to Boris that said 'Vorkuta'?"

"But Aleksandr is dead," said Wade. "I have proof right here in my pocket. So who would send the message, and what would it mean to Boris?"

"Those are the questions," Roald said. "After the witnesses, the dental records, all of Boris's research, he would never have believed Alek was sending him a message. He knew Alek was dead. But maybe Alek hid something in Vorkuta, and a Guardian found it and sent a message to Boris. The Guardian used the old code, knowing that Boris would have to come. He just never got the message."

The nose of the jet dropped suddenly. Water bottles, mugs, whatever was loose flew off the tables. Becca nearly dropped the diary. Overhead lights flickered.

"Whoa!" Darrell said. "What's going on—"

The jet dipped again, this time at a steeper angle,

and the engines shrieked in protest.

"The storm," said Wade. "Maybe the wings are icing over—"

"Stay put!" Roald staggered to the cockpit, throwing the door open. "What's the trouble?"

"Wind shear!" Terence said, working hard to lift the jet back up and keep control. "Unfortunately, we have to head right back into the track of the storm."

"We're close to Greywolf, are we not?" Marceline asked as she studied the chart.

"Very close, I think," Terence said.

"Can you keep going?" Darrell asked, clutching the door frame next to his father. Wade was out of his seat now too, and staggering down the aisle to the front.

"The wings have iced up and are starting to drag us down," Terence murmured. "I don't know how long I can—"

The words were lost under the sound of the crying engines. Lily stared at Becca. They were both clutching their seat handles so tightly neither could move. "Becca, we better not be going to cra—"

"Don't say it! Don't you dare!"

One of the engines began to whine strangely. The jet tilted suddenly. Wade spun down the aisle and landed on the floor in front of Becca. She screamed.

"I have to land!" Terence said. "Brace yourselves; it's going to be rough!"

The next thing Lily knew, everything was bouncing around the cabin. Roald and Darrell slid back into the aisle sideways, then pitched forward again. Paul crawled over to help them. There was a deep groan of metal. The landing gear dropped. The underside of the jet beneath their feet was battered from below. The jet was slicing into the trees.

"I see a clearing—hold tight!"

"We're going down!" Lily yelled.

Branches slapped the wings; then there was a thunderous squeal of metal as the landing gear and the hull of the jet went skidding along the frozen ground. As hard as Lily tried, she couldn't keep herself together. She started screaming.

CHAPTER FORTY-EIGHT

Greywolf

In the large, lead-lined tower of Greywolf, Ebner von Braun observed the miserable form of Sara Kaplan, folded inside the cage at the center of Kronos, shivering like a waif in a storm. It crossed his mind that even if she did not know precisely what awaited her, she must have had an inkling, a premonition, and it was taking its toll on her health. *Expendable.* That was the word Galina had used.

Helmut Bern clacked furiously on his computer, attempting to finish the patch of programming necessary to resuscitate the crude prototype.

Screening out for a moment the machine's pathetic

inmate, Ebner gazed over his own workmanship. If Kronos I was crude, he had to admit that it was also very beautiful. It had survived the terrible fire and suffered four years of disuse, but Helmut, good soldier that he was, had burnished the machine to a brilliant sheen and restored its moving parts to pristine running order.

In a rage since her empty-handed return from Venice, Galina scowled suddenly. "We should send her now! Send her!"

Bern nearly turned himself inside out with shock. "What? No! Please not yet! She'll be destroyed in transit." Then, his breath blooming icily in front of him, he whined, "Miss Krause . . . I beg you . . ."

Galina sneered and looked away. A reprieve for poor Helmut.

"You are an obedient servant, Helmut Bern," Ebner said with, he hoped, a hint of irony.

Kronos was mostly Ebner's own handiwork—based on Galina's fevered vision—and he loved it like a first, awkward child. He was elated to see it humming once more, and horrified to realize that every experiment involving it had claimed at least one life.

The door to the laboratory resounded with a knock. Galina turned. "Enter."

It was Bartolo Cassa, the sunglasses-wearing

muscleman who managed to be everywhere at the same time, like a tabloid celebrity. "Miss Krause," he said, "the injured guard has died of his wounds. Since then, the escaped prisoner must have made contact with the Kaplans. The family has left Saint Petersburg, heading east by jet. They have also had high-level assistance from a Guardian in the FSB."

"Alert the Brotherhood to increase security over every acre of the property," Ebner said. "The family will enter a trap. Is there anything else?"

Cassa nodded. "A report from the Copernicus Room. The messenger Miss Krause eliminated in Venice . . ."

"Yes?" she said.

"The clock she possessed was owned by the courier you neutralized in Prague. The message it likely contained originated elsewhere. It has been traced backward to its source."

Galina merely tilted her head. It was the signal for Cassa to speak.

He did.

One word.

"Vorkuta."

Vorkuta? It was as if Ebner were being punished for thinking he was as cold as he could be. The godforsaken Siberian city of Vorkuta was an iceberg in a land of ice.

"Bring the transport around," she said frostily to Cassa. "We go to the airfield immediately." She turned away from him as if he were no longer there, and in a moment he was not. "Helmut Bern, you will be successful."

The programmer's stubbled head turned to her, his features dappled with sweat, his hands trembling with fear. "Miss Krause, I am working as quickly—"

A frown. "Did I ask you?"

Bern shot a glance at Ebner but must have realized he was floating alone on a frozen sea. "Yes. Of course, Miss Krause," he managed. "That is to say, no, you did not ask, and yes . . . we are on schedule. We will be successful."

Galina smiled icily. "Ebner, we own the best people."

He attempted to match her smile. "We *are* the Teutonic Order."

Galina whipped around and exited the chamber with him, bolting and locking the laboratory from the outside. On the landing, she said, "Greywolf will live up to its name, Ebner. Let the wolves loose in the castle. If the Brotherhood should fail on the grounds, the wolves will protect Kronos until our return."

When they were out the front door, Ebner told the stony-faced local leader of the Red Brotherhood to empty the building except for Bern and the woman and to release the wolves into the fortress. For dramatic effect, he added, "Release the kraken!"

When the guard tilted his head in puzzlement, Ebner pointed wearily to the stables. "Release the wolves into the house!"

"Sir," the guard said, his expression stony once more.

The military transport started up, with the ever-present Bartolo Cassa at its wheel.

"We will be in Vorkuta in three hours, Ebner," Galina said.

Vorkuta, he mused. *Where "warm" is twenty degrees below zero.*

CHAPTER FORTY-NINE

The last thing Wade remembered before he didn't remember anything else was Becca's face, staring into his and screaming. He was on the floor under her seat, and she was screaming at him. Then nothing for a while; then he woke, still under Becca's seat, but she wasn't in it. Pain shot up his legs and into his sides when he tried to stand.

"So . . . we made it . . . ," he said.

"No. We didn't," Darrell grunted from somewhere. "We all died."

Terence Ackroyd had piloted the jet like a bird among the trees, so incredibly precisely that everyone was only banged up, which was still like having been tumbled in a dryer for thirty minutes, but was better than being dead, which he was pretty sure he wasn't, despite Darrell's claim.

But that could change, he told himself.

Marceline Dufort jerked open the cabin door, and the snowstorm flew inside. Bracing themselves, they climbed out into the blinding snow and found themselves in a narrow clearing about fifty feet from a mainly straight road that might have made a better landing strip but had been hidden from above by the trees. Wade and Darrell staggered to their father and the others.

"I'm going to get the radio going," Terence was saying. "I think I can fly us out of here, but NetJet will send a rescue chopper anyway—after the storm passes."

"Wait, no," said Marceline, consulting the aerial photograph. "Look here." The top of the image showed the vague shape of the structure that was Greywolf, but the detective drew her finger to a road winding through the woods at the very lowest edge of the image. "I think this is where we are."

Wade's father stretched, his face grimacing with pain, as he scanned the trees around them. "How far do you think we are from the castle?"

"At the edge of the property, but not too far,"

Marceline said. "Perhaps ten kilometers. And see here. Only one kilometer from Greywolf's landing strip."

"I agree," said her partner, checking a compass and then pointing up into the deeper woods. "The land rises steeply from here on, the forest is thick, and there are ledges and chasms all over the property, many of them man-made to deter intruders."

"What are you saying?" asked Wade.

Paul grunted. "That it will be a hard climb, but I agree that we not wait for a chopper. We lost nearly an hour because of the storm. It is already almost three in the afternoon. If we climb to Greywolf steadily, we can make it by nightfall, with time to spare before the deadline. *If* we don't run into the Brotherhood, a big *if*."

"Are kilometers more or less than miles?" Lily asked.

"Shorter," said Becca.

"Doesn't matter," said Darrell. "We're going on."

"All right then," said Terence. He pulled a handgun from inside the plane and shoved it into his coat pocket.

Wade's father nodded. "Get your gear, everyone. We have a deadline. But first, listen." He brushed snow from his hair and pulled up his hood. "Darrell, you and the investigators know this, but the others don't. During World War Two, Stalin visited Greywolf many times. All the roads on the property were monitored then.

Sometime in the sixties electronic surveillance was installed and probably updated a few times since then. We're entering the enemy camp here. We've never done anything like this before."

"Let's hope we're far enough away that our landing didn't alert the Order," said Terence. "But I guess we have to assume our jet won't be a secret too long."

"Indeed," Marceline added, checking her automatic. "For now we have the element of surprise, as long as we stay smart and keep off the roads. We don't want a firefight, but we must be ready for one."

Darrell swiped on his cell. "Less than nine hours to midnight."

And that was it. They began marching upward in single file, Roald and the children in a group, Terence and the investigators in the lead, armed and fanning out to cover more territory.

Darrell kept his head low. The wind and the blinding snow and ice that had forced the jet down were mercifully less on the ground. The heavy snow seemed to collect in the dense branches above them more than fall on them, but the upward trek was slow and tiring. A half hour—that seemed twice that, Darrell thought—passed without any sense of progress.

Other than the rough track weaving through the trees, the first sign of Greywolf being a "property" and not just wilderness was a head-high stone wall that snaked through a portion of the forest. It looked old. Maybe sixteenth century. Terence and the two detectives studied both directions.

"I'll climb over," Paul volunteered. It was relatively easy for him, an ex-soldier, to clamber up and straddle it, but the moment he reached the crest, he fell hard. The topmost stones were rigged to collapse under pressure. Not only that, but the level of the ground on the far side of the wall was at least three feet deeper than the close side. The earth was chewed up, craggy, and rock-strewn for a swath of fifty feet along the inside of the wall. It had been dug up purposely and the ground left open and treacherous. Using the gap Paul had made, they mounted the wall one by one, dropped down with his help, and kept on climbing. Another grueling half hour of stinging snow and wind came and went. Then a narrow light burst through the swirling gray air. It swept across the snowdrifts ahead of them.

"Patrol! Back off into the trees," Paul barked like a squad commander. He and Roald hustled them all over the rocky ground into a dense cluster of firs. Terence and Marceline looked through their binoculars.

An engine downshifted, and a transport truck camouflaged in white and pale green passed slowly along the road about a mile above them. It had a covered back. Sensors fixed high on the trees on either side of the road blinked in rapid succession as the vehicle crept slowly down the incline. It made a turn and vanished.

"Stay here; we're going forward," Terence said. He darted ahead with Marceline to another copse of trees, then another. A minute later, they returned.

"Galina's in the transport," Marceline hissed breathlessly. "I spied her—"

"Galina? Where is she going?" said Wade.

"Maybe to the airstrip," Paul said. "She'll pass the road not far from us."

After three long minutes, they heard the vehicle again, grinding through the gears. From the sound of the engine, Darrell knew it would weave around to that point in the road in less than two minutes. He borrowed the binoculars from Terence.

And there she was.

Galina Krause, the model-beautiful woman from the Berlin cemetery and the cave in Guam and everywhere they happened to be. Her face was as white as snow, her hair as black as night, a ghostly apparition in an army truck.

"The pale guy with the sunken chest is there, too," Darrell said. "They're jammed in the cab with a guy wearing sunglasses." The transport vanished again among the trees. "Another couple of minutes and we'll see it again."

Suddenly, his stepfather was moving. "Paul, Terence, we need to stop that truck. If Galina has Sara in there, we have to—"

"Rocks, branches, anything, throw them all into the truck's path," said Marceline.

"The bigger the better," said Wade. "Make it look like a landslide or something."

The eight of them heaved rocks and branches down into the road. Before long, headlights flashed at the final turn, and the engine growled into a low gear.

"Pull back; flatten," Marceline said, rolling one last rock down. The truck motored toward the curve. The driver noticed the obstacle and jammed on the brakes. The truck slid to a stop, its rear left tire off the road. He leaped out of the cab, went around the front, and swore loud and long in Spanish. Then he pulled out a pistol and observed both sides of the pass.

Ebner stuck his head out of the passenger window. "Why didn't the rockslide set off the sensors?" he barked, but didn't get out of the cab to help.

"I don't know," Sunglasses replied sharply. "I don't see anyone."

"Clear the road," Galina said. "We must go!"

"Yes, Miss Krause." Holstering his pistol, Sunglasses began heaving the rocks and branches to the roadside.

Darrell rose up to his hands and knees. "If Mom is in the back of the truck, I can check without them seeing me."

His father turned in the snow and held him back with an iron grip. "Darrell, no way."

Before anyone could stop him, Wade slid down the ledge in the truck's blind spot. He lifted up the heavy flap that covered the back opening. Instead of just looking in, he hoisted himself up and crawled inside.

Idiot! thought Darrell. *I should be doing that!*

Then Wade poked his head out and shook it, as if to say, *Sara's not here.*

"Then get out of there!" Becca hissed. "Unless Galina's going for the relic . . ."

Terence grunted under his breath. "Becca may be right. I'll go with Wade. Stay with the investigators. We'll be back."

Lily started moving now. "Galina can't be allowed to steal the relic! I'm going."

"You are not!" Becca said, reaching out for her, but

Lily slid to the end of the ledge and crept down with Terence.

Becca nearly choked on her own breath. Neither Darrell nor his father could move or raise their voices. Paul and Marceline had their pistols out, aimed at the driver with the sunglasses. Then it was too late. Lily and Terence climbed into the back of the truck. Sunglasses hopped into the cabin again and started the engine. He shifted it into gear.

Becca and Roald squirmed away from the rim of the ledge and into the trees with Paul and Marceline, while Darrell gaped, wide-eyed, at the receding truck.

His stepfather urged him back and back and back into the trees, but all Darrell could do was watch the headlights fade and then vanish around the next turn.

CHAPTER FIFTY

Wade hoped his brain wasn't completely wrecked, that it was *merely* the brutal cold, his tumbling in the jet landing, several smacks to the head, his near drowning in the Venice canal, and the specter of a horrifying deadline that had combined to make him think sneaking into Galina's truck was even a thing.

When Lily crawled into the truck hissing, "Are you insane?" he kind of had to admit he was. But then so was she, so he had company.

"Did you think this would help?" she whispered.

"I guess I did."

Then Terence appeared, and Wade didn't know what to believe.

"Your father and stepbrother are rather freaking out back there," Terence said. "I don't know who was holding who back."

"What about Becca? What did she think?"

Lily's mouth fell open. "Are you serious?" She was going to swat him, when the truck bounced suddenly into and out of a pothole, nearly throwing Wade on top of her. He managed to roll off next to a long, narrow case that must have been filled with rocks, because it was as heavy as stone.

"That is a weapon," Terence whispered. "A big one." He unzipped the case. Inside was what looked like a rifle with a huge barrel and canisters alongside. "Ooh, a flamethrower. I burned down a ski lodge with one of these."

Lily choked. "You what?"

"Oh yes. That was chapter seventeen of *The Mozart Inferno*. Hold on, I think I might be able to tweak the fuel line a little bit. . . ." He leaned over the flamethrower and began to pick at the controls with his fingers.

Meanwhile, the truck driver—Sunglasses—seemed to aim for every single bump in the road as if it were his job and he wanted a promotion.

Finally Lily said, "Shh," although neither Wade nor Terence had said anything. "We're slowing down. Listen, I hear engines. Do you hear engines? Shh."

The truck dipped into a half dozen more potholes, then slid to a stop on flat, snowy pavement. The engine turned over for a half minute before giving up in a last cloud of purple smoke, which blossomed into the rear compartment.

Footsteps crunched noisily over the snow away from the truck. No one came around back. Drawing his handgun, Terence peeked out the flap; flakes flew in. "Airfield."

It was a long, straight strip of flat land cleared out of the forest and paved. The engine noise Lily had heard came from two snowplows finishing their work a mile down at the far end. The snowfall and wind had lessened, and they could see a small jet, gray and steely and looking as powerful as it was sleek. It was idling about a hundred feet away, its nose pointing down the strip. Two rough-looking men with hoses sprayed deicing fluid on its wings, while its cargo door hung open, touching the tarmac.

Lily glanced at the black case. "Let's get out of here

before anyone comes for the flamethrower."

"Good idea," whispered Terence, zipping up the case again. "Keep your heads down." He glanced out the back and eased his way to the ground. Lily went next. Wade last. They hurried to the nearest cover, a supply hut at the edge of the airstrip. They crouched behind it.

Galina was busy bullying somebody on her phone as she and Ebner climbed a short ladder into the jet. Sure enough, after checking out the cargo bay, Sunglasses returned to the truck. He removed the long case from the rear compartment, then hitched it onto his shoulder as if it were a violin case. He carried it to the jet and slid it into the cargo hold. Then he stomped over to the hut they were hiding behind. There must have been a phone inside, because Wade heard a chime. Sunglasses spoke a series of quick words. Something, something, Vorkuta. He hung up.

Lily shared a look with Wade and Terence. *Vorkuta*, she mouthed. *The relic!*

The moment Sunglasses ascended to the jet's cabin and the cargo door began lifting, Lily stood up. "We need to get on that jet."

"No," said Terence gently, holding her back. "My jet. We know where she's going, and I'm sure I can get it off the ground. If we can make it back to their truck and drive it to where we landed, we'll only be a few minutes behind her. We have to be careful, though. Those guys with the snowplows are still out there. Come on."

It sounded good. *If* they could get Terence's jet off the ground.

Seventeen minutes after slipping cleanly away from the airstrip, Lily was staring through the cockpit window of Terence's NetJet into a world of white as he tried to get the engines going. The snow was heavy once more. The flakes fell large and wet.

"Won't we just crash again?" she asked.

"Oh, we'll make it," Terence said casually, starting the engines. "It'll be a tad bumpy, of course, bouncing over the ground to the road. And there's a bit of a curve in the road, but if we can get up enough speed on the straight, we'll be okay."

"If?" said Wade.

"Better buckle up," Terence added. "Just in case."

The bounce up to the road was more than a tad bumpy. Twice it felt as if the jet would simply topple over, but Terence finally got it into the rutted tracks. "Here goes!"

and read the screen for a few seconds. "Oh, and double oh. It says . . . 'Duke Vasily many had of alliances. One of with' . . . ack! Guess who?"

"The pope," said Darrell. "Napoleon. Dracula! Final answer!"

She shook her head. "The Demon Master, AVH himself!"

"Seriously?" said Wade. "Duke Vasily's ally was Albrecht von Hohenzollern?"

"'Albrecht of Hohenzollern Prussia,'" Lily read. "The one and only Grand Master of the creepy Knights of the Teutonic Order, and the creepy nemesis of Copernicus!"

The reading room went quiet.

Becca closed the diary, unable to read anymore. "So . . . Copernicus meets Maxim Grek in Padua when they're students. Later, when he has to hide the relics, he remembers his college friend, who is now in Russia, where Maxim quickly becomes the enemy of Vasily *and* Albrecht at the same time. Maxim Grek is very possibly our Guardian!"

Lily smiled. "And because the first will circle to the last, Copernicus leaves the clue in Magellan's dagger, which we only found when Becca cracked it—saving *my* life. In other words, you're welcome."

Darrell eased back to the computer. "It goes on . . .

'War plenty. Maxim prison was after and after for his life. Last years in Saint Sergius monastery inside out of Muscovy. Only after Maxim die is he buried. This can be 1556!'" Darrell blinked. "To translate the translation, Maxim was jailed in one monastery after another and finally spent his last years in a place called Saint Sergius, a monastery 'inside out of Muscovy.' He never made it back to Greece. They buried him in the monastery after he died."

"Here's Saint Sergius." Julian turned a large photographic book around. Spread across two pages was a picture of the massive Saint Sergius monastery. It was an enormous and opulent fortress. Towering over its high white stone walls were dozens of plump domes painted brilliant gold or deep blue and flecked all over with silver stars.

"Can you imagine how many places you could hide a relic there?" asked Lily. "Seriously, it makes sense to start at the end of his life and work backward. It's how we zeroed in on Magellan."

Which Becca realized for the first time was true, as it had been for Uncle Henry, too. It was at the end of *his* life that he had passed the secret on to them.

"Man, I wish I was going with you," said Julian.

"Going with us?" Wade asked. "To Russia? Are we

seriously thinking the relic is in Russia?"

"Go to where he died. That's where I would begin," Darrell said. "Russia. The monastery at Saint Sergius. For which, by the way, *you're* welcome."

"All right, then," said Wade. "It would be totally amazing if we think we've already figured out who the Guardian might be. But I'm getting nowhere on what the double-eyed relic is—"

Julian's cell phone buzzed. He swiped it on and answered it. He nodded once, ended the call, and stood up. "We have to go right now."

"Did the Order find us?" said Darrell. "Are they here? Why do we have to leave?"

"For brunch," Julian said. "Our dads are meeting us in half an hour!"

CHAPTER TWELVE

As a precaution, Lily, Julian, and a guard left the Morgan from the old entrance on Thirty-Sixth Street, while Wade, Becca, Darrell, and another guard exited the brownstone through a pair of glass doors at 24 East Thirty-Seventh Street. They met one another a block east of the museum, on Park Avenue, where a brown four-door Honda sedan was idling at the curb. Dennis, the Ackroyds' driver, sat behind the wheel. He smiled and unlocked the doors, the kids climbed in, and the two guards trotted back to the museum.

"Dennis, how are you feeling this morning?" Julian asked.

"Fine today," he said. "Where to?"

"The Water Club."

"I hope they have food, too," said Darrell.

Wade laughed. Darrell was feeling good. They all were. In a couple of short hours, they had gained a solid idea of who the second Guardian was. That was real progress.

Ten minutes later, after zigzagging from block to block across streets and down avenues, they arrived at a broad, low restaurant overlooking the river. Julian thanked Dennis, who drove off to park nearby.

"Your father will arrive in . . . seventeen minutes," said a man at the desk, checking his watch. "Your table is ready for you now."

The dining room smelled deliciously of hot coffee, fried eggs, bacon, and pastries, and Wade's stomach wanted all of them. They crossed the floor to a large round table by a wide bank of windows. Snowflakes, heavier now, were falling gently and dissolving into the river outside.

Becca took a seat next to him. "What's this river?"

"The East River," said Julian. "You can just make out the Williamsburg Bridge."

"Oh." She shivered. "Better to look at it than be on it."

As soon as they were all seated, Wade drew the star

95

chart from his backpack and unfolded it. "The constellation is here, somewhere," he murmured. "The double-eyed beast has got to be one of Ptolemy's original forty-eight constellations. But which one?"

"There are a dozen or so 'beasts,'" Lily said, making air quotes around the last word. "And I'm including dogs, birds, Hydras, dragons, and bears."

Wade nodded. "But some are profiles. Not all of them have both eyes visible." As he looked at his antique sky map, Wade imagined Uncle Henry's kind, old face, and he felt something shut off in his brain. The table, the windows, the snow vanishing into the river, even Becca and the others around him, seemed to fade into the background. His talent for blocking out noises and distractions—so tested lately—came forward.

He mentally ticked off the constellations that couldn't for an instant be considered "double-eyed." That still left a number of water creatures, centaurs, a lion, bears, a dragon, a horse, and more. Studying the golden and silver constellations, he remembered what his father had taught him about stars, and a small thought entered his mind.

Could *double-eyed* refer to the astronomical phenomenon known as a double star? "Huh . . ."

"Huh, what?" asked Lily.

"Well, maybe Copernicus meant that there's a double star in the constellation's head."

"What's a double star?" Darrell asked. "And don't say two stars."

Wade laughed. "Well, they kind of *are* two stars—"

"I asked you not to—"

"Which is why I did. A double star is really where two stars are so close together that they sometimes appear like one really bright star. It's only when you observe them for a long time that you discover that there are two of them. Lily, can you cross-check double stars against Ptolemy's forty-eight constellations?"

"Smart," she said, her fingers already moving over the tablet's screen, "for a non–intelligence officer, that is. I'm searching, searching, and . . . oh."

"You found something already?" asked Julian.

"Actually, no. There are a ton of double stars in the constellations and a bunch where the eyes could be."

Darrell leaned over Wade's notebook. "Well, then, what about this 'unbound' beast? What does that even mean? A wild beast? A beast out of control?"

"Right," said Julian. "Or maybe it's loose somehow? Not together—"

"You mean like Wade?" said Darrell.

"Good one," said Julian. "I mean like in a bunch of

different parts? Is there a constellation, *one* constellation, in more than one part? That *also* has a double star
in its head?"

Wade studied the star chart carefully before ruling
out one constellation after another. Then he stopped,
shaking his head. He ran through the constellations a
second time. He felt a smile coming on that he couldn't
hide. "You got it, Julian. There *is* one constellation that
has two stars in its head, and it *is* in two separate parts,"
he said. "Just one . . ."

They waited.

"Wade. Seriously," said Becca.

"And they call the name of that constellation . . ."

Lily narrowed her eyes at him. "Tell. Us."

"Serpens," he said, tapping the chart directly on the
constellation appearing in the northern sky. "Serpens.
Which stands for—"

"The Serpent, yeah," Darrell said. "We figured it out.
Let's go find it."

"Except . . . look at it," said Wade. "The Serpens constellation really *is* in two parts. In the west is the serpent
head and in the east is the body. In between is the figure of the guy who's wrestling it—Ophiuchus—and
he's got his own other constellation. Serpens is actually
divided into two parts. It's odd that way."

"You're odd that way," Darrell said, squinting over the chart.

"I get it from you," Wade said. "I'm just hoping the relic isn't in two pieces, each one hidden in a different place."

"We'll still find it," Darrell said. "Both of it."

Wade was wondering what it might really mean if the relic was split and hidden in two places when his father and Terence Ackroyd entered the restaurant. They both wore cautious smiles.

"Paul Ferrere is already on his way back to Paris, certain that Sara is in Europe, probably southern Europe," said Terence. "All other destinations for the two jets have been ruled out, and the detectives are paying particular attention to Madrid's several municipal and private airfields."

"Which is very good," Wade's father added. "Their extensive team of investigators is fanning out across the continent."

"Really good!" said Darrell. "This is soooo good!"

"From this moment on, I will be the go-between for the detectives and you," Terence said. "Now, what did you learn at the Morgan?"

"Maxim Grek."

"Serpens."

99

"Russia."

That's what Wade and the others told his father and Terence. Both men countered their arguments here and there, and the kids countered back. This went on during their three-course brunch, until both men agreed that, given the evidence, they were very likely on the right track.

"Russia," Roald said finally. "As soon as Galina finds out, and she *will* find out, she'll bring Sara to Russia, too. If we have no other leads, then Russia is a start. Don't travel visas take several days to get?"

Julian glanced at his father. "Are you thinking what I'm thinking? Comrade Boris?"

Terence seemed strangely reluctant, then nodded. "I think so, yes. There is a man. A Russian fellow. His name is Boris Volkov. He's lived in London for the past few years. I think you should fly there first and see him. He can likely be of help to you."

"Likely?" said Becca.

"Volkov is a scholar of languages and a historian of Russia's medieval period," Terence said. "I met him when I was writing a book about the treasure the Crusaders brought back from the Middle East. He knows a lot about the Order, perhaps the Guardians, too. Whether he is an agent of one or the other, I can't say.

He's quite cagey about what he reveals. But he may be able to help you get into Russia quickly and aid you while you're there. Boris Volkov seems to have . . . connections."

"Well, we can't afford—" Wade's father began.

Terence waved his hand to stop him. "Think no more about that. I told you, my resources are yours. Since you don't have the authorities on your side, the Ackroyd Foundation will bankroll your continued travels. I'll do everything in my power to help you get Sara back safely and find the relic."

"Awesome," said Lily, smiling at both Ackroyds. "Thank you, again."

Wade's father took a breath, then raised his eyes to the two girls. "There's . . . something else," he said. "Becca, I called your mother this morning, and Lily, your dad, about you going home or going on. You both need to call your parents, not at home, but on their cell phones."

Becca's face fell. "What is it? Oh, I should have answered when I got the call last night. I didn't want to. What's happening—"

Roald held up his hands. "Everyone is fine, they're fine, and in fact Paul Ferrere has already alerted his people in Austin. But there was an incident at Maggie's

101

school the other day, and Lily, your father was followed home from work. Nothing happened, nothing at all, but as of this morning, both of your families have been relocated temporarily."

Lily held one hand over her mouth as she dug furiously for her phone.

Becca did the same. "Maggie, Maggie, I should have answered!"

For the next few minutes, both girls were sitting at different tables, glued to their cell phones, deep in conversation with their parents, while Terence filled in the details.

"The stinking Order," Darrell grumbled.

"Dad—" Wade started.

"I already talked to your mother," his father said, assuring him. "She's fine and traveling in Mexico. She doesn't appear to be on their radar at all."

A weight had been lifted, but Wade realized it had been days since he had spoken with her. "I'll call her right after this."

"Basically," Terence said, "it's best for none of you to return to Austin until we're sure of what we are dealing with. The Order could simply be flexing its muscles. I have no doubt that whatever they are doing comes from Galina herself, but my feeling is that she won't want to spread herself too thin with actions as intimidating as doing anything to the girls' families. Her empire is huge. She will need to focus it."

Wade shared a look with Darrell, who muttered something about Galina that Wade knew he probably shouldn't repeat. That was when his father produced a narrow silver tube from his pocket. It was the size of a fat ballpoint.

"It's a stun gun," he said. "A miniature Taser. Totally legal. The investigators gave one to me."

"Do we each get one?" asked Darrell.

"Absolutely not. And it's for defense only."

"A little something," said Terence. "It can be handy in tight quarters, without being a dangerous weapon."

Minutes later, Lily returned, wiping her cheeks. "They're all right. Way upset, with, like, a million questions, but they don't think I should be there right now." She started crying again behind her hands. "I'm sorry." Darrell put his arm around her shoulders, and she leaned into him.

Becca came back to the table looking like a zombie, blinking tears away from her eyes, unable to sit down. "Maggie's okay, worried like crazy. My parents, too, but they said I should stay with you. I never even thought of going home, and now I really want to, but I guess I should stay. I don't know."

Lily pulled away from Darrell and put her hand on Becca's wrist, and Becca sat. It was like that for a long while, everyone quiet, eyes down, not knowing what to say.

Wade once more remembered his dream of the cave: Becca lying lifeless on the floor. Then the way Markus Wolff had stared at her in San Francisco. He suddenly feared that Becca might be in some particular kind of danger, but he still didn't know how to express it. He just gazed at her, then at Lily, then at Becca again.

Finally, dishes were removed and dessert came, and that seemed to reset things.

"Is Boris Volkov a friend of yours?" Roald asked over a final coffee.

"No, not a friend," Terence said, waving a waiter over and asking for the check. "But he's useful. Listen to what he has to say. He knows many people in Russia who may be able to help you. However, I wouldn't entirely trust him. Boris doesn't do anything for nothing."

Wade felt uneasy to hear those words. But he hoped that the mysterious Russian would shed light on the relic's whereabouts. At the very least, the family was, as his father had hoped, moving forward.

To Russia. To the second relic . . . and Sara.

"In the meantime," Julian said, "Dad and I will focus on finding out what we can from our side. The instant we discover anything, we'll call you."

"Night or day," Roald said, looking around at the children.

With a final firm pledge of assistance, Terence made a call. Seven minutes later, Dennis pulled up outside the Water Club in yet another limo. Their luggage packed and safely in the trunk, the kids and Roald began their roundabout journey to JFK, to await their evening flight to London.

CHAPTER THIRTEEN

Madrid; London
March 19

Ebner von Braun woke to the tinny ascending scale of a digital marimba that suddenly sounded like a skeleton drumming a piano with its own bones. It was a ringtone he was determined to change at his first opportunity.

He blinked his eyes onto a black room.

Where am I?

More marimba.

Right.

Madrid.

He slid open the phone. *"¿Hola?"*

It was an Orc from the Copernicus Room. He listened. *"¿Londres?"* he said. *"¿Cuándo?"* The voice replied. Ebner pulled the phone away from his face. *"¿Quién es el jefe del Grupo de los Seis?"*

"*Señor Doyle.*"

"Then send Señor Doyle."

Click.

The aroma of grilled tomatoes greeted Archie Doyle when he woke up. He gazed through sleepy eyes at the bedroom of his three-room flat at 36B Foulden Road in the Borough of Hackney in London. He yawned.

It was 5:51 a.m., and his wife, Sheila, and his son, Paulie, were already awake.

Ah, family.

He flapped his lips and blew out the stale breath of sleep. "Bbbbbbbbbb!" This habit, and other exercises of the face and vocal cords, were ones he had learned in his unsuccessful years as an actor, which, alas, were all of them. As an actor, a mimic, a stand-up comedian, and the sad clown Tristophanes, in whose guise he appeared at birthday parties and bar mitzvahs, Archie Doyle had struggled.

He was far better at his other calling.

He liked to kill people.

And he'd be getting to do more of it soon. A recent and bizarre auto accident involving no less than three operatives had left Archie next in line to head Group 6 of the East London section of the Teutonic Order, a post he held while Berlin made up its corporate mind about more permanent arrangements.

Archie was determined to make a good impression.

"The rrrrrain in Sppppppain stays mmmmmainly on the pppppplain!"

"That you, dear?" came the call from the kitchen. "Breakfast in five minutes."

"Coming, luv," Archie responded happily. Sitting up, he slid his laptop from the end table onto the bed and opened it. He then typed in seven distinct passwords, and the screen he wanted came up. On it was a photograph of five rather downcast people, a man and four young teenagers, at a departure gate in what his trained eye told him was JFK airport in New York. Did they know they were being tracked? Their expressions suggested they might. It was next to impossible to avoid detection in such places when the Order was after you. On the other hand, a father and four children? Where was Mum?

Mine not to reason why.

Beneath the photograph were the names of the five persons, and these words:

Guardian alert: 19 March. NY flight Virgin Atlantic 004. Arrival 7:25 a.m. Heathrow Terminal 3.

"Oh, brilliant!" he whispered with a smile. There was a standing order to terminate all Guardians when identified as such. Five kills in one day. This would be a rather lovely way to convince his superiors that Archie was the man for the top job.

When he scrolled down a little farther, however, his smile crinkled to disappointment. Beneath the names and destination of the people in the photograph was a series of items with little boxes to be checkmarked as to Archie's course of action.

☐ *Terminate immediately*
☐ *Terminate off site*
☐ *Kidnap and report*
☑ *Follow only and report*

"Blast it all!" he breathed softly. "I am a termination machine!"

Still, a job was a job, and pleasing the Order was far preferable to displeasing them. And by *them* he meant *her*, and by *her* he meant Galina Krause. He'd seen her angry once. He hoped never to see it again.

Pulling up the train schedule, Archie calculated that the journey from his local railway station of Rectory Road to Heathrow would take a total of ninety-four minutes. Just before 6:30, he would snag a seat on the excruciatingly slow one-hour service west to central London, disembark at Paddington Station, dash over to Platform 6 for the 7:30 Heathrow Express to Terminal 3, and arrive twenty minutes later. Given another twenty or so minutes spent deplaning, collecting bags, if any, passport control, bathroom time, etc., the gloomy family couldn't be expected to be out of the arrivals hall until eight a.m. at the earliest, anyway. He checked the time again. Six o'clock.

I do have to get a move on.

Archie Doyle was of normal height and build with features that were, in the best tradition of foreign agents, nondescript. He leaped from bed, cleaned himself up, dressed in a smart wool suit of dark blue and a white shirt with muted tie, and topped it all off with a crisp bowler hat. He then slipped his briefcase onto his dresser and flipped up the lid.

Inside were the tools of his trade: several thicknesses and shades of adhesive mustaches and matching eyebrows, a range of eyeglasses, a tube of rub-on tanner, two false noses, three slender vials of poison, a small pistol and silencer, a stiletto, and assorted untraceable cell phones. It amazed him how many of these items he also used for his party activities. He placed his computer inside and clamped the briefcase shut. Then he slid his brolly—umbrella—from the closet, opened and closed it once, then tapped one of two small buttons inside its handle. With barely a breath, a hollow two-inch needle emerged from the umbrella's tip. Such a weapon could inflict a range of wounds, from a simple annoying scratch to a deadly puncture, if the needle was infused with poison. That was what the second button was for.

Archie wondered for an instant: Who *were* the Kaplans, anyway? Why "follow only and report"? Why not terminate? With no answers coming, he carefully retracted the umbrella's needle, gave his bowler a slap, and was in the kitchen—all in less than ten minutes from the time he woke.

His lovely wife, Sheila, turned to him, her smile like sunshine on the lawn of Hyde Park. In the tiny room with her, and taking up much of the floor space, was a portable crib. Fingers in mouth, sippy cup wedged between his plump legs, sat Paulie Doyle, fourteen months of pudge and drool and grins.

"I'm nearly plating the tomatoes, dear," Sheila said. "Kippers this morning?"

Archie Doyle sighed. "Sorry, dear. Must leap to the office immediately. I'll grab an egg and bacon on the way to the train. Save the tomatoes, though. Should be home for lunch."

"All right, dear," she said. "You have a wunnyful day."

"Thanks, luv," Archie said, kissing her ample cheek. "And bye-bye, Little Prince Paulie." He ruffled the wispy hair on the head of his son on his way to the door.

Archie was out, down the stairs, and on the sidewalk in a flash. Brisk day. Gray but pleasant. A perfect day for a termination—or five—he thought, but good enough to follow only and report.

"We shall see," he murmured, fingering the second button on his umbrella, "what we shall see."

CHAPTER FOURTEEN

London

Knowing there was little escape from airport cameras, Becca emerged head down from the Jetway in the arrivals terminal at London's Heathrow Airport. She trailed Lily, who as usual was acting as a sort of guide through the crowded world of crowds. It was the morning after the flight, and early, only a few minutes after eight a.m. But already the gates and concourses were busy, and Becca couldn't look up without feeling nauseous.

A really annoying personality trait.

It was like shouting, *Hey, everybody, look at me! I'm not looking at you!*

"You'll have to learn to do this one day, you know," Lily said over her shoulder.

"Not if you're always here."

"I just might be!"

Before the flight had left New York the previous evening, both girls had received a second and third round of phone calls from their parents, and Becca had had a very long talk with Maggie, which had managed to settle them both so that by the end they'd been laughing through their tears and whispering promises to each other to be good and safe. Becca felt that for her and Lily, hearing from their families was like Roald, Darrell, and Wade hearing from the investigators: all of them were now more or less assured that things were as okay as they could be for the moment and moving in the right direction. Without that, Becca didn't know how they could possibly focus on the relic and Russia and whatever else was to come. But here they were, on their first leg of the Serpens quest, and they were doing it.

"Oh, brother, now it begins," Lily grumbled as an airport official waved them and a hundred thousand other international passengers into the same skinny line.

There was no hiding here, Becca thought. No possibility of evasive action. Everyone had to go through passport control. And they were undoubtedly being filmed. In San Francisco they'd learned about the Order's awesome "Copernicus servers," with a computer power most first-world countries would envy. The family had probably been spotted at Kennedy airport, back in New York, so the Order *had* to know they were already in London. Eyes were on them. Of course they were.

Nearly an hour of blurring movement and bouncing from one line into another and opening bags and zipping them up and showing documents and squeezing into another line finally ended, and they were out of the terminal, and it was great, but not that great.

London might have been the home of Oliver Twist and Sherlock Holmes, but Becca's first experience outside the terminal was a stabbing downpour of cold, heavy, exhaust-filled, vertical rain.

"Absolutely fabulous, it's not," Lily grumbled. "Who knew it rained in England?"

"Uck, okay. Stay together," Roald urged, and they did, sticking close as he moved them quickly across the lanes of bus and shuttle traffic to the taxi stand, where they piled into a bulbous black cab that looked very much like the old one they'd seen in San Francisco last week. The sight of it started a superfast stream of memories in Becca's mind, culminating with a gun at her head at Mission Dolores, which, thankfully, hadn't gone off. Best not to live those days again. These days were bound to be scary enough.

"We'll be stopping at various places," Roald told the driver from the backseat. "First destination, Covent Garden."

"Certainly."

The taxi, piloted by a very quiet driver who wore a Sikh turban, was soon grinding its way from the airport and up onto a broad highway known as the M4. One of the things both Terence Ackroyd and the investigator had advised, to confuse would-be followers, was to take a roundabout route wherever they went. Terence Ackroyd's private apartment—or "safe flat," as he called it—was near the British Museum, but it would likely be a couple of hours before they actually reached it.

"Evasive maneuvers," Roald called them.

In the same spirit, Darrell and Wade had worked out a set of secret finger gestures on the plane. "To use if something bad is happening but you can't tell anyone," Darrell had said.

Lily gave them a blank look. "Um . . . what?"

"The complete range of bad things can be said with only five fingers," Wade insisted. "You raise them to

116

your face in a casual way, and the rest of us know what to do."

"What?" she said again.

They explained it this way:

One finger: The Order is near—run.

Two fingers: Meet me at (location to be determined).

Three fingers: Create a diversion.

Four fingers: Help.

Five fingers: Just get away from me.

The last one was added by Darrell specifically, he said, for use between the brothers. Becca and Lily spent a long time rolling their eyes, then shrugged and practiced the gestures. Roald woke from a brief nap as the plane was descending and learned them as well, but he thought he might be able to come up with a better set of commands.

"I dare you, Dad," Darrell quipped.

Becca watched out the cab window as they motored swiftly past brick and brownstone neighborhoods with names that exuded Englishness: Cranford and Osterley, Brentford and Shepherd's Bush. She could practically see the sheep grazing in pastures, though that was a scene from old novels and, by now, there weren't many pastures that hadn't been developed and built on.

Still, the slower the taxi went, the more clogged the streets were, and the more Becca began to feel the aura of "London, England" breathing from the sights around her. It came powerfully. All those English novels by English writers! They were written here, about here, and they were everywhere, as if those books had spilled their pages out into the living city. Even the presence of the Sikh driver spoke of the once-great colonial empire that was Great Britain, and how London gathered in its vast geography everyone from everywhere it had ever ruled.

"My first time to London in ten years," said Roald, his neck craning around here and there to catch every moment, just as she was doing. "There was a conference at the University of London. I presented a paper on Europa, one of Jupiter's moons. It was my first international paper."

"So cool," Becca breathed, aware that there was little volume in what she said.

"Only if you don't read the paper," he said with a laugh. "Pretty dull stuff."

"Still," she said. "London."

Trying not to annoy or alarm the driver, Roald gave him several addresses to drive to—as if they were sightseeing—before the final one. After Covent Garden, a bustling market in the heart of the city, they drove through the madly snarled traffic of Piccadilly Circus, around to Selfridges department store, across a bridge to Southwark, and back over another bridge to Saint Paul's Cathedral. When, finally, they motored toward their final stop, Darrell suggested they call the telephone number Terence had given them, "to get things started." Roald tapped a number on the cell phone installed with Julian's homemade alert software.

"Galina probably knows we're in London," Wade whispered; then he frowned. "There's no probably about it. She knows. We have to be supersmart."

Becca shared a grim look with the others. Despite their hopped-up phones, if for some reason Galina Krause *didn't* already know their exact location, she would soon.

"I've never been not smart," said Lily. "An intelligence officer can't afford to be. That witch is out there. Her and her thugs. I'm sure of it."

The Sikh driver half turned. "*Thugs*, miss. This is a word coming from the Hindi term *thuggees*, the name given to some fanatic followers of Kali. The goddess of destruction."

"Thank you," Lily said, her eyes widening. "How weirdly . . . accurate. . . ."

Becca's blood tingled in her veins. The quest was on, and she believed, as they all did, that if Maxim *was* the Guardian, and Serpens *was* the second relic, then Russia was the place, and she hoped Boris Volkov would help confirm it.

"Hallo? Who is?" The voice crackled loudly from Roald's phone.

"Hello. Is this Boris Volkov?"

"Ya. Hallo. Who is?"

"Excuse me," Roald said as they eased deeper into the streets. "This is a friend of Terence Ackroyd's. He told us—"

"Ah, yes, Terry! Dear friend, Terry. Yes, yes. Family Keplen. Come see me. Is Boris. Boris Volkov." There was the sound of ice clinking into a glass on the other end. "You come Promenade. Ten thirty this morning. Dorchester Hotel."

"Uh . . . we would prefer somewhere more private," Roald said.

"No. Public is safe. Witnesses be there. Public only. Bring item with you, yes?"

"Item?" said Roald. "I'm not sure I know exactly—"

"Park Lane. You find? Yes? Good. You come."
Click.

"Dad, what does he want?" Wade asked. "We don't have any *item* for him."

Roald tapped the phone and returned it to his jacket pocket. "I think we'll find out soon enough. Hotel Cavendish, Gower Street," he told the driver.

"Certainly."

CHAPTER FIFTEEN

The Hotel Cavendish was a small boutique hotel near the corner of Gower Street and Torrington Place in the neighborhood surrounding the British Museum. Wade wondered what their rooms were like. He would continue to wonder. When their taxi wove through a series of narrow streets and passages and finally stopped outside, his father paid their driver handsomely. They entered the hotel, where they booked two rooms, made sure the taxi was gone, then turned and walked right back outside, to the bewilderment of the desk clerk, who was dangling two sets of room keys for no one.

believe it was actually wolves. The wolves of Greywolf. But what else could it be—

Something zipped from left to right across the falling snow.

A chunk of tree bark flew off to Darrell's right.

"Everyone down!" Paul hissed, flattening with Marceline, both raising their pistols.

Becca dropped hard into the snow behind the stump of a cracked tree, hurting her wounded arm even more. She stifled a cry. Darrell joined his father behind a rock outcropping. She bit her lip to keep from making noise. The wound ached, throbbed. *Be still!* A spray of gunfire burst among the tree trunks. Paul and Marceline aimed at its source and waited.

"That was a warning!" a voice shouted. "Keplens, surrender. We have you surrounded."

Paul raised himself to his elbows. "No they don't," he whispered. "At the first opportunity, go back down the ridge and around."

"We'll cover you," Marceline added.

Becca watched both detectives settle into the snow and take coordinated aim into the trees. They nodded silently to her and the others as two bursts of gunfire blasted through the tree cover at them. The detectives returned fire, crisscrossing their shots.

"Go!" Marceline whispered.

Darrell crawled on his elbows to Becca. Roald did the same. "Down the ledge," he whispered, nodding behind her. She turned, her arm wet inside her parka. Her wound was bleeding again. *Just move*, she told herself. *No noise, just move.* The gunfire popped and thundered: semiautomatic fire, machine-gun fire, she didn't know what else.

She could die. They could all die. But she kept on, elbowing down the ledge and away from the firefight, from Paul and Marceline.

"Behind the ridge," she said over her shoulder, seeing a path forward. She went first, on her hands and knees initially, then on her feet, running. Darrell was right behind her, Roald last. They were out, away, and heading up again. Seconds stretched to minutes. Longer. The fire was sporadic now.

Then a noise. A whining engine. A snowmobile was heading to the gun battle.

Darrell whispered, "Let's pretend to give up, then steal the snowmobile."

"You're nuts," Becca hissed.

"Actually . . . we need speed," Roald said.

"What? No!"

"Only four hours left," Darrell snapped.

The snowmobile zipped past a knot of trees, fully visible. Suddenly, Roald stood bolt upright in the snow, his hands raised high. The driver was startled; then he recovered and aimed his pistol, slowing his vehicle.

"Stand still," he barked in English. "Both of you!" Darrell reluctantly did as he was told.

Oh, perfect.

The driver reached for his radio transmitter. Becca knew it was up to her. *Something* was up to her. The radio crackled. That was the moment. She jumped to her feet, making sure she registered on the periphery of his vision. She dived down again. It was enough of a distraction. The driver swiveled his head, not his gun, and Darrell and his stepfather flew like ghosts and pushed him off the snowmobile. He hit the ground hard, his gun sinking into the snow. Roald pressed his Taser on the man's neck. It was a low charge. The man continued to grapple with Roald. Darrell pounded his fists on the man's arm. The man jerked his hands loose of them.

The snowmobile rolled, then stopped, still idling. Becca went to it immediately and searched the compartment under the saddle—for what, she wasn't sure. Roald and Darrell wrestled the half-aware driver face-down in the snow and pinned his arms behind him.

"We need to tie him up or something—" Darrell started.

"Wire!" Becca said. "I found wire."

"Take off his coat first," Roald said. "I'll wear it."

"Why?" asked Darrell.

"If we're spotted, they'll think I'm him. It'll buy us time, at least."

"Good idea," said Becca. She knelt next to Darrell and removed the driver's parka, while Roald undid the man's ammunition belt, bound his hands with the wire, jerked him to his feet. He twisted the wire once around a tree before securing it. Darrell stuffed the man's mouth with his own scarf and tied the excess around his head.

The gunfire behind them continued unevenly. Becca knew they had to make the most of the distraction Paul and Marceline were risking their lives to create. After slipping the driver's parka on himself, Roald dug into the snow for the dropped pistol, holstered it in the ammo belt, and tied the belt around his waist.

"Dad . . . ," Darrell said. "Really?"

"Just in case."

Becca watched Roald gaze through the trees up the hill. The fortress still wasn't visible. But now they had the snowmobile. He pulled the parka hood low. "Let's move it."

The firefight was moving too, down the hill and away. Paul and Marceline were in retreat, drawing the Brotherhood away from them. Roald got on the snowmobile, with Darrell behind him and Becca on the back. They had to squeeze, but it felt so good to be sitting on something softer than stone.

"You safe back there?" Darrell asked over his shoulder.

"Maybe."

She clutched the sides of the seat, and Roald twisted the grips on the handlebars. The gunfire started up again, furiously this time but still farther away. Without a pause, the snowmobile lurched forward up the treacherous rise to Greywolf.

CHAPTER FIFTY-FIVE

Vorkuta

When Wade struck the floor, he was sure he cracked his skull. His forehead thundered. His temples burned. His eyeballs ached and saw double when he tried to blink them into focus. Galina was nowhere. The freezing air had turned viciously hot. The room was on fire.

"Lily? Lily!" he cried.

"Help Alek," she coughed.

The doctor moaned and rolled over. "Friends . . ."

Flames had blackened two walls and were scorching the third. Wade scrambled over on his hands and knees. If Galina had shot Aleksandr in the arm or leg, there might have been a way to stop the bleeding. But the wound was just under his sternum, in the stomach, and his ratty clothes were soaked. Aleksandr would bleed to death all too soon.

"How do we get out of here?" Lily asked, searching everywhere.

"There is a passage behind the gas canisters," Aleksandr groaned, his face strangely peaceful. "Do not worry; the canisters are empty." He pointed to the back corner.

"We'll make it out." Wade coughed.

"You, perhaps—"

"All of us."

Together, Lily and Wade rolled the canisters aside and crawled through a low passage into another room, dragging Alek between them.

"There." Alek nodded at a padlocked exit door. "Try to open that. I must tell you about the relic. There may be no time, later."

Wade wrenched the leg off a metal chair. He battered the lock. "What did Galina mean that the relics can't die?"

Aleksandr coughed for a full half minute. "Simply that Copernicus himself tried to destroy them but could not."

"Then where is Serpens now?" he asked for the third time.

401

"Have I told you that there is a morgue at Greywolf?"

"Yes, Alek, you did," said Wade. Was the man losing his mind? Losing his blood *and* his mind? Then it struck him with the power of Galina's punch. "Are you saying you *hid* the Serpens head in the morgue at Greywolf? That it never left?"

Aleksandr gasped. "I did! It never left! It lies bathed in the blood of the dead. The body, however . . ." With difficulty, he lifted up his right pant leg. The leg itself was burned and scarred as badly as his face and neck, but there was something else, too. A section of several square inches of scarred skin covered his calf. It was sewn on one side with haphazard stiches like those on the Frankenstein monster.

"It looks as if you operated on your—" Lily started.

Aleksandr nodded once. "There was no place closer to me than myself."

Using a shard of glass, Aleksandr laboriously slashed away at the stitched skin. It bled little because of the thick scarring. Slowly he pried the wound open. From it, he withdrew a small white capsule, two or so inches long. He wiped it clean and pulled it apart, then tilted the open capsule into his palm.

"Knowing I could no longer protect the relic my father found in the ruins of Königsberg, I sent it to a friend of mine. An Egyptologist in Moscow. He perished last year. Even so, Serpens remains safe. Once, I dared to ask where he hid it. He did not respond until on his deathbed. Then he sent me this. Along with the Magister's own words. You will be happy to hear that the twisted path of the Serpens body ends with this clue. Now I give it to you." He pulled a rolled strip of paper from the capsule and passed it to Wade, breathing out a long, ragged breath.

On the paper was a square box drawn in ink as red as blood. Filling the inside of the box was a large upside-down *V* with a sequence of numbers running up the left side to the top and three question marks running down the right side.

"What does it mean?" Wade asked. "You said he was your friend in Moscow?"

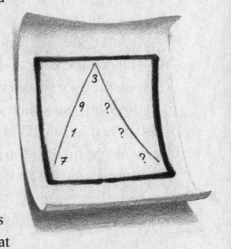

"I never knew the significance. My friend told me just this: no matter how many codes are devised, this will override them all. What that means, I do not know. But if you wish to locate the body of Serpens, this is nearly all the help I can give."

"What were Copernicus's words that your friend told you?" Lily asked.

"'Puteshestvye do kontsa morya dlinoy,'" he whispered. "Which means 'the journey to the end of the sea is long.'"

"Boris told us that!" said Lily. "What does it mean?"

Aleksandr seemed relieved, as if released of a great burden. "It is a quotation we Guardians have always known. As Nicolaus's journey was long in the hiding of the relics, the Guardians' journey is just as long. You will find Serpens soon, but your journey will continue!" Then he began coughing, and his breathing grew rapid, shallow, and labored.

Wade hacked once more at the lock. It broke off. He whipped the door open to find a clear passage, but opening the door sucked the fire into the room.

"Up! Out!" Aleksandr choked. "You cannot die like this!" When he lifted himself up from the floor, he bled freely. Yet he managed to push Wade and Lily ahead of him through the door, into room after room, then hung between them, huffing, "This way . . . no, there! That tunnel! Up. Up! You *must* find the relic before Galina. You must!"

Wade's legs felt like lead. The fire burst into the passages behind them faster than they could run. Aleksandr grew suddenly heavy. Was he dead? "Lily . . ."

Tears cut through the grime on her cheeks. "I feel cold air. That way. That way!"

Together, they pulled Alek up a narrow side passage. There *was* cold air, streaming in on them. A ceiling beam crashed down across the passage. Then two more. They were trapped. A voice shouted from the other side of the fallen beams. No, it was the roar of the fire. No, a voice. A call from so far away that Wade wasn't sure he even heard it. Lily's fingers tightened on his wrist. She stopped her breath to listen.

There was a crash, and the voice yelled, "Stand away. Get back!"

Lily pulled Wade flat with Aleksandr behind the fallen beams as the wall burst in at them. Voices came clearer now, even above the screams of the fire. Terence stumbled in with a stream of Russian police behind him. Wade could tell from their uniforms and the expression on Terence's face that they were real police, not Brotherhood. They threw fire cloaks on the children and Aleksandr.

"Out of here!" Terence cried. "Hurry up!"

And they were running, Terence and the police carrying the limp form of Aleksandr from the burning mine. They tore up a last set of broken metal steps and fell onto the frozen ground as the mine threw up a howling gust of flame.

The entrance collapsed; the rumbling and thundering was now underground. They were out of the mine. Bitter cold rushed over them. They laid the burned man on the ground. He was limp, completely still. His mouth gaped. His eyes stared upward. Terence and two policemen worked over him. Sirens wailed in the distance, coming closer. Ambulances, fire engines. Wade turned to see a plume of black smoke pouring out from the mine in three columns. "Lily, Terence, we have to—"

"Maybe they'll come in time to save him," she said.

"Sure," he said.

The quest for Serpens. We're closer than ever to the center, but we're not done.

Terence helped Lily and Wade to their feet. They left Aleksandr Rubashov on the icy ground surrounded by policemen and medical technicians rushing from their trucks, and ran back across the tundra toward the paved strip.

"To the airport," said Terence. "We'll find a plane. We can be at Greywolf in under three hours."

"No," said Lily. "Alek gave us one last clue. We have to go to Moscow!"

* * *

On the airstrip, an old woman with a mop of white hair bent under the nose of Terence's jet. She supervised a mechanic changing the last of the three blown tires.

"What's going on?" Lily asked. "Who's that?"

"I think she believes she's the new owner of our jet," Terence said, trotting quickly over the tarmac. "While I was with the police, she commandeered it."

The woman was dressed in what looked like ten layers of clothing, and she had a rifle over her shoulder. At the sound of their footsteps, she pulled a hidden revolver from inside her coat. "*Stoy!*" she snarled, a word that obviously meant "Stop!"

"Let me handle this," Terence whispered. "Hello—this—is—our—jet!"

The woman narrowed her eyes at both of them but did not lower the pistol. She shook her head and said a long string of Russian, ending in, "*Nyet.* Is my zhet." Then, without taking her tiny eyes off them, she tapped the gun barrel on the fuselage. The door of the plane squeaked open from the inside, and a young woman poked her head out. "I am Ekaterina," she said. "I speak English."

"This is really our jet, and we need to fly to Moscow right now," Wade said.

The younger woman shook her head. "It *was* your

jet. We are taking it."

"I have an idea," whispered Terence. He offered the Ogienko family, as they called themselves, ten thousand rubles to fly them to Moscow in the jet. They hesitated. When Lily searched the net and discovered that ten thousand rubles was about three hundred dollars, Terence quintupled it, which made the old woman and her family ecstatic.

"But I fly zhet," the old woman insisted. "Is my zhet."

"Fine," said Terence. "Just let's go!"

As soon as they muscled their way into the tiny cockpit, the pilot gunned the engines. A little girl, the English-speaking woman's daughter and the pilot's granddaughter, immediately began to kick Wade in the shins, then laugh as if it were the funniest thing in Russia. Maybe it was.

"We have to tell your dad about the morgue," said Lily.

Wade pulled out his phone. "No service. Excuse me, do you have a radio on board?"

"Yes," said the pilot's daughter. "But you cannot call a cell phone."

"How about FSB headquarters in Moscow?" asked Lily.

The woman's eyes widened. "Do not turn us in."

Terence assured them they would not, and Wade radioed Inspector Yazinsky. He was rerouted and put on hold several times before finally reaching the inspector's answering machine. "This is Wade. Tell my father that the head of Serpens is in the morgue at Greywolf. Aleksandr said it's in the east wing of the fortress. Serpens is 'bathed in the blood of the dead.' Sara is trapped in a time machine. We'll go to the airport with Terence when it's all over, but right now we're flying to Moscow—"

The connection crackled and died.

"The relic is in Red Square," Lily said. "We're going to Red Square."

"What?" said Wade.

"Red Square?" said Terence.

"Pfft!" muttered the old woman.

"Look at it," Lily said, holding up the sketch Alek had given them. "It's a red box. A red square. The body of Serpens is hidden in Red Square!"

"Seat belts. We fly now," said Ekaterina.

Terence offered to copilot the jet, but the old woman refused his help. Without much experience at the controls, the pilot moved the wheel first too much, then too little. The plane lifted, then sank toward the blank gray face of a giant high-rise. She tugged the wheel back again, and they rose but barely gained altitude.

The tires bounced across the icy roof of a second building; the jet dropped off the far side, nearly crashing into a third building until the pilot veered left and the nose lifted at the last second. They cleared the next roof and the next.

At last, the city below them, an unruly mass of streetlights and lighted buildings, surrounded by the vast darkness of the Siberian landscape, began to shrink and fade away.

They were airborne.

CHAPTER FIFTY-SIX

As her Mystère-Falcon shot over the tundra back to Greywolf, Galina studied the satellite image she'd just received on her cell phone. Three figures were running away from the burning Vorkuta mine toward a jet standing on the airfield. There was a force of police and a man lying in the snow. Emergency vehicles surrounded the mine.

"They are charmed, these children," she said softly.

"Rather than charred," Ebner offered.

Bartolo Cassa sat stonily in the pilot's seat. "They would never have escaped without help," he said quietly. "The flamethrower was sabotaged."

"I should have shot them myself," Galina said.

Then why didn't I? Seeing them there, children only a few years younger than herself, she'd found herself unable to take the shot. Did she *want* the children alive? Why would that be? They had followed her, sometimes even led her, to something that was so deeply a part of herself. How could she tolerate such an intrusion?

Was it that . . . one of the children *might* turn out to be . . . the one who . . .

She could not think it.

Calmly, she tapped in a text and waited as the jet climbed. *Triangulate their course.* The cockpit was silent for two minutes until her cell lit up with a single word.

"Moscow," she read. "They are en route to Moscow."

"Shall I change course?" Cassa asked her.

"No. Ebner will return to Greywolf. You will pilot me to Moscow. Ebner, have a troop of the Crows meet me at Sheremetyevo in Moscow, with a transport. The Russian surgeon has obviously given the children a clue. I will follow them. Midnight comes soon. You shall oversee the completion of Bern's programming and the successful transportation of Sara Kaplan to Cádiz in 1517. Complete this mission. We need a body there . . . and then."

The physicist nodded. "It shall be done, Miss Krause."

Galina withdrew a pair of earbuds from a zipped

pocket on her coat and inserted them. She tapped an icon on her cell phone and heard the plaintive andante from Haydn's string quartet opus 33, number 6. It was the same piece that had been playing in the antiquarian's shop five days prior. As the cello's insistent funeral march rolled on and the yearning violins begged fruitlessly for comfort, Galina cradled the miniature portrait from Prague. She stared at the face that breathed as if it were alive even now, five centuries later. Inwardly, if not visibly, tears melted down the inside of her breast. Why she loved old artifacts like this was simple . . . and complicated.

A living portrait, yes, she thought, *but how many years did you actually live?*

The portrait's eyes gazed back as if to ask her the same question.

Chapter Fifty-Seven

Greywolf

The gunfire at Greywolf grew increasingly sporadic until it died under the roar of the wind through the trees. Midnight was only an hour and a handful of minutes away.

The final push to the summit was excruciatingly slow, despite the speed of the snowmobile, and far longer than Becca expected. They had to take a meandering route to avoid the main road, and twice had to shut off the engine as motorized patrols fanned out over the property in response to the gunfire.

They'd heard Galina's jet return, just before it took off once more. It was over an hour since Chief Inspector

Yazinsky had called Roald's cell to relay Wade's message.

"Galina must be following Wade and Lily to Moscow," Roald reported.

"Then why stop here at all?" asked Darrell. "To let someone off . . ."

The jet taking flight again was followed later by a transport returning from the airfield to the fortress, proving Darrell right. The way the transport had shifted its gears on the road above them had told Becca that the summit was near.

Then the air shuddered. A blast rolled up the hill from below.

"That sounded like a bomb," said Roald. "Or a grenade. Keep moving."

Minutes later, the hulking stone fortress loomed into view. It was larger and more menacing than Becca had imagined. A haunted, gloomy pile of stones dotted with black windows and pierced by a frightening tower that flickered with light like a mad scientist's lair. Roald stopped the snowmobile inside the tree line, cut its engine, and scoured every compartment for more ammo, which he took.

The howling began suddenly, and Roald stiffened in fear. "Wolves. In the house."

"Why are they *inside* the house?" Darrell wondered. "That's just sick."

The howling was horrific. The wolves were in some kind of pain. Or maybe they smelled food approaching. Becca imagined their snarling faces, snouts, jaws, fangs.

Roald unholstered the pistol. "The wolves are there to make sure no one gets in before the deadline."

Becca pushed the idea of guns and wolves out of her mind. "Wade said there was a morgue below the operating room. Let's get moving."

Her legs were freezing, barely with feeling, but they moved her forward.

Together, the three hurried across the clearing. They came to rest behind what were likely the original stables, now the garages. The air was unbearably frigid. Becca couldn't move the muscles of her face. Roald's beard was frozen. They kept in motion, shifting their feet, wrapping their arms around themselves for warmth. The chorus of ghostly wails from inside the fortress rose and fell, crisscrossed, subsided, rose again.

"If Galina is after Wade and Lily, then who's still here?" whispered Becca.

"Ebner, maybe," said Darrell. "Or the goon with sunglasses."

Then the sound of a snowmobile sputtered behind

416

the stables. They whirled around, Roald crouching, gun aimed. It was Marceline in the saddle. Marceline alone, an automatic in one hand, a machine gun hitched over her shoulder.

"Paul was shot twice," she whispered. "He is below, out of danger of the Brotherhood. He will survive."

Becca felt her heart sink, her neck go numb, as if she might pass out. She stomped her feet to regain feeling. "Will the Brotherhood come back up here?"

"They will. Though they, too, lost troops. And their transport was destroyed. Still, we must do this quickly."

Roald filled her in on Wade's message while he checked and rechecked his pistol. "Isabella escaped from the back of the castle. That could be the weakest entry point."

"I will go there," Marceline said. "You search for the morgue. Ten minutes exactly is all you have while I create a diversion at the back. Ten minutes. If you have not found Serpens by then, leave it. Once you hear me shooting, you enter the front. I'll do what I can to stop the wolves, then join you in the tower to get Sara out."

That was the end of the talking.

Becca pulled Darrell and his stepfather away from Marceline and hurried to the side of the building. Her heart was pounding. The wolves went crazy against the windowpanes on the ground floor, sensing their presence. Their faces, their teeth, their horrible eyes glimmered in the snow light. Roald skirted the edge of the stables, then loped across the clearing to the back of the house.

"Ten minutes is nine minutes now," said Darrell.

The east wing was a hulk of three freestanding walls, doorless, roofless, and windowless. It hung off the body of the fortress like a ghost limb. But it was free of wolves. Roald pushed into the ruins.

The charred machinery of medicine lay twisted and mangled, a horrifying mess across the floor. The debris was covered by a thick blanket of snow. Rusted poles, girders, ceiling beams, overturned cabinets, and wrecked carts protruded from the white.

"The morgue," Darrell grunted, nodding his head at a portion of the floor that had collapsed, through which they could glimpse a chamber down below. "What did Wade say—bathed in the blood of the dead? The whole morgue is bathed in the—"

He didn't go on—couldn't make himself go on, Becca figured. She found the stairs and climbed tentatively down to the floor below. Four minutes had elapsed since they'd left Marceline.

The morgue was a black pit, a hole, a concrete-lined

grave. It was a crypt for the victims of the Order through the years, the KGB before them. Becca shone her light on the ruined equipment, drills and saws and undertaker tools, mangled with the beds and carts and monitors that had crashed through from the floor above.

"How in the world are we supposed to find anything in this junk?" she asked.

Roald trained his light. "Bathed in blood? It's a riddle. But what does it mean?"

There was a shot, then two more. Roald jerked back. "Marceline? It's too soon."

"Dad, go," said Darrell. "No one's going to find us here. We'll scrounge through the junk, then meet you in the castle. Go!"

"Take this." Roald gave Darrell the Taser. "Be careful when you—" But he was off in the direction of the shots before he finished his sentence.

Becca pushed carefully through the equipment, while Darrell kicked at it angrily. He shoved aside burned-out cabinets and overturned stretchers and the remains of octopus machines with charred hoses dangling from them. He muttered about time and midnight and his mother. Becca tried to find something, anything that could be a hiding place for a handful of jewels, but the morgue was a heap of junk covered in snow and ice.

"Darrell, it could be anywhere."

"We have to find it! We both have to! The Legacy! We have to stop that witch from . . . from . . ." His fingers froze unmoving above the floor. "Becca . . . Serpens is bathed with the blood of the dead."

"I know that! What does that mean?"

"Where does the blood of the dead go in a morgue? The drain. Becca, they wash away the blood down a drain!"

She watched him push across the floor until he came to the very center of the room. He kicked at the snow covering the floor. Then his body jerked in several directions at once. He was frantic, tearing around in the debris until he found something, a tool—a two-foot length of pipe. He slammed it on the floor. The air rang with the sound of metal on metal. He did it again and again, swinging at the floor as if he were chopping down a tree. She heard the chink of metal, and then suddenly the drain—a crosshatched ring of metal—flew up sharply and nearly struck him in the face.

He dropped the pipe, fell to his knees, and drove his hand into the floor, into the drain hole. There must have been so much blood washing down there over the years, but Darrell obviously didn't think of that; he just pushed his fingers into the hole. When he brought them back up, they were twitching and twisting and . . . glistening.

She shone a light on his hand. He held an object, a device. It looked more mechanical than a piece of jewelry. Maybe it was both. It was a delicate construction of silver. Twin blue diamonds gleamed prism-like in the rays of her flashlight.

"It's . . . Darrell, oh my gosh. You found it! The head of Serpens—we have it!"

He rose to his feet and came toward her, the object seeming to draw the light into it while at the same time shooting it back out in a series of flashes or pulses that set the dark room glowing. Darrell's face shone. He blinked at the intensity of the light.

So did Becca. "Is it magic?" she asked. "Is it?"

"No," he said. "Something else. It's heavy. Becca, it's like ten pounds. It's hot and it's heavy and it's humming or something—"

A series of shots cracked the air like multiple explosions. Another and another, followed by the spray of machine-gun fire. There was a thunderous howl, then more shots. Roald and Marceline were at the rear of the house, shooting the wolves, and the wolves were out, charging from the fortress and onto the property.

"Hide the relic. Give me the pipe. Come on!" said Becca firmly.

Darrell wrapped it in his scarf and shoved it into the pocket of his parka. They ran back up the stairs, out of the operating room, and around to the front of the castle. The timbered doors, studded with iron bolts, looked impregnable.

She jumped first up the steps and twisted the pipe into the iron door handles. She pulled it down. The handles squealed. She did it again. They squealed more.

"Together," Darrell said. They both gripped the pipe and pushed up first, wedging it tight; then Darrell kicked it down. The handles groaned awfully and fell. They shouldered into the doors together. They swung in. The wolves were still pouring out the rear of the house. Here in the front rooms, there were none.

"The stairs," Darrell said. "Isabella said Mom is in the tower. Hurry up!"

CHAPTER FIFTY-EIGHT

Moscow

Red Square. The heart of the city. The dead of night. It had all come down to this.

Thirty minutes before, they had landed safely at Sheremetyevo airport. Then, disaster. Terence and the Ogienkos were held in a cramped room for violating Russian airspace without proper clearance—or something—a trumped-up charge they immediately credited to the Red Brotherhood. Irina Lyubov was not on duty. This left Wade and Lily alone and free, which they realized was simply because the Brotherhood planned to tail them directly to the relic.

"Take a roundabout route to Red Square," Terence

423

told them privately before he was led away. "Switch cabs, zigzag, do what you can to lose any pursuers. I trust you'll get there eventually. When you do, stay put. Do nothing. I will meet you. Seriously, do nothing until I get there, understood?"

"Yes," Wade said, then thought, *It's just us again.*

Out on the street, Wade and Lily hailed a cab, awkwardly made their first destination known to the driver, and quickly crossed the city. Two cars were obviously following them. "Stopsky heresky please," Lily blurted out at a busy intersection, which the driver surprisingly understood and forgave, even as she apologized. She overpaid him in euros, then they jumped out and raced down one street, cut through to another, and snagged another taxi before their pursuers could spot them. They left that taxi three dark blocks from the enormous Red Square. Strong winds blew snow in tiny cyclones up and down the empty street. The cab drove away. They waited in the shadows of a deep doorway.

Satisfied that the Brotherhood had not followed them, Wade pulled out the paper Aleksandr had given them, huddled against the wind, and tried to study the drawing. But all he saw in his mind were Sara and Darrell and Becca and his father, and he could only imagine the terror of what was happening at Greywolf. "I hope they're okay. The others, I mean—"

"I know who you mean," Lily said, crouching up against him in the doorway. "I'm thinking about them, too. But we have work here. Come on."

He tried to reset his thoughts and focus on the paper again. "Okay, if you're right, the first clue is Red Square, but what do we do when we get there?"

"Hey, I deciphered the first clue," she said. "Now it's your turn."

"Thanks so much."

"While you think, let's keep moving," she said. "And I mean it. You think."

They marched out of the doorway into the wind, crossed two streets, doubled back, and moved forward until the tunneled arches of the famed Resurrection Gate loomed ahead of them. They waited where they had agreed to meet Terence, but he didn't come and didn't come.

Lily shook her head. "We need to go on. Terence may be hours. We don't have hours. The journey to the end of the sea is long, and we're nearly there. What does the triangle inside the square mean?"

Wade had asked himself the same question. "It's technically an upside down *V*; the bottom isn't closed, as in a triangle."

Lily gave him a face. "Helpful, Einstein. Alek said his Guardian friend was an Egyptologist. They're all about pharaohs and pyramids and deserts and mummies—" She stopped, whipped out her tablet, and powered it on. "I'm searching 'Red Square' and 'Egypt' to see if there's any kind of clue here. What about the numbers? Come on. Figure out the numbers while we walk."

They crept through under the gate's deep archway and came out alongside the bulky, ornate, redbrick State Historical Museum. Its gold awnings were heavy with new snow. They paused at the corner and looked south across the vast, deserted square. It was already covered by a thickening blanket of white; snow was blowing around in more twisters.

"The numbers, I don't get," he said, slowing under the first streetlight. "Forgetting for a second the upside-down *V*, I've been trying to find a pattern in the numbers, but I don't see one. Seven, one, nine, three, blank, blank, blank. If there was a pattern, I might be able to figure out the last three. They might be a combination or an entry code. But I can't find the sequence. Maybe I can use the calculator on the tablet—"

"Oh."

"What?"

She pointed across the square through the squalling

snow. Against the high red wall of the Kremlin fortress stood a stumpy pyramid of red and black stone. "There."

"What about it?" he asked.

"Well, (a) it's a pyramid. And (b) it's the Lenin mausoleum. Not John Lennon, but Vladimir Ilyich Lenin, one of the leaders of the Russian Revolution. And (c) maybe your eyes aren't as good as mine because of all the reading you do, but if you look at the lettering on the front of the tomb, the red lettering against the black, you'll see what I see. It says *Lenin*. Of course, it's in Russian, so the *L* in *Lenin* is not a regular *L*, as in Lily, but an upside-down *V*. Look at it."

He did. Through the whirling flakes he read the letters.

ЛЕНИН

He made a sound. "Whoa . . . is that it?"

"I don't know," she said, tugging Alek's scroll from him, "but if the outside box *does* mean Red Square, then the upside-down *V* could mean a building *in* Red Square. That would make me think that maybe the numbers tell us something *about* the upside-down-*V* building. Maybe that's the way the clue goes. From outside to inside."

From outside to inside? Lily was being pretty brilliant.

Wade studied the tomb. It sat snugly against the Kremlin wall, a squat, five-level pyramid of granite and marble, forty feet tall. It vaguely reminded him of a stepped Aztec temple. In one way it was small, like the foundation of a much taller structure that was never built. In another way, the building was grimly impressive, its multiple levels catching the light of the square in odd and ominous ways.

Because it was the resting place of a maybe-controversial Russian leader, it was heavily guarded. From that distance, it appeared to have eight, maybe ten fully armed soldiers stationed around it.

"Okay, but why there?" he asked.

"Because Lenin is *embalmed*," she said, wagging her tablet. "It says here that every year and a half they redo the embalming to keep him looking fresh and natural. I'm guessing that Alek's Guardian friend was an Egyptologist who knew about embalming, and that he worked on Lenin and hid Serpens in there while he was doing embalming stuff."

"Your face turns green whenever you say *embalming*, you know," Wade said.

"I feel it doing that."

On either side of the tomb and following the Kremlin wall was a loose row of blue spruce trees. They were impeccably trimmed, of nearly identical size, and now ornamented and sagging with heavy late-season snow.

"So . . . the Copernicus relic is in Lenin's tomb?" Wade said.

"One plus one equals Lenin's tomb," she said.

"Speaking of numbers, what *about* the numbers?" he asked.

"That's so your department, math head," she said. "Come on."

They paused close to the facade of the Historical Museum, then darted over the cobblestones to where the Kremlin wall jutted out. They peeked around the abutment to scout out the mausoleum guards.

"Two guards on this side of the tomb and six spread across the front," Lily said. "I don't see any at all covering the back. There are probably two or more on the far side. You know, maybe the numbers are a Russian phone number."

He gave her a look. "I think modern Russian phone numbers have more than seven digits."

"Digits, huh?" She counted the guards again. "Maybe it's an old number."

"Right. Maybe it's Lenin's home phone number from 1924, but nobody knows the last three digits because how do you phone a dead guy?"

She looked at him. "You could try a little harder, you know. We're out of time. We need to do this. Then we need to get out of Russia forever."

At the word *Russia*, Wade's brain twitched. In their time there, he'd never come to terms with the country. His "map" of Russia was false, based on the insane things they'd done over the last few days, the danger they'd been in, the number of times they'd nearly died, the terror about Sara's fate. The dread of what was happening at Greywolf weighed on him like lead. He'd seen Lubyanka and Vorkuta, but he'd never really gotten to know *Russia*. Now, like Lily, all he wanted to do was leave it.

"Our best bet is to make our way behind the trees," Lily said. She slid past him, weaving through a stretch of temporary fencing. They flattened together against the Kremlin wall. Wade figured they were a couple hundred yards from the tomb. His chest ached. This was ridiculous. A movie. What if they were actually spotted? Caught? Fired on?

And yet, the moment the tomb guards looked off toward the cathedral, he trotted down the narrow space between the trees and the Kremlin wall, toward the back corner of the tomb, with Lily right after him.

Ridiculous or not, they were doing it and getting closer to the center of the onion.

Then Lily went to stone. "Look."

There was a narrow set of steps at the back of the structure, leading down several feet from ground level to a steel door at the bottom of the steps.

"A basement."

"Do tombs have basements?" he whispered.

"Maybe. This is Russia. What do we know?" She leaned out as far as she could and stared at the tomb. "Besides, there's something on the wall next to the door. I think it's a keypad. There are your *digits* for you, math boy."

The soldiers shifted slightly, then froze like columns, unmoving, except for their eyes, which were staring forward. The kids waited for some kind of noise distraction, and after a few breathless minutes, it came. A siren blared several blocks away from the square. An ambulance or fire engine, wheeling through the streets, honking and wailing. Then a second one, following the first. Wade and Lily left the cover of the trees and darted the twenty feet to the back corner of the mausoleum and down the narrow steps before the sirens died. The keypad was set at eye level next to the door frame.

"This is where you shine, number boy," she said. "Or get us killed. Your choice."

His chest tightened. His heart didn't stop booming. Keypads. Lily was right. A single wrong entry and they were done for. A squad of Russian soldiers were only yards away, and they probably had orders to shoot to kill, no questions asked.

"Have you figured out the pattern yet?" she asked.

He shook his head. "There are a thousand combinations. Just let me think." And he tried to. He nearly did. But the thought of all the possible combinations froze him. *Key in the wrong numbers and we're dead.* With one unknown number, he might have had a chance to determine the pattern, but *three* unknowns? He stared blankly at the keypad as if it would somehow tell him the answer. It didn't. He looked at the strip of paper for the numbers. He didn't have to. He had memorized the sequence.

7, 1, 9, 3, ? ? ?

He tugged off his glove, then ran his shaking index finger over the keypad, not touching it, but tracing out the first four numbers. Seven. One. Nine. Three. He did it again. A third time. A fourth. Something unfroze in his brain. Something thawed and shifted.

"Your fingers aren't touching the pad, you know," Lily said.

"I know," he said. "But look at this." He repeated the sequence twice for her. "See?"

"Your finger not touching the pad? I do see that."

"No, look again. There's a shape. What shape does it make when you key in seven, one, nine, and three?" He moved his index finger once again over the keys.

"Um . . . *N*," she said. "So seven, one, nine, three is *N*, as in . . . Wait, you're not saying *N* for *Nicolaus*? Are you saying the next three numbers form a *C* for *Copernicus*?"

He found himself grinning at her. "Why not? It's what Brother Semyon did at the monastery, moving the stones in the shape of an *M*, for *Maxim*. It's an old trick, a simple one, but unless you know where and when to do it, you wouldn't guess it. If this *is* it, making the shape of a letter with numbers, the three numbers for *C* would be two, four, and eight. The whole sequence, for *N* and *C* is seven, one, nine, three, two, four, eight. I'm going to do it." He glared at her. "Unless you stop me."

She crossed her arms.

"Okay, then." He raised his trembling finger and tapped in the numbers.

Seven . . .

One . . .

Nine . . .

Three . . .

Two . . .

Four . . .

"Wait!" Lily whispered, clutching his hand suddenly. "It's not eight. It's zero. The last three numbers aren't two, four, eight; they're two, four, zero."

"What? Why?"

"Because of the other clue. The Copernicus quote, remember? 'The journey to the end of the sea is long'? Everybody's been telling us this line, but what if sometimes it isn't *sea*—as in splash-splash—but *C* as in *Copernicus*? The journey to the end of the *C* is long. And the Egyptologist meant it that way, as a trick or a pun. Guardians have to be tricky. So the leg of the *C* doesn't end at eight. It goes as long as it can. All the way down to zero. Do it, do zero now!"

"Did you say 'splash-splash'?"

"Just. Do. It."

Wade lifted his right index finger, held it steady with his left hand, and keyed in the final number.

Zero.

7, 1, 9, 3, 2, 4, 0. For *NC*. Nicolaus Copernicus.

Nothing happened for a full five seconds. Then there came a soft click. It was followed by a slow sequence of sliding bolts and levers behind the door, ending in a dull thud. Wade stared at Lily. She stared at him.

Breathing deeply, they pushed on the door together. It opened soundlessly. And side by side, they slipped into the tomb of Vladimir Ilyich Lenin.

CHAPTER FIFTY-NINE

Greywolf

Wolves howled and guns blasted as Darrell and Becca pushed from hall to room to passage to the center of the fortress. It stank of animals.

"Becca, trade you, the jewels for the pipe. I'll break them."

"Not likely, but yeah." She inserted the relic into the inner pocket of her parka, where Darrell knew she kept the diary. Both relic and diary, he suddenly realized, had belonged to Copernicus.

The man who'd started this quest.

The man who, in a roundabout way, had led them here to Darrell's mother.

"Darrell!" Becca cried. He turned to hear the frantic scampering of paws. Three wolves broke into the room. They were emaciated and gray. They slid across the floorboards, momentarily startled to see the kids. Their growling was like the grinding of gears.

"The door at the top of the stairs," Darrell whispered. "Go!" The wolves leaped up after them, but Roald and Marceline were suddenly there, startling the wolves with gunfire. Two of the creatures bared their fangs and growled, but ran out of the room. The third stood its ground for a second, arched up its hind legs, then ran out, too.

"Go with the children," Marceline said to Roald. "I'll stay here. Go on!"

"Hurry!" Roald snagged their sleeves as he rushed up with them. "She's got ammo, and she's a great shot."

From the top of the stairs, they turned to a mirrored hallway. Darrell ran down the hall and found a final set of stairs. Now that they had the Serpens head, it was all about finding his mother. They climbed to the landing. Roald shot at the locked door, a double-wide set of doors, and pushed into a large circular room. It was the inside room of the tower.

"Sara!" Roald cried out.

Darrell nearly vomited.

His mother hung, limp and drugged, inside a cage of metal bands at the center of a horrifying engine of gears and wheels and pistons. A haggard young man jerked out from behind the machine. He had an enormous handgun trained on them.

"You were never supposed to make it this far," the man said. "You were supposed to die at the hands of the Red Brotherhood. Or at least the wolves!"

"What have you done to her?" Darrell screamed. "Get my mother out of that thing!"

The man barely registered the words, but shot wildly. The bullet ricocheted powerfully off the wall behind them. "Stop or die. I must finish Kronos. I must . . ." His eyes widened, then narrowed, as if his brain was completely fried. Keeping his pistol leveled at the three of them, the man moved his free hand. It scrambled with lightning speed over a keyboard attached by a cable to the machine. The machine resembled a kind of gun, its barrel hinged inward at his mother.

"We're taking her out of there," Roald said, moving toward the machine. The man raised his gun and shot him.

In the forearm. Becca screamed. Roald reeled back, dropping his pistol, but stayed on his feet. It was a graze, not serious. "I'm fine," he said.

Darrell pulled out the Taser. "We're going to get her—"

"Please stop, or I will kill you all!" the man screamed, firing his pistol at the floor in front of Darrell, exploding the flagstones at his feet. "Twelve minutes! Twelve min— No! Eleven! Look! See!" He pointed the gun barrel at a clock mechanism mounted next to Sara. "If you move, I will kill her. And then I will kill you. I must do this."

Darrell heard footsteps coming toward them in the hallway. Marceline? The shooting had stopped. Had she neutralized the wolves?

Marceline Dufort leaped up the stairs and burst into the laboratory, her machine gun raised. The man at the device was startled to see her, and her gun. He thrust his pistol at Sara's head. "Drop your gun. Kick it here. Or she dies right now." Marceline placed her gun on the floor and followed his order.

"You see I *must* do this," the man said, his pistol still trained on Darrell's mother. He moved his free hand back to the keyboard and tapped three times in rapid succession.

The machine made an urgent sound.

One very large wheel began to turn.

Chapter Sixty

Lily quickly pulled the tomb's utility door closed behind them and held her breath. No alarm. The *NC* code had worked. With, naturally, her own brilliant correction.

She and Wade wound through a sequence of basement hallways until they found a cement staircase with a door at the top. They climbed up. The door was locked, but there was another keypad. Assured by Aleksandr that the Guardian code could override any other, they used it again, and the door lock clicked. They opened it and entered the mausoleum.

"Oh, man," Wade breathed.

She totally agreed.

The inside of the tomb resembled a modern hotel lobby more than a crypt, except, of course, for the giant coffin.

There were lights embedded in the ceiling, bare stone walls, marble floors. It wasn't as frigid as outside by any means, but it wasn't room temp, either. *Tomb temp,* Lily thought, then dismissed it. This was a place of reverence, whatever you thought of the man lying there.

Wade was dumbstruck, barely moving. "Where would you hide a relic here?"

"The shorter list is where *couldn't* you hide one," she said. "Serpens could be anywhere." Though not, she hoped, inside the coffin.

Or *sarcophagus*, as the websites had called it. It stood on a raised platform in the center of the large square room. The base was framed in marble. Above it was a bronze sculpture of cloth spilling tastefully out from the open casket. Several feet above the casket itself stood a construction of four tiers of marble and wood. In between were walls of thick glass, angled slightly outward from the base to the larger top. Inside the glass, lying in the casket as still as stone, was the embalmed body of Vladimir Lenin.

She swallowed hard and took a step toward it.

The dead leader's head and shoulders were—nice touch—tilted upward on a dark ruby pillow. To make for better viewing by the daily crowds, she guessed. Lenin's eyes were closed, but the embalming was so good that they looked as if they had just recently shut themselves. His hands were poised individually, not crossing each other at the waist, but separated. They had, if Lily could bring her mind to say it, a kind of personality. The right hand was folded on itself as if holding something. She really hoped it wasn't a diamond serpent. The left hand rested lightly on the upper left thigh.

"Okay, let's get to work," Wade said.

She shook her head to focus her thoughts. "Take two walls. Go over every inch of them. But remember that people are here all the time to pay their respects. So maybe the best hiding place will be a place where people don't go very much."

"Good point," Wade said softly. "I guess we have to be as clever as the Guardian who hid the relic. We have no real information on who he was, but we know the *NC* trick with the keypad. Maybe there's something like that going on inside, too."

"I just hope it's as far away as possible from *him*," she said. "You know, the third person in the room." She thought she heard Wade chuckling.

She hoped it was Wade chuckling.

For his part, Wade wanted to think logically about their search, but Guardian code makers were among the most sophisticated in the world, so it could be devilishly clever. Or devilishly simple. Or intuitive. Or impossible.

The four walls were clean, just flat or stepped marble blocks up to the ceiling, with minimal ornaments and light fixtures, none of which looked like it held a relic, and all of which was far too public anyway. So they moved toward the center of the tomb, or rather Lily did, because Wade found he had stopped moving.

"What's the matter? Outside the obvious one of breaking into a tomb?"

"I don't know." Wade slipped the strip of paper that Alek had given them from his pocket and stared at the simple cleverness of the solution to the entry code. Then he scanned the four corners of the room and the public entrance on the front wall, an entrance that jutted out into Red Square. That entrance was just like the zero on a keypad. He looked down at the floor, then up at the ceiling.

"What are you thinking?" she asked. "Because I hope you're thinking."

"I think I am thinking," he said. "And I'm thinking that the *NC* thing *could* be more than just the entry code. I mean, it's what Aleksandr told us. No matter how many times codes are changed, this will still work. Well, maybe that's the beauty of it. The simplicity. Because look at the layout of the floor. It juts forward, like the zero on the keypad. What if we trace the same two letters in the room, as if they form the same shape as the letters?"

Lily visually took in the four corners, the middle of the back wall, the right wall (from Lenin's perspective), and the entrance. "I don't know what we'll see that way that we didn't see before."

"Maybe it isn't what we see," he said. "Or what *we* see."

"Fine, be cryptical. I don't have a better idea."

Together, they stood under the ceiling light in the lower left corner. It suddenly flickered out. They walked slowly to the upper left corner, making the first "stroke" of the *N*. There was another ceiling light there. It too went out when they stood under it. They made their way around the sarcophagus to the lower right, then finally to the upper right, completing the *N*. There were ceiling lights in both corners, and both went out.

"That was the *N*. Now the *C*," he said. Starting at the

middle of the back wall, where there was also a ceiling light, they went to the middle of the side wall, then down to the entrance—the long journey to the end of the *C*—where there was a final ceiling light. Those three blinked and died, too.

"The lights are sensors!" she said.

All seven lights came on again, and from the center of the room came the sound of something sliding. To Wade, it seemed more mechanical than electronic. The sound continued for another few seconds, then stopped with a click.

"The sarcophagus," he whispered. His arms and legs tingled as he walked slowly to the large glass coffin, but Lily focused on the source of the noise first. She scurried over to the foot of the coffin. The marble molding around the base was unbroken except in one spot, where a short length of black marble was protruding two or three inches. As the ceiling light haloed her face and hair, she knelt and pried at the close-fitting molding.

It slid out another three inches and stopped.

Wade watched as she pushed her fingers behind the molding, and felt around and around, until her whole body quivered.

"Lily?"

From inside she drew a small rectangular item and held it up to the light.

It was a burnished wooden box, two inches deep and as long and wide as two decks of playing cards set end to end.

She gasped. "The box is so heavy. Wade? Could this be it? Omigod, what if Darrell and Becca find the head? We'll have both parts."

"We don't have anything yet," he said. "Open the box."

She let out all her breath. "Okay . . . okay . . ." Holding the bottom of the box in her hand, she undid the simple clasp and tilted the lid.

Silver light bloomed out of the inside of the box. She glanced away, blinked, then looked back. Her face burned with the glow. "Wade . . ."

The body of Serpens was a thing of rods and hinges and wires—coiled and braided into the shape of an angled *S*. It gleamed of silver, tooled and delicately shaped and studded with diamonds of varying sizes and shapes. It shone like a constellation, its own impossible source of brilliant light.

"It's electric, Wade. Or, I don't know."

"It looks like it's moving," he whispered, feeling his fingers reaching for it, wanting to touch it.

"It's hot, and it's humming or something," she said. "And it *will* move after we connect it to the head," Lily breathed. "Oh, man, Wade. After all this, after the whole long journey, I can't believe we actually—"

There was a sudden dull whump from the square outside, a muffled blast, then yelling. This was followed by a distant spray of machine-gun fire. An engine revved noisily. Then another smaller blast, closer this time. Next came a rapid series of concussions. The floor shook beneath them.

"What in the world—" Wade started.

The square outside thundered with explosions and the rumbling of vehicles approaching the tomb swiftly. There was another blast. The walls shook, and a bright spear of light flashed across the room. Alarms sounded as a second entrance at the rear of the tomb swung in and closed quickly with a breath of frigid air.

Lily clamped down the lid of the box. "Wade, no, no, no—"

Before he could move, the room was filled with heavily armed soldiers dressed in black parkas and ski masks. The Brotherhood? FSB? He couldn't tell. They surrounded both of them. One who looked like he might be the leader grabbed the box from Lily and threw her into Wade. She yelled at the man.

"Shut up," he growled. "Get up the stairs. Both of you."

"Stairs?" Wade hadn't seen any.

The other men pushed both kids roughly to the back corner through a narrow hall to a set of marble stairs that led upward. They forced them to climb. Wade felt as if he and Lily were being led to their execution. She shook as she held on to his arm. "Omigod, Wade," she whispered. "What . . . what are they going to do?"

There was a door at the top of the steps. One of the men shot at the handle and kicked the door open. Snow swirled in at them. The air quaked to the sound of gunfire and the heavy rolling of military vehicles.

Wade didn't move, and he held Lily so tightly she couldn't, either.

"Go!" the officer said, and they were suddenly outside on one of the steps of the pyramid. It was a kind of reviewing platform overlooking the square. It had a marble wall about waist high. The square was a battleground. There were at least two military tanks now, several transports, some with military insignia, others unmarked. The army against the Brotherhood.

All at once, the air was different, full of pressure. Through the gunfire and the roar of the wind came a heavy thwack-thwack that overwhelmed every sound.

"A helicopter!" Lily cried.

A small black helicopter thundered out of the storm overhead. Snow flew around them as the chopper hovered a mere two feet from the roof of the top level. Wade clutched Lily to himself, each bracing the other to keep from being blown off, while both were locked in the vise-grip of several Brotherhood troops. They mounted the final steps to the roof itself.

The blades slowed. The door of the helicopter opened. Galina pounced out and calmly received the box from the officer who had taken it.

She turned to Wade. With a surprisingly penetrating voice over the sound of the battle below and the helicopter above, she said, "It turns out to be a good thing you two did not die in Vorkuta. You have found Serpens for me. And now that this relic will lead me to the next one, you have outlived your usefulness."

Galina slid the box lid off.

The object inside shone like a full moon on her face, flashing among the whirling snowflakes and beaming into her two-colored eyes like a spotlight, a laser. In that glow, Wade saw, Galina was more beautiful, if that was possible, than at the coal mine. Pale and pure in a strange way. Unless what he thought was beauty was something else. Electricity? A raw obsession? Hunger?

As if she *had to have* the relics? As if she *needed* the Eternity Machine?

As if there were another deadline that only *she* was under?

A very rare and almost unknown modality of cancer.

Galina drew in a very long, very slow breath. "The body of Serpens. I have recovered what Rubashov's father stole from the tomb of my . . . Grand Master . . . Albrecht von Hohenzollern. . . ."

Wade's chest was frozen. "How did you even know we were here?"

She raised her eyes from the relic. "Once I saw that you had survived Vorkuta, I knew that the good doctor had given you a clue. The Brotherhood followed you from the airport, partway, at least. Your friend Terence Ackroyd managed to set a little ruse for us, too. But I deduced the rest."

The square echoed with the rapid hammering of machine guns, then two unmarked transports exploded in flames. The lead officer stepped forward. "Miss Krause, the tide is turning against us."

Galina drew a gun on Wade and Lily. There was a strange, resigned look on her face. It was the end, Wade thought. They were out of time, unless . . .

All at once, he pushed Lily with all his might off

the edge of the roof. She disappeared over the side, swearing at the top of her lungs. He jumped after her, yelling "Dive-dive-dive!" as bullets flew, ricocheting off the marble walls of the platform below. Lily was on her feet, screaming along the passage, as machine-gun fire thudded the walls above and below them. She tumbled down the passage into the tomb, Wade at her heels. They raced down the stairs all the way to the subbasement just as an explosion thundered against the front wall of the tomb.

They stole out the same door they had used to enter.

Amid the chaos of automatic gunfire and vehicles and wailing sirens and whirling snow, Wade watched the helicopter ascend over the tomb, over the square, and move west across the city. "Galina has it! Lily, she has our relic!"

In the confusion of the final military assault on the Brotherhood, an unmarked car skidded to a stop at the rear corner of the tomb. Chief Inspector Yazinsky was behind the wheel. "In!" he ordered as Terence bolted from the backseat and dragged them both in with steely arms. "We need to leave Moscow right now!"

"What about the others?" Wade cried as he hit the floor with Lily. "Sara? Becca?"

"The city's riot forces are sealing off the square!" the

inspector said. "Not even I shall be able to pass!"

"But what about Sara?" Wade asked.

"There's no news!" said Terence. "We have to leave now."

The car tore away from the crisscrossing fire, racing past the Kremlin wall.

"But Sara," Lily cried. "Tell us!"

"We know nothing!" the inspector cried. "Nothing!"

CHAPTER SIXTY-ONE

Greywolf

Seven minutes to midnight became six minutes to midnight.

The machine—Kronos—shuddered as if it were alive. Darrell heard its clock ticking unceasingly. It had an open mechanism of fine gears and claws spinning rapidly, and hands of a sort that were turning counter-clockwise. The large wheel looked as if it was growing hot, and its barrel . . . was aimed directly at his mother's chest. The whole thing was counting down.

"Take my mother out of there!" he screamed at the man fiddling with the machine's knobs and levers. *"Get her out or I swear—"*

"I'm sorry," said the crazy man, having scooped up Marceline's gun before they could stop him. "I've never hurt anyone. But you see my time is nearly up. I haven't any left. I had a mother once, too, but I must . . . They want 1517, you know. This is unusual. I hope you see that. A master programmer who shoots people."

"He's crazy," Becca whispered to Darrell and his stepfather. "We have to get Sara out by ourselves."

Darrell edged slowly across the room, step by step with Becca and his stepfather, the pipe swinging in his hand like a pendulum. "I'm going to get her out."

"Stop where you are," squealed a voice behind them.

Ebner von Braun was standing by the door. He had a pistol in each hand, one aimed at Becca's forehead, the other at Darrell's chest just below the neck. He sneered. "Your mother is in the hands of Kronos now." His voice was hoarse, weary. "You are too late to do anything but watch her leave us."

Darrell's anger stuck like a knife in his throat. He wanted to tear the bent man limb from limb. But the guy was armed. He was *well* armed.

The machine went into another mode now. Its wheel began to turn quickly.

"Five minutes," Ebner said, his feet firmly planted on the floor. "Isn't it exciting?"

Roald was standing directly behind Darrell. Becca glared at Darrell, as if to get his attention. *I understand,* he thought. *The guy is an insane creep, and you're afraid.*

But that wasn't it. Becca flicked her glance down to the pocket of her jacket. The relic was there. So close to the German he could probably sniff it, if he wasn't such a demon-idiot-creep-troll. Then Becca raised three fingers so only Darrell could see them.

Three fingers! Three fingers mean . . . create a diversion!

Before he could devise anything, he heard a whimper. "Darrell, I love you."

It was his mother. Darrell swung around to see her lift up her pale face.

"I love you . . . ," she repeated.

Her faint voice exploded something inside him, and he knew what the diversion was. He jumped back and jerked the pipe around as far and as fast as he could. Into Helmut Bern's forehead. The man groaned and fell, dropping his gun. Ebner raised his suddenly, when Becca shrieked at the top of her lungs and Roald rammed him like an offensive tackle.

Becca then twirled impossibly and jumped with both feet on Ebner's right arm. His other gun went off. He screamed. His shoe had burst open and was smoking. He'd shot his own foot, the bullet going through and then grazing Marceline in the side. Darrell scrambled for the machine gun. He raised it to the cage lock. "Mom, look away—"

"Give it to me!" cried his stepfather. Taking it from him, he pressed the barrel to the cage lock. He pulled the trigger. The blast was deafening. The chain blew apart.

"Stand away from Kronos! Leave your mother inside!" Ebner had wobbled to his feet, his gun in his bleeding hand, and he had it pressed into Becca's throat. "Move and the girl dies. Then you die. Finish it, Bern. Finish Kronos!"

Bern staggered to his feet, bloody forehead and all, and resecured Sara in the cage. Darrell and the others were frozen where they stood. Bern jammed a quivering finger on the keyboard. "And the code begins to upload. Only three minutes now."

"No!" Darrell cried helplessly. "Please!"

The sound of the machine changed again, growing to a fever pitch. The giant wheel was spinning faster and faster, the barrel glowing with a white heat, while three jagged-edged brass cones located on the base of the machine began to rotate.

Becca couldn't think. As if the oxygen to her brain were shut off. The diversion hadn't worked. If there was a chance, any chance at all, she alone had it.

"Here," she said. "Here, take it."

Darrell turned. "Bec, no . . . no . . ."

Her hands shook. She thrust her fingers into her parka as Ebner stared at her.

"It? *It?*" he screamed.

She removed a small wrapped bundle, held it dangling in front of the bent German's face. "Take it. The head of Serpens. No more killing!"

The troll practically turned inside out, he looked so stunned. "Galina! I have it!" He thrust his hand at the relic, when Becca threw it as hard as she could out the door and down the stairs. "Fool!" he screamed, limping after it with his wounded foot. He was nearly out of the room when Marceline thrust her foot straight out. Ebner tripped out the door and back down the stairs. Everyone else ran toward the machine.

Darrell elbowed the programmer aside. He threw aside the chain, wrenched open the cage. "Mom!" he screamed. "Mom!" But the creep was all bone now, clawing at the controls. Just as Roald reached him, grabbing his fingers, Helmut Bern drove his hand at a blue lever on the console.

"Galina, I did it!" he shrieked. "Kronos is perfect!" Becca pounded his face and hands, then heard a final tick of the clock like a thunderous explosion, and Darrell screamed—"*Mom—Mom—Mom—Mom!*"—and Roald threw his hands toward Sara just as a blinding light flashed across Becca's eyes like a white razor, and then there was nothing.

Nothing but darkness and silence and nothing.

CHAPTER SIXTY-TWO

Bosporus Strait, Turkey
March 24
11:57 a.m.

The old steam-powered ferry rocked gently on the waves.

Galina Krause leaned on the starboard railing and watched in silence as ancient Istanbul shimmered before her eyes. A city of white and glistening gold, beckoning her to pause at the crossroads of Europe and Asia Minor before passing through the strait into the broad Sea of Marmara and beyond, to the Mediterranean.

"Miss Krause."

The voice was deep, icy. She turned. "Markus Wolff."

"You asked me to investigate the Somosierra incident."

"What have you discovered about the driver, Diego Vargas? The young student?"

"You will recall the theory that a time event establishes a hole in the past," Wolff said. "A hole that might linger some amount of time after the event before collapsing."

She trembled. "And?"

Wolff handed her a black-and-white photograph. "This image was taken by the war photographer Robert Capa in Somosierra. It dates from early September 1936. From the same sequence as Capa's famous portrait of the dying soldier."

This print showed a young boy, his jacket in tatters, his face worn by war—or something worse—staring, hollow-eyed, at the camera.

"The Copernicus Room's facial-recognition software has confirmed that this face is that of Fernando Salta, aged eleven years, four months, thirteen days," said Wolff.

"Fernando Salta?"

"The student stranded at Somosierra in 1808," said Wolff. "This photograph is proof that our student has traveled forward from 1808 to 1936. Fernando Salta is making his way back to the present."

Galina stared at the photograph. The boy's dark eyes burned with something. Desire to return? Certainly. But what else? Anger? Revenge? What manner of creature was eleven-year-old Fernando Salta becoming, during his passage through time? And where and when would he turn up next?

"What do you wish me to do now?" Wolff asked.

Galina removed the miniature Holbein portrait from her jacket pocket. She uttered a simple instruction. "London. Discover what can be discovered." Wolff pocketed the portrait and drifted away among the other passengers.

Galina turned to the sparkling cityscape, but her view of the many-towered mosques of the ancient metropolis blurred. Her fingers slipped into the same zipped pocket and removed Serpens's two sections. She connected them with an easy twist at the inner hinges.

The relic, complete for the first time in five centuries, lay in her palm for a moment, then twitched.

Tick . . . tick . . . tick . . .

The very breath was sucked out of her lungs. She felt dizzy, intoxicated by the hypnotic movement of the serpent sliding across her skin. Suddenly, as if it had stung her—cursed her—she unhooked the thing. Her thoughts flashed to Copernicus, disassembling his Legacy, distributing its relics.

Perhaps he'd known the horror of such power after all.

Ebner limped up behind her, a bruised fighter. She knew he was smiling despite his various wounds. "A momentous juncture," he said, leaning heavily on his cane. "On the one hand, the first relic, Vela, will soon be ours. A new effort is being mounted by the gentlemen from Marseille to retrieve it from the Morgan's vault in New York City. And with Serpens in our possession, we will soon locate the third Copernicus artifact. It is only a matter of time before the astrolabe is rebuilt, my dear."

"We are out front once more, Ebner, and sailing into the warm south."

He grinned. "I should tell you that the particle injection Kronos delivered to its passenger is working splendidly. Already our traveler has been located. Alas, not at the precise time and place we hoped—a thousand miles and six months off—but bizarrely close enough."

Galina felt her body flood with a strange glee. "Ebner, I want the Kaplans dead." She turned her eyes to him. "Kill them. All but the one, do you understand?"

Ebner laughed a subtle laugh. He tapped a few

buttons on his cell phone. "I am sending an alert to our man on the scene."

Galina knew that at that instant a message was delivered not only in Berlin, but also to a computer screen in a flat on faraway Foulden Road in London.

☑ Terminate immediately

"You have made Mr. Doyle very happy," he said.

"Collect my bags, Ebner; we are entering port."

As her doting physicist receded, scuffling across the deck on his cane, Galina leaned against the railing. She drew in lungful after lungful of sea air and lightly touched the scar on her neck. It was warm.

Once again, she had nearly died in Russia. She would never set foot there again, if she could help it, and thanks to the children, she would likely not have to. Not in this lifetime, at least.

CHAPTER SIXTY-THREE

London
March 27
9:27 a.m.

Wade Kaplan stared up at the exquisite vaulted ceilings of Westminster Abbey, but he wasn't seeing them. The thousands of footsteps that padded and clicked and scampered and slid over the marble floors of the enormous nave were no more than a blur of echoes, a soft whoosh of noise behind his twisting thoughts.

What happened?

How did it all happen?

Could we have done anything differently?

What do we do now?

Someone touched his shoulder. He looked to see Lily's slender fingers. He didn't want her to remove them. He needed something real to prove to him that they were actually there and that it had happened the way it did.

"You were good back there," she said. "In Russia. You were good. Me, too, of course, but you, too."

"We did what we could, right? There wasn't anything else we could have done, was there?"

"No . . . ," she said, as if maybe there was doubt. Then, more firmly, "No."

As tough as he thought they had become in New York at the beginning of the hunt for Serpens, they were tougher now. Tougher, harder, more steeled for the road ahead. It had been a horrifying week and a half of extremes—of bitter arctic cold, of danger and countless brushes with death—pushing each of them to the brink. It had exhausted every ounce of everything they'd had, but they'd come through it.

Mostly.

Lily and Darrell stood next to him, all three staring quietly into the shadows beneath the gallery of the north transept, where Wade's father leaned over the side of a wheelchair and hugged Sara as if he could lose her again at any minute, as if he were hugging her for the first time ever.

Sara Kaplan was alive and safe and with them again.

Wade recalled the frantic moment when they'd all met in the early morning at the airport in Moscow.

How Sara had wrapped her weak arms around Lily and Wade together and brought Darrell and everyone into it, crying their names over and over, not singling out her real son over anyone else, how soon they were all crying.

Then, on the flight to London, while the kids took turns filling her in about the search for Vela *and* Serpens, Sara was stunned and silent, until she threw herself on all the children, Darrell last and most, then completely lost it, shaking uncontrollably in his father's arms the rest of the long flight. She slept in the London hospital for a day and a half, where she was monitored and nourished. For three days they were in a kind of limbo, waiting on pins and needles until yesterday morning, when she woke up and it was suddenly over. "I want to see London," she said, and that was that.

Of course Sara was weak and she would, her doctors insisted, become exhausted despite herself. They urged Roald to make sure she used a wheelchair for another few days, but they were pleased to say that she would make a complete recovery. Sara's ordeal, everyone was happy to realize, was over.

Wade looked around himself like a panorama camera. "So where's Bec—"

Then there she was, still wrapped in her fur-lined parka, standing quietly to the side of them as if she'd been there the whole time. She wore a puzzled frown on her face, and her eyes were downcast nearly to her feet, while she rocked on the marble tiles as if to keep her balance.

At least since the Moscow airport, Becca had been so quiet—so *quiet*—and had barely spoken a word. He stepped over to her. "Hey. We lost you for a second."

"Lost?"

"I mean, how are you feeling? The headaches. Your fever? Were you crying?"

"What?" she said. "No. Why?" She lifted her hand, apparently surprised to find her cheeks wet and salty. Her puzzled look returned. "Oh. Maybe. It's . . . it's good to have Sara back."

He nodded over and over again, aware he was grinning like a fool but unable to stop. "Oh, yeah, it's good. I feel like crying, too."

Lost . . .

Becca had stood there immobile for many minutes,

467

her eyes throbbing, even in the abbey's diffused light. Her head felt as if it were being bisected by a battle-ax separating the hemispheres in a way that had, three times so far, preceded something like a blackout. The crossbow wound on her arm hurt like never before, too. It might have stung from the hospital antiseptic she'd received here in London, but it felt like it wasn't healing so much as deepening, getting worse.

Around Becca in every direction, the noise of the great stone room crashed into her ears like waves battering a deck in a storm. It brought back to mind scenes from *Moby-Dick*, which she had been reading just last week.

When she stepped after Wade to join his parents, who clung to each other like the lost loves reunited that they actually were, Becca was not aware of the words of her friends or the echo of their feet on the stones so much as the sudden terrible creaking of wood, and an odd forlorn voice in her ears crying, *I am lost . . . lost! Bring me home!*

Lily sidled up to Becca, joining arms with her. "You guys, we are never, *ever* splitting up again. I never want to make big decisions. Ever. Not without all of you there to back me up when I decide something brilliant." Lily held back her tears as well as she could, but she finally had to turn away and rub her cheeks dry. "I know I've said it a billion times since Russia, but I still sort of can't believe we had Serpens and lost it."

"It was worth it," Darrell said softly. "But yeah. We had it, and we gave it away."

The loss of both halves of Serpens was a gnawing ache to them all.

In the coming days, Lily knew, the weirdness of Kronos and Galina and the loss of Serpens and all of it would probably become less a kind of grief and more an alarm, goading them to keep up the hunt. It would force them into their next mission. They were Guardians of the Astrolabe of Copernicus. They were the *Novizhny*. If there had been the slightest doubt about that when they entered Russia, if they'd thought they were really only there to find Sara, there was no doubt now. After what had happened at Greywolf and Vorkuta and Red Square, there could never be any doubt.

Becca stayed mostly quiet about it, but Darrell had given them a stunning second-by-second account of the last moments before the device's clock struck midnight.

"After Ebner bolted for the jewels," Darrell had said, "Helmut Bern tried to keep us from getting Mom out of Kronos. But Becca punched—I'm telling you *punched*— the guy with, like, a movie punch. Bern looked like he'd just been insulted or something; then he fell back at the last second before midnight. Dad and I yanked Mom out of Kronos, the machine went all *ka-boom* on us, the lights and everything went out, and Dad dragged us all out of there, even Marceline, without looking back."

Lily couldn't get enough of the story, partly because she and Wade had had no idea what had happened before they got to the airport, nor that they had both recovered—then given up—their halves of Serpens. Neither Terence nor Inspector Yazinsky had had any news from Greywolf, either about Roald and Sara or about Darrell and Becca. Everyone had kept checking phones, but there had been no word.

Bright morning light streamed in the stained-glass windows of the nave, crisscrossing the floor in shapes of shadow and color. Darrell felt peaceful for the first time since his mother had been kidnapped.

"I keep thinking we should be holding Serpens right now," he said, gazing up at the brilliant gold altarpiece, then back at them. "We should have the relic right here in our hands. Cursed or not, I think we'd be able to deal with it. It's supposed to be ours. I mean . . . well . . . we should have it, end of story."

There wasn't much else to say. They all felt the same.

"I keep wondering if the umbrella man is out there somewhere," Wade said, scanning the vast nave of the abbey. "Not that we'd know it if he's in disguise."

"No problem," said Darrell. "Lily can spot a wig fifty feet away, right, Lil?"

She laughed. "Just one of my talents." Then she sighed. "I guess we go back to Texas now? Just like that?"

Wade grumbled. "No one wants to, but we don't know where to start searching for the next relic, do we? Only Galina does."

In a day or two, their London rest would be over. Lily's and Becca's parents were due to arrive to take them home. There would be all sorts of craziness trying to justify all they'd done, but Darrell knew that when the girls' parents saw his mother safe and heard how she wouldn't be there if not for the two girls' help, they'd realize that there had been no choice. They would all have to work out their individual returns to Austin, however, and even how safe that might be, given how the Order forced them from their homes. That was as big a question as anything else.

But then, only one thing *wasn't* a question.

They'd made a solemn oath, the four of them, that they were "totally and completely and absolutely" committed to the relic quest. And Darrell's mother and stepfather were just as committed. They had no real idea where to start looking for the third relic—a giant obstacle, but they'd overcome obstacles before.

Lots of them.

Wade was the first to see a familiar-looking boy trot across the marble stones to them.

"Thanks for meeting me," Julian Ackroyd said. "All safe and sound?"

"Neither," Darrell said, "but good enough. How's your dad?"

"Fine. He's tied up with the London foundation until tonight, but I've just gotten off the phone with him," Julian said. "Paul and Marceline are back in Paris and doing all right, but both will be out of action for a while. They reported that there's not a stitch of information on Galina Krause right now. When she disappeared from Red Square in the chopper, she might just as well have been swallowed up by the storm. Dad's people are searching, but you know . . ." He trailed off.

"She'll discover where the next relic is," Becca said, as if it pained her to talk. Her brow was furrowed again. "She'll do what she can to rebuild the Eternity Machine. She'll destroy the world."

"We might be able to help with that," Julian said. "Honestly, I've never seen Dad so into anything. Me, either, actually. He's dedicating a whole division of our foundation to stopping Galina Krause. We're not letting this go."

"Thanks for that," said Wade, watching Becca's expression darken as Roald wheeled Sara out of Poets' Corner and across the floor toward them.

"Which brings me to the real reason I wanted to meet you here in London," Julian said. He swiped his phone. "In addition to helping with the London activities of the Ackroyd Foundation, I've been doing some work. I believe you know this man?"

They leaned over the picture to see a tall, white-haired man in a long black leather coat standing by a river. He had close-cropped white hair and a stony expression.

"OMG, that's Markus Wolff!" Lily said. "He killed us in San Francisco! Well, almost!"

"He said he would finish the job if he ever saw us again," said Darrell.

"Markus Wolff," Julian said, "works exclusively for Galina Krause as a sort of personal archaeologist."

"And personal assassin," Lily added.

"There are boats behind him," Becca said. "Where

was this picture taken, and when?"

"This morning on the Thames, not two and a half miles from here," Julian said, closing his phone. "During the current renovations of the historic area, the remains of a trading barge from the early fifteen hundreds have been discovered. The question is, what's so interesting to Galina Krause about an old boat?"

"A boat . . . ," Becca murmured.

Wade stepped next to her. "A clue to another relic. A definite clue."

"You must be Julian!" Sara said softly, raising her hand to him as Wade's father wheeled her to a stop.

"I am!" Julian took her hand with a broad smile. "I'm happy to meet you, Sara Kaplan, and *so* happy to see you up and around."

"No way can you keep my mom down," Darrell said.

"And you won't," Sara said, her voice coming back to her. "Does anyone know where Galina's gone to? I have a score to settle with that . . . young woman."

Wade nearly laughed, then told her about Markus Wolff being seen at the riverside. "If Wolff is there, it has to mean something."

Sara nodded sharply. "All right then." She locked eyes with his father, then with each of the others. "We're going to the river. The hunt is on."

"Yes!" said Darrell, slapping Wade's shoulder and giving Lily a high five. "It's on, all right. It's on until it's done!"

Julian smiled. "My limo is just outside. "We can be there in ten minutes."

As they hurried across the marble floor of the abbey and out into the bustling noisy streets of London, the children knew there would nevermore be an atom of doubt.

They were on their quest once more.

They were the *Novizhny*.

They were Guardians.

EPILOGUE

North Sea
October 30, 1517
Evening

The whole thing was no more than a blur to Helmut Bern's fevered mind.

There'd been a flash, and something like a hundred-foot blade going through his chest, and he'd been sucked through an industrial-strength garbage disposal, ground down to nothing, and his bits reassembled. In the proper order, he hoped.

You there, sir . . .

But where in the world was he? His eyes ached when he glanced around.

You there, sir . . .

He appeared to be on the deck of an ancient sailing vessel. His stomach twisted. The ocean was stupid. As the ship tumbled up and down over ridiculous waves, he shivered under a filthy, mouse-ridden blanket of some kind. He was very cold. And also hot. His face felt like a frying pan. But why wasn't he at Greywolf? And where was the woman? And Kronos?

"You there . . . sir," a voice said in German.

Some tedious man bent over him. He was dressed in a variety of cloaks and sashes and belts as if it were Halloween. *Is that a sword at his waist? Good God!*

"You, there, Brother—"

"Yes? Yes? What's wrong with you?" Helmut snapped. "I hear you. Where the devil am I?"

"Where . . . Brother?"

"Where!" Bern snapped at the man. "As in *at what location*! And why do you keep calling me 'brother'?"

The ship rolled suddenly, lifted like a speedboat, then crashed into the waves again. Lord, the air stank. He tried to sit up but couldn't get his legs unstuck.

"You wear the cloak of a monk, sir," the man said.

Monk? An image flashed across his mind. Yes, yes. He *awoke* some hours ago surrounded by stone, didn't he? A church? Kronos! He saw it. Kronos was in a church. And he had stumbled out of the place and there was the shore, and a ship and . . . He must have blacked out after that, because suddenly he was here.

"What bloody year is this?" Helmut asked.

The Halloween man arched back as if the question were idiotic. He had intelligent, thoughtful eyes, creased with worry and study, perhaps. *A scholar*, Helmut thought. *But a swordsman, too.* The man was pleasantly bearded and tanned, well built, perhaps forty or forty-five, with a slouchy velvet hat perched on his head to complete the costume.

"The year of our Lord 1517, sir."

The gears in Helmut's brain stuttered. 1517? Copernicus had taken a sea journey from Cádiz in Spain in 1517. He himself had programmed the very coordinates into Kronos. But . . . no! It couldn't possibly be! Could it? Had he, Bern, actually done it? Had he actually managed to program Kronos I to send him back safe and sound into the past, with such absolute accuracy? He *was* a genius! Here was the bloody proof!

For the first time, Helmut peered closely at the man standing over him. The look of his face, as clear as it could be through blurry eyes, was as identical to the portraits as any face could be.

"Ha! Ha-ha! You are he!" he cried. "You are Nicolaus Copernicus!"

"Do I know you, sir?" he said. "You rather remind me of someone I once knew."

"When did we leave Cádiz? And where are we bound?"

"Cádiz, sir?" said the man he suspected to be Copernicus. "We did not leave Cádiz."

A cold knife blade of fear entered his spine. "Not Cádiz? But . . . then where is this bloody ship *going*?"

"Brother, we are en route to England."

"England? England!"

Crouching closer, the man set his palm over Helmut's forehead and eyes. "But there will be time for talking later, friend. You are unwell. . . ."

Helmut swatted the hand away and tried to rise, but the deck still refused to let him go. He looked down at the position of his legs. There was something wrong with them. And his fingers were curled, his wrists as weak as rope. He tried to examine them more closely, but seawater kept dripping over his eyes. The skin of his hands was dark red, as if he'd fallen asleep under a sunlamp. His cheeks were raw, and the salt spray stung him. Hot and cold again, both at the same time. "What in the world . . ."

"I know these sores," the man said. "My own brother . . ."

Was Copernicus speaking of his own brother?

The poor Andreas, who everyone knows died of . . . *leprosy*?

It came at Helmut with the force of a tsunami. The journey in Kronos had not only taken him to the wrong place and time, it had done something else to him. The particle injection! The radioisotope! It had sickened him!

Just then a shape moved behind the astronomer. Was this the legendary young assistant, Hans Novak, creeping behind his master?

But it was not Novak. It was not a boy at all. It was a girl. Long brown hair, wet, clinging to her face. A . . . parka . . . a modern parka; her cheeks wet, splashed by salt waves; bearing a crazed, puzzled expression; . . . and . . . *I . . . know her!*

"I know you!" Helmut screamed in English. "The American girl from Greywolf! They called you . . . Becca! What . . . what are you—"

Yet in that instant, just as she focused before his eyes, the girl vanished from the deck, as if the very air and waves had washed her into oblivion. Or back into the future from when she came.

"I am lost! Lost!" Helmut cried at the top of his lungs. "Bring me home!"

"Sir?"

"Bring me home! Bring me home! Bring me home!"

TO BE CONTINUED in *The Copernicus Archives: Becca and the Prisoner's Cross* . . . and *The Copernicus Legacy: The Golden Vendetta.*

AUTHOR'S NOTE

I've always been fascinated by the layering of imagined story and factual research in a novel and how the two finally become (or should become) indistinguishable.

The Serpent's Curse is of course a piece of fiction, though behind (and above and in between) that fiction was woven a good deal of reading, travel, conversation, code making and breaking, artwork, and a host of other oddments.

Of the books that have seeped into the present story, there are a good number; here are some of the main ones: Arthur Koestler's brilliant novel about a man's fight against inhumanity, *Darkness at Noon*, was a constant, not least for supplying me with the name *Rubashov*, but also for a certain sparkling bleakness of tone. Oh, and for the bit about pacing back and forth in a small cell that more than one character does here. *Gulag: A History*, by Anne Applebaum, and *The Gulag Archipelago: 1918–1956*, by Aleksandr Solzhenitsyn, along with *In Siberia*, by Colin Thubron, were the prime sources for the setting of the Siberian work camp. James H. Billington's *The Icon and the Axe* was useful as a starting place for study of the late-medieval period in Russia. Masha Gessen's *Words Will Break Cement* and *The Snowden Files*, by Luke Harding, were helpful with background color and because they recount current events. On the lighter side, I have to mention Daniel Silva's *Moscow Rules* and *The English Girl*, both delightful nightstand companions during the writing of this book.

ACKNOWLEDGMENTS

My thanks go first to my family. They are the foundation upon which I am blessed to be able to write at all. Heartfelt gratitude also goes to Andrew Freeburg for his close reading of the story's Russian pages, for his suggestions, and for correcting my more obvious mistakes in language and setting. Thanks to Patti Woods for her careful reading of the Venice episode; I do not, however, apologize for her subsequent desire to return there. To Kathryn Silsand and Karen Sherman, my copy editors, countless thanks (or rather, six hundred sixty thanks, based on the latest revision). To Karen, especially, who somehow read the story as deeply and fully as I wrote it, I send my best wishes and kindest thoughts and apologies for the length of the book. You are the best. As before and always, to Claudia Gabel, Melissa Miller, and Katherine Tegen, my good companions on this relic quest, my thanks beyond all thanks.

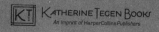